THE PAPERS OF

WOODROW WILSON

VOLUME 64

NOVEMBER 6, 1919–FEBRUARY 27, 1920

SPONSORED BY THE WOODROW WILSON
FOUNDATION
AND PRINCETON UNIVERSITY

THE PAPERS OF
WOODROW
WILSON

ARTHUR S. LINK, *EDITOR*

JOHN E. LITTLE, *ASSOCIATE EDITOR*

MANFRED F. BOEMEKE, *ASSOCIATE EDITOR*

L. KATHLEEN AMON, *ASSISTANT EDITOR*

PHYLLIS MARCHAND, *INDEXER*

Volume 64
November 6, 1919–February 27, 1920

PRINCETON, NEW JERSEY

PRINCETON UNIVERSITY PRESS

1991

Note to scholars: Princeton University Press subscribes to the Resolution on Permissions of the Association of American University Presses, defining what
we regard as "fair use" of copyrighted works. This Resolution, intended to encourage scholarly use of university press publications and to avoid unnecessary applications for permission, is obtainable from the Press
or from the A.A.U.P. central office. Note, however, that
the scholarly apparatus, transcripts of shorthand, and
the texts of Wilson documents as they appear in this
volume are copyrighted, and the usual rules about the
use of copyrighted materials apply.

Printed in the United States of America
by Princeton University Press
Princeton, New Jersey

INTRODUCTION

THE opening of this volume, on November 6, 1919, finds Wilson still bed-ridden and only occasionally able to perform even the minimal duties of the presidency. The Cabinet continues to meet weekly, and the departmental heads concerned with domestic affairs work closely with and through Tumulty to deal with urgent matters, such as the settlement of the nationwide bituminous coal strike and the decision when to return the railroads to private management. In mid-November, Tumulty gains direct access to Wilson's sick room and talks to Wilson from time to time, but he usually uses Mrs. Wilson as the conduit for communication with his chief. Wilson has always insisted upon making all important decisions concerning foreign affairs. Now, in his paranoid distrust of Lansing, he refuses to see his Secretary of State or even, in most cases, to respond to his urgent appeals for guidance and instructions. During the one dangerous crisis of November and December—the possibility of war with Mexico—Wilson rallies enough strength to receive Senators Hitchcock and Fall of the Foreign Relations Committee and, in a public declaration, to end all talk of war.

Grayson manages to retain Wilson's confidence and plays an important role in managing affairs of state. He also undertakes important, if risky, initiatives on his own. Two weeks before this volume opens, he prepares a full public disclosure of Wilson's physical condition; Mrs. Wilson vetoes its issuance. Thus thwarted, Grayson and his consultants continue to give out frequent bulletins about Wilson's health and activities, which give the appearance of steady progress toward recovery. Grayson's most daring gambit is to attempt in mid-January to persuade Wilson to resign for reasons of health. Wilson is willing, but Mrs. Wilson again interposes her veto.

The most urgent task of Wilson's advisers during the period covered by this volume is to persuade him to accept the so-called Lodge reservations to the Versailles Treaty, or a milder version of them, in order to win the consent of two thirds of the senators to ratification of that treaty in a vote scheduled for November 19, 1919. Hitchcock discusses strategy with Wilson only twice before that date. The two men decide to use the threat of a pocket veto of the Treaty by Wilson to attempt to force the Senate to adopt mild reservations. Enough Democrats follow Wilson to prevent a two-thirds vote for consent to ratification with the so-called Lodge reservations. After the failure of any consent resolution to obtain a two-thirds majority on November 19, Wilson thinks first of challenging his opponents in the Senate to go with him before the voters in a special referendum on the Treaty. When this plan proves to be constitutionally infeasible, Tumulty comes forward with the draft of a letter from Wilson to Democrats on Jackson Day, January 8, 1920, saying that if the Senate will not accept mild interpretive reservations, the Democrats should make the election of 1920 a solemn referendum on the ratification of the Treaty. Wilson eagerly grasps the nettle danger and makes the language of Tumulty's draft even more uncompromising than it was.

Public reaction to the Jackson Day message is so overwhelmingly hostile among both Democrats and Republicans that Tumulty, with the help of Wilson's key advisers, now makes one last great effort to persuade Wilson to accept the intent, if not the exact wording, of the so-called Lodge reservations. On January 15, Tumulty submits a new letter accepting reservations along these lines. At this point, Wilson comes down with a severe viral attack and is either unable to call up enough energy to respond to Tumulty's initiative or else falls back upon his earlier position of no significant concessions. At this very moment, however, a bipartisan group in the Foreign Relations Committee, led by Lodge and Hitchcock, is making substantial progress on a set of compromise reservations. Hopes for a settlement that Wilson can accept are blasted by the bitter-end Republican opponents of the Covenant, who, by threatening to bolt the G.O.P., force Lodge to disrupt the bipartisan conferences and to fall back to his original demand for Wilson's acceptance of his reservations. The only way out of this impasse is a new move by Wilson.

Wilson recovers from his viral infection in late January and, in a state of mild euphoria, moves aggressively to regain control of the presidential office. For the first time since his stroke, he begins to dictate on a regular basis to Swem, although his physical resources are still very limited and his clumsy efforts to put himself in charge reveal an intensified paranoia. His first move is to issue a stinging rebuke to Viscount Grey, the recent British Ambassador to the United States, whom Wilson never received, when Grey, in a letter to the *Times* of London, says that it would be better to have the United States in the League of Nations with the so-called Lodge reservations than to have the United States isolated from the major powers. Next, Wilson discharges Lansing for alleged disloyalty to his policies and attempting to usurp the executive prerogative. Finally, Wilson enters the fray of the settlement of the Adriatic dispute by threatening to withdraw the Versailles Treaty from the Senate if the British and French Prime Ministers make good their announced intention to grant sovereignty over the small Italian section of Fiume, the so-called *corpus separatum*, to Italy.

This is the way things stand as this volume ends.

◇

The decision of Dr. Grayson's surviving sons to provide us with all materials in their father's papers relating to this period has given us an opportunity to print for the first time the records of the person who, except for Mrs. Wilson, stood closest at Wilson's side during these months of his severest disability. We call the reader's special attention to the three reports of Dr. Francis X. Dercum on Wilson's physical condition prepared immediately after the onset of Wilson's stroke. We also call the reader's attention to the brilliant analyses of these reports by Doctors Toole and Park. The significance of the Dercum reports lies in the fact that they give us a retrospective view of Wilson's long struggle with cerebrovascular disease. We think that it can now be said definitively that Wilson had long suffered from carotid artery disease, malignant hypertension, and what is called the lacunar state. Dr. Dercum's reports and other evidence from the Grayson Papers and other sources make it clear for the first time that Wilson, on October 2, 1919, suffered a devastating trauma, one so extensive that it would be impossible for him ever to achieve more than a minimal state of recovery. We would suggest that biographers and historians who have written about Wilson during this period as if he had been a reasonably healthy person, one responsible for his actions, might want to reconsider Wilson's behavior during this period with some understanding of its causes.

We would suggest also that the documents in this and the next two volumes ought to lay at rest the legend, so dear to the heart of many publicists and commentators, that Mrs. Wilson "ran" the government of the United States, particularly during the four or five months following Wilson's stroke. As we have said, Mrs. Wilson did make two decisions with monumentally important political implications: first, that no disclosure of Wilson's true condition should be made; and, second, that Wilson should stay on in the White House until the end of his term. But we have found no evidence that she ever tried to "run" the government or ever really acted other than as Wilson's amanuensis.

◇

We extend our sincere thanks to the persons who have given invaluable assistance in the preparation of this volume: James Gordon Grayson and Cary T. Grayson, Jr.; Timothy Connelly, of the National Historical Publications and Records Commission, for indefatigable research in numerous archives and for supplying us with many of the photographs reproduced in this volume; Dr. Bert E. Park, for his essay on the aftermath of Wilson's stroke; Dr. Park and Dr. James F. Toole, for their analyses of the Dercum reports; Mr. and Mrs. John P. Renshaw, for their permission to reproduce the letters from Wilson to McCombs printed as addenda; John Milton Cooper, Jr., William H. Harbaugh, August Heckscher, Richard W. Leopold, and Betty Miller Unterberger of our Editorial Advisory Committee, for carefully reviewing the manuscript of this volume; and Alice Calaprice, our editor at Princeton University Press, for keeping things on track.

We hereby note the retirement on October 31, 1990, of Mrs. Ilse Mychalchyk, our administrative assistant for the past seven years. We will miss her cheerful presence and remember her dedication to the project. We welcome Nancy Plum as her successor.

David Wayne Hirst, Senior Associate Editor, retired on June 30, 1989, after thirty years of service. He joined *The Papers* as Assistant Editor in 1959 and played a principle role for the next four years in the collection, photocopying, and arranging of the great core of our collection. He became Associate Editor in 1965 and was named Senior Associate Editor in 1979. Not least among his notable contributions to *The Papers* was his continued research, from volume to volume, which added thousands of documents to our series. For his scholarly talents and his dedication and contributions to *The Papers*, the scholarly world will be forever indebted. For his friendship and wise counsel, editors across the country, and particularly we ourselves, will always be grateful. We are fortunate to have him nearby as an active colleague.

THE EDITORS

Princeton, New Jersey
November 1, 1990

CONTENTS

Introduction, vii
Illustrations, xix
Abbreviations and Symbols, xxi

The Papers, November 6, 1919-February 27, 1920
Domestic Affairs

Wilson addresses, statements, and press releases
  Armistice Day statement, November 11, 1919, 7
  Draft of a statement rejecting all reservations to the peace treaty, November 19, 1919, 65
  Annual Message on the State of the Union, December 2, 1919, Tumulty draft, 73; message sent, 106
  Draft of a statement on the need to ratify the peace treaty, December 2, 1919, 118
  Statement on the bituminous coal strike, December 9, 1919, 154
  Statement rejecting compromise on reservations, December 14, 1919, 187
  Executive Order establishing the working hours for per-diem federal employees, December 23, 1919, 218
  Proclamation relinquishing federal control of railroads and transportation systems, December 24, 1919, 226
  Press release establishing March 1, 1920, as the date for relinquishing federal control of railroads, December 24, 1919, 228
  Jackson Day message:
    Tumulty draft, January 6, 1920, 247
    Wilson redraft, January 7, 1920, 252
    Jackson Day letter, January 8, 1920, 257
  Convocation of the first meeting of the League Council, January 12, 1920, 272
  Press release on the letter by Viscount Grey, February 5, 1920, 363
  Remarks at a stag dinner, December 28, 1918, 490

Wilson correspondence
  From Wilson to
    Allen E. Barker, 426
    Elizabeth Merrill Bass, 3
    Carrie Clinton Lane Chapman Catt, 396
    Albert Bacon Fall, 152
    Harry Augustus Garfield, 185
    Carter Glass, 52, 339
    Gilbert Monell Hitchcock, November 18, 1919: Tumulty draft, 15; Wilson's revised draft, 51; January 26, 1920: Tumulty draft, 278; letter sent, 329
    David Franklin Houston, 349
    Bert Mark Jewell and Others, 420
    Franklin Knight Lane, 374, 405
    Robert Lansing, 383, 404, 413, 414
    Russell Cornell Leffingwell, 361
    John Llewellyn Lewis, 179
    William C. Liller, 515
    Breckinridge Long, 352
    William Frank McCombs, 521, 522 (3), 523 (3), 524

Frank Lyon Polk, 464
Henry Mauris Robinson, 206
Joseph Patrick Tumulty, 351, 475
Tom C. Waldrep and Martin Edwin Trapp, 466
William Bauchop Wilson, 64
To Wilson from
Joshua Willis Alexander, 142
Newton Diehl Baker, 436
Albert Bacon Fall, 140
Harry Augustus Garfield, 145, 146, 180, 181, 186
Carter Glass, 41, 60, 349, 387, 410
Samuel Gompers and Others, 197
Walker Downer Hines, 188, 223, 406, 411, 467
Gilbert Monell Hitchcock, 70, 93, 312, 466
Edward Mandell House, 89, 96
David Franklin Houston, 349, 475
Bert Mark Jewell and Others, 428
Franklin Knight Lane, 373, 392
Robert Lansing, 41, 91, 103, 167, 183, 310, 388, 408
Russell Cornell Leffingwell, 362
John Llewellyn Lewis, 180
Breckinridge Long, 352
Vance Criswell McCormick, 95
Edwin Thomas Meredith, 330
Alexander Mitchell Palmer, 179, 214, 222
Gifford Pinchot, 354
Henry Mauris Robinson, 246, 393
William Graves Sharp, 285
Thetus Wilrette Sims, 195
Joseph Patrick Tumulty, 15, 238, 467, 479, 480
Oscar Wilder Underwood, 69

Collateral correspondence
Albert Sidney Burleson to Edith Bolling Galt Wilson, 338
Maurice Brice Clagett to Joseph Patrick Tumulty, 21
Frank Irving Cobb to Edith Bolling Galt Wilson, 66
Norman Hezekiah Davis to Joseph Patrick Tumulty, 104
Rudolph Forster to Edith Bolling Galt Wilson, 426
Walker Downer Hines to Joseph Patrick Tumulty, 21, 24
Gilbert Monell Hitchcock to Joseph Patrick Tumulty, 283, 288, 327
Gilbert Monell Hitchcock to Edith Bolling Galt Wilson, 28, 37, 50, 58, 244, 273
Edward Mandell House to Edith Bolling Galt Wilson, 88, 95
Robert Lansing to Frank Lyon Polk, 54
Breckinridge Long to Edith Bolling Galt Wilson, 350
Alexander Mitchell Palmer to Joseph Patrick Tumulty, 215, 296
Key Pittman to Cary Travers Grayson, 127
Henry Mauris Robinson to Edith Bolling Galt Wilson, 392
Oscar Solomon Straus to Joseph Patrick Tumulty, 384
Joseph Patrick Tumulty to Josephus Daniels, 10
Joseph Patrick Tumulty to John Sharp Williams, 156
Joseph Patrick Tumulty to Edith Bolling Galt Wilson, 6, 14, 16, 42, 69, 72,

90, 93, 103, 153, 203, 204, 214, 222, 246, 276, 282, 287, 345, 353, 355,
  391, 396, 419, 467, 473, 474, 475, 480
Thomas James Walsh to Gilbert Monell Hitchcock, 59
Edith Bolling Galt Wilson to Albert Sidney Burleson, 336, 343
Edith Bolling Galt Wilson to Rudolph Forster, 426
Edith Bolling Galt Wilson to Harry Augustus Garfield, 167
Edith Bolling Galt Wilson to Carter Glass, 405
Edith Bolling Galt Wilson to Gilbert Monell Hitchcock, 206 (2), 243, 274
Edith Bolling Galt Wilson to Thomas Davies Jones, 232
Edith Bolling Galt Wilson to Robert Lansing, 119 (2), 389
Edith Bolling Galt Wilson to Alexander Mitchell Palmer, 202
Edith Bolling Galt Wilson to Joseph Patrick Tumulty, 4, 16, 97, 145, 198,
  330, 448
Edith Bolling Galt Wilson to the White House Staff, 322

Notes, reports, and memoranda
  Memorandum by Cary Travers Grayson on a conference between Wilson
    and Gilbert Monell Hitchcock about the treaty situation in the Senate, 43
  Memorandum by Cary Travers Grayson about Wilson's conference with Al-
    bert Bacon Fall and Gilbert Monell Hitchcock, 135
  Memorandum by Cary Travers Grayson on a conversation with Wilson
    about the appointment of Bainbridge Colby, 472
  Miscellaneous notes and memoranda by Cary Travers Grayson, 485, 486,
    487, 488, 490
  Memorandum by Cary Travers Grayson on his testimony at the first Cabinet
    meeting during Wilson's illness, 496
  Draft by Walker Downer Hines of a message to Congress on the railroad
    situation, 17
  Proposed substitute reservations to the peace treaty by Gilbert Monell
    Hitchcock, 29
  Compromise reservation on Article X by Gilbert Monell Hitchcock, 313
  Notes and memoranda by David Franklin Houston about Tumulty's draft of
    a Jackson Day message, 251
  Memorandum by Robert Lansing on Wilson's capacity to perform his offi-
    cial duties, 123
  Memorandum by Robert Lansing on the implications of Wilson's interview
    with Senators Fall and Hitchcock, 139
  Memoranda by Robert Lansing on his desire to resign from the Cabi-
    net, 179, 255, 385
  Memorandum by Robert Lansing on Wilson's refusal to compromise in the
    treaty fight, 192
  Memorandum by Robert Lansing on Wilson's Jackson Day message, 267
  Memorandum by Robert Lansing on his resignation, 415
  Memorandum by Robert Lansing on the "Frazier affair," 451
  Memorandum by Robert Lansing on the Cabinet meetings held during
    Wilson's illness, 454
  Reservations to the peace treaty by Henry Cabot Lodge, 38, 289
  Memorandum by Joseph Patrick Tumulty on a conversation with Wilson
    about the Jackson Day Dinner, 261
  Notes by Edith Bolling Galt Wilson on Wilson's conference with Senators
    Fall and Hitchcock, 133
  List by Wilson and Edith Bolling Galt Wilson of senators opposed to unre-
    served ratification of the Versailles Treaty, 336

Draft by Wilson of a public challenge to the senators opposed to the peace treaty, 199

Memoranda and statements on Wilson's medical condition
    Memoranda by Francis Xavier Dercum, 500
    Statements by Cary Travers Grayson, 497, 511
    Memorandum by Cary Travers Grayson, 507

News reports
    "President Still Gaining," November 8, 1919, 4
    "President, Able to Sit Up, Enjoys an Evening Serenade," November 11, 1919, 6
    "Prince Sees Wilson," November 14, 1919, 31
    "President on Porch in a Wheeled Chair," November 14, 1919, 32
    "Remarkable Improvements by President in Two Weeks," November 15, 1919, 37
    "President Will Pocket Treaty if Passed as Modified," November 17, 1919, 45
    "President Out on Lawn for First Time Since Return," November 17, 1919, 50
    "President, Outdoors Again, Holds Informal Lawn Party," November 18, 1919, 57
    "Hitchcock Called to White House on Treaty Fight," November 24, 1919, 71
    "President Has Thanksgiving Dinner in Bed," November 27, 1919, 93
    "Fails to See Wilson. Hitchcock, at the White House, Waits Vainly for Audience," November 30, 1919, 99
    "President's Health Shows Steady Improvement," December 2, 1919, 105
    "Wilson to See Senators," December 4, 1919, 120
    "Wilson Won't Act on Treaty Now," December 5, 1919, 126
    "Senators See President," December 5, 1919, 129
    "President Jests on Moses Story," December 5, 1919, 132
    "President Makes Proposal to Coal Miners," December 7, 1919, 142
    "Wilson Won't Agree to Lodge Program," December 9, 1919, 165
    "Wilson Walks; Not Paralyzed," December 14, 1919, 187
    "Wilson Reported Much Better; Dercum Stops Regular Visits," December 20, 1919, 211
    "No Third Term Ambition. Wilson Has No Idea of Running Again, Says Palmer," January 10, 1920, 267
    "President's Health Shows Steady Improvement," January 20, 1920, 307
    "Senate Conferees Near Compromise on Resolutions," January 22, 1920, 311
    "Wilson for Peace Prize," January 29, 1920, 342
    "Wilson Narrowly Escapes Influenza," February 3, 1920, 351
    "Wilson, Recovered from Cold, is out on Portico in Storm," February 4, 1920, 361
    "Sees President Near Recovery. Improvement Slow, Sure and Steady, Says Dr. Young of Johns Hopkins," February 10, 1920, 394
    "Public Diagnosis Vexes President," February 11, 1920, 403
    "Dercum Won't Talk," February 11, 1920, 403
    "President Shows Old Form in Talk with Railroad Men," February 13, 1920, 420
    "President Will Never Recover, Is View of Dr. Bevan," February 15, 1920, 432

"Dr. Dercum Declares Mind of President Wilson is Keen, Denying Relapse," February 15, 1920, 433
"Grayson Reports President Still Gaining," February 17, 1920, 435

Diaries
Henry Fountain Ashurst, 62, 252, 256, 263, 384
Ray Stannard Baker, 61, 320, 359, 362, 365, 385, 434
Homer Stillé Cummings, 427
Josephus Daniels, 122, 141, 166, 216, 222
Edward Mandell House, 182, 184, 217, 231, 239, 243, 270, 347, 360, 444
Robert Lansing, 3 (2), 36, 50, 167, 235, 274, 276, 282, 296, 310, 316, 353, 366, 383, 385, 386, 398, 405, 414, 428

Diplomatic, Military, and Naval Affairs

Diplomatic notes
A British-French-American proposal for settlement of the Adriatic dispute, 168
An Anglo-French proposal for settlement of the Adriatic dispute, 264
An Anglo-French-Italian agreement for settlement of the Adriatic question, 298
A note by the Yugoslav government protesting against the Anglo-French-Italian agreement on the Adriatic question, 304
Draft by Lloyd George of a telegram from the Supreme Council on the question of trade with Russia, 308
A protest by the United States Government against the unilateral decisions taken by Great Britain and France on the Adriatic question, 320
A reply by David Lloyd George and Georges Clemenceau to the American protest against a lack of consultation on the Adriatic question, 318
A reply by the Yugoslav government to the Anglo-French-Italian proposal for a settlement of the Adriatic dispute, 331
A note by the Supreme Council on the opening of peace negotiations with Turkey, 344
A protest by the United States Government against the Anglo-French-Italian proposal for a settlement of the Adriatic dispute, 375 (draft), 398
A reply by the British and French governments to the American protest against the Anglo-French-Italian agreement on the Adriatic question, 436
A note by the United States Government affirming its opposition to the Anglo-French-Italian agreement on the Adriatic question, Wilson draft, 445; note sent, 459
A note by the British and French governments emphasizing the possibility of the implementation of the Treaty of London as the only alternative to a speedy settlement of the Adriatic dispute, 481

Wilson correspondence
From Wilson to
Newton Diehl Baker, 375
Julius Howland Barnes, 13, 14
Robert Lansing, 361, 375, 408
Frank Lyon Polk, 445, 448, 470
To Wilson from
Francisco Aguilar Barquero, 153
Newton Diehl Baker, 389
Louis Dembitz Brandeis, 358

Norman Hezekiah Davis, 11, 478
Raymond Blaine Fosdick, 274
Friedrich Wilhelm Viktor August Ernst, 397
Douglas Wilson Johnson, 368
Robert Lansing, 8, 25, 34, 66, 117, 127, 148, 153, 186, 190, 210, 212,
    216, 219, 236, 239, 260 (2), 261, 272, 298, 307, 313, 340, 344, 367,
    371, 372 (2), 380, 381, 382, 390, 407
Frank Lyon Polk, 323, 331, 436, 443, 446, 448, 450, 458, 464, 468, 472,
    480, 483
Joseph Patrick Tumulty, 7, 473
Antoine Velleman and Others, 97
Eleuthérios Kyrios Vénisélos, 157

Collateral correspondence
Julius Howland Barnes to Joseph Patrick Tumulty, 5, 12, 13
Austen Chamberlain to David Franklin Houston (extract), 477
Gilbert Fairchild Close to Edith Bolling Galt Wilson, 297
Richard Crane to the Department of State, 443
Norman Hezekiah Davis to Albert Rathbone, 12
Norman Hezekiah Davis to Joseph Patrick Tumulty, 33
John William Davis to Robert Lansing, 88, 381
Ellis Loring Dresel to Robert Lansing, 364
Raymond Blaine Fosdick to Sir Eric Drummond, 306
Raymond Blaine Fosdick to Joseph Patrick Tumulty, 306
Viscount Grey of Fallodon to Robert Lansing, 33
Edward Mandell House to Edith Bolling Galt Wilson, 53
Douglas Wilson Johnson to Arthur James Balfour (draft), 370
Robert Underwood Johnson to Robert Lansing, 343
Jean Jules Jusserand to Robert Lansing, 101
Alexander Comstock Kirk to Cary Travers Grayson, 90
Robert Lansing to Cary Travers Grayson, 88
Robert Lansing to Jean Jules Jusserand, 102
Robert Lansing to Frank Lyon Polk, 36, 156
Robert Lansing to Joseph Patrick Tumulty, 5, 66, 94, 187, 273
Robert Lansing to Hugh Campbell Wallace, 320, 342, 373, 398
Robert Lansing to Edith Bolling Galt Wilson, 147, 316, 343, 366, 391, 407
David Lloyd George to Viscount Grey of Fallodon, 33
Breckinridge Long to Joseph Patrick Tumulty, 234
William Phillips to Joseph Patrick Tumulty, 157
Frank Lyon Polk to Robert Lansing, 35, 91, 117, 150, 168
Frank Lyon Polk to Joseph Patrick Tumulty, 229
Frank Lyon Polk to Hugh Campbell Wallace, 411, 465
Leo Stanton Rowe to Joseph Patrick Tumulty, 245
Joseph Patrick Tumulty to Raymond Blaine Fosdick, 286, 310
Joseph Patrick Tumulty to Robert Lansing, 87, 91, 153, 182
Joseph Patrick Tumulty to Edith Bolling Galt Wilson, 4, 10, 65, 103, 190,
    233, 245, 358, 397 (2)
Hugh Campbell Wallace to Robert Lansing, 263, 298, 300, 303 (3), 314,
    315, 318, 331, 341
Edith Bolling Galt Wilson to Robert Lansing, 100, 156, 218, 228, 296, 322,
    335, 346, 352, 366
Edith Bolling Galt Wilson to John Barton Payne, 218
Edith Bolling Galt Wilson to Joseph Patrick Tumulty, 87, 97
Sir William Wiseman to Edward Mandell House, 53

Memoranda, reports, and aide-mémoire
  Memorandum by Norman Hezekiah Davis on a British proposal for the cancellation of inter-Allied war debts, 476
  Memorandum by the Division of Western European Affairs on the Anglo-French-Italian proposal for the settlement of the Adriatic dispute, 301
  Memorandum by Robert Lansing on the *Imperator* shipping controversy, 8
  Memorandum by Robert Lansing on issues concerning the Turkish settlement, 25
  Memorandum by Robert Lansing on diplomatic matters requiring Wilson's immediate attention, 65
  Memorandum by Robert Lansing for the Japanese Ambassador on the withdrawal of American troops from Siberia, 219
  Memorandum by William Phillips on diplomatic matters awaiting Wilson's consideration, 52

Personal Affairs

Wilson correspondence
  From Wilson to
    Albert, King of the Belgians, 31, 230
    Alexandra, the Queen Mother, 28, 237
    Gilbert Fairchild Close, 344
    Winthrop More Daniels, 514
    Frederick A. Duneka, 514
    Edward, Prince of Wales, 237
    George V, 231
    James Henry Henderlite, 213
    John Grier Hibben, 213, 519 (2), 520 (2), 521 (2)
    Lucy Day Martin, 24
    William Joseph Martin, 213
    Charles Wellman Mitchell, 515, 516 (3), 517 (2), 518 (4), 519 (2)
    Grace Linzee Revere Gross Osler, 237
    Thomas Ridley, 184
    Woodrow Wilson Sayre, 451
    South Trimble, 97
    Mrs. Young, 214
  To Wilson from
    Albert, King of the Belgians, 30, 61, 230
    Alexandra, the Queen Mother, 27, 235
    Edward, Prince of Wales, 71
    Maurice Francis Egan, 474
    George V, 42, 230
    James Cardinal Gibbons, 237
    John Grier Hibben, 246
    Edward Mandell House, 53
    Robert Lansing, 229
    William Phillips, 204
    Frank Lyon Polk, 227
    Joseph Patrick Tumulty, 233

Collateral correspondence
  Ray Stannard Baker to Edith Bolling Galt Wilson, 326
  Charles Richard Crane to Edith Bolling Galt Wilson, 262, 425
  Francis Xavier Dercum to Cary Travers Grayson, 435, 500

Edward, Prince of Wales, to Edith Bolling Galt Wilson, 36
Cary Travers Grayson to Stockton Axson, 324
Cary Travers Grayson to William Gibbs McAdoo, 492
Cary Travers Grayson to Louis Seibold, 495
William Joseph Martin to Edith Bolling Galt Wilson, 191
Louis Seibold to Cary Travers Grayson, 494
Edith Bolling Galt Wilson to Ray Stannard Baker, 335
Edith Bolling Galt Wilson to Edward Mandell House, 61
Edith Bolling Galt Wilson to Frank Lyon Polk, 235
Edith Bolling Galt Wilson to John Wesley Wescott, 232

Appendix: The Aftermath of Wilson's Stroke (Park), 525
Index, 529

ILLUSTRATIONS

Following page 266

WILSON'S PHYSICIANS

Cary Travers Grayson, on leaving the White House on February 19, 1920
Library of Congress

Francis Xavier Dercum
Thomas Jefferson University

George Edmund De Schweinitz
Princeton University Library

Hugh Hampton Young
Alan Mason Chesney Medical Archives, Johns Hopkins University

Edward Rhodes Stitt
The Stitt Library, National Naval Medical Center

Harry Atwood Fowler
Library of Congress

Sterling Ruffin
Library of Congress

John Chalmers Da Costa
Thomas Jefferson University

◇

Robert Lansing about the time of his resignation
Library of Congress

ABBREVIATIONS

A.C.N.P.	American Commission to Negotiate Peace
A.E.F.	American Expeditionary Forces
AL	autograph letter
ALI	autograph letter initialed
ALS	autograph letter signed
AMP	Alexander Mitchell Palmer
CC	carbon copy
CCL	carbon copy of letter
CLST	Charles Lee Swem typed
EAW	Ellen Axson Wilson
EBW	Edith Bolling Galt Wilson
EBWhw	Edith Bolling Galt Wilson handwriting, handwritten
EMH	Edward Mandell House
FKL	Franklin Knight Lane
FLP	Frank Lyon Polk
FR	*Papers Relating to the Foreign Relations of the United States*
GMH	Gilbert Monell Hitchcock
Hw, hw	handwriting, handwritten
JD	Josephus Daniels
JPT	Joseph Patrick Tumulty
MS, MSS	manuscript, manuscripts
PPC	*Papers Relating to the Foreign Relations of the United States, The Paris Peace Conference, 1919*
RG	record group
RL	Robert Lansing
T	typed
TC	typed copy
TCL	typed copy of letter
TI	typed initialed
TLI	typed letter initialed
TLS	typed letter signed
TS	typed signed
WBW	William Bauchop Wilson
WW	Woodrow Wilson
WWhw	Woodrow Wilson handwriting, handwritten
WWTLS	Woodrow Wilson typed letter signed

ABBREVIATIONS FOR COLLECTIONS AND REPOSITORIES

Following the National Union Catalog of the
Library of Congress

AzU	University of Arizona
CSmH	Henry E. Huntington Library
CSt-H	Hoover Institution on War, Revolution and Peace
CtY	Yale University
DLC	Library of Congress
DNA	National Archives

IGK	Knox College
LDR	Labor Department Records
MdHi	Maryland Historical Society
NcDaD	Davidson College
NjP	Princeton University
NjP-Ar	Princeton Univerity Archives
RSB Coll., DLC	Ray Stannard Baker Collection of Wilsoniana, Library of Congress
SDR	State Department Records
ViU	University of Virginia
WC, NjP	Woodrow Wilson Collection, Princeton University
WP, DLC	Woodrow Wilson Papers, Library of Congress

SYMBOLS

[January 6, 1920]	publication date of published writing; also date of document when date is not part of text
[*December 5, 1919*]	composition date when publication date differs
[[February 12, 1920]]	delivery date of speech when publication date differs
* * * * * * *	text deleted by author of document

THE PAPERS OF

WOODROW WILSON

VOLUME 64

NOVEMBER 6, 1919–FEBRUARY 27, 1920

THE PAPERS OF
WOODROW WILSON

From the Desk Diary of Robert Lansing

Thursday Nov 6 [1919]

British Amb. on Stuart case.[1] Long discussion. He agree[d] to have his name removed from Dip. List & that he not appear at receptions. Charges to be further investigated. Discussed reservations before Senate. To go into matter tomorrow.

Hw bound diary (R. Lansing Papers, DLC).
[1] About which, see n. 1 to the extract from the Lansing Desk Diary printed at Oct. 30, 1919, Vol. 63.

To Elizabeth Merrill Bass

My dear Mrs. Bass: [The White House] November 7, 1919.

The book on the war work of women in America has my endorsement and I am sure that the members of the Cabinet will be equally interested and will do all in their power to assist Mrs. Taylor in the collection of material for the history.[1]

Cordially and sincerely yours,   Woodrow Wilson

TLS (Letterpress Books, WP, DLC).
[1] Mrs. Bass' letter is missing. Mrs. Taylor was Clara Sears (Mrs. Eugene Whitman) Taylor, journalist of Washington, formerly director of the Division of Women's War Work of the Committee on Public Information. Her projected book on the war work of American women was never published.

From the Desk Diary of Robert Lansing

Friday Nov 7 [1919]

Lord Grey by appointment. We went over in detail the reservations in Com. rept. Many of them are very objectionable.

Cabinet meeting—11-12:45. Coal strike.[1] Hines and Garfield present.

Lunch—12:50-1:50. Phillips tells me Hitchcock sure he can kill reservations. After that, time to propose modified reservations.

[1] About which, see n. 1 to the excerpt from the Daniels Diary printed at Dec. 5, 1919.

A News Report

[*Nov. 8, 1919*]

PRESIDENT STILL GAINING.
Grayson Says Visiting Physicians
Note General Improvement.

Washington, Nov. 8.—Dr. Francis X. Dercum, of Philadelphia, paid his regular weekly visit to President Wilson today and held a consultation with Rear-Admirals Grayson and Stitt and Dr. Sterling Ruffin of this city.

After the consultation Admiral Grayson said the visiting physicians were well satisfied with the President's condition and noted a general improvement.

Two bills, one providing indemnity to Colorado citizens whose arms and ammunition were seized by Federal troops during the 1914 coal strike[1] and the other providing for reclamation of arid Nevada lands, became law today with the President's signature.

A number of minor measures also became effective without the President's signature, including that extending Federal steam vessel regulations to Shipping Board vessels and that granting lands for school purposes on Government town sites.

Printed in the *New York Times*, Nov. 9, 1919.
  [1] About this strike, see the index references under "Colorado coal strike" in Vol. 39 of this series.

Edith Bolling Galt Wilson to Joseph Patrick Tumulty, with Enclosures

The White House [Nov. 10, 1919].

The President says tell Mr. Barnes to draw up the proper form of authorization & send it for the President's signature   EBW

ALI (WP, DLC).

E N C L O S U R E   I

Joseph Patrick Tumulty to Edith Bolling Galt Wilson

My dear Mrs. Wilson: The White House 10 November 1919.

You can see how vital is the attached request of the Secretary of State with reference to the relief of Poland.

I hope you can get the President to O.K. this as soon as possible.
                              Sincerely yours,   Tumulty

TLS (WP, DLC).

ENCLOSURE II

Julius Howland Barnes to Joseph Patrick Tumulty

My dear Mr. Secretary: New York October 31, 1919

There will undoubtedly be brought up to you for the President the matter of wheat and wheat flour to Poland. For instance, I enclose you copies of two cables received in this office and you will note that a cable has been sent to the American Polish Mission, and will probably come to you through the State Department.

Mr. Hoover and myself feel that possibly 100,000 tons immediate shipment is more than they actually need for relief of their pressing requirements. More than that, as you know in the case of supplies for non-Bolshevik Russia, my position must be that, since there is an element of economic aid in this, and not a pure matter of commercial operation, that the credit discretion lodged with the Wheat Director ought not to be exercised without the approval and direction of the President, himself.

I quite realize that if the condition is as this cable indicates, and I have no evidence to the contrary, that it would be a serious matter to refuse them this accommodation.

Will you please develop the matter as it is presented to you and call on me for such information or advice as may be desired?
                              Sincerely,   Julius H. Barnes.

TLS (WP, DLC).

ENCLOSURE III

Robert Lansing to Joseph Patrick Tumulty

Dear Mr. Tumulty: Washington November 7, 1919.

With reference to your letter of November 1st, enclosing a letter from Mr. Julius H. Barnes which I return herewith, the Department has received a telegram from Paris dated November 4th, copy of which has been sent to the President, saying that our Minister at Warsaw[1] reports that Paderewski has great difficulty in preserving a majority in the Diet. Mr. Polk feels, and I concur, that our Government should do all it can to strengthen Paderewski's hands and it is quite possible that the fall of his Government may bring about a very dangerous situation in Poland.

In view of the above, I hope that it will be found possible to authorize Mr. Barnes to grant immediate shipment to Poland of the hundred thousand tons of grain which that Government desires, as I deem this of great importance for the peace of eastern Europe.

The Department has already spoken to Mr. Barnes on the telephone in regard to this matter. He states he is willing to accede to the Polish request if he receives the necessary authority from the President.

I am, my dear Mr. Tumulty,
                          Sincerely yours,   Robert Lansing

TLS (WP, DLC).
¹ That is, Hugh Simons Gibson.

Joseph Patrick Tumulty to Edith Bolling Galt Wilson

My dear Mrs. Wilson: The White House 10 November 1919.

Congress will convene in new session on the first day of December, and the President will be required to forward his Message on the day after the opening. Will you please remind him of this?
                          Sincerely yours,   [J P Tumulty]

CCL (J. P. Tumulty Papers, DLC).

A News Report

[Nov. 11, 1919]

President, Able to Sit Up,
Enjoys an Evening Serenade

Washington, Nov. 11.—For the first time since he returned from the West, ill from overwork, President Wilson today sat up in a wheel chair in his room at the White House.

The President remained in his wheel chair for an hour with the consent of his physicians and is declared to have been none the worse for his experience.

Tonight a chorus of community singers gathered on the steps of the Treasury across from the White House to serenade Mr. Wilson.

The President had planned some days in advance to leave his sickbed today as in some measure his own commemoration of the significance of Armistice Day, and reposing in a wheel chair was able to hear part of the program arranged by the singers in his honor.

The President asked to be permitted to sit up for a while after he heard the firing of shots from Lafayette Square, where a salute was being given as part of a celebration of Armistice Day. The President inquired about the firing and when he learned that Armistice Day was being celebrated he informed Rear Admiral Cary T. Grayson, his physician, that he was unable longer to remain in bed with such a celebration in progress.

Printed in the *New York Times*, Nov. 12, 1919.

An Armistice Day Statement[1]

The White House, 11 November, 1919.

To my Fellow-countrymen:

A year ago today our enemies laid down their arms in accordance with an armistice which rendered them impotent to renew hostilities, and gave to the world an assured opportunity to reconstruct its shattered order and to work out in peace a new and juster set of international relations. The soldiers and people of the European Allies had fought and endured for more than four years to uphold the barrier of civilization against the aggressions of armed force. We ourselves had been in the conflict something more than a year and a half.

With splendid forgetfulness of mere personal concerns we remodeled our industries, concentrated our financial resources, increased our agricultural output, and assembled a great army, so that at the last our power was a decisive factor in the victory. We were able to bring the vast resources, material and moral, of a great and free people to the assistance of our associates in Europe, who had suffered and sacrificed without limit in the cause for which we fought.

Out of this victory there arose new possibilities of political freedom and economic concert. The war showed us the strength of great nations acting together for high purposes, and the victory of arms foretells the enduring conquests which can be made in peace when nations act justly and in furtherance of the common interests of men. To us in America, the reflections of Armistice Day will be filled with solemn pride in the heroism of those who died in the country's service, and with gratitude for the victory, both because of the thing from which it has freed us and because of the opportunity it has given America to show her sympathy with peace and justice in the councils of nations.   Woodrow Wilson.

Printed in the *New York Times*, Nov. 11, 1919.
[1] Tumulty or Newton D. Baker undoubtedly wrote this statement. There are no drafts of it in WP, DLC, or in the J. P. Tumulty Papers, DLC, and the N. D. Baker Papers, DLC.

From Joseph Patrick Tumulty, with Enclosures

Dear Governor: [The White House] 11 November, 1919

I have talked to Mr. Davis,[1] and he thinks that we only ought to consent to the immediate return of the "Imperator," and to hold the others for what he calls "trading purposes on the other side." He says you will understand.   Sincerely yours,   Tumulty

The President says he does not know enough about this matter to act upon it & directs that no action be taken until he is well enough to act upon it[2]

TLS (WP, DLC).
  [1] That is, Norman H. Davis.
  [2] EBWhw.

E N C L O S U R E   I

From Robert Lansing

My dear Mr. President: Washington November 5, 1919.

The retention of the IMPERATOR group of ships by the Shipping Board in retaliation for alleged arbitrary action by Great Britain in regard to certain German tankers is causing such friction in our relations with Great Britain that I feel it my duty to call it to your attention.

The matter is explained in the attached memorandum. It was thoroughly discussed in a cabinet meeting at which Judge Payne was present and it was unanimously agreed by the cabinet that the retention of the IMPERATOR group of ships was indefensible and tended to discredit the honor of the United States and the pledged word of its President. The cabinet felt, however, that it could take no action on account of the Shipping Board's position that it was responsible for its acts to you alone.

I consider it of urgent importance in the carrying on of our international relations that the cabinet or myself be empowered by you to require the Shipping Board to transfer the IMPERATOR and other ships of the group to Great Britain or the powers now entitled thereto.

I am,   Your obedient servant,   Robert Lansing

TLS (WP, DLC).

E N C L O S U R E   I I

CONFIDENTIAL

IMPERATOR SHIPPING CONTROVERSY

1. The boats in question are the IMPERATOR, PATRICIA, PRINZ FREDERIC WILHELM, GRAF WALDERSEE, MOBILE and PRETORIA.

2. *History.* These ships at the time of the Armistice were in German ports and were handed over under Brussels Agreement to the A.M.T.E.[1] They were allocated to the United States for repatriation

purposes, understood clearly to be for the repatriation of American troops. In May last an agreement was entered into between President Wilson and Mr. Lloyd George which provided that in consideration of the British recognizing our right to the ships taken at our ports during the war, the United States would give up claim to a share in the final allocation of ships that had been taken from German ports.

On the near completion of rapatriation [repatriation] needs, pursuant to the policy of the Wilson-Lloyd George agreement, the Interim Reparations Commission, at the instance of the American delegates, instructed the A.M.T.E. to plan subsequent provisional allocation of these and other ships on the same basis on which they would be finally allocated. Such a policy was agreed to by the Shipping Board and notification on August 11 was sent to the A.M.T.E. by Judge Payne that the United States did not wish to manage these ships after repatriation needs were satisfied. On written advice of the Shipping Board the War Department was preparing to deliver these ships direct to the transferees appointed by the A.M.T.E. and had notified the A.M.T.E. that the IMPERATOR would be ready for delivery on September 20, and the other boats at different dates all before the 5th of October.

On September 26th, however, the War Department was informed that the Shipping Board would take delivery of the ships themselves, stating no reason for the change of policy. Information was received on the 13th that three of the ships, including the IMPERATOR, had been passed by a joint board of survey as being completely reconditioned and were ready for delivery. The Shipping Board informed the Department that they were taking delivery of the IMPERATOR and other boats on the 14th

Crews for all these boats were sent over here on the basis of the Shipping Board's promise of redelivery of August 11. Great Britain has been caused great inconvenience and expense on account of the difficulty and costs of maintaining these crews in New York. The Shipping Board and the Department did their best to supply quarters for these crews on Ellis Island but the crews refused to go there. It is to be noted that a bill may be rendered to the United States for the expense of maintenance of these crews as a result of the breach of the agreement to hand over the boats.

The Department of State has been orally informed by the Shipping Board that they wish to hold the IMPERATOR group of ships as an act of retaliation for the action of Great Britain in reference to the German tankers and other acts of the British Shipping Ministry. They have further stated that they desire to hold the ships for passenger service under the American flag. They have been instructed that retention of the ships would involve a breach of an agreement made by them and be contrary to the policy formally agreed to by President Wilson and Mr. Lloyd George and further that such an act would be of exceedingly serious nature and highly discreditable to the honor of the United States and its President. In addition it was pointed out to the Board that although the tanker situation was brought to a head by an irregular act of a British official, such act has been ratified by the decision of the Supreme Council in Paris and is now, therefore, an act of the Allied and Associated Powers and agreed to by Mr. Polk and cannot afford justification for a retaliation directed alone against Great Britain.

Three strong notes of protest have been addressed to the Government by the British Embassy.

The Shipping Board has promised to transfer the IMPERATOR and the other ships of the group after they have been used for repatriating Czecho-Slovak troops from Siberia, provided the German tankers are transferred to the American flag. The British have not agreed to this proposal, however, on the ground that it is an attempt to bargain with something to which they are unconditionally entitled.

T MS (WP, DLC).
   [1] The Allied Maritime Transport Executive, or Council. About the Brussels Agreement, see EMH to WW, March 7, 1919, n. 1, Vol. 55.

Joseph Patrick Tumulty to Edith Bolling Galt Wilson, with Enclosure

Dear Mrs. Wilson: The White House, 11 November, 1919

Norman Davis is anxious to know what the President's decision is in the Rathbun [Rathbone] matter. Would you please call it to the President's attention, when you think best?

J P Tumulty C.L.S.

O.K.[1]

TL (WP, DLC).
   [1] EBWhw.

E N C L O S U R E

From Norman Hezekiah Davis

Washington, October 30, 1919.

MEMORANDUM FOR THE PRESIDENT:

As you will notice from attached cables from Messrs. Polk and Rathbone,[1] the British and Belgians have informally requested that the American representative accept the Chairmanship of the Reparation Commission. While they only desire to know whether or not we would accept the Chairmanship after the ratification of the Treaty, I do not feel justified, in view of the importance of such a step and of the attitude of the Foreign Relations Committee of the Senate, in giving any reply without your approval.

My feeling is, that unless the governments represented on the Reparation Commission are willing to adopt a broad, constructive policy and, within six months, agree upon a definite reasonable amount which Germany shall be called upon to pay, as contemplated in the interchange of notes with Germany before the Treaty was signed, then the work of the Reparation Commission will be doomed to failure. As France, for political and other reasons, apparently will be reluctant to adopt such a policy, and as the Chairman will thus be placed in a position of opposing France by pressing for the adoption of such a policy, we might consequently receive more unwarranted criticism and hostility than would be the case if we were not at the head of the Commission. If, however, our Government is convinced that it can do more good by accepting the Chairmanship than by refusing, it is doubtful whether we should refuse because of any unpopularity that might result therefrom.

I am of the opinion that the leaders of the French Government now fully realize the impossibility of collecting from Germany anything like what they have expected; that they will not collect anything of importance unless they fix a definite amount considerably smaller than their published estimates of what Germany can be made to pay; and that the financial stability of the world will require a definite early settlement of Germany's reparation liability. At the same time, I am fearful that they will hold out against such a policy, in an endeavor to force England and the United States to cancel the sums France owes them, in view of France's inability to collect from Germany anything like what she has expected.

For this reason, therefore, it would, in my opinion, be most important that we should not appear as imposing our will upon the Commission, but that if we accept the Chairmanship it should only be upon the official request of all concerned, made after the Treaty is ratified.

The Senate will probably not take any action which would prevent our accepting the Chairmanship of the Commission, unless it should be prematurely and inadvisedly announced that America had consented to accept the post.

I am attaching a proposed cable to Mr. Rathbone[2] embodying the substance of this memorandum which I shall send, if it meets with your approval.[3]   Norman H. Davis

TS MS (WP, DLC).
[1] FLP to RL, Oct. 27, 1919, and A. Rathbone to N. H. Davis, Oct. 24, 1919, both T telegrams (WP, DLC).
[2] "In view of the fact that the Senate has not ratified the Treaty, our friends will undoubtedly understand the position in which we are placed and the impossibility of giving a definite decision at this time as to the Chairmanship of Reparation Commission. If, however, after the Treaty has been ratified, an official request is made by all the governments concerned, possibly including Germany, the President would probably feel inclined in the interest of harmony and the general welfare of the situation, to accede to the request of the various interested parties that the United States accept the Chairmanship." N. H. Davis to A. Rathbone, Oct. 30, 1919, CC MS (WP, DLC).
[3] A JPThw notation on his letter to Mrs. Wilson says that the proposed cable was "Ok'd" by Wilson and returned to Davis on November 13.

Julius Howland Barnes to Joseph Patrick Tumulty, with Enclosure

My dear Mr. Secretary: New York November 11, 1919

In response to your letter of November 10th, I enclose you, for the President's signature, authority to supply the Republic of Poland with 100,000 tons of breadstuffs on credit.

I return you, also, the correspondence, including that from the State Department, on this matter as per your request.

I assume from your letter that the President has already expressed approval of this and will therefore execute the order and that you will return the order to me, immediately, so executed. I will take steps at once to try and arrange immediate shipment.

I ventured to advise Herbert Hoover to-day that, from your letter I think it safe to assume that the President does so approve and have asked Mr. Hoover in negotiations already started with the Polish representative here to arrange some method of paying the ocean transportation, which we are hopeful of doing, immediately.

Thank you, heartily, for facilitating these matters and particularly appreciate the attention the President has given this.
                            Sincerely,   Julius H. Barnes.

TLS (WP, DLC).

E N C L O S U R E

**PROPOSED LETTER FROM THE PRESIDENT TO MR. BARNES
REGARDING POLISH FOODSTUFFS.**

My dear Mr. Barnes:

It has been brought to my attention that the Polish Government has made application to the Grain Corporation to purchase on a credit basis 100,000 tons of wheat and wheat flour, which is urgently needed for the relief of the civilian population of Poland.

I feel that we should do all we can to assist in the establishment and continuance of a stabilized government in Poland, the maintenance of which has a direct influence in protecting our own economic position. I, therefore, consider it of great importance for the peace of Eastern Europe that this food be made available.

Pursuant to the authority conferred upon me by Act of Congress, approved March 4, 1919, I hereby direct and authorize you to sell to the Polish Government on credit or otherwise, the wheat and wheat flour mentioned above on such terms as you may in your discretion determine.   Yours truly,[1]

T MS (WP, DLC).
[1] This was sent as WW to J. H. Barnes, Nov. 14, 1919, TLS (Letterpress Books, WP, DLC).

Julius Howland Barnes to Joseph Patrick Tumulty, with Enclosure

My dear Mr. Secretary: New York November 11, 1919

With the proposed authority sent you herewith for the signature of the President authorizing us to supply Poland on credit with 100,000 tons of breadstuffs, as suggested in your letter of November 10th, I venture to enclose also for presentation to the President an order regarding Armenia.

I do this at the earnest solicitation of Herbert Hoover, supported by the cable enclosed herewith from Haskell,[1] setting forth the very deplorable food situation in that country and the urgency of the need of relief.

Mr. Hoover states that he can arrange with the Rockefeller Foundation or from other sources to pay the ocean freight for the transportation of this quantity of breadstuffs, if the President would feel justified in authorizing the Grain Corporation to sell that quantity on credit.

The President, with his intimate knowledge of conditions there, needs no elaboration of that condition; therefore I venture to enclose the order in anticipation of his approval. If he so approves, will you please secure his signature and return the order to me as authority?

In either event, may I ask you to send me a telegram as to the President's action so that we may by cable advise American representatives in Armenia whether this relief may be definitely expected. Sincerely, Julius H. Barnes.

TLS (WP, DLC).
[1] That is, Col. William Nafew Haskell, U.S.A., head of the United States mission to Armenia. His telegram is missing.

E N C L O S U R E

PROPOSED LETTER FROM THE PRESIDENT TO MR BARNES
REGARDING ARMENIAN FOODSTUFFS.

My dear Mr. Barnes: November 11, 1919

I am informed that the Armenian Government has made application to the Grain Corporation to purchase on a credit basis 35,000 tons of wheat and wheat flour. I understand that this Government is in great distress for these prime foodstuffs, and that they have no available credits which will enable them to pay for this in cash.

I consider it of great importance for the peace of Eastern Europe that this wheat and flour be made available for Armenia, and I desire to aid the Armenian people in the establishment and continuance of a stabilized government, the maintenance of which has a direct influence in protecting our own economic position.

Pursuant to the authority conferred upon me by Act of Congress, approved March 4, 1919, I hereby direct and authorize you to sell to the Armenian Government on credit or otherwise, the wheat and wheat flour mentioned above on such terms as you may in your discretion determine. Yours truly,[1]

T MS (WP, DLC).
[1] This was sent as WW to J. H. Barnes, Nov. 14, 1919, TLS (Letterpress Books, WP, DLC).

Joseph Patrick Tumulty to Edith Bolling Galt Wilson, with Enclosure

Dear Mrs. Wilson: The White House, November 11, 1919.

Will you please read the attached to the President at an opportune time? Sincerely yours, J P Tumulty

TLS (WP, DLC).

From Joseph Patrick Tumulty

Dear Governor: The White House November 11, 1919.

I have to leave for New York on the Congressional and wish to put this suggestion before you with reference to the Treaty situation. I tried to reach Senator Hitchcock to discuss it with him but I failed. It seems to me that the country ought to know what the real purpose of the Republican opposition is to the League of Nations and the Peace Treaty. I think it might be wise to address the following letter to Senator Hitchcock. Doctor Grayson could bring it to him and ask him what he thinks of it. The letter is as follows:

"My dear Senator Hitchcock:

Only grave concern over the possible changes which a majority of the Senators seem incline[d] to make of the Treaty impel me to say to you that these changes will inevitably result in a failure of the Treaty and the postponement of peace with Germany. In that event, this Government will face important decisions, decisions that are fraught with the gravest possible consequences. It will be necessary for us either to ask our associates, consisting of Nations, to reconvene the Peace Conference, or for America to arrange a new treaty with Germany. It is with the full sense of my responsibility that I say to you that it will be impossible for us to ask our associates to agree to vital changes such as the reservations advocated by Senator Lodge contemplate, without giving our associates an opportunity for discussion and drawing the full fire of counter proposals from them. The failure of the Treaty in its effect upon the world is too terrible to contemplate. Each day's delay gives free rein to forces of passion throughout the world that in no way can be checked excepting through the instrumentality of a stabilizing influence like the League of Nations. I have no pride of opinion in the matter of reservations were it a matter between this Government and another Nation. In a normal time we could consider them without risk or danger to anything, but this is not a normal time. The world awaits America's action, and to disappoint the world may lead to chaos and tragedy of the deepest kind. I am sure that you understand the situation and will share in the apprehension I feel."   Tumulty

TLS (WP, DLC).

Joseph Patrick Tumulty to Josephus Daniels

Dear Mr. Daniels: The White House 11 November, 1919

The President is making preparations for the delivery of his December message to Congress, and would appreciate a memorandum from you as to any matters in your Department that you think he ought to call to the attention of Congress.[1]

Sincerely yours,   J P Tumulty

TLS (J. Daniels Papers, DLC).
[1] Tumulty sent similar letters to the other members of the cabinet.

Edith Bolling Galt Wilson to Joseph Patrick Tumulty, with Enclosures

The White House, [c. Nov. 11, 1919]

The President says he cannot do any thing with the R.R situation until he can write something him self to send or deliver to Congress

AL (WP, DLC).

E N C L O S U R E   I

Joseph Patrick Tumulty to Edith Bolling Galt Wilson

Dear Mrs. Wilson: The White House, November 11, 1919.

I am sending you a message to Congress, prepared by the Director General of Railroads. I have gone over this carefully and think it important that it should go to Congress today. If you can have the President sign these two copies today, I shall see that the message is promptly delivered. You will note from Clagett's[1] letter that all of the advisers of the Director General urge that such a message be sent immediately.

The missing figure on Page 2 is to supplied by the Director General.   Sincerely yours,   J P Tumulty

TLS (WP, DLC).
[1] Maurice Brice Claggett, assistant to the Director General of Railroads.

ENCLOSURE II

The White House, November, 1919.

TO THE SENATE AND HOUSE OF REPRESENTATIVES:

In my address to the Congress on December 2, 1918,[1] I referred to the importance and urgency of constructive action upon the question as to how the railroad situation should be dealt with. I stated that it was not fair either to the public or to the owners of the railroads to leave the question unanswered. I added:

"The one conclusion that I am ready to state with confidence is that it would be a disservice alike to the country and to the owners of the railroads to return to the old conditions unmodified. Those are conditions of restraint without development. There is nothing affirmative or helpful about them. What the country chiefly needs is that all its means of transportation should be developed, its railways, its waterways, its highways and its countryside roads. Some new element of policy, therefore, is absolutely necessary—necessary for the service of the public, necessary for the release of credit to those who are administering the railways, necessary for the protection of their security holders. The old policy may be changed much or little, but surely it can not wisely be left as it was. I hope that the Congress will have a complete and impartial study of the whole problem instituted at once and prosecuted as rapidly as possible. I stand ready and anxious to release the roads from the present control and I must do so at a very early date if by waiting until the statutory limit of time is reached I shall be merely prolonging the period of doubt and uncertainty which is hurtful to every interest concerned."

Following the thoughts thus expressed as to the desirability of early relinquishment of the railroads, I stated in my message to the Congress of May 20, 1919,[2] that the railroads would be handed over to their owners at the end of the calendar year. This statement was made in the confident belief that adequate legislation would be enacted by that time and I yet hope that this may be accomplished.

I believe all will agree that it is of the highest importance to obtain at the earliest possible date the adoption of constructive legislation on this subject.

I am greatly concerned as to the ability of the railroads to make the necessary improvements and obtain the necessary additional equipment to enable them to perform satisfactorily the transportation service which the country will require in the calendar year

---

[1] That is, Wilson's Annual Message to Congress, printed at this date in Vol. 53.
[2] Wilson's special message to Congress, printed at this date in Vol. 59.

1920. The conditions created by the war and the uncertainty of the railroad situation since the armistice have made it impracticable to provide the normal amount of improvements and new equipment or to obtain the new capital to pay therefor. If there shall be large crops and a heavy general business in the year 1920, the necessary transportation service cannot be satisfactorily provided without the promptest creation of a definite basis upon which plans can be made and new capital raised to provide these essential additions to the railroad plant. The Director General of Railroads advises me that plans ought at once to be made for the expenditure of not less than $750,000,000, of which amount about [blank] ought to be actually expended in the first seven or eight months of the calendar year 1920 in order to meet satisfactorily the probable heavy transportation demands next fall. The making of these plans and the raising of the necessary funds will require time and will require certainty. I am, therefore, convinced that the public interest imperatively requires definite action at this session of the Congress upon which plans can be made and carried out to insure adequate transportation service next year. As I view the situation, either of the following two courses will completely meet that need:

First, The framing and adoption at the present session of thoroughgoing legislation dealing with all phases of the railroad problem. I do not believe there can be a successful permanent solution of the question until there shall be a reconstitution of the railroad systems and their capitalization with resulting provisions which, on the one hand, will more certainly assure an adequate and steady return to the railroad companies, thereby promoting the public interest through having a railroad credit which will continue to obtain the new capital needed for railroad development, and, on the other hand, will protect and reassure the public against excess earnings being appropriated unduly to private benefit. I also believe that a right understanding cannot be obtained and maintained respecting the inter-related interests of the public, labor and capital without adequate representation of all three of these interests on the managing boards of the railroads. In my address to the Congress on December 2, 1918, I foreshadowed such a general plan as worthy of consideration describing it as "an intermediate course of modified private control under a more unified and affirmative public regulation and under such alterations of the law as will permit wasteful competition to be avoided and a considerable degree of unification of administration to be effected." An elaboration of these ideas was presented to the Senate Committee on Interstate Commerce by the Director General of Railroads last February and in September he submitted a further elaboration of this idea to the House Committee on Interstate and Foreign Commerce. I believe even those who may disagree with me as to the ultimate necessity of all of these steps will agree that a solution cannot be regarded as permanent and satisfactory until there shall have been the fullest and widest opportunity for discussion of these great problems by the legislative representatives of the people.

Second, If it is concluded by the Congress that there is not the time during the present session to adopt such thoroughgoing legislation as I have suggested, there is a great deal in favor of the plan of definitely and positively continuing the present Federal control for a period of not less than one year, pending full opportunity to dispose of those fundamental questions after fullest opportunity for debate and deliberation. Such a course would, undoubtedly, be a stabilizing influence in a time of most serious industrial and economic unrest. Such a course would probably avoid, or at any rate minimize the reconstruction of the rate structure of the country in what is admittedly an experimental period following the war. Such a course would make it necessary to take only a single step from the present temporary Federal control to a scheme of permanent regulation adopted after adequate opportunity for discussion, whereas a turning back of the railroads in advance of such comprehensive solution would probably prove nothing but an intermediate step to be followed later by still another step which would be the result of more comprehensive legislation.

But such a course could not be successful unless it was supported by the affirmative action of Congress in the way of appropriations to enable the Government at once to put into effect and carry forward the plans for improvement necessary in order to render adequate service next year. I have seen no indication of a desire on the part of Congress to maintain the present Federal control under a positive arrangement for the accomplishment of the facts I have here stated, and therefore without positive approval of the Congress and adequate financial provision, I am unwilling to continue the existing form of Goverment control beyond December 31st next.

If it shall develop that there is not adequate time at the present session to debate to a conclusion the important questions undoubtedly involved in a permanent solution of this problem, and if the Congress is unwilling to take affirmative action supporting the positive extension of the present Federal control, pending an opportunity for such consideration at a later date, thereby assuring adequate financial support upon the basis of which the Government can at once make the necessary plans for improvements next year, I then urge upon the Congress the paramount importance of adopting, before the present session expires, legislation sufficiently definite and comprehensive to serve as a reasonable basis of certainty upon which the railroad companies can proceed without delay to make their financial arrangements and their plans for improvements and acquisition of equipment, in order to meet the heavy responsibilities to the public which they must begin to discharge upon reassuming the management of their properties on January 1st next. I take it that a mere temporary guaranty of rental for a few months without other provisions cannot give any such element of certainty. On the other hand, I believe there are various important elements of this matter which have been thoroughly considered in the Senate and House Committees and upon which substantial agreement is practicable, and I urge that every element of the situation which can be reasonably made certain during the present session be so dealt with in order to obtain the maximum basis of certainty upon which provision as nearly adequate as possible can be made for the rendition of the public service during the approaching year. I wish to add that if the Congress proceeds along these lines and if it includes in the legislation adopted any temporary guaranty to the railroad companies, it is highly important to provide that in connection with the payment of such guaranty some appropriate governmental agency shall supervise the expenditures which may be charged to operating expenses, and shall pass upon all proposals to abandon practices which have been adopted during Federal control for the purpose of effecting operating economies, and it is also highly important to provide that rates shall not be reduced during the period of the guaranty except with the approval of the Federal rate regulating authority because otherwise the competition which is likely to ensue upon the restoration of private management may result in improvident rate reductions by individual railroad companies and seriously add to the burden incurred by the Government through its guaranty.

I also believe that it would be decidedly in the public interest for the Congress, if the course just mentioned is pursued, to direct the Interstate Commerce Commission immediately to begin the collection of the necessary facts in connection with the rate structure so that there may be no delay in passing upon any proposals for rate changes which may be submitted by the railroad companies.

In conclusion I wish particularly to emphasize the importance of legislation being finally adopted before the adjournment of the present session. Otherwise the ability to make plans will continue to be suspended until a date so late in the year as largely to defeat any efforts which could then be made to plan intelligently and effectively for the adequate performance of the transportation service of next year.

T MS (WP, DLC).

E N C L O S U R E   I I I

Maurice Brice Clagett to Joseph Patrick Tumulty

My dear Joe: Washington November 10, 1919.

In accordance with my telephone conversation, I enclose herewith a tentative draft prepared by Mr. Hines of a message from the President to the Congress on the railroad situation.

I think he explained to you the other day that he believes there is very strong reason for sending such a message, because the prospect is that Congress will drfit [drift] along on the railroad question and as a result difficulties will eventuate which, to a degree, at least, may be laid at the door of the President.

I may say that all of the advisers of the Director General, including Swagar Sherley,[1] believe very strongly that such a message should be sent. This draft, of course, is in preliminary form and the Director General has asked me to send it to you so that you could consider it immediately before it is put in final shape for submission to the President.

Of course, action along this line should be taken almost immediately.   Sincerely yours,   Brice Clagett

[1] Joseph Swagar Sherley, Democratic congressman from Kentucky, 1903-1919; at this time, director of the Division of Finance of the United States Railroad Administration.

E N C L O S U R E   I V

Walker Downer Hines to Joseph Patrick Tumulty

Dear Mr. Tumulty: Washington November 11, 1919.

It occurs to me in discussing with the President the draft of message which I have sent you, he would probably wish to consider the following points:

The first alternative outlined in the message would be regarded as a commitment on his part against complete Government ownership of the railroads and also against an ownership of them by the employes along the lines of the Plumb plan. Of course if the President wished to reserve his views on these matters he could do so by indicating that the legislation ought at least to be as far-reaching as is suggested in this alternative.

As to the second alternative, the extension of Federal control for a period of not less than one year from January 1, 1920 has to face certain disadvantages. The year 1920 will be a presidential year. The disposition to criticise the Railroad Aministration will be greatly intensified by the partisan temper of a considerable part of the Press, public speakers, etc. The election will come at a period of the year when business is heaviest and most difficult to handle. If the extension shall end at December 31, 1920, we will at the time of election be within two months of the expiration of the period and we will be again having unrest in the railroad organization, speculating on what will happen when the period comes to an end. Of course this will be considerably alleviated if before the end of the next session of Congress permanent legislation shall be adopted. But we must be prepared for the entire matter being dropped as the presidential campaign approaches and we may be in a state of at least as great uncertainty in November, 1920 as we are at present, and it may become necessary for the Congress meeting in December, 1920 to adopt again some eleventh hour extension to give an opportunity for legislation. Perhaps this could be avoided by pressure being put upon Congress next spring either to adopt permanent legislation before adjournment or to grant a further extension. The arguments for this would be so strong that probably Congress could be prevailed upon before adjourning next summer to deal with the matter with finality one way or the other, and in that event the uncertainty next fall would be largely removed. Despite these difficulties, I believe the Railroad Administration could give a good account of itself in the operation of the railroads next year but these difficulties ought not to be overlooked.

I believe it is highly desirable for the President to communicate promptly with Congress on the subject as I think it will aid to clarify the atmosphere and that without such communication there is a prospect that everything will remain in complete uncertainty until the latter part of December and this would be extremely bad for the railroad service.

Another course which would be open to the President would be to say that in view of the changed conditions he is unwilling to release the railroads at December 31st in the absence of comprehensive legislation, and that unless Congress at this session takes sufficiently comprehensive action, he intends to continue to hold the railroads under the discretionary power vested in him in the Federal Control Act and he will also at once take the responsibility of again exercising the powers conferred by that statute, whereunder he can order the railroad companies to make improvements and to acquire equipment necessary in the public interest and so far as may be needful he will, as he is empowered to do by the Act, commit the Government to furnishing the necessary funds, and will call upon Congress in due time for appropriations to cover these commitments. Such a course would make the position of the Executive self-acting and would not be dependent upon action by Congress, being merely subject to change if Congress shall act. My own feeling, however, has been that the public temper is so unfavorable to an extension of Federal control, and the difficulties of operation next year are of such a character as to make it unwise for the President to take such a stand, but on the other hand to adhere to his declaration of last May unless Congress itself shall take action as outlined in the draft of message.

The provision of the Federal Control Act upon the relinquishment of the railroads is as follows:

"Sec. 14. That the Federal control of railroads and transportation systems herein and heretofore provided for shall continue for and during the period of the war and for a reasonable time thereafter, which shall not exceed one year and nine months next following the date of the proclamation by the President of the exchange of ratifications of the treaty of peace: Provided, however, That the President may, prior to July first, nineteen hundred and eighteen, relinquish control of all or any part of any railroad or system of transportation, further Federal control of which the President shall deem not needful or desirable; and the President may at any time during the period of Federal control agree with the owners thereof to relinquish all or any part of any railroad or system of transportation. The President may relinquish all railroads and systems of transportation under Federal control at any time he shall deem such action needful or desirable. No right to compensation shall accrue to such owners from and after the date of relinquishment for the property so relinquished."

I construe this as meaning that the President has clear power to relinquish the railroads prior to the proclamation of the exchange of ratifications of the treaty of peace, although the first part of the Section gives color to the view that Congress assumed that in any event the Federal control would continue during the period of the war. It is quite possible that Labor which is so anxious to have Federal control continued may argue that if the war is still in effect for the purposes of controlling the coal strike under the Lever Act, the war is equally in effect for the purpose of retaining control of the railroads. This argument if valid would be opposed to the idea of relinquishing control December 31st next, as heretofore announced by the President, unless by that date the President had proclaimed the exchange of the ratifications of peace.

The draft of message I sent you contained a rider suggesting that Congress direct the Interstate Commerce Commission to begin an inquiry into what changes ought to be made in the rate structure. It occurs to me it would be better instead of the words "Interstate Commerce Commission" to use the words "such Federal authority as may be vested by the legislation with functions in that regard" because the legislation agreed upon may provide some additional tribunal which will have functions to perform in this regard.   Sincerely yours,   Walker D. Hines.

ENCLOSURE V

Walker Downer Hines to Joseph Patrick Tumulty

Dear Mr. Tumulty: Washington November 11, 1919.

Referring again to the draft of message which I have sent you, the sentence which contains the two blanks and which relates to probable expenditures should be revised to read as follows:

"I am advised by the Director General of Railroads that in order to make the improvements and acquire the equipment desirable for the purpose of performing satisfactorily the country's transportation business next year provision ought to be made at once for capital expenditures approximating $700,000,000."

                    Sincerely yours,   Walker D Hines

TLS (WP, DLC).

To Lucy Day Martin

[The White House] November 12, 1919.

May I not express my deep sympathy and sense of personal grief in the death of your distinguished father?[1] I regarded him as one of my warmest friends and feel that Virginia and the country have sustained a real loss.   Woodrow Wilson.

T telegram (Letterpress Books, WP, DLC).
[1] Senator Thomas Staples Martin had died on November 12.

From Robert Lansing, with Enclosure

My dear Mr. President: Washington November 12, 1919.

I venture to lay before you the summary, as well as copies, of telegrams the Department has received from Mr. Polk and from the Ambassador in London[1] regarding the political and military situation of Syria and the general question of the Turkish Empire, and of mandates.

After a careful perusal of these telegrams, I venture to suggest the advisability, should it meet with your approval, of instructing Mr. Polk and Mr. Davis to inform respectively the Peace Conference and the British Government which has inquired as to our desires in the premises, that since the British feel that everything points to the urgent necessity of settling the question of military occupation as well as the ultimate political status of the component parts of the Turkish Empire, and since, on the other hand, our own present Mission is not prepared to take part in negotiations for such settlement, this Government would, therefore, have no objection to the other powers proceeding with those negotiations.

I should be very grateful for an expression of your views.

Faithfully yours,   Robert Lansing.

Enclosures:
Telegrams
    #3254 October 16, from London
    #3264 October 18, from London
    #4732 October 19, from Paris.
    #4759 October 21, from Paris
    #4807 October 24, from Paris
    #4832 October 26, from Paris.
    Synopsis of above-mentioned telegrams.

TLS (WP, DLC).
[1] That is, John William Davis.

E N C L O S U R E

SYNOPSIS OF TELEGRAMS FROM PARIS AND LONDON.

On the 16th instant Mr. Davis reports Lord Curzon's conversation with him respecting:

1. Emir Faisal's request for the participation of this Government in a conference to decide the military situation of Syria.

2. Urgent necessity to settle at once not only the military occupation, but also the ultimate status of the component parts of the

From London, No. 3254, October 16th.[1]

Turkish Empire. This question, Lord Curzon states has been post-poned awaiting decision in America regarding mandates.

3. The inquiry by the British Cabinet as to whether America would be willing to consider at once in a conference to be held at Paris or London the settlement of the non-Turkish portions of the Turkish Empire.

From London, No. 3264, October 18th.[2]

On the 18th instant Mr. Davis reports that the Emir Faisal called on him to discuss the Syrian military situation and the Anglo-French agreement to divide the Arab countries. The Emir states he understands Mr. Clemanceau objects to the presence of an American officer at the proposed conference on the military question. The Emir protests against the division of the Arab countries; he states any effort to subdivide them or to put them under French rule would be met by force of arms, and suggests that there might be a Turko-Arab cooperation. He intimates he might agree to separate Palestine under British mandate, and states he would do any thing which met with your approval.

From Paris, No. 4732, October 19th.[3]

Referring to the foregoing, Mr. Polk telegraphs on the 19th that he believes French hope to get control of Turkey, through commissionership at Constantinople keeping Turkey in Asia Minor and Europe together. This might satisfy them for not getting what they want in Syria. Mr. Polk thinks the British would probably be unwilling to leave these questions to be conisered [considered] at Paris, and in his opinion should we attempt to settle this issue and the question of military occupation, possibly all three powers would be dissatisfied with us. Moreover, he points out that the present Commission is not equipped to deal with this question.

From Paris, No. 4759, October 21st,[4] and No. 4807, October 24th.[5]

On the 21st instant Mr. Polk reports visit of an agent of the Emir and on the 24th that of the Emir himself. The Emir desires that both the political and military situation in Asia Minor be left to a Committee of four persons, including a British, a French, and an American representative, and the Emir himself. The British accept his suggestion only as far as the military situation is concerned, while Mr. Clemanceau refuses the plan even for the discussion of the military situation. While Faisal makes no threats some of those around him hint at the possibility of a holy war, and a Turko-Arab alliance. The Emir wanted to know whether America would accept a plan for arbitrating question of political and military control. Mr. Polk informed Faisal that he did not think it likely that such a plan would be accepted. Thereupon the Emir wished Mr. Polk to insist upon the French accepting his plan. Mr. Polk did not see how that was possible but intimated that the Emir had the right to apply to the Supreme Council.

Mr. Polk says General Bliss has always been of opinion that the several military occupations will irrevocably fix the future political status of the component parts of Turkey in Asia. He is convinced that American arbitration of this question whether as a political or a military one, will be futile. He believes that this Government should demand prompt consideration of the Turkish problem by a conference which shall not sit in Paris or in London. He thinks that the principle of mandates should be applied and the regions subject to mandate should be agreed upon, America being free to accept or reject any mandate that may be offered her. If the other powers decline to do this, then in General Bliss' opinion, the United States should announce its withdrawal from any further participation after the signature of the present treaties.

From Paris, No. 4759, October 21st.

Mr. Polk anticipates great difficulty in the negotiation of the Turkish Treaty. He feels that Constantinople and Asia Minor should be kept together, making one country responsible for the order and finances. But what country should be charged with this duty? He expresses the wish that there were some way in which we could withdraw from this whole affair. Above all, however, he thinks it essential that this Treaty should not be negotiated in Paris and should not be negotiated by the present Commission, but it should be negotiated very soon.

From Paris, No. 4807, October 24th.

In telegram dated October 26th, Mr. Polk transmits summary of views of the Harbord Mission[6] given by General Harbord arguing that the same power should have mandate over Constantinople, Anatolia, Armenia, and all Trans-Caucasia. After describing the deplorable condition of the countries General Harbord says he is convinced that delay in the settlement is making whole Turkish problem daily more difficult and complex and therefore recommends its immediate consideration by Peace Conference.

From Paris, No. 4832, October 26th.[7]

T MS (WP, DLC).
[1] J. W. Davis to RL, Oct. 16, 1919, T telegram (SDR, RG 59, 763.72119/7282, DNA).
[2] J. W. Davis to RL, Oct. 18, 1919, T telegram (SDR, RG 59, 763.72119/7327, DNA).
[3] FLP to RL, Oct. 19, 1919, T telegram (SDR, RG 59, 867.00/965, DNA).
[4] FLP to RL, Oct. 21, 1919, T telegram (SDR, RG 59, 867.00/967, DNA).
[5] FLP to RL, Oct. 24, 1919, T telegram (SDR, RG 59, 867.00/970, DNA).
[6] About which, see n. 1 to the Desk Diary of Robert Lansing, July 29, 1919, Vol. 62.
[7] FLP to RL, Oct. 26, 1919, T telegram (SDR, RG 59, 860j01/124, DNA).

From Alexandra[1]

Sandringham, November 12, 1919.

I do hope with all my heart that you are feeling stronger now and that the rest after your wonderful work for the benefit of the whole world has given you fresh strength and health for the future. I am so glad you were able to spare a moment to see my precious grandson,[2] and with kindest remembrance to your wife.

Alexandra.

T telegram (SDR, RG 59, 811.001W69/795, DNA).
    [1] The Queen Mother, widow of Edward VII.
    [2] She meant that Wilson would be able to see the Prince of Wales.

To Alexandra

Cablegram

The White House,

Her Majesty Queen Alexandra   [Nov. 13, 1919]

Your Majesties' message gave Mrs. Wilson & me a great deal of pleasure.

The welcome accorded your grandson here[1] is from the heart.

I am happy to say I am steadily improving and Mrs. Wilson & I shall always hope to renew the friendship so delightfully begun. We unite in the most cordial messages & in thanking you for your thought of us.   Woodrow Wilson[2]

EBWhw telegram (WP, DLC).
    [1] About Edward's visit to the White House, see the news report printed at Nov. 14, 1919.
    [2] This was sent as WW to Alexandra, Nov. 13, 1919, T telegram (Letterpress Books, WP, DLC).

Gilbert Monell Hitchcock to Edith Bolling Galt Wilson, with Enclosure

My dear Mrs. Wilson: [Washington] November 13, 1919

In accordance with your suggestion and for the information of the President, I give you this information in brief form of what is going on in the Senate in consideration of the treaty.

One by one we are voting on the Lodge reservations. The republicans are supporting those reservations solidly. We are offering substitutes which are being supported by the democrats with three or four exceptions.

Already the Senate has adopted the first and second reservations[1] and probably by adjournment today will adopt the third reservation relating to Article 10. This reservation is not quite as obnoxious as it was when the President denounced it in Salt Lake,[2] a slight change in phraseology having been made in order to secure the support of four or five "mild reservation" senators. Still it is bad.

It is our plan at the proper time to offer a resolution of unqualified ratification of the treaty as a substitute for Lodge's resolution of ratification with reservations. We shall be beaten on that and shall then offer interpretative reservations to take the place of the drastic reservations proposed by Senator Lodge.

We expect, of course, to be beaten also on this vote but will make the democratic record clear. Senator Lodge will thereupon present for final vote a resolution of ratification including his reservations and it is then proposed by us to cast enough votes against it to prevent it from receiving the necessary two-thirds vote for ratification.

This plan is subject to modification, however, in case when the time arrives we shall determine, or the President shall advise us to vote for the Lodge resolution. Some democrats feel that they would like to have the President's advice at that time and I have promised to submit the matter to him when the day arrives. That may be some time next week.

I enclose copy of the reservations we propose to offer as a substitute for those proposed by Senator Lodge. The first four are in substance in accordance with suggestions made to me by the President[3] and the last one is, I think, in accordance with his views on the true meaning of the league covenant.

Yours very sincerely,   G M Hitchcock

TLS (WP, DLC).

[1] For the text of the first and second so-called Lodge reservations (among others), see the Enclosure printed with GMH to EBW, Nov. 15, 1919.

[2] The Salt Lake City speech is printed at Sept. 23, 1919, Vol. 63. The reservation then read: "The United States assumes no obligation under the provisions of Article X to preserve the territorial integrity or political independence of any other country or to interfere in controversies between other nations whether members of the League or not or to employ the military and naval forces of the United States under any article of the treaty for any purpose unless in any particular case the Congress, which under the Constitution has the sole power to declare war or authorize the employment of the military and naval forces of the United States, shall by act or joint resolution so declare." See W. Phillips to WW, Sept. 22, 1919 (first telegram of that date), Vol. 63.

[3] For the text of which, see Wilson's memorandum printed at Sept. 3, 1919, Vol. 62.

E N C L O S U R E

PROPOSED SUBSTITUTE RESERVATIONS.[1]

To take the place of those Proposed by Sen Lodge[2]

That any member nation proposing to withdraw from the league on two years notice is the sole judge as to whether its obligations referred to in Article I of the League of Nations have been performed as required in said article.

That no member nation is required to submit to the league, its council, or its assembly, for decision, report or recommendation, any matter which it considers to be in international law a domestic question such as immigration, labor, tariff, or other matter relating to its internal or coastwise affairs.

That the national policy of the United States known as the Monroe doctrine, as announced and interpreted by the United States, is not in any way impaired or affected by the Covenant of the League of Nations and is not subject to any decision, report or enquiry by the council or assembly.

That the advice mentioned in Article X of the covenant of the league which the council may give to the member nations as to the employment of their naval and military forces is merely advice which each member nation is free to accept or reject according to the conscience and judgment of its then existing government and in the United States this advice can only be accepted by action of the Congress at the time in being, Congress alone under the Constitution of the United States having the power to declare war.

That in case of a dispute between members of the league if one of them have self-governing colonies, dominions or parts which have representation in the assembly, each and all are to be considered parties to the dispute and the same shall be the rule if one of the parties to the dispute is a self-governing colony, dominion or part, in which case all other self-governing colonies, dominions or parts as well as the nation as a whole shall be considered parties to the dispute and each and all shall be disqualified from having their votes counted in case of any enquiry on said dispute made by the assembly.

T MS (WP, DLC).
¹ Hitchcock introduced these reservations on November 15 (they were ordered to lie on the table) with the following preamble:
"*Resolved (two-thirds of the Senators present concurring therein)*, That the Senate do advise and consent to the ratification of the treaty of peace with Germany concluded at Versailles on the 28th day of June, 1919, subject to the following reservations, understandings, and interpretations, which shall be made a part of the instrument of ratification:
"That the Government of the United States understands and interprets this treaty as follows:"
² GMHhw.

From Albert, King of the Belgians

[On board *U.S.S. George Washington*] 1919 Nov 13

6821: following from USS George Washington. "For the President. Having safely reached our destination after a delightful voyage on board the George Washington, I want to extend to you a last expression of my deep gratitude for the American hospitality and of my heartfelt wish for your health. The Queen joins me in sending to you and Mrs. Wilson our most sincere greetings. Signed Albert."

T radiogram (WP, DLC).

To Albert, King of the Belgians

Cablegram

The White House, [Nov. 13, 1919]

To His Majesty the King of the Belgians

Hearty felicitations to you and the queen and your people on your safe return.

It was a genuine pleasure to receive you here and to have you feel the sincere friendship of the American people

Mrs. Wilson joins in most cordial messages to you & Her Majesty. Woodrow Wilson[1]

EBWhw telegram (WP, DLC).
[1] This was sent as WW to His Majesty, King of the Belgians, Nov. 13, 1919, T telegram (Letterpress Books, WP, DLC).

Two News Reports

[Nov. 14, 1919]

PRINCE SEES WILSON

President Wilson's visit with the rulers of Great Britain in London last spring was returned yesterday afternoon, when Edward Windsor, the future King of England, called at the White House to convey the good wishes of the empire to the head of the American government.

When the prince stepped from the royal automobile and walked up the wide steps, flanked by the slender colonial pillars of the White House veranda, he was greeted by Mrs. Wilson and the President's daughters, Miss Margaret Wilson and Mrs. Francis B. Sayre.

Prince Edward took tea with his hostess, Miss Wilson and Mrs. Sayre, and then proceeded to the sick room on the second floor of the White House. President Wilson was propped up in the mahogany bed in which Baron Renfrew, later King Edward VII, slept when he visited Washington in 1860. Prince Edward bowed punctiliously and then stepped forward to clasp hands with the President.

Soon after the exchange of felicitations had been finished the President noticed that his visitor was observing the massive old mahogany bed, and told him that Baron Renfrew had slept in the bed when he was entertained at the White House by President Buchanan. He added that it was the same bed in which President Lincoln slept during his term of office.

Prince Edward inquired concerning the President's health, and expressed his pleasure when Mr. Wilson told him that he was much improved. The President asked about King George and Queen Mary, and mentioned the pleasure with which he received a cablegram yesterday from the Queen Mother Alexandra.

Edward told the President of some of his experiences since his arrival on the American continent, and the youthful heir to the British throne and the first man of America laughed heartily over the humorous incidents.

The conversation covered a wide range of subjects and the entire meeting was much the same as might take place between any likeable boy with a keen sense of humor and a statesman whose worries have not deprived him of the gift of laughter.

The prince expressed his appreciation for the generous reception accorded him in Washington and regretted that his stay in the United States was to end soon.

Dr. Grayson said, after Prince Edward had left, that the President's spirits had risen as a result of the conversation, and that Mr. Wilson had enjoyed the visit greatly.

Printed in the *Washington Post*, Nov. 14, 1919.

[*Nov. 14, 1919*]

President on the Porch in a Wheeled Chair

Washington, Nov. 14.—Dr. Hugh Hampton Young of Johns Hopkins University, Baltimore, will visit the White House tomorrow for another general consultation on President Wilson's illness. Dr. Francis X. Dercum, neurologist, also will attend the consultation. At the White House it was explained that the visit simply meant that they were coming to make their usual week-end study of the case so as to be able to check up on the President's progress.

The President continues to improve slowly but steadily. On Armistice Day he was able to be up for an hour in a roller chair for the first time since he was brought back to Washington from his Western trip.

Today he was able to go one step further, when he was again

placed in a roller chair and taken to the rear porch of the White House, where he had the benefit of the sunshine and open air.

Printed in the *New York Times*, Nov. 15, 1919.

Norman Hezekiah Davis to Joseph Patrick Tumulty, with Enclosures

Dear Mr. Tumulty: Washington November 14, 1919.

With reference to our conversation regarding the German ships, I am enclosing herewith copy of a letter to the Secretary of State from the British Ambassador with a note from the Prime Minister on the subject.

I am thoroughly convinced that it is not only right but expedient that we should at least turn over the "Imperator" without further delay. We have no right to retain it, we have no use for it, and it is a white elephant on our hands which is an unnecessary risk and expense. If the Shipping Board should immediately turn over the "Imperator" unconditionally on the ground that they do not need it, they would still be left with a considerable amount of German ships which they could retain if they think it advisable pending a settlement of the disposition of the tankers.

Very sincerely yours,   Norman H. Davis

TLS (WP, DLC).

ENCLOSURE   I

Viscount Grey to Robert Lansing

My dear Mr. Secretary: Washington. November 10th, 1919.

I have received the enclosed message from the Prime Minister which I forward to you.

I have of course reported home all that you have said to me, but the continuance of the deadlock is becoming increasingly serious.

Believe me, my dear Mr. Secretary,

Very sincerely yours,   (Signed) Grey V.F.

CCL (WP, DLC).

E N C L O S U R E   I I

I do not wish the President to be troubled about the following matter but I am anxious that it should be considered by the United States Administration.

The present position in regard to the "IMPERATOR" and the 7 other ex-German Passenger Ships under U. S. management is arousing very serious feeling here. There is a sense of broken faith about the transaction. When the German ships were handed over under the Armistice it was agreed that they should be put under the control of the Allied Maritime Transport Council, to be used for Allied purposes connected with the repatriation of troops, and the liquidation of war activities. Eight of the vessels above mentioned were, by Agreement, temporarily allocated by the Council to the United States for the repatriation of American troops subject to their afterwards being allotted to France and Great Britain for similar purposes. American repatriation is now complete but Great Britain still has hundreds of thousands of troops and other passengers to move and urgently needs ships for these purposes. Yet the Shipping Board of the United States refuse to release them. I cannot believe that it is the intention of the United States Government to go back upon their word, especially as it means depriving their associates in the War of ships that they urgently require, in order that they may bring back to their homes troops worn with 5 years of fighting.

The question of the German Tankers which has been introduced is quite a distinct matter on which the Supreme Council has given a decision. If the United States is dissatisfied with the decision it is open to her to submit her case to the Council again. The fact that she wishes to raise a question on this point is not justification for the retention of the Passenger Ships. I confidently rely on the United States Government to give immediate instructions for the delivery of the ships to the seamen who have been long waiting in the United States to receive them.

T MS (WP, DLC).

From Robert Lansing, with Enclosure

Dear Mr. President: Washington November 14, 1919.

I enclose a copy of a telegram, dated November 13th, from Mr. Polk regarding the attitude which the Council proposes to assume towards Roumania in certain eventualities. It seems to me that the attitude of the Council is the only one to take but before sending any instructions to Mr. Polk, I should be grateful for an expression of your views.   Faithfully yours,   Robert Lansing

The President says he approves E.B.W.

TLS (WP, DLC).

E N C L O S U R E

Paris November 13, 1919

5172. Confidential. For the Secretary from Polk. At the meeting of the Council yesterday and again today we discussed the action to be taken on the Roumanian reply to our note of October 20.[1] M. Clemenceau was firmly of the opinion that the note was very unsatisfactory and was even of a nature to cause anxiety. Answer was practically a refusal of all our demands of October 20, the only point on which the Roumanians had even partially agreed was the evacuation of Hungary and this they only accepted as far as the river Theiss. On all other points the answer was evasive and defiant. Both Clemenceau and Pichon stated that their patience was at an end and said that the time had come for final action.

At the meeting this morning we had before us a draft answer prepared by Berthelot[2] which was carefully gone over and modified in certain particulars. The note gives a brief history of the negotiations with Roumania, states that their reply is unsatisfactory and allows them six days in which to definitely accept our demands. If they do not do so we say that they will cease to be an Ally, that we will withdraw our representatives in Bucharest and hence they will no longer be represented at the conference.

A final decision will be taken at the meeting tomorrow[3] and I should be very grateful if you will let me know, as soon as possible, whether I have your authority to commit you to the withdrawal of our representative in Bucharest in the event that the Roumanians refuse our demands. I might add that the French, who have been inclined to act as protectors of Roumania up to the present, are thoroughly convinced that the time has come for final action. They also believe that the Roumanians will come to terms.

Please see my 4062 September 5, 11 p.m.[4] I earnestly recommend that we act in concert with other powers in this matter.

Kindly rush. Polk.

T telegram (WP, DLC).
[1] The note of the Associated Powers insisted upon Rumania's adherence to their decisions on territorial frontiers, Rumania's acceptance of the special minorities treaty in the treaty with Austria, and Rumania's evacuation of Hungary and acceptance of the plan of the Associated Powers to establish a stable government in that country. This

telegram is printed as the Associated Powers to the British Chargé, Bucharest, Oct. 11, 1919, *PPC*, VIII, 583-86. This telegram was sent on October 20. The Rumanian reply of November 2 is printed in *ibid.*, IX, 136-38.

² It is printed in *ibid.*, pp. 154-57.

³ The council agreed to postpone a decision to send the telegram drafted by Berthelot until all the delegates had received instructions from their governments.

⁴ See W. Phillips to RL, Sept. 8, 1919, n. 2, Vol. 63.

From the Desk Diary of Robert Lansing

Friday Nov 14 [1919]

Forster from W.H. phoned Prest approved of threat to sever dip. relations with Roumania.

Robert Lansing to Frank Lyon Polk

Washington, November 14, 1919.

3763 Very urgent and confidential.

For Polk. Your 5172, November 13, 8 p.m.

I have presented this matter to the President who approves of your suggestion in regard to the withdrawal of our representative at Bucharest in the event that the Roumanians refuse the demands of the Council. You are, therefore, authorized to inform the Council that, if the Roumanian Government refuses to comply with the conditions of the note which you state is to be forwarded to that Government, the Government of the United States will withdraw its representative at Bucharest at the same time that the representatives of the other Allied and Associated Governments withdraw their representatives from that city.   Lansing

TS telegram (SDR, RG 59, 763.72119/7765, DNA).

Edward, Prince of Wales, to Edith Bolling Galt Wilson

Dear Mrs. Wilson,   [Washington] *14th Nov. 1919*

I must send you a line before I leave Washington to thank you most sincerely for all your kindness & to tell you how delighted I am to have seen the President. It was a great privilege to have been taken up to his room yesterday & I was much relieved to find him looking better than I had expected from the published reports.

I much regret that my stay here is so short & am very sorry to be leaving Washington this evening; but I look forward to paying another visit on some future occasion to the United States.

Will you please tell the President how greatly I appreciate the warm hearted welcome & hospitality which I have enjoyed here.

Please accept this photograph as a souvenir of my visit.

Hoping that the President may soon be completely restored to health & with my kindest regards to you both I remain

yours very sincerely   Edward P.

ALS (WP, DLC).

A News Report

[*Nov. 15, 1919*]

"Remarkable Improvement"
by President in Two Weeks

Washington, Nov. 15.—President Wilson in the last two weeks has made "remarkable improvement," in the opinion of Dr. Francis X. Dercum of Philadelphia, who told Dr. Grayson so today after paying his weekly visit to the White House.

Late yesterday the President was permitted to sit for a short time on the south portico. He seemed so much benefited that Dr. Grayson expects to repeat the treatment.

Some executive business was brought before the President today.

Printed in the *New York Times*, Nov. 16, 1919.

Gilbert Monell Hitchcock to Edith Bolling Galt Wilson, with Enclosure

My dear Mrs. Wilson: [Washington] November 15, 1919

Great Progress was made today in consideration of the Lodge reservations, the Senate adopting reservations from 4 to 13 inclusive. I think I have already sent you a copy, but I enclose a copy of the Lodge reservations.

We agreed to cloture by an overwhelming vote, only fourteen voting against it, most of whom were republicans.

The Vice President announced that when the time came he would rule that if the Lodge resolution fails to receive a two-thirds vote other resolutions of ratification might be offered. The time to make this decision has not arrived and will not arrive until the Lodge resolution has been voted on. The time is close at hand when I must learn from the President definitely whether in his judgement the friends of the treaty should vote against the adoption of the resolution of ratification containing these Lodge reservations and thus defeat it.

It is our plan to pursue this course unless the President advises us otherwise.

In order to make the democratic vote as nearly solid as possible, however, I would like to have definite word from the President if possible that in his judgment this is the proper course to take. If entirely convenient I could call Sunday afternoon. I am engaged Sunday during the morning and until two thirty but can be summoned after that hour by telephone, North 4418.

I shall probably call a final conference of friends of the treaty Tuesday morning.   Yours very sincerely,   G M Hitchcock

Program he out lines has his approval. He could not accept ratification with Lodge Reservations in any case[1]

TLS (WP, DLC).
  [1] EBWhw on back of envelope enclosing this letter.

ENCLOSURE

66th CONGRESS,
    1st Session.   IN OPEN EXECUTIVE SESSION.
              TREATY OF PEACE WITH GERMANY.
        IN THE SENATE OF THE UNITED STATES.
        November 3 (calendar day, November 6), 1919.
                    RESERVATIONS
    Intended to be proposed by Mr. Lodge to (S. Doc. 85)
              the treaty of peace with Germany.

1. The reservations and understandings adopted by the Senate are to be made a part and a condition of the resolution of ratification, which ratification is not to take effect or bind the United States until the said reservations and understandings adopted by the Senate have been accepted by an ex[c]hange of notes as a part and a condition of said resolution of ratification by at least three of the four Principal Allied and Associated Powers, to wit, Great Britain, France, Italy, and Japan.

2. The United States so understands and construes Article 1 that in case of notice of withdrawal from the league of nations, as provided in said article, the United States shall be the sole judge as to whether all its international obligations and all its obligations under the said covenant have been fulfilled, and notice of withdrawal by the United States may be given by a concurrent resolution of the Congress of the United States.

3. The United States assumes no obligation to preserve the territorial integrity or political independence of any other country or to interfere in controversies between nations—whether members of the league or not—under the provisions of Article 10, or to employ the military or naval forces of the United States under any article of the treaty for any purpose, unless in any particular case the Congress, which, under the Constitution, has the sole power to declare war or authorize the employment of the military or naval forces of the United States, shall by act or joint resolution so provide.

4. No mandate shall be accepted by the United States under Article 22, Part 1, or any other provision of the treaty of peace with Germany, except by action of the Congress of the United States.

5. The United States reserves to itself exclusively the right to decide what questions are within its domestic jurisdiction and declares that all domestic and political questions relating wholly or in part to its internal affairs, including immigration, labor, coastwise traffic, the tariff, commerce, the suppression of traffic in women and children and in opium and other dangerous drugs, and all other domestic questions, are solely within the jurisdiction of the United States and are not under this treaty to be submitted in any way either to arbitration or to the consideration of the council or of the assembly of the league of nations, or any agency thereof, or to the decision or recommendation of any other power.

6. The United States will not submit to arbitration or to inquiry by the assembly or by the council of the league of nations, provided for in said treaty of peace, any questions which in the judgment of the United States depend upon or relate to its long-established policy, commonly known as the Monroe doctrine; said doctrine is to be interpreted by the United States alone and is hereby declared to be wholly outside the jurisdiction of said league of nations and entirely unaffected by any provision contained in the said treaty of peace with Germany.

7. The United States withholds its assent to Articles 156, 157, and 158, and reserves full liberty of action with respect to any controversy which may arise under said articles between the Republic of China and the Empire of Japan.

8. The Congress of the United States will provide by law for the appointment of the representatives of the United States in the assembly and the council of the league of nations, and may in its discretion provide for the participation of the United States in any commission, committee, tribunal, court, council, or conference, or in the selection of any members thereof and for the appointment of members of said commissions, committees, tribunals, courts,

councils, or conferences, or any other representatives under the treaty of peace, or in carrying out its provisions, and until such participation and appointment have been so provided for and the powers and duties of such representatives have been defined by law, no person shall represent the United States under either said league of nations or the treaty of peace with Germany or be authorized to perform any act for or on behalf of the United States thereunder, and no citizen of the United States shall be selected or appointed as a member of said commissions, committees, tribunals, courts, councils, or conferences except with the approval of the Senate of the United States.

9. The United States understands that the reparation commission will regulate or interfere with exports from the United States to Germany, or from Germany to the United States, only when the United States by Act or Joint Resolution of Congress approves such regulation or interference.

10. The United States shall not be obligated to contribute to any expenses of the league of nations, or of the secretariat, or of any commission, or committee, or conference or other agency, organized under the league of nations or under the treaty or for the purpose of carrying out the treaty provisions, unless and until an appropriation of funds available for such expenses shall have been made by the Congress of the United States.

11. If the United States shall at any time adopt any plan for the limitation of armaments proposed by the council of the league of nations under the provisions of Article 8, it reserves the right to increase such armaments without the consent of the council whenever the United States is threatened with invasion or engaged in war.

12. The United States reserves the right to permit, in its discretion, the nationals of a covenant-breaking State, as defined in Article 16 of the covenant of the league of nations, residing within the United States or in countries other than that violating said Article 16, to continue their commercial, financial, and personal relations with the nationals of the United States.

13. Nothing in Articles 296, 297, or in any of the annexes thereto or in any other article, section, or annex of the treaty of peace with Germany shall, as against citizens of the United States, be taken to mean any confirmation, ratification, or approval of any act otherwise illegal or in contravention of the rights of citizens of the United States.

14. The United States declines to accept, as trustee or in her own right, any interest in or any responsibility for the government or disposition of the overseas possessions of Germany, her rights

and titles to which Germany renounces to the Principal Allied and Associated Powers under Articles 119 to 127, inclusive.

15. The United States reserves to itself exclusively the right to decide what questions affect its honor or its vital interests and declares that such questions are not under this treaty to be submitted in any way either to arbitration or to the consideration of the council or of the assembly of the league of nations or any agency thereof or to the decision or recommendation of any other power.

Printed copy (WP, DLC).

From Robert Lansing

My dear Mr. President:　　　　　Washington November 15, 1919.

Mr. Tumulty asked me a few days ago for a list of the vacancies in the diplomatic service, from which I assume that you are contemplating making some appointments in the near future. I hope before any are made that you will review the names which have been suggested to me by various leading Democrats, as some of them seem to me particularly worthy of consideration.

In this connection I am especially anxious to have William Phillips named as Minister to The Netherlands. I have known for some time that he was desirous of returning to the foreign service, and in view of his long and loyal service as Assistant Secretary I feel that we should meet his wish. He will be a very real loss to the Department but we would lose him anyway, as I learn indirectly that his physician has stated that his health requires him to give up the close and confining routine of his present office. He has not been at all well and his wife has been much worried about him for the past year. Loyalty and a high sense of duty have prevented him from leaving the departmental service.

In view of his ability, his experience and his faithfulness as Assistant Secretary I earnestly hope that you will find it possible to appoint him Minister to The Hague, vice Mr. Garrett,[1] resigned.

Faithfully yours,　　Robert Lansing.

TLS (WP, DLC).
[1] That is, John Work Garrett.

From Carter Glass

My dear Mr. President:　　　　　Washington November 16, 1919.

The Governor of Virginia[1] has tendered me an ad interim appointment to the Senate of the United States pending the election of a successor to the late Senator Martin in November of next year. It is a high distinction and a mark of confidence which I deeply appreciate. But, dearly as I love my own State, I cannot fail to realize that my immediate obligation is to you and to the country in your hour of illness.

Hence, if it is your judgment that I would better remain at my post in the Treasury, you may be sure I am quite prepared cheerfully to accept that view. Conversely, if it should seem to you advisable, in all the circumstances, for me to take service again in the legislative branch of the government, I would desire to accept the honor which Governor Davis has been pleased to offer me.

With assurances of unabated devotion and great anxiety for your complete restoration to health, I am, Mr. President,

Sincerely yours,   Carter Glass.

TLS (WP, DLC).
[1] Westmoreland Davis, Democrat.

From George V

[London] (Received Nov. 16, 1919.)

My son has transmitted to me your kind message of greetings and also the good news that you are making satisfactory progress towards recovery at which I rejoice for I have been much concerned at your illness. I deeply appreciate the cordial reception given to my son by everyone in Washington and I shall follow with great interest the further events of his visit to your country. The Queen joins with me in expressing our sincere regards to Mrs. Wilson.   George, R.I.

T telegram (WP, DLC).

Joseph Patrick Tumulty to Edith Bolling Galt Wilson

Dear Mrs. Wilson: The White House 17 November 1919.

Will you get the following information to the President before he sees Senator Hitchcock this morning?

Senator Underwood says that the President ought to insist on his friends in the Senate voting to defeat the Lodge resolution of ratification, and that he should insist upon Senator Hitchcock's favoring a vote on unconditional ratification of the Treaty. Senator Underwood says this will put the President in a position to dictate the terms of settlement between the different forces in the Senate.

Sincerely yours,   [J P Tumulty]

CCL (J. P. Tumulty Papers, DLC).

A Memorandum by Cary Travers Grayson

HITCHCOCK interview with the President
on the Peace Treaty—November 17, 1919.

Senator Hitchcock called at the White House today at 10:30 for a conference with the President concerning the recent developments in the Senate in connection with the ratification of the Peace Treaty. The Senator had sent me a copy of the Lodge resolution, which I read to the President.

The Senator, after exchanging good-morning greetings with the President, asked him if he had read the Lodge resolution, and whether he had anything to suggest concerning it. The President immediately replied: "I consider it a nullification of the Treaty and utterly impossible." He then drew an analogy between this and South Carolina's threat to nullify the Constitution. Senator Hitchcock then called the President's attention to the changes the Senate had made in Article X, to which the President replied: "That cuts the very heart out of the Treaty; I could not stand for those changes for a moment because it would humiliate the United States before all of the allied countries." Senator Hitchcock said: "What would be the effect of the defeat of the Treaty by the Lodge resolution?" The President's answer was: "The United States would suffer the contempt of the world. We will be playing into Germany's hands. Think of the humiliation we would suffer in having to ask Germany whether she would accept such and such reservation!" The President said: "If the Republicans are bent on defeating this Treaty, I want the vote of each, Republican and Democrat, recorded, because they will have to answer to the country in the future for their acts. They must answer to the people. I am a sick man, lying in this bed, but I am going to debate this issue with these gentlemen in their respective states whenever they come up for re-election if I have breath enough in my body to carry on the fight. I shall do this even if I have to give my life to it. And I will get their political scalps when the truth is known to the people. They have got to account to their constituents for their actions in this matter. I have no doubts as to what the verdict of the people will be when they know the facts. Mind you, Senator, I have no hostility towards these gentlemen but an utter contempt."

Senator Hitchcock favored certain compromises with the Republicans. The President said: "With the exception of interpretations, which would not alter the substance, I am not willing to make any compromise other than that we agreed upon at our meeting on [blank]."[1] The President's position was that he would not oppose reservations which were merely interpretations of the Treaty, but that he was irreconcilably opposed to any alteration of the Treaty which would cause a recommitment to council with other nations.

The Senator told the President that he had had a conference with Lord Grey, the British Ambassador, and with Mr. Jusserand, the French Ambassador. They told the Senator that they considered—and relying on official advices from their own countries they knew that their respective countries considered—that Senator Lodge and the Republican party had killed the Peace Treaty and the League of Nations. They also commented on the fact that this view had been published in both English and French papers. They also expressed the belief that their countries would reject a Treaty amended in accordance with the Lodge resolution.

The President interrogated Senator Hitchcock as to what had occurred in the Senate concerning the Treaty in the last month. He said: "I have been lying on my back and have been very weak, and it has fatigued me to read and to discuss matters in my mind, so to speak. I have been kept in the dark to a certain extent except what Mrs. Wilson and Doctor Grayson have told me, and they have purposely kept a good deal from me. I want you to tell me now just everything that has taken place, so I may pick up the threads that were left when I was put to bed." These interrogations were at considerable length, the interview lasting one hour and five minutes. Whenever Senator Hitchcock would bring forth some argument why so and so was done, the President would combat him and ask to be advised why it was done and for what purpose. He said repeatedly: "Senator, I think you have acted very wisely and used good judgment in the circumstances, but why did you do so and so. I am not criticising you but I am asking you for information."

As the interview was drawing to a close the President said: "If it is not too much trouble, will you please send me a little notice of what is transpiring during the day so that at your next visit I may be familiar with what has occurred and be prepared to discuss the situation with you." The Senator replied that he would be very glad to comply with his request.

As the Senator arose to leave the room, he said: "Mr. President, I hope I have not weakened you by this long discussion." And the President smilingly replied: "No, Senator, you have strengthened me against the opponents."

After the Senator and I had left the room, the Senator turned to me and said: "The President is looking remarkably well. He has strengthened so much more physically and mentally since I saw him last. He is very combative today as he sits up there in that bed. On certain compromises he is as immovable as the Rock of Gibraltar." The Senator also said to me: "I would give anything if the Democrats, in fact, all the Senate, could see the attitude that man took this morning. Think how effective it would be if they could see the picture as you and I saw it this morning!"

During the interview the President, in commenting to Senator Hitchcock concerning Senator Hoke Smith, said: "Don't bother about him. That is his usual attitude. He is always wrong in debate but he votes right. You need not pay any attention to him."

T MS (received from James Gordon Grayson and Cary T. Grayson, Jr.).
[1] We know very little about this earlier meeting, except that it took place. The only evidence concerning it is the following excerpt from a memoir by Hitchcock:

". . . The trip was abandoned and he came back to Washington. Instead of reviving he had a stroke and became a helpless bedridden invalid while the fight was raging in the Senate.

"At this time I was apparently the only one permitted to see him. Not even his cabinet officers were admitted. He was afflicted by several maladies besides the stroke. On my first visit I was shocked to see that within a few weeks he had become an old man. As he lay in bed slightly propped up by pillows with the useless arm concealed beneath the cover I beheld an emaciated old man with a thin white beard which had been permitted to grow. But his eye was clear and his resolve strong. When I reported to him that we were defeating the dangerous amendments one by one and would soon have them all out of the way he brightened up. But when I had to tell him we could not ratify the treaty without reservations he became anxious again. He asked how many votes we could get for ratification without reservations. I told him not over forty-five out of ninety-six. He fairly groaned: 'Is it possible, is it possible.' " "Wilson's Place in History," T MS (G. M. Hitchcock Papers, DLC).

Two News Reports

[Nov. 17, 1919]

PRESIDENT WILL POCKET TREATY
IF PASSED AS MODIFIED

Washington, Nov. 17.—The fight in the Senate over the peace treaty with Germany reached an acutely critical stage today with two developments. These were:

President Wilson told Senator Hitchcock, the Democratic leader, at a conference at the White House, that he would "pocket" the treaty if the Lodge resolution of ratification, with the majority reservations as a part of it, were adopted.

The Senate killed the last two reservations on the committee program, one of which rejected participation in the disposal of the German colonies and the other excluded the League of Nations from action affecting the "honor and vital interests" of the United States. Senator Lodge, the Republican leader, announced that he would keep the Senate in session tomorrow until the forty remaining reservations offered by various Senators had been disposed of. He will then move the adoption of his resolution of ratification, which will come up for a vote on Wednesday.

Leaders among the middle ground Republican Senators conferred among themselves over a hint thrown out by Senator Hitchcock that the President might accept the majority reservations if a slight change were made in that on Article X. touching on the guarantee of territorial integrity and political independence of members of the League of Nations, and if Reservation No. 1, originally known as the preamble, requiring the assent of three of the four principal signatories to the reservations, were eliminated.

Senator Hitchcock made it plain, after his conference with the President, that Mr. Wilson was unalterably opposed to the so-called preamble, the President's attitude being actuated, it is understood, by insistent objections raised to it, as cable dispatches have indicated, by Great Britain and France. With the preamble embraced in the resolution of ratification, Mr. Hitchcock said the President would "pigeonhole the treaty."

At the same time Mr. Hitchcock gave what was taken by the opposing forces as a clear indication that President Wilson was willing to compromise with the majority reservationists if the preamble were stricken out and Article X. altered along the line of the substitute reservation offered by Mr. Hitchcock last week.

In talks with newspaper men Mr. Hitchcock said that the President was not opposed to "all the Lodge reservations," but he declined to specify which ones the Executive would accept as a basis of compromise.

That the President had reached the point of acceptance of any of the Lodge reservations came as a surprise to the Republican leaders.

The middle ground Senators, apparently impressed that there was an opportunity of saving the treaty from defeat, seized upon it with the view of determining if agreement actually could be effected.

At the end of the day the treaty situation was more tangled than ever, with the Administration forces saying that they would vote down the Lodge ratifying resolution and the middle-ground Senators apparently undecided what attitude to pursue after that to prevent the treaty from being "pocketed."

Senator Hitchcock asserted unqualifiedly that as an outcome of his conference with the President, the Lodge resolution would be voted down. After that, he said, the Administration forces would endeavor to obtain the adoption of their substitute resolution, with the reservations offered by Mr. Hitchcock. If that were rejected, as the Democrats expect it will be, then, Mr. Hitchcock said, the Senate would be ready to consider compromise steps.

Senator Lodge said that he thought the preamble ought to stay. He told a group of newspaper men tonight that he did not believe that the effort of Democrats to remove it from the resolution of ratification would succeed. While there are a number of Republicans who seem to think that the preamble is superfluous in that the reservations must go to the principal signatories, yet Senator Lodge does not share that opinion.

In the Senate lobbies, however, throughout the afternoon, the talk of compromise was in the air. Radical Senators among the Republicans, discussing the hint that President Wilson would ultimately accept the majority reservations, without the preamble and with Article X. changed, characterized the reported shift in the President's attitude as evidence that he had become convinced that compromise was necessary to prevent the treaty from being sidetracked.

Middle-ground Senators, notably Senator Lenroot of Wisconsin, while declining to say that they actually would bolt the Lodge program and vote to eliminate the preamble, gave unmistakable indication that they were seriously considering such a move.

Senator Lenroot declared, however, that overtures for compromise must come from Senator Hitchcock before they would be taken up by the middle-grounders. Senator Hitchcock, when asked whether the Lodge resolution would be accepted with the two changes indicated, said he was not prepared to say what the basis of compromise "might be." He declined to discuss the talk of President Wilson being willing to accept the treaty with the preamble eliminated.

As to Article X., Mr. Hitchcock remarked that the substitute he had offered differed only slightly from the majority's reservation. To this most of the Republicans agreed, although refusing to admit that the Hitchcock substitute would be accepted in place of that of Mr. Lodge.

The effort for compromise, it was made clear by Mr. Hitchcock, would not be initiated by the Administration forces until after the Lodge resolution was voted down and the minority resolution put before the Senate.

Senator Hitchcock's conference with President Wilson lasted nearly an hour. The Senator said he found the President greatly improved, bright, and cheerful, and fully acquainted with the treaty events as they have developed in the Senate since Mr. Hitchcock's previous visit two weeks ago. The President appeared to be full of fight as [to] the outcome of the Senate's action on the treaty.

"The President told me that he had read and considered the Lodge reservations," said Senator Hitchcock, "He characterized them, as a whole, as a nullification of the treaty and utterly impossible of acceptance. He had not changed his mind as to their effect upon the treaty.

"President Wilson will pocket the treaty if the Lodge program of reservations is carried out in the ratifying resolution. The President did not say, however, that all the Lodge reservations were unacceptable."

"Did he say which reservations he would be willing to accept?" was asked.

"I know the President's ideas on that subject but I do not feel free to quote him," said Mr. Hitchcock. "The one he considered as killing the treaty without any action on his part is the first reservation, requiring three of the four principal Allied Powers to consent to the reservations adopted by specific, formal action. He regards that reservation as being as bad as an amendment."

"How about Article X.?" was asked.

"That is very objectionable to the President," said the Senator.

"Are your statements with reference to these reservations a reflection of the President's ideas?" Mr. Hitchcock was asked.

"I do not like to quote him at this time," was the reply.

Asked what action would be taken if the Lodge resolution of ratification commanded the two-thirds vote necessary to adoption, Mr. Hitchcock said:

"I think the President would like to have the treaty defeated in the Senate rather than to assume all responsibility for its rejection, and I told him that that would be the probable outcome.

"I am satisfied that the President will withdraw the treaty after the Lodge resolution of ratification is defeated, unless the deadlock promises a means of compromise. He could then send the treaty back in the next session of Congress or later."

"Did you discuss any means of ending the war with Germany if the present treaty is rejected?" was asked.

"We did not," replied Mr. Hitchcock. "We did not consider the possibility of passing a joint or concurrent resolution."

Senator Hitchcock went on to say that "no definite conclusion had been reached by the Democrats for rejection of the treaty."

"I expect," said the Senator, "to get the Democratic friends of the treaty together before the Lodge resolution is voted on. When that resolution is out of the way we will try to get together with the Republicans who really want the treaty ratified. All pledges of the Republicans to vote for the Lodge resolution program will be off after that has been rejected. The Republicans will then be released and can treat with us."

Senator Hitchcock thought, he said, that changes would be in order under the closure rule on any resolution of ratification after the Senate had voted adversely upon that of the majority. Under

Vice President Marshall's ruling, he said, new matter could be added to any of the resolutions not acted upon before.

"I told the President that adjournment might occur with the treaty pending," said Senator Hitchcock.

"The President said, 'There is merit in that suggestion. I would like to have some of the Senators go home to their constituents while the treaty is still pending.'"

Senator Lenroot, who voted for the preamble, said he did so because of the agreement reached among the Republican Senators, when compromise was effected among the various elements in the party ranks, to "stand by the Lodge program." This "gentleman's agreement," Mr. Lenroot said, would run only until the vote on the Lodge resolution, after which the Republican Senators would be at liberty to make any agreement they desired. He was careful to say that he would not come to any final decision as to voting to eliminate the preamble until the Lodge resolution was voted down.

Exactly the same attitude was expressed by others of the middle-ground Senators.

While the compromise talk was going on, the Senate, by a vote of 64 to 29, defeated the committee reservation drafted by Senator Shields, Democrat, of Tennessee, to eliminate the United States from participation in the disposition of the German overseas colonies. By a vote of 56 to 36 it rejected the reservation, suggested by Senator Reed, Democrat, of Missouri, providing that questions affecting the "honor and vital interests" of the United States must not be submitted to the League of Nations for consideration, or to any arbitration.

Later a reservation, offered by Senator Owen, Democrat, of Oklahoma, providing that the protectorate of Great Britain over Egypt is "understood to be merely a means through which the nominal suzerainty of Turkey over Egypt shall be transferred to the Egyptian people," and is not to be construed as a recognition by the United States of any sovereign rights of Great Britain over the Egyptian people, was defeated, 45 to 37.

Another reservation by Mr. Owen reaffirming the principle of President Wilson's "Fourteen Points" in the treaty with Germany, was defeated by a viva voce vote.

Senator McCumber, Republican, of North Dakota, offered a reservation to provide that the United States withhold its assent to the labor provisions of the treaty—Article XIII.—without specific action by Congress when its participation under these provisions is sought. This reservation, which went over until tomorrow, is said to have the support of the majority of the Senate.

Senator Lodge gave notice, at the end of the day, that he would hold the Senate in session tomorrow night, if necessary, in an effort to dispose of the remaining reservations.

[*Nov. 17, 1919*]

President Out on the Lawn
For First Time Since Return

Washington, Nov. 17.—For the first time since his return to Washington from his Western tour President Wilson today went outside of the White House. He was rolled in a wheel chair on to the lawn near the south portico and for more than an hour enjoyed the fresh air and sunshine.

Today's event marked one more step in the progress of the President toward health. He is gaining steadily but has not yet reached the point where it is possible for him to take an automobile ride.

Printed in the *New York Times*, Nov. 18, 1919.

From the Desk Diary of Robert Lansing

Monday Nov 17 [1919]

Tumulty phoned that Prest told Hitchcock he would withdraw treaty if Lodge reservations were adopted. I urged him to have Glass resign at once since he intended to accept senatorship. Asked him to call Cabinet meeting tomorrow.

Gilbert Monell Hitchcock to Edith Bolling Galt Wilson, with Enclosure

My dear Mrs. Wilson: [Washington] November 17, 1919

Enclosed please find the draft of a letter which might be addressed to me if it meets with the President's approval.

The Senate today rejected by large majorities the fourteenth and fifteenth reservations proposed by Senator Lodge.

There are additional indications which come to me from hour to hour of uneasiness in the republican camp.

In a parliamentary sense at least I think our position has been considerably improved. At this writing the probabilities are that the democratic conference will not be held until Tuesday afternoon at the earliest and probably not until Wednesday morning. A letter, however, could be forwarded to me at any time to be held until the conference meets.

I trust my visit to the President this morning did not result in any backset.   Yours sincerely,   G M Hitchcock

TLS (EBW Papers, DLC).

E N C L O S U R E

A Draft of a Letter to Gilbert Monell Hitchcock

To Senator Hitchcock[1]

My dear Senator[2]   ⟨A SUGGESTION.⟩[3]

You were good enough to bring me word that the democratic senators supporting the treaty expected to hold a conference before the final vote on the Lodge resolution of ratification and that they would be glad to receive a word of counsel from me.

I should hesitate to offer it in any detail but I assume that the senators ⟨only⟩ desire my judgment *only*[4] upon the all-important question of the final vote on the resolution containing the many reservations by Senator Lodge. On that I can not hesitate, for in my opinion the resolution in that form does not provide for ratification, but rather for ⟨defeat⟩ *the nullification*[5] of the treaty. I sincerely hope that the friends and supporters of the treaty will vote against the Lodge resolution of ratification.

I understand that the door will probably then be open for a ⟨possible compromise agreement on a resolution that will make ratification possible. At least the democratic senators will have made a record in support of the treaty by bringing forward a real⟩ *genuine*[6] resolution of ratification ⟨while those who oppose it will be compelled to bear the responsibility⟩.

I hope therefore that all true friends of the treaty will refuse to support the Lodge resolution.

T MS (EBW Papers, DLC).
  [1] EBWhw.
  [2] *Idem.*
  [3] This and other deletions either by Wilson or Mrs. Wilson.
  [4] EBWhw.
  [5] WWhw.
  [6] *Idem.*

To Carter Glass

My dear Mr. Secretary: [The White House] 17 November 1919.

It was most thoughtful and generous of you to consult my desires in the matter of your selection by Governor Davis for the senatorship from Virginia, left vacant by the death of Senator Martin. Of course you must accept the appointment. While your withdrawal from the Administration as a Cabinet officer is a matter of deep regret to me and to your associates, I feel that your fine ability may again be utilized as a member of the Senate, in advancing the interests of the Nation and the Administration in that great forum.

No President has had a more loyal, a more devoted, or a more resourceful friend than you have been to me. Your work as chairman of the Banking and Currency Committee of the House of Representatives in connection with the establishment of the Federal Reserve Act, and your stout support of the Administration at every turn while a member of the House caused us to rely upon you in every emergency.

While your occupancy of the office of Secretary of the Treasury has been brief, the administration of its affairs under your guidance has moved forward to the highest levels of efficiency and high devotion to the public interest.

Governor Davis has honored the old State of Virginia by paying tribute to so distinguished a son. We shall watch your career in the Senate with affectionate interest and admiration.

Cordially and sincerely yours,   Woodrow Wilson[1]

TLS (Letterpress Books, WP, DLC).
[1] There is a CC of this letter in WP, DLC, with four purely stylistic changes in EBWhw, which would seem to indicate that Tumulty prepared the draft of the letter, that Mrs. Wilson read it to Wilson, and that he dictated the changes.

A Memorandum by William Phillips

[Washington] November 17, 1919.

MEMORANDUM.

Inquiries were made of the White House today, asking whether the President could indicate his answers to the following recent notes from the Secretary:

1. Regarding the negotiations for the Turkish Treaty,
2. Regarding the IMPERATOR.

Mr. Forster tells me that the President indicated that he was not ready to consider either question until he was stronger and that this answer covered both inquiries.   WP

TI MS (R. Lansing Papers, DLC).

Edward Mandell House to Edith Bolling Galt Wilson, with Enclosures

Dear Mrs. Wilson: New York City. November 17, 1919.

I am inclosing a cable which has just come from Sir William Wiseman. If it were not for their economic dependence upon us I have no doubt the Allied Nations would be glad to have an opportunity to say what they think of the Senate's action.

I inclose a note to the President which I hope you will think he is well enough to read now, or before long.

Your friend always,   [E. M. House]

Before Wiseman left I agreed that his cables should be kept in confidence.

CCL (E. M. House Papers, CtY).

E N C L O S U R E   I

[London] November 12th, 1919.

Please deliver following cable personally to COL. HOUSE, and send copy to TYRRELL:

Action of U. S. SENATE in delaying ratification of Peace, and generally using vital international situation for party purposes, has aroused strong feeling of irritation among general public here as well as political circles.

PHILIP KERR asks me to tell you that H.M.G. do not think they will be able to accept any American reservations whatever. League Covenant is admittedly not perfect document, and only basis on which Great Powers can be expected to join is that of mutual trust, looking to the League itself to amend and perfect its own Constitution as experience shows wise.

You can cable me through this channel.

CC MS (E. M. House Papers, CtY).

E N C L O S U R E   I I

From Edward Mandell House

Dear Governor: New York City. November 17, 1919.

This is just a line to tell you how glad I am that you are getting on so finely. It is good to have your steady hand at the helm once more, and I hope no further mishaps may come to you.

After many weeks of painful illness I find myself practically well and of course you know I am always at your service.

Affectionately yours,   [E. M. House]

TCL (E. M. House Papers, CtY).

Robert Lansing to Frank Lyon Polk

PERSONAL AND SECRET:

My dear Frank: Washington November 17, 1919.

By the time this letter reaches you the fate of the Treaty in the Senate will have been decided and so my comments as to the proabablities [probabilities] of its ratification in any form at all acceptable would be of doubtful value. However you may find some interest in the views I hold at the present time.

The treaty when laid before the Senate was tremendously handicapped by two things; first, the Covenant as drafted which certainly from the legal standpoint was open to valid criticism because it apparently was in defiance of certain constitutional provisions; and second, the insensate animosity of a considerable group of Republican Senators to the President personally. This latter feeling enhanced the objections to the League because he with the aid of Colonel House was looked upon as the author of the Covenant or at least its chief sponsor and advocate. If his enemies could practically destroy the League or render it worthless, they were particularly desirous of doing so because they felt that it would humble his pride of authorship and prove to the world that he was by no means so great and powerful as had been supposed. With this end in view the Senate majority began its campaign apparently against the Covenant but really against the President.

The earlier hearings before the Committee on Foreign Relations, among them mine, showed conclusively that it was personal hostility to the President which was the controlling motive, and that the interests of the United States were really secondary to them in importance. It is undeniable that the attempts of the Committee to discredit the President in his conduct of the negotiations at Paris were more or less successful so far as the public were concerned. Unfortunately the President's record was vulnerable and nothing was overlooked by the partisans who were testing every joint of his armor.

There is no doubt that at the outset the great majority of the people were back of the President and the League. I felt that if the President did not assume a defensive attitude he would in large measure retain this popular support, but that, if he began to explain the Covenant, he would unavoidably become involved in arguments which would be subject to attack arousing doubt as to their validity in the public mind. For that reason I strongly advised him, two days after I landed, not to make a speaking tour for the League. He yielded very unwillingly agreeing to postpone his trip, though he would not abandon it.

I had hoped that the postponement would result in abandonment, but as the attacks on the weak points in the Covenant increased in virulence the President became incensed and pugnacious with the result that he was inflexible in his determination to go out and appeal to the people over the heads of the Senators. I attempted again to dissuade him from taking this step, because I felt sure that it would solidify the opposition in the Senate and that instead of being an offensive, which would only amount to abuse anyway, it would be a defense of the Covenant.

You know, if you followed the President's speeches in the West that, while he used some rather undignified expressions about the opposition in the Senate, he sought to defend the Covenant and its various provisions. I am sure the performance lost rather than gained support for the Treaty. It came to me from various sources that the public began to consider that the objections had some merit otherwise the President would not have taken so much trouble to answer them. Prior to his western trip the public were disposed to brush the objections aside on the supposition that they were only put forward to discredit the President rather than the Treaty. Thus, the President's speeches, while they may have won over a few, lost, in my opinion, a great deal of public support, especially as the whole proceeding took on the character of a party issue.

Then, as you know, came the President's physical collapse, his return to Washington, and his elimination from the struggle by reason of his grave illness. While his inability to direct the defense of the Treaty in the Senate may have affected the present situation unfavorably, I am not at all sure that he could have accomplished more than Hitchcock, who has kept his head and shown himself capable and adroit.

The President lost the best chance to compromise on moderate reservations last August. I suggested that policy to him and his jaw shot out and he said that there were going to be no reservations and if the opposition wanted a fight they would "get a damned good one," referring of course to his appeal to the people. With a majority against him on some sort of modification of the Treaty I confess that his course seemed to me a policy which would force the "moderatists" to join the "irreconcilables." Now that is just what has happened and the steam-roller is working smoothly and successfully.

Today Hitchcock had a brief talk with the President, which in his state of health is a dangerous thing to do, and the President said that if the resolution of ratification was passed with the present reservations, he would withdraw the treaty. Both he and Hitchcock think that this step will create a situation where they can dictate moderate reservations which will be acceptable to other nations as well as to the President. Now you understand this is the last stand. The President is with his back to the wall and means to go down rather than surrender. I am not so sanguine of success as he and the Senator seem to be, judging from Tumulty, who is my informant. Many Senators will rejoice if the Treaty is withdrawn and will use all their influence to prevent its revival. These enemies of the document have grown stronger than they were last August and I am not certain by any means that they can be defeated. If this policy succeeds I will certainly have to take off my hat to Hitchcock as a great parliamentary leader. He showed his adroitness in announcing after he left the President, that the Lodge reservations were unacceptable to the President, who would, if they were adopted, "pocket" the treaty. At least he has thrown down the gauntlet and it will be interesting to see the effect.

Meanwhile the industrial unrest and the outbreaks of Bolshevists in this country together with the serious strike of the coal miners, the injunction against the leaders and the present miners' conference here have diverted public attention from the Treaty in large measure. Three months ago everybody talked of it. Now everybody is weary and only desire to have the matter settled one way or the other. They do not seem to care how it is settled. Since the grave problems of domestic nature take up the attention of the people, they have lost interest in the economic condition of the world. The disposition seems to be to attend to our own affairs and let the rest of the nations go to the devil if they want to.

As for assuming a mandate over anything or anybody the present state of the public mind makes the idea almost out of the question. I think that the President will have to abandon any plan that he may have to assume guardianship over Armenia or Constantinople. I believe the Republicans are solid against doing it and that there are many Democrats who feel the same way.

Altogether the outlook for the President's world policies is very gloomy. He cannot, I feel sure, carry them through. Why he cannot seems to me evident. And I think the blame can be placed with almost equal certainty. It causes one, loyal to the President, a feel-

ing of sorrow and regret to see his great reputation as a leader being thus shattered. He reached the zenith of his greatness in January of this year, and since that time he has lost in prestige and
popularity at home and abroad. I shall not go into the reasons but
leave you to judge them as you can do as well as I.

I have heard nothing from Colonel House directly or indirectly
for a month. I cannot find that he is taking any active part in public
affairs. He is sharing the President's character of a target for senatorial sarcasm and curses. I have wondered sometimes what he
thinks of this awful mess and if he sees any way out.

I must close to get this in the pouch. With my affectionate
wishes to you and Mrs. Polk,[1] and my hope to see you in about a
month I am   Faithfully yours,   Robert Lansing.

TLS (F. L. Polk Papers, CtY).
  [1] Elizabeth Sturgis Potter Polk.

A News Report

[*Nov. 18, 1919*]

President, Outdoors Again,
Holds Informal Lawn Party

Washington, Nov. 18.—President Wilson was again able to go
out of the White House today in his wheel chair to the lawn south
of the White House, where he spent some time in the sunshine
and fresh air. The President, in fact, had an informal lawn party
for, while he was enjoying his wheel-chair rides around the paths
of the "back yard" of the White House, Mrs. Wilson, Miss Margaret
Wilson, Rear Admiral Cary T. Grayson, the President's physician,
and the nurses were along as company.

There is a large flock of sheep in the White House grounds, belonging to the President,[1] who bought them several years ago, and
today he was much interested in the flock which came close to the
party. From the windows in the Cabinet room the members of the
Cabinet while in session could see the President in his wheel chair.

Printed in the *New York Times*, Nov. 19, 1919.
  [1] There have been several references in past volumes to the sheep that were grazing
on the White House grounds during the war and to the sale of their clip for the benefit
of the American Red Cross.

To Gilbert Monell Hitchcock[1]

My dear Senator: The White House 18 November, 1919.

You were good enough to bring me word that the Democratic Senators supporting the treaty expected to hold a conference before the final vote on the Lodge resolution of ratification and that they would be glad to receive a word of counsel from me. I should hesitate to offer it in any detail but I assume that the Senators desire my judgment only upon the all-important question of the final vote on the resolution containing the many reservations by Senator Lodge. On that I can not hesitate, for in my opinion the resolution in that form does not provide for ratification, but rather for the nullification of the treaty. I sincerely hope that the friends and supporters of the treaty will vote against the Lodge resolution of ratification. I understand that the door will probably then be open for a genuine resolution of ratification. I trust that all true friends of the treaty will refuse to support the Lodge resolution.

Cordially and sincerely yours,   Woodrow Wilson

TLS (G. M. Hitchcock Papers, DLC).
[1] There is an EBWhw copy of this letter in the J. P. Tumulty Papers, DLC.

Gilbert Monell Hitchcock to Edith Bolling Galt Wilson, with Enclosure

My dear Mrs. Wilson: [Washington] November 18, 1919

Work in the Senate today from ten o'clock this morning until this hour (six o'clock) has not been of any great significance except in the adoption of two rather important reservations, one on the labor question and one on equalizing the voting power in the league. I enclose copies.[1] They are both rather drastic and destructive.

The real significant developments today consist of some indication on the republican side of a disposition to consider a compromise but it has not developed enough yet to give much promise. It was intimated to me that Senator Lodge would be willing to confer with me on the subject and so we had a meeting and discussed this proposition which I made to him:

That after the defeat of the Lodge resolution, which is now generally admitted, Senator Lodge support a motion to reconsider, which being carried, I would propose a resolution of ratification with interpretative reservations, whereupon the Senate would recess for the day to give an opportunity for conference to see whether a compromise could be effected. After discussing the proposition Lodge said he would confer with his associates and advise me. He then advised me he could not accept the proposition unless I could state in advance of the vote on his resolution, or at least in advance of the vote on the motion to reconsider, what compromise we could offer. I told him that could not be formulated in so much of a hurry because I must consult not only the President but democratic members in caucus or conference. So the matter stands at the present time.

I hope it will yet work out, however, that after Lodge's resolution is defeated, enough republicans will support my motion to keep the matter before the Senate in some form, pending a possible compromise. I would be perfectly willing when our proposition is before the Senate to have the Senate adjourn until the first Monday in December, but Lodge does not seem to be disposed to do that.

I am enclosing for the President's consideration a statement by Senator Walsh of Montana expressing his view that even if the present Lodge reservation on Article 10 stands and Article 10 is to that extent mutilated and emasculated there is enough workable machinery derived from other articles to unite the nations in preventing a war of conquest.

I would like to say to the President that many democrats hold the same view that Senator Walsh expresses.

Should it become desirable for me to see the President again I will take the liberty of advising you by telephone.

Very sincerely,   G M Hitchcock

TLS (WP, DLC).

[1] They are missing, but they read as follows:

"The United States withholds its Assent to Part XIII [the labor provisions] of said treaty unless Congress, by act or joint resolution, shall hereafter make provision for representation in the organization established by said Part XIII, and in such event the participation of the United States will be governed and conditioned by the provisions of such act or joint resolution." *Cong. Record*, 66th Cong., 1st sess., p. 8699.

"The United States assumes no obligation to be bound by any decision, report, or finding of the council or assembly in which any member of the league and its self-governing dominions, colonies, or parts of empire in the aggregate have cast more than one vote, and assumes no obligation to be bound by any decision, report, or finding of the council or assembly arising out of any dispute between the United States and any member of the league if such member, or any self-governing dominion, colony, empire, or part of empire united with it politically has voted." *Ibid.*, p. 8739.

E N C L O S U R E

Thomas James Walsh to Gilbert Monell Hitchcock

My dear Senator Hitchcock: [Washington] November 18, 1919.

In connection with such negotiations as you may have hereafter concerning some compromise reservations, I venture to suggest that perhaps we have attached undue importance to Article X. I know I have, and on more than one occasion referred to it as the very soul of the Covenant. Let us consider the situation should it be altogether excised, and I assumed the other nations will not assume its obligations if we do not.

By Article XII all members agree to submit to arbitration or inquiry by the Council any dispute likely to lead to a rupture and not to go to war until three months after the award or report.

By Article XIII the members agree not to go to war with any nation that complies with the report of the council on the submission of a dispute.

Then by Article XVI if any member goes to war contrary to the covenants of the League, the economic boycott goes into effect automatically and it commits an act of war against every other member, which is justified in making, if not required in honor, to make war against the offender. In that case the Council under Article XI might, and in a grave case would, recommend warlike measures, if necessary, thus impelling that course. A war of aggression contemplated by Article X would necessarily be contrary to the Covenant, so that it would bring into operation the economic boycott. Accordingly, though I regret exceedingly seeing Article X emasculated, I have ceased to regard it as vital. The removal of it will make less feasible the reduction of armaments, but if it is necessary to save the Treaty to let it go, and I fear it is, I am willing to concede a reservation such as that adopted, which unquestionably cuts the heart out of it.   Very truly yours,   T. J. Walsh

TLS (WP, DLC).

From Carter Glass

My dear Mr. President: Washington November 18, 1919.

I have your very gracious note of the 17th in response to mine of the 16th instant, having reference to my appointment by Governor Davis to the United States Senate as ad interim successor of the late Senator Martin. In agreement with your judgment I shall accept the appointment and I hereby tender my resignation as Secretary of the Treasury to take effect as soon as you may find it convenient to name my successor.

With a very deep sense of appreciation of all your kindness, believe me, my dear Mr. President,

Faithfully yours,   Carter Glass

TLS (WP, DLC).

From Albert, King of the Belgians

Bruxelles (Received Nov. 18, 1919.)

I thank you heartily for your cordial congratulations and your kind appreciation of the steadiness of the Belgian people.[1] The Queen and myself form warmest wishes for your health and send Mrs. Wilson our sincere greetings. Albert.

T telegram (WP, DLC).
[1] WW to Albert, Nov. 13, 1919.

Edith Bolling Galt Wilson to Edward Mandell House

My dear Col. House: The White House Nov. 18, 1919

I read your letter and the cable enclosed to the President, and he asks me to tell you how sorry he is to know you have been ill. As I wrote you he knew nothing of your illness, but when I read him what you said about it, he said, "oh! poor fellow I am so sorry."

He did not ask me where you wrote from, so I fancy he still thinks you are in Paris.

Please thank Mrs. House for her little note with Mr. White's article enclosed.[1] I had not seen it, and have intended every day writing to thank her for sending it. My hands now are so full that I neglect many things.

But I feel equal to anything that comes now that I see steady progress going on, although it is very, very slow.

With good wishes for your own complete recovery, believe me with remembrances from us both

Faithfully, Edith Bolling Wilson

ALS (E. M. House Papers, CtY).
[1] It is missing in both WP, DLC, and the EBW Papers, DLC.

From the Diary of Ray Stannard Baker

New York. Nov. 18, 1919

Went up to luncheon with Colonel House & had a long talk. He had been reading "The Friendly Road"[1] & asked me to autograph it. He is much worried over the present situation & the desperate plight of the treaty. I expected to find him looking very ill: but he looks in fact very well. He philosophized upon the chief asset of the politician. It was not money. Money did not get most men. It was the ability to play upon men's vanity. The compliment of consultation. . . .

Roosevelt had this gift: but Wilson has it not. He never plays on the vanity of anyone: he simply does not know the modern Machievellianism. He consults with no one to flatter his vanity: but only to learn: or to detect.

It is a very curious thing, my own reaction toward the Colonel. I like him very much: he interests & attracts me. I see him playing also on *my* vanity, and remark it to myself—for what can better flatter a writer's vanity than to have a man like his book, buy a beautiful copy of it bound in fancy leather & ask an autograph?—I see this and note it, and like the man very much. For there is beneath it a basis of real sincerity: he does like people, he does enjoy winning them, he does enjoy raising them in their own estimation & he has really read & I think liked my books! This genius for appealing to men's vanity is never wholly artifice. No flatterer who was all flatterer ever succeeded. There has to be a basis of human interest, a foundation of sincere friendliness. It was so with Roosevelt. He, too, played the game (I remember so well the White incident!)[2] but meant a good deal of it. So with the Colonel—who was absolutely ingenuous to-day in revealing his secret of political success. Smooth people along: keep contacts: play on vanities—

No doubt the President has kept House close to him because he recognized that he possessed the arts in which he himself was wanting.

The President is stark in his simplicity, directness, his want of artifice: but those qualities—his true greatness—will not be regarded until he is dead.

There is this also about the Colonel: he is an *instinctive* liberal. He does not think it out, but it is the reaction of his nature. He is a very useful man for that reason alone.

Hw bound diary (R. S. Baker Papers, DLC).
[1] David Grayson [Ray Stannard Baker], *The Friendly Road: New Adventures in Contentment* (Garden City, N. Y., 1913).
[2] Baker probably referred to William Allen White's first meeting with Theodore Roosevelt in June 1897, when Roosevelt so entranced White that ever afterward he thought that Roosevelt was the most splendid man he had ever known. "He overcame me. . . . He poured into my heart such visions, such ideals, such hopes, such a new attitude toward life and patriotism and the meaning of things, as I had never dreamed men had." *The Autobiography of William Allen White* (New York, 1946), p. 247.

From the Diary of Henry Fountain Ashurst

November 19, 1919.

Breakfasted early and went direct to the Capitol, to attend the caucus called by Democratic Leader Hitchcock upon the Lodge Resolution of Ratification. The breeze from my motor-car stirred the dead leaves strewn about, and I knew that President Wilson's Treaty would soon be as dead as those leaves.

Every Democratic Senator who favored the Treaty was present at the caucus except Senator Culberson of Texas, who for months has been ill. Senator Underwood moved that the Democratic Senators vote against the Lodge Resolution of Ratification. Democratic Leader Hitchcock then drew from his breast pocket and read the following letter from President Wilson: . . .[1]

Examining the letter I perceived that it was not signed by President Wilson but that the words "Woodrow Wilson" were affixed thereto by a rubber stamp facsimile in purple ink.

At noon the Senate convened and within ten minutes newspapers containing W.W.'s letter to the caucus were brought into the Senate Chamber. Senator Lodge read the letter into the Congressional Record. The Democratic Senators were astounded that the letter had been given publicity; it enraged the "Mild Reservationists" and two or three of them let off oaths in an undertone.

Roll call on the Lodge Resolution of Ratification. Result:

Ayes	39
Noes	55
Absent	1
Vacancy from Va.	1

On this vote all the Senators who attended today's Democratic caucus voted against the Lodge Resolution of Ratification. Senator Reed, Missouri, moved to reconsider the vote; his motion carried. The administration Senators sought an adjournment but were defeated, whereupon the Vice President held that the motion to reconsider which had just been carried, placed the Treaty before the Senate in a posture, where it was subject to amendment, and where further reservations could be offered. Senator Lodge appealed from the decision and the Chair was overruled; the Pro-Leaguers voting to sustain, and the Anti-Leaguers voting to overrule the Chair, and within ten minutes the Chair was overruled two more times by the same "line-up." In vain the Pro-League senators attempted adjournment; in vain they proposed motions to recommit, and tried to effect compromises with the "Mild Reservationists," but the time for compromises had gone. The Pro-Leaguers had sinned away their day of grace by failing to compromise last August. After parliamentary maneuvering another vote was taken on the Lodge Resolution of Ratification and three Democrats, to wit, Myers, Owen, and Pomerene voted with the Lodge Reservationists, but all other Pro-League Democrats stood against the Lodge Resolution of Ratification.[2] Senator Underwood then asked unanimous consent for a vote upon the ratification of the

Treaty *as it came from the President's hands.* A roll call was had without debate and the naked Treaty without reservations received thirty-eight votes.[3] Thus the Versailles Treaty which has been ratified by the principal allied and associated powers, mustered but thirty-eight votes in the Senate.

T MS (AzU).
[1] Here follows the text of WW to GMH, Nov. 18, 1919.
[2] The second vote on the Lodge resolution was forty-one to fifty.
[3] The vote on this resolution was thirty-eight to fifty-three.

To William Bauchop Wilson

My dear Mr. Secretary: The White House 19 November, 1919.

In accordance with the suggestion given me by the Public Group of the recent industrial conference, I am calling a new body together to carry on this vitally important work, and I trust you will give me the pleasure of naming you as one of its members.

Guided by the experience of the last conference I have thought it advisable that in this new body there should be no recognition of distinctive groups, but that all of the new representatives should have concern that our industries may be conducted with such regard for justice and fair dealing that the workman will feel himself induced to put forth his best effort, that the employer will have an encouraging profit, and that the public will not suffer at the hands of either class. It is my hope that this conference may lay the foundation for the development of standards and machinery within our industries by which these results may be attained.

It is not expected that you will deal directly with any condition which exists today, but that you may be fortunate enough to find such ways as will avoid the repetition of these deplorable conditions.

The conference will meet at a place to be hereafter designated in this city on the 1st of December next.

Cordially and sincerely yours,   Woodrow Wilson[1]

TLS (LDR, RG 174, DNA).
[1] A draft of this letter, prepared by Franklin K. Lane, is printed as Enclosure V with JPT to EBW, Nov. 4, 1919, Vol. 63. Wilson sent the same letter, *mutatis mutandis,* to Thomas Watt Gregory, George Woodward Wickersham, Oscar Solomon Straus, Henry Mauris Robinson, Frank William Taussig, Samuel Walker McCall, Herbert Clark Hoover, Martin Henry Glynn, Henry Carter Stuart, William Oxley Thompson, Richard Hooker, George Theron Slade, Julius Rosenwald, Owen D. Young, Henry Jackson Waters, Stanley King, and Cyrus Hall McCormick, Jr.; all dated November 19, 1919, except for that to McCormick, which was dated November 21, 1919; all TLS (Letterpress Books, WP, DLC). Those persons not previously identified in this series were Slade, a railroad executive who had most recently served as Deputy Director of Transportation with the A.E.F., and Waters, managing editor of the *Weekly Kansas City Star.*

A Draft of a Statement

The White House [c. Nov. 19, 1919]

This Treaty not a particular compact between us & the other Signatory Powers but a general (chiefly European) settlement with the Central Powers, which the associated governments by high valor & the unutterable sacrifices of their people won the right to exact but whose terms they determined in constant conference with us, with unfailing defference to our views & with an honest effort to make them square with the principles we had laid down as the guiding principals of the conflict.

Reservations in effect redifinitions of responsibilities & duties undertaken by us under the Treaty.

This is the field & function of nego[ti]ation not of ratification

EBWhw MS (WP, DLC).

Joseph Patrick Tumulty to Edith Bolling Galt Wilson, with Enclosure

Dear Mrs. Wilson: The White House, 19 November 1919.

Secretary Lansing handed me the enclosed memorandum. Will you speak to the President of it?

Sincerely yours,   J P Tumulty

TLS (WP, DLC).

E N C L O S U R E

MEMORANDUM: FOR MR. TUMULTY.   November 18, 1919.

Matters urgently requiring immediate decision:

1. Participation of the United States in the negotiations for a treaty with Turkey. (See letter to the President, dated November 12th.)

2. Status of the Imperator. (See letter to the President, dated November 5th.[1]

3. Recognition of Costa Rican Government. (See letter to the President, dated November 4, 1919.)[2]

T MS (WP, DLC).
[1] Printed as Enclosure I with JPT to WW, Nov. 11, 1919.
[2] Printed as an Enclosure with JPT to EBW, Nov. 5, 1919 Vol. 63.

Frank Irving Cobb to Edith Bolling Galt Wilson

Dear Mrs. Wilson: New York. November 20, 1919.

I most earnestly hope that the President has not taken the temporary defeat of the treaty too seriously, and that he is not worrying.

The Senate's action may turn out to be the best thing that could have happened short of unqualified ratification, which was impossible in the circumstances.

Anyway, it is still a beautiful fight, and the most important thing is that the President should continue to make steady gains toward complete recovery. The rest will take care of itself.

Mrs. Cobb[1] joins me in sending sincerest regards and best wishes to both of you.   As ever yours,   Frank I. Cobb.

ALS (WP, DLC).
[1] Margaret Hubbard Ayer Cobb.

Robert Lansing to Joseph Patrick Tumulty, with Enclosure

My dear Mr. Tumulty: Washington November 21, 1919.

I am sending to you a letter addressed to the President in an unsealed envelope. After reading, if you have no comment to make upon it, will you be good enough to seal it and deliver it?
                    Very cordially yours,   Robert Lansing.

Dear Mrs. Wilson,
I leave it to your judgment as to what to do with this letter.
                        Sincerely,   Tumulty

TLS (WP, DLC).

E N C L O S U R E

From Robert Lansing

My dear Mr. President: [Washington] November 21, 1919.

Mr. Tumulty, after seeing you yesterday, telephoned me that you opposed any statement being made at the present time in regard to the Senate's refusal to ratify the treaty but at the same time desired matters abroad to continue as they are, which I assume means that we should keep our unofficial representatives in Paris to act as advisers and observers in connection with the various commissions provided for in the treaty and also that our representative should sit on the Supreme Council and that our commissioners should sign the Bulgarian treaty.

As to the omission of any statement at this time I do not think there is any argument in favor of making one.

The continuance of our unofficial activities in Paris is more or less a question of expediency. The removal of our people would unquestionably affect adversely commercial and financial interests in this country. They would enter protests against this course and could be met by the justifiable statement that in view of the Senate's action we could not continue. The consequence would be, I believe, indignation toward the Senators and strong pressure upon them to reverse their action. Already I am beginning to receive evidences of the apprehension with which our business men and financiers view the situation in which the Senate has left American interests. It might be well to increase this resentment against the opponents of the treaty by not attempting to relieve the difficulties of commerce and trade by continuing to participate unofficially in the relations created by the provisions of the treaty. The blame is bound to fall, as it should, upon the Senate in insisting on nullifying reservations.

On the other hand, if we continue the activities in which we have been engaged, the Senate may raise some question as to the propriety of our doing so, and refuse to make the necessary appropriation to pay for the men employed. The Emergency Fund, already overtaxed by royal visits and the regular work of the Department, is quite inadequate to meet this expense, and its use for the proposed continuance is open to question. It will require an appropriation. I am doubtful if that can be obtained if the expenditures are predicated on a final ratification of the treaty. Before the action of the Senate on the treaty they could make no complaint, but now the conditions are different and they may and probably would refuse to reimburse the fund, which would seriously cripple the necessary work of the Department. Of course this does not apply to work under the terms of the armistice.

In view of this state of affairs I believe that careful consideration should be given as to whether it would not be politic to withdraw our men from Europe and let the people draw the conclusion, which would be the right one, that we had done so because of the Senate's action.

As to our representative on the Supreme Council I think that he should be continued—at least until ratifications are deposited by three of the Principal Powers, when, naturally, the functions of the Supreme Council will be in large measure ended, although I antitipate [anticipate] that he will be less influential than he has been

prior to the Senate's action, because foreign governments will undoubtedly assume that the American Government is divided as to
questions of policy. Possibly this question of continuance requires
no consideration as there is a general intention on the part of the
Council to dissolve early in December, since the members feel,
particularly the American and British, that their usefulness is at an
end. They have made all their arrangements for departure and, as
I felt that the work they are now doing, could be done as well, if
not better, through regular diplomatic channels, I have not discouraged them.

In regard to the Bulgarian Treaty and our participation in it as a
signatory there is a clear question of policy. We never were at war
with Bulgaria and we never broke off diplomatic relations with her.
We took part in the negotiations on the theory that under Article X
we were bound to guarantee the settlements and therefore should
have a voice in reaching them and should also be a party to the
treaty. We did take part in the negotiations and were able, I believe,
to obtain more just treatment for Bulgaria than she could have obtained if left to the rapacity and hatred of her neighbors. With the
treaty ready for signature our chief service has been rendered.
Ought we in view of the Senate's action to proceed further and
sign the treaty? So far as the effect on Bulgaria is concerned I do
not see that it makes the least difference whether we do or not, but
it may have an effect on the situation here if we proceed on the
assumption that the reason for continuing is as strong now as it
was before the Senate refused to ratify the treaty with Article X in
it. Personally I am uncertain which policy is the wiser and more
expedient. There is of course no legal reason why we should not
be a party to the treaty regardless of what has taken place, but it is
for you to decide whether or not it is politic to do so in view of what
has occurred.

I am sorry, Mr. President, to disturb you with so long a letter, but
I feel that I should know your views in order that I may carry out
your policy. I hope most sincerely that your recovery from now on
will be speedy; and you may be sure that I will endeavor so far as
I am able to avoid annoying you with the vexatious questions
which seem to multiply rather than decrease because of the inex-
cusable delay in the ratification of the treaty and even more because of the disturbed political and economic state in so many
countries.   Faithfully yours,   [Robert Lansing]

CCL (SDR, RG 59, 763.72119/8126½A, DNA).

Joseph Patrick Tumulty to Edith Bolling Galt Wilson, with Enclosure

Dear Mrs. Wilson: The White House November 21, 1919.

Enclosed is the letter from Senator Underwood which I was to get for the President.   Faithfully yours,   J. P. Tumulty

ENCLOSURE

From Oscar Wilder Underwood

My dear Mr. President: [Washington] November 21, 1919.

This morning, I had a conversation with Mr. Tumulty in reference to the conditions that confront the ratification of the treaty of peace, since the efforts of the Republicans to defeat it on last Wednesday. Mr. Tumulty suggests to me that I write this letter as a memorandum to to [sic] you as to the way I view the situation.

First, the treaty is not dead in the Senate, as Mr. Lodge says it is, but it is before the Senate, where a majority of the Senators can act upon it if they desire to do so. The only thing that can kill it is the direct effort of the Republican majority to destroy it.

I think the vote on Wednesday last will prove to be a distinct shock to the country. The people of America believed that in some way the treaty would be ratified. Its defeat by the Republican majority will shortly produce a reaction in favor of the treaty, in my opinion.

There are in the Senate at present twenty or twenty-five men who are determined to defeat the treaty, by direct or indirect methods. The membership of the Senate is ninety-six. This leaves from seventy-one to seventy-six men, and out of that number we must get sixty-four votes to pass a resolution of ratification—not an easy task at best.

In my judgment, before the time the Senate meets, many of the Republicans will be prepared to compromise, but I fear that they will insist on a compromise that, in the end, if accepted, would destroy the treaty. Unless Article X lives, in its integrity, we will have no league of nations. Of course, I do not suggest a compromise as coming from you. It should be proposed from the other side, and when proposed it can be weighed and considered on its merits.

The suggestion that I made to Mr. Tumulty is this: In the event that no honest compromise can be made that will preserve the life of the league of nations, as a last resort you might accomplish the result by adopting a more or less drastic method—say to the Congress that the people of the country expect peace; that war conditions are intolerable and cannot be maintained further; that the league of nations is not a theory today, but a living entity; that if this Government is not willing to accept the league of nations for itself, it should not destory [destroy] it for the balance of the world; that a compromise of destruction is unthinkable, but that a compromise where we alone go to the wilderness and leave the balance of the world with the league of nations to guard them, would only be a sacrifice for ourselves and not of the high ideals for which we have stood; that, as a last resort, we would consent to a resolution that ratified the treaty of peace in its integrity for the balance of the world, and by a reservation eliminating Article I, the league of nations, from binding effect on us and our Government alone; and then propose to go to the country on the issue as to whether or not the people of the United States would elect a Congress that would ask the permission of the other nations that we might hereafter become a member of the league in its full integrity, and not an emasculated league, such as the Republicans propose.

Pardon me for imposing these suggestions upon you. My viewpoint may be entirely wrong in reference to the matter. My only desire is to preserve the league of nations in its integrity, that the world in the future may live at peace and not at war. I am prepared to stand shoulder to shoulder with you in the fight, and hope you will keep me advised as to your position in reference to the matter.

Hoping that you may soon be restored to strength and health, I am Sincerely and cordially yours, O W Underwood

TLS (WP, DLC).

From Gilbert Monell Hitchcock

My dear Mr. President: [Washington] November 22, 1919.

I am leaving for a flying trip to Omaha expecting to be back next Saturday.

The situation in which we now find ourselves in the Senate is not a defeat, but only a dead-lock in my opinion. When the Senate meets in December we will have eighty-one senators who favor or pretend to favor ratification in some form and I am more than hopeful that we shall be able to secure a combination of sixty-four on some particular form of ratification, notwithstanding Senator Lodge's expressions to the contrary.

If at any time you would like to have any suggestions from me I shall, of course, be glad to offer them. Meanwhile, I wish you a rapid recovery. Yours sincerely, G M Hitchcock

TLS (WP, DLC).

From Edward, Prince of Wales

H.M.S. RENOWN, via YD., Boston, Mass., Nov. 23, 1919

I cannot leave the United States without expressing to you my deepest appreciation of the generous hospitality offered to me by the United States government during my stay, and of the friendly welcome accorded to me by the American people wherever I have been. I have greatly enjoyed my first visit to the United States and I hope to return at the first convenient occasion for I can never forget the universal kindness bestowed on me. It was a great pleasure and privilege to me to have been able to see you at the White House. I am using no conventional phrase. I wish you a speedy return to health, since as head of one of the world's greatest states you represent an influence and an authority indispensable in the settlement of the grave problems bequeathed by the war.

Kindest regards to Mrs. Wilson.   Edward P.

T radiogram (WP, DLC).

A News Report

[*Nov. 24, 1919*]

HITCHCOCK CALLED TO WHITE HOUSE ON TREATY FIGHT
Wilson Summons Him for Saturday—
Expected to Confer on Message to Senate.
COMPROMISE MOVE STRONG

Washington, Nov. 24.—An appointment has been made for Senator Hitchcock, acting leader of the Senate minority, to confer with President Wilson over the treaty situation Saturday, when Mr. Hitchcock will return to Washington from Nebraska. At that time, it is expected, the policy of the minority respecting the treaty at the next session of Congress, which begins the following Monday, will be agreed upon. Word of the President's desire to see Mr. Hitchcock was conveyed to the Senator today.

By the time Mr. Hitchcock returns to the capital the sentiment of the country will have been sounded out by Senators as to ratification of the treaty with such reservations as the Administration might accept. That the country is anxious to have the treaty ratified was asserted by Mr. Hitchcock before he left the Capitol on Saturday. Mr. Hitchcock felt, he said, that the Republicans who voted against ratification without the majority reservations would discover a strong sentiment at home in favor of a reasonable compromise.

President Wilson has given no intimation of the attitude he will take as to the treaty at the next session, but there are undercurrents which convey the impression that he may advocate an agreement based on reservations that would not eliminate any vital phase of the treaty, while at the same time meeting the viewpoint of Senators among the Republican forces who argue that some reservations must be embraced in the ratifying resolution.

While President Wilson, it is stated, will decline to yield his insistence that the majority reservations virtually kill the treaty, he is understood to be in sympathy with Mr. Hitchcock's position that friends of the treaty ought to find the way to an agreement.

Senator Hitchcock's assertion that "reservations in the ratification of the treaty are inevitable" has been accepted at the Capitol as reflecting the opinion of the President as to the policy that must be pursued.

The President, it is understood, will go over with Mr. Hitchcock that part of his message to Congress which will deal with the treaty, and the policy to be outlined by Mr. Wilson will guide the Administration forces when the Senate reconvenes.

There is a distinct feeling on the part of many leaders at the Capitol, Democrats and Republicans alike, that agreement will not seem so difficult, once the Senators are back next Monday. It is believed that, with opportunity for reflection upon the gravity of the situation, Senators who held out against compromise in the final hours of the last session will be found in a more yielding mood.

Although Senator Lodge appears to be anxious to have the treaty put into the next political campaign as an issue, the feeling is apparent on the part of many Republican Senators that the question ought to be decided now, so that Congress in the next few months can devote itself to pressing after-war legislation, which, because of the treaty, was neglected during the session ended last week.

Printed in the *New York Times*, Nov. 25, 1919.

Joseph Patrick Tumulty to Edith Bolling Galt Wilson, with Enclosure

Dear Mrs. Wilson: The White House [Nov. 24, 1919]

I am sending you a draft of a proposed message to Congress by the President. You will notice that I followed the spirit at least of the President's Western speeches in many of the things I say.

There are some repetitions in it that we can, of course, take care of.   Sincerely, Tumulty

TLS (WP, DLC).

E N C L O S U R E

A Draft of an Annual Message[1]

Gentlemen of the Congress:

I sincerely regret my inability to be present at the opening of the session of the Congress. There are many questions, both of international and domestic concern, that are pressing for solution ⟨at the hands of the Congress⟩. ⟨The most pressing and the most important, because of its effect upon the world and our own domestic situation, is of course the ratification of the Treaty of Peace. The whole world awaits America's action and America's answer to the call of duty. There can be no peace or settled order in the world until the Treaty is finally ratified. We have the alternative, armed isolation or peaceful participation. If there is not to be settled peace through the instrumentality of a league of nations, then America must arm herself against the contingencies of the future. If America is to stand alone and withdraw herself from the concert of nations, it means that we shall arm as Germany was armed, that we shall submit our young men to the kind of constant military service that the young men of Germany were subjected to; it means that we shall pay not lighter but heavier taxes; it means that we must have a larger standing army and a large navy ever ready to defend America's rights and her honor. It means that we shall play a lone hand and trade in a world in which we are suspected and watched and disliked, instead of in a world which is now ready to trust us, ready to follow our leadership, as men who are welcome, as men who bring goods and ideas for which the world is ready and for which the world has been waiting. It means that we are going to substitute for Pan-Germanism a sinister Pan-Americanism, and that means taking care of ourselves, being armed and ready, having a chip on our shoulder, thinking of nothing but our own rights, never thinking of the rights of anybody else, thinking that we were put into this world to see that American might was asserted and forgetting that American might ought never to be used against the weak, ought never to be used in an unjust cause, ought never to be used for aggression, ought to be used with the heart of humanity beating behind it. If the United States should stand off from this thing, we must have the biggest army in the world. There would be no one else that cared for our fortunes. We should have to look out for ourselves. There would have to be universal conscription. There would be taxes such as even yet we have

---

[1] Deletions in angle brackets by EBW or WW; words in italics EBWhw.

not seen. We would have to have a staff like the German staff, and you would have to center in the Commander-in-Chief of the Army and Navy the right to take instant action for the protection of the nation.⟩

There is a matter of vital interest, regarding which there has been no definite legislation up to this time, and that is the matter of the railroads. In my message delivered at a joint session of the two houses of Congress on the second of December,[2] I called attention to the necessity for legislation in ⟨the following words:⟩ *terms which I will not burden you by repeating.*

⟨"The question which causes me the greatest concern is the question of the policy to be adopted towards the railroads. I frankly turn to you for counsel upon it. I have no confident judgment of my own. I do not see how any thoughtful man can have who knows anything of the complexity of the problem. It is a problem which must be studied, studied immediately, and studied without bias or prejudice. Nothing can be gained by becoming partisans of any particular plan of settlement.

⟨"It was necessary that the administration of the railways should be taken over by the Government so long as the war lasted. It would have been impossible otherwise to establish and carry through under a single direction the necessary priorities of shipment. It would have been impossible otherwise to combine maximum production at the factories and mines and farms with the maximum possible car supply to take the products to the ports and markets; impossible to route troop shipments and freight shipments without regard to the advantage or disadvantage of the roads employed; impossible to subordinate, when necessary, all questions of convenience to the public necessity; impossible to give the necessary financial support to the roads from the public treasury. But all these necessities have now been served and the question is, what is best for the railroads and for the public in the future.

⟨"Exceptional circumstances and exceptional methods of administration were not needed to convince us that the railroads were not equal to the immense tasks of transportation imposed upon them by the rapid and continuous developments of the industries of the country. We knew that already. And we knew that they were unequal to it partly because their full cooperation was rendered impossible by law and their competition made obligatory, so that it has been impossible to assign to them severally the traffic which could best be carried by their respective lines in the interest of expedition and national economy.

[2] In Wilson's Annual Message of December 2, 1918, printed at that date in Vol. 53.

〈"We may hope, I believe, for the formal conclusion of the war by treaty by the time spring has come. The twenty-one months to which the present control of the railways is limited after formal proclamation of peace shall have been made will run at the farthest, I take it for granted, only to the January of 1921. The full equipment of the railways which the federal administration had planned could not be completed within any such period. The present law does not permit the use of revenues of the several roads for the execution of such plans except by formal contracts with their directors, some of whom will consent while some will not, and therefore does not afford sufficient authority to undertake improvements upon the scale upon which it would be necessary to undertake them. Every approach to this difficult subject matter of decision brings us face to face, therefore, with this unanswered question: What is it right that we should do with the railroads, in the interest of the public and in fairness to their owners?

〈"Let me say at once that I have no answer ready. The only thing that is perfectly clear to me is that it is not fair either to the public or to the owners of the railroads to leave the question unanswered and that it will presently become my duty to relinquish control of the roads, even before the expiration of the statutory period, unless there should appear some clear prospect in the meantime of a legislative solution. Their release would at least produce one element of a solution, namely, certainty and a quick stimulation of private initiative.

〈"I believe that it will be serviceable for me to set forth as explicitly as possible the alternative courses that lie open to our choice. We can simply release the roads and go back to the old conditions of private management, unrestricted competition and multiform regulation by both state and federal authorities; or we can go to the opposite extreme and establish complete government control, accompanied, if necessary, by actual government ownership; or we can adopt an immediate [intermediate] course of modified private control, under a more unified and affirmative public regulation and under such alterations of the law as will permit wasteful competition to be avoided and a considerable degree of unification of administration to be effected, as, for example, by regional corporations under which the railways of definable areas would be in effect combined in single systems.

〈"The one conclusion that I am ready to state with confidence is that it would be a disservice alike to the country and to the owners of the railroads to return to the old conditions unmodified. Those are conditions of restraint without development. There is nothing affirmative or helpful about them. What the country chiefly needs is that all its means of transportation should be developed, its railways, its waterways, its highways, and its countryside roads. Some new element of policy, therefore, is absolutely necessary,—necessary for the service of the public, necessary for the release of credit to those who are administering the railways, necessary for the protection of their security holders. The old policy may be changed much or little, but surely it cannot wisely be left as it was. I hope that the Congress will have a complete and impartial study of the whole problem instituted at once and prosecuted as rapidly as possible. I stand ready and anxious to release the roads from the present control and I must do so at a very early date if by waiting until the statutory limit of time is reached I shall be merely prolonging the period of doubt and uncertainty which is hurtful to every interest concerned."

⟨With reference to the return of the railroads to private ownership, I can only repeat that it will be my duty to relinquish control on the first day of January, 1920, unless there should appear some clear prospect in the meantime of a legislative solution. In the event of the return of the railroads by Presidential Proclamation, I shall of course ask Congress to expedite the enactment of legislation to make this possible and to meet the obligations of the Government toward the railroads by adequately safeguarding the rights of the security holders and the public interest.

⟨I ask the Congress again to give careful consideration to the condition of the public service in the great departments in Washington. The greatly multiplied business of the Government cannot be conducted with efficiency and economy unless there be attracted to and retained in the public service a group of highly trained, well paid and permanent officials of supervisory and technical grades. Uncertainty of tenure and inadequacy of compensation have closed the public service to men of the best type or forced them out of the public service at the moment of their greatest usefulness. The war has increased the public debt twenty-five or thirty fold and has increased the function and activities of the Government in many ways. It must be our business to eliminate all unnecessary government expenditure with the utmost possible speed. It is not, however, to be hoped that expenditures of the Government will ever return to the pre-war standard. The interest and sinking fund payments in respect to the public debt alone will be fifty per cent in excess of the entire pre-war expenditures of the Government. Under these conditions the failure to take such action as may be necessary to attract and retain in the public service men of exceptional ability and of real distinction in their fields can result only in grave burdens to the taxpayers and possible disaster.

Already the transaction of the business of the Government is hampered by deficiencies of personnel due to the return to private life of many men of exceptional ability who during the period of active warfare were glad to serve their country at a great personal sacrifice. Only prompt action by the Congress to build up a permanent and dignified civil service which will include men of great ability and high attainments, can prevent mistakes and failures in the trasnaction [transaction] of the public business, the consequences of which may be disastrous.)

I hope that Congress will definitely proceed to consider the preparation and enactment of legislation for the establishment of a budget system. That there should be one single authority responsible for the making of all appropriations and that appropriations should be made not independently of each other, but with reference to one single comprehensive plan of expenditure properly related to the Nation's income, there can be no doubt. I believe the burden of preparing the budget must, in the nature of the case, if the work is to be properly done and responsibility concentrated instead of divided, rest upon the executive. The budget so prepared should be submitted to and approved or amended by a single committee of each House of Congress and no single appropr[i]ation should be made by the Congress, except such as may have been included in the budget prepared by the executive or added by the particular committee of Congress charged with the budget legislation.

Another and not less important aspect is the ascertainment of the economy and efficiency with which the moneys appropriated are expended. Under existing law the only audit is for the purpose of ascertaining whether expenditures have been lawfully made within the appropriations. No one is authorized or equipped to ascertain whether the money has been spent wisely, economically and effectively. The auditors should be highly trained officials with permanent tenure in the Treasury Department, free of obligations to or motives of consideration for this or any subsequent administration, and authorized and empowered to examine into and make report upon the methods employed and the results obtained by the executive departments of the Government. Their reports should be made to the Congress and to the Secretary of the Treasury.

I trust the Congress will give its immediate consideration to the problem of future taxation. The Revenue Act of 1918, approved February 24, 1919, imposed taxes calculated to produce revenue in respect to the fiscal year of 1919 of upwards of $6,000,000,000 and in respect to the fiscal year of 1920 of upwards of $4,000,000,000. No further reduction than this in the total amount of revenue to be produced can, so far as at present appears, be looked forward to in the immediate future if the Government is to persist in the sound policy of meeting its current expenditures, including interest and an adequate sinking fund upon the war debt, from taxation. A departure from this policy can only retard the restoration of conditions of normal and healthy economic life ⟨and burden the people with all the evils of inflation⟩.

With reference to the details of the Revenue Law, the Secretary of the Treasury and the Commissioner of Internal Revenue will lay before you for your consideration certain amendments necessary or desirable in connection with the administration of the law. The practice of retrospective taxation imposes an undue burden of uncertainty upon business and upon the Treasury of the United States. On the other hand, I hope that the appropriate committees of Congress will immediately engage in the consideration of amendments to the Revenue Bill with a view to more fundamental changes in respect to taxation for the calendar year 1920. It may well be doubted whether the higher rates of income and profits taxes can in peace times be effectively productive of revenue and whether they may not, on the contrary, be destructive of business activity and productive of waste and inefficiency. There is a point at which in peace times high rates of income and profits taxes discourage energy, remove the incentive to new enterprise, encourage extravagant expenditures and produce industrial stagnation with consequent unemployment and other attendant evils. It will be for the Congress to consider means of producing the necessary revenue, the amount of which cannot, as I have indicated, wisely be decreased, in such a way as to avoid the evils to which I have called attention.

The problem is not an easy one. A fundamental change has taken place with reference to the position of America in the world's affairs. The prejudice and passions engendered by decades of controversy between two schools of political and economic thought,— the one believers in protection of American industries, the other believers in tariff for revenue only,—must be subordinated to the single consideration of the public interest in the light of utterly changed conditions. Before the war America was heavily the debtor of the rest of the world and the interest payments she had to make to foreign countries on American securities held abroad, the expenditures of American travelers abroad and the ocean freight charges she had to pay to others, about balanced the value of her pre-war favorable balance of trade. During the war America's exports have been greatly stimulated and increased prices have increased their value. On the other hand, she has purchased a large proportion of the American securities previously held abroad, has loaned some $9,000,000,000 to foreign governments, and has built her own ships. Our favorable balance of trade has thus been greatly increased and Europe has been deprived of the means of meeting it heretofore existing. Europe can have only three ways of meeting the favorable balance of trade in peace times: by imports into this country of gold or of goods, or by establishing new credits. Europe is in no position at the present time to ship gold to us nor could we contemplate large further imports of gold into this country without concern. The time has nearly passed for international governmental loans and it will take time to develop in this country a market for foreign securities. Anything, therefore, which would tend to prevent foreign countries from settling for our exports by shipments of goods into this country could only have the effect of preventing them from paying for our exports and therefore of preventing the exports from being made. The productivity of the country greatly stimulated by the war must find an outlet by exports to foreign countries and any measures taken to prevent imports will inevitably curtail exports, force curtailment of production, load the banking machinery of the country with credits to carry unsold products and produce industrial stagnation and unemployment. If we want to sell we must be prepared to buy. Whatever, therefore, may have been our views during the period of growth of American business concerning tariff legislation, we must now adjust our own economic life to a changed condition growing out of the fact that American business is full grown and that America is the greatest capitalist in the world.

No policy of isolation will satisfy the growing needs and opportunities of America. The provincial standards and policies of the past, which have held American business as if in a strait-jacket, must ⟨yield and⟩ give way to the needs and exigencies of the new day in which we live, a day full of hope and promise for American business, if we will but take advantage of the opportunities that are ours for the asking. The recent war has ended our isolation and thrown upon us a great duty and responsibility. The United States does not view itself as the competitor of any country but as a sharer of an expanding world market. The United States desires ⟨nothing⟩ *no artificial advantage* for itself, only equal opportunity with the other nations of the world, and it believes that through the process of friendly discussion and cooperation the legitimate interests of the nations concerned can be successfully and equitably adjuoted.

There are other matters of importance upon which I urged action at the last session of Congress which are still pressing for solution. I am sure it is not necessary for me again to remind you that there is one immediate and very practicable question of labor that we should meet in the most liberal spirit. That is the matter of relief to our soldiers. I can do no better than to quote from my last message[3] urging this very action:

"We must see to it that our returning soldiers are assisted in every practicable way to find the places for which they are fitted in the daily work of the country. This can be done by developing and maintaining upon an adequate scale the admirable organization created by the Department of Labor for placing men seeking work; and it can also be done, in at least one very great field, by creating new opportunities for individual enterprise. The Secretary of the Interior has pointed out the way by which returning soldiers may be helped to find and take up land in the hitherto undeveloped regions of the country which the Federal Government has already prepared or can readily prepare for cultivation and also on many of the cutover or neglected areas which lie within the limits of the older states; and I once more take the liberty of recommending very urgently that his plans shall receive the immediate and substantial support of the Congress."

⟨Another matter, in this time of readjustment and preparation for peaceful pursuits, most urgently pressing for solution is that of the final disposition of our merchant ships. We have now, in our shipyards and on the high seas, a merchant tonnage second to none in the world. (?) These ships will prove immensely serviceable to every maritime people in restoring much more rapidly than would otherwise be possible the tonnage wantonly destroyed in the war. It ought to be part of our commercial preparedness to establish a fixed policy with reference to the use and control of these ships so that our business throughout the world may be expanded and not checked by unfriendly rivalry. All our legislation looking to the best use of this most necessary instrumentality of trade and accommodation should be friendly.⟩

In the matter of tariff legislation, I beg to call your attention to the statements contained in my last message[4] urging legislation with reference to the establishment of the chemical and dyestuffs industry in America:

"Among the industries to which special consideration should be given is that of the manufacture of dyestuffs and related chemicals. Our complete dependence upon German supplies before the war made the interruption of trade a cause of exceptional economic disturbance. The close relation between the manufacture of dyestuffs, on the one hand, and of explosives and poisonous gases, on

---

[3] His special message to Congress, printed at May 20, 1919, Vol. 59.
[4] *Ibid.*

the other, moreover, has given the industry and [an] exceptional significance and value. Although the United States will gladly and unhesitatingly join in the programme of international disarmament, it will, nevertheless, be a policy of obvious prudence to make certain of the successful maintenance of many strong and well equipped chemical plants. The German chemical industry, with which we will be brought into competition, was and may well be again, a thoroughly knit monopoly capable of exercising a competition of a peculiarly insidious and dangerous kind."

I would call your attention to the widespread condition of political restlessness in our body politic. The causes of this unrest, while various and complicated, are superficial rather than deep seated. Broadly, they arise from or are connected with the failure on the part of our Government to arrive speedily at a just and permanent peace permitting return to normal conditions, from the transfusion of radical theories from seething European centers pending such delay, from heartless profiteering resulting in the increase of the cost of living, and lastly from the machinations of passionate and malevolent agitators. With the return to normal conditions, this unrest will rapidly disappear. In the meantime, it does much evil. It seems to me that in dealing with this situation Congress should not be impatient or drastic but should seek rather to remove the causes. It should endeavor to bring our country back speedily to a peace basis, with ameliorated living conditions under the minimum of restrictions upon personal liberty that is consistent with our reconstruction problems. And it should arm the Federal Government with power to deal in its criminal courts with those persons who by violent methods would abrogate our time-tested institutions. With the free expression of opinion and with the advocacy of orderly political change, however fundamental, there must be no interference, but towards passion and malevolence tending to incite crime and insurrection under guise of political evolution there should be no leniency. Legislation to this end has been recommended by the Attorney General and should be enacted.[5] In this direct connection, I would call your attention to my recommendations on August 8th,[6] pointing out legislative measures which

[5] Palmer, on November 15, had sent to the Senate a lengthy letter in which he said that existing federal law was insufficient to deal with radical sedition and subversion in the United States. He enclosed a draft bill which defined sedition and its promotion very broadly and provided penalties for sedition of fines of up to $10,000 and/or imprisonment for up to twenty years, and for the promotion of sedition of fines up to $10,000 and/or imprisonment for up to ten years. The draft bill further provided that aliens convicted of sedition or its promotion could be deported and that naturalized citizens so convicted could be stripped of their citizenship and deported. Most of the text of Palmer's letter and the full text of the draft bill were printed in the *New York Times*, Nov. 16, 1919.

[6] In his address to Congress printed at that date in Vol. 62.

would be effective in controlling and bringing down the present cost of living, which contributes so largely to this unrest. On only one of these recommendations ⟨have you⟩ *has the Congress* acted.[7] If the Government's campaign is to be effective, it is necessary that the other steps suggested should be acted on at once.

I renew and strongly urge the necessity of the extension of the present Food Control Act as to the period of time in which it shall remain in operation. The Attorney General has submitted a bill providing for an extension of this Act for a period of six months. As it now stands it is limited in operation to the period of the war and becomes inoperative upon the formal proclamation of peace. It is imperative that it should be extended at once. The Department of Justice has built up extensive machinery for the purpose of enforcing its provisions; all of which must be abandoned upon the conclusion of peace unless the provisions of this Act are extended.

During this period the Congress will have an opportunity to make similar, permanent provisions and regulations with regard to all goods destined for interstate commerce and to exclude them from interstate shipment, if the requirements of the law are not complied with. Some such regulation is imperatively necessary. The abuses that have grown up in the manipulation of prices by the withholding of foodstuffs and other necessaries of life cannot otherwise be effectively prevented. There can be no doubt of either the necessity or the legitimacy of such measures.

As I pointed out in my last message, publicity can accomplish a great deal in this campaign. The aims of the Government must be clearly brought to the attention of the consuming public, civic organizations and state officials, who are in a position to lend their assistance to our efforts. You have made available funds with which to carry on this campaign, but there is no provision in the law authorizing their expenditure for the purpose of making the public fully informed about the efforts of the Government. Specific recommendation has been made by the Attorney General in this regard. I would strongly urge upon you its immediate ⟨passage⟩ *adoption*, as it constitutes one of the preliminary steps to this campaign.

I also renew my recommendation that the Congress pass a law regulating cold storage as it is regulated, for example, by the laws of the State of New Jersey, which limit the time during which goods may be kept in storage, prescribe the method of disposing of them if kept beyond the permitted period, and require that goods

---

[7] About which, see n. 1 to the remarks to railway shopmen printed at Aug. 25, 1919, Vol. 62; n. 2 to the second news report printed at Oct. 11, 1919, Vol. 63; and the news report printed at Oct. 22, 1919, *ibid.*

released from storage shall in all cases bear the date of their receipt. It would materially add to the serviceability of the law, for the purpose we now have in view, if it were also prescribed that all goods released from storage for interstate shipment should have plainly marked upon each package the selling or market price at which they went into storage. By this means the purchaser would always be able to learn what profits stood between him and the producer or the wholesale dealer.

I would also renew my recommendation that all goods destined for interstate commerce should in every case, where their form or package makes it possible, be plainly marked with the price at which they left the hands of the producer.

We should formulate a law requiring a federal license of all corporations engaged in interstate commerce and embodying in the license, or in the conditions under which it is to be issued, specific regulations designed to secure competitive selling and prevent unconscionable profits in the method of marketing. Such a law would afford a welcome opportunity to effect other much needed reforms in the business of interstate shipment and in the methods of corporations which are engaged in it; but for the moment I confine my recommendations to the object immediately in hand, which is to lower the cost of living.

No one who has observed the march of events in the last year can fail to note the absolute need of a definite programme to bring about an improvement in the conditions of labor. There can be no settled conditions leading to increased production and a reduction in the cost of living if labor and capital are to be antagonists instead of partners. Sound thinking and an honest desire to serve the interests of the whole nation, as distinguished from the interests of a class, must be applied to the solution of this great and pressing problem. The failure of other nations to consider this matter in a vigorous way has produced bitterness and jealousies and antagonisms, the food of radicalism. The only way to keep men from agitating against grievances is to remove the grievances. An unwillingness even to discuss these matters produces only dissatisfaction and gives comfort to the extreme elements in our country who endeavor to stir up disturbances in order to provoke governments to embark upon a course of retaliation and repression. The seed of revolution is repression. The remedy for these things must not be negative in character. It must be constructive. It must comprehend the general interest. The real antidote for the unrest which manifests itself is not suppression, but a deep consideration of the wrongs that beset our national life and the application of a remedy.

Congress has already shown its willingness to deal with these industrial wrongs by establishing the eight-hour day as the standard in every field of labor. It has sought to find a way to prevent child labor. It has served the whole country by leading the way in developing the means of preserving and safeguarding ⟨the⟩ lives and health in dangerous industries. It must now help in the difficult task of finding a method that will bring about a genuine democratization of industry, based upon the full recognition of the right of those who work, in whatever rank, to participate in some organic way in every decision which directly affects their welfare. It is with this purpose in mind that I called a conference to meet in Washington on December 1st, to consider these problems in all their broad aspects, with the idea of bringing about a better understanding between these two interests.

The great unrest throughout the world, out of which has emerged a demand for an immediate consideration of the difficulties between capital and labor, bid us ⟨to⟩ put our own house in order. Frankly, there can be no permanent and lasting settlements between capital and labor which do not recognize the fundamental concepts for which labor has been struggling through the years. The whole world gave its recognition and endorsement to these fundamental purposes in the League of Nations. The statesmen gathered at Versailles recognized the fact that world stability could not be had by reverting to industrial standards and conditions against which the average workman of the world had revolted. It is, therefore, the task of the statesmen of this new day of change and readjustment to recognize world conditions and to seek to bring about, through legislation, conditions that will mean the ending of age-long antagonism between capital and labor and that will hopefully lead to the building up of a comradeship which will result not only in greater contentment among the mass of workmen but ⟨will⟩ *also* bring about a greater production and a greater prosperity to business itself.

To analyze the particulars in the demands of labor is to admit the justice of their complaint in many matters that lie at the*ir* basis ⟨of their complaint⟩. The workman demands an adequate wage, sufficient to permit him to li⟨f⟩*ve* in comfort, unhampered by the fear of poverty and want in his old age. He demands the right to live and the right to work amidst sanitary surroundings, both in home and in workshop; surroundings that develop and do not retard his own health and well-being; and the right to provide for his children's wants in the matter of health and education. In other words, it is his desire to make the conditions of his life and the lives of those dear to him tolerable and easy to bear.

The establishment of the principles regarding labor laid down in the League of Nations offers us the way to industrial peace and reconciliation. No other road lies open to us. Not to pursue this one is longer to invite enmities, bitterness, and antagonisms which in the end only lead to industrial and social disaster. The unwilling workman is not a profitable servant. An employee whose industrial life is hedged about by hard and unjust conditions, which he did not create and over which he has no control, lacks that fine spirit of enthusiasm and volunteer effort which are the necessary ingredients of a great producing entity. Let us be frank about this solemn matter. The evidences of world-wide unrest which manifest themselves in violence throughout the world bid us pause and consider the means to be found to stop the spread of this contagious thing before it saps the very vitality of the nation itself. Do we gain strength by withholding the remedy? Or is it not the business of statesmen to treat these manifestations of unrest which meet us on every hand as evidences of an economic ⟨disease⟩ *disorder* and to apply constructive remedies wherever necessary, being sure that in the application of the remedy we touch not the vital tissues of our industrial and economic life? There can be no recession of the tide of unrest until constructive instrumentalities are set up to stem that tide.

Governments must recognize the right of men collectively to bargain for humane objects that have at their base the mutual protection and welfare of those engaged in all industries. Labor must not be longer treated as a commodity. It must be regarded as *the activity* [of] human beings, possessed of deep yearnings and desires. The ordinary business man gives his best thought to the repair and replenishment of his machinery, so that its usefulness will not be impaired and its power to produce may always be at its height and kept in full vigor and motion. No less regard ought to be paid to the human machine, which after all propels the machinery of the world and is the great dynamic force that lies back of all industry and progress. Return to the old standards of wage and industry in employment is unthinkable. The terrible tragedy of war which has just ended and which has brought the world to the verge of chaos and disaster would be in vain if there should ensue a return to the conditions of the past. Europe itself, whence has come the unrest which now holds the world at bay, is an example of standpatism in these vital human matters which America might well accept as an example, not to be followed but studiously to be avoided. Europe made labor the differential, and the price of it all is enmity, antagonism and prostrated industry. The right of labor to live in peace and comfort must be recognized by governments. America should be the first to lay the foundation stones upon which industrial peace shall be built.

Labor not only is entitled to an adequate wage, but capital should receive a reasonable return upon its investment and is entitled to protection at the hands of the government in every emergency. No government worthy of the name can "play" these elements against each other, for there is a mutuality of interest between them which the government must seek to express and to safeguard at all cost.

The right of individuals to strike is inviolate and ought not to be interfered with by any process of government, but there is a predominant right and that is the right of the government to protect all of its people and to assert its power and majesty against the challenge of any class. The government, when it asserts that right, seeks not to antagonize a class but simply to defend the right of the whole people as against the irreparable harm and injury that might be done by the attempt by any class to usurp a power that only government itself has a right to exercise as a protection to all.

In the matter of international disputes which have led to war, statesmen have sought to set up as a remedy arbitration for war. Does this not point the way for the settlement of industrial disputes, by the establishment of a tribunal, fair and just alike to all, which will settle industrial disputes which in the past have lead to war and disaster? America, witnessing the evil consequences which have followed out of such disputes between these contending forces, must not admit itself impotent to deal with these matters by means of peaceful processes. Surely, there must be some method of bringing together the counsels of peace and amity of these two great interests, out of which will come a happier day of peace and ⟨reconciliation⟩ *cooperation*, a day that will make men more hopeful and enthusiastic in their various tasks, that will make for more comfort and happiness in living and a more tolerable condition among all classes of men. ⟨Shall we show ourselves blind to the processes of history and prefer economic war to the healing processes of peace?⟩ Certainly human intelligence can devise some acceptable tribunal for adjusting the differences between capital and labor.

This is the hour of test and trial for America. By her prowess and strength, and the indomitable courage of her soldiers, she demonstrated her power to vindicate on foreign battlefields her conceptions of liberty and justice. ⟨Shall her⟩ *Let not her* influence as a mediator between capital and labor be weakened and her own failure to settle matters of pure domestic concern be proclaimed to the world⟨?⟩. There are those in this country who threaten direct action to force their will upon a majority. Russia today, with its blood and terror, is a ⟨fine⟩ *painful* object lesson of the power of minorities. It makes little difference what minority it is; whether capital or labor, or any other class; no sort of privilege will ever be permitted in this country. ⟨It is⟩ *We are* a partnership or ⟨it is a mockery⟩ *nothing that is worthwhile*. ⟨It is⟩ *We are* a democracy, where the majority are the masters, or all the hopes and purposes of the men who founded this government have been defeated and forgotten. In America there is but one way by which great reforms can be accomplished and the relief soubht [sought] by classes obtained, and that is through the orderly processes of *representative* government. Those who would propose any other method of reform are enemies of this country. America will not be daunted by threats nor lose her composure or calmness in these distressing times. We can afford, in the midst of this day of passion and unrest, to be self-contained and sure. The road to economic and social reform in America is the straight road of justice to all classes and conditions of men. Men have but to follow this road to realize the full fruition of their objects and purposes. Let those beware who would take the shorter road of disorder and revolution. The instrument of all reform in America is the ballot. The right road is the road of justice and orderly process.

T MS (WP, DLC).

Joseph Patrick Tumulty to Robert Lansing

Personal.

Dear Mr. Lansing: The White House 24 November 1919.

Mrs. Wilson this morning sent me the following memorandum[1] with regard to the matter contained in your letter of the 21st instant to the President:

"The President says he agrees with the Secretary as regards to withdrawing our representatives in Paris, and of retaining our member of the Supreme Council.

"About the signing of the Treaty with Bulgaria, he thinks if the American representatives are still in Paris, they could sign, but does not advise their remaining for that purpose."

Sincerely yours,   J P Tumulty

TLS (SDR, RG 59, 763.72119/8127½, DNA).
[1] EBW to JPT, [Nov. 24, 1919], EBWhw MS (WP, DLC).

Robert Lansing to Cary Travers Grayson, with Enclosure

PERSONAL AND VERY CONFIDENTIAL

Dear Admiral Grayson: [Washington] November 24, 1919.

I enclose a paraphrase of a telegram I have just received from Ambassador Davis in regard to Lord Grey's support of Major Stuart.[1] Lord Grey casually mentioned something of the kind to me but I did not take it seriously.

I presume that the Ambassador has returned from New York after seeing the Prince off on Saturday. When he makes an appointment with me, as I expect he will this week, I am going to ask you to be present. My own disposition is to insist on Stuart's severance of his relations with the Embassy, whatever the effect on Lord Grey's continuance as Ambassador may be as I think he is taking a very wrong attitude and that we should not establish the precedent of having imposed upon us an attaché of a foreign embassy who is *persona non grata* by the threat of an Ambassador to resign unless the demand for his recall is withdrawn.

If you think is it advisable of course you can show this letter to the President and see whether or not he agrees with my views.

Cordially yours,   [Robert Lansing]

CCL (SDR, RG 59, 701.4111/303, DNA).
[1] About this matter, see n. 1 to the extract from the Lansing Desk Diary printed at Oct. 31, 1919, Vol. 63.

E N C L O S U R E

London November 22, 1919

Urgent. 3434. Personal for Lansing from Davis: Curzon tells me informally that Grey is much exercised about request to dismiss Crawford Stewart and has threatened to resign if compelled to part with him. Represents that services at Embassy are essential to his comfort.   Davis.

T telegram (SDR, RG 59, 701.4111/303, DNA).

Edward Mandell House to Edith Bolling Galt Wilson, with Enclosure

My dear Mrs. Wilson—   [New York] Nov. 24, 1919.

You can never know how long I have hesitated to write to the President about anything while he is ill, but it seems to me vital that the Treaty should pass in some form. His place in history is in the balance. If the Treaty goes through with objectionable reservations it can later be rectified. The essential thing is to have the Presidents great work in Paris live.

Your sincere friend,   E. M. House

ALS (WP, DLC).

E N C L O S U R E

From Edward Mandell House

Dear Governor: New York City. November 24, 1919.

I hesitate to intrude my views upon you at such a time, but I feel that I would be doing less than my duty if I did not do so since so much depends upon your decision in regard to the Treaty. Its failure would be a disaster not less to civilization than to you.

My suggestion is this: Do not mention the Treaty in your message to Congress but return it to the Senate as soon as it convenes. In the meantime, send for Senator Hitchcock and tell him that you feel that you have done your duty and have fulfilled your every obligation to your colleagues in Paris by rejecting all offers to alter the document which was formulated there, and you now turn the Treaty over to the Senate for such action as it may deem wise to take.

I would advise him to ask the Democratic Senators to vote for the Treaty with such reservations as the majority may formulate, and let the matter then rest with the other signatories of the Treaty. I would say to Senator Hitchcock that if the Allied and Associated Powers are willing to accept the reservations which the Senate see fit to make, you will abide by the result being conscious of having done your full duty.

The Allies may not take the Treaty with the Lodge reservations as they now stand, and this will be your vindication. But even if they should take them with slight modifications, your conscience will be clear. After agreement is reached it can easily be shown that the Covenant in its practical workings in the future will not be seriously hampered and that time will give us a workable machine.

A great many people, democrats, progressives and republicans, have talked with me about ratification of the Treaty and they are all pretty much of one mind regarding the necessity for its passage with or without reservations. To the ordinary man, the distance between the Treaty and the reservations is slight.

Of course, the arguments are all with the position you have taken and against that of the Senate, but, unfortunately, no amount of logic can alter the situation, therefore, my advice would be to make no further argument but return the Treaty to the Senate without comment and let Senator Hitchcock know that you expect it to be ratified in some form, and then let the other signatories decide for themselves whether they will accept it.

The supreme place which history will give you will be largely because you personify in yourself the great idealistic conception of a league of nations. If this conception fails, it will be your failure. Today there are millions of helpless people throughout the world who look to you and you only to make this conception a realization.

Affectionately yours, E. M. House

TLS (WP, DLC).

Joseph Patrick Tumulty to Edith Bolling Galt Wilson

Dear Mrs. Wilson,   The White House [c. Nov. 25, 1919].

I have completed the memorandum[1] you desire to lay before the President. I have added a paragraph with reference to the work of the Farmers during the war. Not to have mentioned his work would cause a great deal of criticism.

The information used with reference to farmer was obtained from Sec'y of Agriculture   Yours Sincerely   Tumulty

ALS (WP, DLC).
[1] That is, a revision of Tumulty's draft of an Annual Message printed as an Enclosure with JPT to EBW, Nov. 24, 1919. This revised draft is missing in WP, DLC, and the J. P. Tumulty Papers, DLC, probably because it is the one that was sent to the Public Printer.

Alexander Comstock Kirk to Cary Travers Grayson, with Enclosure

PERSONAL AND VERY CONFIDENTIAL:

My dear Admiral Grayson: [Washington] November 25, 1919.

The Secretary directs me to send you a paraphrase of another message which he has received in regard to the Major Stuart matter and to say that it in no way affects his views.

He asked me to state further that Lord Grey is to call upon him tomorrow (Wednesday) morning at eleven-thirty, and he hopes you will find it possible to be present at that time.

Sincerely yours,   [A. C. Kirk] Secretary.

CCL (SDR, RG 59, 701.4111/304, DNA).

E N C L O S U R E

London Nov. 24, 1919.

Urgent. 3442. Strictly confidential for the Secretary of State from Polk. "Curzon and Reading have both spoken to Davis and myself in regard to Crawford Stewart. They seem to fear that Grey would come home if we insist on Stewart being withdrawn. I know nothing of the situation at Washington in regard to this case but unless you consider it a matter of importance it would seem advisable to let matters stand rather than create another cause of possible irritation."   Davis.

T telegram (SDR, RG 59, 701.4111/304, DNA).

Joseph Patrick Tumulty to Robert Lansing, with Enclosure

Personal

Dear Mr. Secretary: The White House November 26, 1919

I return your letter of November 26th, asking instructions as to the unofficial participation of the United States in the work of the Reparation Commission, and beg to invite your attention to the President's notation of approval thereon.

Sincerely yours,   J. P. Tumulty

TLS (SDR, RG 59, 763.72119/8631, DNA).

E N C L O S U R E[1]

From Robert Lansing

My dear Mr. President: [Washington] Nov. 26, 1919.

I should like further instructions as to the handling of reparation affairs in Paris in the present circumstances. The necessity of our close association with the handling of questions of reparation even though the treaty should fail of ratification, becomes apparent when it is considered what an important part the Reparation Commission can play for good or for ill in economic reconstruction, and when it is further realized that all German assets available for the satisfaction of United States war claims are pledged by the treaty to the Reparation Commission for distribution.

It would seem whether or not the treaty is ratified by the United States, reimbursement for the expenses of our Army of Occupation during the Armistice period and thereafter must be satisfied, if at all, through the Reparation Commission. So also the guarantee of our proportional share of the distribution of the German merchant ships, including those ships taken in our ports. Through an arrangement which amounts practically to a pre-execution of the dye option, we are purchasing dyes from Germany through the Reparation Commission at present and for the protection of our dye consumers, should claim when the treaty comes in force, our full share of the dye option.

Should the treaty be not finally ratified the validity of the confiscation of German assets in this country for the payment of our pre-war damage claims may be questioned under international law. Indeed, it is understood that certain other powers maintain the view that German assets in non-signatory countries are available to the Reparation Commission. If such view prevailed, damage claims which amount to considerable sum arising before and during the war would have to be satisfied through the Reparation Commission.

The Allies consider us necessary parties to any solution of the serious economic situation in Austria and the plan suggested by the Powers contemplates its execution through the Reparation Commission.

It is necessary that our interests in the German tanker ships, which are subject to the jurisdiction of the Reparation Commission, be watched and protected.

The Reparation Commission in its function as practical receiver of the German and Austrian assets has tremendous power over commercial relations with those countries. For our protection it would seem necessary to closely watch the use of these powers.

It is suggested as a policy necessary to the protection of American interests that you authorize me to continue our present unofficial association with reparation affairs. I should cable instructions as soon as possible on account of meetings of the Reparation Commission.   Faithfully yours,   Robert Lansing

(sgd) Approved W.W.

TCL (J. F. Dulles Papers, NjP).
    [1] There is a CC of this letter in SDR, RG 59, 763.72119/8045a, DNA. The original copy is missing in all files.

A News Report

[*Nov. 27, 1919*]

President Has Thanksgiving Dinner In Bed

Washington, Nov. 27.—Thanksgiving Day was observed generally today in Washington with Government departments closed
and many officials absent. Secretary Daniels and many high naval
officials attended the Navy football game here, but other Cabinet
officers who were in town had no special plans.

President Wilson ate his Thanksgiving Day dinner propped up
in bed. South Trimble, clerk of the House, again supplied turkeys
for the White House from his Kentucky farm, but Rear Admiral
Grayson would not permit the President to eat turkey. He had
quail.

Before dinner Mr. Wilson was wheeled out to the south lawn at
the White House, where he spent an hour with Mrs. Wilson and
his daughter, Miss Margaret Wilson. The only guest at the White
House was little Miss Lucy Maury of Roanoke, Va., a niece of Mrs.
Wilson.

Printed in the *New York Times*, Nov. 28, 1919.

Joseph Patrick Tumulty to Edith Bolling Galt Wilson, with Enclosures

Dear Mrs. Wilson: The White House, November 27, 1919.

Will you not bring to the attention of the President the enclosed
letters from Senator Hitchcock and Secretary Lansing?

Sincerely yours,   Tumulty

E N C L O S U R E   I

From Gilbert Monell Hitchcock

My dear Mr. President: Omaha, November 24, 1919.

Since writing you on the day I left Washington, I am more than
ever disposed to believe that a settlement of the treaty by Christmas is reasonably possible.

I suggest that it may be wise not to send it back to the Senate
until about December 6th.

That will give us time to work up a compromise. It can then be
referred to the Committee with instructions to report it within a
certain time.

I have talked with several reservation republicans, and find enough of them desirous of a compromise to give good promise that we can control the Senate to start with when we reassemble.

The republican senators who may be counted on can be divided into three groups:

Urgent for settlement
McCumber
Nelson
McNary
Colt
Kellogg
Keyes

Also desirous of compromise
Lenroot
Stirling [Sterling]
Edge
Townsend
Spencer

Willing to compromise under conditions
Kenyon
Cummins
Jones of Washington
Capper
Hale
Warren
Smoot
Calder

There are some others who will come if we get a working majority so we can control senate procedure.

We can lose Reed and Gore in my opinion and still win, providing we can make such concessions as will be substantial and still leave the league in good working order.

I shall take the liberty of submitting by mail to you tomorrow one or possibly two suggestions as a reservation on Article Ten.

I shall leave here Thursday evening, and reach Washington Saturday morning.   Very sincerely,   G M Hitchcock

ENCLOSURE II

Robert Lansing to Joseph Patrick Tumulty

Dear Mr. Tumulty: Washington November 26, 1919.

Referring to my letter of November 4 to the President,[1] I would very much appreciate it if you could find an opportunity to intimate to the President that delay of recognition of the Costa Rican Government will tend to undermine the authority of that Government and make its existence very precarious.

In this matter the President's policy has been completely vindicated, the constitutional government has been established, the Costa Rican Constitution of 1871 has again been put in force and we have all reason to consider the Government of Francisco Aguilar Barquero to have the backing of the great majority of Costa Rican people. I therefore hope that prompt recognition can be accorded in order to maintain the stability of the present gratifying situation.   Sincerely yours,   Robert Lansing.

TLS (WP, DLC).
¹ That is, the Enclosure printed with JPT to EBW, Nov. 5, 1919, Vol. 63.

From Vance Criswell McCormick

My dear Mr. President   Harrisburg Pa. Nov. 27 1919
Admiral Grayson conveyed to me yesterday afternoon your message in regard to my accepting the appointment of Secretary of Commerce. While I am deeply grateful for this additional evidence of your confidence in me, after most careful consideration, I feel compelled for personal and other reasons to decline this great honor.

Knowing as you do my deep affection and loyalty to you, you will I know appreciate that my action is not altogether selfish but really for what I believe to be for the best interests of all concerned.

As you know I am with you heart and soul and my fondest desire is to continue to help you as I have always tried to do and it is therefore particularly distressing to me to be unable to accept your most generous offer.

Again thanking you from the bottom of my heart and regretting that I must forego this honor
I am   Your very sincere friend   Vance C. McCormick

ALS (WP, DLC).

Edward Mandell House to Edith Bolling Galt Wilson, with Enclosure

Dear Mrs. Wilson—   [New York] Nov. 27, 1919.
May I trouble you again with another letter to the President. I am afraid that I did not make myself altogether clear in my last

one. I feel that if he understands the suggestion as I have it in mind, he will approve it.   Sincerely yours,   E. M. House

ALS (WP, DLC).

E N C L O S U R E

From Edward Mandell House

Dear Governor: New York City. November 27, 1919.

I am wondering if I made myself clear to you in my letter of the other day.

I wish to emphasize the fact that I do not counsel surrender. The action advised will in my opinion make your position consistent and impregnable. Any other way out that now seems possible of success would be something of a surrender.

Practically everyone who is in close touch with the situation admits that the Treaty cannot be ratified without substantial reservations. You need not be a party to those reservations. You stood for the Treaty as it was made in Paris, but if the Senate refuses to ratify without reservations, under the circumstances, I would let the Allies determine whether or not they will accept them.

This does not mean that no effort will be made by those Senators and others who favor the Treaty as it is to make the reservations as innocuous as possible. Neither does it mean that the Allies will accept the Treaty as the Senate majority have desired it.

If you take the stand indicated, it will aid rather than hinder those working for mild reservations. It will absolutely insure the passage of the Treaty and probably in a form acceptable to both you and the Allies.

I did not make the suggestion until I had checked it up with some of your friends in whom I felt you had confidence, for the matter is of such incalculable importance that I did not dare rely solely upon my own judgment.

In conclusion, let me suggest that Senator Hitchcock be warned not to make any public statement regarding your views. When the Treaty is ratified, then I hope you will make a statement letting your position become known.

I feel as certain as I ever did of anything that your attitude would receive universal approval. On the one hand your loyalty to our Allies will be commended, and, on the other, your willingness to accept reservations rather than have the Treaty killed will be regarded as the act of a great man.

Affectionately yours,   E. M. House

TLS (WP, DLC).

Edith Bolling Galt Wilson to Joseph Patrick Tumulty

Mr. Tumlty   [The White House, c. Nov. 28, 1919]
The President wishes to appoint to this office
    Chas. A. Talcott
      Utica
        New York[1]   E.B.W.

ALI (WP, DLC).
[1] "By direction of the President I am returning the nomination of Edward Murphy to be an additional United States Judge for the northern district of New York, together with the memoranda which accompanied it. The President wishes to appoint Charles A. Talcott of Utica to this position and would be glad to have you send over a nomination accordingly." JPT to AMP, Nov. 28, 1919, CCL (WP, DLC).
    The Editors have been unable to identify Murphy. He was probably a Democratic lawyer from upstate New York. Charles Andrew Talcott was Wilson's old friend and classmate at Princeton University.

To South Trimble

My dear Mr. Trimble: [The White House] 29 November, 1919
    You were very generous again to send us a turkey, and I wish to give myself the pleasure of thanking you warmly for your thoughtful kindness.
    With regard,
             Cordially and sincerely yours,   Woodrow Wilson

TLS (Letterpress Books, WP, DLC).

Edith Bolling Galt Wilson to Joseph Patrick Tumulty, with Enclosure

Dear Mr. Tumlty   [The White House, c. Nov. 29, 1919]
    The President says will you send an answer to this letter expressing his regret at not being able to welcome them in person— & also thank them for a box of flowers which came with the letter—& say how much he values their thoughts   EBW

ALI (WP, DLC).

ENCLOSURE

From Antoine Velleman and Others

Mr. President,   Washington, D.C. Day of Thanksgiving, 1919
    The Labor Conference, which brought us from Switzerland to Washington as members of the Secretarial Staff, is drawing to a

close, and we shall probably soon leave this country, in the hopes, that the work done by this Conference may be the beginning of some better understanding between Labor and Capital.[1]

It has certainly been a disappointment to us, not to have the Initiator of the Conference appear at any of its meetings, but we were particularly sorry to think that it was illness that stood in your way.

We do not wish to return to Europe without paying you our respects and expressing our heartiest good wishes for your speedy and complete recovery, so that you may soon be able to again attend with full strength to the great national and world's problems that are awaiting you, problems towards whose solution you have brought a new spirit, which we trust will be a turning point in the history of Mankind, and become the Spirit of the World.

May we add that, as citizens of Switzerland, we have not forgotten the particular interest that you have shown in, and the help you have bestowed upon, our country, in time of trouble.

We do not think that we can thank you better than by trying to help, to the best of our abilities, the New Spirit to come to victory, and it will be our constant effort to do so.

Believe us, Mr. President, in high esteem and sincere admiration.

Yours obediently
Antoine Velleman, of Geneva,
Chief Interpreter to the Conference,
Dr. Maurice C. A. Frondichmann of Geneva,
Interpreter.
Edward Thommen, of Basel,
Interpreter.
Robert Fatio, of Geneva
Interpreter

ALS (WP, DLC).

[1] The first International Labour Conference had met in Washington from October 29 to November 29, 1919. Delegates from thirty-nine countries were present. Among the countries not participating for one reason or another were Soviet Russia, Germany, Austria, Hungary, Bulgaria, and Mexico. The United States was represented unofficially by Samuel Gompers, who attended only from October 29 to November 5. William B. Wilson, who had been nominated by Woodrow Wilson, served as chairman of the conference as a private citizen rather than in his official capacity as Secretary of Labor. The conference devoted much of its time to the establishment of the International Labour Organization and the rules of procedure for future conferences. However, it also drew up six conventions dealing with hours of labor, unemployment, the night work of women, the night work of young persons, the age of admission of children to industrial employment, and the employment of women before and after childbirth. In addition, it adopted numerous recommendations and resolutions on other labor subjects. See International Labour Office, *Draft Conventions and Recommendations adopted by the International Labour Conference during its First Session held at Washington 1919* (Geneva, 1922); James T. Shotwell, ed., *The Origins of the International Labor Organization* (2 vols., New York, 1934), I, 285-330; and the *New York Times*, Oct. 30-Nov. 30, 1919, *passim.*

A News Report

[Nov. 30, 1919]

Hitchcock, at the White House,
Waits Vainly for Audience.

Despite assurances from Dr. Cary T. Grayson, President's personal physician, and Joseph P. Tumulty, the President's secretary, that the President was improved in health, the impression prevailed here last night that his condition is giving cause for increased anxiety. This impression was largely created by the failure of the White House to make an appointment yesterday for Senate Minority Leader Hitchcock to see the President and get his instructions with respect to the treaty.[1]

Senator Hitchcock returned to the city yesterday morning and through his secretary made application for an appointment, the senator was notified late in the afternoon that the President would be unable to see him. At 5:15 o'clock last evening Senator Hitchcock appeared at the executive offices, and said he was there to see Mr. Tumulty. The latter, at that time, was at the White House. The senator waited 30 minutes, then went home without seeing the President's secretary.

When Mr. Tumulty returned from the White House he was asked to explain the situation created by Senator Hitchcock's failure to see the President, and also the many rumors that were in circulation throughout the day concerning the President's illness.

"Just as soon as the President is in shape to see Senator Hitchcock he will see him," was Mr. Tumulty's reply. "The President has made wonderful improvement. When I telephoned over to the White House this morning, Mrs. Wilson said that until after the physicians saw the President this afternoon she thought it unwise for him to hold a long conference with Mr. Hitchcock or anyone else. The President is better than he has been for months. Dr. Dercum said he was absolutely surprised to see the improvement in his condition. The only thing is it was inadvisable to make the appointment for today."

Dr. Grayson last night was persuaded to issue an official bulletin on the condition of the President. It was as follows:

"The President's improvement steadily continues. He is improving slowly. He is considerably better than he was several weeks ago."

While Senator Hitchcock was waiting for Mr. Tumulty he told newspaper correspondents that he really had had no appointment with the President for yesterday and that there was no reason why he should see him immediately.

The senator said that Mr. Tumulty told him over the telephone earlier in the day that after the conference of the physicians at the White House he would inform him whether or not it would be possible for the President to grant him an audience.

"I told Mr. Tumulty I would drop in to see him anyway on my way home," said the senator. Then glancing at the clock, he said: "Well, it's getting on to 6 o'clock. I'm tired of waiting."

Earlier in the afternoon, when information from the Capitol was to the effect that Senator Hitchcock was waiting in his office for some word from the White House as to whether or not he could see the President, Dr. Grayson was sought for an explanation. The physician said he had not heard of the reported appointment, but that he considered the President well enough to see the senator.

The President, despite the fact that it was cold and rainy, was wheeled out in the open yesterday morning. His chair was taken to a sheltered part of the portico in the rear of the White House, and he sat in the open for about an hour.

As regards Senator Hitchcock's impending visit to the White House, Mr. Tumulty last night placed the greatest emphasis in the statement that "only the friendliest and warmest relations existed between Senator Hitchcock and the President." He said the senator and the President had been in communication all week, and that the senator would probably see the President either today or tomorrow.

The President is understood to have taken little if any part in the coal crisis, and the Mexican situation, both of which have been outstanding subjects of importance in the past week.

Printed in the *Washington Post*, Nov. 30, 1919.

[1] Hitchcock obviously wanted to discuss with Wilson the strategy laid out in his letter to Wilson of November 24. JPT to EBW, Dec. 1, 1919 (first letter of that date), implies that Wilson refused to see Hitchcock.

Edith Bolling Galt Wilson to Robert Lansing, with Enclosure

[The White House, Dec. 1, 1919]

The President wishes me to say he adheres to his original decision—in regard to the withdrawing of our American Commissioners.　　　　　　　　　　　　　　　　　　　　　　E.B.W.

ALI (SDR, RG 59, 763.72119/8217½, DNA).

ENCLOSURE

Jean Jules Jusserand to Robert Lansing

My dear Mr. Secretary,   Washington November 29, 1919.

As agreed this morning, I am sending you herewith a brief summary of what I said, commending it to your most serious and friendly attention.

My Government who has every reason to count on American goodwill, considers that the departure at the present juncture of the American delegation in Paris would have a deplorable effect. The fact that the treaty is held here in abeyance, its fate being doubtful, and no action having been taken with the French one, has awakened among the Germans the hope that our intimacy and therefore our force is on the wane. The ratifications which were to be exchanged by us with them on December first have been postponed by them and new and unexpected objections raised to our requests for a strict observance of the clauses of the armistice.[1]

If now, when important questions remain to be solved, and will be in a short time, your delegates were to shake the dust of France off their feet the Germans would feel still more encouraged, and your allies the reverse.

There are more than one question the solving of which may be delayed and for which there would be no need for your delegates to stay: the Russian, the Turkish or even the Italo-Adriatic ones. But others, of the gravest import, will be settled in a few days, and no one would understand our being left before that moment. Of that number are, the exchange of ratifications with Germany which will mark the real beginning of the peace; the signing, which seems imminent, of the Austrian and Bulgarian treaties, by the Serbs and the Roumanians, the signing of the Hungarian treaty greatly desired by the American delegation: a new democratic Government has been established in Hungary;[2] its delegates are soon expected in Paris and no difficulties are foreseen.

A brief delay would surely suffice for all this work, and the continued presence of your representatives would cause the enemy to understand that they vainly hoped that there was any friction between us and they could take advantage thereof. They would cease to refuse for instance, handing to us for judgment those men whose names we know, who captured some honorable French girls and sent them away to be used as white slaves. No worse crime can be imagined.

My government cannot believe that, when you have done so much with such splendid effect, this little supplementary help will be denied us and it wants me to beseech you to grant it. "No one in France, my telegram reads, where the gratitude is profound towards the United States as well as the trust in them, would understand their failing at this juncture the cause which they have so nobly defended."

Hoping that you will see your way to grant us a favor which I solicit in the most earnest fashion, I beg you to believe me, my dear Mr. Secretary,   Most sincerely yours,   Jusserand

TLS (SDR, RG 59, 763.72119/8216½, DNA).
  [1] The German government had ratified the Versailles Treaty on July 9. However, the exchange of ratifications with the Principal Allied Powers was at this time being held up on account of German refusal to accept the protocol described in n. 2 to the draft of Wilson's statement printed at December 2, 1919. Ratifications were finally exchanged on January 10, 1920.
  [2] The Supreme Council had recently been negotiating for the establishment of a new and more liberal government to replace the regime of Stephen Friedrich (about which, see n. 1 to Lansing's memorandum printed at Aug. 20, 1919, Vol. 62). The Rumanian army left Budapest on November 14; and two days later, Sir George Russell Clerk, the British Minister to Czechoslovakia, sent by the Supreme Council on special mission to Budapest, persuaded Friedrich to give way to a coalition government. Karoly Huszár, a Christian Socialist who had served as Minister of Education in Friedrich's cabinet, became the new Prime Minister, and Friedrich remained in the new government as Minister of War. The Supreme Council, on December 1, invited the Huszár government to send a delegation to Paris to negotiate a peace treaty. About these events and their background, see Francis Déak, *Hungary at the Paris Peace Conference: The Diplomatic History of the Treaty of Trianon* (New York, 1942), pp. 116-73.

Robert Lansing to Jean Jules Jusserand

My dear Mr. Ambassador: [Washington] December 1, 1919.

I submitted to the President your personal note of November 29th, containing a statement of the earnest desire of your Government that our Commissioners should remain in Paris beyond December 6th; and I have just received a communication from him returning your letter and stating that he "adheres to his original decision in regard to the withdrawing of our American Commissioners."

I am telegraphing to Mr. Polk the President's decision and requesting him to advise M. Clemenceau of it.

As I told you on Saturday last, I realize the reasons for your Government's desire, and regret that other reasons, which are more imperative in my opinion, compel this Government to withdraw from Paris as originally planned. Anything which might affect the ratification of the Peace Treaty by the United States would be most unwise, and I am not alone in the belief that the continuance of our Commissioners at Paris after the Senate's action at its last session would injuriously affect the plan of campaign to secure ratification at an early date.

I am, my dear M. Jusserand, as always
                    Very sincerely yours,   Robert Lansing

CCL (SDR, RG 59, 763.72119/8217½, DNA).

Two Letters from Joseph Patrick Tumulty to Edith Bolling Galt Wilson

Dear Mrs. Wilson: The White House, 1 December 1919.

Senator Hitchcock still insists upon seeing the President. Also, Secretary Glass who says he must soon leave the Treasury, and therefore, his desire to see the President.

Sincerely yours,   [J P Tumulty]

Dear Mrs. Wilson: The White House, 1 December 1919.

Just talked to Mr. Lansing about the Sayre matter.[1] He said nothing *radical* would be done in Mexico without consulting the President. His justification for sending "stringent" notes was to forestall Congressional action.[2]

Sincerely yours,   [J P Tumulty]

CCL (J. P. Tumulty Papers, DLC).

[1] Tumulty must have said or meant the Jenkins affair, about which see n. 1 to the news report printed at Dec. 4, 1919.

[2] About this, see RL to WW, Dec. 5, 1919.

From Robert Lansing

My dear Mr. President: Washington December 1, 1919.

As I wrote you some time ago Mr. Phillips is very anxious to return to the diplomatic field as soon as possible. He has served so long and so faithfully as Assistant Secretary of State and previously as Third Assistant Secretary that I feel it to be only a matter of justice that he should be suitably rewarded by giving him a foreign mission. I need not elaborate upon his loyalty, his zeal and his ability. I am sure that you appreciate them as I do. His personal devotion to you has been unfailing and I am personally indebted to him for the service he has rendered me in the Department.

In view of this and of the fact that his physician insists that he should give up the routine work at once if he is to preserve his health, I earnestly urge you to authorize me to ask Mr. Phillips if he would accept the appointment as Minister to the Netherlands, feeling sure that post would appeal to him more strongly than any other if it was tendered to him. Indeed I feel so deeply about it that I ask this authorization as a personal favor, and I hope that I can receive it speedily because of Mr. Phillips' need of an immediate change of work.   Faithfully yours,   Robert Lansing.

TLS (RSB Coll., DLC).

Norman Hezekiah Davis to Joseph Patrick Tumulty

Dear Mr. Tumulty: Washington, December 1, 1919.

Evidently ratification of the Treaty cannot be obtained without reservations, but it will be possible, in my opinion, to throw the opponents on the defensive and eliminate the most objectionable reservations. I believe the President would increase his prestige and have the support of all right-thinking men if he were now to take the position that the votes of the Senators before adjournment were a necessary test to determine just exactly what the situation there was, and that he is ready to recognize the consequence of those votes, and, as much as possible to subordinate his own opinions to the necessities of the world's crisis, which has been accentuated by the delay in the ratification of the Treaty. The situation in Europe is so grave and the danger of a catastrophe there resulting from starvation and cold is so immediate that every other consideration should, if possible, be subordinated to the paramount necessity of reaching an agreement upon reservations which will be accepted by two-thirds of the Senate and which would enable the President to file at once our ratification of the Treaty.

Holding these views, I would suggest that the President write a letter to the Senate Minority Leader[1] substantially to the effect that, while his own opinion that reservations are neither necessary nor advisable remains unchanged, and while in justice to himself and in loyalty to his associates representing the Principal Powers who had cooperated with him in preparing a Treaty which was finally signed by twenty-seven nations, he could not have agreed to any modifications to that document without making every effort to maintain it intact, he is now reluctantly convinced that two-thirds of the Senate do not agree with his views and that many of the Senators consider reservations to be necessary, and he has come to the conclusion that this fact, together with the desperate situation in the world today, which affects the United States in the gravest way, requires that every effort should be made to reach a meeting of minds among those Senators who, whatever their views as to the specific terms of the Treaty or specific reservations, are in accord in believing that the Treaty should be ratified at the earliest possible date.

Several of our friends with whom I have discussed this matter are in thorough accord with my views. Some, however, were of the opinion that the President should write a letter or send a message explaining in detail what reservations he will accept, and what reservations he cannot accept, and why. I do not share this view, because I believe that the fight of those who have blocked ratification is not so much upon any specific reservations as it is an effort to kill the Treaty and oppose or humiliate the President. I regret to say that, in my opinion, if the President should propose in writing to accept the Lodge reservations in toto, but couched in different language, the Senate majority would refuse his offer. Unfortunately, the reservations as presented have an innocent appearance and appeal to many Americans who are in favor of the Treaty as a reasonable precaution to avoid any misunderstanding in the future, and discussions of technical points obscure the great principles really involved.

I am of the opinion that too much emphasis cannot be laid on the fact that the President did not write this Treaty, that he fought desperately for six months to uphold American ideals, and that, although the Treaty was in some respects a compromise, he was most fortunate in being able to obtain a Treaty as sound and constructive as this is.

On account of my intense interest in this great question and natural desire to be of any service, I have presumed to express my views in the hope that they may be of some worth.

Very sincerely yours,   Norman H. Davis[2]

TLS (WP, DLC).
  [1] The position was vacant on account of Senator Martin's death, but Davis probably thought, as many other people did, that Hitchcock was Minority Leader.
  [2] A transcript of a shorthand note at the top of this letter reads: "Ask Mrs. Wilson if she cares to read this to the President."

A News Report

[Dec. 2, 1919]

President's Health Shows Steady Improvement
Despite Many Rumors and He Is Doing More Work

Washington, Dec. 2.—According to those close to President Wilson, the condition of his health is improving steadily. During the last week he has signed a great number of nominations for transmission to the Senate, worked on his annual message and written and dictated letters.

There has been a marked improvement in the steadiness of the President's handwriting, as shown by his signature to recent communications. He was sitting in a chair in his bedroom today when the official copies of his annual message were brought to him and he signed them on a pad held before him.

The shorthand notes made by the President in composing his annual message and other writings[1] are said to be extremely clear and unwavering, and this and other evidence exist to show that his nerves are well under control.

Some uneasiness is being shown in the Senate and House over the President's prolonged lack of participation in public activities. A considerable number of Congressmen believe that the President is in much worse condition than his physicians have indicated, while others assert that whatever the state of his health it is time that Congress and the country should know the facts.

Another reason advanced for the widespread belief that the President is in a serious state of health is his failure to keep his engagement with Senator Hitchcock, minority leader of the Committee on Foreign Relations, who led the Administration forces in the Senate in the contest over the ratification of the Versailles Treaty of Peace.

In spite of all these reports, those in a position to know the President's condition of health insist that he is getting along excellently. No prediction is made as to when he may be expected to be up and about, but it is said that the serious aspect of his illness has disappeared and that his gradual complete recovery is assured.

Printed in the *New York Times*, Dec. 3, 1919.
    [1] We have not found these in WP, DLC.

An Annual Message on the State of the Union

The White House, 2 *December, 1919*

To the Senate and House of Representatives:

I sincerely regret that I cannot be present at the opening of this session of the Congress. I am thus prevented from presenting in as direct a way as I could wish the many questions that are pressing for solution at this time. Happily, I have had the advantage of the advice of the heads of the several executive departments who have kept in close touch with affairs in their detail and whose thoughtful recommendations I earnestly second.

In the matter of the railroads and the readjustment of their affairs growing out of federal control, I shall take the liberty at a later date of addressing you.

I hope that Congress will bring to a conclusion at this session legislation looking to the establishment of a budget system. That there should be one single authority responsible for the making of all appropriations and that appropriations should be made not independently of each other, but with reference to one single comprehensive plan of expenditure properly related to the nation's income, there can be no doubt. I believe the burden of preparing the budget must, in the nature of the case, if the work is to be properly done and responsibility concentrated instead of divided, rest upon the executive. The budget so prepared should be submitted to and approved or amended by a single committee of each House of Congress and no single appropriation should be made by the Congress, except such as may have been included in the budget prepared by the executive or added by the particular committee of Congress charged with the budget legislation.

Another and not less important aspect of the problem is the ascertainment of the economy and efficiency with which the moneys appropriated are expended. Under existing law the only audit is for the purpose of ascertaining whether expenditures have been lawfully made within the appropriations. No one is authorized or equipped to ascertain whether the money has been spent wisely, economically and effectively. The auditors should be highly trained officials with permanent tenure in the Treasury Department, free of obligations to or motives of consideration for this or any subsequent administration, and authorized and empowered to examine into and make report upon the methods employed and the results obtained by the executive departments of the Government. Their reports should be made to the Congress and to the Secretary of the Treasury.

I trust that the Congress will give its immediate consideration to the problem of future taxation. Simplification of the income and profits taxes has become an immediate necessity. These taxes performed indispensable service during the war. They must, however, be simplified, not only to save the taxpayer inconvenience and expense, but in order that his liability may be made certain and definite.

With reference to the details of the Revenue Law, the Secretary of the Treasury and the Commissioner of Internal Revenue will lay before you for your consideration certain amendments necessary or desirable in connection with the administration of the law—recommendations which have my approval and support. It is of the utmost importance that in dealing with this matter the present law should not be disturbed so far as regards taxes for the calendar year 1920, payable in the calendar year 1921. The Congress might well consider whether the higher rates of income and profits taxes can in peace times be effectively productive of revenue, and whether they may not, on the contrary, be destructive of business activity and productive of waste and inefficiency. There is a point at which in peace times high rates of income and profits taxes discourage energy, remove the incentive to new enterprise, encourage extravagant expenditures and produce industrial stagnation with consequent unemployment and other attendant evils.

The problem is not an easy one. A fundamental change has taken place with reference to the position of America in the world's affairs. The prejudice and passions engendered by decades of controversy between two schools of political and economic thought,— the one believers in protection of American industries, the other believers in tariff for revenue only,—must be subordinated to the single consideration of the public interest in the light of utterly changed conditions. Before the war America was heavily the debtor of the rest of the world and the interest payments she had to make to foreign countries on American securities held abroad, the expenditures of American travelers abroad and the ocean freight charges she had to pay to others, about balanced the value of her pre-war favorable balance of trade. During the war America's exports have been greatly stimulated, and increased prices have increased their value. On the other hand, she has purchased a large proportion of the American securities previously held abroad, has loaned some $9,000,000,000 to foreign governments, and has built her own ships. Our favorable balance of trade has thus been greatly increased and Europe has been deprived of the means of meeting it heretofore existing. Europe can have only three ways of meeting the favorable balance of trade in peace times: by imports into this country of gold or of goods, or by establishing new credits. Europe is in no position at the present time to ship gold to us nor could we contemplate large further imports of gold into this country without concern. The time has nearly passed for international governmental loans and it will take time to develop in this country a market for foreign securities. Anything, therefore, which would tend to prevent foreign countries from settling for our exports by shipments of goods into this country could only have the effect of preventing them from paying for our exports and therefore of preventing the exports from being made. The productivity of the country greatly stimulated by the war must find an outlet by exports to foreign countries and any measures taken to prevent imports will inevitably curtail exports, force curtailment of production, load the banking machinery of the country with credits to carry unsold products and produce industrial stagnation and unemployment. If we want to sell, we must be prepared to buy. Whatever, therefore, may have been our views during the period of growth of American business concerning tariff legislation, we must now adjust our own economic life to a changed condition growing out of the fact that American business is full grown and that America is the greatest capitalist in the world.

No policy of isolation will satisfy the growing needs and opportunities of America. The provincial standards and policies of the past, which have held American business as if in a strait-jacket, must yield and give way to the needs and exigencies of the new day in which we live, a day full of hope and promise for American business, if we will but take advantage of the opportunities that are ours for the asking. The recent war has ended our isolation and thrown upon us a great duty and responsibility. The United States must share the expanding world market. The United States desires for itself only equal opportunity with the other nations of the world, and that through the process of friendly cooperation and fair competition the legitimate interests of the nations concerned may be successfully and equitably adjusted.

There are other matters of importance upon which I urged action at the last session of Congress which are still pressing for solution. I am sure it is not necessary for me again to remind you that there is one immediate and very practicable question resulting from the war which we should meet in the most liberal spirit. It is a matter of recognition and relief to our soldiers. I can do no better than to quote from my last message urging this very action:

"We must see to it that our returning soldiers are assisted in every practicable way to find the places for which they are fitted in the daily work of the country. This can be done by developing and maintaining upon an adequate scale the admirable organization created by the Department of Labor for placing men seeking work; and it can also be done, in at least one very great field, by creating new opportunities for individual enterprise. The Secretary of the Interior has pointed out the way by which returning soldiers may be helped to find and take up land in the hitherto undeveloped regions of the country which the Federal Government has already prepared or can readily prepare for cultivation and also on many of the cutover or neglected areas which lie within the limits of the older states; and I once more take the liberty of recommending very urgently that his plans shall receive the immediate and substantial support of the Congress."

In the matter of tariff legislation, I beg to call your attention to the statements contained in my last message urging legislation with reference to the establishment of the chemical and dyestuffs industry in America:

"Among the industries to which special consideration should be given is that of the manufacture of dyestuffs and related chemicals. Our complete dependence upon German supplies before the war made the interruption of trade a cause of exceptional economic disturbance. The close relation between the manufacture of dyestuffs, on the one hand, and of explosives and poisonous gases, on the other, moreover, has given the industry an exceptional significance and value. Although the United States will gladly and unhesitatingly join in the programme of international disarmament, it will, nevertheless, be a policy of obvious prudence to make certain of the successful maintenance of many strong and well-equipped chemical plants. The German chemical industry, with which we will be brought into competition, was and may well be again, a thoroughly knit monopoly capable of exercising a competition of a peculiarly insidious and dangerous kind."

During the war the farmer performed a vital and willing service to the nation. By materially increasing the production of his land, he supplied America and the Allies with the increased amounts of food necessary to keep their immense armies in the field. He indispensably helped to win the war. But there is now scarcely less need of increasing the production in food and the necessaries of life. I ask the Congress to consider means of encouraging effort along these lines. The importance of doing everything possible to promote production along economical lines, to improve marketing, and to make rural life more attractive and healthful, is obvious. I would urge approval of the plans already proposed to the Congress by the Secretary of Agriculture, to secure the essential facts required for the proper study of this question, through the proposed enlarged programmes for farm management studies and crop estimates. I would urge, also, the continuance of federal participation in the building of good roads, under the terms of existing law and under the direction of present agencies; the need of further action on the part of the States and the Federal Government to preserve and develop our forest resources, especially through the practice of better forestry methods on private holdings and the extension of the publicly owned forests; better support for country schools and the more definite direction of their courses of study along lines related to rural problems; and fuller provisions for sanitation in rural districts and the building up of needed hospital and medical facilities in these localities. Perhaps the way might be cleared for many of these desirable reforms by a fresh, comprehensive survey made of rural conditions by a conference composed of representatives of the farmers and of the agricultural agencies responsible for leadership.

I would call your attention to the widespread condition of political restlessness in our body politic. The causes of this unrest, while various and complicated, are superficial rather than deep seated. Broadly, they arise from or are connected with the failure on the part of our Government to arrive speedily at a just and permanent peace permitting return to normal conditions, from the transfusion of radical theories from seething European centers pending such delay, from heartless profiteering resulting in the increase of the cost of living, and lastly from the machinations of passionate and malevolent agitators. With the return to normal conditions, this unrest will rapidly disappear. In the meantime, it does much evil. It seems to me that in dealing with this situation Congress should not be impatient or drastic but should seek rather to remove the causes. It should endeavor to bring our country back speedily to a peace basis, with ameliorated living conditions under the minimum of restrictions upon personal liberty that is consistent with our reconstruction problems. And it should arm the Federal Government with power to deal in its criminal courts with those persons who by violent methods would abrogate our time-tested institutions. With the free expression of opinion and with the advocacy of orderly political change, however fundamental, there must be no interference, but towards passion and malevolence tending to incite crime and insurrection under guise of political evolution there should be no leniency. Legislation to this end has been recommended by the Attorney General and should be enacted. In this direct connection, I would call your attention to my recommendations on August 8th, pointing out legislative measures which would be effective in controlling and bringing down the present cost of living, which contributes so largely to this unrest. On only one of these recommendations has the Congress acted. If the Government's campaign is to be effective, it is necessary that the other steps suggested should be acted on at once.

I renew and strongly urge the necessity of the extension of the present Food Control Act as to the period of time in which it shall remain in operation. The Attorney General has submitted a bill providing for an extension of this Act for a period of six months. As it now stands it is limited in operation to the period of war and becomes inoperative upon the formal proclamation of peace. It is imperative that it should be extended at once. The Department of Justice has built up extensive machinery for the purpose of enforcing its provisions; all of which must be abandoned upon the conclusion of peace unless the provisions of this Act are extended.

During this period the Congress will have an opportunity to make similar, permanent provisions and regulations with regard to all goods destined for interstate commerce and to exclude them from interstate shipment, if the requirements of the law are not complied with. Some such regulation is imperatively necessary. The abuses that have grown up in the manipulation of prices by the withholding of foodstuffs and other necessaries of life cannot otherwise be effectively prevented. There can be no doubt of either the necessity or the legitimacy of such measures.

As I pointed out in my last message, publicity can accomplish a great deal in this campaign. The aims of the Government must be clearly brought to the attention of the consuming public, civic organizations and state officials, who are in a position to lend their assistance to our efforts. You have made available funds with which to carry on this campaign, but there is no provision in the law authorizing their expenditure for the purpose of making the public fully informed about the efforts of the Government. Specific recommendation has been made by the Attorney General in this regard. I would strongly urge upon you its immediate adoption, as it constitutes one of the preliminary steps to this campaign.

I also renew my recommendation that the Congress pass a law regulating cold storage as it is regulated, for example, by the laws of the State of New Jersey, which limit the time during which goods may be kept in storage, prescribe the method of disposing of them if kept beyond the permitted period, and require that goods released from storage shall in all cases bear the date of their receipt. It would materially add to the serviceability of the law, for the purpose we now have in view, if it were also prescribed that all goods released from storage for interstate shipment should have plainly marked upon each package the selling or market price at which they went into storage. By this means the purchaser would always be able to learn what profits stood between him and the producer or the wholesale dealer.

I would also renew my recommendation that all goods destined for interstate commerce should in every case, where their form or package makes it possible, be plainly marked with the price at which they left the hands of the producer.

We should formulate a law requiring a federal license of all corporations engaged in interstate commerce and embodying in the license, or in the conditions under which it is to be issued, specific regulations designed to secure competitive selling and prevent unconscionable profits in the method of marketing. Such a law would afford a welcome opportunity to effect other much needed reforms in the business of interstate shipment and in the methods of corporations which are engaged in it; but for the moment I confine my recommendations to the object immediately in hand, which is to lower the cost of living.

No one who has observed the march of events in the last year can fail to note the absolute need of a definite programme to bring about an improvement in the conditions of labor. There can be no settled conditions leading to increased production and a reduction in the cost of living if labor and capital are to be antagonists instead of partners. Sound thinking and an honest desire to serve the interests of the whole nation, as distinguished from the interests of a class, must be applied to the solution of this great and pressing problem. The failure of other nations to consider this matter in a vigorous way has produced bitterness and jealousies and antagonisms, the food of radicalism. The only way to keep men from agitating against grievances is to remove the grievances. An unwillingness even to discuss these matters produces only dissatisfaction and gives comfort to the extreme elements in our country which endeavor to stir up disturbances in order to provoke governments to embark upon a course of retaliation and repression. The seed of revolution is repression. The remedy for these things must not be negative in character. It must be constructive. It must comprehend the general interest. The real antidote for the unrest which manifests itself is not suppression, but a deep consideration of the wrongs that beset our national life and the application of a remedy.

Congress has already shown its willingness to deal with these industrial wrongs by establishing the eight-hour day as the standard in every field of labor. It has sought to find a way to prevent child labor. It has served the whole country by leading the way in developing the means of preserving and safeguarding lives and health in dangerous industries. It must now help in the difficult task of finding a method that will bring about a genuine democratization of industry, based upon the full recognition of the right of those who work, in whatever rank, to participate in some organic way in every decision which directly affects their welfare. It is with this purpose in mind that I called a conference to meet in Washington on December 1st, to consider these problems in all their broad aspects, with the idea of bringing about a better understanding between these two interests.

The great unrest throughout the world, out of which has emerged a demand for an immediate consideration of the difficulties between capital and labor, bids us put our own house in order. Frankly, there can be no permanent and lasting settlements between capital and labor which do not recognize the fundamental concepts for which labor has been struggling through the years. The whole world gave its recognition and endorsement to these fundamental purposes in the League of Nations. The statesmen gathered at Versailles recognized the fact that world stability could not be had by reverting to industrial standards and conditions against which the average workman of the world had revolted. It is, therefore, the task of the statesmen of this new day of change and readjustment to recognize world conditions and to seek to bring about, through legislation, conditions that will mean the ending of age-long antagonisms between capital and labor that will hopefully lead to the building up of a comradeship which will result not only in greater contentment among the mass of workmen but also bring about a greater production and a greater prosperity to business itself.

To analyze the particulars in the demands of labor is to admit the justice of their complaint in many matters that lie at their basis. The workman demands an adequate wage, sufficient to permit him to live in comfort, unhampered by the fear of poverty and want in his old age. He demands the right to live and the right to work amidst sanitary surroundings, both in home and in workshop, surroundings that develop and do not retard his own health and well-being; and the right to provide for his children's wants in the matter of health and education. In other words, it is his desire to make the conditions of his life and the lives of those dear to him tolerable and easy to bear.

The establishment of the principles regarding labor laid down in the covenant of the League of Nations offers us the way to industrial peace and conciliation. No other road lies open to us. Not to pursue this one is longer to invite enmities, bitterness, and antagonisms which in the end only lead to industrial and social disaster. The unwilling workman is not a profitable servant. An employee whose industrial life is hedged about by hard and unjust conditions, which he did not create and over which he has no control, lacks that fine spirit of enthusiasm and volunteer effort which are the necessary ingredients of a great producing entity. Let us be frank about this solemn matter. The evidences of world-wide unrest which manifest themselves in violence throughout the world bid us pause and consider the means to be found to stop the spread of this contagious thing before it saps the very vitality of the nation itself. Do we gain strength by withholding the remedy? Or is it not the business of statesmen to treat these manifestations of unrest which meet us on every hand as evidences of an economic disorder and to apply constructive remedies wherever necessary, being sure that in the application of the remedy we touch not the vital tissues of our industrial and economic life? There can be no recession of the tide of unrest until constructive instrumentalities are set up to stem that tide.

Governments must recognize the right of men collectively to bargain for humane objects that have at their base the mutual protection and welfare of those engaged in all industries. Labor must not be longer treated as a commodity. It must be regarded as the activity of human beings, possessed of deep yearnings and desires. The business man gives his best thought to the repair and replenishment of his machinery, so that its usefulness will not be impaired and its power to produce may always be at its height and kept in full vigor and motion. No less regard ought to be paid to the human machine, which after all propels the machinery of the world and is the great dynamic force that lies back of all industry and progress. Return to the old standards of wage and industry in employment are unthinkable. The terrible tragedy of war which has just ended and which has brought the world to the verge of chaos and disaster would be in vain if there should ensue a return to the conditions of the past. Europe itself, whence has come the unrest which now holds the world at bay, is an example of standpatism in these vital human matters which America might well accept as an example, not to be followed but studiously to be avoided. Europe made labor the differential, and the price of it all is enmity and antagonism and prostrated industry. The right of labor to live in peace and comfort must be recognized by governments and America should be the first to lay the foundation stones upon which industrial peace shall be built.

Labor not only is entitled to an adequate wage, but capital should receive a reasonable return upon its investment and is entitled to protection at the hands of the government in every emergency. No government worthy of the name can "play" these elements against each other, for there is a mutuality of interest between them which the government must seek to express and to safeguard at all cost.

The right of individuals to strike is inviolate and ought not to be interfered with by any process of government, but there is a predominant right and that is the right of the government to protect all of its people and to assert its power and majesty against the challenge of any class. The government, when it asserts that right, seeks not to antagonize a class but simply to defend the right of the whole people as against the irreparable harm and injury that might be done by the attempt by any class to usurp a power that only government itself has a right to exercise as a protection to all.

In the matter of international disputes which have led to war, statesmen have sought to set up as a remedy arbitration for war. Does this not point the way for the settlement of industrial disputes, by the establishment of a tribunal, fair and just alike to all, which will settle industrial disputes which in the past have led to war and disaster? America, witnessing the evil consequences which have followed out of such disputes between these contending forces, must not admit itself impotent to deal with these matters by means of peaceful processes. Surely, there must be some method of bringing together in a council of peace and amity these two great interests, out of which will come a happier day of peace and cooperation, a day that will make men more hopeful and enthusiastic in their various tasks, that will make for more comfort and happiness in living and a more tolerable condition among all classes of men. Certainly human intelligence can devise some acceptable tribunal for adjusting the differences between capital and labor.

This is the hour of test and trial for America. By her prowess and strength, and the indomitable courage of her soldiers, she demonstrated her power to vindicate on foreign battlefields her conceptions of liberty and justice. Let not her influence as a mediator between capital and labor be weakened and her own failure to settle matters of purely domestic concern be proclaimed to the world. There are those in this country who threaten direct action to force their will upon a majority. Russia today, with its blood and terror, is a painful object lesson of the power of minorities. It makes little difference what minority it is; whether capital or labor, or any other class; no sort of privilege will ever be permitted to dominate this country. We are a partnership or nothing that is worth while. We are a democracy, where the majority are the masters, or all the hopes and purposes of the men who founded this government have been defeated and forgotten. In America there is but one way by which great reforms can be accomplished and the relief sought by classes obtained, and that is through the orderly processes of representative government. Those who would propose any other method of reform are enemies of this country. America will not be daunted by threats nor lose her composure or calmness in these distressing times. We can afford, in the midst of this day of passion and unrest, to be self-contained and sure. The instrument of all reform in America is the ballot. The road to economic and social reform in America is the straight road of justice to all classes and conditions of men. Men have but to follow this road to realize the full fruition of their objects and purposes. Let those beware who would take the shorter road of disorder and revolution. The right road is the road of justice and orderly process.

Woodrow Wilson.

Printed in *Message of the President of the United States . . . December 2, 1919* (Washington, 1919).

From Robert Lansing, with Enclosure

My dear Mr. President: [Washington] December 2, 1919.

I feel that I must call your attention to this telegram from Mr. Polk which reached me late last night.

I do not think that it changes the matter in the least but in view of the last paragraph I feel a reply should be immediately sent to Mr. Polk saying that your decision of yesterday was final and that we expect the Commission to sail on the sixth as planned.

Will you please let me know at once if I am not correct in this so that I can telegraph Mr. Polk to that effect?

Faithfully yours,   Robert Lansing

CCL (SDR, RG 59, 763.72119/8074, DNA).

ENCLOSURE

Paris December 1st 1919.

Extra Priority A. 5517. Most urgent and confidential for the Secretary of State from Polk.

In connection with the German refusal to deposit ratifications and sign protocol Clemenceau made an earnest appeal to me today begging that we postpone our departure. He said that not only would our departure encourage the Germans to stand out against the other powers but it would be construed by the French as an abandonment of the French in their hour of need. He said in his opinion it was one of the most serious crises that had confronted France and begged that we stay until Germany had deposited ratifications. I tried to reassure him and tried to point out that if the Ambassador were charged with the power he could act for the United States but Clemenceau and the British both feel it would not be the same thing.

I have consulted my colleagues and we have come to the conclusion that there is a great deal of justice in the position the French have taken and that a delay of our departure for two or three days would impress the Germans with our intention to stand by our allies and at the same time give us an opportunity for discussion and making up our minds what course should be pursued. Clemenceau is most insistent that I should stay until ratifications deposited, but I believe that if General Bliss were charged with the duty of staying here until the Germans consented to sign the protocol the French people would be satisfied and the Germans would be impressed with our intention to support the allies.

I can see that the republicans might object to our remaining

here to influence the Germans to accept the treaty which the senate has refused to ratify but in my opinion it should be put on the
ground that we should stand with our allies in compelling the enemy to carry out the armistice terms if they refuse to put treaty
through effectively.

In view of the situation we have agreed to delay our departure
until the ninth unless you see objection. I beg however that in view
of the strong feeling on the part of the French we be permitted to
remain until the ninth and that you give careful consideration to
the advisability of requesting General Bliss to remain to represent
this Government. He would have a sufficient staff with the men
assigned to the Embassy to do all that is necessary for him. I will
report fully tomorrow after a further conversation with Clemenceau. Polk.   American Mission

T telegram (SDR, RG 59, 763.72119/8074, DNA).

A Draft of a Statement

[c. Dec. 2, 1919]

Unless civilization can have the benefit of the full & prompt
adoption & execution as formulated at Paris by representatives of
all the beligerant nations for the purpose of rectafying the gross
wrongs committed by Germany[1] It is undoubtedly for these reasons that Germany is even now refusing to deposit at Paris as required by the Treaty the notification of her ratification of the
Treaty—& that she has point blank refused to sign the Protocol
which is necessary to the completion of the Treaty & which she
had agreed to at Paris[2] There are even hints that she will ignore
the terms of the Treaty itself—treating it as only one more "scrap
of paper" She will respect no Treaty which has not the united force
of the free nations behind it.

The action of the Senate has convinced her that no force or influence of America will be put behind the execution of the treaty

EBWhw MS (WP, DLC).
   [1] Unfinished sentence or missing page.
   [2] Wilson was confusing two different protocols. The one which Germany "had agreed
to at Paris" was the protocol signed at the same time as the peace treaty on June 28,
1919. About this protocol, see n. 1 to the extract from the Lansing Desk Diary printed
at July 30, 1919, Vol. 62. The second protocol was formulated by the Council of Heads
of Delegations in Paris in late October and presented in a note to the German government on November 1. This protocol listed various obligations which Germany had accepted in the Armistice Agreement of 1918 but had not as yet carried out, and it indicated how these obligations were being dealt with. However, this protocol also included
the significant new demand that Germany make specific reparation for the ships destroyed at Scapa Flow (about which, see n. 8 to the Minutes of the Council of Four
printed at June 21, 1919, 3:45 p.m., Vol. 61), as well as for several submarines destroyed

at other times since the Armistice. The German government was to turn over five light cruisers named in the protocol, as well as floating docks, floating cranes, tugs, and dredges equivalent to a total displacement of 400,000 tons. The protocol concluded with the threat that, if Germany did not comply with these new obligations within the time specified, the Allied and Associated Powers reserved the right "to take all military or other measures of coercion which they may consider appropriate." The protocol is printed in *PPC*, XIII, 743-48. For the discussions of the Council of Heads of Delegations on the protocol, see *ibid.*, VIII, 803-805, 830-33, 847-55, 874, and 878-80.

It was rumored in Paris as early as November 9 that the German government would object to making reparation for the vessels sunk at Scapa Flow. *New York Times*, Nov. 10, 1919. The German delegation in Paris raised questions about the protocol and specifically about the Scapa Flow provisions in a meeting with Allied representatives on November 20 (*PPC*, IX, 287-90), and it was erroneously reported in the press that they had refused to sign the document. *New York Times*, Nov. 23, 1919. The Associated Press reported from Berlin on November 28 that the German government would refuse to pay at least part of the reparation demand for Scapa Flow (*ibid.*, Nov. 29, 1919). It was only on November 27 that Baron Kurt von Lersner, president of German delegation at Paris, sent to Clemenceau a memorandum on the Scapa Flow affair in which the German government stated explicitly that it was "obliged to refuse to agree in any way to execute obligations which might be imposed on it on account of the scuttling of the German battleships." The memorandum argued that the German government could not be held responsible for the act of a German admiral in British captivity with whom it was forbidden to communicate and over whom it had no control. It suggested that the matter be referred to the Court of Arbitration at The Hague. *PPC*, IX, 414-17. This development was reported in the newspapers of November 30; see, for example, the *New York Times* for that date. Baron von Lersner reiterated the position of his government in a meeting with Paul-Eugène Dutasta on December 1, which the latter recorded as follows: "What we absolutely refuse is 1st) the demands presented as compensation for the scuttling of the German fleet at Scapa Flow; 2nd) the eventual military measures provided for in the last paragraph. For us, they are unacceptable." *PPC*, IX, 438. This interview was reported in the *New York Times*, Dec. 4, 1919.

Two Letters from Edith Bolling Galt Wilson to Robert Lansing

The White House, Dec. 2, 1919

The President feels it will do no harm to delay the departure until the 9th but advises that all of the Commission leave at that date and that this be made final.   EBW

ALI (SDR, RG 59, 763.72119/8218½, DNA).

The White House, Dec. 2, 1919

In regard to Diplomatic appointments the President is sorry to be obliged to insist that they all wait until his recovery.

But this is without the least prejudice to the suggestion you make with regard to the Hague.   E.B.W.

ALI (RSB Coll., DLC).

A News Report

[*Dec. 4, 1919*]

WILSON TO SEE SENATORS

Washington, Dec. 4.—At the end of a prolonged conference to-day the Senate Foreign Relations Committee, by a vote of 6 to 5, the Republicans voting yes and the Democrats no, decided to appoint a sub-committee of two to confer with President Wilson on the Mexican crisis and ascertain his views upon any action the Senate might take in regard to a break in relations with the Mexican Government.[1]

Senator Fall, Republican, of New Mexico, who has recently returned from an investigation of the Mexican situation at the border, and Senator Hitchcock, ranking Democratic member of the committee, were appointed on the sub-committee by Senator Lodge.

Dr. Grayson said tonight there was nothing in the present condition of the President likely to make it impossible for him to receive the Senators, but that the hour when the Senators might see the President would naturally depend on his condition. According to one report he saw no reason why the committee could not call tomorrow.

Senator Hitchcock said tonight that he had no doubt that the President would see Fall and himself. "But I do not think it will be as early as tomorrow," he went on. "I think he will see us within two or three days."

The action of the committee was taken by Senate leaders, aside from its bearing on the Mexican situation, as bringing to a focus an effort which has been under way at the Capitol to ascertain whether the President is able to perform the functions of his office. Many Republicans, as well as a few Democratic Senators, have been insisting for some time that the President was not fit to discharge his duties and that Congress ought to be informed as to the situation.

The Democratic Senators, Hitchcock, Swanson, Shields, Pittman, and Williams, who voted against having the sub-committee confer with the President, were actuated by the feeling that the committee was unnecessarily putting the President to the task of taking up the Mexican crisis when there was no real occasion to impose it upon him, at least until the reply to the last note to Mexico is received.

The Republican members, Lodge, Borah, Fall, New, Johnson, and Moses, maintained that the Mexican situation had become so serious that the President must be consulted. If a war juncture is at hand and the Senate felt it to be its duty to pass the resolution offered by Senator Fall, calling for a severance of diplomatic relations with Mexico, or, at least approve the State Department policy, they argued, the President's attitude ought to be ascertained first.

That there is a strong tendency to adopt the Fall resolution in the Senate was asserted by Republican leaders. Action upon it by the committee was deferred, it was said, only through a desire to learn how far President Wilson wished Congress to go at this time.

Not until the sub-committee confers with the President, or, failing that, some definite word comes from Mr. Wilson indicating his attitude on Mexico will the resolution be pressed.

The committee's decision concerning the conference with the President was reached after it had heard Ambassador Fletcher and Secretary Lansing in secret session. Mr. Fletcher was before the committee two hours in the morning and Mr. Lansing appeared in the afternoon, remaining with the committee an hour and a half. Both officials laid intimate facts before the committee bearing upon the crisis.

Secretary Lansing is understood to have approved that part of Senator Fall's resolution indorsing the action of the State Department's handling of the Mexican situation since the capture and detention of Jenkins, but he urged that that portion of the resolution, counseling a withdrawal of recognition of Caranza as President of Mexico and a severance of diplomatic relations with the Mexican Government be abandoned, for the present.

Mr. Lansing argued that it would be inadvisable for the Senate to urge intervention while the State Department's negotiations with Mexico were pending.

In reply to questions of Republican members, Secretary Lansing said that he had not conferred with President Wilson as to any of the recent phases of affairs with Mexico. He stated that as far as he knew, no State Department official had talked about Mexico with the President since his return from his Western trip.[2]

Printed in the *New York Times*, Dec. 5, 1919.

[1] About the movement led by Senator Albert B. Fall and others to bring about military and/ or political intervention in Mexico, see W. Wiseman to A. J. Balfour, Aug. 4, 1919, n. 1, Vol. 62. Fall and his associates soon decided that the best means of arousing public opinion in favor of some form of intervention in Mexico would be a well-publicized Senate investigation of Mexican-American relations. Senator William H. King, on July 1, 1919, introduced S. Res. 106, which called for such an investigation; the Senate adopted an amended version on August 8. *Cong. Record*, 66th Cong., 1st sess., pp. 2145, 3714. Lodge appointed a subcommittee of the Committee on Foreign Relations consisting of Fall as chairman, Frank B. Brandegee, and Marcus A. Smith to conduct the investigation. The subcommittee began hearings on September 8, 1919, and concluded its work on May 10, 1920. It assembled two large volumes (totaling 3,551 pages) of testimony and documents, all designed to demonstrate the alleged perfidy and iniquity of the Carranza government in its dealings with the United States and its citizens. *Investigation of Mexican Affairs: Preliminary Report and Hearings of the Committee on Foreign Relations United States Senate*

Pursuant to S. Res. 106 . . . , 66th Cong., 2d sess., Sen. Doc. No. 285 (2 vols., Washington, 1920). The proceedings of the subcommittee through November 25, 1919, filled 766 pages.

Two events in the late autumn of 1919 played into the hands of Fall and his associates in their campaign for intervention. In a new move to implement the provisions of Article 27 of the Mexican Constitution of 1917 (about which, see n. 2 to the extract from the diary of C. P. Anderson printed at March 8, 1917, Vol. 41, and n. 5 to the Enclosure printed with RL to WW, April 15, 1918, Vol. 47), Carranza in August refused to grant drilling permits unless oil companies signed an agreement to comply with forthcoming legislation in regard to Article 27. Because American oil companies refused to obtain drilling permits and drilled without them, the Mexican army, on November 12, began seizing wells drilled without permit; five days later, Carranza ordered the seizure of all such wells.

The second incident, which seemed to bring the United States and Mexico close to war, began with the kidnaping, on October 19, of the United States consular agent at Puebla, Mexico, William Oscar Jenkins. It was suggested, both at the time and later, that Jenkins had arranged his own abduction to create an incident between the United States and the Carranza government over the latter's alleged inability or unwillingness to protect United States citizens in Mexico. The suspicion increased a few days later, when Jenkins suddenly paid off his captors and was released. On November 19, a Puebla court indicted Jenkins for giving false information to investigators of the affair, ordered his incarceration, and set his bail at $500. Jenkins, on the advice of an official of the American embassy in Mexico City, refused to post the bail and called upon the United States Government to secure his freedom. Lansing sent several strong notes to the Carranza government demanding Jenkins' release and told the Mexican Ambassador, Ignacio Bonillas, on November 28 that, if Jenkins was not freed immediately, a "tide of indignation" among the American people might prevent further diplomatic discussion and force a break in relations which would almost inevitably mean war.

Fall, having just returned from a trip to the West, conferred with Lansing on the Mexican situation at the latter's home on December 1. Lansing gave the Senator copies of his recent diplomatic correspondence with Mexico and told him that he was acting on his own initiative, without Wilson's knowledge. Fall told Lansing that his subcommittee would make an official report on Mexican affairs to the Senate and that he would introduce a resolution supporting Lansing's actions. On December 3, Fall presented two different drafts of a concurrent resolution to Ambassador Henry P. Fletcher, whom Lansing had designated as the State Department's liaison with Fall's subcommittee. Fletcher selected one of the two, and Fall introduced it, Senate Concurrent Resolution 21, in the Senate later that day. It read as follows: "*Resolved by the Senate (the House of Representatives concurring)*, That the action taken by the Department of State in reference to the pending controversy between this Government and the Government of Mexico should be approved; and, further, that the President of the United States be, and he is hereby, requested to withdraw from Venustiano Carranza the recognition heretofore accorded him by the United States as President of the Republic of Mexico and to sever all diplomatic relations now existing between this Government and the pretended government of Carranza." *Cong. Record*, 66th Cong., 2d sess., p. 73.

This narrative is based upon Clifford W. Trow, " 'Tired of Waiting': Senator Albert B. Fall's Alternative to Woodrow Wilson's Mexican Policies," *New Mexico Historical Review*, LVII (April 1982), 159-82; C. W. Trow, "Woodrow Wilson and the Mexican Interventionist Movement of 1919," *Journal of American History*, LVIII (June 1971), 46-72; Charles C. Cumberland, "The Jenkins Case and Mexican-American Relations," *Hispanic American Historical Review*, XXXI (Nov. 1951), 586-607; and RL to WW, Dec. 19, 1919, and Jan. 3, 1920.

[2] It was this statement by Lansing that caused the Republican members of the Foreign Relations Committee to insist upon the appointment of what has been called the "smelling committee."

From the Diary of Josephus Daniels

December Thursday 4 1919

Long talk with Tumulty on coal & Mex. He told L that WW would not go to war with Mexico & he ought not to make the movement. If there is war, let the Reps do it.

Saw Lansing who said Mexican Embassy here was propaganda headquarters for red literature & Fall was right. He told Com he had not consulted Wilson about J arrest & imprisonment. Fall & Hitchcock named to confer with the President about Mexican policy. Rec'd letter from Lansing enclosing letter from Justin Mc-Grath[1] asking ships be sent to Mexico & telegraph from Wm. Randolph Hearst urging such course Lansing requested ships be sent.

Hw bound diary (J. Daniels Papers, DLC).
[1] Washington editorial correspondent of the Hearst newspapers and the Universal News Service.

A Memorandum by Robert Lansing

December 4, 1919.

THE PRESIDENT'S CAPACITY TO PERFORM HIS DUTIES.

The question as to whether the President is actually and generally performing his official duties and whether he is mentally and physically capable of doing so is growing more and more insistent.

I think that his annual message, which went to Congress two days ago, brought the matter more or less to a head, and my statement to the Senate Committee on Foreign Relations that I had not consulted the President in the Jenkins case did not help matters.

There has been a great deal of speculation as to the authorship of the President's message. It is pointed out that many phrases are Wilsonian in style, but there are portions which seem to be written by another hand. In a way the document as a whole seems to lack the strength and consistency of thought so characteristic of the President's state-papers. I remarked to Burleson, who came in to see me, that the paper did not appear to me to be written by the President though he may have changed some of the words. He replied that it was a "Wilson message" all right, because it was made up from sentences and phrases which he had used in previous addresses. I said: "The loose stones are there but the cement is not that usually used by the President." He laughed and said that very few would get onto that. Burleson's statement showed me very clearly that the President did not write the message. Someone, probably Tumulty, thoroughly familiar with the President's utterances clipped appropriate ones out of speeches and arranged them to make what seemed a new document. If this was the way of it, it was certainly cleverly done, for much of the language would be the President's and the peculiarities of literary structure would mark it as Wilsonian. Burleson evidently considered the deception put over on Congress and the people as a fine piece of political work. I cannot agree with him. If it ever gets out it will make a fine scandal.

This confession or boast of the Postmaster General explained why the President in his message did not touch on the present state of foreign affairs or on the ratification of the Treaty. Conditions had so materially changed since he became ill that none of his former utterances were applicable. The result was that what he ought to have put first in his message and what the public expected to be there does not appear even by allusion.

Burleson—and I am assuming that he knew the truth—showed that the President must still be very weak, since he would permit anyone else to write a message for him. The presumption is that, while the President may act in a few cases, someone as a rule is acting for him and thinking for him too if the subject is complex or detailed. I had gained this impression from certain things that had happened so I did not put up the Jenkins case to the President as I knew Tumulty was opposed to taking a strong stand with Mexico. He telephoned me that he and Mrs. Wilson felt I ought to put the matter up to the President before I went very far. I told him that I would when I felt that the situation was critical. Then I went my own way for I did not want Tumulty and Mrs. Wilson to decide the policy in that case which I feared would be the result if I sent it to the President. Of course this may have been an unjust suspicion, but it was so strong that I retained the Jenkins case in my own hands.

Senator Spencer of Missouri was another caller this morning. After we had settled the business which he came to see about, he began on the question of the possible disability of the President and the danger of his pretending to act if he was unable to do so. He said that he could not understand why his physicians did not come out frankly and tell the whole story of his illness "in language that any country doctor could understand"; and that all this secrecy was having the effect of making people think that he must be wholly incapacitated and that someone was acting in his stead who had no legal right to do so.

He said that this continued silence was producing a fine crop of stories as to the trouble of the President; that some said that he was entirely paralyzed below the waist; others, that he was mentally unbalanced; others, that there was a liason [lesion] of a blood vessel in the brain and he might die suddenly at any time; and others still that he had lost the sight of an eye and was paralyzed on the right side (a few said, the left side). Spencer felt that nothing would satisfy the public except a plain straightforward statement by his medical attendants, and that Congress considered the situation so serious that there was talk of an investigation to determine whether the policies of the Government were actually being determined by the President.

He pointed out that in a signature of the President's which he had seen the "Woodrow" could not have been read if one covered up the "Wilson," and that it all looked like the writing of a child. He thought that a man who could not write better than that would have a hard time making stenographic notes of a message as Tumulty said the President did of his annual message. He said that the story from the same source that the President was learning to write with his left hand was nonsense and concocted to explain these illegible signatures and also to disprove that his left side was paralyzed. The Senator said that no one was fooled by the statements for Hitchcock had told how the President in greeting him had grasped him firmly with his *right* hand, and if his right hand was all right there was no reason to use his left. He said Tumulty's stories were making people all the more suspicious.

With gossip like this in the smoking rooms at the Capitol and with such remarks as "Well, here's another message from Tumulty" and "We've a batch of some more of Tumulty's nominations to act on," being made, it is not to be wondered at that Congress is getting impatient at being kept in ignorance as to the truth.

This afternoon about 5:30 Tumulty telephoned me that the Foreign Relations Committee had directed Senators Fall and Hitchcock to ask an interview with the President in regard to Mexico. (This followed my statement to the Committee that I had not consulted the President since his illness on Mexico.) Tumulty was much perturbed by the request judging from his voice and said that he believed all they were after was to find out whether the President was competent to do business. He said that he did not think that they ought to be allowed to see him. I replied that being ignorant myself of the President's malady and condition I did not know what to advise, but that, if he was as well as appeared by the daily reports, it would be difficult to excuse a refusal to so reasonable a request. Tumulty said with some heat, "Well, it's a shame to put us over here in such a position. If I say they can't see him, then there'll be the devil to pay; and, if I say they can, I don't know what Fall will give out. Hitchcock ought not to have let the Republicans put it over him like that." He stopped a moment and then added, "Well, think it over anyway."

Now what was the natural conclusion from this conversation to one who did not know the real state of facts? Certainly that Tumulty was afraid to have Fall see the President lest he should find a man much weaker and less capable than Grayson and Tumulty had been giving out to the press. However I believe that Fall and Hitchcock will see the President and that his strong will will be able to stand the test.

T MS (R. Lansing Papers, DLC).

A News Report

[*Dec. 5, 1919*]

WILSON WON'T ACT ON TREATY NOW

Washington, Dec. 5.—President Wilson intimated to Senator Hitchcock today that he would wait awhile before making any move regarding the Peace Treaty. Mr. Hitchcock asked the President about his intentions with respect to the treaty, just as he was leaving the Mexican conference.

"The President," said Senator Hitchcock, "said that he regarded responsibility for the treaty as having been shifted from his shoulders to others, and that he was disposed to let it rest there awhile."

Mr. Hitchcock said he took this to mean that the President would do nothing at all for the present, leaving the Senate to work out a compromise or not, as it saw fit. He will not even withdraw the treaty from the Senate files with a view to its resubmission and is in no hurry about writing a message on it, in Mr. Hitchcock's opinion.

In the interim, Mr. Hitchcock said, he believed public opinion would gradually work up such a demand for ratification that it would be brought about without the President having to take an active hand in the efforts at adjustment.

The suggestion was heard today that Mr. Wilson might elect to submit the Austrian treaty before attempting to revive the Versailles agreement. Since the Austrian treaty also contains the League of Nations covenant, the compromise on reservations, with the single exception of the Shantung provision, would be possible in that treaty. Once worked out on that, a compromise could quickly be applied to the German treaty, it was pointed out.

Talk of pushing the Lodge resolution[1] declaring peace has virtually died out. So much opposition developed within Mr. Lodge's own party, both in the House and the Senate, that the plan is deemed inopportune. Senator Lodge is now being urged to bring before his committee the tripartite agreement between the United States, Great Britain, and France for special defensive measures against any new German aggression. Mr. Lodge said he intended to get this agreement before the committee at the earliest opportunity.

Printed in the *New York Times*, Dec. 6, 1919.

[1] This concurrent resolution, introduced by Lodge on November 19, simply stated that, in the light of certain events, "the said state of war between Germany and the United States is hereby declared to be at an end." *Cong. Record*, 66th Cong., 1st sess., p. 8804. The resolution was referred to the Foreign Relations Committee, which never acted upon it.

From Robert Lansing

My dear Mr. President: Washington December 5, 1919.

Mr. Tumulty informs me that you are to see Senators Hitchcock and Fall this afternoon in regard to the Mexican situation. I have not troubled you with the Jenkins case which is of considerable complexity as to facts and as to law because there was no possibility of that case developing a situation which could possibly warrant intervention in Mexico. As to this I am sure that the Foreign Relations Committee is in entire accord.

The real Mexican situation is the whole series of outrages and wrongs which Americans in Mexico have suffered during the Carranza administration. There is no doubt that the complaints are numerous and justified and that the indictment which can be drawn against Carranza will appeal very strongly to the people and arous[e] a very general indignation. The danger is that Congress, in view of the facts which will be reported undoubtedly by Senator Fall's sub-Committee on Mexico, will demand drastic action or put us in a position where it will be very difficult to treat the matter with a proper deliberation.

I have seen this coming for some time, knowing the vast amount of material collected by the Fall Committee and it was with that purpose that I sought to divert attention to the Jenkins case which I knew could not possibly result in a rupture between the two Governments.

I thought before you saw these two Senators you should be advised as to the real question which is, as I have said, Carranza's past record of hostility toward this Government and not the Jenkins case, which can be handled by the Department without endangering our relations with Mexico.

Faithfully yours,   Robert Lansing.

TLS (WP, DLC).

Key Pittman to Cary Travers Grayson

From Senator Pittman to Admiral Grayson:

Dear Admiral: At the Executive Office, December 5, 1919.

I beg you not to interfere any more than you have to with the opportunity that the President is offered to kick Senator Fall in the "slats." He and some of those with him who seek immediate war with Mexico are using every scheme and force that they can command to force immediate action upon the Fall Resolution before the Jenkins matter may be settled. This was clearly demonstrated by Fall's action before the Foreign Relations Committee yesterday. Mr. Lansing expressed to the Committee that he was very hopeful that the Jenkins matter would be satisfactorily settled in a few days. It is true that it was only a hope, but with this in mind he requested delay of action on the Fall Resolution. Fall became furious and threatened to wash his hands of the whole matter as Chairman of the Sub-Committee, which has been investigating matters for two months, unless the Committee acted immediately. Moses, unconsciously, by reason of his jealous hatred of the President and his desire to magnify himself, moved that a committee of two be appointed to call upon the President, if he would grant the interview, and request his advice upon the Fall Resolution. This motion was made and carried by the Republicans in the belief that the President would resent the interference by Congress in his Constitutional functions and would decline to receive the committee.

What we desire is delay. The settlement of the Jenkins matter will end the Mexican case.[1] All the vast amount of evidence of Mexican outrages committed during the past several years which Fall has collected will be of no value. The Foreign Relations Committee have requested Fall to file his report as Chairman of the Sub-Committee in writing on or before Monday. It is a voluminous report. The President could end the interview in three minutes. He could simply ask Senator Fall to file with him a written copy of the report which he (the Senator) is to file with the Foreign Relations Committee, and, at the same time, could state to Senator Fall and Senator Hitchcock that he would obtain a report from the State Department and would then reply to the communication transmitted to him through the committee appointed by the Foreign Relations Committee. That ends the interview as far as I can see. There is nothing to discuss because the President has not up to the present had an opportunity to review the evidence that has been obtained by the State Department and the Sub-Committee of the Foreign Relations Committee, which has been working in harmony and in conjunction with the State Department. The Foreign Relations Committee will hardly dare force the resolution out of committee until after the President has had a reasonable time in which to review a report of the Sub-Committee and the report of the State Department with regard to the matter.

I would urge nothing, of course, that would retard in the slightest the rapid recovery of the President but I am satisfied he will enjoy this opportunity to block the demagoguery and also the dangerous move of some thoughtless Senators.

TL (WP, DLC).

¹ Jenkins was released from prison on December 5, when his bail was paid, without his knowledge or consent, by a United States citizen otherwise uninvolved in the affair. The Jenkins case dragged on in the Mexican state and federal courts until December 1920, when Jenkins was exonerated by the federal district court of Puebla. Cumberland, "The Jenkins Case," pp. 598-605.

Two News Reports

[*Dec. 5, 1919*]

SENATORS SEE PRESIDENT
Fall and Hitchcock Report That
His Condition is Excellent.

Washington, Dec. 5.—The Special Committee, consisting of Senators Fall and Hitchcock, named by the Senate Committee on Foreign Relations to seek a personal interview with President Wilson on the Mexican situation, was received by the President at 2:30 o'clock this afternoon. The conference lasted forty minutes.

This personal interview disposed of rumors that President Wilson was in no condition to direct American action in the perturbing state of affairs that has developed between the United States and the Carranza government. The two Senators who interviewed the President with the ill-concealed purpose on the part of members of the Foreign Relations Committee to ascertain the truth or falsity of the many rumors that he was in no physical or mental condition to attend to important public business, came away from the White House convinced that his mind was vigorous and active.

One of these Senators, Mr. Fall, Republican, of New Mexico, has been a severe critic of President Wilson. It was he who offered the resolution to withdraw American recognition of the Carranza Government that brought about the effort to get first-hand information as to the state of the President's health.

A dramatic touch was given to the interview between the President and the two Senate emissaries by the sudden appearance of Rear Admiral Grayson, the President's physician, with the announcement that Jenkins, around whose imprisonment the Mexican crisis centered, had been freed last night. The President was lying propped up in bed. The two Senators sat by his bedside.

"Pardon me for interrupting, gentlemen," said Dr. Grayson, as he entered the sick room, "but Secretary Lansing has asked me to tell you immediately that Jenkins has been released."

The message concerning Jenkins had come to the State Department while the conference was on. Secretary Lansing telephoned to the White House that he desired the information to be given to the two Senators immediately. Dr. Grayson confided to some of his friends that the news of Jenkins's release fitted into the situation so dramatically that he felt like an actor making a sensational entrance as he broke in upon the deliberations of the President and his visitors.

Senator Fall represented the Republican critics of the President at the conference, Senator Hitchcock was chosen as the President's friend. The Foreign Relations Committee had learned from Secretary Lansing that President Wilson had not been informed of the critical aspect of the Jenkins case in the dealings between the Carranza Government and the United States. The whole delicate matter had been handled by the State Department, under Mr. Lansing's direction and following a policy previously determined upon.

But when Senators Hitchcock and Fall entered the sick room at the White House they found that the President had become acquainted with the main features of the Jenkins case and had some idea of the general charges against the Carranza Government that had been made by Senator Fall.

The two Senators were with the President for forty minutes. They found him cheerful and inclined to joke about the alarmist reports of the nature of his illness. It was evident that he had been told of the gossip about the state of his health. Senator Hitchcock said after the interview that the President looked much better than when he saw him recently.

The request for the interview had been made to Joseph P. Tumulty, the Secretary to the President, who had referred it to Rear Admiral Grayson. The request was granted after Admiral Grayson had consulted Mrs. Wilson. Both were satisfied that the President would be able to stand the physical strain that would come from discussing an important public question with the official emissaries of the Senate.

Before entering the White House the two Senators asked Admiral Grayson how long they might remain with the President. Admiral Grayson set no time limit. As a result, there was a full and free discussion of the Mexican situation.

Senators Hitchcock and Fall were with the President from 2:35 until 3:15 o'clock. For the first time since the President's illness newspaper representatives were permitted to enter the White House grounds and wait for the two Senators on the main portico. There was apparently an effort to have it appear that those around the President wanted the fullest publicity.

In order to save the President all possible fatigue, Admiral Grayson had directed that he should go to bed. He was propped up on pillows when the Senators entered. Mrs. Wilson was in the room and remained throughout the conference. The President greeted his callers cheerfully, and they took seats near the bed.

When the two Senators emerged from the White House after the conference, Senator Hitchcock was smiling broadly. The two had agreed beforehand that Mr. Hitchcock should make a statement and in response to a request for information, he said:

"We had a pleasant chat with the President. Senator Fall did most of the talking and presented a very good summary of conditions to which the President gave deepest attention.

"The President looks much better than when I last saw him. He was sitting up in bed, wearing a dark brown sweater. His color was good. He was clean shaven. I understand he now shaves himself.

"He was mentally most alert, and physically seemed to me to have improved greatly. He shook hands with us with his right hand, and used both hands freely in picking up and laying down a printed copy of Senator Fall's resolution. He also made stenographic notes occasionally during the conference.

"While we were in the midst of our talk a message came that Jenkins had been released. It was quite dramatic. In fact, the stage was so well set that the dramatic effect was perfect."

At this both Senators smiled.

Continuing, Senator Hitchcock said:

"The President said that the possibilities of the Mexican situation were too numerous and grave, even terrible, to warrant haste either in expression or action. He stated the problem demanded the fullest consideration, which, he said, he would give it.

"At the end of the conference the President told us a couple of funny stories. The President said the discussion of the Mexican problem had reminded him of Hennessy, who, upon being asked whether he thought the United States should intervene and take Mexico, replied: 'Mexico is so contagious to us that I'm thinkin' we'll have to take it.' "[1]

When questioners turned to Senator Fall he said that Mr. Wilson had agreed to go over a memorandum[2] prepared by Mr. Fall and then give the Foreign Relations Committee some expression of his views concerning the Fall resolution, and possibly on the whole Mexican question.

"The President said he would try to give us this expression by Monday, when the committee meets," said Senator Fall. "I expect to submit my memorandum to him tonight. It will cover the facts I laid before him this afternoon, and, like my statement to him to day, will very closely follow my report to the Foreign Relations Committee on recent events."

"Did the President's condition seem to you to be such that he is capable of handling the Mexican situation?" Senator Fall was asked.

"Do you mean his mental condition?" he inquired.

"Yes."

"In my opinion, Mr. Wilson is perfectly capable of handling the situation," replied Mr. Fall. "He seemed to me to be in excellent trim, both mentally and physically, for a man who has been in bed for ten weeks. Of course, I am not an expert, but that's how it appeared to me."

Senator Fall said the President did not express an opinion on the Fall resolution.

"I did not ask him to and he did not volunteer any," said the Senator. "I asked him no questions, and he did not ask me any. You see, I did most of the talking, and he had to listen."

"Did the President appear to you to be conversant with details of the Jenkins case and the whole situation?" he was asked.

"As I say, no questions were asked," was the reply. "I merely made a statement, and the President promised to consider the facts and let us know his judgment."

Mr. Fall concurred in detail with Senator Hitchcock's description of the President's physical appearance.

At the Capitol, where the result of the conference had been awaited with the keenest interest, the frank statement of both Senators that Mr. Wilson appeared to be in mental and physical trim to meet emergencies as they arose created a deep impression. The committee's mission was generally regarded as one of inquiry into the President's condition, and it was that portion of their report which was most commented upon. Their unanimity and freedom from hesitation in telling how active the President was mentally and how improved physically was accepted as silencing for good the many wild and often unfriendly rumors of Presidential disability.

[*Dec. 5, 1919*]

President Jests on Moses Story.

Washington, Dec. 5.—Senator Fall after the conference with the President today said Mr. Wilson commented on the published statement of Senator Moses, Republican, New Hampshire, some weeks ago that Mr. Wilson had suffered a brain lesion.[3]

"The President said that as a result of the conference the Senator would be reassured, although he might be disappointed," said Senator Fall.

When the Senator greeted the President and asked him how he felt, the President replied: "I'm feeling fit."

Senator Fall gave a detailed account of the White House visit. He said Dr. Grayson received them and took them up to the President's bedroom where Mrs. Wilson shook hands with each Senator.

"Then the President shook hands with each of us," Senator Fall continued. "He was lying in bed flat on his back. His shoulders were propped up slightly. His bed was in a shaded portion of the room. He greeted us pleasantly, and while his articulation seemed somewhat thick during the entire conference I could understand perfectly every word he said.

"I think he was covered up to the chin, with his right arm out. I sat a little to one side and slightly below him, near a table, and he frequently turned his head to talk to me. He also reached over the table several times to secure papers on it."

Asked regarding the President's physical appearance, Senator Fall said he was "not an expert" but would not judge that the Executive had lost any weight. He continued that Senator Hitchcock opened the discussion by stating that he personally had nothing to present but accompanied Senator Fall, who desired to submit some information.

Announcement of Jenkins's release, it was said by those present, gave the conference its only dramatic turn. All of those present expressed satisfaction at the news, and then Senator Fall resumed his statement. He told the President of much of the evidence turned up by the Mexican inquiry, especially regarding the alleged activities of Mexican officials in spreading Bolshevist propaganda in this country.

Printed in the *New York Times*, Dec. 6, 1919.

[1] Finley Peter Dunne had written several "Mr. Dooley" satires on Mexico and Mexican-American relations. We have not found the piece in which Hennessy, Mr. Dooley's friend, is thus quoted.

[2] See A. B. Fall to WW, Dec. 5, 1919.

[3] See the third news report printed at Oct. 11, 1919, Vol. 63.

Notes taken when Senator Fall called on the President in his bedroom at the White House. Taken by EBW[1]

[Dec. 5, 1919]

F I hope you will consider me sincere. I have been praying for you Sir.[2]

H The committee on Foreign relations has passed a Resolution, which [blank]

F. I hope we will forget any fight. We have been making an investigation of Mex affairs cooperating with the State Dept, thinking it would be helpful to do so.

I left here to attend wedding on the 20, & [was] telegraphed from my committee that the situation owing to the Jenkins affair was critical   So stayed 1 day, & went to El Paso to get reports

The Reports were somewhat startling. We discovered through the Embassy here & elsewhere a lot of propaganda by an Australian—was interfearing with a Liberal Gov—were interfearing with the gov. & as an agent of Doheny We discovered Caranza was in touch with these parties The 3 men of the U. S. brought with them a plan by the favor of Mexican. We secured from the British Embassy City of Mexico.

They attended the meetings & the B. also. That on Nov. 15 a strike would be in the U. S. & with the assistance of the Mexicans they would set up a gov. in Cal. & return to Mex. the border states[3]—Enter Grayson, saying Excuse me But the State Dept. telephones Jenkins has been released.

Blue book Caranza[4] showing how he has won every fight, & showing great animosity to Pres. W. Miss L's book, called the "Caranza [undecipherable word]."[5] He directs her to conclude the book in which she is to dwell upon the fact that he has tried to prevent Amer. & Brit. capital to come in to Mexico & to show Wilson's animosity to Mexico.

Oil note, Caranza[6]

The Sec. was quoted as saying Amer. citizens had no more right than any others. Caranza reitereated his Now has troops who have seized mines & peoples houses & tools. Even upon private property His decree is to the affect that they must have a permit, which is correct, but adds that they must agree to abide by any law made

Upon Fall's arrival in Wast [Wash], was sent for by Lansing who said he had not discussed the situation with the Pres. & wanted Fall's council

Fall advised a withdrawal of recognition of Caranza by this Gov, & perhaps Gonzalez[7] might be elected, but that was spec.

He wants (Caranza) to get up just as close to the line as possible, & then say to his people to do away with Elections & leave it to him.

The reason for introducing the Resolution was that Lansing had suggested Fletcher act as Liasone officer, & Fall submitted the Res. to Fletcher, & he decided on the *one* of the 2 Res. he had formulated. Fall thinks the adoption of this Reso. would strengthen the Pr. hands in dealing with Mexico—"I hope you understand that I

P Thank you very much for your statmt Sen. It is very full. We are dealing with a question which affects

H. How the Dem. view the matter without knowing the Pres. views. Lansing came before the Com. & stated that he did

F Now about the conditions in Mexico there is a very strong feeling against militarism. Private opinion is in favor of peace.

80 or 85 per cent of the people would welcome interfearence by America

Papers (Mexican) are saying such things with out interfearance from Caranza, who does not dare try to suppress.

EBWhw MS (WP, DLC).
  [1] EBWhw on envelope enclosing Fall's memorandum.
  [2] Mrs. Wilson later recalled that Wilson responded to this remark with the question: "Which way, Senator?" Edith Bolling Wilson, *My Memoir* (Indianapolis and New York, 1938), p. 299. Wilson himself described the incident to David F. Houston in February 1921 as follows: "After the committee had discussed certain matters with me and had, I think, discovered that I was very much all here, the committee turned to leave. Senator Fall paused a moment and said: 'Mr. President, I want you to know that I am praying for you.' " Wilson did not mention his alleged retort but instead commented to Houston: "If I could have got out of bed, I would have hit the man. Why did he want to put me in bad with the Almighty? He must have known that God would take the opposite view from him on any subject." David F. Houston, *Eight Years with Wilson's Cabinet, 1913 to 1920* (2 vols., Garden City, N. Y., 1926), II, 141.
  [3] The Plan of San Diego, about which, see n. 1 to A. B. Fall to WW, Dec. 5, 1919.
  [4] Cited in n. 1 to the Enclosure printed with RL to WW, Aug. 21, 1919, Vol. 62.
  [5] Actually, Hermila Galindo. Her book is cited in n. 2 to the letter cited in the preceding note.
  [6] This may refer to Carranza's decree of July 31, 1918 (printed in *FR 1918*, pp. 752-54), which provided for taxes on oil production and on oil-bearing lands or to any of the subsequent decrees and regulations in 1918 and 1919 which sought to enforce the decree of July 31, 1918, for which see *ibid.*, pp. 754-92, *passim*, and *FR 1919*, II, 591-613, *passim*. See also n. 1 to the news report printed at Dec. 4, 1919.
  [7] Gen. Pablo Gonzáles, who, along with Gen. Álvaro Obregón, was a candidate to succeed Carranza as President of Mexico.

A Memorandum by Cary Travers Grayson[1]

Friday, December 5, 1919.

From the time the President was taken sick necessitating the abandonment of the Western trip, the Republican majority in the Senate took advantage of every possible opportunity to belittle his illness. They made no effort to fight in the open, contenting themselves with a campaign of innuendo and "whispering slander." The general feeling among the Republicans was that the President must certainly be the big issue in the next Presidential campaign, and they were willing to go any length if possible to disarm him. A score of Senators, notably New and Watson of Indiana, Poindexter of Washington, Johnson of California, Sherman and McCormick of Illinois, Lodge of Massachusetts, Hale of Maine, Penrose of Pennsylvania, and Moses of New Hampshire took occasion every time they conversed with the newspaper correspondents to declare that the President was unable to discharge his duties under the Constitution. The wish always was father to the thought. On several occasions these Senators made statements privately that had they been made publicly it would have driven them out of public life.

Moses wrote a letter to a constituent in which he declared that the President had suffered a brain lesion and that his right side was paralyzed; but it was not alone the political opponents of the President who sought to mislead the public in statements regarding the actual illness of the Executive. Washington's "high society," always on the alert for morsels of misleading information, took great delight in declaring that the President's sickness was far more serious than I had indicated in any of my bulletins. Many of these so-called leaders of society professed to have information that came directly from the White House showing that the President would never again be able to resume work. These people took it upon themselves to declare that I had been the leader in a conspiracy to keep the actual truth from being known by the people. Some of them even went so far as to say that the President had not received the King and Queen of the Belgians or the Prince of Wales when they visited him in the White House. Although fully aware of the various stories that were in circulation, I made no effort to deny them. I had my own plan to meet this situation when the time came. The opportunity of putting the plan of campaign into operation was averted when the Foreign Relations Committee took it upon itself to interfere with the Executive handling of the Mexican situation. A Consular official named Jenkins had been kidnapped in Mexico and released upon the payment of a ransom. The Mexican government, through the instrumentality of President Carranza, had Jenkins arrested on a charge that he himself had conspired to bring about the kidnapping in order to discredit the government. A demand for his release had been made in the regular diplomatic manner. Senator Fall, of New Mexico, introduced a resolution calling on the President to sever diplomatic intercourse with the Carranza government. When the resolution came up in the Senate Foreign Relations Committee, the Republican members seized upon it as a vehicle, if possible, to discredit the President. They adopted a resolution directing that a committee composed of Senator Fall and Senator Hitchcock (the Democratic leader in the Senate) call upon the President and ask him what action he wanted taken upon the Fall Resolution, and at the same time commissioned Senator Fall to give certain information he claimed to have dealing with Mexico to the President direct. This resolution was not adopted in an open manner. It was part of a deliberate conspiracy on the part of Senator Lodge and other Senators to endeavor to put the President in the position of refusing to receive a committee of the Senate.

Senator Moses was the prime spirit in initiating the plan. Moses wanted to vindicate his pulished statement that the President was unable to transact business.

I made no public statement as to what the President would or would not do. In fact, I adopted a non-committal attitude that had the effect of making a number of Republicans believe that I would not let the President receive the committee. Meanwhile, however, I had told the President about the entire proposition, and he had said that he would be very glad to receive the committee.

In consequence, when the committee sent word to the White House that Senators Fall and Hitchcock were desirous of seeing the President, the former was dumfounded when I let it be known that I had no objection to their coming, and that the President would be very glad to receive them. I had told all who asked me that the President was undergoing a rest cure and that personally I would prefer that he be not compelled to devote attention to anything of a controversial nature, but that if it was necessary there was no real reason why the President could not transact any business, he having responded so wonderfully to the continued treatment previously referred to.

When the Senators asked what time they were to come to see the President, they were told "2:30 this afternoon." They had said that they would be willing to wait until Monday, when the committee was to resume its consideration of the Fall Resolution, but there was no real reason for delay.

Consequently, the two Senators put in an appearance at 2:30 in the afternoon. When I met them, Senator Fall wanted to know how long they could stay. I had no intention of taking any responsibility for Senator Fall's actions, so I told him that he would be the best judge of that. This was another staggering blow, because there is no doubt the Republican majority of the Senate was hopeful that I would, even if I permitted the committee to see the President, limit the time and make it very brief. In consequence of my failure to fix any limit the two Senators were with the President for more than forty-five minutes.

The President received the Senators reclining in his bed. By his direction, all of the electric-lights in the room were turned on so that there would be plenty of opportunity for the Senators to see everything that was to be seen. It was a gloomy day outside but very bright in the President's bed-room.

The President conversed with the two Senators at great length.

He accepted from them the papers which they submitted, and they admittedly were amazed at his wonderful grasp of the entire Mexican problem and his complete knowledge of even the most minute developments.

When they entered the room Senator Fall shook hands with the President and told him that he hoped that he was getting along well and that he would soon recover. The President laughingly assured the Senator that he was getting along nicely and expressed the opinion that he soon would be able to get on his feet and go to the Capitol and take up personally problems affecting the Government. He then told Senator Fall that he hoped he would convey this information to his colleague, Senator Moses, laughingly saying that he hoped the New Hampshire Senator would be "reassured" although he might be "disappointed." Senator Fall told the President that he wanted him to know that he was not one of this group. The New Mexico Senator declared that he was in earnest when he told the President that he was praying for him daily.

After the two Senators went back to the Capitol they issued a statement in which they described the President's condition as reassuring. Senator Fall took occasion specifically to declare that the Presdident was mentally alert and that it was plain to be seen that he was capable of handling any problem of government that might be brought before him. Senator Fall's action in emphasizing the clearness of the President's mental processes had the effect of completely puncturing the various rumors that had been so carefully circulated by the Senators throughout the Capitol. Not alone this, but it also had the effect of destroying a reputation for "inside information" possessed by certain Washington social leaders. In this connection, the Washington POST carried a very interesting article showing just how this was done.

There was no question whatever that the manner in which the conference between the Senators and the President was indulged had been of enormous benefit to the nation at large. There had been so many word-of-mouth lies circulated, professing to tell the exact facts in connection with the President's illness, that many sane Americans had been misled. When the truth came out as the result of what Senator Fall saw and what he afterwards told he saw, many of these scandal-mongers suffered a very material loss in their reputation for truth and veracity.

One of the incidents of the conference that gave me a little personal satisfaction was to be called to the telephone while the President was talking with Senators Fall and Hitchcock and to be informed by the State Department that it had received word that Consul Jenkins had been released last night (December 4th). I interrupted the conference long enough to impart this information to the President and the two Senators. It developed afterwards that the release of Jenkins ended that particular phase of the Mexican crisis.

T MS (received from James Gordon Grayson and Cary T. Grayson, Jr.).
  ¹ This memorandum was probably written retrospectively, but not long after the events described therein.

A Memorandum by Robert Lansing

December 5, 1919.

Well, the President received Senators Fall and Hitchcock as I thought he would. Fall did most of the talking but the President took a keen interest in what was said and closed the interview with a laugh. Fall on leaving the White House stated frankly that he considered the President to be capable mentally to perform his duties. His assurance has relieved the present tension of public doubt and ended the stories that his mind is in any way affected. As far as it goes that is a good thing all around.

But I am not sure that that ends the business. People are surely going to ask about the President's physical condition, and whether it permits him to use his mind except at occasional intervals. Fall says that the President received him and Hitchcock lying flat on his back in bed and moved none of his limbs except his right arm. This may mean nothing or it may mean a good deal. The interviewers came away no wiser as to whether his legs or his left side was paralyzed. They may be for all they could tell. He may be suffering from great weakness. They could not tell.

If his physical condition of his nerves are in bad shape his physicians would prohibit him from too much mental exertion. I am convinced that this is what they have done, and that they reluctantly consented to his seeing Fall and Hitchcock to silence gossip as to his mental state. I am sure too that Grayson was fearful of the ordeal upon the President and would have avoided it if he did not fear an investigation by Congress.

In view, therefore, of the ignorance of the public as to the character of the President's malady, though relieved of the rumors as to his mental disability, I feel that the secrecy which has prevailed should come to an end. Until this is done by a complete statement from his physicians, stories will continue to circulate and the question will arise as to whether he is physically able to do his work properly, even though he may now and then pass on a simple question.

I think that the American people are entitled to know and the Cabinet ought to know the truth. It is not a matter of invading the privacy of an individual. It is not Woodrow Wilson but the President of the United States who is ill. His family and his physicians have no right to shroud the whole affair in mystery as they have done. I would not blame Congress if they instituted an investigation to ascertain the facts. It would not be an unreasonable thing for them to do.

T MS (R. Lansing Papers, DLC).

From Albert Bacon Fall

My dear Mr. President: [Washington] December 5, 1919.

In accordance with my promise, I am herewith handing you by special messenger an uncorrected transcript of the report[1] which I made to you verbally this afternoon. You will pardon the shape in which this document appears under the circumstances.

I am convinced that you are as desirous of having it at the earliest possible moment as I am that you may have an opportunity to look it over.

As I stated to you, the Committee will meet on Monday, and of course, if entirely consistent, I will be glad to have from you either to myself, or Chairman Lodge, the Chairman of the Committee, an indication of your desire with reference to the pending resolution.

Very truly yours,   [Albert B. Fall]

CCL (A. B. Fall Papers, CSmH).
[1] The enclosure was a very rough draft (CC MS, WP, DLC), which briefly set forth numerous examples of the alleged efforts of the Carranza government to spread radical propaganda among left-wing groups in the United States and to promote a revolution among dissatisfied elements, mostly Mexican Americans, in the states of the Southwest. The report contained several references to the Plan of San Diego, a document purportedly signed by nine individuals in the small town of that name in Duval County, Texas, on January 6, 1915. It called for a revolutionary uprising of Mexican Americans and blacks to proclaim the independence of Texas, New Mexico, Arizona, Colorado, and California, with an eye to their later incorporation into Mexico. For a detailed discussion of the origins of this scheme and its subsequent effects on relations between the United States and Mexico, see Charles H. Harris III and Louis R. Sadler, "The Plan of San Diego and the Mexican-United States War Crisis of 1916: A Reexamination," *Hispanic American Historical Review*, LVIII (Aug. 1978), 381-408. A copy of the "report" that Fall sent to Wilson is printed in *Investigation of Mexican Affairs . . . Pursuant to S. Res. 106*, I, 843D-843J.

From the Diary of Josephus Daniels

1919 Friday 5 December

Cabinet—Long session. Palmer said Judge Anderson had taken case in his hands—had summoned the Grand Jury, and it looked like he was going to imprison many miners for contempt because they had not gone back to work.[1] He was trying to prevent this as it was unjust to punish these small fellows & would react. As matter of fact there has been reaction because people were being thrown out of employment because they could not get coal to carry on industries. Public thinks Cabinet approves Garfields statement that 14% increase is right.[2] Operators offered 20%—decided to refer matter to the President, as I had urged at former meeting.[3] Glass, Palmer & Houston to take matter up & get statement from Wilson, Garfield and Hines and then prepare suggestions to the President who would act. Tumulty had suggested a committee of such men as Judge Gray, Straus, & Endicott[4] to try to get operators and miners together.

[1] About the beginning and progress of the strike of the coal miners and the injunction issued by Judge Albert Barnes Anderson ordering the leaders of the United Mine Workers to rescind their strike order no later than November 11, see n. 1 to the extract from the Daniels Diary printed at Nov. 4, 1919, Vol. 63. As noted therein, although John L. Lewis did rescind the strike order on November 11, most miners remained on strike. Dan W. Simms, a Special Assistant United States District Attorney appointed to oversee the enforcement of the injunction, made a statement in Indianapolis on November 17, in which he warned that any individual miner who refrained from working in order to continue the strike was in violation of the terms of the injunction, which forbade union officers, miners, or anyone else from doing anything whatsoever toward the furtherance or continuation of the strike. Simms issued another warning on November 29, in which he said that coal had to be mined and that every miner, operator, or any other person who had knowledge of the injunction and who thereafter violated its terms would be cited for contempt. On December 3, charges of criminal contempt were filed in the United States district court in Indianapolis against John L. Lewis and some eighty other officials of the United Mine Workers who were, it was alleged, in fact encouraging the strike despite their claims to the contrary. Simms announced that these were only the first of the contempt proceedings and that the government would in due time act against all persons encouraging the strike. Judge Anderson, on December 4, ordered a special session of a federal grand jury to investigate all aspects of the coal strike with the ultimate goal of prosecuting all violators of the Lever Act, the Sherman Antitrust Act, and the court's injunction. See the *New York Times*, Nov. 18 and 30 and Dec. 1, 3, 4, and 5, 1919.

[2] Garfield had read a lengthy statement to a meeting of coal mine operators and union representatives in Washington on November 26, in which he declared that the miners should receive an increase in wages "commensurate with the increase in the cost of living" since 1913 and that, by his calculations, this would amount to an average increase of 14 per cent. The operators declared themselves willing to accept this proposal, but the union leaders rejected it with open contempt. *New York Times*, Nov. 27, 1919. For a detailed statement of Garfield's reasoning, see the Enclosure printed with H. A. Garfield to WW, Dec. 7, 1919.

[3] At the cabinet meeting on November 26, following a meeting on the preceding day. For a detailed account, see Lansing's memorandum, "THE MEETINGS OF THE CABINET ON THE STRIKE OF THE COAL MINERS," T MS (R. Lansing Papers, DLC).

[4] That is, George Gray, Oscar Solomon Straus, and Henry Bradford Endicott.

From Joshua Willis Alexander[1]

My dear Mr. President: Washington, D. C. December 6, 1919.

I wish to express to you my sincere appreciation of the very high honor you are conferring upon me by selecting me for a place in your cabinet as Secretary of Commerce.[2]

I will spare no pains to discharge the duties of the office in a manner to meet your approval and with credit to your administration.

Sincerely hoping that you may soon be restored to health and strength and that I may soon have the privilige of expressing to you in person my appreciation of the great honor conferred upon me, and with very best wishes, I am, Sir,

Yours very sincerely,   J. W. Alexander

TLS (WP, DLC).
[1] Democratic congressman from Missouri since 1907.
[2] Alexander's nomination was sent to the Senate on December 5, and he was confirmed six days later. He served as Secretary of Commerce until March 4, 1921. There are no documents in WP, DLC, or the J. P. Tumulty Papers, DLC, relating to his appointment. The *New York Times*, Dec. 3, 1919, commented on Alexander's appointment as follows:
"The offer of the Cabinet post was a surprise to official Washington and to nobody more than to Mr. Alexander. Several days ago, while he was visiting his home in Missouri, he received a telegram from Joseph P. Tumulty asking him to call at the White House today [December 2]. When he appeared there Secretary Tumulty informed him that the President wished him to enter the Cabinet as Secretary of Commerce."

A News Report

[Dec. 7, 1919]

PRESIDENT MAKES PROPOSAL TO COAL MINERS; LEADERS ACCEPT, STRIKE LIKELY TO END.

Washington, Sunday, Dec. 7.—Attorney General Palmer announced at 1 o'clock this morning that President Wilson has made to the coal miners a definite concrete proposal looking to a speedy termination of the strike and an adjustment of the entire controversy,[1] and that Acting President Lewis and Secretary Green of the miners would urge its acceptance at a meeting of the Scale Committee, called to meet in Indianapolis Tuesday.

The President's terms were submitted to Acting President Lewis and Secretary Green at a meeting yesterday at the Department of Justice, which was attended also by Joseph Tumulty, secretary to the President. Mr. Palmer had previously gone over the whole coal situation with the President.

Mr. Lewis and Mr. Green, whose presence in Washington was unknown until the announcement was made, indorsed the terms and will submit them at the meeting at Indianapolis Tuesday.

The nature of the new offer has not been disclosed.

Mr. Palmer's announcement was as follows:

A conference was held at the Department of Justice, in Washington, on Saturday, at which were present the Attorney General, Secretary Tumulty, John Lewis, Acting President, and William Green, Secretary-Treasurer of the United Mine Workers of America, with a view to reaching an understanding between the Government and the miners which would result in a settlement of the coal strike situation.

At this conference there was submitted a definite concrete proposition from the President looking to a speedy termination of the strike situation and an adjustment of the entire controversy. The officers of the United Mine Workers, in response to the suggestion of the President, agreed, and have called a meeting of the General Scale Committee, the representatives of all the district organizations and the International Executive Board of the United Mine Workers to be held in Indianapolis on Tuesday, Dec. 9, at 2 o'clock P.M., at which time the President's proposal will be considered and its acceptance by the miners urged by Mr. Lewis and Mr. Green.

The Attorney General will be in Indianapolis on Tuesday.

It is accepted here as a foregone conclusion that this announcement means the speedy termination of the strike, and with that the withdrawal of the injunction proceedings which were brought before Judge Anderson in Indianapolis.

The decision of the leaders of the mine workers was reached after President Wilson had personally passed upon the situation created by the strike and had decided that the Government must stand firm in the position it had taken.

This is taken to mean that the Government will stand by the Garfield program for an increase of 14 per cent to the miners at this time, with the understanding that a committee to be appointed by President Wilson and headed by Secretary Franklin K. Lane will make a thorough review of the situation, with a view to making readjustments, if such are warranted.

The new negotiations were carefully guarded by officials and there was no intimation given, until the formal announcement was made at 1 o'clock this morning, that Lewis and Green were in Washington.

It is understood that the Government did not request the leaders to come to Washington through the Department of Justice, at least. It could not be determined whether Lewis and Green had come on their own initiative or whether the move was made through some agency, not associated with that department.

The Attorney General was at the White House at about 1 o'clock yesterday afternoon and had a conference with the President lasting a few minutes. While this was going on Tumulty was closeted with Lewis and Green.

It is understood that the Attorney General placed the facts before the President, sketching the status of the injunction proceedings and the arguments made by miners and operators, as well as the stand taken by Mr. Garfield. It is reported that President Wilson gave his assurance of support to the Garfield program and told the Attorney General that he also would have the full support of the Government. But the word was also to be carried to the leaders of the miners that the Government would see to it that no injustice was done to them in the final review of the case.

The Attorney General and Secretary Tumulty then met jointly with Mr. Lewis and Mr. Green and placed before them in detail the proposal of the President. The first conference between the four began at 2 o'clock in the afternoon, and they were not concluded until very late at night. The statement given out by the Attorney General was then drawn up and agreed to by all of the conferees.

Up to the time the announcement was issued the Department of Justice had stood firmly to the position that there would be no change in the Government's policy in treating with the strikers and that its agents were going to Indianapolis to handle the proceedings in the Federal Court.

But this was before the Department of Justice was able to announce that Lewis and Green would urge upon their members the acceptance of the Government's program.

In the conferences which took place between Palmer and Tumulty for the Government and Lewis and Green for the miners, all the points at issue were reviewed. The situation among the miners in the Central Competitive field were discussed and the opinion formed, it is understood, that most of them would quickly go back to work, once the announcement was made that Lewis and Green were satisfied and that the President demanded that such a result be brought about.

As an upshot of the conference it was decided that Mr. Palmer should go to Indianapolis to attend the meeting called by the miners for Tuesday. Pending the outcome of that meeting the injunction proceedings will be stayed.

It is understood here that the decision of President Wilson was predicated on his conviction that the higher increase could not be granted to the miners at this time without greatly increasing living costs, and that the line must be drawn where wage increases, other than those absolutely necessary to prevent suffering among workers, must no longer have Governmental sanction. This point was brought home to the miners in the conference by the representatives of the Government.

The decision of the mine leaders came, it is said, after it was made plain that such was the Government's position and that the officials of the Government directing the fight against the coal miners, was backed by the White House.

The Attorney General, it is understood, held that for the miners to continue their strike after the President had approved a basis of settlement, would put them in the position of defying the Government, despite the fact that the Government had promised a careful review of all complaints and further readjustments where the justice of their claims were made evident.

The officials who had worked all day and night to bring about the agreement by the leaders of the mine workers were elated after the decision was reached and were confident that the end of the strike was now in sight.

Printed in the *New York Times*, Dec. 7, 1919.
    [1] The statement that Wilson signed is printed as an Enclosure with JPT to EBW, Dec. 8, 1919.

Edith Bolling Galt Wilson to Joseph Patrick Tumulty

Dear Mr. Tumlty   [The White House, c. Dec. 7, 1919]

The President says will you see the Sec. of Labor & ask him to let him know if the Federal Gov. is still carrying on any investigation in the Mooney case in California[1]   EBW

ALI (WP, DLC).
    [1] William B. Wilson's reply was WBW to WW, Dec. 8, 1919, TLS (WP, DLC). In this memorandum, Secretary Wilson stated that Luigi Galleani, whom he identified as "one of the leading anarchists in the United States," had said in the course of his deportation hearing on November 23, 1918, that he had "the mathematical certitude" that Tom Mooney was innocent of the crime for which he had been convicted. About the Mooney case, see WW to W. D. Stephens, May 11, 1917, n. 2, Vol. 42. At a later date, Galleani said further that he knew the man who had actually thrown the bomb and that the person had told him about it after the event. The Labor Department had since been trying to run down this "clue" but had so far been unsuccessful. "That is all," Secretary Wilson concluded, "the Department of Labor is at present doing in connection with the Mooney case."

From Harry Augustus Garfield, with Enclosure

Dear Mr. President: Washington, D. C. December 7, 1919

Referring to your statement concerning the bituminous coal strike handed to the Attorney General yesterday, am I not correct in assuming that you intend the commission, which may be appointed to readjust wages and prices, should be governed by the principle set forth in the last paragraph but one of my letter to you of December 5?

　　For your convenience, I herewith attach a copy of my letter.
　　　　　　Cordially and faithfully yours,　H. A. Garfield
　　　　　　　　United States Fuel Administrator

　　I of course welcome your suggestion for a commission to review my findings, the above principle being accepted, but the public should not be allowed to confuse this commission with the permanent advisory body proposed by me & referred to in the fifth paragraph of your statement.　　　　　　　　H.A.G.

TLS (WP, DLC).

ENCLOSURE

From Harry Augustus Garfield

Dear Mr. President:　　[Washington] December 5, 1919

　　The statements and conclusions presented by me to the operators and mine workers on the 24th and 26th of last month, copies of which are attached hereto,[1] and the arguments offered at Cabinet meetings in support of my position may be summed up as follows:

　　The increase in the cost of living since 1913 has been 79.8%.

　　The wages of the several groups of bituminous mine workers have been increased since 1913 as follows:

1. Machine miners, loaders, and cutters		56.1%
2. Pick miners		34.8%
3. Tracklayers		81.3%
4. Pipemen		77.0%
5. Trappers (boys)		100.8%
6. Tracklayers, cagers, drivers, trip runners, haulers, timbermen, wiremen and motormen		76.1%
Weighted average of all mine workers		57.6%

The mine workers receiving the lowest total annual wage are found among the last four groups. It will be observed that the increase of wages of the mine workers in groups 5, 4 and 6 (excluding boys) already substantially equals the increased cost of living. The average wage of the lowest paid group, except boys, is about $950 per annum, that is, nearly $80 per month for twelve months, working, however, only about 200 days in the year. These are unskilled day laborers. The similar class of laborers on the railroads receive about $900 per annum working about 300 days in the year.

14% added to the average increase of wages above shown (57.6%) will bring the average wages of mine workers as a whole up to the percentage of increase in cost of living (79.8%) without doing substantial injustice to those at present receiving the smallest annual wage.

It is necessary as a practical matter to preserve the present wage differentials, that is to say, neither the mine workers nor the operators would be content to bring each of the six groups above named to 79.8%. If Secretary Wilson's proposal is followed, namely, to bring the pick miners up to 79.8%, and all others by the same per cent of increase, thus preserving the wage differential, the average wages of the mine workers would be advanced 107% or $238,000,000 as against $107,000,000, if the average wages are increased 14%.

There is here presented a difference in principle which is of fundamental importance, namely, that the public ought not to be asked to pay more for its fuel than is necessary to bring the average wages of labor up to a point sufficient to cover increased cost of living, when, as in the present case, the wages of the lowest paid group furnish them a livelihood and place them on a parity with laborers of corresponding groups in other industries.

I am satisfied that the operators can absorb this 14% increase. If they are willing to agree to pay more, they are of course free to do so but they should not be permitted to load any part of it on the public now or hereafter.

Cordially and faithfully yours,   [H. A. Garfield]

CCL (WP, DLC).
 [1] They are missing in WP, DLC.

Robert Lansing to Edith Bolling Galt Wilson, with Enclosures

My dear Mrs. Wilson—   Washington December 7, 1919.

This is a matter of such immediate importance that I am going to ask you the great favor to read the enclosed letter to the President at the earliest moment possible in order that I may instruct Mr. Polk accordingly.

I would spare the President in every way possible from matters of this sort but this question is one of such high policy as well as expediency that I do not like to act without his full approval.

Will you please convey to the President my affectionate regard and believe me   Faithfully yours   Robert Lansing.

ALS (EBW Papers, DLC).

ENCLOSURE   I

From Robert Lansing

My dear Mr. President: Washington December 7, 1919.

In view of the insistence of Mr. Polk in the enclosed message (No. 5592), which was received in four sections, I feel that I should lay before you for immediate decision the question of dealing with the present critical situation in Paris as a result of the withdrawal of our Commissioners and the failure of the Germans to sign the protocol.[1]

I have considered the subject with sympathetic appreciation of the French attitude toward our withdrawal and at the same time with a realization that to continue a representative on the Supreme Council in view of the Senate's action would be to relieve that body of a responsibility which they ought to bear and which will become all the more evident if we do not proceed as if they had not rejected ratification.

To me the latter course seems much the more important and the European press as well as the American press is beginning to blame the Senate, as it should do, for the present situation. To Mr. Polk, on the other hand, the importunity and arguments of the French seem of first importance, and he suggests a means of meeting their wishes. While we thus differ as to the essential factor in deciding the problem, I am in a measure willing, if it meets your views, to go part way in relieving French anxiety, provided it can be done without removing the blame which today rests upon the Republican Senators for the present situation.

I suggest two possible methods of handling the problem:

First: To direct Ambassador Wallace to sit in on the Supreme Council as an observer and not as a participant, and to instruct him to take no action and to express no opinion on any subject discussed; to report the proceedings to Washington and await instructions; and to issue to him full powers to sign the Hungarian and Roumanian (minority) treaties.

Second: For me to ask a hearing before the Foreign Relations Committee or interview with Senator Lodge, lay the whole situation before them, and say to them frankly that the Senate's action has placed us in this dilemma and that, therefore, they should decide whether or not we should continue to co-operate with the Allies in having even a silent representative on the Supreme Council.

Personally I do not favor either suggestion, but, if either is to be adopted, the first seems to me the better because I do not like the idea of even indirectly giving the impression that the Senate has the right to control in any way our foreign affairs except as to its constitutional power in relation to treaties. I think that the principle outweighs the expediency of forcing the Republican majority to express an opinion as to the wisdom of retaining an inactive member on the Supreme Council. It would of course seriously embarrass them; but, on the other hand, if they favor such representation, they would be relieved in part at least from the tide of public complaint and criticism which is constantly growing higher as the consequences of their failure to ratify the treaty become more apparent to everybody.

As our Commissioners leave Paris Tuesday night, I think this matter should be settled immediately; otherwise it will be too late to communicate with Mr. Polk before his departure, and he ought to be able, before leaving, to tell the French what we intend to do.

I would like also to have your decision as to whether our troops in the Rhineland should take part in the reported operations instituted by Foch to force Germany to sign the protocol.[2] As the protocol has to do in fact with the deposit of ratifications, should we permit our men to participate in the present coercive measures? And yet, since it may be claimed that the sinking of the German ships at Scapa Flow was a violation of the armistice and the protocol was drawn to recompense the Allies for the loss due to the violation, the failure to permit our troops to be used might be open to criticism. I never liked the terms of the protocol, but as it was agreed to by the Supreme Council I do not see how we can reopen the case on the merits. I confess that I do not blame the German Government for doing so. The only thing is how far ought we to go in allowing our armed forces to be used in compelling the Germans to submit.

Viewed strategically the longer the protocol remains unsigned by Germany so much the more blame will be put on the Senate and so much the more pressure will be put on that body to ratify the Treaty.

As the newspapers are announcing, on what authority or information I do not know, that our troops are participating in Foch's movement across the Rhine, I think that a decision in this matter ought to be reached without delay.

Faithfully yours, Robert Lansing.

TLS (SDR, RG 59, 763.72119/8218½B, DNA).
[1] About this protocol, see n. 2 to the draft of a statement printed at Dec. 2, 1919.
[2] There had been repeated reports in the newspapers that General Foch would soon order an advance of the Allied armies beyond the Rhine to compel the German government to sign the protocol. See, for example, the *New York Times*, Dec. 2 and 5, 1919; the *Washington Post*, Dec. 6, 1919; and the New York *World*, Dec. 7, 1919.
As it turned out, the Council of Heads of Delegations and the German delegation negotiated a compromise on the carrying out of the terms of the protocol in late December. See *PPC*, IX, 667-70, 686-87, 703-704, 711-14, and 721-26. The Germans signed the document on January 10, 1920. *Ibid.*, pp. 819-20; *New York Times*, Jan. 11, 1920.

Paris, December 6, 1919.

Double priority 5592. Strictly confidential and personal for the Secretary of State only from Polk to be delivered at the Secretary's residence immediately. Your 3975, December 5, 3 p.m.[1]

I will let you know in a later telegram about the Rhine Commission, Teschen and funds for Bandholtz. I know how busy you are and how many irritating and trying questions are before you and I hesitate to add one more worry but at the present time I hope you will forgive me if I again urge upon you the necessity of letting some one finish the work in the Supreme Council which will be pending on the day of our departure. We will be in the position of working until arrival of an arbitrary day and then taking our departure leaving the other four powers to go on with the work that we have actually been engaged in preparing with no representative of the United States.

End Section one. Polk.

Double priority. Section two. 5592, December 6, 8 p.m.

In regard to Germany you already have my views and also in regard to the Hungarian treaty, the minorities treaty, and the Austrian treaty, but I must again beg you to consider the position in which we are placing ourselves by not completing our uncompleted tasks. In view of the fact that we have been largely instrumental in framing the Hungarian treaty and making it possible for the Hungarians to form a government, I cannot see that the Senate or anyone could object to our being present when the treaty is presented, provided the decision of the Senate is not to be treated as final. The same is true of the minorities treaty with Roumania. The powers have presented an ultimatum to Roumania to sign[2] and it seems to me that no one could criticise our standing by until the Roumanian minority treaty is signed particularly as the treaty was imposed on the Serbs, Poles and Greeks. Neither the Hungarian treaty nor the Roumanian treaty would require the Ambassador to exercise any discretion as all the details are complete.

End Section two. Polk.

Double priority. Section three. 5592.

In regard to the German protocol I personally think Germany will sign, yet nothing will convince the French that we have not abandoned them in an emergency if we pull out while the negotiations are still going on. In this matter too it seems to me the Senate could not object to our sitting in the conference, for in the event of the Germans refusing to sign it would be only fair that the other governments should know what position if any we intend to take under the armistice. I think it is thoroughly understood by the powers that the Supreme Council as such can only function in connection with these matters and that it would be very easy to impress on them the fact that the Ambassador would in each case have to refer to his government for instructions.

We leave Tuesday evening at eight o'clock and Clemenceau is still hoping something can be done to save the appearance of our arbitrarily leaving.

End Section three. Polk.

Section Four. Double priority. 5592.

I am convinced that he is disturbed not only on account of the effect of our withdrawal on Germany but he also sees that our withdrawal practically throws the European situation into the lap of Great Britain which will be the only power strong enough to assume leadership.

Let me again apologize for being so persistent but on every side, from the French, Americans and British, I get the impression that this is one of the critical moments in the diplomatic history of the United States and on your decision, in a great measure, rests the prestige of the United States. Men like himself are urging me to present this point of view to you, for they cannot see what our position will be on Wednesday with business to be done and no one to represent us whereas on Tuesday we were represented. Why should we change our position by our departure Tuesday night particularly as the business we were discussing Tuesday morning is unfinished. Again I apologize for bothering you but we are in an embarrassing position.

End of message.   Polk.   American Mission.

T telegram (SDR, RG 59, 763.72119/8153, DNA).

[1] RL to FLP, Dec. 5, 1919, printed in *PPC*, XI, 689-90. Lansing asked Polk's opinion as to whether the Armistice Commission would cease to exist when the peace treaty went into effect and whether Pierrepont B. Noyes and his staff could be continued at Coblenz as "a special commission from this Government in the occupied area, during the time between the coming into force of the treaty and our ratification." He also asked Polk's opinion of the qualifications and availability of Arthur Wood Du Bois to serve as chairman of the Teschen Plebiscite Commission, should Poland and Czechoslovakia ask the United States to nominate an American citizen to that post. Lansing also agreed to Polk's suggestion that Brig. Gen. Harry Hill Bandholtz, U.S.A., continue for the time being as the American military representative in Budapest but asked what expense this would entail.

[2] For the background of this ultimatum, see the Enclosure printed with RL to WW, Nov. 14, 1919, and the notes thereto. For the text of the note sent by the Council of Heads of Delegations to the Rumanian government on November 15, see *PPC*, IX, 182-84.

To Albert Bacon Fall[1]

My dear Sir: The White House 8 December, 1919

Thank you very much for your kind promptness in complying with my request that you send me a copy of the memorandum report of the Sub-Committee on Mexican Affairs of the Committee on Foreign Affairs. I shall examine it with the greatest interest and care. What you told me of the investigation, on Friday last, prepares me to find in it matter of the greatest importance.

You ask an indication of my desire with regard to the pending resolution to which you and Senator Hitchcock called my attention on Friday, and I am glad to reply with the utmost frankness that I should be gravely concerned to see any such resolution pass the Congress. It would constitute a reversal of our constitutional practice which might lead to very grave confusion in regard to the guidance of our foreign affairs. I am confident that I am supported by every competent constitutional authority in the statement that the initiative in directing the relations of our Government with foreign governments is assigned by the Constitution to the Executive, and to the Executive only. Only one of the two Houses of Congress is associated with the President by the Constitution in an advisory capacity, and the advice of the Senate is provided for only when sought by the Executive in regard to explicit agreements with foreign governments and the appointment of the diplomatic representatives who are to speak for this government at foreign capitals. The only safe course, I am confident, is to adhere to the prescribed method of the Constitution. We might go very far afield if we departed from it.

I am very much obliged to you for having given me the opportunity to express this opinion.[2]

                    Very truly yours,   Woodrow Wilson

TLS (A. B. Fall Papers, CSmH).

[1] It seems safe to say that Wilson did not write this letter, although he probably went over it and probably added sentences such as "We might go very far afield if we departed from it." Wilson probably would not have called the Committee on Foreign Relations the Committee on Foreign Affairs, and he never used the construction "on Friday last." The only two copies of this letter are the one in the Fall Papers and a letterpress copy in WP, DLC.

[2] This letter effectively killed the Fall Resolution. After reading the letter and conferring about it with Fall and Brandegee, Lodge spoke briefly to reporters on December 8 as follows: "Of course the committee will do nothing now. The President desires complete responsibility for the Mexican situation to rest on him. Let it rest there. We desired only to assist him; he does not wish us to do so. He does not even allow us to express our support or to make a suggestion. The committee will not again consider the resolution. We are through." *New York Times*, Dec. 9, 1919.

From Robert Lansing

My dear Mr. President: Washington December 8, 1919.

On November 11 Mr. F. Aguilar Barquero, the President of Costa Rica, telegraphed as follows:

"His Excellency the President of the United States of America, Washington, D. C.

"This day represents the principle of the Peace which the world now enjoys and in the conquest of which the people of your great Nation had so glorious a part. So on this day I send effusive greetings to Your Excellency and make most sincere wishes for the prosperity of your country and the complete recovery of Your Excellency's health.

"(Signed) F. Aguilar Barquero, President of the Republic of Costa Rica."

On November 12 Mr. Tumulty wrote me as follows:

"Will you not be good enough to have appropriate acknowledgment made of the enclosed message from the President of the Republic of Costa Rica?"

I have not as yet however acknowledged the message from Mr. Aguilar as I have deemed that it would be more appropriate to await your decision as to whether this Government should recognize the present Government of Costa Rica.

I enclose the draft of a telegram for your signature to Mr. Aguilar[1] and will be glad to be informed as to whether you wish it sent at this time.   Faithfully yours,   Robert Lansing.

TLS (WP, DLC).
[1] T MS (WP, DLC). It acknowledged Aguilar's message with generous thanks but did not explicitly recognize the Aguilar government. Wilson did not return the telegram, and it was not sent.

Joseph Patrick Tumulty to Edith Bolling Galt Wilson, with Enclosure

Dear Mrs. Wilson: The White House, 8 December 1919.

I have re-read the statement the President signed Saturday night with reference to the coal mining situation.[1] Frankly I do not find any limitation in it embodying the paragraph in Mr. Garfield's letter, which the President called to my attention.

At his leisure the President might peruse the statement again.

I hope that until favorable action is taken, the President will allow me to hold up his approval of the Garfield principle. It would be disastrous to any possible settlement for Mr. Garfield to say that through the President he has put a limitation upon any settlement.

Sincerely yours,   Tumulty

TLS (WP, DLC).
[1] The cabinet, on December 5, had asked Glass, Palmer, and Houston to draft the following statement. See the extract from the Daniels Diary printed at Dec. 5, 1919, and R. Lansing, "RECORD OF THE CABINET MEETINGS HELD DURING THE PRESIDENT'S ILLNESS," dated Feb. 23, 1920 (T MS, R. Lansing Papers, DLC): "The next meeting took place on Friday, December 5th. We discussed the strike situation for two hours and forty minutes finally appointing Glass, Palmer and Houston a committee to prepare a statement which the President could issue if he approved."

E N C L O S U R E

I have watched with deep concern the developments in the bituminous coal strike and am convinced there is much confusion in the minds of the people generally and possibly of both parties to this unfortunate controversy as to the attitude and purposes of the Government in its handling of the situation.

The mine owners offered a wage increase of twenty per cent conditioned, however, upon the price of coal being raised to an amount sufficient to cover this proposed increase of wages, which would have added at least $150,000,000 to the annual coal bill of the people. The Fuel Administrator in the light of present information has taken the position, and I think with entire justification, that the public is now paying as high prices for coal as it ought to be required to pay and that any wage increase made at this time ought to come out of the profits of the coal operators.

In reaching this conclusion, the Fuel Administrator expressed the personal opinion that a 14% increase in all mine wages is reasonable because it would equalize the miners' wages on the average with the cost of living, but he made it perfectly clear that the operators and miners are at liberty to agree upon a larger increase, provided the operators will pay it out of their profits so that the price of coal would remain the same.

The Secretary of Labor, in an effort at conciliation between the parties, expressed his personal opinion in favor of a larger increase. His effort at conciliation failed, however, because the coal operators were unwilling to pay the scale he proposed unless the Government would advance the price of coal to the public and this the Government was unwilling to do.

The Fuel Administrator has also suggested that a tribunal be created in which the miners and operators would be equally represented to consider further questions of wages and working conditions, as well as profits of operators and proper prices for coal. I shall, of course, be glad to aid in the formation of such a tribunal.

I understand the operators have generally agreed to absorb an increase of 14 per cent in wages, so that the public would pay not to exceed the present price fixed by the Fuel Administrator, and thus a way is opened to secure the coal of which the people stand in need, if the miners will resume work on these terms pending a thorough investigation by an impartial commission, which may readjust both wages and prices.

By the acceptance of such a plan, the miners are assured immediate steady employment at a substantial increase in wages and are further assured prompt investigation and action upon questions which are not now settled to their satisfaction. I must believe that with a clear understanding of these points they will promptly return to work. If, nevertheless, they persist in remaining on strike they will put themselves in an attitude of striking in order to force the Government to increase the price of coal to the public, so as to give a still further increase in wages at this time rather than allow the question of a further increase in wages to be dealt with in an orderly manner by a fairly constituted tribunal representing all parties in interest.

No group of our people can justify such a position and the miners owe it to themselves, their families, their fellow workmen in other industries and to their country to return to work.

Immediately upon a general resumption of mining, I shall be glad to aid in the prompt formation of such a tribunal as I have indicated to make further inquiries into this whole matter, and to review not only the reasonableness of the wages at which the miners start to work but also the reasonableness of the Government prices for coal. Such a tribunal should within sixty days make its report, which could be used as a basis for negotiation of a wage agreement. I must make it clear, however, that the Government cannot give its aid to any such further investigation until there is a general resumption of work.

I ask every individual miner to give his personal thought to what I say. I hope he understands fully that he will be hurting his own interest and the interest of his family and will be throwing countless other laboring men out of employment if he shall continue the present strike, and further, that he will create an unnecessary an[d] unfortunate prejudice against organized labor which will be injurious to the best interests of working men everywhere.

(Signed)   Woodrow Wilson.[1]

T MS (WP, DLC).

[1] This statement was printed, e.g., in the *New York Times*, Dec. 10, 1919.

Joseph Patrick Tumulty to John Sharp Williams

Dear Senator: The White House 8 December 1919.

I asked Mrs. Wilson to read to the President the postscript on your letter of the fifth instant.[1] She tells me that it amused him very much.   Sincerely yours,   J P Tumulty

TLS (J. S. Williams Papers, DLC).
  [1] "P.S. Tell Mrs. Wilson to tell the President how proud I was of the way he is letting the enemies of the peace of the world 'stew in their own grease' & of his manner of checkmating the venomous purpose in the appointment of the 'visiting committee.' " J. S. Williams to JPT, Dec. 5, 1919, TLS (WP, DLC).

Edith Bolling Galt Wilson to Robert Lansing

The White House Monday 8.15 a.m. [Dec. 8, 1919]

My dear Mr. Secretary:

Your note with enclosures I have just submitted to the President and he wishes me to say that he still agrees with you that the Mission should leave Paris as arranged but that the plan you suggest (no, *one*) of having Ambassador Wallace sit in etc he is willing to adopt.

Then, in regard to the matter of our troops in the Rhineland, the President says he will leave that to Gen. Bliss, and make his judgment concerning it, his own.

I am returning your letter that you may have it for reference. Also Mr. Polk's cable.

Thank you for your message to the President. He is gaining every day now. Please remember me as well to Mrs. Lansing.[1]

Faithfully   Edith Bolling Wilson

ALS (SDR, RG 59, 763.72119/8219½, DNA).
  [1] Eleanor Foster Lansing.

Robert Lansing to Frank Lyon Polk

Washington, December 8, 1919.

3997. Double Priority.

Confidential From the Secretary for Polk. Your 5592 December 6, 10 p.m.

In the circumstances the President has agreed that Ambassador Wallace may sit on the Supreme Council on behalf of the United States as an observer and not as a participant. Ambassador Wallace is being instructed in this sense and is likewise being instructed to take no action and to express no opinion on any subjects discussed; to report the proceedings to Washington and await instructions.

The Department is likewise issuing to Ambassador Wallace full powers to sign the Hungarian Treaty and the Roumanian Minority Treaty.

Ambassadors Jusserand and Gray are being informed of the above.   Lansing

T telegram (SDR, RG 59, 763.72119/8153, DNA).

William Phillips to Joseph Patrick Tumulty, with Enclosure

My dear Mr. Tumulty: Washington December 8, 1919.

Mr. Frazier,[1] who was acting as Colonel House's Confidential Secretary in Paris, sent to the Department last week the enclosed letter to the President from Mr. Venizelos.

The letter, as you will observe, is dated September 27th, and the delay in its delivery to the White House is apparently due to the fact that Colonel House intended to hand it to the President personally.

I am holding the documents annexed to the letter at this Department, but will, of course, send them to you at once if the President desires to have them.

Very sincerely yours,   William Phillips

TLS (WP, DLC).
[1] That is, Arthur Hugh Frazier, Counselor of Embassy in Paris.

ENCLOSURE

From Eleuthérios Kyrios Vénisélos

My dear Mr. President: Paris, September 27th, 1919.

The message which you so very kindly sent me through Mr. Polk on the 24th instant,[1] confirms what I had all along believed, namely: that your refusal to approve the cession of Thrace to Greece was based chiefly—if not altogether—on the assumption that the Greek element in Thrace does not possess "a clear ethnical preponderance."

For this reason, I deem it important that I should especially lay before you the proofs of this preponderance.

[1] See WW to RL, Sept. 19, 1919 (second telegram of that date), Vol. 63.

To begin with, however, one point must be made clear, viz: what date should be considered as the basis for the examination of such a preponderance?

It is a well-known fact that shortly after the Treaty of Athens, by virtue of which the Balkan War between Greece and Turkey was ended, that is to say, from the early months of 1914, the Turkish Government inaugurated a systematic and violent persecution against the Greek element in Thrace and Western Asia Minor, by confiscating the property of the Greeks and by forcibly expelling them from their homes and soil. The number of those who took refuge in Greece, fleeing from this persecution amounted to about 400,000 people who for the last five years have been doomed to live in exile subsisting with the exile's ration and who today most impatiently await the signing of peace with Turkey, so that they may return to their homes and be reinstalled in their possessions.

Moreover, in addition to these refugees in Greece, a great number of the remaining Greeks—especially those inhabiting the littoral of Propontis and of Western Asia Minor—have been deported during the war into the interior of Asia Minor. The number of these deportees is estimated by the Chief Representative of the Inter-Allied Mission at Constantinople at 480,000, and approximately half of these have perished as a result of the sufferings they endured, according to the opinion of the above mentioned Mission (Appendix A).[2]

I firmly believe that these wholesale expulsions and deportations should be taken into consideration by the Conference in its estimate of the ethnological status of Thrace, in order not to legalize such criminal actions.

Whatever be the decision of the Conference as to the future political status of Thrace, its primary duty should be to assure to these unfortunate exiles their return to their homes and their resettlement in their possessions. Such an act is not only dictated by justice but it is also a philanthropic duty towards those evicted from their homes and deported.

Moreover, it is dictated by the political and economic interests of the country, because according to the above mentioned report of the Chief Representative of the Inter-Allied Mission at Constantinople, "the Greek population of Turkey forms the most progressive and prosperous factor in the country, and the repatriation of the evicted Greeks in their homes will be far the soundest way of restoring prosperity in the country."

[2] This appendix and the others mentioned below not printed.

While all those who have been expelled from Thrace to Greece will be able to return to their homes, with the exception of comparatively few who have succumbed to privations, it is unfortunately true that of those deported into the interior of Turkey a very great number has perished from privation. On the other hand if one takes into consideration the losses which the Turkish element sustained on the battlefield and on account of epidemic, it may be stated that the comparative strength of the Turkish and Greek elements has not materially changed. At all events one can positively contend that the number of the Greeks of Thrace who have perished owing to the Turkish atrocities should be now added to the number of the living.

It was for these reasons that I submitted to the Conference the comparative strength of the respective elements as they stood in the 1912 statistics compiled by the Oecumenical Patriarchate.

It is, however, evident that these numbers cannot be accepted by the Conference as absolutely accurate unless some additional proof of their accuracy could be brought forward.

The proof of the accuracy of the Patriarchate's figures is contained in the official Turkish statistics of the year 1894, published at that time by the Vilayet of Adrianople. I have submitted the text of these statistics to the American Delegation in Paris and I am attaching herewith (Appendix B) phototyped pages of same.

By comparing the aforesaid Turkish statistics with those of the Oecumenical Patriarchate the proof is established that the numbers of the latter are not only genuine but accurate as well. (Appendix C.)

Whereas according to the Patriarchate's statistics of 1912, the Greek element of Thrace exceeded the Turkish by 40,000, the Turkish statistics assert that 20 years earlier the Greeks had a preponderance of about 32,000 over the Turks.

The apparent discrepancies between these two statistics are chiefly due to the interval of time which separates them, during which period the respective populations have increased.

As regards the Bulgarian element the differences are chiefly due to the migrations of the Bulgarians who in many parts of Thrace had not as yet had permanent abodes, being for the most part landless agricultural workmen.

I consider, therefore, that there is absolutely no doubt that even on the eve of the Great War the Greek element in Thrace was the preponderant one.

In addition to the above, I think that I am justified in invoking, in support of the disposition of Thrace, as I have claimed it, certain historical arguments supplied to me by the work of Mr. Rizoff the Bulgarian Minister at Berlin,[3] published during the war in 1917 and entitled "The Bulgarians in their Historical, Ethnological and Political frontier." (Appendix D.)

Indeed, if one would glance over the historical maps published in that book (vide pp. 2, 4, 6, 8, 10, 12, 14, 18,) he will notice that, during the whole period of nearly seven centuries which elapsed from the settlement of the Bulgarians in the Balkans to the Turkish conquest, the Bulgarians even during the time of their greatest expansion (Czars Symeon, Boris, Samuel and Kaloyanis) were never masters of the Thrace we claim. There is only one instance of their having attained some mastery over it for a period of 17 years, and this during the Frankish conquest of Constantinople, when the seat of the Greek Empire was removed to the city of Nicea in Asia Minor. This was the first occasion when the Greeks and Bulgarians allied themselves against the Franks, the second being during the First Balkan War when, owing to their alliance with the Greeks, they were enabled to occupy the Thrace Greece claims.

Moreover, the map which appears on page 22 of Mr. Rizoff's work, shows very clearly that on the eve of the coming of the Turks the southern boundaries of Bulgaria, far from crossing the frontiers now claimed by Greece in Thrace, were even lying to the north of them. The Greco-Bulgarian frontier as it then existed was indicative of the respective ethnical preponderance of the Greek and Bulgarian elements, prior to their subjection to the Turks. And it is noteworthy to remark that the aforesaid respective ethnical preponderance of the two elements underwent no change during the whole period of the Turkish conquest, as it is proved by the ethnographical maps appearing on pages 26, 32, 38 of Rizoff's work. The first of these three maps was drawn by Ami Boué in 1847; the second by Lejean in 1861; and the third by MacKenzie and Irby in 1867.[4] It is well proved by these three maps—whose authenticity and accuracy are proclaimed by Rizoff himself—that at as a recent a date as fifty years ago, Eastern Thrace was inhabited almost exclusively by Greeks with the exception of a few and small islets of Turkish population. The rapid increase since that period of the Turkish element in Eastern Thrace to such an extent as to come short today of the Greek element only by 60,000 or 100,000—ac-

---

[3] Actually, Dimitŭr Rizov only wrote a preface to *Die Bulgaren in ihren historischen, ethnographischen und politischen Grenzen (Atlas mit 40 Landkarten)* (Berlin, 1917).

[4] Ami Boué (1794-1881) and Guillaume-Marie Lejean (1828-1871) were French geographers, both of whom published books on Turkey-in-Europe. Georgina Mary Muir Mackenzie (1833-1874) and Adeline Paulina Irby (1831-1911) were English women who traveled in European Turkey from 1861 to 1864 and published a report of their journeys in G. Muir Mackenzie and A. P. Irby, *Travels in the Slavonic Provinces of Turkey-in-Europe* (London and New York, 1866).

cording to the Turkish or Greek statistics—is due to the fact that
since the Russo-Turkish war of 1878 the Turkish Government settled Thrace with many thousands of Turks, whom she instigated
to migrate there, from those parts of the Balkans which were lib-
erated from Turkish suzerainty as a result of the aforementioned
war.

It follows, therefore, from the above, that Eastern Thrace, which
had been almost exclusively inhabited by Greeks from the coming
of the Bulgarians in the Balkans till the Turkish conquest, retained
its pure Hellenic character during the whole period of the Turkish
era up to the Russo-Turkish war; and even since that period to the
eve of the Great War there has existed in Eastern Thrace a great
ethnical preponderance in favour of the Greek element. Even if we
add to Eastern Thrace that part of Western Thrace which has been
left outside the new Bulgarian frontiers, and in which the Turkish
element predominates over the Greek, there still remains a clear
ethnical preponderance in favour of the Greek element for the
whole of Thrace.

If the above facts leave no doubt in your mind as to their accuracy, Mr. President, I am sure that you will not hesitate, even for a
moment, to recognize the justice of the Greek claims on Thrace.

The argument which is being brought forward to the effect that
the Power which will undertake the mandate for Constantinople
will be subjected to heavy expenses for the covering of which a
proportionate hinterland is necessary, is not an argument that can
be brought forward by President Wilson, who has enunciated to
the world the noble political principle that the right of a people to
choose their own political status and government transcends all
other considerations, brought to bear by the economic interests of
others, and that a people are no more to be used "as pawns and
tools."

Constantinople can very well meet the expenses of its administration, even without the Thracian Hinterland. Moreover, it can
very well—if necessary—incorporate larger territories around the
sea of Marmora, and in Asia Minor, where there exists a Turkish
majority, that is to say, a majority belonging to a nation characterized both by the conscience of Humanity, and by the Supreme
Council of the Conference, as altogether incapable of governing
foreign races. (Appendix E.) And in the last resort the expenses of
Constantinople could be borne—if necessary by the League of
Nations, for it would be unjust that Greece should be doomed to
bear them by being prevented from including within her boundaries by far the most excellent part of her national inheritance.

It would be doubly unjust to Greece, if, in addition to not being given Constantinople—by reason of the great international interests which center in that city—she be deprived as well of Thrace, for the simple purpose of increasing the revenue of the State of Constantinople. The disappointment which Hellenism will feel in such a case, will indeed be a most bitter one.

This injustice against Greece will be all the more severe when one takes into consideration the fact that all the other Allied nations of Eastern and Central Europe—Czechoslovakia, Jugoslavia, Poland and Rumania—will include within their new boundaries nearly the whole of their national strength, whereas Greece, even with the incorporation of Thrace, will have 30% of her co-nationals in Europe and Asia Minor outside her boundaries. And if we take into consideration the Greeks who live outside of Europe, the Hellenic nation in such a case will but include within its frontiers 65% of its national family.

Neither will the non-restoration of Thrace to Greece serve in any way the interests of peace in that part of Europe. The Bulgarians of course will rejoice at seeing their hereditary opponents unjustly treated by the Conference. But it does not follow that they will accept with the spirit of sincerity the peace which is being imposed upon them. When, at the end of the First Balkan War, the Greeks and the Serbians, for the sake of attaining a pacific settlement of the Balkan question, were offering to Bulgaria the whole of Thrace as far as the Enos-Midia line, the whole of Eastern Macedonia, part of Central Macedonia as far as the left bank of the Vardar, and at the same time Serbia was acquainting Bulgaria with her readiness to submit the question of Monastir to the arbitration of the Czar, the Bulgarians rejected this Greco-Serbian offer and preferred to wage the Second Balkan War, because that which they were seeking was nothing less than the establishment of an absolute Bulgarian hegemony in the Balkans.

And again, when in 1915 the Allied Powers were offering to Bulgaria the very same concessions and South-Dobroutza in addition, Bulgaria rejected this offer and participated in the Great War, identifying herself in an absolute alliance of spirit and purpose with the Central Powers and with Turkey, for the purpose of dismembering Serbia and imposing her hegemony.

In view of the repeated experience of the past, Mr. President, is it justifiable to believe today that Bulgaria will accept a peace which forever mars her imperialistic dreams with but the most profound bitterness, keeping herself in readiness to conspire once more against peace as soon as she feels capable of doing so? Therefore, since Bulgaria will accept peace with such a vindictive feeling, will the cause of peace be at all served if the Greek nation comes out of the Conference with a feeling that its national interests have been overlooked by the very Powers at the side of which it has fought the good fight?

May I also be permitted to mention another complaint which the Greek nation will be justified in having? When on the first week of last February, the Council of Ten referred the Greek claims to the Commission on Greek affairs, this Commission pronounced itself in favour of the Hellenic claims on Thrace almost in their entirety.[5] (Appendix F.) And I am glad to state that the American member of this Commission was in full accord with his French and English colleagues[6] on this subject. It was therefore, quite natural for me, Mr. President, to consider since then that the Thracian question would be settled in favour of Greece. Moreover, as I was aware that for the purpose of imposing this solution on the Bulgarians and the Turks, the only available allied army would be the Greek one, not only did I not proceed to demobilize it after the signing of the Armistice, but on the contrary I increased its strength from ten divisions—its total on the day of the Armistice—to twelve divisions on a war footing. The upkeep of such a large force for a whole year since the armistice, has caused an extra item of 1,400,000,000 drachmae in the Greek budget, which is a most serious burden for a small nation to bear. Had there been no favourable report on the Thracian question, Greece would have at least proceeded to a partial demobilization, keeping at most five divisions on a war footing instead of twelve.

This economic aspect bears a far greater importance in view of the fact that the Conference in obliging Bulgaria to pay 2,250,000,000 Frs. for reparations, cancelled at the same time all the debts contracted by Bulgaria in Germany and Austria-Hungary, for the purpose of carrying on the war—a sum which indeed exceeds the total to be exacted from her for reparations. Thus, Greece is subject to emerging from this war with a greater public debt than that of Bulgaria. And whereas the latter country, having undergone no enemy invasion, emerges from this war with her productive sources altogether unimpaired and flourishing, Greece, in addition to having had one of her richest provinces—Eastern

---

[5] For the discussions of the Greek claims in the Council of Ten, see the minutes of that body printed at Feb. 3, 1919, and n. 1 to the extract from the Diary of Dr. Grayson printed at Feb. 4, 1919, both in Vol. 54. The Committee for the Study of Territorial Questions Relating to Greece recommended in its report of March 6, 1919, that all of western Thrace and that part of eastern Thrace which might be left out of the proposed state of Constantinople should belong to Greece. See N. Petsalis-Diomidis, *Greece at the Paris Peace Conference (1919)* (Thessaloniki, 1978), pp. 153-58.

[6] The members of this commission were Jules Martin Cambon, who served as president, and Jean-Étienne-Paul Gout of France; William Linn Westermann and Clive Day of the United States; Sir Robert Borden and Sir Eyre Crowe of the British Empire; and Giacomo de Martino and Fortunato Castoldi of Italy.

Macedonia—devastated by the Bulgarian invasion, has also had her "cheptel"[7] diminished by half as a result of the three year presence on her soil of the Army of the Orient.[8] Moreover, whilst Greece possessed at the beginning of the war a merchant marine of a tonnage of 860,000 t., she found herself at the signing of the Armistice with a tonnage amounting to only 270,000 tons. So, Greece emerges from this war with two of the chief sources of her national wealth—the merchant marine and the "cheptel"—most seriously paralyzed.

Concerning the question of a commercial outlet to the Aegean Sea, this can be fully assured to her by placing Dédéagatch under the League of Nations which may appoint a Commission for the Administration of the City, of the port and of the railway. Greece, however, is disposed to [grant] Bulgaria a commercial outlet through Cavalla under the guarantee of the League of Nations and moreover to construct at her own expense a railroad line between Cavalla and the Bulgarian frontier. In fact, this commercial outlet is incomparably more profitable to Bulgaria than the one through Dédéagatch, as Bulgaria herself has always declared, having used this very same argument at the time she was claiming Cavalla.

If you will do me the honour, Mr. President, to read the chapter on Thrace as contained in my first Memorandum to the Conference (Appendix G) you will find in it the proof of my conciliatory policy towards Bulgaria, and you will be convinced, I am sure, that I have always had the courage of assenting to very painful national sacrifices only for the sake of assuring the success of the higher general interests of the peoples of the Peninsula. But, I am equally certain that any sacrifice of the Hellenic interests today will in no way serve the higher interests of mankind. For, I venture to believe, that my policy during the Great War has been one based on the higher conception of political morality. Should this policy, therefore, be judged by the Greek people and the rest of the world as having failed to be crowned with success, in spite of the full victory of the Allied effort, such a verdict would in no way contribute towards the strengthening of the moral principles guiding the governing of peoples.

I have taken the liberty to submit the above to your kind consideration, awaiting with full confidence your judgement on this very vital question of Hellenism.

Believe me, my dear Mr. President,

Cordially and faithfully yours,   E. K. Vénisélos

TLS (SDR, RG 59, 763.72119/10927, DNA).

[7] The French word for livestock.

[8] That is, the Allied Army of the East, which had operated in Macedonia from a base at Salonika from October 1915 to December 1918.

A News Report

[*Dec. 9, 1919*]

WILSON WON'T AGREE TO LODGE PROGRAM
Wants Some Reservation Phrases Softened
and the Preamble Cut Out.

Washington, Dec. 9.—President Wilson has intimated to Administration leaders in the Senate that no compromise on the Peace Treaty would be acceptable to him so long as it included anything to be interpreted as an acceptance of the Lodge reservation program.

This became known today, although Democratic leaders, in explaining the President's position, said that they themselves were not clear whether the President meant that a compromise could not be worked out along the line of the Lodge reservations or whether he was opposed to accepting the reservations as phrased. The Democratic leaders are convinced that the President will soon inform the Senate in a formal way, or permit those in charge of the treaty fight for him to know in a more definite way just what is in his mind.

Inasmuch as Senator Hitchcock, Administration leader, denied reports that he had been forbidden by Mr. Wilson to entertain compromise proposals or to seek to reach an adjustment of the differences which prevented treaty ratification, it is believed that the President is not opposed to considering compromises which will soften some phrases in the Lodge reservations and eliminate the preamble.

It is plain to Mr. Wilson, the Administration leaders say, that the treaty cannot be ratified without including reservations in some form. The Republicans classed as "mild reservationists" are not opposed to considering changes in the reservations, and a move on the part of the President that does not overlook sentiment existing in the Senate for some form of reservations would turn his treaty fight into a victory.

After his return from Europe, President Wilson told members of the Foreign Relations Committee[1] that he was not opposed to interpretations, but did not see the necessity for reservations which would destroy the fabric of the treaty. Since that time he has learned that the foreign powers would not be adverse to some of the reservations made by the Senate, and that they are eager for the United States to ratify the treaty. It is believed that the President is willing to make some concession to Republican opposition in the Senate, but just how far he will go in meeting the Lodge proposals cannot be learned. His attitude is generally interpreted as that of willingness to accept some of the Lodge reservations if the harsh phrases are softened and the preamble eliminated.

Democratic Senators are of the opinion that the President will finally propose that the preamble be eliminated from the Lodge reservations. This requires three of the chief powers allied with America in the war to accept the reservations before the United States is bound by the terms of the treaty.

The treaty situation is that the door is still open to negotiations, but the President insists that the Republicans surrender much more than they are now prepared to do.

Printed in the *New York Times*, Dec. 10, 1919.
[1] In his interview with members of that committee printed at Aug. 19, 1919, Vol. 62.

From the Diary of Josephus Daniels

1919 Tuesday 9 December

Long cabinet meeting. Lansing had been told by Garfield that WW had approved G's stand on the coal situation which would defeat the idea of a commission to look into whole matter already approved by the President & accepted by Lewis and Greene.[1] At last session[2] we had appointed Glass, Palmer and Houston to receive statements from [William B.] Wilson, Garfield & Hines & present to the President & then to act for the cabinet. Garfield had, after learning of WWs approval, wh. was in a sense taking out of his hands sole power, sent a letter to the President[3] which if approved would have favored nothing over 14% no matter what was established after study & investigation. Houston was appointed to go see WW. He went over, saw Mrs. W—& she brought back dictated letter to Garfield withdrawing his approval. We had dictated a joint note which Houston took over.

Reported that WBW had decided to resign because the Cabinet, after authorizing him to negotiate had repudiated his action & sided with Garfield in coal matter. Every member expressed himself that it would be a calamity & asked me to see Wilson & assure him of our feeling. Wilson showed me letter he had drafted and I urged him that it was his duty to stick. He promised to take no action until I returned to city Friday

[1] See the news report printed at Dec. 7, 1919.
[2] See the extract from the Daniels Diary printed at Dec. 5, 1919.
[3] See the Enclosure printed with H. A. Garfield to WW, Dec. 7, 1919.

From the Desk Diary of Robert Lansing

Tuesday Dec 9 [1919]

Cabinet meeting 11-1:10. Discussed coal strike situation; Prest's proposal of settlement; and Garfield's letter approved by Prest. Unanimously agreed that publication of Garfield's letter might endanger settlement, so I sent a letter to Prest for Cabinet on subject. Sec. Houston directed to see Mrs. Wilson at once with letter. Tumulty said he heard Wilson was to resign from Cabinet after settlement of strike. Daniels to see him.

From Robert Lansing

Dear Mr. President: Washington, D. C. 9 December 1919.

We did not understand in drafting the memorandum of Sunday night that the Commission therein proposed should be controlled by anything other than the facts gathered by them. Therefore we think that the approval of Dr. Garfield's letter of Thursday might result in a misunderstanding and imperil the prompt settlement of the strike upon the basis of the statement made by you Saturday night.

We would therefore ask that Dr. Garfield be informed by telephone, if possible, that you will defer action upon his letter of the seventh of December.

Sincerely yours,   Robert Lansing.   For the Cabinet.

TLS (WP, DLC).

Edith Bolling Galt Wilson to Harry Augustus Garfield

My dear Dr. Garfield,   The White House Dec. 9, 1919

The President has asked me to say that upon more intimate knowledge of the situation as a whole he deems it wise to withold his approval of the letter you sent him on Dec. 7th.

He fears that any qualification, at this stage, of the terms of his letter of Saturday suggesting the creation of a Commission would bring about a sereous setback in the whole settlement and thinks that the best course is to leave the Commission perfectly free and, for the present, say nothing further.

With kindest regards, and the Presidents confidence that you will understand, believe me

Faithfully yours   Edith Bolling Wilson

ALS (H. A. Garfield Papers, DLC).

Frank Lyon Polk to Robert Lansing

Paris December 9, 1919.

Urgent (First Section) 1727, December 9, 12 pm.

Confidential from Polk. The following memoranda were signed by Clemenceau, Crowe and myself at the close of the meeting of the Supreme Council at Quai d'Orsay this morning:

At the moment when the Peace Conference is entering what it is hoped may be the last stage of its labors for the conclusion of peace with Germany Austria and Hungary, the territorial settlement still remains incomplete in respect of regions which the (?) [state of][1] uncertainty is calculated to affect gravely the vital interests of the countries directly involved and might easily endanger the peace of Europe and of the world.

Being persuaded that this danger could only grow in intensity if the Peace Conference were to terminate before an agreement had been reached among the Principal Allied and Associated Powers concerning the Adriatic question, the representatives of the Conference of America, Great Britain and France desire to call the attention of their Italian colleague to the urgent necessity of finding a solution. They realize fully the difficulties with which the Italian Government is confronted in dealing with this problem but it is precisely for this reason that they believe that it would be unjust to all the parties concerned, and in the first place to Italy herself, were they any longer to delay putting frankly before the Italian Government a statement of the position such as they see it after many months of examination and reflection. The friends of Italy therefore feel impelled to make a further effort to reach a settlement which would be the fulfillment of her legitimate aims and aspirations with the equitable claims of the neighboring states as well as with the supreme interests of the peace of the world.

The three representatives, accordingly, venture to invite the Italian Government to proceed to a fresh survey of the field in the light of the statement which they have now the honor to make.

The British and French representatives have followed with earnest and sympathetic attention the negotiations which have passed between the Italian Government and the President of the United States. If they have hitherto refrained from tendering their direct advice to the Italian Government in the matter, it was because they had hoped the Italian Government would be able to reach an

---

[1] Corrections and additions from the text in U. S. Department of State, Division of Foreign Intelligence, Series M, No. 167, *The Adriatic Question: Papers Relating to the Italian-Jugoslav Boundary* (Washington, 1920).

agreement with President Wilson to which the British and French Governments could readily subscribe. It will be remembered that the British and French Governments have already, more particularly by their note communicated to President Wilson on September 10th, used their best efforts to promote such an agreement which the President's answer to that note gave every reason to hope could be brought about.[2] Though a complete agreement has not so far been arrived at, the points of difference still outstanding have been so much reduced as to justify an expectation that complete accord will now be reached.

It is well, with this view, to place on record, in the first place, the chief points on which agreement has been reached. This is all the more desirable as it would appear from recent official Italian statements that some misapprehension may exist in regard to matters which can readily be cleared up, such, for instance, as the exact description of what is generally referred to as President Wilson's line. The points of agreement are, in the main, embodied in the American memorandum communicated to the Italian Delegation in Paris on October twenty seventh.[3]

One. With regard to Istria, President Wilson had, from the first, agreed to a frontier running from the Arsa River to the Karawanken Mountains which widely overstepped the recognized ethnical line between Italy and Yugo Slavia and which would have, as a result, to incorporate in Italy more than three hundred thousand Yugo Slavs. Italy's geographical position, as well as her economic requirements, was held to justify this serious infringement of the ethnic principal and President Wilson, anxious to give the fullest value to these important considerations, went still further in agreeing to an extension eastward in such a way as to give to Italy the region of Albona in spite of the considerable additional number of Yugo Slavs thereby incorporated.

Moreover, to strengthen the strategic security of Italy, President Wilson, in agreement with the Italian Government, has indorsed the creation of a buffer state between the Italian territory in Istria and the Serb-Croat-Slovene Kingdom in which some two hundred thousand Yugo Slavs, as against less than forty thousand Italians, will be placed under the control of the League of Nations. Anxious to remove any conceivable strategic menace that Italy might fear from the Serb-Croat-Slovene state, President Wilson has agreed,

[2] It is printed in W. Phillips to WW, Sept. 11, 1919, Vol. 63; Wilson's reply is printed in JPT to W. Phillips, Sept. 13, 1919, ibid.

[3] About Lansing's note to Tittoni of October 27, 1919, which was a reply to Tittoni's so-called Third Project, and Lansing's note to Nitti of November 12, 1919, mentioned below, see René Albrecht-Carrié, *Italy at the Paris Peace Conference* (New York, 1938), pp. 250-55.

and the British and French Governments are glad to associate themselves with this agreement, that the so called Assling region shall be permanently demilitarized. The three representatives would be happy to learn from the Italian Government whether slight modification of the demilitarized zone between the Arsa River and Cape Promontore are deemed necessary to safeguard the security of the defenses on Italian territory.

Two. There is complete agreement concerning the creation, in the interest of Italy, of the buffer state to be known as the (free state of Fiume) and its control by the League of Nations. Ethnic considerations would demand that this state, containing two hundred thousand Yugo Slavs, should be afforded an opportunity by plebiscite to decide its own fate. In deference to Italy's objection that the incorporation of this region in the Serb-Croat-Slovene state by free act of the inhabitants might create a real menace, it is now agreed that the determination of the whole future of the state shall be left to the League of Nations which, in conformity with Italian requirements, shall not fail to provide the full measure of autonomy which the city of Fiume enjoyed under Austro-Hungarian rule.

Three. The three representatives are glad to record their appreciation of the wisdom and moderation which have marked the attitude of the Italian Government towards the difficult question of Dalmatia. They feel that the Italian Government have acted on an enlightened view of their higher interests in officially withdrawing territorial claims to an area where, to enforce them, would have meant permanent discord with the inhabitants of the Serb-Croat-Slovene state and prevented all possibility of friendly relations with them. In order, however, to safeguard every Italian racial and sentimental interest it has been agreed that the City of Zara shall enjoy a special regime. Its geographical position indicates Zara as part of the Yugo Slavs' state but, provided the town is left within the Yugo Slavs' customs union, it is to be given complete sovereignty under the League of Nations and freedom to control its own affairs.

Four. The same wisdom and moderation as that which had marked the attitude of the Italian Government towards the Dalmatian question have characterized their attitude as regards the islands in the Adriatic. The Italian Government appears to be as one with President Wilson in realizing the necessary racial, geographic and political connection of the Dalmatian coastal islands with the Yugo Slavs' state. On the other hand the possession of certain outlying islands, though ethnically Yugo Slav and economically connected with Yugo Slavia, are considered by the Italian

Government necessary to Italy's strategic control of the Adriatic and the reasonableness of this claim has been accepted, the following islands being accorded to Italy on a demilitarized status namely: A. The Pelagosa group, B. Lissa and the small islands west of it, C. Lussin and Unie. These islands are to pass in full sovereignty to Italy who, on her part, is to make an agreement with the Slav population of Lissa providing for their complete local autonomy.

Second section 1727.

Five. Italy is to receive a mandate for the administration of the independent state of Albania under the League of Nations. Attached to the present memorandum is an outline of the form which, in the opinion of the three representatives such a mandate should take. The frontiers of Albania on the north and east at present will be those fixed by the London conference in 1813 [1913], the southern frontier is still a matter for negotiation. In order, however, not to delay a general settlement by such negotiations the following provisional arrangement could be adopted: Greece shall occupy the territory west and south of a demarcation line which shall run as follows (reference one million two hundred thousand Austrian staff map): from Mount Tumba on the northern boundary of Greece northwestward along the crest of the Nemercha Ridge to the Vojusa River thence down that river to Teleleni, Mirica to point 98. Thence south passing between the villages of Lopsi-Martolozit and Zemblan thence through points 1840 and 1225 to a point about two miles south by east of 1225 thence westward passing just north of Poljana, thence southeast to point 1669 thence west and northwest to point 2025 thence south westward to the coast just south of Asprhyonruga. The triangle of territory from point 98 on the Vojusa River, between Baba and Sinanaj, northeastward to Lake Malik and southward to the Greek frontier and the demarcation line mentioned above should be the subject of later negotiation between the three Allied representatives on the one hand and Italy and Greece on the other, the three Allied representatives acting for Albania.

Six. The city of Valona together with such hinterland as may be strictly necessary to its defense and economic development is to be granted to Italy in full sovereignty.

The above six points in their general aspects are those on which, after many months negotiation, the Italian Government have happily reached an agreement with the President of the United States. They afford to Italy full satisfaction of her historic national aspirations, based on the desire to unite the Italian race; they give her the absolute strategic control of the Adriatic; they offer her complete guard against constitutional guarantees against whatever aggressions she might fear in the future from her Yugo Slav neighbors, an aggression which the three representatives on their part consider as most improbable if the lines of a just and lasting settlement are reached. They have even carried their concern for Italian security to the point of neutralizing the Dalmatian Islands and adjacent waters from the northern border of the Ragusa region to Fiume. The three representatives therefore venture very earnestly to urge on the Italian Government in the most friendly spirit that they should reflect on the great advantages which the above settlement, following on that which gave to Italy the frontiers of the Alps, would bring her and the great moral and material triumph with which its successful conclusions would now provide the Italian Government.

Anxious however to give the most sympathetic consideration to every Italian interest or sentiment the three representatives have carefully examined in all their bearings certain further demands which the Italian Government have presented under the following four heads: A. Control by Italy of the diplomatic relations of Zara. B. An arrangement by which the city of Fiume the so called (corpus separatum) should be dissociated from the free state of Fiume and made completely independent though its port and railway should be left to the free state. C. Direct connection of the city of Fiume with the Italian province of Istria by the annexation to Italy of a long narrow strip of territory running along the coast from Fiume to Volosca between the railway and the sea, the Italian frontier in Istria being pushed eastwards so as to include the whole peninsula within Italy. D. Annexation to Italy of the Island of Lagosta.

With regard to the first point, the representation of Zara, there ought to be no difficulty in satisfying the national Italian demand that this small historic Italian town shall preserve its Italian character both in its internal administration and in its representation abroad. It is already conceded that (beyond such connection with Yugo Slavia as Zara shall have by its incorporation in the Serb Croat Slovene customs union) the city shall be completely independent under the League of Nations. The city will therefore be entirely free to decide, subject to the approval of the League of Nations, how it shall be diplomatically represented abroad. If, as is contended, the city is completely Italian, its choice will naturally be made in accordance with the Italian claims and it is hoped that in this way entire satisfaction will be given to the desire of the Italian Government. The Italian proposal to withdraw from the city of Fiume, except its port from the free state, is one which has been found seriously perplexing. The main object of the creation of a buffer state between Italy and Yugo Slavia was precisely to guarantee on the one hand Italian strategic security and on the other the prosperity and development of Fiume. It is not understood how it would be possible for the so called buffer state to exist without Fiume and still less how it would be possible for Fiume to exist except within the buffer state. Fiume and the buffer state are absolutely dependent one on the other and any arrangement which removed Fiume from the buffer state would put an end to the prosperity alike of the city and of its hinterland. Mindful of the sentimental feeling aroused in Italy by the question of Fiume, the three representatives have always believed that a practicable plan could be devised whereby the city of Fiume within the buffer state should enjoy a privileged position. With this object in view they propose for Fiume precisely the same degree of autonomy as the city had under Austro Hungarian rule. It is believed that this provision and the watchful and sympathetic interest of the League of Nations will guarantee to Italy full protection for the Italian ethnic and cultural elements at Fiume. With absolute sovereignty vested in the League of Nations and with Italy represented in the council of the League every Italian interest will be fully safeguarded. Moreover to separate the city of Fiume from the buffer state could not fail to lead to a protest against the very establishment of such a buffer state which under such conditions would be inhabited entirely by Yugo Slavs.

With respect to the new Italian proposal for the annexation to Italy of the long narrow strip of coast from Fianona to the gates of the city of [Albona] there are difficulties of a practical nature. The reason for which the Italian Government have made this demand is stated to be a purely sentimental one, namely the desire that the city of Fiume should not be separated from Italy by any intervening foreign country. No doubt such a sentimental reason may be of great importance in the eyes of the Italian Government but it would appear to rest on a misapprehension of the real position of Fiume. The creation of the buffer state which is to be completely independent of Yugo Slavia was, among other reasons, probably intended to safeguard the position of Fiume; and the free state of which Fiume must as indicated in the preceding paragraph form an essential part is already in direct contact with the Kingdom of Italy not only by sea but by a long land frontier of approximately a hundred miles. Full effect therefore is already given to the sentimental considerations to which the Italian Government attach so much value. In fact the new Italian plan would not achieve this object so well, as in practice it is to be feared that it would be quite unworkable. The Italian Government does not propose to interfere with the railway connecting Fiume with the north which they admit is to remain within the free state. This railway runs for a considerable distance along coast and the Italian proposal amounts so far as this region is concerned to cutting off from the free state and incorporating with Italy the line of sandy and barren beach intervening between the railway and the sea. Whilst the injury to the free state which would in this eccentric way be entirely cut off from its only seaboard is obvious and unmeasurable, it is not easy to understand what would be the benefit to Italy unless it be considered a benefit to her that the free state should be so crippled. Nor does it seem necessary to dwell on the extraordinary complexities that would arise as regards customs control, coast guard services and cognate matters in a territory of such unusual configuration.

Third Section. 1727.

The plan appears to run counter to every consideration of geography, economics and territorial convenience, and it may perhaps be assumed that if these considerations were overlooked by the Italian Government this was due to their having connected it in their mind with the question of annexing to Italy all that remains of the Yugo-Slav portion of the peninsula of Istria.

This question of further annexation of Yugo-Slav territory is raised quite unambigously both by the demand for the whole of Istria and by the proposal to annex the Island of Lagosta. In neither case do even considerations of strategy arise. For the strategical command of the Adriatic is already completely assured to Italy by the possession of Trieste, Pola, the islands facing Fiume, Pelagosa and Valona. Additional security is afforded by the proposed demilitarization of the whole free State of Fiume together with a large zone lying to the north of it and of the small portion of Istria remaining to the free (*) [state] of Fiume.

Economic considerations being equally excluded there remains nothing but a desire for further territory. Now the territories coveted are admittedly inhabited by Yugo-Slavs. They contain practically no Italian elements. This being so it is necessary to refer to the way in which President Wilson with the cordial approval of Great Britain and France has met every successive Italian demand for the absorption in Italy of territories inhabited by peoples not Italian and not in favor of being absorbed. On this point the following passage may be quoted from a telegram addressed to Signor Tittoni by the Secretary of State at Washington on November 12.

"Your excellency cannot fail to recognize that the attitude of the American Government throughout the negotiations has been one of sincere sympathy for Italy and of an earnest desire to meet her demands. Italy claimed a frontier on the Brenner Pass and the demand was granted in order to assure to Italy the greatest possible protection on her northern front although it involved annexing to Italy a considerable region populated by alien inhabitants. Italy demanded further a strong geographic eastern frontier and this likewise was granted in order to assure her abundant protection although it involved incorporation within Italian boundaries of further territory populated by alien inhabitants. Italy demands the redemption of her brothers under foreign sovereignty and every effort was made to meet this wish even in certain cases where, by so doing, much greater numbers of foreign races were brought within Italian sovereignty. Italy demanded complete naval control of the Adriatic and this was granted by according her the three keys of the Adriatic: Pola, Valona and a central island base. When all this failed to satisfy Italian claims there was added concession to concession at Sextan Valley, at Tarvis, at Albona, in the Lussin Islands, in the terms of the Fiume free state and elsewhere. In our desire to deal generously, even more than generously, we yielded Italy's demand for an Italian mandate over Albania, always hoping to meet from Italy's statesmen a generous response to our efforts at conciliation."

To the considerations thus urged by Mr. Lansing the three representatives desire to add another argument. In doing so they trust the Italian Government will not credit them with any desire to give advice on questions of Italian high policy on which the Italian Government will rightly claim to be the best judge. But an appeal to an historical argument may be permitted to the representatives of three countries to whom the liberation of Italian territories from foreign domination has been a matter of unwavering concern and sympathy through generations of noble and often terrible struggles. Modern Italy won the place in the hearts of all liberty loving peoples which she has never since lost by the pure spirit of her patriotism which set before her people the generous aim of uniting under the Italian flag those extensive provinces formerly within the ancient Italian boundaries which were and have remained essentially Italian territories in virtue of their compact Italian population. The sympathies of the world have accompanied Italy's advance of the outer borders of Italia Irredenta, in pursuit of the sacred principle, the self determination of the peoples. This principle is now invoked by other nations. Not invariably is it possible owing to the complicated interaction of racial, geographical, economic and strategical factors to do complete justice to the ethnic principle. Small isolated communities surrendered and outnumbered by populations of different race cannot in most cases be attached to the territory of their own nation from which they are effectively separated. But the broad principle remains that it is neither just nor expedient to annex as the spoils of war territories inhabited by an alien race, anxious and capable to maintain a separate national state of irridentism exactly analogous in kind to that which justified the demand of Italia Irridenta for union with the Italian State.

The three representatives venture with all deference to express the opinion that in declining to agree to the incorporation of more Yugo-Slav territory they are acting in the highest interest of the Italian nation itself.

From this point of view the inclusion in Italy of purely Yugo-Slav territories where neither security nor geographical or economical considerations compel annexation is not in itself a commendable policy. It would be bound to create within the Italian borders a compact body.

The three representatives would make an earnest appeal to the Italian Government to seize the present most favorable of opportunities for arriving at a friendly agreement with them for the immediate conclusion and permanent guarantee of the definite settlement on lines which they venture to think fully realize all the legitimate national aspirations of Italy, and fully safeguard her preeminent position in the Adriatic. A settlement based on the foundations which Italy, in conjunction with her allies, could thereby lay would have given a means of reconciling interest at present divergent and of offering Italy an opportunity for rendering more cordial and solid her relations with the new nations, who are her neighbors, and to whom she could furnish such valuable assistance and economic support as her resources and experience entitle her to offer.

The spirit of moderation which was characterized in the recent attitude of the Italian Government leads the three representatives to hope that this appeal from Italy's American, British and French Allies will not pass unheeded and that the Italian Government will, by assuring definite agreement with their Allies, place on firm foundations the great moral and material triumphs to which Italy's efforts and sacrifices throughout the war have so justly entitled her.

Section four 1727.

Memorandum as to the form of the Albanian mandate.

The United States, British and French Governments desire to recognize the independence of the Albanian State. They consider that the State of Albania will require to the extent indicated in paragraph 4 of Article 22 of the covenant of the League of Nations

"The Administrative advice and assistance" of the Great Powers. For this task Italy by her geographical situation and economic capacity is primarily indicated.

The United States, British and French Governments are anxious therefore to entrust to Italy a mandate over the state of Albania under the conditions implied in the covenant of the League of Nations. They consider that these conditions should form the basis of Italy's acceptance of this mandate and should be in a convention to be concluded between the Italian Government and the Governments of the Principal Allied and Associated Powers. The headings of such a convention would be the following:

One. Albania is recognized as an independent State within the frontiers indicated in the body of the covering memorandum.

Nothing in these stipulations shall however prevent the Albanian State from negotiating with the Serb Croat Slovene state such region rectifications as may be in accord with local ethnographic and economic requirements.

Two. The Serb Croat Slovene Government shall have the right to construct and operate railways through Northern Albania north of parallel 41 degrees 15 and otherwise to enjoy full privileges of international purport across Northern Albania.

Three. The right to control the development of the Boyana river shall be vested in the Council of the League of Nations with power to delegate the work to either Italy or the Serb Croat Slovene State under proper restrictions. It is assumed for this purpose that Montenegro will form part of the Serb Croat Slovene State.

Four. A commission shall forthwith be established consisting of a representative of the Italian Government, a representative of the League of Nations and a representative of the Albanian State who shall be designated by the Principal Allied and Associated Powers for the purpose of elaborating (A) the terms of the mandate to be entrusted to Italy over Albania and (B) the organization of the future state of Albania. This commission shall terminate its labors within five months from the signature of this convention and will address a report thereon with the necessary recommendation to the Council of the League of Nations. The final decision as to the terms of the mandate and the organization shall be made by the Council of the League acting by a majority vote.

Five. The Commission foreshadowed in the above paragraph shall base its deliberations not only on the considerations above outlined but also on the following principles:

(A) The freedom of conscience and the free and outward exercise all forms of worship, the complete liberty in education and linguistic matters of all the inhabitants of the State of Albania.

(B) The organization in so far as may be compatible with the tradition of the country and the exercise of efficient administration of legislative and administrative bodies representing all sections of the population.

(C) The prevention of the exploitation of the country or its colonization in a manner liable to militate against the interests of the native inhabitants. Under this heading would be included any recommendations which the commission might make as to improvements in the existing system of land tenure.

(D) The eventual creation of gendarmerie the senior officers of which may be Nationals of the mandatory power. The mandatory power shall have the right for a period of two years from the date of which the mandate is conferred and pending the organization of the native gendarmerie the request for armed forces in the country. After that period the State of Albania shall be permanently demilitarized and no power shall be allowed to maintain regular forces in the country without the sanction of the Council of the League of Nations.

As no complete record exists of various conversations on the subject and particularly in view of recent demarches by the Italian Ambassador in London, we deemed it desirable to present the foregoing to the Italian delegation. These memoranda were carefully drawn by Bowman and Leeper[4] and revised by Sir Eyre Crowe and myself. They are entirely without the scope of the memorandum handed to Tittoni by me on October 27 (See 4850 Oct. 28). They are not to be considered as constituting the final word on this subject but rather as a summary review of the points of agreement between us and the French and the British. The presentation of the question in this form enables our Ambassadors and the French and the British Foreign Offices to discuss the question in a precise and unified manner with the Italian representatives, a thing hitherto impossible. It is considered a peculiarly timely statement in view of the present developments in the Adriatic and in view of the possibility afforded Italian Government for publishing, if it so desires, a diplomatic document of this kind as an aid to the settlement of the Fiume question. Copies have been sent to our Ambassadors in London and Rome. End of section four and message.

Wallace[5]

T telegram (SDR, RG 59, 763.72119/8216, DNA).

[4] Isaiah Bowman, the geographer of Johns Hopkins, and Alexander Wigram Allen Leeper of the British Foreign Office.

[5] The State Department sent a copy of this telegram to Wilson as soon as it was received, and Polk sent him another copy on January 24, 1920. Wilson may never have read the entire telegram, but he was certainly aware of its main contents by the latter date.

From Alexander Mitchell Palmer

Indianapolis, Indiana, December 10, 1919.

Miners conference by decisive vote accepts your proposal exactly as written. They also refused to take action looking to the calling of a convention. I have the fullest confidence that mining operations will be promptly resumed everywhere. Your commission of course should not be appointed until general resumption about which I will advise you later.   Palmer.

T telegram (WP, DLC).

A Memorandum by Robert Lansing

December 10, 1919.

MY INTENSE DESIRE TO RETIRE FROM THE CABINET.

I don't know how I am going to stand the present state of affairs much longer. It has become almost intolerable. Even if he cannot run things himself, I think the President is well enough to choose my successor. He is certainly well enough to interfere with or nullify everything that I attempt to do. He shows in many ways that he distrusts me and, I believe, dislikes me. I don't care a rap about his good will but I do care about his preventing me from properly conducting our foreign affairs.

I wish something would happen so that I could resign without being subject to the charge of disloyalty, as I would undoubtedly be if I retired today.

I must continue for a while at any rate, though the irrascibility and tyranny of the President, whose worst qualities have come to the surface during his sickness, cannot be borne much longer. I suppose no one dares cross him for fear of another paralytic stroke, so his violent passions and exaggerated ego have free rein.

I shall seize the first opportunity, which will give me a plausible excuse, to lay down my task. I earnestly hope that it will soon come and that I will be free.

T MS (R. Lansing Papers, DLC).

To John Llewellyn Lewis[1]

[The White House] December 11, 1919

May I not express to you and, through you, to the other officers of your organization, my appreciation of the patriotic action which you took at Indianapolis yesterday? Now we must all work together to see to it that a settlement just and fair to everyone is reached without delay.   Woodrow Wilson

T telegram (Letterpress Books, WP, DLC).
    ¹ "I think it would be wise if the President would send this message to Mr. Lewis." JPT to EBW, Dec. 11, 1919, TL (WP, DLC). The same letter contains the following Hw notation by Irwin H. Hoover: "The President says alright—I.H.H."

From John Llewellyn Lewis

Indianapolis, Ind., December 11, 1919.

I am honored in the receipt of your message wherein you commend as patriotic the action of the mine workers conference of yesterday. Your recognition of this fact I am sure will be echoed by the American people. The mine workers are profoundly impressed with the assurances of fair dealing which you have extended. The sincere cooperation of myself and associates will be given to the end that the final settlement will comprehend every element of justice and right.   John L. Lewis.

T telegram (WP, DLC).

From Harry Augustus Garfield, with Enclosure

Confidential

Dear Mr. President: Washington, D. C. December 11, 1919

In my letter of Sunday, December 7, replying to your message of that morning, I conveyed to you my apprehension of the danger inherent in the proposed commission of review, and I was greatly relieved Monday noon to have your approval of my position.¹ The enclosed letter is dictated by my understanding of your message of Tuesday,² communicated by the courtesy of Mrs. Wilson, withholding that approval.

As I think you know, the proposal of a commission with power, in place of an advisory body, was submitted to you without my knowledge or approval. A commission with power should be composed of representatives of the public only. On the other hand, a commission composed of representatives of the three parties in interest,—the public, represented by government, capital, and labor,—ought to be advisory only, in view of the fact that the representative of the public could always be outvoted by the other two. The reported arrangement of last Saturday night, confirmed by a formal statement published in yesterday's papers, leaves no room for doubt that you are expected to appoint a commission on which the three parties are represented. This question was fully discussed last February at the conference between operators, mine workers, and the Fuel Administration, and all agreed that such a body should have advisory powers only. If the powers of the commission now agreed upon are not limited before the sittings begin by a statement of principles to be followed or by some other efficient check, there is the strongest probability of a compromise finding. I have given most careful consideration to the whole matter, desiring to embarrass you as little as possible, and I reach the conclusion that my resignation should be accepted now rather than later.

Please rest assured that no difference of opinion between us on any public matter can possibly disturb the regard and affection which I have for you.

As always,

Cordially and faithfully yours,   H. A. Garfield.

¹ Perhaps this message was conveyed by telephone or in a note from Mrs. Wilson, which is missing in both the Wilson and Garfield Papers.
² EBW to H. A. Garfield, Dec. 9, 1919.

E N C L O S U R E

From Harry Augustus Garfield

Dear Mr. President: Washington, D. C. December 11, 1919

In December, 1918, I placed my resignation of the office of United States Fuel Administrator in your hands.¹ I think the time has now come when I may ask you definitely to signify your acceptance of it.

When I was asked by the Cabinet, some six or seven weeks ago, to return to Washington, the records of the Fuel Administration, including the data relating to production costs and prices of coal, had been transferred to the Department of the Interior in accordance with your Executive Order, and I had no organization or means of establishing one. An acute emergency existed and, as the Railroad Administration alone had the machinery through which coal could be distributed, the Director General of Railroads was authorized to perform that function. This was done with the approval of the Attorney General, and I have since delegated to the Director General the power to make conservation regulations. The enforcement of Fuel Administration regulations is in the hands of the Department of Justice. The proposed commission is not the consultative tribunal recommended, but is clothed with full power to readjust and fix prices and the principles upon which prices are made.

In these circumstances, there can be no inconvenience to you nor detriment to the public service involved in my withdrawal, and the circumstances surrounding the agreement between the government and the mine workers under which this commission with power is to be appointed as well as the questions of principles involved render it impossible for me to continue.

Cordially and faithfully yours,   H. A. Garfield.

TLS (WP, DLC).
    [1] Citing his need to devote more time to the presidency of Williams College, Garfield had presented his formal resignation, to take effect at Wilson's pleasure, in H. A. Garfield to WW, Dec. 1, 1918, TLS (WP, DLC). He also said in the same letter that, by April 1, 1919, "the end of the coal year," it should be possible to wind up the affairs of the Fuel Administration. Wilson formally accepted the resignation in WW to H. A. Garfield, Dec. 3, 1918, printed at that date in Vol. 53. However, both men obviously agreed, probably in conversation, that Garfield would continue to spend at least part of his time in Washington to conclude the affairs of the Fuel Administration. As it turned out, the organization did not entirely cease to function until June 30, 1919.
    Garfield returned to Washington to assist in dealing with the coal strike crisis on October 26 and remained there until December 13. For his own summary of events from December 1918 to December 1919, see Harry A. Garfield, *Final Report of the United States Fuel Administrator, 1917-1919* (Washington, 1921), pp. 10-19.

Joseph Patrick Tumulty to Robert Lansing[1]

My dear Mr. Secretary: The White House December 11, 1919.

The President has asked me to return to you the enclosed letter from Mr. Venizelos, which accompanied Mr. Phillips' letter of December 8th, and which belongs with the papers pertaining to Thrace. The President wishes to take up this question with you as soon as you and he can discuss it.

Sincerely yours,   J P Tumulty

TLS (SDR, RG 59, 763.72119/10927, DNA).
    [1] EBW to [JPT], c. Dec. 11, 1919, AL (WP, DLC), refers to the Vénisélos letter as follows: "Please return to the Sec. of State & say this letter belongs with the papers pertaining to Thrace, which question he wishes to take up with the Sec. as soon as they can discuss it."

From the Diary of Colonel House

December 11, 1919.

Senator Hitchcock, who has charge of the Treaty in the Senate, came to see me yesterday to discuss the situation. I tried to put some courage into him and urged him to lead. He constantly returned to the President's uncompromising attitude and said he was afraid anything he might do would not be sanctioned by the Pres-

ident. He also thought the republicans would question every proposal he made, wishing to know if they yielded whether the President would accept the compromise. He outlined a speech he
intended to make last night at the Southern Society Dinner which,
by the way, is an excellent one.

Tuesday, Lamont called up Grayson to say that he regretted the
President was taking such an uncompromising attitude as indicated in Hitchcock's remarks after he and Senator Fall had seen
the President.[1] Grayson promised to talk to the President about it
and to let Lamont know the result today. He telephoned Lamont
this morning, giving a message from the President to the effect
that Hitchcock had misrepresented him and he was irritated over
what had been given out. The President indicated that after the
holidays he would take the matter up again and that he was not
pleased at the report of his uncompromising attitude.

The truth is, the President is in no condition physically to direct
important business. He undoubtedly told Hitchcock what he,
Hitchcock, gave to the press. The Senator told me the President
showed signs of irritability which is often a consequence of serious
illness.

T MS (E. M. House Papers, CtY).
    [1] See the news report printed at Dec. 9, 1919.

From Robert Lansing

My dear Mr. President: Washington December 12, 1919.

The Cabinet have instructed me to inform you that this morning
at a session which lasted over two hours they considered the railroad question and the advisability of returning the roads to the
owners on December 31st of this year. Mr. Hines was present and
urged most earnestly that you should defer the return in view of
the assurances which he had received that Congress would shortly
pass legislation in regard to the railroads and that it would seriously
affect the public interest if the roads were returned before such
legislation had been passed.

All the members of the Cabinet expressed decided resentment
that Congress had not acted before this but felt that the public interest was of first importance.

After debating the subject and viewing it from the political as
well as the general point of view the members reached the following conclusions:

First: That it was wise, if it met with your approval, to issue as
soon as possible a proclamation as to when the railroads would be
returned to their owners.

Second: That Secretaries Glass, Daniels, Lane, Houston, Alexander and I agreed in the opinion that there should be a postponement in the delivery. To this opinion the Postmaster-General dissented.

Of those holding the opinion that there should be a postponement on account of the present conditions of legislation and the difficulties surrounding the return of the railroads affecting labor, rates, and financing, all but Secretary Daniels favored a return on March 1st, next. Secretary Daniels was in favor of February 1st, believing that would give sufficient time to adopt the necessary legislation. The other members of the Cabinet favorable to a postponement based the extension to March 1st on Mr. Hines' statement that after the legislation had been adopted there should be a certain lapse of time before the roads were returned.

As I said at the outset I am sending this letter at the request of the Cabinet.   Faithfully yours,   Robert Lansing.

TLS (WP, DLC).

To Thomas Ridley[1]

My dear Mr. Mayor: [The White House] 12 December, 1919

May I not ask you to express to the members of the Council of Carlisle my warm thanks for the honour you have bestowed upon me in making me a citizen of your city, which is so filled with the tender associations with my mother.

My visit to Carlisle[2] will always be one of the happiest incidents in my memory, and I am proud to feel that I am one of you. The very interesting casket which I have just received will always be a valued souvenir, together with the emblazoned copy of the resolutions which I have hung by the one you so thoughtfully sent me some years ago of my mother.[3]

With renewed appreciation, believe me,
            Cordially and sincerely yours,   [Woodrow Wilson]

CCL (WP, DLC).
    [1] There is an EBWhw copy of this letter in WP, DLC.
    [2] About this visit, see the extract from the Diary of Dr. Grayson printed at Dec. 29, 1918, Vol. 53.
    [3] Both resolutions are missing in WP, DLC.

From the Diary of Colonel House

December 12, 1919.

Gregory telephoned from Washington to tell several things of interest. Secretary Wilson had his resignation written ready to send to the President. Gregory persuaded Wilson not to do so not alone on account of the President's illness but because of the Industrial Commission now sitting.

Gregory told of how Alexander happened to be appointed Secretary of Commerce. I have been interested in this appointment. I did not believe the President made it himself but thought it had been suggested by Tumulty either at the instigation of McAdoo or Mitchell Palmer. McAdoo denied all knowledge of the matter yesterday and Gregory tells me that the President first offered it to Vance McCormick. This was before the President became so ill. McCormick declined it. The President then picked up a Congressional Record, looked over the Committee on Shipping and Commerce, and selected Alexander because his name came first among democrats on that committee.

Alexander is on bad terms with both Champ Clark and Senator Reed and is the friend of nobody in particular, and did not want the place. It gives two Cabinet officers from Missouri and, if McCormick had taken it, it would have given three to Pennsylvania, a rockribbed republican State, one the democrats in no circumstances could hope to carry.

To Harry Augustus Garfield

My dear Garfield: [The White House] 13 December, 1919

Your conviction in the matter is evidently so clear that I do not feel at liberty to withhold my acquiescence in your retirement at such date as you may deem necessary from the duties of Fuel Administrator. But we have always dealt with each other with absolute frankness, and I feel bound to say that I think your judgment in this matter is not justified in proposing a retirement in the midst of a vital settlement which must inevitably affect the fuel supply of the whole country and of a very large part of the world.

Let me say I think the whole country has profited by your administration of the office of Fuel Administrator, and express my own personal thanks and warm appreciation. It was a very onerous office which you undertook at my solicitation and I know what it cost you of effort and anxiety.

    Always

        Cordially and faithfully yours,   Woodrow Wilson

TLS (Letterpress Books, WP, DLC).

From Harry Augustus Garfield

Dear Mr. President: Washington, D. C. December 13, 1919

I am deeply grieved that our judgments do not travel together with respect to the settlement of the coal strike. If it were not that my judgment leads me to believe that the principles offended go to the very foundation of our institutions, I should abide by your wish and remain in office for the present. As it is, I must bear with whatever criticism may come from retiring at the present time and, as you consent to my retirement at such date as I may deem necessary, I will indicate the present moment as the time.

As always,

Cordially and faithfully yours, H. A. Garfield.

TLS (WP, DLC).

From Robert Lansing

My dear Mr. President: Washington December 13, 1919.

Events have transpired in Costa Rica since my letter of November 4,[1] which lead me to lay before you certain facts relating to the present situation. You will recall that with the downfall of the Tinoco regime, the Constitutional system of Costa Rica was re-established and the orderly succession to the Presidency was secured through the designation of the Honorable Aguilar Barquero as Provisional President. In accordance with the terms of the constitution of 1871, which was re-established after the downfall of Tinoco, new presidential elections have been held, and I am certain that it will be a source of very real satisfaction to you to learn that these elections were conducted in an orderly and legal manner. There were but two candidates:—Julio Acosta and Jose Maria Soto. The latter was a strong supporter of Tinoco and the erstwhile adherents of Tinoco rallied to the support of Soto. The elections resulted in an overwhelming victory for Julio Acosta. He will not take office until May 1920, and I deem it, therefore, a matter of very great importance to the stability and tranquillity of Costa Rica that we should squarely place ourselves back of the present Constitutional Government and thus discourage any conspiracies or subversive movements on the part of the former adherents of Tinoco. In view of the fact that we have secured in Costa Rica the complete vindication of your policy, it would, I feel, be most unfortunate if a delay in recognition were unfavorably to affect the prestige of the present government. Sincerely yours, Robert Lansing.

TLS (WP, DLC).
[1] The Enclosure printed with JPT to EBW, Nov. 5, 1919, Vol. 63.

A News Report

[Dec. 14, 1919]

WILSON WALKS; NOT PARALYZED

President Wilson overruled his physicians in arising from his bed and walking about his room, Dr. Cary T. Grayson said yesterday when it became known that the President had been up.

That the President's walk resulted in no ill effects, however, was shown by the announcement of Dr. F. X. Dercum, Philadelphia neurologist, who said, after his weekly visit to the White House yesterday, that the President is markedly better than he has been since he was ordered to bed October 1.

White House officials said the President's walk effectually set at rest rumors that his right leg was paralyzed.

With announcement of the President's improvement, administration leaders were hopeful that he might take some hand in politics, as well as official business. Democratic party chiefs revived hope that they may yet seat the President as the guest of honor at the Jackson day banquet here January 8.

Printed in the *Washington Post*, Dec. 14, 1919.

A Statement[1]

[*Dec. 14, 1919*]

It was learned from the highest authority at the executive offices today that the hope of the Republican leaders of the Senate that the President would presently make some move which will relieve the situation with regard to the treaty is entirely without foundation.

He has no compromise or concession of any kind in mind, but intends, so far as he is concerned, that the Republican leaders of the Senate shall continue to bear the undivided responsibility for the fate of the treaty and the present condition of the world in consequence of that fate.

Printed in the *New York Times*, Dec. 15, 1919.
[1] JPT to EBW, Dec. 16, 1919, seems to say that Wilson dictated this statement. There are no copies of it in WP, DLC, or the J. P. Tumulty Papers, DLC.

Robert Lansing to Joseph Patrick Tumulty

My dear Mr. Tumulty: Washington December 15, 1919.

Lord Grey is returning to England and will cease to be British Ambassador. He sails, I think, on the third of January from New

York. He has not been received by the President in order to present his credentials, and while an opportunity to present his credentials cannot be asked, not only because of the President's illness, but because of the fact that there are several other Ambassadors and ministers who have been waiting longer than Lord Grey to present their credentials, still I feel it would be most appropriate for the President to receive him informally, just in order that he might say goodbye.

Will you not take this up with the President at the earliest opportunity and try to get his consent? The appointment should be as soon as possible after Christmas, in order that he may depart from New York several days before his boat leaves.

If you will advise me the President's pleasure I will be glad to see that his desires are complied with.

Yours very sincerely,   Robert Lansing.[1]

TLS (WP, DLC).
[1] "What shall I say?" JPT to EBW, c. Dec. 15, 1919, ALI (WP, DLC).

From Walker Downer Hines

Dear Mr. President: Washington December 15, 1919

I regret exceedingly to burden you with another communication on the railroad problem, but I feel that I cannot meet my responsibility in the circumstances without presenting to you the critical need for an announcement on the matter.

1. The legislative situation appears to require such an announcement. Your message to Congress on the 2nd instant indicated your purpose to communicate with Congress somewhat later as to the railroads. The leaders of both Houses are awaiting announcement as to your position before undertaking to pass temporary legislation which will be essential to prevent a chaotic financial condition if Federal control should be relinquished at December 31st. There is widespread uncertainty, which, if it continues, may easily be made the basis of unfair manipulation of the prices of railroad securities. The time remaining for the adoption of such temporary legislation is so brief that such legislation will at best be highly unsatisfactory. If relinquishment of control at December 31st should be decided upon, and if, in order to protect the financial situation, Congress should pass hasty and unsatisfactory legislation giving a temporary guaranty, there would arise the dilemma [dilemma] whether such enactment should be permitted to become a law or whether it should be vetoed, with the result that the railroads would go back to private control at December 31st without any temporary protection at all.

2. The labor situation is exceedingly difficult. The employes are pressing for further consideration of their demands for a general increase in wages. The situation is likely to become immediately acute if Federal control is relinquished at December 31st, because it will be impossible in any temporary legislation to provide machinery for dealing with the demands of labor. On the other hand the situation will be at least temporarily tranquillized by an announcement that a relinquishment will not take place at December 31st. Representatives of some of the principal labor organizations are now pressing me for a conference on this matter and I cannot speak with confidence until I know whether the roads will or will not be turned back at December 31st.

3. Operating problems are of the most pressing character. We need to make plans at once for the maintenance of the property after December 31st and yet we cannot do this until we know that Federal control will not be relinquished on that date. Contracts for cross ties and some other sorts of material should be made at once if the necessary supplies are to be forthcoming. Numerous important questions of operating organization are pressing for decision.

All the developments since my former communications to you confirm the conviction I have expressed that it is in the public interest that Federal control shall not be relinquished at December 31st, and, further, that it is in the public interest that the way shall be left open for the development of a sentiment in favor of a retention of Federal control, with adequate congressional support, pending an opportunity for more deliberate consideration of general legislation.

The subject is so pressing and so important that I would like very much to have the opportunity of a few moments conversation with you in the event any doubts occur to you as to the course which ought to be pursued, because I feel such an interview would materially aid in expediting a conclusion with the least tax upon your time.

I am sure you will acquit me of any undue insistence in this matter, because the urgency is such as to constitute a justification.

Cordially yours,   Walker D Hines[1]

TLS (WP, DLC).
[1] "I am bound to send you the enclosed for the President." JPT to EBW, Dec. 16, 1919, TL (WP, DLC).

From Robert Lansing

My dear Mr. President: Washington December 15, 1919.

The Senate, on December 8th, passed without amendment the House Bill (H.R. 9822), authorizing you to call and to participate in an International Conference to consider all aspects of international communications, and appropriating $75,000 for this purpose.

The bill is in the form proposed by the Department of State with the addition of two amendments suggested by the House Committee. The first of these makes it necessary that the Senate confirm appointments of representatives to participate in the Conference; the second forbids the expenditure of any of the $75,000 for the purposes of entertainment, medals or badges.

In view of your interest in this conference, I venture to bring the matter to your attention with a view to appropriate early action.

Faithfully yours,   Robert Lansing

The President will be obliged if the Secretary will formulate the "Call" for the Conference E.B.W.[1]

TLS (WP, DLC).
[1] EBWhw written on notepaper and pasted on Lansing's letter. This message was conveyed in JPT to RL, Dec. 17, 1919, TLS (SDR, RG 59, 574D1/13, DNA).

Joseph Patrick Tumulty to Edith Bolling Galt Wilson

Dear Mrs. Wilson: The White House, 16 December, 1919.

The President's statement Sunday was a body blow. Of course, its immediate effect will be to call forth the bitter criticism and antagonism of our enemies and the indifferent friends we have on the Hill, many of whom are ready to swallow anything as long as it is called a League of Nations. It was a brave, audacious thing to do. Tell the President that in my opinion it will cleanse and purify the merky [murky] atmosphere which has surrounded the whole situation.

I thought you might like to read the enclosed letter.[1]

Sincerely,   [J P Tumulty]

CCL (J. P. Tumulty Papers, DLC).
[1] It is missing.

William Joseph Martin[1] to Edith Bolling Galt Wilson

My dear Mrs. Wilson: Davidson, N. C. December 16, 1919.

I am saying to you what I would be glad to say to Mr. Wilson if he were not ill, but what I hope you can convey to him in your own way.

Davidson College will always feel proud of the fact that your distinguished husband was a student in this institution and the College rejoices in the knowledge that Mr. Wilson remembers the College with kindness, believes in its work, and has faith in its future.

We have been deeply distressed over his illness. Never do I conduct the morning chapel service without a petition for his complete and speedy restoration to health.

We are likewise distressed, and indignant too, over the treatment of him by a certain sect of the opposition in matters connected with the League and Treaty.

We want to do all we can to support his hands and show our faith in him.

The College has had three professorships endowed within the last three weeks, each for fifty thousand dollars. One of these was endowed by the First Presbyterian Church of Gastonia, North Carolina,[2] of which Rev. J. H. Henderlite,[3] D.D., is pastor. The President has no more loyal supporters than the officers of that church, many of whom are most successful cotton mill manufacturers. They, knowing Mr. Wilson's relation to Davidson College, and desiring to express their faith in and admiration for him, have requested that the Chair be called "The Woodrow Wilson Chair of Economics and Political Science," and they have written me that a letter has gone forward to you stating their action.[4] May I not join them in the earnest request through you that Mr. Wilson will honor the College by consenting to the name selected and saying so in a short message to the Gastonia Church? I would not tax him further for the College than to ask his consent that his name be given the Chair, the incumbent of which will always be a Christian man who will do all he can to inculcate the Spirit of Christ in his students as they face the vexed problems that must come up in Economics and Political Science. Tell your husband that Davidson looks forward to a bright future and enlarged service and will always hold him in high regard and affection.

When his cares of office are laid aside, after that he shall have won a sure victory for righteousness and World peace, will you not bring him to see us again and let him give us a message of counsel and hope?

I have just today showed three visiting gentlemen his old room

in Chambers, where he spent the days of his college life in Davidson, and told them the stories of his student life as he told them to
you when he visited his old quarters a few years ago.[5]

May God grant your heart's desire in his speedy restoration to
health and give him the fruition of his great hope of "Peace on
Earth, Good Will among Men."

Remember me to him if possible and accept for him as well as
for yourself my high regards and cordial good will.

Very sincerely yours,   Wm. J. Martin

TLS (WP, DLC).

[1] President of Davidson College.

[2] This church had pledged this amount for a Woodrow Wilson professorship, as part
of the Synod of North Carolina's Million Dollar Campaign. The reports of the treasurer
of Davidson College do not subsequently mention receipt of any funds for the Wilson
professorship. The Gastonia church's contribution was probably insufficient to endow
the chair, and it was probably added to the college's general endowment fund. The
trustees established the Woodrow Wilson Chair of Economics and Political Science on
March 30, 1920. Archibald A. Currie held it until his death in 1942, when it was either
abolished or allowed to lapse. Mary Beaty to A. S. Link, Oct. 4, 1989, TLS (WC, NjP).

[3] James Henry Henderlite.

[4] Henderlite's letter is missing; for Wilson's reply to it, see WW to J. H. Henderlite,
Dec. 22, 1919.

[5] The Wilsons had visited Davidson College on May 20, 1916, following a speech by
Wilson in Charlotte.

A Memorandum by Robert Lansing

December 16, 1919.

THE PRESIDENT'S POLICY OF
"NO CONCESSION AND NO COMPROMISE."

The President's formal announcement published day before yesterday that he was not considering making any concession or compromise in the matter of ratification of the Treaty has had a most
depressing effect on many of the Democrats in the Senate, and
some of them are very near to uniting against the leadership of the
President, whom they have up to now loyally supported though
doubtful as to the wisdom of his course.[1]

Coming as it did the day after Senator Underwood's concilliatory
speech in favor of an agreement to restore a legal state of peace,
the President's announcement seems to be a repudiation of Underwood and favorable to Hitchcock as leader, since the latter has im-
plicitly obeyed the President throughout the long battle in the Senate. Just how this will affect the contest for Senate leadership is
hard to say, because offsetting the President's apparent support of
Hitchcock is the popular demand that peace be restored in some
way and the increasing popular resentment that the political quarrel between the President and the Senate should prevent this demand being granted.

At the Cabinet meeting today the President's announcement was defended by Carter Glass, who bitterly attacked Lodge and other leading Republicans. He would not listen to any expressions of doubt as to the way the public might interpret the President's bald defiance of those who sought to compose the differences as to the Treaty, asserting with his usual sullen vehemence that the President had all along said that he would accept interpretive reservations, and the present announcement must be read in the light of what he had previously said. Both Lane and I said that this ought to be made clear to the people in some authorat[at]ive way otherwise they would not understand the President's position and would blame his obstinacy for non-ratification.

Glass showed a lot of temper in replying to this suggestion, saying "Lodge and his gang ought to be allowed to stew in their own juice" and that he was not in favor of doing anything toward meeting them even half way. It was perfectly evident that he was willing to sacrifice the interests of this country and of the world rather than recede one step in the political battle going on in the Senate. His narrow and unstatesmanlike attitude and his vicious language showed that it was useless to debate the question with him.

The Postmaster General with his chronic partisanship and usual political optimism, which so often is ill-founded, declared emphatically that the Democrats had the Republicans "on the hip," that they would have "to come across" in the end, and that he considered the situation better than at any time. He and Glass talked much the same language and showed about an equal amount of sanity, which was mighty near zero.

Baker and Daniels approved without qualification the President's announcement and thought it needed no explanation. *After* the President has taken action, these two always endorse it. They seem to have no minds when the President has made up his. They act as if he could not possibly make a mistake. This form of flattery, for that is what it is, gives them much popularity with their chief and results in an intimacy which those who show independence of judgment do not enjoy. Their way of dealing with the President reminds one of the shrewd way that Colonel House gained and held the good will of the President. To me this course is inconsistent with manliness, with self-respect and with a true sense of public duty. However, it cannot be denied that these two gentlemen are in high favor with the President, who is very responsive to praise of his conduct and policies, but so are most men for that matter.

Palmer and Wilson were not present at the meeting, and I do not recall that Houston or Alexander took part in the discussion. At any rate Lane and I felt rather lonely.

It will be interesting to see the effect of the announcement on the struggle between Underwood and Hitchcock, which may be settled this week. I should not be surprised if Hitchcock calls the meeting late in the week, because Underwood's supporters being in the south and east are apt to have gone home already, while the western Senators, on whom Hitchcock relies, are not likely on account of the distances to leave Washington at all. Possibly though Hitchcock may not take such an unfair advantage of his opponent.

My own view is that Underwood is the stronger personality and that he would be a more fearless and more aggressive leader, while as a parliamentarian he has few equals. His independence of opinion and his frankness of expression may not be pleasing to the President. He will cooperate with the White House but not subordinate himself to the judgment of another if they disagree. In this he differs from Hitchcock. Hitchcock will obey orders. Underwood prefers to give them. One is a lieutenant; the other, a commander.

T MS (R. Lansing Papers, DLC).

[1] The *Washington Post*, Dec. 16, 1919, reported that the statement had "brought open resentment" into the ranks of Democratic senators. "Signs of revolt," it continued, "against continued advocacy of the no-compromise slogan were manifest among administration senators, many of whom expressed themselves in no uncertain terms. The proposal to declare peace by legislation or ratify the treaty without the league of nations may get added support from the Democrats unless the atmosphere is cleared before Senator Knox's resolutions are put to the test. The chief objection to the President's announced attitude is that it pledges Democratic senators to an obviously lost cause, according to these senators themselves, and in addition, makes them responsible for delaying peace. There has developed a pronounced sentiment among the Democratic senators, led by Senator Underwood, to arrive at some practical solution of the deadlock over the treaty and restore the economy to a normal basis. Representatives of business interests of the country, and of the cotton growing States of the South, want to see quarrel and controversy give way to peace and they see no possible hope in following the original peace plan laid down by the President. Consequently, they are behind Senator Underwood in his compromise efforts and they are behind Senator Knox in his resolution to ratify the treaty and leave the league to be decided later. A peace on this basis is admittedly not the peace which the administration senators hoped to procure, but it is now regarded as the best available and certainly better than no peace at all."

The news report went on to quote remarks of Democratic senators who had previously supported Wilson.

Thomas J. Walsh: "The Democratic senators are inwardly seething over the position taken by the President. They are all wondering whether the statement was really written by the President or by some cheap politician assuming to speak the President's mind."

Charles S. Thomas: "I think the statement of the President is very unfortunate."

Atlee Pomerene: "Eighty senators voted in favor of ratification of the treaty in some form or other. In my humble judgment the public has a right to expect these 80 senators to make concessions, one to the other, which will lead to the adoption of a resolution of ratification with the required two-thirds majority."

The reference above to the "Knox resolutions" was to the Knox Resolution of June 1919 (about which, see JPT to WW, June 11, 1919, Vol. 60), now defunct. About the contest between Hitchcock and Underwood for the position of Minority Leader, see GMH to EBW, Jan. 13, 1920, and EBW to GMH, Jan. 13, 1920.

From Thetus Wilrette Sims

My dear Mr. President: Washington, D. C. December 17, 1919.

If I did not feel that it was my duty to do so I would not put you to the trouble of reading a letter from me at this time. But, without any reference to what effect it may have upon any of the numerous suggested "Plans" for railroad legislation, I sincerely believe that the public interest cannot be best served by any kind of railroad legislation that may be passed during the year of 1920, nor in fact earlier than after March 4, 1921. I do not believe that the Esch bill as it passed the House ought to become a law, and I even more strongly believe that the Cummins bill as reported to the Senate should not become a law.[1]

The fact that active political agitation is now present and will grow stronger continuously until after the election in November next, makes it impossible in my judgment to secure comprehensive legislation dealing with all questions that necessarily ought to and must be dealt with in any comprehensive plan without being more or less injuriously affected by reason of such prevailing conditions. No doubt the two principal political parties in their respective national conventions will take positions on this all important subject. The results of the election no doubt will shed much light as to public opinion relative to this matter, but the short three months' session of the present Congress would not be sufficient even then to properly consider this all-important legislation.

For these reasons and many others I think it best for the country, best for the railroads and best for security owners that Federal control of railroads should continue until legislation can be had by the Sixty-seventh Congress. An extra session no doubt will be called early after the fourth of March, 1921, and the railroad question can then be dealt with with the least possible political embarrassment. The situation would be similar to that of the enactment of the Federal Reserve Banking law in the extra session which you called immediately following your inauguration.

I do not believe it will be possible for the railroads to serve the country under private ownership as efficiently as it can be served by the present unified government control. The people have more confidence in the ability of the railroads operated by a single head and as a single system to best serve the country's transportation needs than can possibly be done by competing systems even though they may be reduced in number. Furthermore, it is perfectly evident that the railway employees as a whole have more confidence in just treatment by the government railway administration than by the respective railroads being operated competitively by their owners. Conditions will certainly be more stable, and labor will have grown more tranquil by the time I have suggested than can possibly be hoped for should the railroads be returned to their owners during 1920. The consuming and shipping public has every confidence that there will be no further general increase in rates, fares and charges during further federal control, but they are very apprehensive of additional general increases in rates if the railroads are returned to their owners.

The present Congress has had from May 19, to the present hour to legislate on this subject. It had full knowledge that you intended to return the railroads at the end of this year, and at this late hour nothing has been done in the way of enabling legislation preparatory to such return. As late as yesterday at 1.30 o'clock, or about that time, I was in the Senate chamber when the so-called Cummins bill was being considered. There was only one republican senator in the chamber; to wit, Senator Poindexter,[2] and he was making a speech on the bill. There were only seven democrats in the chamber at the time. As Senator Poindexter was discussing the "Long and short haul" clause of the Commerce Act,[3] in which I was particularly interested, I remained in the chamber not less than five minutes, during which time no other senator entered the chamber. It is perfectly evident that railway legislation is failing to receive the consideration of senators to the extent that its importance demands; and that if the so-called Cummins bill is passed by the Senate, the legislation will, in fact, have to be practically provided by conference committee rather than by either chamber.

Therefore, I sincerely believe that no comprehensive legislation attempting to solve the railway problem should be attempted, at least until after the election in November next; and I believe most earnestly that the country cannot possibly be as well served by any legislation that it will be possible to enact during the year, 1920, as it can and will be if the railroads continue under the control and operation of the government.

Very sincerely yours,   T. W. Sims[4]

TLS (WP, DLC).
[1] Cummins had introduced S. 3288 on October 23, 1919. In addition to providing for the complex process of returning the railroads to private control, the bill set forth a comprehensive program for the future of American railroads. It proposed their eventual consolidation into not less than twenty or more than thirty-five regional systems. This was to be done in a manner that would provide adequate profit to all lines while maintaining competition on the more profitable routes. A new federal transportation board would both set up the new systems and share the oversight of them with the Interstate Commerce Commission. Pending the completion of this consolidation, for which the bill allowed up to seven years, the I. C. C. was empowered to set rates according to an elaborate scheme set forth in the measure, which was designed both to protect the public interest and to insure the survival of the weaker existing railroads. The bill also contained provisions for coordinating rail and water transportation under federal control. The most controversial sections of the bill were those dealing with railway workers.

They included an antistrike provision which forbade any individual from preventing the operation of trains or railway service, with penalties of fines and/or imprisonment for violators. Labor disputes were to be settled by several boards composed of representatives of employers and employees similar to those existing during the period of federal control. For a summary of the important provisions of the Cummins bill, see the *New York Times*, Oct. 23, 1919. A more detailed summary is in 66th Cong., 1st sess., Senate Report No. 304.

Esch had introduced H.R. 10453 in the House of Representatives on November 8, 1919. His bill was much less ambitious than the Cummins measure. The Esch bill was primarily concerned with a smooth transition of the railroads from federal to private control and attempted to deal with the railroads' recurring financial problems through a series of provisions which were to be carried out by the I. C. C. It contained no antistrike clause but attempted to prevent strikes by an elaborate system for the settlement of labor disputes, including a requirement for cooling-off periods and final appeals to a Railway Board of Labor Appeals made up of representatives of management, labor, and the public. The bill was approved by the House on November 17 in an amended form. It replaced the labor section with a new one favored by organized labor, which provided for the settlement of disputes by several boards composed of representatives of employers and employees, but no public representatives, and which in effect conceded the right to strike by failing to provide for any compulsory awards or decisions. About the Esch bill, see the *New York Times*, Nov. 10, 15, and 18, 1919, and the editorial "The Railway Bills" in *ibid.*, Nov. 17, 1919. For the bill as introduced on November 8, see 66th Cong., 1st sess., House Report No. 456.

[2] Miles Poindexter, Republican of Washington.

[3] The Interstate Commerce Act of 1887.

[4] "I thought the President might want to have this view from Congressman Sims." JPT to EBW, c. Dec. 17, 1919, TLS (WP, DLC).

From Samuel Gompers and Others[1]

Dear Mr. President: Washington, D. C., December 17, 1919.

Proponents of the Cummins Bill for the immediate return of the railroads with a high guaranteed compensation are attempting to justify this bill by asserting that it is your plan to return the railroads to their owners by January 1st, 1920, and that some legislation providing for such return must be enacted immediately.

We believe that this assertion is a great injustice to you. As you will doubtless know, an overwhelming majority of the farmers, of the members of the American Federation of Labor, of the Railway Brotherhoods, as well as the general public favor an extension of the period of government operation of the railroads for at least two years, in order that a fair test may have been made of government operation and a plan may be worked out for the ultimate disposal of the railroads which would be fair to all interests involved. Such recommendation was made by Mr. McAdoo when Director General of the Railroads, who urged a five year extension of government operation while members of the Interstate Commerce Commission have also urged extension.

Director General Hines and members of the Interstate Commerce Commission have shown clearly that the return of the railroads will involve an increase in freight revenue of close to a billion dollars, the rates being increased 25 to 50 per cent. This increase in rates, according to these same authorities, will be reflected in an increased cost of living of at least four billion dollars a year, possibly five billion. The American people cannot and should not stand such increase.

Government operation, as reported by Director General Hines, showed a net profit at the rate of $168,000,000 a year for the three months prior to the coal strike.

The Senate is now being asked to investigate serious charges against certain officials of railroads during the period of Federal Control, that they had committed sabotage and had wilfully and purposely attempted through unfair methods while presumably serving the Government, to discredit government operation.

We respectfully request, Mr. President, on behalf of the farmers, the American Federation of Labor and the Railway Brotherhoods, as well as the general public, that you stop the rumors that you plan to return the railroads to private control, and that in view of the changed conditions and the prevalent industrial unrest you re-establish public confidence by advocating that the period of government operation be continued for at least two years, so that under peace conditions there may be a more thorough and more consistent trial of government operation, and that a carefully considered plan for the ultimate disposal of the railroads may be worked out and adopted.   Yours respectfully,

Saml. Gompers.
Geo. P. Hampton
Warren S Stone
Timothy Shea
L E Sheppard[2]

TLS (WP, DLC).
[1] "I think this is important enough to read to the President." JPT to EBW, Dec. 18, 1919, TLS (WP, DLC).
[2] George P. Hampton, managing director of the Farmers' National Council; Warren Sanford Stone, Grand Chief Engineer of the International Brotherhood of Locomotive Engineers; Timothy Shea, acting president of the Brotherhood of Locomotive Firemen and Enginemen; and Lucius Elmer Sheppard, president of the Brotherhood of Railway Conductors.

Edith Bolling Galt Wilson to Joseph Patrick Tumulty

[The White House, c. Dec. 17, 1919]

The President returns this[1] requesting the Sec. to say "It is incompatible with the Public interest."   E.B.W.

ALI (WP, DLC).
[1] This was in reply to RL to WW, Dec. 15, 1919, TLS (WP, DLC). Lansing informed Wilson that the Senate had passed a resolution (S. Res. 221) on October 28, which

requested Lansing to send to the Senate a copy of the report of the United States mission to Poland headed by Henry Morgenthau, "if it is not incompatible with the public interest." Lansing submitted to Wilson copies of Morgenthau's report and a second report made by Brig. Gen. Edgar Jadwin, U.S.A., and Homer Hosea Johnson, the other members of the commission. These reports are missing in WP, DLC.

Wilson authorized publication of the Morgenthau report on about Janaury 8, 1920. See RL to WW, Jan. 8, 1920 (first letter of that date). Lansing's letter of December 15, 1919, was then redated January 14, 1920, and sent to the Senate the next day, along with copies of the two reports. The letter and the reports are printed in *FR 1919*, II, 773-800.

The Morgenthau mission, established by the A.C.N.P., was in Poland from July 13 to September 13, 1919. Lansing, on June 30, had instructed it to inquire into all aspects of relations between Jewish and non-Jewish elements in Poland, including alleged pogroms, economic boycotts, and "other methods of discrimination against the Jewish race." *Ibid.*, p. 774. Morgenthau's report was dated October 3, 1919. Jadwin and Johnson, who had been held up by other duties, completed their report on October 31. Both reports detailed the history and nature of anti-Semitic activity in Poland since the Armistice. Both downgraded the estimated number of Jewish deaths in incidents of anti-Semitic violence to three hundred or less, but both gave extensive evidence of widespread anti-Jewish prejudice and activity. Morgenthau was more sympathetic to the plight of Polish Jews but reported that the government of Piłsudski and Paderewski was doing its best to prevent or punish outrages and improve relations between Jews and gentiles. He also said that conditions for Jews would improve greatly once the boundaries of the Polish state were finally determined and economic conditions returned to normal. Jadwin and Johnson were more inclined to blame the Polish Jews themselves for the extent of their problems and indicated that the Jews would have to recognize and accept Polish citizenship as their primary allegiance. They, too, believed that determination of Poland's boundaries and a return to normal economic life would greatly improve the situation.

A Draft of a Public Letter[1]

My Fellow Countrymen: [c. Dec. 17, 1919]

It is unthinkable that at this supreme crisis and final turning point in the international relations of the whole world, when the results of the great war are by no means determined but still questionable and dependent upon events which no one can foresee or count upon, the United States should withdraw from the concert of progressive and enlightened nations by which Germany was defeated and all similar governments, if the world be so unhappy as to contain any, warned of the certain consequences of any attempt at a like iniquity; and yet that is the effect the course ⟨of⟩ the Senate of the United States has taken with regard to the Treaty of Versailles.

Germany is beaten but we are still at war with her and the old stage is re-set for a repetition of the old plot. It is now ready for the resumption of the old offensive and defensive alliances which made settled peace impossible. It is now open again to every sort of intrigue, and the old spies are free to resume their former abominable activities. They are again at liberty to make it impossible for governments to be sure what mischief is being worked among their own people, what internal disorders are being fomented.

None of the objects we professed to be fighting for has been se-

cured or can be without the Treaty⟨,⟩. ⟨w⟩Without the covenant of
the League of Nations⟨.⟩ ⟨T⟩there may be as many secret treaties
as ever to destroy the confidence of governments in each other and
their validity cannot be questioned. Without the Treaty Germany
may make no reparation for any of the criminal wrongs she in-
flicted; Alsace and Lorraine need not be returned to France; Germany may retain all her threatening armaments and renew all her
former designs.

Is there any wonder German agents are already busy representing that the combinations against Germany have already broken
up in alienation and divergency of purpose, and that in particular
the United States and France are no longer united in any kind of
friendship which need give Germany any concern; that the English speaking peoples no longer offer any obstacle to Germany's
ambitions; in brief, that the results of the war are already undone
and Germany free as ever to work out the purposes of Wilhelm-
strasse?

I do not believe that this is what you wish or will be satisfied
with. I have asserted from the first that an overwhelming majority
of the people of the country desire the ratification of the Treaty,
and my impression to that effect has recently been confirmed by
the unmistakable evidences of public opinion received during my
visit to seventeen of the States. But my assertions with regard to
your wish and opinion have not been credited. It has been assumed that I am no longer your spokesman; that I no longer enjoy
the confidence you so generously expressed in me in the autumn
of 1916.

There is but one way to settle such questions, and that is by
direct reference to the voters of the country. I have, as you know,
repeatedly professed my adherence to the principle of the referendum and recall, and I could wish both that you might have an early
opportunity to express *at the ballot box* your sovereign wish with
regard to the treaty ⟨at the ballot box⟩, and that you might, if you
desire, also have an opportunity to recall your commission to me to
act and speak in your name and on your behalf.

I am sorry the Constitution provides no method or machinery for
such a reference; but I have a method to propose which I am sure
is perfectly legal and feasible and which I hope may have your
united and outspoken approval and support.

I challenge the following named gentlemen, members of the
Senate of the United States, to resign their seats in that body and
take immediate steps to seek re-election to it on the issue of their
several records with regard to the ratification of the Treaty:

The Honorable John H. Bankhead of Alabama

The Honorable William F. Kirby of Arkansas
The Honorable Hiram W. Johnson of California
The Honorable Charles S. Thomas of Colorado
The Honorable Lawrence C. Phipps of Colorado
The Honorable Frank B. Brandegee of Connecticut
The Honorable George P. McLean of Connecticut
The Honorable L. Heisler Ball of Delaware
The Honorable Park Trammell of Florida
The Honorable Hoke Smith of Georgia
The Honorable William E. Borah of Idaho
The Honorable Lawrence Y. Sherman of Illinois
The Honorable Medill McCormick of Illinois
The Honorable James E. Watson of Indiana
The Honorable Harry S. New of Indiana
The Honorable Albert B. Cummins of Iowa
The Honorable William S. Kenyon of Iowa
The Honorable Charles Curtis of Kansas
The Honorable Arthur Capper of Kansas
The Honorable Bert M. Fernald of Maine
The Honorable Frederick Hale of Maine
The Honorable Joseph I. France of Maryland
The Honorable Henry Cabot Lodge of Massachusetts
The Honorable David I. Walsh of Massachusetts
The Honorable Charles E. Townsend of Michigan
The Honorable Truman H. Newberry of Michigan
The Honorable Frank B. Kellogg of Minnesota
The Honorable James A. Reed of Missouri
The Honorable Selden P. Spencer of Missouri
The Honorable George H. Moses of New Hampshire
The Honorable Henry W. Keys of New Hampshire
The Honorable Joseph E. Frelinghuysen of New Jersey
The Honorable Walter E. Edge of New Jersey
The Honorable Albert B. Fall of New Mexico
The Honorable James W. Wadsworth, Jr., of New York
The Honorable William M. Calder of New York
The Honorable Asle J. Gronna of North Dakota
The Honorable Warren G. Harding of Ohio
The Honorable Thomas P. Gore of Oklahoma
The Honorable Charles L. McNarry of Oregon
The Honorable Boise Penrose of Pennsylvania
The Honorable Philander C. Knox of Pennsylvania
The Honorable LeBaron B. Colt of Rhode Island
The Honorable Thomas Sterling of South Dakota
The Honorable John K. Shields of Tennessee

The Honorable Reed Smoot of Utah
The Honorable William P. Dillingham of Vermont
The Honorable Carroll S. Page of Vermont
The Honorable Wesley I. Jones of Washington
The Honorable Miles Poindexter of Washington
The Honorable Howard Sutherland of West Virginia
The Honorable Davis Elkins of West Virginia
The Honorable Robert M. LaFollette of Wisconsin
The Honorable Irving L. Lenroot of Wisconsin
The Honorable Francis E. Warren of Wyoming
The Honorable John B. Kendrick of Wyoming

For myself I promise and engage if all of them or a majority of them are re-elected, I will resign the presidency. I am authorized by the Vice President to say he will also in such case resign the vice-presidency.

The office of president would then, under existing law, devolve upon the Secretary of State; and it is my purpose in the meantime to invite one of the acknowledged leaders of the Republican party to accept that office.

CC MS and T MS (WP, DLC).
[1] There are two drafts of this letter in WP, DLC—a carbon copy (the first draft) and a T MS (the second draft), which includes the list of senators. The two versions conform when the first draft is read en clair, except, of course, for the list of senators. Words in angle brackets deleted by Mrs. Wilson in the carbon copy; words in italics added by her.
     We think that Tumulty drafted the first letter along lines suggested by Wilson.
     As Kurt Wimer, "Woodrow Wilson's Plan for a Vote of Confidence," *Pennsylvania History*, XXVIII (July 1961), 279-93, has said, the idea of a national referendum on the League of Nations was undoubtedly Wilson's. Tumulty later referred to it as Wilson's "larger plan." JPT to WW, Jan. 2, 1920. Wilson's plan to challenge opposition senators to resign was of course legally and politically infeasible, but the document that we print below became the basis for another public letter—the Jackson Day message of January 8, 1920—and another effort by Wilson to obtain a national referendum on the League.
     Tumulty, or whoever prepared the list of senators for him, was careless. In order to be a candidate for that list, a senator should either have voted for the Lodge resolution for consent to ratification with the so-called Lodge reservations or against the Underwood resolution for consent to ratification without any reservations, or both. By this criterion, Bankhead and Kirby did not belong on this list: both had voted against the Lodge resolution and for the Underwood resolution. Kendrick's name also did not belong on the list. He voted against the Lodge resolution. He was paired with the absent Senator Fall in the vote on the Underwood resolution but announced that he would have voted for it except for his pair. We have not corrected errors in the spelling of these names.

Edith Bolling Galt Wilson to Alexander Mitchell Palmer[1]

My dear Mr. Attorney General: The White House Dec. 18, 1919

The President wants me to ask you to let him have an answer to the following question at your early convenience

"What affect would the resignation of the United States Senator have in each of the several following states.

Alabama	Massachusetts
Arkansas	Michigan
California	Missouri
Colorado	New Hampshire
Connecticut	" Jersey
Delaware	" Mexico
Florida	" York
Georgia	North Dakota
Idaho	Ohio
Illinois	Oklahoma
Indiana	Pennsylvania
Iowa	Rhode Island
Kansas	South Dakota
Maine	Tennessee
Maryland	Utah

Vermont Washington West Virginia Wisconsin Wyoming.

Would the Governor select their successors, or would the people elect by popular Election?"

Will you have a memorandum made as to the law in the States above.

Sincerely and Cordially yours   Edith Bolling Wilson.

ALS (A. M. Palmer Papers, DLC).
¹ There is an EBWhw draft of this letter in WP, DLC.

Joseph Patrick Tumulty to Edith Bolling Galt Wilson, with Enclosure

Dear Mrs. Wilson: The White House 18 December, 1919

When you get a chance to talk to the President, will you please tell him that Senator Hitchcock sent for me yesterday, and wanted to know "whether the President would look with favor upon any effort on his part to make an adjustment with the mild reservationists by which to soften the Lodge reservations and thus avoid splitting the Democratic party." He said that some weeks ago, when he discussed this with the President, he was told "to go on and do the best he could." He says 'that the Lodge preamble can be knocked out.

Would you let me know if the President has decided whether he will receive Sir Edward Grey?

I am calling your attention to a letter from William Phillips which he asked me personally to hand to the President.

Sincerely,   Tumulty

E N C L O S U R E

From William Phillips

Dear Mr. President: Washington December 17, 1919.

I hesitate more than I can tell you to intrude a personal matter upon you at this time, yet I do not want to do anything which might possibly seem to convey a wrong impression. I do, however, want you to understand just how I am fixed.

It has become necessary for my wife[1] to sail immediately for England to see her mother[2] who is dying from an incurable illness. Under the painful circumstances I naturally hesitate to have her go over alone. I am planning, therefore, to sail with her on January 3d. I am reluctant to leave the Department at a time when so many important things are happening. At the same time my doctors tell me that I must have a change from the Departmental grind, and I realize that this is only too true.

I am thankful to hear that you are rapidly being restored to health, and am glad of this opportunity to thank you again for the kindness and consideration which you have always shown me and which I assure you are very deeply appreciated.

I am, my dear Mr. President,

Faithfully yours,   William Phillips

TLS (WP, DLC).
[1] Caroline Astor Drayton Phillips.
[2] Charlotte Augusta Astor Drayton (Mrs. George Ogilvy) Haig.

Joseph Patrick Tumulty to Edith Bolling Galt Wilson

Dear Mrs. Wilson: The White House 18 December, 1919

Please don't think I am trying to crowd you or to urge immediate action by the President, but I thought it would help you if you could have before you a list of matters that at intervals the President might wish to have presented to him for discussion and settlement.

I submit such a list, as follows:

Message as to railroads, if any.

Recognition of Costa Rica.

Selection of commission to settle miners' strike.

Appointments as follows:

Secretaryship of the Treasury.

Secretaryship of the Interior.[1]

Assistant Secretaryship of Agriculture.

Action upon Secretary Lansing's recommendation of William Phillips for Holland.

Oklahoma appointments recommended by the Attorney General, now before the President (The President has objected to these because of his desire to know whether Senator Gore approved these appointments. I took the matter up with Senator Owen and he says they are friends of his and not of Gore's and he desires the President to okeh them.)

Civil Service Commission—vice Galloway,[2] resigned, Sept. 7, 1919

Federal Trade Commission—term expiring Sept. 25, 1921— vice Davies,[3] resigned (Democrat)

Interstate Commerce Commission—term expiring Dec. 31, 1925—vice Harlan[4] (Democrat)

United States Shipping Board—vice Robinson,[5] resigned (Republican vacancy)

United States Tariff Commission—term of 12 years expiring Sept. 8, 1928, vice Taussig,[6] resigned (Republican)

War Finance Corporation—Director—term expiring 1920, vice Leonard,[7] resigned.

Waterways Commission—seven persons

One at least from active or retired list, Engineer Corps, U.S.A.

One expert hydraulic engineer from civil life.

Five to be chosen either from civil life or public service.

Members from civil life to receive $7,500 per annum.

Rent Commissioners, under Act of October 22, 1919[8]—three.

Vacancies in Diplomatic Corps:

Bulgaria

China

Costa Rica, if recognized and if Hale[9] resigns as requested.

Italy—ought not to be named until Adriatic question settled.

Netherlands (Lansing recommends William Phillips)

Salvador

Siam

Switzerland—after February, 1920.

Sincerely, Tumulty

TLS (WP, DLC).

[1] Lane intended to resign and wished to do so at the earliest possible time. See the extract from Lansing's Desk Diary printed at Oct. 4, 1919, Vol. 63.

[2] That is, Charles Mills Galloway.

[3] That is, Joseph Edward Davies.

[4] That is, James Shanklin Harlan.

[5] That is, Henry Mauris Robinson.

[6] That is, Frank William Taussig.

[7] Clifford Milton Leonard.

[8] About this Act, see n. 2 to the second news report printed at Oct. 11, 1919, Vol. 63.

[9] That is, Edward Joseph Hale.

A Draft of a Letter from Edith Bolling Galt Wilson to Gilbert Monell Hitchcock

Dec. 19, 1919 answer to Hitchcock

The President asks me to thank you very warmly for consulting him as you do in your letter of _____ he is clear in the conviction that it would be a serious mistake for him, or for our side to *propose* any thing—any proposition must come from those who prevented the ratification of the Treaty

His interview with the Foreign Rela. Com. of the Senate made perfectly clear the interpretations he himself puts upon each provision of the Treaty, & he would of course feel obliged to accept any action which meerly embodied those interpretations & did not touch the substance of the Treaty

He hopes that no proposal or intimation of compromise or concession will come from our Caucus.

EBWhw MS (WP, DLC).

Edith Bolling Galt Wilson to Gilbert Monell Hitchcock

My dear Senator Hitchcock: The White House Dec. 19, 1919

The President asks me to thank you very warmly for consulting him as you do through your interview with Mr. Tumulty, a memorandum of which he has just reccived.[1]

He is clear in the conviction that it would be a serious mistake for him (or for our side) to *propose* anything.

Any proposition must come from those who prevented the ratification of the Treaty.

His interview with the Foreign Relations Committee of the Senate made perfectly clear the "interpretations" he himself puts upon each provision of the Treaty and he would, of course, feel obliged to accept any action which merely embodied those interpretations and did not touch[2]

AL (G. M. Hitchcock Papers, DLC).
  [1] See JPT to EBW, Dec. 18, 1919.
  [2] The last page of this letter is missing.

A Draft of a Letter to Henry Mauris Robinson[1]

My dear Mr. Robinson: [The White House] December 19, 1919

On October 6, 1917, with the official approval and sanction of the United States Fuel Administration, an agreement (since known as the "Washington Wage Agreement") was entered into between the operators and the union miners and mine workers of the so-called "Central Competitive Bituminous Coal Fields," composed of Western Pennsylvania, Ohio, Indiana and Illinois, which provided for an increase in the production of bituminous coal and an increase in wages to the miners and mine workers from the then existing scale of compensation. The agreement contained the following clause:

"Subject to the next biennial convention of the United Mine Workers of America, the mine workers' representatives agree that the present contract be extended during the continuation of the war and not to exceed two years from April 1, 1918."

Subsequently, on January 19, 1918, this agreement was approved by the convention of the International Union United Mine Workers of America.

At the fourth biennial convention of the International Union United Mine Workers of America, held in Cleveland, Ohio, from September 9 to September 23, 1919, the so-called Scale Committee submitted a report recommending, among other things, that the convention demand a sixty per cent increase applicable to all classifications of day labor and to all tonnage, yardage and dead work rates throughout the central competitive field; that all new wage agreements replacing existing agreements should be based on a six-hour work day from bank to bank, five days per week; the abolition of all automatic penalty clauses; that all contracts in the bituminous field should be declared to expire on November 1, 1919; and that "in the event a satisfactory wage agreement is not secured for the central competitive field before November 1, 1919, to replace the one now in effect, the international officers be authorized to and are hereby instructed to call a general strike of all bituminous miners and mine workers throughout the United States, the same to become effective November 1, 1919."

Subsequently conferences were held between representatives of the operators and of the miners, at which the miners' demands were submitted and declined on the part of the operators. The officers of the International Union United Mine Workers of America then issued so-called strike orders to all of their local unions and members, requiring them to cease work in the mining of bituminous coal at midnight on Friday, October 31st.

On October 15, 1919, the Secretary of Labor called a conference between the operators and miners of the bituminous mines in the central competitive field, which conference also resulted in failure to reach an agreement. In a letter to Secretary Wilson, which was submitted to the conference, I said:[2]

"If for any reason the miners and operators fail to come to a mutual understanding, the interests of the public are of such vital importance in connection with the production of coal that it is incumbent upon them to refer the matters in dispute to a board of arbitration for determination and to continue the operation of the mines pending the decision of the board."

Subsequently, on October 25, 1919, I issued a statement[3] in which I said that a strike in the circumstances therein described "is not only unjustifiable; it is unlawful," and added:

"I express no opinion on the merits of the controversy. I have already suggested a plan by which a settlement may be reached and I hold myself in readiness, at the request of either or both sides, to appoint at once a tribunal to investigate all the facts with a view to aiding in the earliest possible orderly settlement of the questions at issue between the coal operators and the coal miners, to the end that the just rights, not only of those interests but also of the general public may be fully protected."

Despite my earnest appeals that the men remain at work, the officers of the United Mine Workers of America rejected all the proposals for a peaceful and orderly adjustment and declared that the strike would go on. Accordingly, at my direction, the Attorney General filed a bill in equity in the United States District Court at Indianapolis, praying for an injunction to restrain the officers of the United Mine Workers of America from doing any act in furtherance of the strike. A restraining order was issued by the court, followed by a writ of temporary injunction on November 8, 1919, in which the defendants were commanded to cancel and revoke the strike orders theretofore issued. These strike orders were accordingly revoked in a form approved by the Court, but the men did not return to work in sufficiently large number to bring about a production of coal anywhere approaching normal.

On December 6, 1919, I issued a statement[4] in which I restated the Government's position, appealed to the miners to return to work and renewed my suggestion that upon the general resumption of mining operations a suitable tribunal would be erected for the purpose of investigating and adjusting the matters in controversy between the operators and the miners. This statement was submitted to a meeting of the officers of the International Union United Mine Workers of America, having authority to take action, which meeting adopted as its act a memorandum prepared by the Attorney General and approved by me, embodying the suggestions contained in my statement of December 6th. I am informed also that the operators have generally agreed to the plan therein outlined. I enclose for your information a copy of my statement of December 6, 1919, and the memorandum just referred to.

There has now been a general resumption of operation in all parts of the bituminous coal fields sufficient to warrant the appointment of a commission such as is referred to in the memorandum of the Attorney General, and I have accordingly appointed you; Mr. Rembrandt Peale, a mine owner and operator in active business; and Mr. John P. White, a practical miner, as a commission with the powers and duties as set forth in the memorandum agreed to and adopted by the miners and operators, who conducted all the prior negotiations. If a readjustment of the prices of coal shall be found necessary, I shall be pleased to transfer to the commission, subject to its unanimous action, the powers heretofore vested in the Fuel Administrator for that purpose.

I am sure it is not necessary for me to call your attention to the tremendous importance of the work of this commission or the great opportunity which it presents for lasting service to the coal industry and to the country. If the facts covering all the phases of the coal industry necessary to a proper adjustment of the matters submitted to you shall be investigated and reported to the public, I am sure that your report, in addition to being accepted as the basis for a new wage agreement for the bituminous coal miners, will promote the public welfare and make for a settled condition in the industry. No settlement can be had in this matter, permanent and lasting in its benefits, as affecting either the miners, the coal operators, or the general public, unless the findings of this body are comprehensive in their character and embrace and guard at every point the public interest. To this end, I deem it important that your conclusion should be reached by unanimous action. Upon your acceptance of this appointment, I shall be pleased to call an early meeting of the commission in Washington so that you may promptly lay out plans for your work.   Sincerely yours,

CCL (J. P. Tumulty Papers, DLC).
¹ This letter was written either by Tumulty, William B. Wilson, or Palmer, or by all of them. Palmer made a few changes in the text. The same letter was sent to Rembrandt Peale, a Pennsylvania coal operator, and John Philip White, former president of the United Mine Workers of America and now an executive of the Haynes Powder Company. See the *New York Times*, Dec. 21, 1919. Palmer must also have chosen Robinson, Peale, and White, probably in consultation and with William B. Wilson and Tumulty's approval.
² It was conveyed in JPT to WBW, Oct. 24, 1919, Vol. 63.
³ Printed at that date in *ibid*.
⁴ See the news report printed at Dec. 7, 1919.

From Robert Lansing

Dear Mr. President: Washington December 19, 1919.

I enclose a memorandum[1] reviewing the general features of the oil controversy with the Mexican Government.

As the Carranza Government has refused to allow the American companies to put down any wells, unless they formally agreed to accept the provisions of the new petroleum code, which will attempt to nationalize oil lands acquired before adoption of the new constitution and as the oil companies refused to bind themselves in advance to accepting a law, the provisions of which are not now known, and further as a result of this controversy the American companies are being denied the use, enjoyment and development of lands legally acquired according to Mexican law, and still further, as a result of this and the further fact that their older wells are failing in production, a serious crisis has arisen with respect to oil supplies from Mexico.

The memorandum shows that the oil companies appealed to the courts for relief from the exactions of the Carranza decrees attempting to nationalize their private owned lands. These appeals are still pending in the Mexican courts and the Carranza Government has made no direct effort to enforce them up to this time. It is now seeking indirectly, by a questionable exercise of the police power, to enforce upon the American citizens the recognition of its pretention to ownership. The question now arises as to whether the attitude consistently maintained by this Department in support of the claims of the American companies to the use and enjoyment of their vested rights lawfully acquired in Mexico, shall be supported. The Carranza Government has entirely ignored the representations made by this Department looking toward the granting of permits to drill. He has stopped, by the use of military forces, such drilling operations and other development work, such as laying of pipe lines, et cetera, which were undertaken without permit of his Government. The limit of diplomatic pressure in regard to this whole matter seems to have been reached. I have carefully refrained from making any demands or threats, although in our note of April 2, 1918,[2] at the outset of the difficulty, the Mexican Government was solemnly warned that

"In the absence of the establishment of any procedure looking to the prevention of spoliation of American citizens and in the absence of any assurance were such procedure established, that it would not uphold in defiance of international law and justice the arbitrary confiscations of Mexican authorities, it becomes the function of the Government of the United States most earnestly and respectfully to call the attention of the Mexican Government to the necessity which may arise to impel it to protect the property of its citizens in Mexico divested or injuriously affected by the decree above cited."

I respectfully request your directions as to such further steps which you may wish taken in this matter and I think I ought to state that I am convinced that Mr. Carranza will go up to the point of a definite break with this Government before abandoning the policy which he has adopted in regard to the oil lands. If nothing further shall be done by this Government, the Carranza Government will undoubtedly gain its point, which entirely aside from all questions of loss of prestige, may seriously affect the supplies of oil to this country with great loss not only to those who have invested in this industry, but to many of our great public services and the oil using industries, generally, throughout the United States.

Faithfully yours,   Robert Lansing.

TLS (WP, DLC).
    ¹ Actually, two documents: "BRIEF REVIEW OF CARRANZA'S EFFORTS TO CONFISCATE AMERICAN OWNED OIL PROPERTIES IN MEXICO," Dec. 4, 1919, and "CHRONOLOGY. MEXICO'S ATTEMPT AT CONFISCATION. MEXICO'S ASSURANCES THAT CONFISCATION WOULD NOT BE EFFECTED," both T MSS (WP, DLC). Both documents detailed the efforts by the Carranza government to bring foreign oil properties and operations under strict control in accordance with Article 27 of the Mexican Constitution. The second document also listed diplomatic protests by the United States Government against these efforts.
    ² H. P. Fletcher to C. Aguilar, April 2, 1918, printed in FR 1918, pp. 713-14.

A News Report

[Dec. 20, 1919]

Wilson Reported Much Better;
Dercum Stops Regular Visits

Washington, Dec. 20.—Dr. Dercum, the Philadelphia specialist who has been visiting President Wilson every Saturday and who saw the President today, has decided to discontinue his regular consultations with Rear Admiral Grayson because of the improvement in the President's condition, it was said at the White House this afternoon.

In making this announcement Admiral Grayson said that hereafter the visits of Dr. Dercum would be made at "indefinite" periods, and that there had been a marked improvement in the state of the President's health. Today the President was wheeled out for an airing on the snow covered White House grounds.

Mr. Wilson will eat Christmas dinner in his room and there will be no Christmas tree at the White House this year.

Printed in the New York Times, Dec. 21, 1919.

From Robert Lansing

My dear Mr. President: Washington December 20, 1919.

I am considerably disturbed with respect to the attitude of the Shipping Board regarding the seven ships of the IMPERATOR group which it has, in my opinion, arbitrarily seized and held pending a solution of an entirely unrelated question. The British Government has twice protested against this action, and I am at a loss to know what reply to make, inasmuch as I think their protest is entirely warranted.

The Supreme Council, in September, made an allocation (rightly or wrongly) among certain Allied Powers of several tank steamers owned by a German corporation, all the stock of which is alleged to be owned by the Standard Oil Company. This allocation was provisional and without prejudice to the rights of the interested parties. The Standard Oil Company appears to have laid the matter before the Shipping Board and to have induced it to seize the IMPERATOR group of ships (of which one, the IMPERATOR, has since been released) in retaliation for this action of the Supreme Council, and as a pledge for the allocation of all of these tank steamers to the Standard Oil Company. The seized ships have been held in American ports for several weeks at a very heavy expense, which I have no doubt will be the basis of a claim by Great Britain against the United States.

I have had the matter up several times with the Shipping Board, and have discussed the matter with the Chairman himself, but without avail. In order that the responsibility of this Department in the matter may be of record and that the Shipping Board be apprised of the possible results of its action, I desire to send the enclosed letter to the Chairman in reply to his of December 16, 1919.[1] Without your direction I am unable to bring myself to make the reply to the British Government which Mr. Payne's letter of December 16th suggestions [suggests].

Will you be good enough to approve the enclosed letter to the Shipping Board, or to advise me of your views in the premises. I enclose the current correspondence.[2]

Faithfully yours,   Robert Lansing.

TLS (WP, DLC).

[1] RL to J. B. Payne, n.d., CCL (SDR, RG 59, 862.85/963, DNA). Lansing went over the case again, insisted that the British were right, requested that the ships be turned over to them forthwith, and said that Wilson had read and approved this letter.

[2] J. B. Payne to A. A. Adee, Dec. 16, 1919, TLS, and R. C. Lindsay to RL, Dec. 19, 1919, CCL, both in SDR, RG 59, 862.85/963, DNA.

To John Grier Hibben

My dear President Hibben: The White House 22 December, 1919

The big table which was in the study at Prospect when I left Princeton, and which I assume to be there still, is not the property of the University. It was not purchased with funds supplied by the University for the purpose, but paid for out of my own pocket. It may therefore fairly be said to be mine. Would you be kind enough to have it properly crated and shipped in my care here? I would esteem it a real kindness on your part if you would. The table would be most serviceable here in the White House. Of course, I shall hope that you will let me have a memorandum of any cost you may be put to in the crating and shipment.

Very truly yours, Woodrow Wilson

TLS (NjP-Ar).

To James Henry Henderlite

My dear Dr. Henderlite: [The White House] 22 December, 1919

It will always be a matter of profound gratification to me that the officers and people of the Gastonia Church should have deemed me worthy of the great honor they have conferred upon me in endowing at Davidson College a professorship to bear my name. Such evidences of friendship and confidence are a great tonic to one in the midst of difficult affairs, and I am keenly conscious of standing in need of the support of thoughtful people and of the understanding regard of my fellow citizens.

Cordially and sincerely yours, Woodrow Wilson

TLS (Letterpress Books, WP, DLC).

To William Joseph Martin

My dear President Martin: The White House 22 December, 1919

I am very much obliged to you for consulting me about the Woodrow Wilson Chair of Economics and Political Science and asking my permission that it should bear that name. I am more than willing, I am highly honored, that my name should have been connected with it. I have taken pleasure in writing to the Gastonia Church to express my deep appreciation.

With best wishes for Davidson and for the success of the occupants of the chair,

Cordially and sincerely yours, Woodrow Wilson

TLS (NcDaD).

To Mrs. Young[1]

My dear Mrs. Young: [The White House] 22 December, 1919

After having been confined to the house for several months by illness, I am beginning to hope that I may have a vacation in Bermuda, and I am writing to ask if it would be possible for you to let us have Glencove during the months of February and March. I know of no house in which we could be more comfortable or enjoy Bermuda more, and it would be a great joy if you found it convenient to let us have it.

With much respect and pleasantest memories of my former occupancy of Glencove, and with cordial regards to your husband,
Cordially and sincerely yours,   [Woodrow Wilson]

CCL (WP, DLC).
  [1] We have been unable to find Mrs. Young's full name. She was presumably still the owner of Glencove, a house in Paget West, Bermuda, which the Wilsons had rented for a vacation after the election of 1912. There is no reply from Mrs. Young in WP, DLC.

Joseph Patrick Tumulty to Edith Bolling Galt Wilson

Dear Mrs. Wilson: The White House, 22 December, 1919.

I hope you will let the President read the enclosed papers from Secretary Glass,[1] when the opportunity presents itself.
Sincerely,   J P Tumulty

Of course the President would attend if he were able—but he fears that he will not be able to, but will be glad to okeh any arrangments Mr. Glass makes.   EBW

TLS (WP, DLC).
  [1] C. Glass to WW, Dec. 19, 1919, TLS (WP, DLC). Glass reminded Wilson that the Second Pan American Financial Conference was to meet in Washington on January 12, 1920. He hoped that Wilson would confirm the arrangements he had made in a tentative way for Wilson's attendance at the formal opening session of the conference. Glass wanted Wilson to say "a few words of personal greeting" at the meeting. He enclosed a tentative outline of topics to be discussed at the conference. T MS (WP, DLC).

From Alexander Mitchell Palmer

Dear Mr. President: Washington, D. C. December 22, 1919.

In answer to your request, as contained in the note from Mrs. Wilson, I beg to say the Governor of the State is duly authorized, pursuant to Article XVII of the Federal Constitution, by enactment of the state legislature, to temporarily appoint a United States Senator in place of one resigned, in the following States mentioned in your note: Alabama, Delaware, Georgia, Idaho, Illinois, Indiana,

Iowa, Maryland, Michigan, New Hampshire, New Jersey, New Mexico, New York, Ohio, Oklahoma, Pennsylvania, South Dakota, Utah, Vermont, and Missouri; and in Arkansas, if the vacancy occurs within twelve months of an approaching general state and county election; and in Tennessee, if necessary to avoid a vacancy in the office while Congress is in session.

I find no such express authority duly reposed in the Governor in the other states mentioned in your note: California, Colorado, Connecticut, Florida, Kansas, Maine, Massachusetts, Rhode Island, Washington, West Virginia, Wisconsin, Wyoming, and North Dakota. An enactment of the legislature of West Virginia dating from before Article XVII of the Federal Constitution provides for temporary senatorial appointments by the Governor; and the constitutions of 1889 of North Dakota and Wyoming provide for appointment by the Governor to fill a vacancy in any office from any cause; and I am informed that the Governor of Kansas made a senatorial appointment in 1906 without express authority and without objection by the United States Senate. But since Article XVII of the Federal Constitution made a fundamental alteration in the manner of selecting United States Senators, there may be a question whether previous provisions or established practice covering such appointments would be controlling under Article XVII.

In any case, the appointment by the Governor to fill the vacancy is only until a successor may be selected by popular election, for Article XVII of the Federal Constitution provides for the issuance in all cases of writs of election to fill such vacancies; and many of the States have enactments providing for holding such elections at general or special elections.

Very cordially,   A Mitchell Palmer

TLS (WP, DLC).

Alexander Mitchell Palmer to Joseph Patrick Tumulty

Dear Joe: Washington, D. C. December 22, 1919.

I have your note saying that the President desires to appoint Charles A. Talcott, of Utica, to be United States Judge for the Northern District of New York, and that he has directed you to return to me the nomination of Edward Murphy for that place.

I wish you would kindly call to the President's attention the fact that Mr. Talcott was born June 10, 1857, and is, therefore, sixty-two years of age and offends against the rule which the President has insisted upon, that no persons over sixty years of age should be appointed Federal Judge. We have insisted on this rule so many times recently that it will embarrass us greatly if it is broken now. I am quite sure the President is not aware of the fact that the suggested appointment of Mr. Talcott would be in violation of his rule. Will you let me know as soon as possible what the President says about it?   Sincerely yours,   A Mitchell Palmer

The President says he feels the Attorney Gen. is right, & he will with draw the appointment[1]

TLS (J. P. Tumulty Papers, DLC).
[1] EBWhw. Wilson later changed his mind. See AMP to JPT, Jan. 19, 1920.

From Robert Lansing

Dear Mr. President: Washington December 22, 1919.

The American members of The Hague Arbitration Tribunal have been Elihu Root, George Gray, John Bassett Moore and Oscar S. Straus. Mr. Root's term expired in December, 1916. The terms of Judge Gray and Mr. Moore expired last March. Mr. Straus' term will expire in January, 1920.

A recent telegram from our Chargé at The Hague states that the first case to come before the Tribunal since the war was to be submitted on September 28. It therefore becomes important that we should have our full quota of members of the Tribunal. Is it your desire that the same gentlemen be re-appointed for another term of six years?

I am, my dear Mr. President,
        Faithfully yours,   Robert Lansing[1]

TLS (WP, DLC).
[1] "Yes approved by the President. Reappoint the same." EBWhw on JPT to EBW, Dec. 23, 1919, TLS (WP, DLC). Tumulty conveyed this message in JPT to RL, Dec. 24, 1919, TLS (SDR, RG 59, 500A1a/709, DNA).

From the Diary of Josephus Daniels

December Monday 22 1919

Talked to Tumulty. Troubled about the President. Five important missions to be fill[e]d—& unless named soon nobody would regard it as desirable to accept, Reps. might refuse to confirm. Also half a dozen other important places.

Grayson came in. President improving slowly. T[umulty] if he had [died?] when brought the treaty home it would have let him loom larger in history.

From the Diary of Colonel House

December 22, 1919.

Gregory came to dinner last night and remained until nearly eleven o'clock. We reviewed the Washington situation in detail. He tells the same story of chaotic conditions and deprecates the fact that Marshall was not made acting President when Wilson first fell ill. He believes, like every sensible friend of the President, that he has been crucified by trying to perform the functions of his office when totally unfit to do so. Gregory thinks no country except the United States could have survived such a condition without anarchy and revolution. I asked if he thought I was doing right in remaining quiescent. He did not think I could do otherwise.

Sir William Tyrrell came this afternoon and remained for nearly two hours. We reviewed the situation in Washington. He believes the Crauford Stuart incident has been dropped. Grey, he said, is going home fairly satisfied with his venture over here. This is because of the improvement in his eyesight and the assurance that it will not grow worse, and because the trip has revived his interest in people and life. I told him how gratified I was to hear this since I felt responsible for his visit. He said too that Grey would return as Ambassador, he thought, if the President recovered and resumed his relations with me, otherwise he would not come since it would be useless.

Tyrrell said there was much indignation in Washington on account of the situation at the White House. Vice President Marshall told him Thursday that he had been trying to see the President for two months without success and during that time "people had access to him who should be properly in jail." This is a strong statement and I wondered if Tyrrell repeated it accurately. Marshall expressed himself as being thoroughly tired of the delay in ratifying the Treaty and spoke with emphasis when he declared it would certainly be ratified within the next thirty days; that if there was an attempt to hinder it he, Marshall, would break his silence and make a public statement.

Edith Bolling Galt Wilson to Robert Lansing, with Enclosure

Enclosure

My dear Mr. Secretary: The White House [c. Dec. 23, 1919]

I have just sent the following letter to Judge Payne for the President, and he asks me to send you a copy—as a reply to your letter on the subject of the "Imperator" groups of ships.

Faithfully   Edith Bolling Wilson

ALS (SDR, RG 59, 862.85/976, DNA).

E N C L O S U R E

Copy

My dear Judge Payne

The President asks me to send you the enclosed unsigned letter[1] submitted to him by the Sec. of State for his approval—and to say that much to his regret he finds no ground for differing from the Sec. of States' judgement in this important matter.   EBW.[2]

Copy.

EBWhw MS (SDR, RG 59, 862.85/976, DNA).
  [1] Cited in RL to WW, Dec. 20, 1919, n. 1.
  [2] There is an EBWhw draft of her letter to Payne in WP, DLC.

An Executive Order

The White House 23 December, 1919.

It is hereby ordered that on December 24th and December 31st, 1919, four hours, exclusive of time for luncheon, shall constitute a day's work for all per diem employees of the Federal Government and the Government of the District of Columbia, in the said District of Columbia.

Provided, however, that this Order shall not apply to any bureau or office of the Federal Government, or the District of Columbia, or to any of the per diem employees thereof, that may for special public reasons be excepted therefrom by the head of the Department having supervision or control of such bureau or office, or where the same would be inconsistent with the Provisions of existing law.

Woodrow Wilson

TS MS (Letterpress Books, WP, DLC).

From Robert Lansing, with Enclosure

My dear Mr. President: Washington December 23, 1919.

I enclose a memorandum which I ask your authority to read to the Japanese Ambassador.[1] It means the withdrawal of all our forces from Siberia. I heartily recommend it for your approval. The Secretary of War has read it and is in thorough accord. He informs me the MOUNT VERNON is now approaching Vladivostok and is large enough to carry all our troops.

The truth of the matter is the simple fact that the Kolchak Government has utterly collapsed; the armies of the Bolsheviki have advanced into Eastern Siberia, when [where] they are reported to be acting with moderation. The people seem to prefer them to the officers of the Kolchak regime. Further, the Bolshevik army is approaching the region where our soldier[s] are, and contact with them will lead to open hostilities and to many complications. In other words, if we do not withdraw we shall have to wage war against the Bolsheviki.

I ask your early and earnest consideration and your authority to proceed.   Faithfully yours,   Robert Lansing.

TLS (SDR, RG 59, 861.00/6107, DNA).
[1] Kijuro Shidehara.

E N C L O S U R E

December 23, 1919.

The Government of the United States has given the most careful consideration to the subject matter of the communication from the Japanese Government which was read to the Secretary of State by the Japanese Ambassador on the 8th day of December,[1] and which concerned the recent unfavorable development of the military situation with which Admiral Kolchak's forces have been confronted, and which proposes three alternative courses for the Allied and Associated Powers to take.

The Government of the United States agrees that for it to send a reinforcement of sufficient strength and to act on the offensive in cooperation with Anti-Bolsehvik [Bolshevik] forces is impracticable.

The Government of the United States believes that to continue to guard the districts now under Allied military protection, without assuming the offensive against the Red Army is also impracticable, for the reason that an agreement to send reinforcement to such extent as may be required, with a view to maintain the status quo, might involve the Government of the United States in an undertaking of such indefinite character as to be inadvisable. The amount of reinforcement, which it might eventually develop would be necessary for the execution of such an agreement might be so great that the Government of the United States would not feel justified in carrying [it] out. Further than that, such a plan might lead to warlike activity against the Bolsheviki and the Government of the United States has not declared war against them.

The alternative presented by the Government of Japan to avoid direct contact with the troops opposing Admiral Kolchak, and to affect [effect] entire or partial withdrawal of the Allied troops now on Siberian soil appears to the Government of the United States the only reasonable course.

It will be recalled by the Japanese Government that it was agreed that American soldiers cooperate with those of Japan for the purpose to aid the Eastern movement of the Czechoslovaks, to give such aid to the Russians in such efforts toward self-government as they themselves might initiate, and to guard the military supplies which were assembled at Vladivostok and which it was feared might fall into the hands of Germany against the Government of which the United States and Japan were at that time engaged in hostilities. Following the entry of American and Japanese soldiers into Siberia it developed that the maintenance of communication and transportation along the route of the Trans-Siberian and Chinese Eastern railroads was the most effective means of stabilizing the conditions in Siberia and in affording the Russians there an instrumentality necessary for economic and industrial rehabilitation in Siberia, and for furthering such efforts at self-government as the people themselves might initiate. The governments of the United States and of Japan entered into a cordial understanding for the purpose of operating the system of railroads, and did operate it with considerable success.

It seems to the Government of the United States that conditions have now entirely changed. In the first place all the aid and encouragement which it has been possible for the United States to give to the Siberian people in their efforts for self-government have been given. In the second place the Army of the Czechoslovaks, which after remaining for a long time in Central Siberia have now moved Eastward and reached Eastern Siberia. In the meantime arrangements have been made in Paris for the repatriation of these soldiers and plans are now proceeding for their return to their native land. The advance of the armies opposed to the Kolchak forces, which have caused the authorities operating from Omsk to withdraw eastward as far as Lake Baikal, have caused the abandonment of the protection, operation, and control of the Allied forces over that part of the Trans-Siberian railroad which lies west of Lake Baikal. Of those branches which lie east of Lake Baikal, the Chinese Eastern is practically all within Chinese territory. Only a small portion from Manchuli to Chita lies westward of China, and but a very few miles of it are between the eastern border of Manchuria and Vladivostok. The forces operating under the direction of the authorities in control of Trans-Baikal should be numerically sufficient to protect and maintain the operation of that portion of the railroad from Irkutsk to Manchuli. Consequently the proper joint activities of the governments of the United States and of Japan seem, as a result of these developments to have been restricted to a field so small in extent that it seems to the Government of the United States to be inadvisable to continue to maintain its military forces in Siberia for the purpose which grew out of the original arrangement to send troops into Siberia, and it seems to the Government of the United States that the only practical step in the present circumstances is to effect as soon as possible entire withdrawal of its troops from Siberia.

As regards the suggestion of the Government of Japan that the Government of the United States may find it possible to cooperate with them in approaching the governments at London and Paris, the Government of the United States can only answer that the arrangement to cooperate in Siberia was made with the Government of Japan, and the Government of the United States having come to the conclusions which have been expressed and having reached the decision that it is wise to withdraw its troops from Siberia it would seem to be unnecessary to approach the governments at London and at Paris on this subject, but it will be glad to notify those governments of its decision in the form of a communication identical to the one being now expressed to the Government of Japan.

Authorized W.W.[2]

T MS (SDR, RG 59, 861.00/6107, DNA).
[1] An aide-mémoire with the RLhw date of "12/8/19," T MS (SDR, RG 59, 861.00/6109, DNA). It does not appear that Lansing had either sent a copy of this memorandum to Wilson or enclosed one in this letter. An extensively revised version of Lansing's aide-mémoire printed here, was dated January 9, 1920, and sent as an enclosure in RL to K. Shidehara, Jan. 9, 1920. It is printed in FR 1920, III, 487-90.
[2] WWhw.

Joseph Patrick Tumulty to Edith Bolling Galt Wilson

Dear Mrs. Wilson: The White House 23 December 1919.

I received the President's note[1] about the railroad matter.

This morning in discussing with me the advice he had received from the President that the railroads must be returned by December 31st, the Director General told me of a conversation which he had with Judge Brandeis yesterday, in which the Judge was emphatic that it would be seriously injurious to the public interest to return the railroads on the 31st of December, saying that "indeed, in view of the circumstances that had recently developed" he believed that the public would regard the return of the railroads on the thirty-first of the month as highly unjustifiable and unwise.

Sincerely yours,   [J P Tumulty]

CCL (J. P. Tumulty Papers, DLC).

[1] It is missing in both WP, DLC, and the J. P. Tumulty Papers, DLC. However, as will soon be evident, Wilson said in it that the railroads should be returned to private ownership. Hines came at once to the White House (undoubtedly at Tumulty's call) and protested against Wilson's decision. Tumulty then talked with Mrs. Wilson, either in person or over the telephone, and relayed Hines' arguments in favor of returning the railroads on March 1, 1920. The cabinet then met from 11:00 a.m. to 12:45 p.m. to discuss the matter, and Palmer then sent the letter printed below.

Mrs. Wilson's notes of her conversation with Tumulty are an EBWhw MS in WP, DLC.

From the Diary of Josephus Daniels

1919 Tuesday 23 December

Cabinet JPT had note from WW that the RR would go back to their owners Jan 1, as he had stated seven months ago. Hines thought time should be longer and some proposed that Prest be asked again to extend it. Not in face of his plain statement. Grayson said he refused to even talk RR. Proclamation to be sent over with date for turning over left blank. General opinion was that 30 days after signing proclamation should elapse before RRs go back to owners.

From Alexander Mitchell Palmer, with Enclosures

Dear Mr. President: Washington, D. C. December 23, 1919.

I attach hereto draft of proclamation relinquishing the railroads from federal control and a separate proclamation relinquishing the property of the American Railway Express Company from federal control.[1]

I also enclose a letter from Mr. Hines, presenting a new and important phase of the question. In order that you may give consideration to the views of Mr. Hines and so that you may decide whether seven days' notice seems sufficient under all the circumstances, at the suggestion of the Cabinet, which considered the matter this morning, I am leaving blank the date for the proclamations to take effect.

Faithfully yours,   A Mitchell Palmer

[1] A T MS (WP, DLC). It provided for the relinquishment of federal control over the American Express Company, with blanks for the dates. Mrs. Wilson inserted "first" and "March" in the blanks later in the day.

E N C L O S U R E   I

From Walker Downer Hines

Dear Mr. President: Washington December 23, 1919

In accordance with advice which I received from the White House this morning, I inclose draft of Proclamation relinquishing the railroads from Federal control and separate Proclamation relinquishing the property of the American Railway Express Company from Federal control.

Without discussing the merits of virtually immediate relinquishment, let me put before you certain important considerations relating to the vital question whether seven days' notice from the date of the Proclamation is reasonable and adequate.

While your message last May[1] stated that the railroads would be handed back to their owners at the end of the calendar year, and while since then I have repeatedly stated that you had not qualified that announcement, it is a fact that all interested classes—railroad employes, security holders, railroad executives and the general public—believed that the progress made toward legislation at the end of November, coupled with the abnormal conditions created by the coal strike (which cannot be readjusted by January 1st) would result in your weighing, in the light of those developments, the reasons for and against immediate relinquishment. This impression was strengthened by the statement in your message to Congress on December 2nd that you would address Congress at a later date in the matter of the railroads and the readjustment of their affairs growing out of Federal control. Senate leaders repeatedly asked me, following your message on December 2nd, as to whether in fact the railroads would be relinquished at January 1st, stating that if so, they would, prior to the recess of Congress, pass temporary legislation to protect the situation. Since I had submitted to you a full report with recommendation that the roads be not relinquished, and since I understood you were holding this matter for further consideration with a view to sending your additional message to Congress, I was not in position to say anything publicly except that I had submitted the entire matter for your consideration. Undoubtedly this likewise strengthened the impression that the question was being reviewed by you in the light of the recent rapid developments. This impression became more pronounced as the Senate progressed with its Bill. (My view of the matter that I could not give positive notice of relinquishment at December 31st was confirmed by the fact that the Cabinet asked for my views on the subject and on December 12th sent you the recommendation of a majority of its members that the public interest required that relinquishment should not take place until March 1st.[2] This, of course, was not made public but I mention it as emphasizing the situation which prevented my undertaking to speak as to the date on which relinquishment would happen.) When Congress took a recess last Saturday, after both Houses had passed Bills and appointed a Conference Committee to consider them, I am satisfied the fact is that all interested parties, including Congress, believed that a new notice would be given prior to relinquishment and did not regard the matter as finally disposed of by the statement made by you in your message last May.

Having lived in the atmosphere of this situation through the recent weeks filled with so much discussion and speculation, I know, and I would be false to my trust to you if I did not state that knowledge, that all interests involved would regard a Proclamation now issued, with only seven days' notice of relinquishment, as being a notice too short to protect the situation. The employes have been earnestly hopeful that Congress would yet take affirmative action prolonging control. Congress is in recess until January 5th and, of course, cannot in the meantime adopt temporary legislation. Such legislation would undoubtedly have perpetuated existing rates pending legislation, whereas a return, prior to the adoption of even temporary legislation, is likely to cause serious uncertainty as to the legality of existing intrastate rates which are, of course, much higher than the rates established prior to Federal control by State authority, in many instances by the Legislatures themselves.

I therefore respectfully suggest that any Proclamation now issued should give not less than thirty days' notice of the date upon which Federal control will terminate, and for this reason I submit the Proclamation with the date of relinquishment left blank. Of course it would be far more convenient to have the date correspond with the beginning of a month.

Let me further suggest a way in which the railroads could be handed back to their owners at the end of the calendar year, and at the same time a month's notice be given before the protection of Federal control shall wholly terminate. That way is to issue the Proclamation effective at 12.01 A.M. February 1st, 1920, and for you or me at the same time to make an announcement that effective 12.01 A.M. January 1st, the railroads will be handed back to their owners, but will be operated by the owners as agents for the Government during the month of January, at the expiration of which time Federal control shall cease as specified in the Proclamation. This course would meet with general approval, has been frequently suggested, and undoubtedly would facilitate the transition which at best will be exceedingly complicated. It would entirely remove the feeling that Federal control had been terminated without adequate notice.

I cannot too strongly state my conviction that the termination of Federal control on January 1st, in advance of the adoption of even temporary legislation, will create conditions of a most chaotic character, both financially and in an administrative sense.

While my organization has been working steadily throughout the summer and fall to prepare for a complete termination of Federal control at January 1st, the task has been so enormous, involving perhaps the greatest accounting problem that has ever arisen, that it has been impossible to get matters into satisfactory shape for a transfer at January 1st. The difficulties thus incident to winding up the affairs on that date will constitute an added reason for the feeling that a somewhat longer period ought to be allowed. The preservation of Federal control through the month of January, either with the railroads turned back to their owners for operation or not, would enormously improve this difficult situation.

I have devoted the foregoing discussion exclusively to what is reasonable notice, in view of the recent developments, and have not undertaken to rediscuss the general merits which I have presented in my previous letters and which have led me to express the unqualified opinion that the public interest makes it needful and desirable to retain Federal control for the time being, without specifying any date of relinquishment.

Cordially and sincerely yours,   Walker D Hines

TLS (WP, DLC).
[1] Wilson's special message to Congress printed at May 20, 1919, Vol. 59.
[2] RL to WW, Dec. 12, 1919.

E N C L O S U R E   I I

[Dec. 24, 1919]

By the President of the United States of America
A PROCLAMATION
Relinquishment of Federal Control of Railroads and Systems of Transportation.

WHEREAS, in the exercise of authority committed to me by law, I have heretofore, through the Secretary of War, taken possession of and have, through the Director General of Railroads, exercised control over certain railroads, systems of transportation and property appurtenant thereto or connected therewith; including systems of coastwise and inland transportation, engaged in general transportation and owned or controlled by said railroads or systems of transportation; including also terminals, terminal companies and terminal associations, sleeping and parlor cars, private cars and private car lines, elevators, warehouses, telegraph and telephone lines, and all other equipment and appurtenances commonly used upon or operated as a part of such railroads and systems of transportation; and

WHEREAS, I now deem it needful and desirable that all railroads, systems of transportation and property now under such Federal control, be relinquished therefrom;

NOW, THEREFORE, under authority of Section 14 of the Federal Control Act approved March 21, 1918, and of all other powers and provisions of law thereto me enabling, I, Woodrow Wilson, President of the United States, do hereby relinquish from Federal control, effective the first[1] day of March[2] 1920, at 12:01 o'clock A.M. all railroads, systems of transportation and property, of whatsoever kind, taken or held under such Federal control and not heretofore relinquished, and restore the same to the possession and control of their respective owners.

Walker D. Hines, Director General of Railroads, or his successor in office, is hereby authorized and directed, through such agents and agencies as he may determine, in any manner not inconsistent with the provisions of said Act of March 21, 1918, to adjust, settle and close all matters, including the making of agreements for compensation, and all questions and disputes of whatsoever nature arising out of or incident to Federal control, until otherwise provided by proclamation of the President or by Act of Congress; and generally to do and perform, as fully in all respects as the President is authorized to do, all and singular the acts and things necessary or proper in order to carry into effect this proclamation and the relinquishment of said railroads, systems of transportation and property.

For the purposes of accounting and for all other purposes, this proclamation shall become effective on the first[3] day of March[4] 1920, at 12:01 o'clock A.M.

IN WITNESS WHEREOF, I have hereunto set my hand and caused the Seal of the United States to be affixed.

Done by the President, through Newton D. Baker, Secretary of War, in the District of Columbia, this 24th day of December the year of our Lord[5] 1919 and of the Independence of the United States the One Hundred and Forty Fourth.

Woodrow Wilson

TS MS (WP, DLC).
  [1] EBWhw.
  [2] *Idem.*
  [3] *Idem.*
  [4] *Idem.*
  [5] "24th," "December," and the second "19" of "1919" written in an unknown hand.

From Frank Lyon Polk

My dear Mr. President: Washington December 23, 1919.

I arrived in Washington last night, and wish to take this opportunity of expressing my delight at the good reports I hear as to your steady improvement. I suppose it is hardly necessary for me to tell you how keenly anxious everyone abroad was for news, and how devoutly thankful they all were to read from time to time the encouraging reports from Washington.

Of course, I shall be only too glad of an opportunity to see you and report, but quite understand that there is really very little I can tell you, as I am sure you have probably read the reports we have sent over, and probably Mrs. Wilson and your doctors do not wish you to waste your time with unnecessary visitors. If, however, you would care to see me, or care to have me report on any particular point in writing, I am entirely at your disposal.

I was charged by Clemenceau particularly to express to you his good wishes.

Please remember me to Mrs. Wilson, and believe me,

Yours faithfully,   Frank L. Polk

TLS (WP, DLC).

A Press Release

STATEMENT BY SECRETARY TUMULTY:

[Dec. 24, 1919]

Last May in his message to the Congress the President announced that the railroads would be handed over to their owners at the end of this calendar year. It is now necessary to act by issuing the proclamation. In the present circumstances, no agreement having yet been reached by the two Houses of the Congress in respect to legislation on the subject, it becomes necessary in the public interest to allow a reasonable time to elapse between the issuing of the proclamation and the date of its actually taking effect. The President is advised that the railroad and express companies are not organized to make it possible for them to receive and manage their properties if actually turned over to them on December 31st, and if this were done it would raise financial and legal complications of a serious character. The railroad and express companies should be given ample opportunity to adequately prepare for the resumption of their business under the control and management of their own stockholders, directors and officers. Therefore, the transfer of possession back to the railroad companies will become effective at 12:01 A.M., March 1, 1920.

Approved   Woodrow Wilson[1]

T MS (J. P. Tumulty Papers, DLC).
  [1] Stamped signature.

Edith Bolling Galt Wilson to Robert Lansing

My dear Mr. Secretary: The White House 24 December, 1919

The President asks me to say that he does not think it necessary that the call of the conference should be delayed until we have appointed our delegates,[1] though he does agree with you that our delegates should be appointed as soon as possible, in order that they may make such preparations for the conference as you suggest. He is clear in his judgment that the delegates should be headed by the Postmaster General, and that Admiral Benson and Mr. Walter Rogers should be among the delegates. He thinks that these three gentlemen, when appointed, should suggest the technical advisors. He asks me to add that if he should act upon your suggestion that all the governmental dealings with questions of communication should be assembled in a single Department, he feels that that Department should be the Postoffice.

Sincerely yours,   Edith Bolling Wilson

TLS (SDR, RG 59, 574D1/150, DNA).
  ¹ Mrs. Wilson was replying to RL to WW, Dec. 23, 1919, CCL (SDR, RG 59, 574D1/
13, DNA), about the appointment of the United States delegates to the conference on
international communications. Lansing suggested the appointment, among others, of
Admiral Benson and Walter Stowell Rogers and the advisability of giving one department responsibility for "general control of the situation."

From Robert Lansing

My dear Mr. President—   Washington December 24, 1919.

Permit me to send you my sincerest good wishes for Christmas
and the approaching New Year. It has been with a thankful heart
that I have learned of the continued improvement in your health,
and I earnestly hope that your full recovery is not far distant. The
whole nation has watched with anxious concern the progress of
your illness and have expressed in no uncertain voice its relief and
joy over the assurance that early in the coming year you will be
able again to assume entire guidence [guidance] of the affairs of
state as you have in past years.

I have received many letters of inquiry and sympathy concerning you and it has been a gratification to be able to reply to the
writers that all is going well.

With the season's greeting to you and Mrs. Wilson from Mrs.
Lansing and me, and with the continued desire to releive [relieve]
you of every responsibility that I can in these days of grave problems I am, my dear Mr. President,

                    Faithfully yours   Robert Lansing.

ALS (WP, DLC).

Frank Lyon Polk to Joseph Patrick Tumulty

Dear Joe: Washington December 26, 1919.

I know everyone is after the President urging action on various
matters, and I am going to try to be merciful, but there is one matter I really wish, if possible, you could bring to his attention, and
that is the question of the recognition of Costa Rica.

Apparently everything has worked out as we could wish. Tinoco
has gone. They have a government there now which is strictly constitutional. I am afraid that if we delay recognition, the strength of
this government may be seriously undermined, and I am also
afraid that if we delay recognition, our friends on the Hill who are
friendly to Tinoco might try to find some way of being disagreeable
to this present government.

The reason I bring this up is that if we could recognize them now, we could ask them to send delegates to the Financial Congress to be held in January. Everyone has been asked, including Mexico, except Costa Rica. We would have just time to get an invitation down there and get a response, if the President could give this matter consideration.

I would not urge this matter if there were anything, as far as I could find out, that would require an investigation on his part, as I naturally would not wish to burden him with anything that was controversial.   Yours faithfully,   Frank L Polk[1]

TLS (WP, DLC).
    [1] JPT to EBW, Dec. 30, 1919, TLI (WP, DLC): "Will you look over the enclosed, and lay it before the President when an opportunity presents itself?" Neither Wilson nor Mrs. Wilson replied to Polk's letter.

From Albert, King of the Belgians

Brussels Received December 27, 1919.

On the occasion of your birthday the Queen and myself congratulate you heartily. We form the most sincere wishes for the complete restoration of your precious health.   Albert.

T telegram (WP, DLC).

To Albert, King of the Belgians

[The White House] 27 December 1919.

May I not express to Your and to Her Majesty the Queen my warm appreciation of your birthday message and wish for you both from Mrs. Wilson and myself the happiest blessings of the season.
Woodrow Wilson.[1]

T telegram (Letterpress Books, WP, DLC).
    [1] There is an EBWhw draft of this telegram in WP, DLC.

From George V

London, December 27, 1919.

On the occasion of your birthday, Mr. President, I hasten to offer to you my cordial congratulations together with my earnest good wishes for your welfare and happiness and for your full and speedy restoration to health   George R.I.

T telegram (WP, DLC).

From the Diary of Colonel House

December 27, 1919.

We spent a delightful Christmas. The weather was good, we were all well and it has been a long while since conditions were so conducive to contentment and happiness.

Lansing came in unexpectedly this morning and remained for an hour or more. He unburdened himself as to conditions in Washington. He knows no more about the President's condition or state of mind than I do—hardly as much because his sources of information do not seem to be as close. He declared his intention of running the State Department as he thought best and of making decisions without reference to the President because of the uselessness of such a procedure. He said the matters he referred to him came back from Mrs. Wilson with notations in her own handwriting. He believes the President is much sicker than the public is led to believe. He does not think the President is writing any of the papers purporting to come from him. Lansing himself wrote the Thanksgiving Proclamation,[1] and it came back unchanged with the President's signature, I understood him to say, on the top instead of at the end. The signature was almost illegible.

Lansing made several attempts to get the President to act upon some of the foreign appointments. Word finally came back from Mrs. Wilson that the President would not consider these appointments until he was entirely well. He confirmed the Vice President's dissatisfaction over the trend of affairs. We discussed the Mexican situation. He says in the Jenkins matter he did more than send a peremptory note demanding Jenkins' release. He told the Mexican Ambassador if he was not released, we would send troops at once into Mexico.

[1] It is printed at Nov. 4, 1919, Vol. 63.

To George V

[The White House] December 28, 1919.

Your thoughtful and cordial congratulations for my birthday are warmly appreciated and Mrs. Wilson joins me in wishing for you and for Her Majesty the Queen every happiness in the new year.
Woodrow Wilson.

T telegram (Letterpress Books, WP, DLC).

Edith Bolling Galt Wilson to Thomas Davies Jones[1]

My dear Mr. Jones: The White House Dec. 28, 1919

This afternoon the President asked me to write you for him and *dictated the following—*

"Will you permit me to nominate you Secretary of the Interior? and thus complete my official family and fulfill my dearest birthday wish"—

I am sure you have seen from the papers that Mr. Lane wants to resign, and is only waiting until my husband is better before making it definite. I am sure you feel that with you at the head of this Department the President would rest secure knowing your splendid ability and loyalty. Just now he needs this assurance, for he has so many things that necessarily must come directly to him, that he longs to have you, and those like you, to depend on, while he is convalescing

I am writing you frankly, because I know I can, and will you be good enough to let him hear as soon as you can—for it will greatly relieve his anxiety.

Please address the letter to me, as otherwise it would be opened in the office.

We send you every good wish for 1920—and the sincere hope that you are quite well. I have written in the midst of interruptions so please pardon repetition.

                              Faithfully   Edith Bolling Wilson

ALS (Mineral Point, Wisc., Public Library).
[1] Wilson's old friend, former trustee of Princeton University, president of the Mineral Point Zinc Company and of the New Jersey Zinc Company. Jones' reply to this letter is missing; however, he did not accept.

Edith Bolling Galt Wilson to John Wesley Wescott[1]

My dear Judge Wescott: The White House [c. Dec. 28, 1919]

Thank you for your thoughtful suggestion that you will let us read what you have written about my husband.[2] Naturally anything connected with him claims the first interest from me, and when it is from the pen of a warm friend, as he counts you, it needs nothing to stimulate my desire to read it.

The President wants to send his appreciation with mine, and we both wish for you the happiest New Year.

I feel that you can feel reassured as to my husband's improvement, for it is gratifying and steady—but slow, owing to the nature of all nervous troubles. The doctors tell me that to have gone down so far to the "bottom of the hill" his assent [ascent] thus far is marvelous so we feel very happy about him.

Looking forward to a glimpse of your "temple," believe me

Faithfully yours   Edith Bolling Wilson

ALS (J. W. Wescott Coll., NjP).
    [1] Wilson's old friend from Camden, N. J., who had nominated him for the presidency at the Democratic national conventions of 1912 and 1916. After serving as Attorney General of New Jersey from 1914 to 1919, Wescott had returned to the practice of law in Camden and Philadelphia.
    [2] Wescott's letter is missing. However, he had probably promised to send Wilson a draft of John W. Wescott, *Woodrow Wilson's Eloquence* [Camden, N. J., 1922].

From Joseph Patrick Tumulty

Dear Governor: The White House 28 December, 1919

I send you my warmest greetings on your sixty-third birthday. So much has happened in the year that has passed that it seems hard to realize that twelve months have gone by since you went abroad. It has been the hardest year of your life and one that will live in history. It may take time but you will be vindicated. Slowly the world is recognizing that the great plan for a partnership of some kind between nations is the only hope for a settled life among the peoples of the world. You have made an admirable effort for liberalism. It is not your fault that for the moment the forces of hysterical reaction seem to have the upper hand. But it is a specious hold they have, and when the after-the-war clouds of confusion pass, the country will see clearly that the hand that must guide America must apply the noble principle of equality and freedom which you have set forth. Be of good cheer, Governor, the clouds are going to pass and the memory of your work will stand as an everlasting monument to liberalism and the highest ideals of Christianity.   Faithfully,   Tumulty

TLS (WP, DLC).

Joseph Patrick Tumulty to Edith Bolling Galt Wilson, with Enclosure

Dear Mrs. Wilson: The White House 29 December 1919.

Will you kindly read the enclosed letter from Honorable Breckenridge Long, rela[ting] to Mr. Hapgood's resignation as Minister at Copenhagen? I hope this can be done.

Sincerely yours,   Tumulty

The President says please have the State Dept. accept Mr. Hapgood's resignation.   E.B.W.

E N C L O S U R E

Breckinridge Long to Joseph Patrick Tumulty

My dear Mr. Tumulty: Washington December 27, 1919

Mr. Norman Hapgood, during November, telegraphed to the President his resignation as Minister at Copenhagen.[1] The Senate adjourned without having confirmed it.[2] Mr. Hapgood finds himself in a very embarrassing position, and has just written me that he would like to be free in order that he might reply to the stories which Colonel Harvey and others have circulated about him.[3] He will be in Washington on Monday morning. No one here, of course, is authorized to accept his resignation, and I think he would appreciate it if the President would authorize the Secretary of State to notify him that his resignation is accepted.[4]

I have talked this over with Mr. Polk, and, because of the urgency of the matter, am asking you to take it up with the President. I think we owe at least this to Mr. Hapgood, and I know it would do my heart good to have him take a fall out of Colonel Harvey.

Will you let me know if possible some time Monday morning if anything can be done so that I can be guided in my conversation with him.

I am, my dear Mr. Tumulty,
Very sincerely yours,   Breckinridge Long

TLS (WP, DLC).

[1] N. Hapgood to WW, Nov. 16, 1919, T telegram, enclosed in RL to WW, Nov. 17, 1919, TLS, both in WP, DLC. Hapgood explained the situation as follows: "The period of my interim appointment runs out with the present session of Congress. No action has been taken by the Senate Committee on Foreign Affairs. Certain members of that Committee have raised the issue that I am a Bolshevik. My opinions on Russia have been widely known for two years, and have not changed. I do not wish to involve the administration in my personal controversies, especially at a time when so many more important things are at stake, and also at a time when all your friends wish to save your strength for these larger issues. Therefore, with the highest appreciation and thanks, I take the liberty of requesting that I be not reappointed but be allowed to return to America." Lansing asked Wilson to indicate the nature of the reply he wished to have sent to Hapgood's telegram. Apparently, no reply was sent at all.

Hapgood and his family left Copenhagen for the United States on about December 5 and arrived in New York on December 23. The State Department stated repeatedly during this period that Hapgood had not resigned or been recalled but was returning to the United States at his own volition to report to the government on conditions in Soviet Russia. *New York Times*, Dec. 5, 6, 20, and 24, 1919.

[2] That is, the Senate had adjourned on November 19, without confirming Hapgood's appointment as Minister to Denmark.

[3] "Minister Hapgood Returns," *Harvey's Weekly*, II (Dec. 20, 1919), 6-7. In this editorial, George B. M. Harvey asserted that Hapgood was in fact returning home to explain to the Senate Foreign Relations Committee "his own activities as a plenipotentiary of Messrs. Lenine and Trotzky, and to tell to what extent and by what authority he has

misused the American Legation at Copenhagen as a trading-post for the Soviet Government." Harvey also alleged that, before sailing for Copenhagen in late May, Hapgood had visited Wall Street. "There," Harvey continued, "he sought an interview with a group of men representing great interests, and invited them to finance the Bolsheviki. He explained that his post at Copenhagen, in such close proximity to Bolshevik headquarters, would present ideal opportunities for dealing with Messrs. Trotzky and Lenine, and that the business men might rest assured that their venture would mean much profit. Luckily for America, if unluckily for the American Minister to Denmark, Mr. Hapgood chose the wrong group of bankers. They were Americans. Of course they were shocked at the proposal, and spurned his repeated overtures."

[4] The State Department issued a public statement on December 29 which revealed that Hapgood was no longer in the diplomatic service. On the following day, Hapgood gave out a detailed statement in rebuttal of Harvey's charges. *New York Times*, Dec. 30 and 31, 1919.

Edith Bolling Galt Wilson to Frank Lyon Polk

My dear Mr. Polk: The White House [c. Dec. 29, 1919]

Your letter to the President gave him much pleasure and he joins me in a hearty welcome

Warm wishes for the coming year, believe me

Faithfully   Edith Bolling Wilson

ALS (F. L. Polk Papers, CtY).

From Alexandra

Sandringham, Dec. 29, 1919.

With all my heart I pray God to bless you to-day on your birthday and give back your health and restore you in full to the benefit of the whole world and God grant us soon an everlasting peace. Remember me kindly to your wife.   Alexandra.

T telegram (WP, DLC).

From the Desk Diary of Robert Lansing

Monday Dec 29 [1919]

Tumulty phoned much disturbed that Prest was not to see Grey. Hoover at W H phoned asking me to see Mrs. Wilson at noon. . . .

Conferred with Mrs. Wilson on Prest seeing Lord Grey and Prest's offense at Grey's failure to send Major Stuart home. Tried to smooth matters over & have Prest see Grey. Urged on her necessity of immediate recognition of Costa Rican Govt. 12-12:40

From Robert Lansing

My dear Mr. President: Washington [Dec. 30, 1919]

I am enclosing herewith a formal engrossed letter to the President of the Republic of Finland[1] in response to a letter which he addressed to you upon his assumption of office. There is enclosed also an authorization to me to cause to be affixed the seal of the United States.[2]

In regard to this I should like to add that we extend to Finland only a de facto recognition. England and France and some of the other governments, as it now developes, without consultation with us and without our knowledge, have extended to Finland a recognition de jure. This leaves us in the situation of being the only important government in the world which has not recognized the de jure existence of Finland. However, I am inclined to think that the phraseology of our original recognition[3] can be interpreted to mean de jure recognition. As the date of this recognition was anterior to the dates of the recognitions of the other governments concerned, I feel that we could now simply assume that our original communication was a recognition de jure.

If you will sign this letter to the President of Finland I should like, after having transmitted it, to incorporate its text in a communication which I propose to send to the Minister of Finland in response to a note recently received from him[4] in which he discusses the nature of our recognition.

I endorse the extension to Finland of full recognition because of the encouragement it would give that Government, not only by way of strengthening their authority in their internal political operations, but as a means which will contribute to building up in a border state a substantial organization in opposition to the radicalism of Russia.   Faithfully yours,   Robert Lansing.

TLS (WP, DLC).
  [1] Kaarlo Juho Ståhlberg, who had assumed office on July 25, 1919.
  [2] A typed notation by the White House staff on a separate page reads as follows: "Letter and Warrant to affix seal signed and sent to State Dept. Jan. 3, 1920—dated Dec. 30, 1919."
  [3] The United States had extended *de facto* recognition to the Finnish government on May 7, 1919.
  [4] Armas Herman Saastamoinen to RL, Dec. 20, 1919, printed in *FR 1919*, II, 224-26.

To Alexandra

[The White House, Dec. 31, 1919]

Your gracious birthday message has warmed my heart and brightened the day for me. Mrs. Wilson joins me in wishing for you & yours health and happiness in the New Year

Woodrow Wilson

EBWhw MS (WP, DLC).

From James Cardinal Gibbons

Baltimore, Md., Jan. 1, 1920.

From my sick bed I send you my heartfelt thanks for your solicitude in my regard[1] and I pray God may bring you every blessing in this New Year.   Cardinal Gibbons.

T telegram (WP, DLC).
[1] Wilson's message is missing in WP, DLC, and in the Gibbons Papers, Baltimore Cathedral Archives.

To Edward, Prince of Wales

[The White House] 1 January 1920.

Your message[1] assuring me of your good wishes opens the New Year most happily. Mrs. Wilson joins me in appreciation and the hope that 1920 will be a very glad year for you.

Woodrow Wilson.

T telegram (Letterpress Books, WP, DLC).
[1] It is missing.

To Grace Linzee Revere Gross Osler

[The White House] 1 January 1920.

May I not express my heartfelt sympathy with you in the loss of your distinguished husband.[1] His death is a great loss to science and to humanity.   Woodrow Wilson.

T telegram (Letterpress Books, WP, DLC).
[1] Sir William Osler, Regius Professor of Medicine at Oxford University, who had died on December 29, 1919. Wilson had come to know Osler well during his annual sojourns in Baltimore to lecture at The Johns Hopkins University from 1889 to 1897. Osler had been at that time Professor of the Principles and Practice of Medicine at the Hopkins See WW to EAW, Aug. 23, 1908, n. 1, Vol. 18.

From Joseph Patrick Tumulty

Dear Governor: [The White House] 2 January, 1920

I know you will believe me sincere when I tell you that in my opinion we cannot longer adhere to the position we have taken in the matter of the Treaty. The people of the country have the impression that you will not consent to the dotting of an "i" or the crossing of a "t." In fact, these words have appeared in nearly every report of the interview Senator Hitchcock had with you at the White House. The result is that the country is slowly coming to the belief that we will accept no offer of compromise, even as to interpretative resolutions.

The plan I would propose will not in its final result be at all inconsistent with the larger plan you already have in mind. Briefly, it is this: That you take the proposed substitute reservations offered by Mr. Hitchcock in the Senate on November fifteenth[1] and make them your own, with the necessary modifications—adding whatever you think necessary to complete them. For instance, you might add a clause with reference to mandates—that no mandate shall be accepted by the United States without the consent of Congress. Senator Hitchcock informs me that before he introduced these reservations he consulted you and that they met with your approval. I have looked them over and attach hereto a copy of them.

Frankly, the only objection to a plan like this is that we have yielded to the reservation idea and that you have given up the position which you took in the statement issued by you on Sunday, three weeks ago.[2] But therein lies the very virtue of the thing I propose. It would force the mild reservationists to come to your side and would put upon Lodge the whole responsibility of defeating the Treaty, and thus you would be in a position to go to the country in the way that you have in mind. In proposing these reservations, you could make a public statement outlining your reasons for doing so, and the country will applaud your effort by a reasonable compromise to reach a settlement. If you will look over the Hitchcock reservations, you will find that they follow the terms of your Denver speech[3] and the other speeches you made in the West.   Sincerely,   [J P Tumulty]

CCL (J. P. Tumulty Papers, DLC).
    [1] They are printed in the Enclosure with GMH to EBW, Nov. 13, 1919.
    [2] Wilson's statement is printed at Dec. 14, 1919.
    [3] Printed at Sept. 25, 1919, Vol. 63.

From the Diary of Colonel House

January 2, 1920.

We gave a dinner at the Colony Club last night in honor of Lord Grey. There were fifty-eight guests. I took out Madame Clemenceau-Jaquemaire,[1] Clemenceau's daughter, and made her with Grey one of the guests of honor. I append a list of the guests.

Grey came this morning and we had a long and final conference before he sails for England. He sails tomorrow. He claims to have no feeling because he was not received, either directly or indirectly, at the White House, but I can see that he is chagrined and I do not wonder. If Mrs. Wilson had shown him some attention, even if he had not seen the President, it would have made matters better.

He said he had two appointments with Tumulty and both times Tumulty failed to come. Tumulty excused himself by saying he had to be at the Capitol on some mission for the President. The fact that such a man as Tumulty should have thought it possible to treat anyone of Lord Grey's distinction in such a way is beyond belief. Mrs. Wilson, too, seems not to realize that there has been no visitor to America during the President's two administrations of Grey's distinction, yet no one has been treated with such discourtesy.

I have a lurking suspicion that one of the causes for this action is because of his friendship for me, although the Crauford Stuart-Baruch-Grayson incident is the main cause. Nevertheless, it is a fact that this great statesman and friend of the United States has been treated in a manner which should cause every American to blush with shame. There is no man in all the world more modest, more unselfish and none I have met with finer courage or greater nobility of soul.

[1] Clemenceau's oldest child, Madeleine, born in 1870, widow of Numa Jacquemaire, a lawyer of Paris. Mme. Jacquemaire maintained a famous literary salon in Paris and was herself a writer of some prominence.

From Robert Lansing

My dear Mr. President: Washington January 3, 1919 [1920].

As you are aware our relations with Mexico have been for several months considerably strained over various attempts against the lives or persons of American citizens in that country and over the efforts of the Mexican government to oust or confiscate the rights of Americans lawfully acquired to property in Mexico, particularly the right of oil companies to develop oil lands held by them under lease or otherwise. While the acuteness of the Jenkins case has for the moment passed, other assaults have come to notice and I do not believe that the security of life in Mexico has been or will for long be advanced. In respect to property rights there appears to be no amelioration of the policy of President Carranza to claim the right of the Government to nationalize the sub-surface deposits without compensation to owners of rights therein.

In view of the acuteness of our pending difficulties with Mexico as a whole, I propose for your consideration or approval the following plan:

(a) That the American Ambassador be instructed to return to Mexico and to make the following proposals to President Carranza:

(1) That the Mexican Government formally agree to take more effective means for protection for the lives, rights and property of Americans in Mexico than the means now employed,

(2) That the Mexican Government agree, by treaty, to constitute a joint American-Mexican Commission, or as an alternative, a Mixed Commission with a third party Umpire, to adjudicate all claims of American citizens against Mexico, and all claims of Mexican citizens against the United States,

(3) That the Mexican Government agree, by treaty, to submit to the Hague Tribunal the question of the effect of the Mexican Constitution of 1917, and the laws, decrees and regulations issued thereunder or during the prior revolution upon all property rights of American citizens acquired in Mexico prior to the promulgation of this Constitution, and that pending the final decision of this question by such arbitral tribunal the Mexican Government will suspend forthwith the enforcement of all laws, decrees and administrative or judicial proceedings directly or indirectly based upon the new Constitution or upon revolutionary laws or decrees affecting such previously acquired rights; provided, however, that the Mexican Government may continue to collect, as at present, production and export taxes which are not prohibitive in nature and which apply to all foreigners equally and without discrimination. That the two Governments agree that the decision of the said arbitral tribunal as to the question of all such previously acquired property rights including the title to the sub-soil deposits and the right to develop them or to reduce them to possession shall be binding and conclusive.

(b) That the American Ambassador be authorized and instructed to await a reasonable time, say four weeks, after the foregoing proposals have been presented to President Carranza for their acceptance in principle, and that if they are not accepted within such reasonable period of time, he is to notify the Mexican Government formally that, unless the above proposals shall be accepted by it within a further period of one week, the United States Government will be forced reluctantly to the conclusion that further efforts to settle the pending controversies between the two Governments by diplomatic means are hopeless, and that the Ambassador is authorized to ask for his passports, to turn over the care of American interests in Mexico to the diplomatic representative of some foreign Power to be designated by the Secretary of State of the United States, and to return forthwith to the United States.

My observations on the foregoing plan follow.

On the point of protection of Americans in Mexico, the Mexican Government will undoubtedly refer to our embargo on arms and ammunition If so, I would suggest that the American Ambassador be authorized to agree, in case the above proposals are accepted by Mexico, that the United States will immediately lift the embargo as to all arms and ammunition which have been purchased and held in storage in this country by the Mexican Government, and that the Ambassador be further authorized to promise orally that if conditions with respect to the protection of American citizens improve in consequence of the lifting of the embargo mentioned, further supplies may be purchased in this country by the Mexican Government for purposes of "pacification" and exported from the United States.

As to the question of submitting to the Hague Tribunal the effect of the Constitution of 1917 and the revolutionary laws, it may be said that if, as the Mexican Government contends, Americans did not acquire any rights in the sub-soil deposits under then existing Mexican laws, it is clear that the Mexican Government can adopt such laws and regulations as it chooses with regard to these deposits. If, on the other hand, American citizens did acquire legal rights in these deposits they should be protected from direct or indirect attempts to give retroactive effect to the theory of national ownership enunciated in the new Constitution and underlying certain pre-Constitutional decrees of General Carranza during the revolution.

An objection to making these proposals to Mexico is that it will afford the Mexican Government an opportunity to engage in a prolonged diplomatic discussion and argument, but in my opinion the case should not admit of such dilatory treatment, and five weeks seems to me ample for the Mexican Government to decide whether it will accept the proposals. If it does not accept them, I think it will be clear to the entire world that the Mexican Government is indifferent to its obligations as a civilized State, and that its President is determined to put through his policy of nationalization without regard to the rights of foreigners involved.

As to the effect of the severance of diplomatic relations, it is fair to say that many people believe intervention must follow as a matter of course; though admitting this as a possibility, I do not think it is a necessary consequence for the American consuls and American citizens will remain in Mexico and our diplomatic representations which have been lately entirely disregarded and ignored will be made by the diplomatic representative of a friendly American government [a]nd will probably be more effective in the circumstances than our own representations at present. Moreover, it is probable that the severance of relations would check the hostile attitude of the Carranza Government towards Americans. In fact it is possible that severance of relations would have the effect finally of eliminating President Carranza as the head of the Mexican Government by the action of the Mexicans themselves, as the election of his successor will take place next June; although Carranza has a year yet to serve as President. Finally, should relations be severed now we will be in a position to renew diplomatic relations with a new President upon an entirely just basis and upon such conditions and assurances as may be deemed advisable. I understand that candidates for the Presidency are in practically all instances convinced that the Carranza attitude toward the United States has been disastrous for Mexico, and many patriotic Mexican people believe that the novel provisions of the new Constitution are a great obstacle to economic progress to Mexico and her credit abroad, and that the new Constitution will be amended.

In conclusion, I desire to say that I am absolutely convinced that it will be useless to make these proposals to Mexico unless our Ambassador has full authority to terminate his mission in the event of a non-acceptance by Mexico within the time specified in his instructions. I may add however that I have reason to believe that the proposed plan will not meet with cordial approval of the oil companies whose rights are affected by the nationalization policy of the Carranza Government.

Faithfully yours,   Robert Lansing.[1]

TLS (WP, DLC).
[1] Wilson never answered this letter.

From the Diary of Colonel House

January 3, 1920.

Billy Phillips had a sad story to tell. Lansing is insulted daily by the White House and does not resent it. His attitude is that he will not resign until the President has sufficiently recovered to indicate whether he wishes him to do so. Phillips said Lansing went to the White House the other day to tell Mrs. Wilson how necessary it was to take some action in some pressing matters which he had already brought to the attention of the President. Mrs. Wilson replied to him curtly, "The President does not like being told a thing twice." The State Department also received a rebuke from Tumulty's office to the effect that there was no use trying to go to the President through Mrs. Wilson, and if they desired action matters should come to him, Tumulty. This was notice, so the State Department believe, that Lansing was no longer *persona grata* with the President and Mrs. Wilson.

January 4, 1920.

T. W. Gregory was my only important caller during the day. He is just from Washington and is terribly distressed over the situation there. He believes it grows steadily worse. He had a long conference with Frank Polk who was much at sea as to what should be done. He is disturbed over Lansing's strained relations with the White House. It is difficult to determine how to act in the circumstances when his immediate chief is disagreeably involved with the President.

Edith Bolling Galt Wilson to Gilbert Monell Hitchcock

My dear Senator: The White House Jan. 5th, 1920

The President asks me to ask you to send him a copy of the memorandum he gave you last Summer,[1] but he also asks that you allow no one else to see it. So, knowing what a busy person you are, I suggest—if agreeable to you—that you send me the original and let me make the copy and return the original to you.[2] Will you address it to *me,* as then I can return it to you promptly.

With good wishes for the New Year, believe me
                    Faithfully yours   Edith Bolling Wilson

ALS (G. M. Hitchcock Papers, DLC).
  [1] It is printed at Sept. 3, 1919, Vol. 62.
  [2] She returned her copy: an EBWhw MS in the G. M. Hitchcock Papers, DLC.

Gilbert Monell Hitchcock to Edith Bolling Galt Wilson

My dear Mrs Wilson: Washington, D. C. Jan 5, 1920

As requested I send you herewith by the kindness of Admiral Grayson the memorandum or suggestion which the President handed to me before his trip.

I used it as the basis for the first four reservations of the enclosed resolution of ratification which I offered and which received 41 votes.

The 5th. reservation I drafted as the result of conversations with the president in which he advised me that such would be the interpretation in practice.

The President may be interested in hearing my analysis of the republican situation in the senate:

Of the 49 republican senators 14 voted against ratification in any form and would do so again. Of the remaining 35 probably 15 but certainly 12 are sincerely desirous of a compromise and adjustment, but they are not able to budge Lodge from his position.

Nothing will move him to a real compromise in my opinion unless the 12 moderate republicans actually rebel which they won't or unless they get enough recruits, say 8, to constitute with loyal democrats the necessary 64 votes to ratify. Then I believe Lodge would come over and bring 9 or 10 more. He is a cold blooded calculating politician, much more interested in holding his party together than in serving his country. He knows Borah will lead 15 or more republicans in revolt if a compromise for ratification is made with the democrats and so he merely dallies and trifles with the moderate republicans to keep them quiet. He always promises them that enough democrats will surrender finally. So far he has succeeded except for about a dozen republicans in keeping them quiet.

It seems to me our policy should be to do everything that will help increase that dozen to twenty. Then Lodge or no Lodge we could send the treaty to the President with reservations that he might accept even if not entirely satisfactory. To increase that dozen to twenty however means concessions and as yet I have little encouragement from the President to make them.

Public opinion is strong for compromise as well as for ratification

Yours sincerely   G M Hitchcock

ALS (WP, DLC).

Joseph Patrick Tumulty to Edith Bolling Galt Wilson, with Enclosure

Dear Mrs. Wilson: The White House 5 January, 1920

I am embarrassed about this letter and leave it to your discretion to say what is to be done.   Sincerely,   J. P. Tumulty

Nothing at present   W.W.[1]

[1] WWhw.

E N C L O S U R E

Leo Stanton Rowe[1] to Joseph Patrick Tumulty

Personal and Confidential.

My dear Mr. Tumulty: Washington, D. C. January 3, 1920.

A difficult and embarrassing situation has been created by reason of our inability to extend an invitation to Costa Rica to be represented at the forthcoming Pan American Financial Conference. As you are fully aware, the policy of the President with reference to Costa Rica has been completely vindicated. Constitutional order has been completely reestablished, the Constitution of 1871 again put in force and orderly elections held for President. Thus every trace of the Tinoco regime has been eliminated.

Our failure to extend recognition to the new Government of Costa Rica has made it impossible to extend an invitation to send delegates to the Financial Conference. Invitations have been extended to every other country of the American continent, including Mexico, and we are therefore placed in the position of refusing to Costa Rica representation at the Conference at a time when her Government needs our support. This exclusion cannot but create comment when the Conference assembles. Our exclusion of Costa Rica will furthermore tend to undermine the existing Government of that country as it will inevitably be interpreted as an indication of disapproval of the existing regime in that country.

If the President is willing to extend recognition to the new Government of Costa Rica, an invitation can immediately be cabled and it is possible that a delegation will be able to reach Washington prior to the assembling of the Conference.

Sincerely yours,   L S Rowe

TLS (WP, DLC).
[1] Distinguished Latin Americanist, Chief of the Latin American Affairs Division of the State Department.

Joseph Patrick Tumulty to Edith Bolling Galt Wilson, with Enclosure

Dear Mrs. Wilson: The White House 5 January, 1920

This matter was discussed at a conference between the Attorney General and Director General Hines. They both feel that the President ought to accede to the request of the Commission,[1] so that there may be representatives of the public present.

Sincerely,   J P Tumulty

The President felt that in appointing this Commission of 3 they were to represent the Public, & he does not feel that any other appointments are necessary

[1] That is, the Bituminous Coal Commission, about the appointment of which, see WW to H. M. Robinson, Dec. 19, 1919.

ENCLOSURE

From Henry Mauris Robinson

Dear Mr. President: Washington 3 January, 1920.

The Commission expects to begin its hearings Monday, January 12.

The mine workers have stated that at these meetings they intend to present their position through a committee.

It is expected that the operators will adopt a like plan, and possibly that both workers and operators will employ counsel.

In order that all of the interested parties may be more nearly on a parity in this investigation and at these hearings, I feel it is my duty as the one chosen to represent the public interest to ask that you, in your discretion, select four or five men, preferably connected with the Government, as a committee to represent the public's interest in all matters before the Commission.

It is possible that such a Committee should have authority to select counsel.   Respectfully yours,   Henry M. Robinson

TLS (WP, DLC).

From John Grier Hibben

My dear Mr. President: Princeton, N. J. January 6th, 1920.

I am enclosing you a freight receipt for the table which was shipped to you on January 2nd.[1] This receipt has just been sent up to me, or it would have been forwarded to you before.

I hope that the table will reach you in good condition. It has been very carefully crated at the University storeroom. The charges have been paid and I hope that you will allow the University this priviledge of delivering the table to you at Washington.

Yours very truly,   John Grier Hibben

TLS (WP, DLC).
¹ See WW to J. G. Hibben, Dec. 22, 1919.

Tumulty's First Draft of a Jackson Day Message

[Jan. 6, 1920]

My dear Mr. Chairman: 8 January, 1920

It is with keenest regret that I find that I am to be deprived of the pleasure and privilege of joining you and the other loyal Democrats who are to assemble tonight to celebrate Jackson Day and renew their vows of fidelity to the great principles of our party, the principles which must now fulfill the hopes not only of our own people but of the world.

The United States enjoyed the spiritual leadership of the world until the Senate of the United States failed to ratify the treaty by which the belligerent nations sought to effect the settlements for which they had fought throughout the war. It is inconceivable that at this supreme crisis and final turning point in the international relations of the whole world, when the results of the great war are by no means determined and are still questionable and dependent upon events which no man can foresee or count upon, the United States should withdraw from the concert of progressive and enlightened nations by which Germany was defeated and all similar governments (if the world be so unhappy as to contain any) warned of the certain consequences of any attempt of any like iniquity, and yet that is the effect of the course the Senate of the United States has taken with regard to the Treaty of Versailles. Germany is beaten, but we are still at war with her, and the whole stage is reset for a repetition of the old plot. It is now ready for the resumption of the old offensive and defensive alliances which made settled peace impossible. It is now open again to every sort of intrigue. The old spies are free to resume their former abominable activities. They are again at liberty to make it impossible for governments to be sure what mischief is being worked among their own people, what internal disorders are being fomented. None of the projects we professed to be fighting for has been secured, or can be without the Treaty. Without the Covenant of the League of Nations there may be as many secret treaties as ever, to

destroy the confidence of governments in each other, and their validity cannot be questioned. Without the treaty Germany need
make no specific reparation for any of the criminal wrongs she in-
flicted; Alsace and Lorraine need not be returned to France; Germany may retain all her threatening armaments and renew all her
former designs. Is it any wonder that German agents are already
busy representing that the combinations against Germany are already broken up in altercation or diminished of purpose, and that
in particular the United States and France are no longer united by
any kind of friendship which need give Germany concern; and that
the English-speaking peoples no longer offer any obstacle to Germany's purposes? In brief, that the results of the war are already
undone and Germany free as ever to work out the purposes of Wil-
helmstrasse?

I do not believe that this is what the people of this country wish
or will be satisfied with. Personally, I do not accept the action of
the Senate of the United States as the decision of the nation. I have
asserted from the first that the overwhelming majority of the people of this country desire the ratification of the treaty, and my impression to that effect has recently been confirmed by the unmistakeable evidences of public opinion given during my visit to
seventeen of the States. But no assertions with regard to the wish
and opinion of the country are credited. There is only one way to
make certain of them, and that is by a direct referendum; and in
my opinion, Mr. Chairman, it is our duty as a party to give the next
election the form of a great and solemn referendum to the voters
of the country in this great matter, a referendum as to the part the
United States is to play in completing the settlements of the war
and in the prevention in the future of such outrages as Germany
attempted to perpetrate, and these are matters of such supreme
importance that they can be settled only by the sovereign voice of
the voters of the Republic. Our fidelity to our associates in the war
is in question, and the whole future of mankind. It will be heartening to the whole world to know the attitude and purpose of the
people of the United States.

I spoke just now of the spiritual leadership of the United States,
thinking of international affairs. But there is another spiritual leadership which is open to us and which we can assume. The world
has been made safe for democracy, but democracy has not been
finally vindicated. All sorts of crimes are being committed in its
name, all sorts of preposterous perversions of its doctrines and
practices are being attempted. This, in my judgment, is to be the
great privilege of the democracy of the United States, to show that
it can lead the way in the solution of the great social and industrial

problems of our time, and lead the way to a happy settled order of life as well as to political liberty. The program for this achievement we must attempt to formulate, and in carrying it out we shall do more than can be done in any other way to sweep out of existence the tyrannous and arbitrary forms of power which are now masquerading under the name of popular government.

Whenever we look back to Andrew Jackson, we should draw fresh inspiration from his character and example. His mind grasped with such splendid definiteness and firmness the principle of national authority and national action. He was so indomitable in his purpose to give reality to the principles of the government, that this is a very fortunate time to recall his career and to renew our vows of faithfulness to the principles and the pure practices of democracy. I rejoice to join you in this renewal of faith and purpose. I hope that the whole evening may be of the happiest results as regards the fortunes of our party and the nation.

With cordial regard,   Sincerely yours,

Hon. Homer S. Cummings,

Chairman, Democratic National Committee,

Washington, D. C.[1]

CC MS (J. P. Tumulty Papers, DLC).

[1] Houston tells the story of the revision of this draft as follows:

"Shortly before Jackson Day (January 8th), I was informed that the President would prepare and send to those present at the Jackson Day banquet in Washington, a letter dealing mainly with the Treaty situation. Tumulty spoke to me about it after Cabinet meeting Tuesday, January 6th, and stated that he wished to bring the Attorney General and the Under-secretary of State [Polk] to my office to go over the letter with me. He did so at 4:30. He read the letter at the conference. It was unsatisfactory. The President said in it that he could not accept the Senate's action, that its action and the delay left the stage set for the old plots, that the world was left without a treaty, that Germany was free to become a menace once more, and that she need not give up armaments, or Alsace-Lorraine, or make reparation. I did not say so, but I doubted if the President had had anything to do with the preparation of this letter. I could not understand how he could make such statements. I suggested that the letter be changed. It contained erroneous statements. There was a Treaty. All the other powers had agreed to the Versailles Treaty. The fact was that we only had not accepted it. Germany was not free to become a menace. She would have to give up armaments and surrender Alsace-Lorraine and properly make reparation. Germany's armament was already largely gone; her fleet was gone, and France already had Alsace-Lorraine. The letter, as it stood, I said, would arouse great adverse comment and would irritate the Allies.

"The statement that the only course left was for the nation to have a referendum on the Treaty at the next election was, I thought, unwise. It was a flat declaration, in effect, against further attempts to agree on reservations and would, if assented to, make the Treaty a partisan issue in an election, while the people were in bad humour and might be interested in many other things besides the Treaty. The conference asked me to revise the address.

"In the circumstances, I agreed to do what I could to alter the letter. I realized that it would be difficult to do more than reshape the statements which contained errors of fact or interpretation. I knew that it would be impossible to avoid saying that our acceptance of the Treaty should be left to a referendum. I revised the letter to indicate plainly that the President was not opposed to reservations of an interpretative character but that if the Senate did not accept the Treaty outright or with such reservations, the only course left would be to submit the matter to the people.

"I sent the revised letter to Tumulty at twelve o'clock Wednesday. On the afternoon of the eighth, I called him up and asked if there was any news. He replied that everything was fine and that the letter as revised would be substantially accepted." Houston, *Eight Years With Wilson's Cabinet*, II, 47-48.

In addition, see the memorandum by Lansing printed at January 10, which says that Polk and Palmer also read this draft and were vehement in their criticism of it.

Notes and Memoranda by David Franklin Houston

[Jan. 7, 1920]

NOTE

Memorandum *No. A* is to be substituted on p. 2 line 6., after the words: *"what internal disorders are being fomented."* The object is to indicate what will happen if this nation does not ratify this treaty and enter into the Covenant. There is no question of *"No treaty"* or of the world's being "without the Treaty." Five nations have ratified it. It is simply a quest. of our wholehearted entry and of what will happen if we do not enter.

This is the form and direction the speeches on the trip assumed.

It would be particularly unfortunate to say, in any event, that Germany "need make no specif. reparation," that "Alsace-Lorraine need not be returned to France," and that "Germany may retain all her threatening armaments." Alsace and Lorraine are already France's and can be recove[re]d only by war. Germany's forces and armament are already dispersed and lost. Her fleet is sunk.

NOTE 2.

I suggest *Mem. B.* to be inserted on p. 3 as a substitute for the sentence beginning on line 5: ["]There is only one way," and ending on line 13 with the words "the Republic."

The object is to make clear again what has already been said that *Interpretative reservations* are not objectionable, but that amendments are, to throw the responsibility where it belongs, and to indicate that final resort may have to be had to the people. Except for the last suggestion, that is in line with the declarations made heretofore.

For illustrations of what was said in the speeches as to our failure to ratify and our objects in going to war, see the volume of addresses, pp. 46, 79, 123, 124, 341 and 357.[1]

Hw MS (J. P. Tumulty Papers, DLC).

[1] Houston's references are to *Addresses of President Wilson: Addresses Delivered by President Wilson on his Western Tour, September 4 to September 25, 1919, on the League of Nations, Treaty of Peace with Germany, Industrial Conditions, High Cost of Living, Race Riots, Etc.*, 66th Cong., 1st sess., Sen. Doc. 120 (Washington, 1919).

Mem. A

None of the projects [objects] we professed to be fighting for has been secured or can be made certain of without this Nation's ratification of the treaty and its entry into the covenant. This Nation entered the great war to vindicate its own rights and to protect and preserve free governments. It went into the war to see it through to the end and the end has not yet come. It went into the war to make an end of militarism, to furnish guarantees to weak nations, and to make a just and lasting peace. It entered it with noble enthusiasms. There is no question of a covenant and a treaty. Five of the leading belligerents have accepted the treaty and formal ratifications will soon be exchanged. The question is whether this country will enter and enter whole-heartedly. If it does not do so it and Germany will play a lone hand in the world. Without the adherence of the United States to the covenant, the covenant can not be made effective. To state it in another way, the maintenance of the peace of the world and the execution of the treaty depend upon the whole-hearted participation of the United States. I am not stating it as a matter of power. The point is that the United States is the only nation which has sufficient moral force with the rest of the world. It is the only nation whose guarantee will suffice to substitute discussion for war. If we keep out of this arrangement, if we do not give our guarantee, then another attempt will be made to crush the new nations of Europe.

Mem. B.

I have endeavored to make it plain that if the Senate wishes to say what the undoubted meaning of the league is I shall have no objection. If, in other words, it does not propose to change that undoubted meaning I have no objection. There can be no reasonable objection to interpretations accompanying the act of ratification, provided they do not form a part of the formal ratification itself. But when the treaty is acted upon I must know whether it means that we have ratified or rejected it. We can not rewrite this treaty. We must take it without changes which alter its meaning or leave it, and then after the rest of the world has signed it, we must face the unthinkable task of making another and separate kind of treaty with Germany. If this becomes the issue, there will be only one way out, and that is to submit this great matter for determination at the next election to the voters of the Nation, to give the next election the form of a great and solemn referendum, a referendum as to the part the United States is to play in completing the settlements of the war and in the prevention in the future of such outrages as Germany attempted to perpetrate. In the event of unsatisfactory action by the Senate, the matters are of such supreme importance that they must be submitted for settlement to the sovereign voters of the Republic

T MS (J. P. Tumulty Papers, DLC).

From the Diary of Henry Fountain Ashurst

January 7, 1920.

'Phoned Dr. Grayson at the White House; told him to caution the President *against* sending to the Jackson Day Banquet a demand for the Ratification of the Versailles Treaty *without reservation*; and that if the President sent such letter to the banqueters it would drive the wedge still further between the factions in the Senate. Doctor Grayson replied: "The President is *not* going to send such a letter to the banqueters."

Redraft of a Jackson Day Message

[Jan. 7, 1920]

My dear Mr. Chairman: 8 January, 1920

It is with keenest regret that I find that I am to be deprived of the pleasure and privilege of joining you and the other loyal Democrats who are to assemble tonight to celebrate Jackson Day and renew their vows of fidelity to the great principles of our party, the principles which must now fulfill the hopes not only of our own people but of the world.

The United States enjoyed the spiritual leadership of the world until the Senate of the United States failed to ratify the treaty by which the belligerent nations sought to effect the settlements for which they had fought throughout the war. It is inconceivable that at this supreme crisis and final turning point in the international relations of the whole world, when the results of the great war are by no means determined and are still questionable and dependent upon events which no man can foresee or count upon, the United States should withdraw from the concert of progressive and enlightened nations by which Germany was defeated and all similar governments (if the world be so unhappy as to contain any) warned of the certain consequences of any attempt of any like iniquity, and yet that is the effect of the course the Senate of the United States has taken with regard to the Treaty of Versailles.

Germany is beaten, but we are still at war with her, and the ⟨whole⟩ *old*¹ stage is reset for a repetition of the old plot. It is now ready for the resumption of the old offensive and defensive alliances which made settled peace impossible. It is now open again to every sort of intrigue. The old spies are free to resume their former abominable activities. They are again at liberty to make it impossible for governments to be sure what mischief is being worked among their own people, what internal disorders are being fomented. Without the Covenant of the League of Nations, there may be as many secret treaties as ever, to destroy the confidence of governments in each other, and their validity cannot be questioned. None of the ⟨projects⟩ *objects*² we professed to be fighting for has been secured or can be made certain of without this nation's ratification of the treaty and its entry into the covenant. This nation entered the great war to vindicate its own rights and to protect and preserve free government. It went into the war to see it through to the end, and the end has not yet come. It went into the war to make an end of militarism, to furnish fuarantees [guarantees] to weak nations, and to make a just and lasting peace. It entered it with noble enthusiasms. Five of the leading belligerents have accepted the treaty and formal ratifications will soon be exchanged. The question is whether this country will enter and enter whole-heartedly. If it does not do so, the United States and Germany will play a lone hand in the world. The maintenance of the peace of the world and the effective execution of the treaty depend upon the whole-hearted participation of the United States. I am not stating it as a matter of power. The point is that the United States is the only nation which has sufficient moral force with the rest of the world to guarantee the substitution of discussion for war. If we keep out of this arrangement, if we do not give our guarantee, then another attempt will be made to crush the new nations of Europe.

I do not believe that this is what the people of this country wish or will be satisfied with. Personally, I do not accept the action of the Senate of the United States as the decision of the nation. I have asserted from the first that the overwhelming majority of the people of this country desire the ratification of the treaty, and my impression to that effect has recently been confirmed by the unmistakeable evidences of public opinion given during my visit to seventeen of the States. I have endeavored to make it plain that if the Senate wishes to say what the undoubted meaning of the League is, I shall have no objection. There can be no reasonable objection to interpretations accompanying the act of ratification itself. But when the treaty is acted upon, I must know whether it means that we have ratified or rejected it. We cannot rewrite this treaty. We must take it without changes which alter its meaning, or leave it and then after the rest of the world has signed it, we must face the unthinkable task of making another and separate kind of treaty with Germany. But no mere assertions with regard to the wish and opinion of the country are credited. If there is any doubt as to what the people of the country think on this vital matter, the clear and single way out is to submit it for determination at the next election to the voters of the nation, to give the next election the form of a great and solemn referendum, a referendum as to the part the United States is to play in completing the settlements of the war and in the prevention in the future of such outrages as Germany attempted to perpetrate. *We have no moral right to refuse now to take part in the execution & administration of these settlements than we had to refuse to take part in the fighting of the last few weeks of the war which brought victory & made it possible to dictate to Germany what the settlements should be*[3] Our fidelity to our associates in the war is in question, and the whole future of mankind. It will be heartening to the whole world to know the attitude and purpose of the people of the United States.

I spoke just now of the spiritual leadership of the United States, thinking of international affairs. But there is another spiritual leadership which is open to us and which we can assume. The world has been made safe for democracy, but democracy has not been finally vindicated. All sorts of crimes are being committed in its name, all sorts of preposterous perversions of its doctrines and practices are being attempted. This, in my judgment, is to be the great privilege of the democracy of the United States, to show that it can lead the way in the solution of the great social and industrial problems of our time and lead the way to a happy settled order of life as well as to political liberty. The programme for this achievement we must attempt to formulate, and in carrying it out we shall do more than can be done in any other way to sweep out of existence the tyrannous and arbitrary forms of power which are now masquerading under the name of popular government.

Whenever we look back to Andrew Jackson, we should draw fresh inspiration from his character and example. His mind grasped with such splendid definiteness and firmness the principle of national authority and national action. He was so indomitable in his purpose to give reality to the principles of the government, that this is a very fortunate time to recall his career and to renew our vows of faithfulness to the principles and the pure practices of democracy. I rejoice to join you in this renewal of faith and purpose.

I hope that the whole evening may be of the happiest results as regards the fortunes of our party and the nation.

With cordial regard,   Sincerely yours,

Hon. Homer S. Cummings, Chairman,
Democratic National Committee,
Washington, D. C.

CC MS (J. P. Tumulty Papers, DLC).
¹ WWhw deletion and substitution.
² *Idem.*
³ EBWhw. This addition was pasted on the bottom of page 3 of this draft.

A Memorandum by Robert Lansing

January 7, 1920.

DETERMINATION TO RESIGN.

Things are going from bad to worse in our foreign affairs and I do not intend to stand it much longer. My mind is becoming more and more enmeshed in perplexities. I am struggling along and making no headway. The exasperation of the foreign diplomats is constantly increasing and I do not wonder. The President's failure to act on the most important questions and his apparent resentment that I dare to advise him are producing a practically impossible situation.

I believe that the time has come when in the interest of public affairs I ought to resign so that the President may appoint a Secretary of State in whom he has sufficient confidence to permit him to run the Department of State.

Ever since the way the President ignored me in Paris and openly humiliated me I have longed to resign as I felt that he viewed with suspicion, if not with resentment, nearly every suggestion that I made. Only a sense of loyalty and a desire to avoid causing a crisis in the negotiations at Paris and in the bitter controversy in Washington over ratification of the treaty have caused me to continue in office.

Now that the President seems sufficiently recovered to pass judgment on international questions I feel that my personal desire to get out of the Cabinet corresponds with my duty. I have, therefore, been at work on a statement setting forth clearly my reasons for resigning. This statement I intend to incorporate soon in a letter to the President.

I confess that I cannot fathom the President's mind. I have endured many mortifications only out of a sense of duty. I have endeavored to be entirely loyal in word and deed, but I cannot subordinate my independence of thought or refrain from telling him frankly that I do not agree with him. This mental independence he seems to resent. With an appearance of suavity he arrogantly demands that his Secretary of State shall be merely a rubber stamp, who accepts his declarations as those of a divinely-inspired superman. I think this is the result of the tremendous popular enthusiasm with which he was received in Europe. He came to believe then in his own infallibility and considered it sacrilege not to fall down and worship him.

No man, convinced of this intolerance of contrary opinion and possessed of any self-respect, could continue in office under him longer than a sense of public duty required. I certainly cannot and do not intend to do so.

My regret is that in giving up my commission I must leave to my successor such a legacy of confusion in our international affairs, a confusion due solely to the President's inability under present conditions to act intelligently or to listen to my advice. The situation is unbearable. I am at my wits' end. It is only a question as to when I should send in my letter of resignation. I cannot wait much longer.

T MS (R. Lansing Papers, DLC).

From the Diary of Henry Fountain Ashurst

January 8, 1920.

If the interest shown in the Jackson Day Banquet to be held to-night be symptomatic of the coming campaign it will have no dull moments, as the banqueters now number two thousand, and two hotels (the New Willard and the Washington) are scarcely commodious enough to entertain them. The speakers will "orate" at both hotels, that is, as soon as they finish a speech at one banquet hall they will proceed to the other Hotel and repeat.

W.J.B.[1] came to town early yesterday morning, bubbling and healthy.

At four o'clock pm, Dr. Grayson 'phoned me that W.W. requested *him* to assure *me* that I "need have no misgivings" as W.W. would *not*, in his letter to be read to the banqueters tonight, demand that the peace treaty be ratified *without* reservations.

[1] That is, William Jennings Bryan.

A Jackson Day Message[1]

The White House,
My dear Mr. Chairman: Washington, January 8, 1920.

It is with keenest regret that I find that I am to be deprived of the pleasure and privilege of joining you and the other loyal Democrats who are to assemble to-night to celebrate Jackson Day and renew their vows of fidelity to the great principles of our party, the principles which must now fulfill the hopes not only of our own people but of the world.

The United States enjoyed the spiritual leadership of the world until the Senate of the United States failed to ratify the treaty by which the belligerent nations sought to effect the settlements for which they had fought throughout the war. It is inconceivable that at this supreme crisis and final turning point in the international relations of the whole world, when the results of the Great War are by no means determined and are still questionable and dependent upon events which no man can foresee or count upon, the United States should withdraw from the concert of progressive and enlightened nations by which Germany was defeated, and all similar Governments (if the world be so unhappy as to contain any) warned of the consequences of any attempt at a like iniquity, and yet that is the effect of the course which the United States has taken with regard to the Treaty of Versailles.

Germany is beaten, but we are still at war with her, and the old stage is reset for a repetition of the old plot. It is now ready for a resumption of the old offensive and defensive alliances which made settled peace impossible. It is now open again to every sort of intrigue.

The old spies are free to resume their former abominable activities. They are again at liberty to make it impossible for governments to be sure what mischief is being worked among their own people, what internal disorders are being fomented.

Without the Covenant of the League of Nations there may be as many secret treaties as ever, to destroy the confidence of governments in each other, and their validity can not be questioned.

None of the objects we professed to be fighting for has been secured, or can be made certain of, without this nation's ratification of the treaty and its entry into the covenant. This Nation entered the Great War to vindicate its own rights and to protect and preserve free government. It went into the war to see it through to the end, and the end has not yet come. It went into the war to make an end of militarism, to furnish guaranties to weak nations, and to make a just and lasting peace. It entered it with noble enthusiasm.

Five of the leading belligerents have accepted the treaty and formal ratifications will soon be exchanged. The question is whether this country will enter and enter whole-heartedly. If it does not do so, the United States and Germany will play a lone hand in the world.

The maintenance of the peace of the world and the effective execution of the treaty depend upon the whole-hearted participation of the United States. I am not stating it as a matter of power. The point is that the United States is the only Nation which has sufficient moral force with the rest of the world to guarantee the substitution of discussion for war. If we keep out of this agreement, if we do not give our guaranties, then another attempt will be made to crush the new nations of Europe.

I do not believe that this is what the people of this country wish or will be satisfied with. Personally, I do not accept the action of the Senate of the United States as the decision of the Nation.

I have asserted from the first that the overwhelming majority of the people of this country desire the ratification of the treaty, and my impression to that effect has recently been confirmed by the unmistakable evidences of public opinion given during my visit to seventeen of the States.

I have endeavored to make it plain that if the Senate wishes to say what the undoubted meaning of the League is I shall have no objection. There can be no reasonable objection to interpretations accompanying the act of ratification itself. But when the treaty is acted upon, I must know whether it means that we have ratified or rejected it.

We cannot rewrite this treaty. We must take it without changes which alter its meaning, or leave it, and then, after the rest of the world has signed it, we must face the unthinkable task of making another and separate treaty with Germany.

But no mere assertions with regard to the wish and opinion of the country are credited. If there is any doubt as to what the people of the country think on this vital matter, the clear and single way out is to submit it for determination at the next election to the voters of the Nation, to give the next election the form of a great and solemn referendum, a referendum as to the part the United States is to play in completing the settlements of the war and in the prevention in the future of such outrages as Germany attempted to perpetrate.

We have no more moral right to refuse now to take part in the execution and administration of these settlements than we had to refuse to take part in the fighting of the last few weeks of the war which brought victory and made it possible to dictate to Germany what the settlements should be. Our fidelity to our associates in the war is in question and the whole future of mankind. It will be heartening to the whole world to know the attitude and purpose of the people of the United States.

I spoke just now of the spiritual leadership of the United States, thinking of international affairs. But there is another spiritual leadership which is open to us, and which we can assume.

The world has been made safe for democracy, but democracy has not been finally vindicated. All sorts of crimes are being committed in its name, all sorts of preposterous perversions of its doctrines and practices are being attempted.

This, in my judgment, is to be the great privilege of the democracy of the United States, to show that it can lead the way in the solution of the great social and industrial problems of our time, and lead the way to a happy, settled order of life as well as to political liberty. The program for this achievement we must attempt to formulate, and in carrying it out we shall do more than can be done in any other way to sweep out of existence the tyrannous and arbitrary forms of power which are now masquerading under the name of popular government.

Whenever we look back to Andrew Jackson we should draw fresh inspiration from his character and example. His mind grasped with such a splendid definiteness and firmness the principles of national authority and national action. He was so indomitable in his purpose to give reality to the principles of the Government, that this is a very fortunate time to recall his career and to renew our vows of faithfulness to the principles and the pure practices of democracy.

I rejoice to join you in this renewal of faith and purpose. I hope that the whole evening may be of the happiest results as regards the fortunes of our party and the Nation.

With cordial regards, Sincerely yours,   Woodrow Wilson.

To Hon. Homer S. Cummings,
Chairman, Democratic National Committee,
Washington, D.C.

Printed in *Cong. Record*, 66th Cong., 2d sess., p. 1249.
¹ Tumulty, presumably, made a few minor literary changes in the penultimate draft (CC MS in the J. P. Tumulty Papers, DLC) before giving out the following text. There is no copy of the text given out in WP, DLC, or in the J. P. Tumulty Papers, DLC.

Three Letters from Robert Lansing

My dear Mr. President: Washington January 8, 1920.

I am enclosing a copy of a letter addressed to me by Prince Lubomirski,[1] Minister of Poland, as well as a memorandum on the subject of this letter prepared by Mr. Polk in which he suggests that in the circumstances, it might be wise if you could reconsider your decision against publishing Mr. Morgenthau's report.[2] I feel that the situation revealed by Prince Lubomirski's letter is a serious one and that steps should be taken to quiet the agitation of which he complains. I have, furthermore, reason to believe that an effort is being made by certain Jewish elements to prevent the publication of Mr. Morgenthau's report. For these reasons I quite agree with Mr. Polk's suggestion.

Faithfully yours,   Robert Lansing.

Publication authorized Woodrow Wilson[3]

TLS (SDR, RG 59, 860c.4016/184, DNA).
[1] Prince Kazimierz Lubomirski to RL, Dec. 22, 1919, TCL (SDR, RG 59, 860c.4016/184, DNA). Lubomirski said that, since his arrival in the United States, he had refrained from any comment on "Jewish conditions" in Poland before the publication of the Morgenthau report. "To my astonishment, however," he continued, "I have been reading now for two weeks or more in the newspapers of this country public speeches on alleged Jewish conditions in Poland by one of the official representatives of the United States Government on the Mission. I cannot allow these statements, which do not represent the true situation as I know it, to pass uncontradicted, but as I am particularly anxious to avoid anything which could be considered as a manifestation even approaching an unsympathetic attitude toward the United States Government, I find myself obliged to inquire as to whether or not I am to consider these speeches as official manifestations of the American people on the Jewish situation in Poland."
[2] [FLP] to RL, Jan. 5, 1920, TL (SDR, RG 59, 860c.4016/184, DNA). Polk revealed that the "speeches on alleged Jewish conditions in Poland" had been made by Morgenthau himself. "It is rather curious," he continued, "that Morgenthau's statements in the press are rather unfriendly toward Poland, whereas the report itself is more or less a vindication. If not a vindication, at least it is a contradiction of the exaggerated stories put out by the Jewish propaganda."
For examples of Morgenthau's public comments on anti-Semitic activity in Poland, see the New York Times, Dec. 3 and 15, 1919. On the reports of the Morgenthau mission and Wilson's earlier refusal to allow their publication, see EBW to JPT, Dec. 17, 1919, and n. 1 thereto.
[3] WWhw.

My dear Mr. President: Washington January 8, 1920.

I am enclosing herewith a copy of a telegram from the American Ambassador at Paris, dated January 7, 1920,[1] the second part of the first paragraph of which relates to a conversation which Mr. Wallace had with Mr. Clemenceau and in which the latter gave his views in regard to the Fiume question which is to be discussed in Paris during the coming week.

In connection with this telegram I have likewise received a message from Mr. Wallace stating that a settlement of the Adriatic situation would probably be discussed at a meeting of the Heads of States in Paris in the near future and inquiring what attitude he should assume in regard to the matter. In reply to this inquiry I have instructed Mr. Wallace to adopt the role of an observer only but to report fully to Washington and to refer to me any point upon which his colleagues particularly desire an expression of opinion from this government.   Faithfully yours,   Robert Lansing

[1] H. C. Wallace to RL, Jan. 7, 1920, T telegram (WP, DLC). The main subject of Wallace's telegram was his effort to persuade Clemenceau to curb anti-American sentiment in the French press. However, he also reported briefly on Clemenceau's comment on the Fiume situation: "He added that Lloyd George's attitude with regard to Fiume was too abrupt and that he wanted to give in to Nitti but for himself he would stand by the promise he had made to the President and would support his views to the end. He had nothing to say regarding so-called settlement."

My dear Mr. President: Washington January 8, 1920.

I have just received a telegram from the American Ambassador at Paris, dated January 7, 1920,[1] in which he states that it is possible that discussions regarding the Turkish Treaty will commence this week in Paris between the Heads of Governments. He likewise inquires as to the attitude which he should adopt should he be invited to attend these meetings.

In regard to the above I am instructing Mr. Wallace to attend the meetings of the Heads of Governments should he be invited to do so, but to make it clear to those present at the meetings that he is participating in them unofficially and as an observer and that all questions upon which they may desire an expression of views from this government will have to be referred by him to Washington.[2]

Faithfully yours,   Robert Lansing.

TLS (WP, DLC).
[1] H. C. Wallace to RL, No. 58, Jan. 7, 1920, T telegram (SDR, RG 59, 763.72119/8592, DNA).
[2] Lansing sent such instructions to Wallace on January 9: RL to H. C. Wallace, No. 62, Jan. 8 [sent Jan. 9], 1920, T telegram (SDR, RG 59, 763.72119/8592, DNA).

A Memorandum by Joseph Patrick Tumulty

The White House
Memorandum by Mr. Tumulty: 9 January 1920.

This morning I talked with the President at great length about the happenings at the Jackson Day banquet last night, and especially Mr. Bryan's attitude toward the League of Nations.[1] The

President evidenced a vigour of mind and an acute understanding of the whole situation with reference to the Treaty.

In the conversation he requested me to instruct the Attorney General to prepare a proclamation lifting the ban on liquors, and declaring demobilization at an end. I discussed with him briefly the unfortunate results of such action at this time, laying before him the fact that there was just an interval of one week in which liquors could be taken out of bond; and the result would be a grand debauch throughout the country.

I told him I favored very strongly the lifting of the ban some weeks ago, but that it would be unwise to do it now. I told him that his power to act was doubtful, whereupon he requested me to confer with Justice Brandeis.

I conferred with the Judge at his home on Saturday, January tenth. The Judge and I discussed the matter at great length. He was of the opinion, and requested me so to inform the President, that the President had no power to lift the ban.[2]

T MS (J. P. Tumulty Papers, DLC).
[1] Approximately 800 persons attended the portion of the Jackson Day dinner held at the Willard Hotel, and seven hundred more dined at the Washington Hotel. All thirteen speakers addressed both groups, and Wilson's message was read aloud at both gatherings. The *New York Times* and the New York *World*, January 9, 1920, both reported that Wilson's message was received with great enthusiasm by both audiences.
Bryan was one of the speakers. He said at the beginning of his speech that he had prepared its text and given it to the newspapers before he knew the contents of Wilson's letter. Wilson, he said, had succeeded far better in Paris than anyone had had a right to expect. He, Bryan, had stood with Democratic senators for unqualified ratification of the treaty. But Democrats faced a new situation: they either had to accept compromise reservations or else go to the country on the issue of ratification. The latter course would mean a delay of fourteen months, even if they could win a two-thirds majority in the Senate. Democrats could not accept responsibility for such delay. Moreover, the Republicans enjoyed a majority in the Senate, and the majority had the right to dictate the terms upon which the treaty would be ratified. The Democrats had no right to prevent ratification on these terms. A text of Bryan's speech is printed in *The Commoner*, XX (Jan. 1920), 8.
[2] This paragraph was obviously added on January 10 or later.

Charles Richard Crane to Edith Bolling Galt Wilson

Dear Mrs Wilson   Washington, D. C. January 9th 1920

Thank you for letting me come and for treating me so much like one of you. I am sure you understand my anxiety and devotion.[1]

Before I go, however, I want to make one little suggestion. Your own responsibility is so great that I hope this suggestion will lighten it just a bit.

When you feel doubtful or need help about any important decision having a political bearing, think about Secretary Houston. His loyalty, wisdom and experience are unquestionably supreme here in Washington.

With affectionate messages to you both,

                    Always devotedly   Charles R. Crane

ALS (WP, DLC).
[1] Crane was in Washington briefly and was staying at the Cosmos Club.

From the Diary of Henry Fountain Ashurst

January 9, 1920.

Set out in a "box" on the front page of morning papers in heavy type is an extract from W.W.'s letter sent to the banqueters in which he says:

"We cannot rewrite this Treaty. We must take it without changes which alter its meaning, or leave it.

"If there is any doubt as to what the people of the country think on this vital matter, the clear and single way out is to submit it for determination at the next election to the voters of the nation, to give the next election the form of a great and solemn referendum, a referendum as to the part the United States is to play in completing the settlement of the war."

Thus W.W. makes the Versailles Treaty the issue in the campaign. This gives the campaign of 1920 an unusual feature to wit, we know now in advance what will be the result.

Hugh Campbell Wallace to Robert Lansing

Paris, Jan. 9, 1920.

Rush 82, January 9, 7 p.m.

Secret from American Mission. At the close of the regular meeting of the Supreme Council this morning session in camera.

Following were present: Clemenceau, Berthelot, Lloyd George, Curzon, Bonar Law, Nitti, Scialoja, Matsui, Leef,[1] Hankey, a French and Italian secretary, myself and Harrison.[2]

Lloyd George stated that he had had conversations with Nitti in London on the whole Adriatic situation. Nitti had made certain suggestions regarding which Lloyd George has consulted his colleagues. They would suggest for the moment an alternative which he would now put forward. This suggestion was made by the signatories of the Pact of London as the United States was not at the present time in a position to discuss the matter. They considered themselves bound by that Treaty and had so informed President Wilson and Signor Orlando. At that time they had also stated that if Italy should insist, they would comply with their obligations under the Treaty. However, he would point out that the Treaty was not applicable to present conditions and that his proposal was submitted on that basis.

Lloyd George observed further that the question of Fiume had become a sort of flag in Italy nothing more. Every days delay in reaching a settlement increased danger for Italy, for the Yugo-Slavs, and for all Europe. They could be no longer responsible for such a situation. He believes that his proposal was the best possible settlement that could be found. If it were accepted by Nitti it would then be submitted immediately to the Yugo-Slavs.

Nitti stated that he would examine the proposal and undertake to make reply at the next meeting which was fixed for tomorrow morning at 11:30.

The British-French proposal reads as follows:

"Secret.

"The Adriatic situation. Joint memorandum by Mr. Clemenceau and Mr. Lloyd George.

"The British and French governments have consistently declared their willingness to abide by the Treaty of London. They cannot forget that Italy voluntarily came to the aid of the Allies at a critical and dangerous moment in the war and that in spite of the very gallant and memorable fight put up by the Servian Nation it was mainly through the courage, the self sacrifice, and the endurance of the Italian people and army that the Croatian and Slovene people have won that independence and freedom from German and Magyar domination which they now enjoy. They are prepared, should the Italian Government require it, to abide by the terms of the treaty they have signed. If, however, the Italian Government agree in thinking that, owing to the disappearance of the Hapsburg Monarchy, the rise of national states in its place, the great uprising of Italian feeling in Fiume, and the other great events which have occurred since 1915, the Treaty of London no longer constitutes a satisfactory settlement of the Adriatic question they are willing, subject to the amendments set forth below, to adopt as the basis of settlement the memorandum presented to Signor Scialoja by the representatives of France, the United States of America and Great Britain, on December 9th, 1919,[3] and modified by proposals made to them by Signor Nitti on January 6th, 1920.[4] They advance these amendments to Signor Nitti's memorandum in the conviction that while they are wholly consistent with Italy's vital interests they are essential to lasting peace and good relations between Italy and its neighbors which the British and French Governments have so much at heart and which they regard as their duty to promote. The

British and French Governments therefore would propose to the Conference the following settlement of the Adriatic question:

"1. There should be constituted a 'free state of Fiume according to President Wilson's plan' but the delineation of the boundary frontier of the proposed state should in the south be moved eastwards. As, however, it is vital that the railway running northward from Fiume should be wholly within the free state it is proposed that the frontier should run as follows:

"The line should leave the coast at Punta Kolova and run through points 6.42, 10.95 and 11.42 up to Mount Planik, thence northwards. It would follow the red line shown on the map.

"2. 'The city of Fiume with its district corpus separatum should be guaranteed by a statute effective safeguarding its Italianita.' This would be fully attained by conferring upon the corpus separatum the same degree of autonomy within the free state as it enjoyed under Austro-Hungarian rule. Both the privileges of Fiume corpus separatum and the free state itself should be placed under the guarantee of the League of Nations. The international character of the port together with full facilities for its development in the interest of all nations concerned and especially of Yugo-Slavia, Hungary and Roumania, must also be secured under the guarantee of the League of Nations.

"3. Inasmuch as the preponderant population of the Island of Cherso is Slav there are serious objections to the removal of the island from the free state of which it is an integral part. The Island of Lagosta, however, should be ceded to Italy should the Italian government consider it necessary for strategic reasons.

"4. The free state of Zara should be governed by a high commissioner advised by a council, representative of the inhabitants, which should select its own diplomatic representatives. Arrangements should also be made governing the economic relations of Zara with the rest of Dalmatia which falls to the Yugo-Slav state. Zara will therefore be within the Serb-Croat-Slovene customs unit.

"5. The Italian proposals for the effective neutralization of all the islands of the Adriatic should be accepted by the proposal to neutralize mainland Dalmatia as well, involving as it must the prohibition to an independent state of all measures of self defense, is one which can hardly be forced upon a friendly ally. Therefore should ask the Italian Government to be content with the neutralization of all the islands which, together with the other most important safeguards conceded under the present arrangements, would seem to give as absolute security as they can reasonably demand.

"6. The Italians of Dalmatia should be free to choose Italian citizenship without leaving the territory. In view of the fact, however, that Fiume is to be set up as a corpus separatum within the free state under guarantee of the League of Nations, it is not possible to extend the arrangement to the citizens of Fiume.

"7. Existing economic enterprises in Dalmatia should have their security safeguarded by an international convention.

"8. There must also be a discussion of the boundaries of Albania. In conclusion the British and French Governments would point out that the present proposal involving the severance of the free state containing an overwhelming majority (200,000) of Yugo-Slavs from their mother land, the modification of its western frontier in favor of Italy, the concession of islands containing a Slav majority, and other points, are very great conditions to ask of a state which is now a friendly ally. The British and French Governments are prepared to ask the Serb-Croat-Slovene State to make these great concessions for the sake of an amicable and prompt settlement of a question which now threatens the peace and progress of Southern Europe. But they can go no further and they earnestly trust that the Conference and the Italian Government will accept them."   Wallace.

T telegram (SDR, RG 59, 763.72119/8623, DNA).
    [1] Actually, Alexander Wigram Allen Leeper.
    [2] That is, Leland Harrison.
    [3] See FLP to RL, Dec. 9, 1919.
    [4] These proposals, the so-called Nitti compromise, in reply to the British-French-American memorandum of December 9, 1919, read as follows: "Italy asks for the fulfillment of the Pact of London. In order to eliminate the difficulties subsequently arisen and to reach a general agreement without any further delay the Italian Government is prepared to accept the following compromise: (1) Free state of Fiume according to Wilson's plan, but with the frontier of the Pact of London in its southwestern part toward Italy; (2) but in the free state, the city of Fiume with its district, *corpus separatum*, must be guaranteed by a statute efficaciously safeguarding its 'Italianita' which, owing to the great Slav majority in the free state, would be more threatened than it was under Hungary; (3) to the *corpus separatum* of Fiume within the free state must be assigned the road to the west with the surrounding strip of territory up to the Italian frontier; (4) the islands of Cherso and Lagosta, besides those already assigned by Wilson, to be assigned to Italy; (5) Zara, free town, with freedom to select its diplomatic representation, guarantees for the relations of the citizens of Zara with the Dalmatian Territory; (6) effective neutralization of the islands and also of the whole coast and of the ports of the eastern Adriatic coast from Fiume down to the mouth of the Vojussa; (7) the Italians of the city of Fiume and Dalmatia to have the freedom of choosing Italian citizenship without leaving the territory; (8) guarantees for the existing economic enterprises in Dalmatia." F. S. Nitti to D. Lloyd George, Jan. 6, 1920, printed in *The Adriatic Question*, p. 38.

Cary Travers Grayson, on leaving the White House on February 19, 1920

Francis Xavier Dercum

George Edmund De Schweinitz

Hugh Hampton Young

Edward Rhodes Stitt

Harry Atwood Fowler

John Chalmers Da Costa

Sterling Ruffin

Robert Lansing about the time of his resignation

A News Item

[*Jan. 10, 1920*]

NO THIRD TERM AMBITION.

Wilson Has No Idea of Running Again, Says Palmer.

Philadelphia, Jan. 10.—Attorney General A. Mitchell Palmer was quoted here tonight by newspaper interviewers to the effect that persons in close touch with President Wilson were certain that he would not seek re-election.

"The President," Mr. Palmer is quoted as saying, "realizes that there is a certain sentiment throughout the country against a Chief Executive running for a third time, and, while he has not made any definite declaration that he will not be candidate this year, his personal friends know he will not even consider it."

Printed in the *New York Times*, Jan. 11, 1920.

A Memorandum by Robert Lansing

January 10, 1920.

THE PRESIDENT'S LETTER AND
BRYAN'S SPEECH ON JACKSON DAY.

The President's letter read at the twin dinners on Jackson Day and Mr. Bryan's speech on that occasion have certainly started a fine rumpus in the Democratic camp. The general feeling seems to be one of bewilderment, nobody appears to know where they are at or where they ought to go next. The party loyalists, particularly the Bryanites, are greatly distressed. They want to applaud Bryan but they are equally anxious to support the President. They stand first on one foot and then on the other like turkeys on a hot stove. It really is amusing to see their antics.

The efforts to harmonize the Wilson policy with the Bryan policy are pitiful. The simple fact is that the President opposes ratification with any actual reservations and declares that the treaty should be *the* issue in the approaching presidential campaign, while Bryan favors ratification with the weakest reservations that can be obtained by compromise and opposes injecting the treaty into the campaign. How any sensible man can honestly believe that these two radically different ideas as to political policy can be made to accord is beyond my comprehension. However there is a lot of grey matter being wasted over a way to solve this insolvable puzzle.

I am sure that the President's letter will be filed under the heading "Blunders" as were his letters of October, 1918,[1] and of November, 1919.[2] He is certainly unhappy in his letter-writing. When one comes to dissect his plan the folly of it as a practical, working policy is only too manifest.

If the treaty-ratification could be made the *single* issue in the campaign and could be submitted to the voters in a question which could be fully answered by a "yes" or a "no," it would be possible to get a popular decision. But this is certainly impossible at a presidential election. A score of other issues will be involved. Each of these will have a greater importance to thousands, than the treaty, who will vote accordingly. How then would the election of President and Senators determine whether the people favor or oppose the Covenant?

A practical method of submitting the question, even in the form of a referendum, if that could be constitutionally done, appears impossible. There are several grades of reservations, interpretative, slightly modifying, radical, and nullifying. How can these various lists of reservations be laid before the people in a way that they can understand? It seems to me that the whole scheme of obtaining the popular judgment either by election or referendum is absurd and utterly unworkable.

While I believe that ratification without reservations is stronger than many think, I am sure that if the direct issue of "reservations or no reservations" was raised, the advocates of the latter would have the advantage. It would be a campaign of protecting national interests. The great bulk of the people are not going to study the merits. Time, in most cases, and ability, in many, are lacking for any analysis of the subject. To the majority it would seem a struggle for an American or an international policy, and of course Americanism would win.

But then what good would it do to elect a President on the ratification issue if two-thirds of the Senators were not of the same mind? The same deadlock as now exists would continue and the effort to break it without compromising would be futile. I have looked over the list of Senators who are to be elected next November, and the greatest Democratic landslide in all history would never carry enough seats to give the necessary two-thirds.

What nonsense it is to talk about a popular decision at the polls. To butt one's head against a granite wall on the theory that mind is more powerful than matter hardly sounds rational, but it is certainly as rational as to try to force the Senate to accept the treaty without reservations by making it an issue in the presidential campaign. The very suggestion seems to come from an illogical mind.

It is manifest too that any advocacy of the present half-war half-peace conditions for another fourteen months would cause bitter indignation throughout the country. Yet that is the way the President's proposal would be interpreted. If the Democratic Party adopts his plan, it is beaten already.

Viewed from every standpoint little can be urged for the plan. Expediency, political sagacity, the psychology of the situation and plain commonsense are all against it. How the President ever came to write such a letter I cannot conceive.

The other course, proposed by Mr. Bryan in his usual loose way of thinking, consists of obtaining the necessary votes by compromise and concession. It is the sensible point of view and if followed will unquestionably bring about ratification. The Democratic Senators will, I believe, adopt some such policy because, as practical politicians, they must see the danger of being blamed for further delay.

I know that the President wrote a letter much more drastic than the one he sent.[3] It was shown to Polk, Palmer and Houston by Tumulty. They were simply aghast at the statements made. They were most vehement in their criticisms to Tumulty and pointed out numerous errors. The consequence was that the letter was rewritten. This indicates to me that the President is by no means as strong mentally as he was, and that he is more susceptible to his emotions than when in good health. The letter first drafted and to a less degree the letter sent appear to have been dictated by personal chagrin and bitterness at the Senate's opposition, while his natural pugnacity is shown in the attacks which he launches against the enemies of the treaty.

Whether he wants to or not the President *must* compromise or he will wreck the party. As a Democrat I am going to try and get him to recede from his present untenable position. I believe that the best channel to reach him will be through Tumulty. A week from now he may be over his present fit of rage and more willing to listen to reason; and yet I am not sanguine of success because his illness may affect his judgment and make him as unyielding as granite. At any rate I shall not attempt to influence him directly because he knows I am not strong for the Covenant anyway and would conclude that in proposing compromise I was seeking to defeat the Covenant in fact. Of course that would be fatal. The proposal must come from one whom the President believes to be whole-heartedly for the League as planned. That one is Tumulty because the political opportunity and the President's reputation will appeal to him beyond Covenant, League or Treaty.

In any event it is worth trying, for nothing can make the situation worse than it is.

T MS (R. Lansing Papers, DLC).
    [1] That is, Wilson's appeal for the election of a Democratic Congress, printed at Oct. 19, 1918, Vol. 51.

² WW to GMH, Nov. 18, 1919.
³ Lansing, without knowing who the author was, referred to Tumulty's first draft of the Jackson Day message printed at Jan. 6, 1920.

From the Diary of Colonel House

January 11, 1920.

Frank Polk was an interesting caller today. He remained over an hour and told of Cabinet and departmental news. He told Tumulty that the tales of a break between the President, Lansing and me were doing the President infinite harm. Tumulty agreed but said he was more or less helpless. He complained of the Baruch White House visit and said Grayson was responsible for the hurtful publicity.¹ This reminds me to say that Baruch rings me up every day to assure me of his friendship.

Polk spoke more definitely of Lansing's position. Mrs. Wilson is white-hot with indignation and wishes him to resign, but Lansing refuses believing that as long as the President is ill he ought to stick to his post and wait until the President is quite ready before he takes action. Polk said when he [Lansing] heard the President intended writing a letter for the Jackson Day Dinner he insisted that Tumulty show it to him. Tumulty declined to do this but Polk advised him against any radical action. As a result, the letter was sent back to the President and he modified it. Polk and I are both wondering what it was like in its original form since it was finally what it was.

I cannot understand how a man of the President's perception could have thought that a democratic caucus was a place to make remarks regarding the Treaty. It puts his action almost on par with his pre-election letter in the Autumn of 1918 which was so disastrous in its results. The press excoriated him even the faithful New York World.²

Thos. Lamont tells me he talked over the telephone with Grayson and Grayson claimed that the letter would not prevent a compromise. He intimated it was the best they could do with the President. I have my doubts as to whether any effort was made to soften him, for Tumulty told Polk it was a fine letter, although he did not express approval of its timeliness. I take it Mrs. Wilson was the President's only adviser, though Grayson knew of it and possibly Tumulty.

Polk regretted the terrible state of affairs in Washington. The Mexican situation grows steadily worse, and all other matters of importance are held up. He believes the President is in worse condition than the White House indicates. I hope Grayson is right when he states the President will be as well as ever by February first.

[1] We have not found anything about this visit.

[2] "RATIFY THE TREATY!" New York *World*, Jan. 10, 1920. This editorial, undoubtedly written by Frank I. Cobb, Wilson's preeminent editorial supporter, follows in full:

"The treaty of peace is not a personal issue between President Wilson and Senator Lodge, nor is the covenant of the League of Nations a personal issue between these two eminent scholars in politics.

"There are 100,000,000 other Americans who have a direct stake in this controversy, and there are hundreds of millions of people in other countries whose interest is no less important.

"President Wilson's letter to the Jackson Day dinner of the Democratic leaders is immediately followed by an expression of defiance from Senator Lodge. The President showed no disposition whatever to compromise. He again expressed his readiness to accept interpretations which would not alter the meaning of the treaty, but 'if there is any doubt as to what the people of the country think on this vital matter, the clear and single way out is to submit it for determination at the next election to the voters of the Nation, to give the next election the form of a great and solemn referendum.'

" 'The issue is clearly drawn,' replies the Senator. 'The President places himself squarely in behalf of internationalism against Americanism.'

"With due respect to President Wilson and to Senator Lodge, who seem to have an infinite capacity for getting on each other's nerves, both of them are talking nonsense, and very dangerous nonsense at such a time as this. There is no way in which the differences between the President and the Senate majority can be submitted to a referendum next fall. How are the American people at the polls going to differentiate between reservations which alter the meaning of the treaty and interpretations which do not alter the meaning of the treaty? The President and Senator Lodge cannot even agree on that question and there is no unanimity of opinion on either side.

"The United States Senate has a great constitutional duty to perform in relation to the treaty, and it should discharge that duty without further delay. The President's hope of an unqualified ratification of the treaty cannot be realized, much to our regret. Senator Lodge's reservations have been decisively beaten, much to our delight. But there is left a great middle ground of compromise, and it is the business of the two factions to reach an agreement for which sixty-four Senators can vote, mindful of their responsibility.

"The Senate cannot evade that duty, nor is it under obligations to run to the White House every time it wishes to change a comma in the treaty. Nevertheless, it is under obligations to take into consideration all the objections that the President has raised to changes in the treaty and to make the resolution of ratification as wholehearted a response on the part of the United States as the situation permits.

"When the Senate has done its duty the responsibility again rests with the President. He can refuse to exchange ratifications if he believes that in effect the treaty has been rewritten and its great aims and objects perverted, but no President would take such a step for light and trivial reasons. What the President does with the treaty after sixty-four Senators have voted for a resolution of ratification is no affair of the Senate. It will have discharged its constitutional function, and the final decision in any event rests with him.

"President Wilson will not reject an honest compromise. No President can ever reject such a compromise. Least of all could President Wilson submit such a rejection to the American people and ask them for their approval. But it must be a fair compromise. Mr. Bryan's advice to the Democrats to take anything that is offered and get the treaty out of the way is merely a revelation of his crass ignorance and of his moral bankruptcy so far as any matter of real principle is concerned.

"For ten months Senator Lodge has posed as an irresistible force, but events have demonstrated that he is not irresistible. President Wilson is now posing as an immovable body, but if the Senate does what the vast majority of the American people expect it to do, events will demonstrate that the President is not immovable.

"The moral prestige of the United States throughout the world must not be further sacrificed to this quarrel."

According to *The Literary Digest*, the reaction of editors across the country to Wilson's message was mixed, but with most newspapers saying that the immediate necessity was to secure ratification of the treaty; that ratification with the so-called Lodge reservations would not preclude the success of the League; and that Wilson should unite with Republican moderate reservationists to put the treaty through. Some editors also doubted the possibility of making the election of 1920 any sort of meaningful referendum on American membership in the League of Nations. Southern Democratic newspapers tended to support Wilson in what they interpreted as a struggle between him and Bryan for control of the Democratic party. "THE BRYAN–WILSON SPLIT ON THE TREATY," *Literary Digest*, LXIV (Jan. 17, 1920), 11-13.

From Robert Lansing, with Enclosure

My dear Mr. President: Washington January 12, 1920.

I have just received from the American Ambassador in Paris, a cable stating that the first meeting of the Council of the League of Nations would take place at the Quay d'Ors[a]y on Friday, January 16, at 10:30 A.M.

Inasmuch as Article V of the Treaty of Versailles provides that you shall convoke this first meeting and inasmuch as you assured me some time ago that you would be willing to issue thie [this] convocation whenever it might be necessary, I am today sending out in your name, an invitation for the first meeting to the following Powers: Great Britain, France, Italy, Japan, Belgium, Brazil and Spain. I would likewsie have sent an invitation to Greece but inasmuch as that nation has not as yet ratified the Treaty I felt it would be wiser to withhold the invitation until the act of ratification had been completed.

The text of the attached invitation was approved on October 24, 1919 by Senator Hitchcock after consultation with certain of his colleagues. It was thereafter submitted to the Council of the Heads of Delegations in Paris and received the approval of that body. It is my present intention to make it public tomorrow.

Faithfully,   Robert Lansing

TLS (WP, DLC).

E N C L O S U R E

"In compliance with Article 5 of the Covenant of the League of Nations which went into effect at the same time as the Treaty of Versailles of June 28, 1919, of which it is a part, the President of the United States, acting on behalf of those nations which have deposited their instruments of ratification in Paris, as certified in a proces verbal drawn up by the French Government dated January 10, 1920, has the honor to inform the Government of [blank] that the first meeting of the Council of the League of Nations will be held in Paris at the Ministry of Foreign Affairs on Friday, January 16, 10:30 A.M.

The President earnestly ventures the hope that the Government of [blank] will be in a position to send a representative to this first meeting. He feels that it is unnecessary for him to point out the deep significance attached to this meeting or the importance which it must assume in the eyes of the world. It will mark the beginning of a new era in international cooperation and the first great step toward the ideal concert of nations. It will bring the League of Nations into being as a living force, devoted to the task of assisting the peoples of all countries in their desire for peace, prosperity and happiness. The President is convinced that its progress will accord with the noble purpose to which it is dedicated."

T MS (WP, DLC).

Robert Lansing to Joseph Patrick Tumulty

Dear Mr. Tumulty: Washington January 12, 1920.

In accordance with the President's pleasure as stated in your letter of December 24,[1] the Permanent Court of Arbitration at The Hague has been notified of the designation of Messrs. Root, Gray, Moore and Straus as United States members of the Court for another term. I have also advised the gentlemen mentioned.

I am, my dear Mr. Tumulty,

Sincerely yours, Robert Lansing

TLS (WP, DLC).
[1] See RL to WW, Dec. 22, 1919, n. 1.

Gilbert Monell Hitchcock to Edith Bolling Galt Wilson

My dear Mrs Wilson [Washington] Jan 13, 1920

Day after tomorrow at 10:30 a.m. the democratic caucus meets to elect a leader.

The contest is rather close between Mr Underwood and myself.

Because I have stood firmly by the League of nations I am opposed by

Gore
Reed
Shields
Wa[l]sh of Mass
and perhaps Hoke Smith.

I lay this matter before you with the suggestion that if something can be done today or tomorrow to influence Senator Harris of Georgia to support me I shall feel quite sure of the result. He is not unfriendly but is influenced by local interests to favor Underwood.

Yours sincerely G. M. Hitchcock

ALS (WP, DLC).

Edith Bolling Galt Wilson to Gilbert Monell Hitchcock

My dear Senator Hitchcock   The White House Jan. 13, 1920

The President is so profoundly convinced that he ought never to give the slightest ground for the accusation that he has acceeded the proper bounds of Executive authority and influence that he feels he is bound in conscience to take no part in the choice to which you refer in your letter to me today.[1]

At the same time he particularly requests me to express again his profound gratitude and admiration for the leadership you have exercised in the great matter of the Treaty.

With warm regards believe me,

Faithfully yours   Edith Bolling Wilson[2]

ALS (G. M. Hitchcock Papers, DLC).
[1] The voting in the Democratic senatorial caucus on January 15 ended in a tie, nineteen to nineteen, when Hoke Smith refused to vote. Underwood was finally elected Minority Leader on April 27, 1920, after Hitchcock's withdrawal from the contest on April 23.
[2] There is a EBWhw draft of this letter in WP, DLC.

From the Desk Diary of Robert Lansing

1920 Tuesday 13 January

Mrs. Wilson phoned me asking about Prest's call of League Council announced in N[ews]. P[apers]. Told her form agreed to in Oct and approved by Senator Hitchcock. Copy sent Prest yesterday not received.

Cabinet meeting—11-12:30. Burleson delivered a lecture on the power of 'catch' phrases in presidential campaigns and the way heart should be put into Democrats this year. Lane and I discussed with Tumulty latter's efforts to get Prest to accept defeat and to put Lodge in a hole by proposing "interpretations." Thinks he has made headway. Time is the essence of the situation.

From Raymond Blaine Fosdick[1]

My dear Mr. President: Washington January 14, 1920

As you will perhaps recall, Sir Eric Drummond last June appointed me Under Secretary General of the provisional organization of the League of Nations. In this capacity I worked with him in London until November, when I returned to represent him at the meeting of the International Labor Conference here in Washington. When the Conference completed its work and my duties in connection therewith were finished, I did not go back to London because I was fearful that with the critical condition existing in the Senate, any publicity as to the connection of an American with the League might prove harmful. This appeared, too, to be the judgment of Secretary Lansing. During the interim, therefore, I have endeavored to keep Sir Eric Drummond in intimate touch with the situation in America, so that he and his associates could gauge the drift of events.

My connection with the Secretariat has consequently been kept quiet, and as a result my position has been too much that of a "pussy footer" to be comfortable. The fact that my salary has been paid from moneys contributed to the League by the French, Belgian and English governments, whereas America has made no contribution, has added decidedly to my feeling of embarrassment. However, Sir Eric Drummond has been anxious that I should stay on, and has refused to consider my offer of resignation, unless I should press it for reasons arising out of the situation in America.

I feel, however, that with the League holding its first Council meeting this coming Friday, my position will be increasingly embarrassing. It is entirely possible that some announcement will be made from Paris as to the personnel of the Secretariat, and I am not at all sure what the effect of such announcement will be in the Senate. What would you advise me to do? Now that the League has become a going concern rather than a provisional organization, will my continued connection with the Secretariat jeopardize the cause? Am I justified in accepting a salary from a fund to which America has not contributed? I may say in this connection, perhaps, that I accepted the position last June only because I felt that it was an obligation from which I could not conscientiously escape. Resignation would relieve me of the burden of serious sacrifices which I have been obliged to make. On the other hand, because I believe the League of Nations is the biggest idea that has been presented to my generation, I am anxious to serve it to the utmost.

There are, perhaps, half a dozen other Americans on the Secretariat who find themselves in a similar position. Mr. Arthur Sweetser, who is attached to the Public Information Section of the Secretariat,[2] is with me here in Washington. Captain Gilchrist,[3] my assistant, is in London with Sir Eric Drummond. The other Americans actively serving on the Secretariat at present are Manley Hudson, attached to the Legal Section, Miss Florence Wilson, Assistant Librarian, Howard Huston, Establishment Officer, and one or two others in positions of lesser importance.

I have naturally hesitated to intrude on your illness with such a detail as this, but the question concerns others than myself, and may have important consequences. May I take this opportunity, as one who has been proud to call himself your friend and follower from old Princeton days, to express the wish, shared, I believe, by the entire world, that your return to health and vigor may not be delayed.   Ever cordially yours,   Raymond B. Fosdick

TLS (WP, DLC).
[1] Fosdick had discussed with Tumulty the problem which he describes below. Tumulty, Fosdick recalled shortly thereafter, had expressed "his belief that the President was not aware of the fact that there were any Americans still connected with the Secretariat" and advised Fosdick "to put the whole thing up to the President in a letter, and ask his advice." R. B. Fosdick to EMH, Jan. 19, 1920, printed in Raymond B. Fosdick, *Letters on the League of Nations* (Princeton, N. J., 1966), p. 106. Writing to another correspondent on the same date, Fosdick said that Tumulty believed that "the President did not know that there were Americans aside from myself serving on the Secretariat." R. B. Fosdick to H. Gilchrist, Jan. 19, 1920, *ibid.*, p. 108.
[2] Former assistant director of the press section of the A.C.N.P.
[3] Capt. Huntington Gilchrist, U.S.A., formerly with the A.C.N.P.

From the Desk Diary of Robert Lansing

January Wednesday 14 1920

Left at 4:30 and went to Ex. Offices. There, conferred 45 min with Tumulty on proposed letter of Prest to Hitchcock suggesting reservations. If the Prest will send this letter the Treaty will be soon ratified

Joseph Patrick Tumulty to Edith Bolling Galt Wilson, with Enclosure

Dear Mrs. Wilson: The White House 15 January 1920.

It now appears that without any initiative on the part of the President, efforts are being made in the Senate to reach a compromise on the Peace Treaty.[1] Those negotiations will soon approach a point at which both sides will reach their irreducible minimum. It is at this psychological moment that action must be taken—if it is to be taken at all—in making clear that the President is not insisting upon an unqualified adoption of the Treaty without the crossing of a "t" or the dotting of an "i." If we say nothing, and a compromise is reached, it will be too late to revise or change the agreement inasmuch as the country will say this thing has been reached after a good deal of struggle—why quibble now—take it; get the thing over with.

Therefore, it would seem to me to be wise to interject at the proper moment, if negotiations have seemed to reach a compromise—our own interpretation of the Treaty.

In the accompanying letter, I have sketched what the President might use as the basis of a communication to Senator Hitchcock. The letter was framed after carefully eliminating the obnoxious parts of all the resolutions proposed by the majority and minority in the Senate Foreign Relations Committee, and by including, of course, the main thread running through the President's western speeches and the proposals made from time to time by Senator Hitchcock.

As the Springfield Republican said the other day, "It is the President's duty to remove every obstacle and locate the responsibility, thus making the road clearer for the great object he has in mind; namely, the National referendum."

Action along the lines suggested in this letter would make the issue clear and clean-cut and remove from the President's shoulders the burden of the responsibility which would be his for a seeming unyielding attitude.

If the President wishes to place full responsibility squarely upon Lodge and the Republicans, this, in my opinion, is the way. It has in it, the great opportunity of obtaining speedily a ratification of the Treaty.   Sincerely yours,   Tumulty

TLS (WP, DLC).
¹ A small group of Democratic and Republican senators were meeting on this same day in the first of a series of bipartisan conferences which were to continue through January 30. For the composition of the group and a description of the results of the first meeting, see GMH to JPT, Jan. 16, 1920. About these conferences, see Thomas A. Bailey, *Woodrow Wilson and the Great Betrayal* (New York, 1945), pp. 229-32; Lloyd E. Ambrosius, *Woodrow Wilson and the American Diplomatic Tradition: The Treaty Fight in Perspective* (Cambridge, New York, etc., 1987), pp. 228-32; and Herbert F. Margulies, *Senator Lenroot of Wisconsin: A Political Biography, 1900-1929* (Columbia, Mo., and London, 1977), pp. 297-300.
Tumulty talked with Mrs. Wilson before he wrote this letter on January 15. She made notes of this conversation (EBWhw MS, WP, DLC) as follows: "Hitchcock with a Rep. Senator write a letter asking your ideas on interprative Reservations—Quote what you said to Foreign Rel. Com. & what you said in your Western speeches—& in your Jackson dinner letter in regard to always being willing to discuss Lodge Reservation in a gen way—stating 5 of these these nullify the Treaty & would require resubmission to Paris The other 9 are local things which affect this country & can be dealt with by our own people. Therefore for the sake of the peace of the World & the magnitude of the Treaty you are willing to accept them if the Senate accept intepretive reservations."
Mrs. Wilson may have urged Tumulty to write his letter of January 15.

ENCLOSURE[1]

My dear Senator:

You have asked me to tell you frankly what interpretations I had in mind when I wrote the letter of January eighth, saying:

"I have endeavored to make it plain that if the Senate wishes to say what the undoubted meaning of the League is, I shall have no objection. There can be no reasonable objection to interpretations accompanying the act of ratification itself."

I am very glad indeed to tell you, so that you may inform your Democratic and Republican colleagues who desire an early ratification of the Peace Treaty, what I would construe as reasonable interpretations. I fully agree with you that delay is most unfortunate and that if there is an opportunity to obtain an agreement on the part of those who sincerely desire to see the Treaty ratified, we should make every effort, in a spirit of accommodation, to accomplish that result as quickly as possible. Each day's delay brings an unsettlement of conditions throughout the world which not only invites disaster to our sorely-tried associates, but brings the contagion of world unrest nearer our own shores.

I have had from the first no doubt about the good faith of our associates in the war; nor have I had any reason to suppose that any nation would seek to enlarge our obligations under the Covenant of the League of Nations, or would seek to commit us to lines of action which under our Constitution only the Congress of the United States can in the last analysis decide, but if any doubts remain in the minds of Senators that in future generations ambiguous constructions may be placed upon various clauses in the Treaty, I am glad to summarize what seem to me reasonable interpretations on the points which have been the subject of controversy in the Senate for many months.

⟨1. It is evident that when ratifications have been deposited, the

[1] Deletions by Wilson in the following document in angle brackets; words in italics, WWhw.

Tumulty drafted this letter on January 14 and sent copies to Lansing and Houston. Lansing went through his copy (it is a CC MS in the J. P. Tumulty Papers, DLC) and made changes and marginal comments in the text. Newton D. Baker also read Lansing's copy and made at least one suggestion. Houston's copy is missing. He apparently returned to Tumulty only a one-page memorandum (Hw MS in *ibid.*) with four rather insubstantial suggestions for revision. Tumulty and Swem then incorporated Lansing's changes and Houston's suggestions in a new copy, which is now in the C. L. Swem Coll., NjP. Swem then typed up what he called a "Corrected" copy. Swem kept a carbon copy of this, and the ribbon copy was sent as the Enclosure which we print. Tumulty sent a copy of the "corrected" copy to Lansing, who returned it with the attached note: "Seems excellent. Have no suggestions. RL 1/15/20." CC MS with Hw note, J. P. Tumulty Papers, DLC.

interpretations set forth by the United States therein will thereby become a part of the Treaty of Peace, so far as the interests of the United States are concerned.⟩

2. The United States is of course able to withdraw from the League of Nations, under Article I of the Covenant, and being a sovereign state, is naturally the sole judge of whether all its international obligations have been fulfilled at the time of withdrawal.[2] But, in my judgment, it would seem to be wiser to give to the President of the United States in the future the right to act upon any such resolution as may be adopted by Congress giving notice of withdrawal, and it would seem, therefore, advisable to make it necessary that any resolution giving notice of withdrawal shall be a joint instead of a concurrent resolution. I doubt whether the President can be deprived of his veto power under the Constitution, even with his own consent. This would permit the President of the United States, who is charged by the Constitution with the conduct of foreign policy, to have a voice in saying whether so important a step as withdrawal from the League of Nations shall be accomplished by a simple majority vote or by a two-thirds vote, which would be the case if he vetoed the resolution. Our fathers provided that whenever the legislative body was to be consulted in treaty-making, a two-thirds vote was required, and it seems to me that there should be no departure from the wise course which they outlined at the beginning of this Republic.

3. With respect to the much-discussed Article X, it seems to me to be clearly a question of whether the moral influence which the Executive branch of the Government of the United States, under this or future administrations, can always exert for the preservation of peace shall not be diminished, but that, on the other hand, it should be clearly understood by our associates at all times that whenever the employment of military or naval forces is recommended by the League of Nations, the power of the Congress of the United States to accept or reject such a recommendation is inviolate. And there must be no misunderstanding at any time on the part of our associates in the League if any President of the United States in the exercise of his constitutional functions submits the matter for decision by Congress before casting the vote of the United States. Disregard of the right of Congress in this respect was never contemplated by the members of the American Peace Commission in Paris, nor was it misunderstood by our colleagues, who were as jealous as we were to guard their own sovereignty and preserve the right of their own legislative parliaments

---

[2] Wilson drew two vertical lines in the left-hand margin here.

to participate in momentous decisions involving the use of military or naval forces.

4. I see no objection to the frank statement that the United States shall not become a mandatory in any part of the globe under Article XXII, part I, or any other provision of the Treaty of Peace with Germany, except by action of the Congress of the United States.[3]

5. As to the sovereign right of the United States to determine what questions are within its domestic jurisdiction, the Covenant expressly excludes interference with domestic questions relating wholly or in part to internal affairs. Therefore, I have no strong objection to stating that immigration, the tariff, the suppression of the traffic in opium, or any other questions which the United States may by its sovereign rights determine are domestic in character, shall not be submitted in any way either to arbitration, inquiry or decision without our consent. The danger in listing them is that this constitutes a limitation by exclusion.

6. With respect to the Monroe Doctrine, the Covenant expressly states that nothing shall impair the validity of such regional understandings as the Monroe Doctrine. I see no objection to an even more specific declaration, if it is desired by the Senate, to the effect that any question which in the judgment of the United States depends upon or relates to our long-established national policy, commonly known as the Monroe Doctrine, shall be interpreted by the United States alone and declared entirely unaffected by any provision contained in the Treaty of Peace with Germany.

7. Clearly, the desire of those who do not approve of the so-called Shantung settlement must be, not merely to condemn, but to do something salutary which will assist in the future settlement of this troublesome question.[4] Therefore, I can see no objection to a declaration reserving to us full liberty of action with respect to any controversy that may arise under Articles 156, 157 and 158 between the Republic of China and the Empire of Japan, if the pledges made by the Japanese delegation, and which are contained in the minutes of the Conference *of the principal powers* at Paris, are not fulfilled.

8. There is no necessity, in my judgment, to insert in the Treaty of Peace provisions that relate entirely to the method by which the United States will provide for the appointment of the representatives[5] of the United States in the Assembly and Council of the League, since each nation must retain its sovereign right of selecting those representatives in whatever way it shall choose. The ap-

[3] *Idem.*   [4] *Idem.*   [5] *Idem.*

pointment of individuals to conduct the foreign policy of the United States is fully covered in the Constitution of the United States, and Congress is authorized to pass laws appropriating or refusing to appropriate money for the maintenance of such representation. Congress can always pass laws forbidding participation by citizens of the United States on commissions of the League of Nations if those citizens have not already been duly appointed as representatives of the United States in accordance with the laws of the United States.

9. With respect to the Reparation Commission and the functions of the American commissioner, it is obvious that the commerce of the United States can be regulated under the Constitution only by the Congress, but that this in no way impairs the power of the Executive branch of the Government to negotiate commercial agreements with foreign powers, subject, of course, to the approval of our legislative body.

10. Those questions which relate to whether or not the United States shall be obliged to contribute to any expenses of the League of Nations unless and until an appropriation of funds for such expenses shall have been made by the Congress of the United States are, of course, in line with what has been recognized would be our practice, and is the practice, of parliamentary governments in all parts of the world who control foreign policy by means of the budget.[6] So, there can be no objection to notifying foreign governments that appropriations for the maintenance of American representation in the Secretariat or on commissions organized under the League of Nations can be made only by the Congress of the United States.

11. No programme for disarmament has as yet been adopted by any of the powers. Provision alone has been made for inquiry into this subject. It is to be expected that when any definite programme is finally presented to the United States for approval or disapproval by the League, this country, of course, reserves the right to say under what conditions, such as when threatened with invasion or when engaged in war, the United States would feel justified in increasing those armaments.

12. It was the unanimous opinion of the men who framed the League of Nations Covenant that in no circumstances should one member have greater voting power than any other. So, I have no objection to stating specifically, as it has been stated in the Senate, that in case of a dispute between members of the League, if one of them have self-governing colonies, dominions or parts which have

[6] *Idem.*

representation in the Assembly, ⟨each and⟩ ? all are to be considered as one party to the dispute, as is evidenced by the parties named in the Treaty.

I sincerely hope, my dear Senator, that the interpretations which I have set forth will be of use in bringing about an early ratification of the Peace Treaty, so that we may take our place alongside the great nations who helped to fight the war to a successful conclusion and who bound themselves together by the solemn terms of the Armistice to establish a concert of power of free nations that would preserve the peace of the world. The only stabilizing influence left to bring order out of this chaos of distress is the League of Nations, whose power and effectiveness would be more or less nullified by the refusal of America manfully to accept her full measure of responsibility with her associates. If there have been any mistakes in the making of the Peace Treaty, the League of Nations furnishes the means for revision in the future. America covets the opportunity to serve humanity and to help save the world. She must not be denied this great opportunity.

Sincerely yours,

Hon. Gilbert M. Hitchcock,
United States Senate.

T MS (WP, DLC).

From the Desk Diary of Robert Lansing

1920 Thursday 15 January

Received draft letter Prest to Hitchcock. Sent it back without suggestion.

Joseph Patrick Tumulty to Edith Bolling Galt Wilson

Dear Mrs. Wilson: [The White House] 16 January, 1920

I submitted the draft of the proposed letter to Secretary Houston. He has examined it very carefully and has dictated the following memorandum which he requested me, through you, to submit to the President:

"I have given much thought to the pending treaty situation. I believe that the President should make clear what he has many times said as to interpretations and reservations. I have read the proposed draft of the letter and it seems to me to cover the situation admirably. It is reasonable and will appeal to the good sense of the American people. I am inclined to believe that it will force a speedy ratification of the treaty and put the full responsibility for delay on the Republicans in the Senate." Sincerely,   [J P Tumulty]

CCL (J. P. Tumulty Paper, DLC).

Gilbert Monell Hitchcock to Joseph Patrick Tumulty

My dear Mr. Tumulty: [Washington] January 16, 1920

I think it might be desirable for me to keep the President advised of suggested compromises that are discussed at various meetings. Hence this letter.

Yesterday by arrangement of Senator Owen a little meeting was held in the rooms of the foreign relations committee. Lodge selected for his supporters in that meeting Lenroot and New, who are almost as irreconcilable as Lodge himself, and Kellogg who is more reasonable. I brought with me Senator Walsh of Montana, McKellar of Tennessee and Simmons of North Carolina, as well as Senator Owen who arranged the meeting. In other words, I was accompanied by senators who desire a compromise and Senator Lodge was accompanied by rather an uncompromising lot except for Kellogg. On someone's suggestion the Lodge reservations were taken up one by one. The first suggestion was that the objectionable part of the preamble should be stricken out. Lodge indicated that this probably could be arranged. The second suggestion was that in reservation No. 1 the notice of withdrawal from the league should be by a joint instead of by a concurrent resolution. Lodge and his friends did not seem to think there would be much difficulty about that.

On Lodge's second reservation which related to Article 10, Senator Simmons presented for discussion the following reservation as a substitute:

"The United States assumes no obligation to employ the military and naval forces of the United States under the provisions of Article 10 or any other article of the treaty to preserve the territorial integrity or political independence of any other country or interfere in controversies between nations, whether members of the league or not, unless in any particular case the Congress shall by act of joint resolution so provite [provide]."

Lodge and New both indicated that they thought it would be very difficult to procure support for this substitute.

Senator McKellar suggested certain changes in the Lodge reservation on Article 10 which after his amendments would read as follows:

"The United States assumes no obligation to preserve by its

military or naval forces the territorial integrity or political independence of any other country, or interfere by its military or naval forces in controversies between nations, whether members of
the league or not, under the provisions of Article 10, or to employ
the military or naval forces of the United States under any article
of the treaty for any purpose until the Congress, which under
the constitution has the sole power to declare war or authorize
the employment of the military or naval forces of the United
States, shall by act or joint resolution so provide."

The underscored words in the above reservation are those which
McKellar proposes to insert. The word "until" takes the place of
the words "unless in any particular case" in the Lodge reservation.

Both of these substitutes go further in yielding to Lodge than I
am ready to go and I have not committed myself to them, but
Lodge indicated that they could not be assented to by his side.

Proposed changes in Lodge's fourth reservation are not important, nor are the proposed changes in reservations 5 and 6.

It is proposed in reservation 7 to make a great condensation so
as to merely state that the Congress is to provide by law for the
appointment of representatives of the United States in the league,
that their duties shall be defined by law and that they shall be appointed by the President with the consent of the Senate.

In the case of the eighth reservation the suggestion made was
that the United States understands that the Reparation Commission will not discriminate against the commerce of the United
States in regulating imports and exports of Germany.

In Lodge's ninth reservation the suggestion was that we should
except the secretariat at least from the expenses of the league that
we were not responsible for until authorized by Congress.

We did not reach for consideration the fourteenth reservation relating to the plural votes of the British Empire. I stated that at the
proper time I should make the proposal that any reservations
adopted should be put in the form of interpretations and understandings of the league.

The republicans present made no suggestions at all and Lodge
merely stated that he would submit the suggestions made by
Owen, Simmons, McKellar and Walsh to a republican conference
today. We are to meet again Saturday morning.

I inserted in the Congressional Record today the striking showing of the vote in several hundred colleges of the country on special
ballots O.K'ed by Lodge and myself January 13th.[1] Lodge and
some of his colleagues seemed to be rather indignant that I
brought the subject up as I did in the Senate but I think it is just
as well to emphasize the weakness of the Lodge reservations in
public opinion.   Yours truly,   G M Hitchcock

TLS (WP, DLC).

¹ *Cong. Record*, 66th Cong., 2d sess., pp. 1603-1604. Hitchcock himself had summarized the results to date of the not yet completed poll of students and faculty of approximately 400 American colleges and universities: 46,259 votes for unqualified ratification of the treaty; 33,304 for ratification with a compromise between the Lodge reservations and the "Democratic reservations"; 23,577 for ratification with the Lodge reservations; and 11,690 opposed to ratification in any form. In addition to a ballot with these four options, the voters had before them printed arguments by Lodge for ratification with his reservations and by Hitchcock for ratification after a compromise between the Lodge reservations and his own "Democratic" reservations. *Ibid.*, p. 1603.

From William Graves Sharp¹

Dear Mr. President: Elyria, Ohio January 16, 1920.

I want to tell you how strongly your recent letter to the Jackson Day banqueters appealed to me, and how accurately you sized up the public mind when you declared: "Personally I do not accept the action of the Senate of the United States as the decision of the Nation. I have asserted from the first that the overwhelming majority of the people of this country desire the ratification of the treaty"—

If my judgment, based upon the talk which I have heard coming from all classes of people, of a number of the middle States, is worth anything, you can rest assured that an appeal to the people would result in an overwhelming support of all the essential principles embraced within the treaty. Of course, the politicians of the opposition—those who are striving for party prestige—are quite united in insisting on material reservations or its entire rejection. Under the slogan of a sham patriotism, they are shouting "Americanism" as the coming issue, but at heart are as afraid as of death of having the treaty made an issue, and especially its feature of the League of Nations.

Every churchman and many college men are very strong in endorsing your position on this question. It is also true that many of the rank and file of the Republican party, who have no axes to grind, have been outspoken to me in their opposition to the tactics used by the Senate majority.

While I have been earnestly hoping that such a compromise could be reached as would not impair reciprocal obligations of the treaty, and at the same time satisfy the pride of the majority leaders—though I am forced to believe it is far more discreditable than pride on the part of some of them—yet neither in moral obligation, expediency or the precepts of international law, rests the power in the Senate to now alter the meaning of the treaty.

None of the messages that you have sent to the American people, as well as to those of other nations, in which I have had reason so often to take pride, have set forth more clearly our accepted and bounden obligation than this last one. I am sure, too, that your observations upon our domestic conditions will exert a profound impression on the people. Each day we are getting further away from our old time conservatism, which, whether I am right or wrong in my view, furnishes infinitely better conditions for true progress than some of the many experimental remedies now being tried. Most of them seek the fiat of law rather than the establishing of moral convictions of man's duty to his fellowmen. Only a revival, national in its scope, of such convictions, and a determined and persistent effort to enforce a higher standard of education among the masses of the youth of our country, have within themselves any substantial hope of bettering the condition of our people. Your own consistent purpose and endeavor in leading thought to these higher things I am sure has its reward in the abounding confidence of your countrymen despite the venom of jealous political partisanship.

At a time when this sort of opposition has reached its heighth— or shall I better say its lowest depth—I have felt that as one enjoying, as I believe, your confidence in the past, it was my duty to write you this message. With the many cares and responsibilities upon you and your long continued illness, which I pray God may soon be a thing of the past, I do not wish you to take the time to make the merest acknowledgment of my letter.

With my best wishes for your continued progress toward good health, I am, believe me, Mr. President,

Very truly yours,   Wm. G. Sharp.

TLS (WP, DLC).
[1] Democratic congressman from Ohio, 1909-1914; Ambassador to France, 1914-1919.

Joseph Patrick Tumulty to Raymond Blaine Fosdick

Dear Mr. Fosdick: The White House 16 January 1920.

The President has carefully read your letter of the 14th of January, and has asked me to say to you that he feels he cannot decide the question it contains as he thinks it is one which should be left to you and the gentlemen associated with you to take counsel together and determine in concert what it is right to do.

Sincerely yours,   J P Tumulty

TLS (R. B. Fosdick Papers, NjP).

Joseph Patrick Tumulty to Edith Bolling Galt Wilson

Dear Mrs. Wilson: The White House 17 January, 1920.

The psychological moment is approaching when the President could strike with great force along the lines suggested in the letter to Senator Hitchcock. The happenings of today (Saturday) will determine whether there is to be an approach to an agreement on the Treaty or a deadlock. This will give the President, in my opinion, his great opportunity.

The enclosed editorial from the Springfield Republican, containing a discussion of Article X.,[1] is interesting, as is the article from the New York World, charging Lodge with unfair tactics.[2]

Sincerely,   Tumulty

TLS (WP, DLC).

[1] It is missing, but it was "A Dispute Over What?" *Springfield*, Mass., *Republican*, Jan. 16, 1920. This editorial began with the observation that the dispute over the Lodge reservation to Article X was reported to be the chief obstacle to a Senate compromise and consent to ratification of the peace treaty. "From the beginning," it declared, "this controversy has had very much of the appearance of unreality. The prolonged contest now has the appearance of a struggle to 'save face' for somebody, or to enable some great leader to crow over another great leader when the end comes." If the principle at stake in the Lodge reservation to Article X was that it would imply no obligation to bind the United States to use its armed forces to prevent external aggression against any nation without the prior consent of Congress, then, said the editorial, there need not have been any dispute at the beginning. "No treaty can affect the constitutional control of the war-making power by Congress inasmuch as no treaty can possibly change the constitution." However, the editorial continued, the Lodge reservation to Article X might in practice prove ineffective: "The Senate by a reservation to a treaty cannot take away from the executive constitutional powers which he already has. A president always has interfered, when he wanted to, and always may 'interfere' in controversies between other nations by diplomatic methods short of war. For the president controls the channels of diplomatic intercourse with other nations. As for this treaty, once the United States ratifies it, it becomes constitutionally 'the supreme law of the land,' in so far as it does not violate the constitution; and the president may take diplomatic action short of war to see that the treaty is enforced even if that means 'interference' in controversies between other signatory states. How is he to be prevented from doing it?"

"In so far as the Lodge reservation would do what its author designed it to do," the editorial concluded, "it would of course paralyze executive initiative in helping to protect any foreign state against 'external aggression' by diplomatic methods, provided there was a Senate majority politically hostile to the administration. This is the key, perhaps, to the Lodge reservation. He is obsessed by the spectacle of a democratic president and must hobble him at any cost. But republican presidents may also be in power when democratic majorities control Congress. What would then be the Lodge view? We might have a righteous president trying to safeguard the peace of the world as against a wicked democratic Congress and an obstreperous Senate seeking partisan advantage."

[2] Also missing, but it was Charles Michelson, "LODGE BLOCKS PACT COMPROMISE, ITS FRIENDS INSIST," New York *World*, Jan. 17, 1920. Michelson described a number of attempts by moderate Republican and Democratic senators to reach some compromise, the latest being the bipartisan conference. Lodge, he believed, was steering all these efforts from the Republican side in such a way that none could reach fruition. "In other words," he wrote, "Senator Lodge has kidnapped the conciliation movement and, for the moment, at least, is guiding it along channels that lead nowhere."

Gilbert Monell Hitchcock to Joseph Patrick Tumulty, with Enclosure

My dear Mr. Tumulty: [Washington] January 17, 1920

I enclose herewith a marked copy of the Lodge reservations which in effect gives the record of the day's conference with Lodge and his associates. No final agreement was reached on anything though tentative agreements were reached on a number of things. We only got as far as Article 10. We shall have another meeting on Monday.   Yours very truly,   G M Hitchcock

TLS (WP, DLC).

Second day (Jan. 17, 1920.)

[Committee Print.]

66TH CONGRESS,
1ST SESSION. }   IN OPEN EXECUTIVE SESSION.

TREATY OF PEACE WITH GERMANY.

IN THE SENATE OF THE UNITED STATES.

RESOLUTION.

1   *Resolved (two-thirds of the Senators present concurring*
2   *therein),* That the Senate advise and consent to the ratifica-
3   tion of the treaty of peace with Germany concluded at Ver-
4   sailles on the 28th day of June, 1919, subject to the follow-
5   ing reservations and understandings, which are hereby made
6   a part and condition of this resolution of ratification which
7   ratification is not to take effect or bind the United States until
8   the said reservations and understandings adopted by the Sen-
9   ate have been accepted by an exchange of notes as a part and
10 a condition of this resolution of ratification by at least three of
11 the four Principal Allied and Associated Powers, to wit,
12 Great Britain, France, Italy, and Japan:

★

Passed over for the present

2

1   1. The United States so understands and construes

2   Article 1 that in case of notice of withdrawal from the

3   league of nations, as provided in said article, the United

4   States shall be the sole judge as to whether all its inter-

5   national obligations and all its obligations under the said

6   covenant have been fulfilled, and notice of withdrawal by

7   the United States may be given by ~~a concurrent resolution~~ *the president or by*

8   ~~of the Congress of the United States.~~ *a majority of both houses* x

By Lodge

9   2. The United States assumes no obligation to preserve

10   the territorial integrity or political independence of any other

11   country or to interfere in controversies between nations—

12   whether members of the league or not—under the provisions

13   of Article 10, or to employ the military or naval forces of

14   the United States under any article of the treaty for any

15   purpose, unless in any particular case the Congress, which,

16   under the Constitution, has the sole power to declare war or

17   authorize the employment of the military or naval forces

18   of the United States, shall by act or joint resolution so

19   provide.

Passed over for the day

20   3. No mandate shall be accepted by the United States

21   under Article 22, Part 1, or any other provision of the treaty

22   of peace with Germany, except by action of the Congress

23   of the United States.

24   4. The United States reserves to itself exclusively the

25   right to decide what questions are within its domestic juris-

O.K. except as to form

3

1 diction and declares that all domestic and political questions

2 relating wholly or in part to its internal affairs, including im-

3 migration. labor, coastwise traffic, the tariff. ~~commerce~~, the   *internal*   *by Kellogg*

4 suppression of traffic in women and children, and in opium   *within, into and from the U.S.*

5 and other dangerous drugs. and all other domestic questions.   *by Walsh*

6 are solely within the jurisdiction of the United States and

7 are not under this treaty to be submitted in any way either

8 to arbitration or to the consideration of the council or of the

9 assembly of the league of nations, ~~or any~~ agency thereof,   *or any*   *By Walsh*

10 ~~to the decision or recommendation of any other power.~~

11   5. The United States will not submit to arbitration or

12 to inquiry by the assembly or by the council of the league

13 of nations. provided for in said treaty of peace. any ques-

14 tions which in the judgment of the United States depend   *no*

15 upon or relate to its long-established policy, commonly   *change*

16 known as the Monroe doctrine; said doctrine is to be in-

17 terpreted by the United States alone and is hereby declared

18 to be wholly outside the jurisdiction of said league of nations

19 and entirely unaffected by any provision contained in the

20 said treaty of peace with Germany.

21   6. The United States withholds its assent to Articles

22 156, 157, and 158, and reserves full liberty of action with

23 respect to any controversy which may arise under said   *O.K.*

24 articles ~~between the Republic of China and the Empire of~~

25 ~~Japan.~~

4

1   7 The Congress of the United States will provide
2 by law for the appointment of the representatives of the
3 United States in the assembly and the council of the
4 league of nations, and may in its discretion provide for the
5 participation of the United States in any commission, com-
6 mittee, tribunal, court, council, or conference, or in the
7 selection of any members thereof and for the appoint-
8 ment of members of said commissions, committees, tribu-
9 nals, courts, councils, or conferences, or any other representatives under the treaty of peace, or in carrying out
its provisions, and until such participation and appointment have been so provided for and the powers and
duties of such representatives have been defined by law,
no person shall represent the United States under either
said league of nations or the treaty of peace with Germany or be authorized to perform any act for or on behalf
of the United States thereunder, and no citizen of the
United States shall be selected or appointed as a member
of said commissions, committees, tribunals, courts, councils,
or conferences except with the approval of the Senate of
21 the United States.

22   8. The United States understands that the reparation
23 commission will not so regulate or interfere with exports from the
24 United States to Germany, or from Germany to the United
25 States. only when the United States by Act or Joint Reso-
as to discriminate against the United States.

Substitute by Walsh favorably considered

By Hitchcock but not favorably considered

4

1   7 The Congress of the United States will provide

2   by law for the appointment of the representatives of the

3   United States in the assembly and the council of the

4   league of nations, and may in its discretion provide for the

5   participation of the United States in any commission, com-

6   mittee, tribunal, court, council, or conference, or in the

7   selection of any members thereof and for the appoint-

8   ment of members of said commissions, committees, tribu-

9   nals, courts, councils, or conferences or ___ ___ ___

Substitute by Walsh favorably considered

11

12   Substitute for Lodge's 7th reservation, favorably
                               considered.

13

14   No person is or shall be authorized to represent the
     United States nor shall any citizen of the United States
     be eligible as a member of any body or agency established
     or authorized by said treaty of peace with Germany except
     pursuant to an act of the Congress of the United States
     providing for his appointment and defining his powers and
     duties.

                         ___ ___ except with the approval of the Senate of

21   the United States.

22   8. The United States understands that the reparation

23   commission will *not so* regulate or interfere with exports from the

24   United States to Germany, or from Germany to the United

25   States, only when the United States by Act or Joint Reso-
     as to discriminate against the United States

By Hitchcock but not favorably considered

5

1   ~~lution of Congress approves such regulation or interference.~~

2   9. The United States shall not be obligated to con-

3   tribute to any expenses of the league of nations, or of the *except for salaries and ordinary office expenses of such secretariat*

4   secretariat, or of any commission, or committee, or confer- *(By Walsh.)*

5   ence, or other agency, organized under the league of nations

6   or under the treaty or for the purpose of carrying out the

7   treaty provisions, unless and until an appropriation of funds

8   available for such expenses shall have been made by the

9   Congress of the United States.

10   10. If the United States shall at any time adopt any plan

11   for the limitation of armaments proposed by the council of

12   the league of nations under the provisions of Article 8, it

13   reserves the right to increase such armaments without the

14   consent of the council whenever the United States is

15   threatened with invasion or engaged in war.

16   11. The United States reserves the right to permit, in

17   its discretion, the nationals of a covenant-breaking State, as

18   defined in Article 16 of the covenant of the league of nations,

19   residing within the United States or in countries other than

20   that violating said Article 16, to continue their commercial,

21   financial, and personal relations with the nationals of the

22   United States.

23   12. Nothing in Articles 296, 297, or in any of the

24   annexes thereto or in any other article, section, or annex of

25   the treaty of peace with Germany shall, as against citizens

6

1 of the United States, be taken to mean any confirmation,

2 ratification, or approval of any act otherwise illegal or in

3 contravention of the rights of citizens of the United States.

4   13. The United States withholds its assent to Part

5 XIII (Articles 387 to 427, inclusive) unless Congress by

6 Act or Joint Resolution shall hereafter make provision for

7 representation in the organization established by said Part

8 XIII, and in such event the participation of the United

9 States will be governed and conditioned by the provisions

10 of such Act or Joint Resolution.

11   14. The United States assumes no obligation to be

12 bound by any election, decision, report, or finding of the

13 council or assembly in which any member of the league

14 and its self-governing dominions, colonies, or parts of em-

15 pire, in the aggregate have cast more than one vote, and

16 assumes no obligation to be bound by any decision, report,

17 or finding of the council or assembly arising out of any

18 dispute between the United States and any member of the

19 league if such member, or any self-governing dominion,

20 colony, empire, or part of empire united with it politically

21 has voted.

C

From the Desk Diary of Robert Lansing

1920 Monday 19 January

Tumulty phoned Prest had decided on certain dip. apptments. Said some of them were "terrible." Wished me to hold them up till Wed. as he was going out of town.

Edith Bolling Galt Wilson to Robert Lansing

My dear Mr. Secretary: The White House Jan. 19, 1920

During the last few weeks the President has given a great deal of thought to the more important vacancies in the Diplomatic Service and has come to some mature conclusions as to who should fill them.

Of these he asks me to apprise you.

He has decided to send to Rome, Mr. Robert Underwood Johnson, of New York, whom every Italien in the United States knows as an ardent and useful friend of Italy

To China, Mr. Chas. R. Crane of Ill. & N. Y. whose familiarity with oriental affairs is unrivaled and whose experience in dealing with oriental questions qualifies him as no one else is qualified.

To the Hague, Mr. Wm. Phillips, as you suggested, because he esteems him as highly as you do.

To Switzerland Mr. Breckinridge Long, whose Character he has learned to value very highly.

To Siam Ex. gov. Hunt of Arizona[1]

Faithfully yours   Edith Bolling Wilson

ALS (RSB Coll., DLC).
  [1] That is, George Wylie Paul Hunt, Democratic Governor of Arizona, 1912-1919.

Alexander Mitchell Palmer to Joseph Patrick Tumulty

Dear Joe: Washington, D. C. January 19, 1920.

I understand from you that the President desires to appoint Charles A. Talcott as United States District Judge for the Northern District of New York, despite the fact that he is about 63 years of age and his appointment would break the rule which we have insisted upon everywhere in the country.

I wonder if the President recalls that in the Ohio case he refused to appoint Mr. Johnson,[1] who was recommended by Senator Pomerene, because of this rule, although Johnson was only a little past 60. In South Carolina and in Georgia, we took a similar strong stand against the recommendations of our friends. If the rule is broken now, of course it will make trouble for us not only with those Senators and others whom we have turned down, but in several other districts where appointments are to be made soon we will not have that rule to protect us against the insistence of our friends that older men should go on the bench.

I would like very much to have this matter settled definitely and finally. If the President feels that he wants to make this appointment despite the rule, it ought to be made immediately. In that event, I think we can solve the problem of the vacant judgeship in the Fifth Circuit by the appointment of Alexander C. King,[2] now Solicitor General. Mr. King has been urged by many lawyers from the South as the best fitted man in the circuit for this place. He is one of the unquestioned leaders of the southern bar. He is 62 years old, however, and I therefore have not considered him; but with the rule gone his appointment would meet with general approval.

Won't you please ask the President about this matter so that we can get both these judgeships settled promptly? I will appreciate it.   Yours truly,   A Mitchell Palmer

Talcott now.[3] I will see the Atty Gen'l about the other at the very earliest hour I feel able   W.W.

TLS (WP, DLC).
[1] Probably Simeon Moses Johnson, prominent lawyer of Cincinnati, active in Democratic party affairs, who became sixty years of age on March 18, 1919.
[2] Alexander Campbell King of Atlanta, Solicitor General of the United States.
[3] See EBW to JPT, Jan. 24, 1920.

Gilbert Fairchild Close to Edith Bolling Galt Wilson

Dear Mrs. Wilson: The White House 19 January, 1920

Professor Edward Capps, of Princeton, and the four other college professors whose names are signed to the enclosed letter[1] called at the White House on Saturday to present to the President the attached petition signed by about 200 prominent college professors with regard to the settlement of the Thracian question from the point of view of the rights of the Greeks of Thrace.[2] The list of signatures is headed by Dr. Eliot, former President of Harvard. I am sending it over to you so that you may call it to the President's attention if you think best.

                              Sincerely yours,   Gilbert F. Close

TLS (WP, DLC).
[1] F. Capps et al. to WW, Jan. 17, 1920, TLS (WP, DLC).
[2] Charles W Fliot et al to WW, c. Jan. 17, 1920, TLS (WP, DLC). This petition, after briefly summarizing the recent history of Thrace, urged that the region be united with Greece. If, however, Thrace was to be governed under a mandate, the wishes of the Greeks and "other civilized peoples" in the region "should be a principal consideration in the selection of the mandatory."

From Robert Lansing, with Enclosures

My dear Mr. President: Washington January 19, 1920.

There are attached the cables from Paris giving the latest Adriatic proposal of Clemenceau and Lloyd-George. It is stated that they were "finally successful in securing Nitti's acceptance" and the memorandum was then telegraphed to Belgrade by Trumbitch for the approval of his Government. In handing the proposal to Trumbitch the statement was made that if it were not accepted the Treaty of London would be applied in its entirety.

While presenting an equally wide departure from the American position, this new proposal differs in many essential points from the other recent proposals. There is attached a brief outline of its essential features. There are also attached two cables from Paris (No. 134 and No. 141, January 14th) which foreshadow the new turn negotiations have taken and also the telegram (Paris, No. 156, January 16th) which transmits Trumbitch's appeal to yourself.

Faithfully yours,   Robert Lansing

TLS (WP, DLC).

E N C L O S U R E   I

Clemenceau-Lloyd George Proposal[1]
Paris January 15, 1920

Urgent. 155. Mission. Confidential. Referring to my number 82, January 9, 7 p.m.[2] and subsequent telegrams regarding Adriatic question.

Am informed that, after several meetings, Clemenceau and Lloyd George were finally successful in securing Nitti's acceptance of a plan of settlement as set forth in the following document which has been telegraphed to Belgrade by Trumbich for the approval of his Government. The document is marked secret. Entitled: "The Adriatic Question, (revised proposals handed to M. Trumbich and Mr. Pachitch by Monsieur Clemenceau at a meeting held at the Quai d'Orsay on the afternoon of January 14th 1920).

"One. The corpus separatum of Fiume to be an independent state under the guarantee of the League of Nations with the right to choose its own diplomatic representation. The town of Sushak to go to the Serb Croat-Sloven[e] state, it being understood the whole port and the railways terminating there with all facilities for their development to be handed over and to belong to the League of Nations which will make such arrangements as it may see fit in the interests of the Serv-Croat-Sloven state *dag* [Hungary][3] and Transylvania as well as of the town itself.

Two. The free state to disappear and the boundary between Italy and the Serb-Croat-Sloven state to be drawn in (a) so as to provide a connection by road along the coast within Italian territory but to leave the whole of the railway from Fiume northwards through Adelsberg within the Serb-Croat-Sloven state; where the railway from Fiume passes along the border, the coast by this is drawn between the road and the railway (B) so as to provide for the protection of Trieste involving a readjustment of the Wilson line in the region of Senosecchia, (C) otherwise (line?) to be drawn as marked by the blue line on the map attached so as to leave purely Jugo-Slav districts in the Serb-Croat-Slovene state.

Three. Zara, within the limits of the municipality, to be an independent state under the guarantee of the League of Nations, with the right to choose its own diplomatic representation.

Four. Italy to retain Valona as provided for in the Treaty of London and in addition to have a mandate over Albania. The boundaries of northern Albania to be readjusted as shown on the map attached. The Albanian districts which will thus come to the (?) by the Serb-Croat-Sloven state will enjoy a special intercessor [regime] as an autonomus province similar to that provided under the Treaty with the Czecho-Slovak Republic for the autonomus safety of province of Czecho-Slovakia [for its autonomous provinces]. The southern boundary of Albania *Belgravia* [shall be], the line proposed by the French and British delegations on the Greek affairs commission leaving Argyro Castro[n] and Koritza to Greece.

Five. The following island groups to be assigned to Italy: Lussin, Pelagosa and Lissa; the remainder of the islands to be under the sovereignty the Serb-Croat-Sloven state.

Six. All the islands of the adriatic to be demilitarized.

Seven. Special waivers will be made permitting batteries in Dalmatia to work for Italian nationality without leaving the territory [Italians in Dalmatia to choose, without leaving the territory, Italian nationality].

Eight. Existing economic enterprises in Dalmatia should have their security safe guarded by an international convention."

End of section one of this telegram. January 16, 7 p.m.

Wallace.

[1] WWhw printing.
[2] H. C. Wallace to RL, Jan. 9, 1920.
[3] Additions and corrections from the copy printed in *The Adriatic Question*, pp. 13-14.

ENCLOSURE II

Comment on Clemencea-Lloyd George Proposal[1]

Paris Jan. 16, 1920

Rush. 161. Secret. Mission. Second section of telegram number 155 January 16, noon.

Beg to submit the following comments on paragraphs of Allied proposal of January 14.

One. Alternative of free state offered by President Wilson and accepted by the Italians is entirely done away with, the corpus separatum of Fiume is placed on a par with the municipality of Zara. The entire port of Fiume, instead of being placed under the control of the League of Nations, is given out and out to the League. The phrase "and the railways terminating there" is rather ambiguous but apparently does not imply that the League should own the railroad in all its length. I am informed that this ambiguity was brought to the attention of Lloyd George who did not wish to have it changed: apparently he was interested in safeguarding an outlet (*) Hungary and it is probable that special provisions will be arranged guaranteeing the transit of Hungarian goods over the railroad which will now pass through Yugo-Slav territory in all its length with the exception of the town. The person by whom the paragraph was drawn admitted its ambiguity and expressed the view that should the proposal be accepted it would have to be referred to a special committee to work out the matter.

Two. A. Italy is given the coastal strip demanded by Tittoni and the boundary will run practically as shown on the map handed to Mr. Polk by Tittoni late in October. B. From north of Volosca the line, although not definitely determined, runs in a general northwesterly direction to some five kilometres east of the Wilson line and then northwards but instead of bending to the west in the region of Senosecchia it will bend to the east in that region joining the Wilson line immediately to the north.

Three. I understand that although it was intimated to Nitti that concessions might be granted as regards the size of the independent state of Zara the Italians preferred to have the state confined practically to the city limits and hence the statement "within the limits of the municipality." The Italians undoubtedly wish to include as few Yugo-Slavs as possible within the independent state.

Four. I am informed that the boundary of northern Albania is drawn south of the valley [of] the Drin. I have been promised the map and will telegraph a description of the southern boundary as soon as obtainable. That Venizelos was consulted on this point and that it was largely due to the position taken by Lloyd George that

Arghyro Castro and Koritza are given to Greece. I am inclined to believe that some of the experts are not satisfied with this arrangement and possibly the question of Koritza may be reconsidered.

Five. Nitti made a fight for the island of Lagosta, but was finally refused.

Six. I am informed that in one of Nitti's memoranda a reference was made to a possible Italian naval base on the island of Lissa. This is now impossible.

Seven. Lloyd George stood out quite strongly against this Italian demand. The Yugo-Slavs however accepted it without question possibly for the reason that they claim there are not more than 6,000 Italians in Dalmatia.

Eight. The Yugo-Slavs made no objection to this Italian proposal.

While it is frankly admitted that the present proposal giving Italy the eastern coast of Istria and the strip of shore up to the corpus separatum of Fiume is bad, nevertheless, I am assured that it was absolutely necessary in order to obtain Nitti's acceptance and is outweighed by the advantages which have been gained, particularly the withdrawal of the Italian demand for the demilitarization of the entire Dalmatian coast and for the Island of Lagosta. The modification of the Wilson line does not entail the transfer of many Yugo-Slavs to Italy and the Italian demand for a rectification of the boundary in the region of Senosecchia in order to protect Trieste is not thought unreasonable. As regards the Yugo-Slavs on the other hand it is pointed out that the present arrangement does away with the free state to which they have always objected. January 16, 11 PM.   Wallace

(*) Apparent Omission

T telegrams (WP, DLC).
  ¹ WWhw printing.

ENCLOSURE   III

Division of Western European Affairs

MEMORANDUM—The Adriatic Question.

The latest proposal of Clemenceau and Lloyd-George is, in certain fundamental points, a new proposition. It does away with the *Free State of Fiume* and establishes the *Free City of Fiume* with a status similar to that proposed for Zara. Much of the territory of the proposed Free State of Fiume is assigned to Jugoslavia, but Italy's territory in Istria is also increased by moving the Wilson line eastward.

An important feature of the present scheme is the effort to satisfy the Belgrade Government by giving to Jugoslavia, in further return for the concessions to Italy, territory in northern Albania, including the valley of the Drin and Scutari, the plea being that Scutari would be as effective an economic outlet for Jugoslavia as Fiume (in this connection see Paris, #134 and #141, January 14).

The various points of the new memorandum are as follows:

1—The Free State of Fiume is to disappear; the corpus separatum of Fiume is to be a free city under the guarantee of the League of Nations, the port and railways to be owned by the League of Nations. Contiguity of the Free City of Fiume with Italian territory is included by means of a corridor along the coast.

2—The Wilson line is to be moved eastward and so arranged as to provide the connection along the coast, as mentioned above. The further description of the line (referred to as "the blue line on the map attached") is unintelligible. The disappearance of the Free State makes this line the boundary between Italy and Jugoslavia. The memorandum merely states that the line is so drawn as to leave the whole of the railway from Fiume northward within Jugoslavia and to assign purely Jugoslav districts to the Serb-Croat-Slovene State.

3—The status of Zara is the same as in previous memoranda.

4—Italy is assigned Valona and the Albanian mandate. The boundaries of northern Albania are to be so re-adjusted as to assign to Jugoslavia Scutari and the valley of the Drin; the Albanian districts thus given to Jugoslavia are to enjoy a special status as an autonomous province similar to that provided by the Treaty in the case of Czecho-Slovakia.

5—Lussin, Pelagosa, and Lissa are given to Italy; the rest of the islands to Jugoslavia (thus Italy renounces Lagosta and apparently Unie).

The remaining points (6, 7, 8) are the same as in the previous memoranda—and refer to the demilitarization of all the Adriatic islands, the right of Italians in Dalmatia to choose Italian citizenship, and the safeguarding of existing economic enterprises in Dalmatia by an international convention.

In handing the above proposal to the Jugoslav delegate the statement was made that if it were not accepted the Treaty of London would be applied in its entirety.

T MS (WP, DLC).

ENCLOSURE   IV

Scutari to Jugoslavia[1]
Paris January 14th 1920

Urgent. 134. Confidential. Mission. In conversation with Berthe-lot last night he said that the question of a solution of the Adriatic problem now lay entirely between the Italians and the Yugo-Slavs and he added "the moment the Italians and Yugo-Slavs are able to reach an agreement the Adriatic question will be settled." From another source I learn that it is not impossible that such an agree-ment may be reached based on the attribution of Scutari and the Valley of the Drin to the Yugo-Slavs.   Wallace

[1] WWhw printing; underlining below by Wilson.

ENCLOSURE   V

Scutari to Jugoslavia[1]
Paris January 14, 1920

141. Secret. Mission. Referring to last paragraph of my telegram number 134 of the 14. During informal conversation members of Foreign Office stated that while now the struggle for Fiume had forced into the background an equally important question; namely that of Scutari which from many points of view was just as impor-tant as an economic outlet for Jugo-Slavia as Fiume, old Servians such as Pashitch were more interested in the question of Scutari than the Croatian port of Fiume. It was pointed out that after all the French count much more on the old Serbs as allies than on the Jugo-Slavs of the new kingdom.

The person in question was personally strongly in favor of giving Scutari to the Jugo-Slavs and felt hopeful that if this were done it would be possible to find a solution of the Fiume question which would be acceptable to all concerned. January 15, 11 a.m.

Wallace.

[1] WWhw printing; underlining below by Wilson.

ENCLOSURE   VI

Jugoslav Appeal to The President[1]
Paris January 16th 1920.

Rush. 156. Confidential. Mission. Mr. Trumbitch called on me this morning. He stated that his delegation had been heard twice by the Council on Saturday and Monday with regard to the Adriatic question. On Tuesday they had been handed by Monsieur Clemenceau first proposal to which they had made certain objections on Wednesday. An amended proposal was handed them with the statement that if it were not accepted the treaty of London would be applied in its entirety. His delegation had not been prepared to accept the proposal and had referred it to Belgrade.

He then handed me the following document which he requested me to transmit immediately to President Wilson "(Green) Monsieur Clemenceau and Mr. Lloyd George in agreement with M. Nitti communicated on the 14th instant to the Jugo Slav delegation the following plan for the solution of the Adriatic problem. '(Here follow the first six paragraphs of the mandate proposal transmitted in my telegram number 155 of January 16th Noon).' The original draft of this plan gave to Italy full sovereignty over Fiume and its port, the Jugo Slav delegation having objected to this plan and pointed out that even M. Tittoni's plan did not claim to recognize sovereignty, Monsieur Clemenceau and Mr. Lloyd George have taken this observation into account and abandoned the claim to the Italian Sovereignty over Fiume.

Monsieur Clemenceau in his own name and the name of Mr. Lloyd George who was present declared on the 14th instant to the Jugo Slav delegation that the treaty of London will be applied and that they have given the necessary authorization to M. Nitti to this effect. In the case that the Jugo Slav delegation declines to accept the above plan, he declared that in such case Italy would obtain all that was promised her in the treaty of London while Fiume would be assigned to Jugo Slav. Furthermore Monsieur Clemenceau declared that M. Nitti had undertaken to evacuate Fiume in favor of Jugo Slavia (?) (?) the treaty of London. M. Nitti was not present at this meeting neither was he present at any other meeting at which the Yugo Slav delegates were present. The Yugo Slav delegates demanded that in the first section of the proposed solution where there is a question of Sushak it should be added that the port of Baros [Porto Baross] will form a part of Sushak. This port is used for the export of timber from Croatia and is separated from the real port of Fiume by a broad pier. Furthermore it forms physically as well as by reason of its commercial function a component part of Sushak. All timber yards are in Sushak while the railway line passes through it. A bifurcation of this railway line terminates at the quay of the port Baros while the other goes from Sushak to Fiume. The port Baros would be the only commercial outlet owned by Yugo Slavia. M. Clemenceau and M. Lloyd George to both of whom as it has been seen this question is a new one have taken no account of this demand declaring that the port of Baros will belong to the League of Nations. The Yugo Slav delegation reserved its reply until the receipt of instructions from its Government. The Yugo Slav delegation intends to demand satisfaction at least in the following questions: One. The port of Baros like Sushak to belong unconditionally to Yugo Slavia; two, The Italian frontier in Carnelia [Carniola] and Istria to follow the Wilson Line, Italy to have no territorial continuity with Fiume; three, the free town of Waken [Zara] to be expressly limited to the city of Waken only and to form part of the Yugo Slav customs union, Yugo Slavia to administer the customs. Concerning the boundary of this free town stated [in] above mentioned plan the term 'within the limits of the municipality' is used. This is not quite clear and may be interpreted broadly in the sense of the commune of Waken which embraces not only the city of Waken but two islands and a large strip of territory on the mainland as well. Where there are no Italians in Dalmatia the term 'municipality' does not exist, commune only is named and used; four, the free states: Fiume without the port and railway and Waken to be under the sovereignty of the League of Nations and to have no right to choose their own diplomatic representation. If they chose the Italian diplomatic representation that would mean disguised annexation of sovereignty in Foreign powers; five, the Island of Lissa to have its own autonomy and within its judisdiction to be included all affairs of local interest and especially the right of language in schools and local administration. The Yugo Slav delegation beg President Wilson kindly to support its aforementioned demands which represent a minimum and to object to the application of the Treaty of London. The delegation stands on the basis of President Wilson's plan."

In reply to the question as to what he thought would be the outcome should his Government refuse to accept the present proposal, M. Trumbitch stated that he did not believe that the Treaty of London would be applied. He thought Clemenceau's statement in this regard was used simply as a means to bring pressure of work on the Yugo Slav. It was evidently a purpose of Clemenceau and Lloyd George to force him to accept their plan which would be in fact an arrangement between the Italians and the Yugo Slavs and which it would then be difficult for the President to refuse to recognize. He thought it extremely unwise to depart from the line proposed by the President as any change in favor of Italy would inevitably lead to conflict in the future. January 16th 6 P.M.

Wallace

T telegrams (WP, DLC).
[1] WWhw printing.

Raymond Blaine Fosdick to Joseph Patrick Tumulty, with Enclosure

Dear Mr. Tumulty: Washington January 19, 1920

I have your letter of January 16th in reply to my letter to the President of the 14th. Under the circumstances I feel that there is but one thing for me to do, and that is to tender my resignation as Under Secretary General of the League. This is the advice that I get from all the President's friends with whom I have talked. You will understand, I am sure, that the question is not in any sense a personal one. I feel that my position as Under Secretary General exposes the League to the possibility of an attack, which at the present critical juncture might do great harm, and I do not believe that I ought myself to assume the responsibility of continuing in a relationship which might help further to imperil the cause. I have therefore cabled my resignation to Sir Eric Drummond, and I am enclosing a copy of it herewith.

Cordially yours,   Raymond B. Fosdick

TLS (WP, DLC).

ENCLOSURE

Now that the League of Nations is no longer a provisional organization, but has become established as a going concern, the continued lack of decision as to America's course places me personally in a position of peculiar embarrassment. In order, therefore, to avoid any confusion or misunderstanding as to my position as Under Secretary General of the League, it seems best for me to tender my resignation. I do this with deep regret because I do not like to appear to be abandoning those with whom I have been associated for the past few months just at the moment when their responsibilities and opportunities are becoming real. The League is now approaching the point where it can begin to carry out the world's hopes for disarmament, arbitration, the protection of backward people, the furthering of international health projects and all the other humanitarian issues upon which we have been working for the past six months. I feel sure, however, that you will appreciate the reasons which have led up to my decision and will recognize that if as an American I now feel forced to withdraw from official connection with the Secretariat, it is not for lack of faith in the League.

T MS (WP, DLC).

A News Item

[*Jan. 20, 1920*]

President's Health Shows Steady Improvement;
Warmly Wrapped, He Takes a Winter Outing

Washington, Jan. 20.—President Wilson is steadily improving, according to information from the White House today. He was taken out of doors this morning, bundled up warmly, and took the air for an hour or so.

While it is stated daily at the White House that the President is making progress toward recovery, no assurance is given there as to when he will be up and about. The statement made in Chicago by Mrs. George Bass of the women's section of the Democratic Committee that the President would be back at work next week seems to be too optimistic.

There are indications, however, that the President is taking a keener interest in public affairs. He is anxious to be informed of what is taking place in Congress and elsewhere, and he is personally attending to official business.

William G. McAdoo, President Wilson's son-in-law, is a guest at the White House. Mr. McAdoo delivered an address before the Pan-American Financial Congress this afternoon.

Printed in the *New York Times*, Jan. 21, 1920.

From Robert Lansing, with Enclosure

My dear Mr. President: Washington January 20, 1920.

I beg to inform you that at a meeting of the Supreme Council on the 19th instant, Mr. Lloyd George proposed that M. Clemenceau, as President of the Conference, should send a telegram to the United States Government with regard to the question of the exchange of goods with Russia. I enclose herewith a copy of the draft which Mr. Lloyd George submitted and which will be considered at the next meeting of the Council.

May I ask for an expression of your views with respect to the points which are raised in Mr. Lloyd George's proposed communication?

In this connection I should like to invite your attention to the report on the Russian situation which I submitted to you under date of December 4, with the recommendation that it be forwarded to Congress under cover of a special message.[1] Events which have occurred since that report was drafted have naturally nullified certain portions of it, but I believe that the major recommendations contained therein are still worthy of your consideration in connection with the situation which has now arisen. It would be particularly helpful to know your views with respect to the revival, as proposed in the report in question, of the Russian Bureau, Incorporated,[2] as a means of supporting American trade with Russia during the reconstruction period.

Faithfully yours,   Robert Lansing

TLS (WP, DLC).

[1] RL to WW, Dec. 4, 1919, TLS, enclosing RL to WW, Dec. 3, 1919, TS MS, both in WP, DLC. The report of December 3, 1919, is printed, with the omission of a brief section summarizing American economic and military aid during 1919 to the areas of Russia controlled by the anti-Bolsheviks, in *FR 1920*, III, 436-44. In his covering letter of December 4, 1919, Lansing described his report as follows: "I am enclosing for your consideration a report upon the Russian situation which sets forth the present conditions, their causes, their importance to other nations and the necessity of correcting these conditions so far as possible, together with certain suggestions as to means which would seem practicable for the accomplishment of this change. I believe the time has come when it is important to lay the whole matter before Congress and to obtain, if possible, the necessary legislation to aid in the economic rehabilitation of the Russian nation. I would suggest therefore, if it meets with your approval, that this report to you be transmitted to Congress with a recommendation that it should receive its consideration and such action as is necessary."

[2] About which, see n. 4 to the extract from the Diary of Col. House printed at Sept. 24, 1918, Vol. 51.

E N C L O S U R E

DRAFT OF TELEGRAM TO UNITED STATES GOVERNMENT

The collapse of Admiral Kolchak and General Denikin has driven the Allied Governments once more to consider the main question for it is now evident that the attempt to overthrow the Bolshevik regime by the anti-Bolshevik forces hitherto supported by the allies has definitely failed. After careful consideration the allies have come to two conclusions in the first place after hearing the representatives the Russian Cooperative Societies, which are the only organizations which have withstood Bolshevik destruction and which have twenty five million members, they have decided to permit free interchange of articles required by the Russian peasants from allied countries in return for wheat, flax, hides and other raw materials of Russia. They are informed by the representatives of the Russian Cooperative Societies that the last year's harvest in South Russia is a record and that very large quantities of foodstuffs and other raw materials would be available for export if transportation facilities could be organized and goods could be introduced into Russia for which the peasants would be willing to exchange their products. These foodstuffs are urgently needed in Europe in order to meet the acute shortage of food which exists there and which is the principal encouragement to Bolshevism in the west. At the same time the Russian cooperatives are convinced that the best counter to Bolshevism is the restarting of trade. They point out that it is possible for a government in time of war to deprive the populations of many of the necessaries of life but that once the war pressure is removed the population will insist on their government making it possible for them to sell their products and to buy clothes, boots, machinery and so forth in exchange. Now that the defeat of Kolchak and Denikin has taken away the Bolshevik argument that they are fighting for the defense of the revolution and the protection of the peasants' land, the pressure on Bolsheviks to cease war, restore normal conditions and to abandon the repressive measures justified on the score of war will become immensely greater. In their judgment the reorganization of trade is the best means of destroying the extreme reforms of Bolshevism in Russia itself.

This interchange of products will imply no negotiations between the Allied Governments and the Soviet Government, no recognition of the Bolsheviks and no permission for Russian representatives to enter any allied country. It simply implies the granting of facilities whereby the Russian cooperatives who have long had their agencies in the capitals of Europe will be able to organize an exchange of goods with allied countries. The scheme of course depends upon the Russian Cooperatives being able to secure the consent and assistance of the Soviet authorities, especially in the matter of transport but for reasons already given they believe that the internal pressure is so great that they will readily agree. So far as this first step is concerned, the United States is not directly affected because they have never been parties to the blockade and the Allied Governments have therefore little doubt that the United States Government will fully approve of it.

The second conclusion which the Allied Governments have reached is that they ought to announce that they are agreed so far as the future is concerned on their policy of non-intervention inside the boundaries of Russia, but that they have recognized the independence of the neighboring states to which they now added Georgia, Azerbaidjan and Armenia and that in the event of the Bolsheviks refusing to make peace with them and endeavors infringe the independence these communities by force of arms, the allies will give them all the support in their power. The allied Governments are most anxious to know whether the United States will agree to this policy.

T MS (WP, DLC).

From the Desk Diary of Robert Lansing

1920 Wednesday 21 January

Polk on dip. appointments. President's condition and almost impossible situation of govt. Polk told Fletcher that he had no business to resign at this time. . . .

Fletcher brought in his letter of resignation for Jany 31.[1] I do not think that he is treating us fairly.

[1] It is missing in all files and collections known to the Editors. The *New York Times*, January 28, 1920, printed a front-page story on the resignation, datelined Washington, January 27. It said that informed persons said that Fletcher was convinced that a continuation of the efforts he had made during the past four years to bring the Carranza government into accord with the United States Government on the issue of protection of American lives and property in Mexico would be futile. Lansing informed the American embassy in Mexico City on February 11, 1920, that Wilson has just accepted Fletcher's resignation. RL to Amembassy, Mexico City, Feb. 11, 1920, TS telegram (SDR, RG 59, 123F63/206a, DNA).

From Robert Lansing

My dear Mr. President: [Washington] January 21, 1920.

I enclose herewith Mr. Fletcher's resignation as Ambassador to Mexico, and also his memorandum to me setting forth the reasons for his retirement.   Faithfully yours,   Robert Lansing

CCL (R. Lansing Papers, DLC).

Joseph Patrick Tumulty to Raymond Blaine Fosdick

Dear Mr. Fosdick: The White House 21 January, 1920.

It was with regret that I received your letter of the 19th of January, telling me that you had tendered your resignation as Under Secretary General of the League of Nations. However, I understand your position.

With best wishes.   Sincerely yours,   J P Tumulty

TLS (R. B. Fosdick Papers, NjP).

A News Report

[*Jan. 22, 1919*]

SENATE CONFEREES NEAR COMPROMISE ON RESOLUTIONS
Both Republicans and Democrats Are Hopeful After Discussion of Article X.
LODGE LOOKS FOR RESULTS

Washington, Jan. 22.—Republican members of the bi-partisan treaty conference tonight reversed the diagnosis of the compromise situation which they made yesterday, and announced that conditions are now more favorable for an agreement than at any time since the discussions began. Whereas yesterday they were predicting a break in the negotiations almost any moment, they are unanimous tonight in the declaration that very important progress was made at today's session, and that things look bright, very bright, indeed.

The sudden change in the situation, they explained, occurred during discussion of Article X, and announcements made after the session in Senator Lodge's office, while confined to the progress made, indicated that tomorrow would probably bring an agreement on Article X. No information as to details of the proposal which provides ground for a compromise or whether Democrats or Republicans have made the concessions was forthcoming.

It seems fair to assume, however, that some proposal submitted by the Democratic conferees is the basis of the expected agreement because the Democrats at a meeting preceding the general conference drew up three proposals for a compromise on Article X, all of which they submitted. Senator Hitchcock drew one, Senator Owen another, and Senator Simmons a third. Senator Simmons, whom his friends describe as "a born compromiser," previously submitted a draft of an Article X reservation to Democratic and Republican Senators, which met with some favor.

Senator Lodge said so many proposals were submitted by both sides that he could not remember the number of them or their languages, but added that he believed "the thing is going to work out."

Senator New, who yesterday gloomily forecast a complete rupture of negotiations, said:

"This much can be said: At no time in the discussions has the possibility of agreement appeared so bright as it is tonight."

It was considered significant by some Senators that the revival of hope followed closely a futile effort by Senators Lodge and New to get Senator McNary to agree that the mild-reservationists will not throw the treaty back into the Senate and reopen debate by moving to take up the treaty again for discussion.

The two Senators invited Senator McNary to see for himself the progress made. They told him in detail of the work they have done and asked him to hold off so that the negotiations may not be spoiled at their most delicate stage. Senator McNary's reply was couched in graphic Western idiom, but did not constitute a promise to hold off. In effect it was that unless more than mere hope comes out of Senator Lodge's office ere long, things will begin to happen on the Senate floor.

The Democratic conferees hurried away tonight after the discussion for further revision of their proposals, and the Republicans remained with Mr. Lodge for a last-minute discussion of the situation. The nine Senators will meet again tomorrow afternoon.

A disagreement tomorrow need not break up the conference, Senators said, as both agreements and disagreements are being regarded as tentative and subject to change, hence failure to agree now might only mean, they said, that discussion of Article X would be dropped for a time and another reservation taken up.

While the conferees were meeting today a report reached the Capitol that President Wilson had conveyed word indirectly to leading Democrats that if they are able to reach a reasonable settlement with the Lodge group, he will not stand in the way of its ratification by the Senate. Confirmation of this report was lacking, however.

Printed in the *New York Times*, Jan. 23, 1920.

From Gilbert Monell Hitchcock, with Enclosure

My dear Mr. President: [Washington] January 22, 1920.

The conferences between Lodge and his three associates and myself and four democratic senators have now reached the sixth day.

On Article X the effort to reach a compromise has now reached a state where both sides are seriously considering a proposition as indicated by the enclosed clipping.

We resume consideration of it tomorrow afternoon.

                              Yours truly,   G M Hitchcock

TLS (WP, DLC).

E N C L O S U R E

2. The United States assumes no obligation to ⟨preserve⟩ *employ its military or naval forces or the economic boycott to preserve* the territorial integrity or political independence of any other country ⟨or to interfere in controversies between nations— whether members of the league or not—⟩ under the provisions of Article 10, or to employ the military or naval forces of the United States under any *other* article of the treaty for any purpose, unless in any particular case the Congress, which, under the Constitution has the sole power to declare war ⟨or authorize the employment of the military or naval forces of the United States,⟩ shall by act or joint resolution so provide. *Nothing herein shall be deemed to impair the obligation of Art 16 concerning the economic boycott*[1]

Printed copy (G. M. Hitchcock Papers, DLC).

[1] Hitchcock appended the following handwritten note to this document in his papers: "I submitted above to Pres Wilson & received from him the reply dated Jan 26, 1920. "We were considering this reservation as above amended when Lodge left us & thus ended the bipartizan conference."

In the document printed above, words in angle brackets deleted by Hitchcock; words in italics added by him.

For the events of January 23, which caused the breakup of the bipartisan conference, see GMH to JPT, Jan. 26, 1920, n. 2.

From Robert Lansing, with Enclosures

My dear Mr. President: Washington January 22, 1920

On January 19th I transmitted to you certain cables from Paris explaining the latest proposal of Lloyd George and Clemenceau in the Adriatic matter. They state that this proposal is made by the signatories of the Pact of London since "the United States is not at the present time in a position to discuss the matter." They indicate that they have been "finally successful in securing Nitti's acceptance" and, in handing the report to Trumbitch, told him that if it were not accepted, the "Treaty of London would be applied in its entirety." The terms of the memorandum depart widely from the American position in the matter. I also transmitted at the same time the memorandum of Trumbitch, enumerating the points in which he must demand satisfaction, and asking for the support of the American Government.

Cables received this morning from Paris convey the urgent request of Trumbitch that he may be informed of the attitude of the United States Government, and express his concern at the ultimatum of the Supreme Council which calls for a favourable reply from his Government by Saturday, January 24th, or in event of its refusal to accede the enforcement of the Treaty of London. The

American Ambassador at Paris expresses his belief that the Jugo Slavs will give in on Saturday unless the American Government intervenes.

Copies of these cables are accordingly enclosed herewith for your consideration and an expression of your views.

I am, my dear Mr. President,

Very sincerely,   Robert Lansing.

TLS (WP, DLC).

ENCLOSURE I

Paris January 21, 1920

208. Confidential. Mission. The Heads of Governments met yesterday afternoon. M. Clemenceau in the chair. M. Millerand present.[1] Matsui[2] and I also attended.

After discussing the question of the troops of occupation of plebiscite areas, reported in another telegram the Council considered (memorandum?)[3] submitted by the Serb-Croat-Slovenes delegations in reply to the proposal handed them on the 14th instant. The text of the memorandum will be telegraphed in full. Briefly stated the demands set forth were the same as those mentioned in my telegram number 156, January 16, 4 p.m.

Nitti stated that his stipulated concessions to the Yugo-Slavs had been given in the proposal of January 14th. He could go no further if the Yugo-Slavs did not accept. He asked that the Pact of London should be applied. He then left for his train.

Pachitch and Trumbich were introduced and Clemenceau asked whether the last word of their Government was given in the memorandum. He informed them that Nitti had asked for the fulfillment of the Pact of London if the proposal of January fourteenth were not accepted without modification. If the present compromise settlement was not made according to the articles, he and Lloyd George would carry out the Pact of London. He appealed to them to accept it. Pachitch stated that he could do no more than advise his Government of Clemenceau's statement. The latter asked him how long it would take to get a reply from Belgrade. Pachitch estimated four days. Trumbitch endeavored to argue the matter but without success. As the matter now stands the Yugo-Slavs are given four days to say yes or no, if no the treaty of London will be applied. Trumbitch has been particularly anxious to know whether any answer has come in reply to his message transmitted in my telegram number 156 January 16th 4 p.m. He is evidently hoping *fop* (for?) some support from the President. Should there be no developments by Saturday I should not be surprised if the Yugo-Slavs were forced to accept.

In this connection I am receiving almost daily visits from the various members of the Albanian delegation appealing for the intervention of the United States and protesting against an Italian mandate. This morning the bishop of Valessio (?) their last hope lay with America. He seemed to not fear participation and was bitter against the Entente for tearing up the London Conference of 1913. He admitted that an Italian mandate for a united Albania would be preferable to the proposed solution giving northern Albania to the Jugo-Slavs, Valona and its hinterland to Italy, and Argyro Castro and Koritza to Greece. He was evidently very discouraged and repeatedly appealed for our interventions. January 21, 7 p.m.   Wallace

---

[1] Alexandre Millerand, the new French Prime Minister, who had assumed office on January 19.

[2] Keishiro Matsui, the Japanese Ambassador to France.

[3] See the Enclosure printed with FLP to RL, Jan. 26, 1920.

E N C L O S U R E   I I

Paris January 21, 1920

RUSH 213 Confidential. Mission. Referring to my telegram 208, January 21.

Trumbich called upon me this afternoon and inquired as to the attitude of the United States Government in the event of a refusal on the part of the Yugo-Slav Government to accept the proposal handed them on the fourteenth instant and the consequent application of the Pact of London. I informed him that I was not in a position to answer his question. He requested that I refer the matter to you and asked that your answer be sent direct to Belgrade as well as to me.

Trumbich is evidently much perturbed by the ultimatum given him last evening.[1] He is evidently at a loss to know what reply his Government should make. He points out that the decision rests with the Conference and not with the British and French. He quotes Orlando as having informed his Parliament to the effect that the decisions of the Council must be unanimous. He is hoping for our aid and intervention.

At the same time, he seems to fear that the Treaty of London will be applied should his Government refuse the proposal of January 14.

I am inclined to think that the Yugo-Slavs will give in unless you intervene before Saturday.

January 21, 11 pm.   Wallace

T telegrams (WP, DLC).
  [1] Wilson's underlining.

From the Desk Diary of Robert Lansing

                                        1920 Friday 23 January

Polk on diplomatic appointments. Went over letter to Mrs. Wilson in answer to hers as to Italy, China, Netherlands, Switzerland and Siam. . . .

Letter to Mrs. Wilson on Prest's selections for foreign posts.

Robert Lansing to Edith Bolling Galt Wilson

My dear Mrs. Wilson: Washington January 23, 1920.

I am in receipt of your letter of the 19th stating the decision of the President as to certain diplomatic appointments.

Although I of course understand that these appointments are practically settled, I think that I should lay before him the names of those who have been urged for these posts with more or less insistence. I do this with no purpose of changing his declared wishes but in order that I may be able to say to the supporters of the various candidates that I submitted the names before any appointments were made and that the President gave them consideration.

If I am not able to say this, I will be placed in a most embarrassing position as in nearly every case I promised to present the name to the President before he selected his appointee for the desired post, but that I presumed no appointments would go in until the President had "fully recovered." You may recall that you sent me a memorandum to that effect a few weeks ago.[1] For that reason I did not send the list before. It seems to me that I would be severely criticized if I had to admit that I had delayed sending in the names before the appointments were made. I hope, therefore, that the President can say that, after giving consideration to the names on the enclosed list, he decided finally upon these contained in your letter.

In regard to the proposed appointment of Mr. Breckenridge Long to Switzerland I wonder if the President knows that he is seeking the nomination for Senator Spencer's seat, that he has announced his candidacy and has issued a public statement as to his principles and policies. The President's decision to name him as Minister came to me as a surprise, as I have never heard that he desired to enter the diplomatic service. I have wondered whether the President communicated with him before deciding to appoint him.

At present Mr. Long is in Missouri in connection with the contest for the congressional seat made vacant by the appointment of Judge Alexander as Secretary of Commerce. I am, therefore, unable to advise him of the President's wishes and to determine whether he desires to abandon his campaign for the Democratic nomination as Senator. I know that he has already written many letters to his political friends, but whether or not he has gone so far that he cannot withdraw I am unable to say. He is expected back on February 2d.

On receipt of your letter I at once telegraphed Mr. Phillips asking him if he would accept the appointment to The Netherlands as the President desired to name him. I have received his answer, a copy of which I enclose.[2]

I assume that the President has communicated with Mr. Crane before deciding to appoint him. May I ask if the same course has been taken with Mr. Johnson and Governor Hunt? If not, should I make the inquiry?

Does the President desire me to speak to the Senators from the states, of which the appointees are residents? This, as you know, is the customary practice and has a tendency to smooth the way of confirmation by putting salve on the senatorial pride.

In the list enclosed[3] I have included Costa Rica as one of the vacant posts although we have not yet recognized that Government. I earnestly urge speedy recognition as the President's policy has been entirely successful. Tinoco and his whole party are out, but may revive again if stability is not given to the financial and economic situation by this Government's renewal of full diplomatic relations.

I should also add that we have just received a telegram stating that Mr. T. Sambola Jones, our Minister to Honduras, now home on leave, is stated by the President of Honduras to be no longer *persona grata*. Of course he cannot be sent back. So that makes another post to fill.

I also enclose a letter which Mr. Polk has sent in behalf of Joseph C. Grew,[4] who would make an excellent minister.

Faithfully yours,   Robert Lansing.

TLS (WP, DLC).
    [1] FBW to RL, Dec. 2, 1919 (second letter of that date).
    [2] W. Phillips to RL, Jan. 22, 1920, T telegram (WP, DLC). Phillips accepted the appointment "with deep appreciation."
    [3] T MS (WP, DLC). This list included separate sheets for all vacant diplomatic posts with brief biographical sketches of all persons who had been suggested for each post.
    [4] FLP to RL, Jan. 23, 1920, TLS (WP, DLC). He recommended Grew for Switzerland.

Hugh Campbell Wallace to Robert Lansing

Paris January 23, 1920

Rush. 241. Mission. Following note dated January 23rd received this evening from the British delegation:

"His Britannic Majesty's Ambassador presents his compliments to His Excellency the United States Ambassador and has the honor to state that he has been charged by Mr. Lloyd George and M. Clemenceau to hand to Mr. Wallace the enclosed telegram drawn up by Mr. Lloyd George and M. Clemenceau before their departure, in reply to the telegram from Mr. Lansing, which Mr. Wallace handed to Mr. Lloyd George and M. Clemenceau on the 20th instant.[1] Lord Derby would be grateful if the telegram now enclosed could be transmitted to Mr. Lansing at the earliest opportunity."

Telegram from Clemenceau and Lloyd George reads as follows:

"The French and British Prime Ministers have given their careful attention to the memorandum communicated to them by the American Ambassador in regard to the Russian and Italian negotiations. As to the Russian question, they had previously sent a statement of their views for the consideration of the United States Government inviting their consent and cooperation.[2]

As regards the Italian question, the absence of the United States has never been regarded by the French and British Governments as more than temporary and they have never lost sight of the American point of view on this question on the right solution of which the future of the world so largely depends. The French, British and Japanese Governments have never had the intention of making a definite settlement of the questions raised without obtaining the views of the American Government. They therefore took up the Adriatic question at the point at which it was left on the departure of Mr. Polk for Washington. Signor Nitti transmitted certain proposals in modification of the joint memorandum handed to Signor Scialoja by the request of the United States, France and Great Britain on December 9th 1919. On the assembly of the conference in Paris a fortnight ago, M. Clemenceau and Mr. Lloyd George immediately resumed negotiations between the Italian Government and the representatives [of] Jugo-Slavia and finally arrived at what they considered an arrangement which was the best available reconciliation of the Italian and Jugo-Slav points of view. The details of this settlement are appended. The French and British Governments are glad to think that practically every important point of the joint memorandum of December 9th 1919 remains untouched and has now been indorsed by the Prime Minister of Italy. Only two features undergo alterations and both these alterations are to the positive advantage of Jugo-Slavia.

1. The free state of Fiume which would have separated two hundred thousand Jugo-Slavs from their fatherland disappears. Three quarters of these people are at once and forever united with Jugo-Slavia, a source of perpetual intrigue and dispute is done away with, and if in return Jugo-Slavia has to agree to the transfer of territory to Italy, including some 18,000 Jugo-Slavs in addition to those already included under the Wilson proposals, the balance is clearly to the benefit of Jugo-Slavia. Fiume becomes an independent state under the guarantee of the League of Nations and the authority of the League of Nations over the port becomes absolute and immediate in the interests of all concerned.

2. As regards Albania, an attempt has been made to afford satisfaction to the necessary requirements of all parties concerned. The details of the administration of this country by Jugo-Slavia, Italy and Greece have yet to be elaborated but in working to this end, sight will not be lost of the feelings and future interests of the Albanian people and every endeavor will be made to carry out the arrangements in full consultation with them. The French and British Governments consider that the above is a fair settlement of a difficult and dangerous question and have informed Italian, Jugo-Slav Governments that in the event of its not being accepted they will be driven to support the enforcement of the Treaty of London which is satisfactory to nobody. Had a plenipotentiary representing the United States Government been in Paris, M. Clemenceau and Mr. Lloyd George would have cordially welcomed his full cooperation in these negotiations, but in the absence of anyone who could speak on behalf of the United States and in view of the vital inportance of arriving (*) the settlement of a question which has inflamed southeastern Europe for more than a year and which, if it is not promptly composed, may not only impede the recuperation and reconstruction of two countries greatly exhausted by the war, but may lead to war itself. The Prime Ministers of France and Great Britain felt that no other course was open to them but to proceed to dispose as quickly as possible of difficulties between two of their allies in close and continuous consultation with both while they were all in Paris together. In doing this they have not intended to show the slightest discourtesy to the United States Government nor have they wished to conceal their action in any way from the latter. They are indeed sure that the President would not have desired them to make a settlement impossible during the necessarily short stay of the Prime Ministers in Paris by requiring every phase of the negotiations to be communicated to Washington in order to obtain his consent to the proposals when he had not heard the arguments and could not interview the principals concerned. In their judgment the only plan was to proceed with the negotiation as rap-

idly as possible and to submit the results to the United States Government as soon as a definite conclusion had been reached."

Wallace

T telegram (SDR, RG 59, 763.72119/8779, DNA).
    [1] RL to H. C. Wallace, Jan. 19, 1920.
    [2] "Please take up with Mr. Clemenceau and Mr. Lloyd George the question of the way
the Russian and the Italian problems have been handled and ascertain their point of
view. The United States is being put in the position of having the matter disposed of
before the American point of view can be expressed, as apparently Mr. Clemenceau and
Mr. Lloyd George have sought only the views of the Italian and Jugoslav Governments
before ascertaining the views of the United States Government. Is it the intention of
the British and French Governments in the future to dispose of the various questions
pending in Europe and to communicate the results to the Government of the United
States? There are features in connection with the proposed Fiume settlement which
both Mr. Clemenceau and Mr. Lloyd George must realize would not be acceptable to
the President.
    "As it was pointed out by Mr. Polk before his departure, the Dalmatian and other
questions should be taken up through regular diplomatic channels, and the fact that
you are not charged with full powers could have no bearing on the question. As no
American official could be sent to these gatherings that could have the same authority
as the Prime Ministers of the three Governments in question, it is manifestly impossible
for the United States Government to be represented at the meetings of the Prime Ministers." RL to H. C. Wallace, Jan. 19, 1920, printed in *The Adriatic Question*, p. 14.

From the Diary of Ray Stannard Baker

New York January 23 1920

I was in Washington yesterday: down by the night train Wednesday night, back by the night train last night. I lunched at the White
House with Mrs. Wilson, Miss Margaret, John Wilson, a cousin
from Pennsylvania, and Dr. & Mrs. Grayson were there. I did not
see the President but he sent me out a cordial message. They are
all pleased with my book.[1] The President directed that a number
be sent to friends & Miss Margaret said she sent away 25. No out-
siders are seeing the President now: Grayson found that, although
he was vigorous mentally, the strain made him nervous & held him
back. Mrs. Wilson says he improves every day: sleeps better, eats
heartily & walks a little more. Grayson says that he is perfectly
calm about everything that comes up *except* the treaty. That stirs
him: makes him restless. He tried some days ago to write out his
views in regard to the various reservations proposed but soon gave
it up.[2] Grayson has got him an Atlantic City board-walk chair &
provided a fur foot-muff so that he can get his exercise in comfort.

I had a long talk with Mrs. Wilson who impressed me again with
her sound good sense, her real understanding of the difficulties of
the present situation & her eagerness to help. I told her just what
I thought the people felt—that while they were whole heartedly
behind the President in their support of the *spirit*, the *reality* of

the league, they were profoundly disturbed by the differences over minor matters: and that they were inclined to blame Mr. Wilson as much as Mr. Lodge. I made the point as diplomatically as I could but she came out quite bluntly: "They think him stubborn," she said.

"So much hangs on this issue," I responded, "possibly the very existence of a League."

"I know" she said "but the President still has in mind the reception he got in the west, and he believes the people are with him."

That is the trouble. He has been ill since last October & he cannot know what is going on. He sees almost nobody: & hears almost no direct news. He consulted nobody about his Jackson-day dinner message—the "solemn referendum" message—but called Close & dictated it to him, & let it go.[3] What chances of mistake, even disaster, are bound up in this situation! This sick man, with such enormous power, closed in from the world, & yet acting so influentially upon events! It is plain that Grayson cannot move him: and also clear from what Mrs. Wilson says that she can do nothing either. I found her in full accord with my suggestion that the President make some great gesture that would thrust aside the trivialities & demand the united response of the country upon the Senate in getting a League & getting it quickly. He would have everyone with him in such a move. Yet he hardens at any such suggestion: the very moment of yielding anything to the Senate seems to drive him into stubborn immovability.

Was there ever such a situation in our history! Everything must come through one over strained woman! Dr. Grayson, of course, is very close to the President, but everything of importance is handled by Mrs. Wilson. I think of this lonely sick man, attacked from all sides, and compare him with the man I saw in Paris & Brussels with thousands of people cheering him, making his triumphal way through the city streets. Surely he has known the extreme vicissitudes of life! When the question of the treaty was up the other day he said to Grayson:

"It would probably have been better if I had died last fall."

Washington is full of the most outrageous & slanderous stories: apparently there is nothing too bitter & low for people to say about this sick man in the White House.

I offered to help in any way I could and made a number of definite suggestions to Mrs. Wilson which she said she would give to the President. Later while I was at dinner with the Graysons she called up & said that it seemed impossible now to do anything. I am not, however, going to give up! The cause is too great! Any effort is worth while to prevent a failure of the nation to undertake its responsibilities toward the future organization & peace of the world.

The impotency of Congress: & the Senate particularly: is appalling.

I had quite a talk with former Atty. General Gregory & with Norman Davis, but spent nearly all day at the White House.

[1] Ray Stannard Baker, *What Wilson Did at Paris* (Garden City, N. Y., 1919).
[2] That is, Wilson gave up trying to revise the Enclosure with JPT to EBW, Jan. 15, 1920.
[3] Baker was of course mistaken here; he had probably been misinformed.

Edith Bolling Galt Wilson to Robert Lansing

My dear Mr. Secretary: The White House Jan. 24, 1920

In reply to your letter of the 22nd, with enclosures, the President asks me to say he has never discussed with Mr Long the appointment in the Diplomatic Service—and made it only because of his friendship and feeling that he merited the confidance—by his loyal service in his present office.

As you suggest it will be well for you to ask him, Mr. Johnson and Gov. Hunt before forwarding their appointments to the President for signature.

In regard to consulting the Senators from their respective States—the practice being customary you state, the President has no objection if you wish to do so.

We are both very happy that Mr. Phillips can serve at the Hague. In regard to the other vacancies the President will take them up as soon as possible.   Faithfully   Edith Bolling Wilson

ALS (RSB Coll., DLC).

Edith Bolling Galt Wilson to the White House Staff

[The White House, c. Jan. 24, 1920]

The President wishes to know if Mr. Talcott has been consulted in regard to this?[1]

EBWhw MS (WP, DLC).
[1] Typed and printed nomination form (WP, DLC), undated but signed by Wilson and initialed by A. Mitchell Palmer. It nominated Charles A. Talcott for United States District Judge for the Northern District of New York and also reappointed Clayton L. Wheeler as United States Marshal for the same district. An attached T MS, dated Jan. 24, 1920, reads as follows: "Nothing has been said to Mr. Talcott about this. Shall the Attorney-General be requested to consult him?" A pencil notation just below reads: "File away." Talcott died on February 27, 1920.

From Frank Lyon Polk

My dear Mr. President: Washington January 24, 1920

Supplementing Mr. Lansing's letters of January 19th and January 22d regarding the settlement of the Adriatic question, I am now enclosing a copy of a telegram from the American Ambassador at Paris[1] advocating certain modifications of the latest British-French proposals with a view to their submission to the Italians and the Jugoslavs as a compromise which the American Government could accept. You will note that while certain features of Mr. Wallace's proposal are an improvement over the British-French text, they nevertheless still contain a provision for contiguity between the free state of Fiume and Italian territory, which you have always considered objectionable.

Assuming that acceptance by the United States of this British-French proposal is out of the question, even as modified by Mr. Wallace, it appears to me that we are faced with the choice of two courses of action:

1. Withdrawal from the deliberations on the Adriatic question after, possibly, a final effort to secure the adhesion of the other powers to the solution contained in the note of December 9, signed by Clemenceau, Crowe, and myself, (copy of which is enclosed).[2]

2. Insistence by this Government on the settlement as embodied in that note with a statement to the Italian Government that this solution is the final concession that this Government is willing to make, and hint that unless the Italian Government sees its way to accede thereto within a specified length of time, the United States might be constrained to consider whether or not the Italian Government still desires to receive the cooperation and assistance of the United States in economic matters.

As an immediate settlement of the Adriatic question is essential in the interest of the entire European situation, it would appear to be desirable that this Government refrain from the responsibility of adopting any attitude which might prolong the controversy. It should be considered in this connection that the Department has been advised that this Government is not, as a matter of fact, in a position to bring any serious economic pressure to bear on Italy. Aside from the proposed funding of the interest on the advances already made to Italy, which it would be to the advantage of this country to grant, no further advances to Italy are in contemplation; such coal shipments to Italy as might be stopped are not considerable; and an attempted economic blockade of Italy by this Government might have the most far reaching and unfortunate developments in both countries and would undoubtedly encourage the existing notable pro-German sentiment in Italy.

In these circumstances, I am inclined to believe that this Government cannot go further than to endeavor to persuade the Italian Government by force of argument of the justice and desirability of the American solution of the Adriatic question. I believe that a final appeal should be made to the French, British, and Italian Governments to adhere to the American plan of settlement accompanied by the intimation that if this fails of acceptance, this Government cannot further modify its views, and if a different solution is desired, it must be arrived at without the approval of the United States. In order that the Jugoslav Government should not labor under any misapprehension, it should be advised accordingly.

I am, my dear Mr. President,

Very sincerely yours,   Frank L Polk

TLS (SDR, RG 59, 763.72119/8833, DNA).
¹ It is printed as Enclosure II with RL to WW, Jan. 19, 1920. Perhaps Polk sent him another copy of this telegram.
² FLP to RL, Dec. 9, 1919.

Cary Travers Grayson to Stockton Axson

Dear Doctor: The White House January 24, 1920.

Wagner¹ and I have missed you a great deal since your departure. We have done some work but not as much as we should have accomplished. So far the New Year has been an unusually busy one for me. We are now getting settled down and hope to make considerable progress the next few weeks. Wagner has run off the first part of the "Personality" and I am sending it to you herewith.²

You will be interested, I know, to learn of a conversation I had with the President just today. Briefly it was about as follows:

He and I spend an hour or so almost every afternoon in conversation. Today we discussed medicine and the future of the medical profession; individuals with whom he and I had come in [con]tact since he became President—we discussed them from their political and personal sides; and reminisced about the various public characters we met in Paris and abroad. The President expressed the wish that I had kept notes on many of the incidents that I personally had observed and told him about; that his memory about many of them was poor and that he had forgotten them. I told him that I had kept some notes.³ He said: "I am awfully glad to hear that; they will be very valuable." I said: "I have no definite plan for the use of these notes; my plans are vague. I want you to have them in case you want them at any time for any purpose. The chief good they would be to you would be to refresh your memory in case you wanted to write." He said: "That is very fine and I appreciate it, but

I think you could write it very effectively." I said: "A great many of these notes would have to be withheld for a long time in the public interest and in the interest of good taste." He said: "Well, Gordon and Cary[4] would be able to publish them, or their sons." He added: "I would rely on your judgment as to what should be published and what should not." And he reiterated: "I am very glad that you made notes." I told the President that I was going to get you to look over some of these notes with a view to correcting them and getting your ideas, and he said: "That's fine. You could not get a better man." This conversation took place this afternoon while I sat on his bed.

The President has given us quite a little uneasiness the last few days. He contracted a sharp attack of the "flu." It gave him a very uncomfortable night. He suffered from nausea, vomiting, severe headaches, sweats and chills and high temperature. At this writing his temperature, pulse and blood pressure are normal and most of his symptoms have subsided. Today he is fairly comfortable. His appetite is returning and he is in good spirits. I feel that with careful nursing and watching, he will soon be all right again. His other condition is improving slowly but steadily. Every week shows a decided gain in strength. He can now walk to the bath-room and back with little assistance. No one outside of Mrs. Wilson and Miss Margaret knows about this recent attack, and since he is responding to treatment so quickly, I have decided not to make any announcement of it. To mention it would, as you can well imagine, bring forth exaggerated reports.

I hope you received the copy of Baker's book, "What Wilson did at Paris."[5] I think it will be of interest to you to read it altogether, and, at the same time, bring forth some valuable ideas.

Mrs. McAdoo was here recently for a ten-day visit and brought little Ellen with her. The President enjoyed their stay very much. Miss Margaret left yesterday for a visit of about two weeks to Asheville, North Carolina. Mrs. Grayson has been away for a week in New York. While there she had several very pleasant visits with Miss Helen Bones.

The atmosphere is saturated with politics—the favorite sons and various candidates for President are under discussion. In the language of our friend, Carter Glass: "That dad bum old political pianola[6] came to town to be present at the Jackson Day dinner, and the damned old thing was out of tune." The tide for Hoover is running very strong just at present, but whether it is strong enough to last the whole route, I do not know. General Wood still seems to be well up in the front, and the others are scattered over the field.

Washington right now has an epidemic of the influenza. It is much less serious, however, than the epidemic a year ago. The weather since the first of January has been miserable—rain and sleet and snow. The streets today are more slippery than I have ever known them to be. I hope you are enjoying the balmy air of the Sunny South, and that you are getting exercise and taking care of yourself. Let me hear from you frequently as to how you are. Also any suggestions that you may have along our line of work. If there is anything in which I can be of assistance to you, call on me. You know I am yours to count on always.

    With warm regards,   Faithfully yours, [Cary T. Grayson]

CCL (received from James Gordon Grayson and Cary T. Grayson, Jr.).

  [1] Charles C. Wagner of the White House Staff, who served as secretary to Dr. Grayson.

  [2] Axson and Grayson had agreed to write a joint biography-memoir of Wilson. This chapter by Axson was on the personality of Woodrow Wilson. The Axson-Grayson manuscript is now in the possession of Arthur S. Link.

  [3] Grayson referred to various notes and memoranda, many of which we have printed, and probably also to the extensive diary he had kept at the Paris Peace Conference and on the western tour of 1919, all of which we have printed in this series.

  [4] That is, James Gordon Grayson and Cary T. Grayson, Jr.

  [5] R. S. Baker, *What Wilson Did at Paris* (Garden City, N. Y., 1919).

  [6] W. J. Bryan.

Ray Stannard Baker to Edith Bolling Galt Wilson

                               The City Club of New York
My dear Mrs. Wilson: Sunday. January 25 '20.

    Since our talk of Thursday, I have had the present situation very deeply upon my mind. I have the feeling that all the President went to France to fight for—for which he fought so nobly—is being swept away: that the chance for world reorganization, which is the President's high purpose, is more and more threatened. And I feel so strongly that if the President were not ill—(*if he were himself*)—he could and would save the situation. I believe the people of the country are in just the mood to respond to the kind of moral appeal which the President, beyond any other living man, is best able to make. The people want the league: they are for the reality—the spirit—which lives in the idea: but they are bitterly confused over the present minor disagreements. Their thoughts go straight to the heart of the matter—which is to get something started quickly. Some going organization to meet the problems of the world. They know that no document can be final, and that a real League will grow as it begins to function.

    As you know, I have been travelling about the country a good deal in the last two or three months—west and east—and have been talking with all kinds of people. It has been my business all my life to try to understand and estimate public opinion. I can say honestly that the great majority of the people of America are with the President in his great main contention—the spirit, the reality, of a world league, but that many doubt his position in standing so firmly upon the letter of the Covenant.

I am certain he could tap this great well of moral conviction if he could come out now and declare that it was the spirit of the League he was defending, and that all he desired was to prevent changes that limited the realization of the fundamental idea bound up in the League—which is the co-operation of nations in facing the new problems of the world. He could tap this moral enthusiasm and throw all the blame for delay and trivial criticism upon the Senate, where it belongs. People in the future will forget about the minor disagreements, if the thing itself comes into being.

I had thought, as I suggested to you, that I might myself present this situation in a strong and sympathetic light—if the President were willing—by writing an article for immediate publication in all newspapers. While it would not be necessary to quote him, the article would, of course, have to bear absolutely the evidence of his approval and authority. There are other ways of doing it (and I am just as willing to serve without appearing in any way personally, if the President desires) but this seemed the best way to get the most sympathetic support for the President in this crisis.

I should not write this, Mrs. Wilson, if I did not have the matter so deeply at heart.   Sincerely yours,   Ray Stannard Baker

I enclose an editorial from yesterday's New York *Evening Post*[1] which conveys nearly the idea I have in the matter.

ALS (EBW Papers, DLC).
[1] It is missing, but it was "One Way with Sedition," New York *Evening Post*, Jan. 23, 1920, which said in part: "We find it impossible to believe that Woodrow Wilson, who went to Europe with a great ideal, will allow that ideal to be shattered by waging war upon the Senate over textual unrealities when he may have the reality of peace and the League for the asking. We find it impossible to believe that the Senate could withstand or would be in the mood to withstand a clear offer from the President to abandon all limited issues and to concentrate on the fundamentals of peace and the League. The President and the Senate face a single and common duty."

Gilbert Monell Hitchcock to Joseph Patrick Tumulty

My dear Mr. Tumulty: [Washington] January 26, 1920.

I return herewith the manuscript left at my house,[1] with apoli gies for the delay.

I think the situation in the treaty matter is still hopeful, notwithstanding the uproar within the Republican ranks during the last few days.[2] We shall know more, of course, after today's conference.

Sincerely,   G M Hitchcock

TLS (J. P. Tumulty Papers, DLC).

[1] A draft of WW to GMH, Jan. 26, 1920, T MS (WP, DLC), which Tumulty probably drafted. The draft that Hitchcock returned and the letter sent conform entirely. It seems likely that Tumulty prepared the draft of this letter before January 26, perhaps on the day before, or even soon after receipt of GMH to WW, Jan. 22, 1920.

[2] Republican "irreconcilables," led by Borah and Johnson, had become greatly concerned over reports in the newspapers on January 22 that the members of the bipartisan conference were about to reach a compromise on reservations, especially that to Article X. On the next morning, Borah and Johnson circulated among their senatorial colleagues, gathering information about the activities of the bipartisan conference and also insinuating that Lodge was "weakening" on his own reservations, particularly that to Article X. The two men then called a meeting in Johnson's office, deliberately timed to coincide with a meeting of the bipartisan conference that afternoon. The other senators at the meeting in Johnson's office were Knox, Brandegee, Moses, McCormick, Sherman, and Poindexter. They summoned Lodge and New from the bipartisan conference meeting, which was first delayed and then canceled.

Reports differ on exactly what took place in Johnson's office on January 23. Lodge himself said to reporters afterwards that he and New had been "hearing some gentlemen who wished to protest against any change in the reservations." He refused, however, to give any details of the meeting. Johnson was also reticent in speaking to reporters, but he did say that he did not see how there could be any compromise on the reservations which Lodge himself had earlier called an "irreducible minimum." Sherman, according to the *New York Times*, had made a "vigorous speech" during the meeting in which he charged that "Wall Street financial interests had obtained control of certain Republican Party leaders, preventing them from taking a stand against the League of Nations." He said, both in the meeting and to reporters afterward, that he would bolt the Republican party in the election of 1920, even to the extent of supporting a third party, if there was any compromise on the so-called Lodge reservations. The *New York Times* report also had the following general comments on the meeting: "It was learned that most of those attending the conference expressed the opinion that the bipartisan conferences should never have been begun and that they should immediately stop, on the ground that no compromise of an irreducible minimum was possible. One Senator said that the meeting was 'lively all the way through,' and another said that it approached 'the parting of the ways.' " This report concluded that the meeting "did not produce any definite results." However, it did quote one senator as saying: "We think that we have put out the fires of compromise, at least for the present." *New York Times*, Jan. 24, 1920.

Borah, in 1937, gave a melodramatic account of his confrontation with Lodge during the meeting. He recalled Lodge leaning against a wall for support and remembered the dialogue as follows:

Lodge: "Can't I discuss this matter with my friends."
Borah: "No, Cabot, not without telling your other friends."
Lodge: "Well, I suppose I'll have to resign as majority leader."
Borah: "No, by God! You won't have a chance to resign! On Monday I'll move for the election of a new majority leader and give the reasons for my action."

Bailey, *Woodrow Wilson and the Great Betrayal*, pp. 230-31.

Bailey himself suggested that Borah's story "was no doubt improved by him with repeated telling." But, as Bailey points out, the result of the meeting was that the bipartisan conference did not meet again until January 26, and no further progress toward a compromise was made before the talks broke off on January 30. *Ibid.*, pp. 231-32.

For other brief accounts of the protest meeting, see Ambrosius, *Woodrow Wilson and the American Diplomatic Tradition*, p. 230; Margulies, *Senator Lenroot of Wisconsin*, p. 299; John A. Garraty, *Henry Cabot Lodge: A Biography* (New York, 1953), pp. 385-87; and Ralph Stone, *The Irreconcilables: The Fight Against the League of Nations* (Lexington, Ky., 1970), pp. 156-58.

To Gilbert Monell Hitchcock

My dear Senator Hitchcock: The White House 26 January, 1920

I have greatly appreciated your thoughtful kindness in keeping me informed concerning the conferences you and some of your colleagues have had with spokesmen of the Republican Party concerning the possibility of ratification of the Treaty of Peace, and send this line in special appreciative acknowledgment of your letter of the twenty-second. I return the clipping you were kind enough to enclose.

To the substance of it I, of course, adhere. I am bound to. Like yourself, I am solemnly sworn to obey and maintain the Constitution of the United States. But I think the form of it very unfortunate. Any reservation or resolution stating that "the United States assumes no obligation under such and such an Article unless or except" would, I am sure, chill our relationship with the nations with which we expect to be associated in the great enterprise of maintaining the world's peace.

That association must in any case, my dear Senator, involve very serious and far-reaching implications of honor and duty which I am sure we shall never in fact be desirous of ignoring. It is the more important not to create the impression that we are trying to escape obligations.

But I realize that negative criticism is not all that is called for in so serious a matter. I am happy to be able to add, therefore, that I have once more gone over the reservations proposed by yourself, the copy of which I return herewith, and am glad to say that I can accept them as they stand.

I have never seen the slightest reason to doubt the good faith of our associates in the war, nor ever had the slightest reason to fear that any nation would seek to enlarge our obligations under the Covenant of the League of Nations or seek to commit us to lines of action which, under our Constitution, only the Congress of the United States can in the last analysis decide.

May I suggest that with regard to the possible withdrawal of the United States it would be wise to give to the President the right to act upon our Resolution of Congress in the matter of withdrawal? In other words, it would seem to be permissible and advisable that any Resolution giving notice of withdrawal should be a Joint rather than a Concurrent Resolution. I doubt whether the President can be deprived of his veto power under the Constitution, even with his own consent. The use of a Joint Resolution would permit the President, who is of course charged by the Constitution with the conduct of foreign policy, to merely exercise a voice in saying whether so important a step as withdrawal from the League of Nations should be accomplished by a majority or by a two-thirds vote. The Constitution itself providing that the legislative body was to be consulted in treaty-making and having prescribed a two-thirds vote in such cases, it seems to me that there should be no unnecessary departure from the method there indicated.

I see no objection to a frank statement that the United States can accept a mandate with regard to any territory under Article XIII, Part 1, or any other provision of the Treaty of Peace, only by the direct authority and action of the Congress of the United States.

I hope, my dear Senator, that you will never hesitate to call upon me for any assistance that I can render in this or any other public matter.   Cordially and sincerely yours,   Woodrow Wilson[1]

TLS (G. M. Hitchcock Papers, DLC).
  [1] Mrs. Wilson enclosed a note with this letter, the text of which follows: "The President's present judgment is that it would not set matters forward to publish this communication of his at this time, but he confidantly leaves to your own judgment the use to be made of it. EBW" EBWhw MS (G. M. Hitchcock Papers, DLC). Wilson's letter was published in the *New York Times*, Feb. 8, 1920.

Edith Bolling Galt Wilson to Joseph Patrick Tumulty

My dear Mr. Tumlty   [The White House, c. Jan. 26, 1920]

The President wants you to know he has asked Sec. Houston to be Sec. of the Treasury & he has accepted. Will you send him his nomination to sign.

He is also telegraphing Mr. Meredith of Iowa[1] to accept Houston's portfolio.   Hastily   E.B.W.

ALI (I. H. Hoover Papers, DLC).
  [1] Edwin Thomas Meredith, publisher and editor of the Des Moines *Successful Farming*. Active in Iowa politics, he had been the unsuccessful Democratic candidate for United States senator in 1914 and governor in 1916. He held numerous federal appointments during the war and was of course well known to Wilson, Tumulty, and administration leaders.

From Edwin Thomas Meredith

Miami, Florida, January 26, 1920.

I am at your service always to do anything of which you may deem me capable. Your suggestion overwhelms but if it is your wish I will be only too glad to accept and do my very best. I cannot say to you how much I appreciate your confidence or put into words my sincere thanks. Will you please advise me Hotel Royal Palm, Miami, Florida, your further pleasures. I earnestly hope you are continuing rapid recovery and soon may be restored to complete health.   E. T. Meredith.

T telegram (WP, DLC).

From Frank Lyon Polk, with Enclosure

My dear Mr. President: Washington January 26, 1920

Supplementing my letter of January 24th relative to the Adriatic question, I beg to transmit herewith the Jugoslav reply to the British-French proposal of January 14th.[1] You will note that it concedes the disappearance of the Free State; accepts under certain provisions the Free City of Fiume; refuses the moving eastward of the Wilson line, as well as the corridor along the Istrian coast establishing contiguity of Fiume with Italian territory; accepts the Free State of Zara, but insists that its diplomatic representation, as well as that of Fiume, shall be assigned to the League of Nations and reserves the right to remove from Zara the Bank of Dalmatia and all matters pertaining to provincial administration; concedes Lussin and Pelagosa to Italy, but refuses Lissa, which all proposals since September have conceded Italy; prefers for Albania the administration established by the Conference of London in 1913, but demands a certain rectification of the Northern border if portions of Albania are attributed to other states. The other points of the British-French proposal are accepted. This Jugoslav memorandum does not alter the situation as presented to you in my letter of January 24th, but is transmitted for your further information.

I am, my dear Mr. President,
                    Very sincerely yours,   Frank L Polk

TLS (SDR, RG 59, 763.72119/8833, DNA).
[1] Printed as Enclosure I with RL to WW, Jan. 19, 1920.

E N C L O S U R E

                              Paris January 23, 1920

Urgent. 231. Mission.

Confidential. Referring to my telegram number 208, January 21, 5 P.M.[1] Following is English translation of memorandum containing reply of the Yugo Slav delegates to the proposals handed them on January 14 in regard to the settlement of the Adriatic question

"One. The corpus separatum of Fiume would not be under Yugo

[1] Printed as Enclosure I with RL to WW, Jan. 22, 1920.

Slav sovereignty and in principle the independence of Fiume is accepted.

"(A). The corpus separatum of Fiume, without the railroads and without the port will be an independent state under the sovereignty of the League of Nations. Fiume's diplomatic representation will also be under the League of Nations. The port of Fiume, inclusive of the great pier and the terminal railroads of Fiume, as well as the installations connected with these services, will be the property of the League of Nations and will be placed under the management of the Serb-Croat-Slovene State. The railroad system of Fiume, which part is the only Servian commercial outlet by water, belongs to the Serb-Croat-Slovene State. The S.C.S. State will have the right to develop the port and the railways and is to conclude arrangements with Roumania, Yugo Slavia, and Hungary for the development of the commerce of these countries. In case of a disagreement the question will be settled by the Council of the [League] of Nations. The City of Souchak and the port of Baros, which form an integral whole and which were constructed exclusively for the lumber trade of Croatia, will be attributed to the S.C.S. Kingdom as its property. This small port would be the only (#) from a commercial point of view, on the entire Adriatic coast which would be the exclusive property of Yugo Slavia.

"Two. The frontier between Italy and Yugo Slavia established by the Wilson Line from the Julian Alps as far as the Arsa is the only frontier which corresponds with the geographic, strategic and economic conditions and it is entirely in favor of Italy. This frontier is accepted, although by according 40,000 Yugo Slavs to Italy, it greatly prejudices the principle of nationalities. This enormous sacrifice, greater than any other allied state has been asked to accept, is nevertheless, agreed to by the Yugo Slav people in the interests of accord and peace. The unjustifiable annexation of purely Yugo Slav territories beyond the Wilson Line would bring about a new and flagrant violation of the principle of nationalities. It would inevitably create a permanent hotbed of irredentism within the frontiers of Italy of a nature precisely analagous to that which was held as a justification of the claims of 'Italia Irredenta' in which its return to the mother country was demanded, as was so excellently emphasized in the 'London Memorandum.'[2] Stipulations concerning the territory on which the railway line from Fiume runs along the coast, if it were attributed to Italians, insurmountable difficulties would occur daily.

"With reference to the customs control, the coast services and

[2] That is, the Anglo-French-American memorandum transmitted in FLP to RL, Dec. 9, 1919. It was delivered to Scialoja in London on December 9, 1919.

other analagous services effecting a successive land of irregular configuration of but a few metres width between the sea and the railway line which constitutes the Yugo Slav frontier, this would inevitably create a source of daily misunderstandings.

"(B). The aggrandizement of Italian territory to the east of the Wilson Line in the Senozetche region.[3] An extension of the frontier a few kilometers to the east can not be justified on the ground of better protection for Trieste. On the contrary, such a measure would result in according a further part of Yugo Slav territory on the Senozetche plateau to Italy and bringing the Italian frontier to within five or six kilometers of the important Saint Pierre Railroad Junction. This railway line, which is the Vienna artery of the Yugo Slav countries, would be thus directly menaced.

"(C). The districts of a purely Yugo Slav character comprise not only those located along the *beneficiaries* line traced on the map attached to the draft, but also those located to the south of Senozetche and extending as far as the sea, which compose a territory almost in the form of a triangle. By the cession of this territory 60,000 more persons of Jugo Slav nationality would be attributed to Italy. The coast extending from Arsa to Boloska [Volosca], more than fifty kilometers in length, dominates the Fiume Gulf, in which Italy has no legitimate interests. On the other hand, the Fiume Gulf is essentially necessary to the existence of Yugo Slavia as it is her only economic outlet. By the cession of this territory to Italy the entire Hinterland, which, as well as the coast, is inhabited by a purely Yugo Slav population, would be separated from the sea.

"Three. As to Zara, although a population of only 12,000 inhabitants and representing but an isolated point in the middle of the Yugo Slav territory from which it acquires its means of existence, the delegation does not insist on its demand that that city be placed under Yugo Slav sovereignty and accepts the principle of its independence.

"Consequently, Zara (the city only, exclusive of the rest of the territory of the Zara commune) will become an independent state under the sovereignty of the League of Nations, to which will also appertain its diplomatic representation.

"It can not be admitted that Fiume and Zara should have the right to choose their diplomatic representation. If this choice laid with Italy it would amount to a disguised annexation.

"However, we wish very seriously to again call attention to the fact that Zara, which possesses no independent means of existence, would be economically ruined if it were separated from the

[3] In Italian: the Senosecchia region.

rest of Dalmatia and constituted an independent state, because for centuries it has been the administrative center of Dalmatia. In view of the fact that nothing opposes a solution of the question by according complete administrative autonomy to Zara under the protection of the League of Nations, its constitution as an independent state which would separate local offices from the rest of Dalmatia is unjustified.

"If, nevertheless, it is decided to create this state the S.C.S. State would have the right to transfer the Crédit Foncier Bank of Dalmatia, the provincial administrations, the archives, the administration library, and all matters pertaining to provincial administration from Zara.

"Four. As to Albania, the S.C.S. Delegation wishes to remark again, as it has done repeatedly since the beginning of negotiations, that the best solution would be to confine the administration of Albania, as was established by the Conference of Ambassadors at London in 1913, to a local autonomous government without interference on the part of any outside power. In the event that this solution is not accepted and if the plan to attribute portions of Albanian territory to other states, now under consideration, is permanently adopted, it will be necessary to submit the proposed frontier of Northern Albania to the modifications indicated on the map hereto annexed. The Albanian districts will enjoy, as the provinces, a special regime analagous to that which is stipulated by the terms of the Peace Treaty with the Czecho Slovak Republic relative to the autonomous Ruthenian Province of Czecho Slovakia. In order to facilitate the solution the S.C.S. State would accept eventually the de-militarization of the Islands, thus making a great sacrifice, but on condition that the island of Lisher [Lissa], which is purely Slav and which from an economic point of view is indissolubly united with Dalmatia shall be attributed to the S.C.S. Kingdom. Consequently the Lussin and Pelagruza [Pelagosa] Islands would remain Italian and would be de-militarized like the other islands of the Adriatic. The de-militarization will consist of an interdiction to fortify the islands. War vessels, however, will be able to move freely in these waters.

"Six. The S.C.S. State recognizes that the Italians of Dalmatia have full liberty to opt for Italian nationality without leaving the territory of the S.C.S. Kingdom.

"Seven. An international convention will guarantee the rights acquired by Italian subjects relative to their industrial enterprises in Dalmatia.

"Eight. Recognition of full and entire protection relative to the national language and that economical and intellectual development nationality Yugo Slav population remaining in Italy will be guaranteed.

"Nine. The question of the division of the Austro-Hungarian war and commercial fleets is closely connected with the Adriatic problem concerning the commercial fleet. It is necessary that Yugo Slavia and Italy immediately be authorized to effect a division of these ships on the basis of the decision which was adopted by the Supreme Council on November 22, 1919. As to the war fleet, the delegation demands, in conformity with its letters of June 2, 1919, and January 8, 1920, copies of which are annexed hereto, that the ships mentioned therein which are indispensable for the elementary defense of the Yugo Slav coasts may be attributed to the S.C.S. Kingdom."   Wallace

(#) Apparent omission.

T telegram (SDR, RG 59, 763.72119/8797, DNA).

Edith Bolling Galt Wilson to Ray Stannard Baker

My dear Mr. Baker: The White House Jan. 26, 1920
I have read with great interest your letter which reached me this morning, and I am convinced that you have the right idea as regards the preservation of the "spirit" of the document, and if you bring out that idea, as you can do so well, it may help as much as your little book is helping.

I asked Dr. Grayson to tell you the day you were here how sincerely my husband appreciates your wish to help, and now I am repeating it that you may know how sincere it is. He asks me to say to you that unless he could talk with you himself he finds it difficult to make suggestions but we all feel you are in such close sympathy & touch with him that you need no further hint. I am writing in great haste to catch the mail, but my warmest thoughts go forward with you.   Cordially   Edith B. Wilson

ALS (R. S. Baker Papers, DLC).

Edith Bolling Galt Wilson to Robert Lansing

My dear Mr. Secretary: The White House 27 January, 1920
Regarding the Adriatic question, concerning which you sent a recent memorandum outlining certain proposals of the British and French Governments,[1] the President requests me to say that the decision last communicated to you (from the train, I believe, while

he was on his recent trip to the West)[2] remains his final conclusion, and that he wishes the French, English, and Italian Governments to understand that, so far as he is concerned, the subject
will not be re-opened.

Sincerely yours,   Edith Bolling Wilson

TLS (SDR, RG 59, 763.72119/8833, DNA).
  [1] See Enclosure III printed with RL to WW, Jan. 19, 1920.
  [2] See JPT to W. Phillips, Sept. 13, 1919, and WW to FLP, Sept. 21, 1919, both in Vol.
63.

Edith Bolling Galt Wilson to Albert Sidney Burleson, with Enclosure

The White House
My dear Mr. Postmaster General: 28 January, 1920

At the President's request, I am sending you the enclosed list of
Senators who hindered or did not assist the ratification of the
Treaty. He asks that you be kind enough to go over it for him with
Senators Hitchcock and Underwood, and that after you have done
so you let him know your joint judgment in answer to these two
questions: (1) Is it fair? (2) Is it complete? He will speak to you
personally about it some time when it is possible for him to see you,
but would in the meantime very much appreciate a brief memorandum on these two points.

Sincerely yours,   Edith Bolling Wilson

TLS (A. S. Burleson Papers, DLC).

E N C L O S U R E

The Honorable William F. Kirby of Arkansas√
The Honorable Hiram W. Johnson of California
The Honorable Charles S. Thomas of Colorado
The Honorable Lawrence C. Phipps of Colorado
The Honorable Frank B. Brandegee of Connecticut
The Honorable George P. McLean of Connecticut
The Honorable L. Heisler Ball of Delaware
The Honorable Park Trammell of Florida√
The Honorable Hoke Smith of Georgia
The Honorable William E. Borah of Idaho
The Honorable Lawrence Y. Sherman of Illinois
The Honorable Medill McCormick of Illinois
The Honorable James E. Watson of Indiana

The Honorable Harry S. New of Indiana
The Honorable Albert B. Cummins of Iowa
The Honorable William S. Kenyon of Iowa
The Honorable Charles Curtis of Kansas
The Honorable Arthur Capper of Kansas
The Honorable Bert M. Fernald of Maine
The Honorable Frederick Hale of Maine
The Honorable Joseph I. France of Maryland
The Honorable Henry Cabot Lodge of Massachusetts
The Honorable David I. Walsh of Massachusetts
The Honorable Charles E. Townsend of Michigan
The Honorable Truman H. Newberry of Michigan
~~The Honorable Frank B. Kellogg of Minnesota~~√
The Honorable James A. Reed of Missouri
The Honorable Selden P. Spencer of Missouri
The Honorable George H. Moses of New Hampshire
The Honorable Henry W. Keys of New Hampshire
The Honorable Joseph E. Frelinghuysen of New Jersey
The Honorable Walter E. Edge of New Jersey
The Honorable Albert B. Fall of New Mexico
The Honorable James W. Wadsworth, Jr., of New York
The Honorable William M. Calder of New York
The Honorable Asle J. Gronna of North Dakota
The Honorable Warren G. Harding of Ohio
The Honorable Thomas P. Gore of Oklahoma
~~The Honorable Charles L. McNarry of Oregon~~√
The Honorable Boise [Boies] Penrose of Pennsylvania
The Honorable Philander C. Knox of Pennsylvania
The Honorable LeBaron B. Colt of Rhode Island √
The Honorable Thomas Sterling of South Dakota
The Honorable John K. Shields of Tennessee
The Honorable Reed Smoot of Utah
The Honorable William P. Dillingham of Vermont
The Honorable Carroll S. Page of Vermont
The Honorable Wesley I. Jones of Washington
The Honorable Miles Poindexter of Washington
The Honorable Howard Sutherland of West Virginia
The Honorable Davis Elkins of West Virginia
The Honorable Robert M. LaFollette of Wisconsin
? The Honorable Irving L. Lenroot of Wisconsin
The Honorable Francis E. Warren of Wyoming

T MS (WP, DLC).

Albert Sidney Burleson to Edith Bolling Galt Wilson

My dear Mrs. Wilson: Washington January 28, 1920.

Last evening I received your communication, to which was attached a list of certain Senators, purporting to be those who "hindered or did not lend assistance" toward the ratification of the Treaty of Peace. You ask, at the request of the President, that I go over the list with Senators Hitchcock and Underwood, with a view to giving our joint judgment as to whether the list is "fair and complete."

Senator Underwood is ill at this time, in consequence thereof is confined to his home and I have been unable to see him. I have conferred with Senator Hitchcock, and after going over the list with great care we reached the following conclusions:

The vote on the Lodge Resolution ratifying the Treaty of Peace with certain reservations, in our opinion, affords a fair index of those who were really for the Treaty and those who were willing to hinder and delay its ratification. I hand you herewith copy of the Congressional Record of date November 19, on page 9304 of which you will find the vote on the Lodge Resolution. You will note that on the list attached to your letter to me are the names of the republicans who voted for this resolution, and also the names of Senators Gore, Shields, Smith of Georgia, and Walsh of Massachusetts, democrats who voted for it. In addition thereto, you will find voting against the Lodge Resolution certain Senators who constitute what is termed the "Irreconcilables," or the so called "Battalion of Death," being so designated because they are opposed to the ratification of the Treaty on any terms. These Senators are Borah, Brandegee, Fernald, France, Gronna, Johnson of California, Knox, La Follette, McCormick, Moses, Norris, Poindexter, Reed and Sherman. In addition to these last named Senators and the republicans and democrats who are embraced in your list, you will find the names of Senators Norris, Nelson, McCumber, McNary and Kellogg, who must be included in the category of those who sought to hinder and did not lend their efforts towards the ratification of the Treaty. I find on the list of names inclosed with your letter, which list I am returning herewith, the names of Senators Kirby, Trammell and Thomas. In my opinion it is not fair, and in this view Senator Hitchcock concurs, to class these Senators with those who hindered and did not lend assistance towards the ratification of the Treaty. Senator Kirby voted for the ratification of the Treaty without amendment; Senator Trammell voted against the Lodge Resolution and voted with those who were undoubted friends of the Treaty on every proposition save one, and is now regarded by Senator Hitchcock as an earnest supporter of ratification; Senator Thomas voted against the Underwood Resolution ratifying the Treaty without amendment or reservation, as shown on page 9321 of the Congressional Record; Senator Hitchcock informs me that this vote was based upon Senator Thomas' opposition to the paragraph of the Treaty dealing with the Labor Question.

There are certain republicans who are and have been at all times classed as "Mild Reservationists": They are Senators Colt, Hale, Jones of Washington, Kellogg, Kenyon, Keyes, McCumber, Mc-Nary, Nelson, Spencer, Sterling and Townsend. Again, there are certain republican Senators who desire to see the ratification of the Treaty without emasculation, provided that in bringing this about no injury results to the Republican Party. These Senators are designated by Senator Hitchcock as "Lodge Reservationists," meaning thereby that they are more anxious to promote the welfare of the Republican party than they are to secure the ratification of the Treaty.

I believe this fully answers the two queries propounded in your note to me. To summarize, and to answer the two queries directly: The list you submit is not fair in that it includes the names of Senators Kirby, Trammell and Thomas in the category of those who hindered and did not lend assistance towards the ratification of the Treaty; it is not complete in that it fails to include the names of Senators Norris, Nelson, McCumber, McNary and Kellogg, who did quite as much as the other republican Senators to hinder the Treaty when they voted for the Lodge Resolution.

In all the statements and conclusions I here express with reference to the list and the Senators names thereon, and likewise as to those names hereinbefore mentioned who are not on the list, Senator Hitchcock is in full concurrence.

Trusting that this will give the President the information he desires, and prayerfully hoping that he continues to improve in his health, I beg to remain,

Respectfully and sincerely yours,   A. S. Burleson

TLS (WP, DLC).

To Carter Glass[1]

My dear Mr. Secretary: [The White House] 28 January 1920.

With considerable regret I have noticed from the press that Congress is delaying the granting of authority for the extension of prompt and generous relief to the stricken portions of Europe, the urgency and importance of which, especially in respect to Poland, Austria and Armenia, you have fully explained to the Ways and Means Committee. It is unthinkable to me that we should withhold from those people who are in such mental and physical distress the assistance which can be rendered by making available on credit a small proportion of our exportable surplus of food which would alleviate the situation. While I am sure that you must have explained fully to the Ways and Means Committee the appalling situation in those parts of Europe where men, women and children are now dying of starvation and the urgent necessity for prompt assistance, I beg of you that you make another appeal to Congress. I am informed that through the published reports of hearings before the Ways and Means Committee, the Congress has now been furnished with incontrovertible facts showing the necessity for immediate affirmative action. This prosperous republic ought not to bear any part of the responsibility for the moral and material chaos that must result from an unwillingness on our part to aid those less fortunate than ourselves. We cannot, merely to husband a small proportion of our surplus, permit the happening of this great catastrophe.

Cordially and sincerely yours,   Woodrow Wilson

TLS (Letterpress Books, WP, DLC).
    ¹ Glass prepared a draft of this letter on January 27. It is a T MS in the C. Glass Papers, ViU. It was retyped on White House stationery and slightly edited by Wilson: T MS with EBWhw emendations, J. P. Tumulty Papers, DLC.

From Robert Lansing, with Enclosure

My dear Mr. President: Washington January 28, 1920

    I am in receipt of your letter of today¹ regarding the Adriatic question and have communicated your decision to the interested governments. If the British, French, and Italian Governments fail to adhere to your solution of the settlement, it would seem that this Government would be immediately confronted with the problem as to what course it should pursue. If you concur in the view which has been advanced that the United States could not bring any economic or other pressure to bear to secure their adherence to the American plan of settlement, would it not be advisable confidentially to inform the Jugoslav Government so they could direct their policies accordingly.

    There is enclosed herewith a copy of a further telegram on the subject from Ambassador Wallace in which Mr. Trumbitch is reported to have said to Mr. Wallace that the Jugoslav Government will neither accept nor reject the Allied proposal of January 14th, but will probably indicate its willingness to abide by any decision taken by the United States, Great Britain, and France in common accord. In this connection I shall assume that any further conferences with the British and French, as suggested by Mr. Trumbitch, which might have as their object a plan of settlement different in any material respect from that embodied in your solution of *yes*[2] the question would be useless and undesirable.

I am, my dear Mr. President,

Very sincerely yours,   Robert Lansing

TLS (WP, DLC).
[1] He meant EBW to RL, Jan. 27, 1920.
[2] EBWhw.

E N C L O S U R E

Paris. January 27, 1920.

Priority A. 273. Secret. Mission.

According to information secured from Mr. Trumbich it would appear that in replying to the Allied proposal of January 14 the Yugo-Slav Government will neither accept nor reject the proposal but will probably state their willingness to abide by any decision taken by the United States, Great Britain and France in common accord.

Trumbich has received a telegram from Washington in which Mr. Grouitch[1] reported a conversation with Mr. Polk on or about the twenty-third and stated that the United States had lodged a protest with the British and French Governments and inquired whether it was intended to settle the Adriatic question without the concurrence of the United States, that the Allied proposal of January 14th did not conform to the views of the United States and that the United States had never agreed to the pact of London or to its enforcement by the conference. Trumbich was unable to confirm the report in LE MATIN this morning to the effect that (delegate?) was requesting a further extension of time which expires tomorrow evening. He may, however, receive instructions. He again stated that it was quite impossible for his Government to accept the proposal of January 14th. He doubted whether Italy would be prepared to annex by proclamation the territory given her in the guaranteed (*) of London but admitting she could do so. He personally felt that the pact was preferable to the Allied proposal as it gave Yugo-Slav Fiume and this (?) an economic out (*) to the Adriatic it would never be possible for Italy to hold Dalmatia.

In reply to a question as to what had been the attitude of his Government and the people of Yugo-Slav towards the joint memorandum of December 9 which had been published in Trieste but not in Italy, he stated that the general attitude had been favorable. The only comment he made was to point out the absence of a provision in the joint memorandum for the holding of a plebiscite throughout the entire neutral states. If such a provision were not inserted his Government would be opposed to the neutral state as they feared that it would become a refuge for (?) deserters and a perpetual source of trouble between Yugo-Slav and Italy. Trumbich inquired whether I had received any reply to his question transmitted in my telegram number 213 January 21st, 9 p.m. January 27, 11 p.m.   Wallace.

(*) Apparent Omissions.
Note: Repetition requested garbled sections.

T telegram (WP, DLC).
    [1] Slavko Y. Grouitch, or Grujić, Yugoslav Minister to the United States.

A News Item

[*Jan. 29, 1920*]

WILSON FOR PEACE PRIZE.
Swedish Socialists Recommend the
President to the Nobel Committee.

Stockholm, Jan. 29.—The Inter-Parliamentary Socialist group in the Riksdag, including [Karl] Hjalmer Branting, the Socialist leader, has decided to recommend to the Norwegian Storthing Nobel Committee that it support President Wilson and Christian Lange, Secretary of the Inter-Parliamentary Union, as the candidates for the 1919 and 1920 Nobel peace prizes.[1]

Printed in the *New York Times*, Jan. 30, 1920.
    [1] See also the Enclosure printed with JPT to EBW, March 2, 1920.

Robert Lansing to Hugh Campbell Wallace

Washington, January 29, 1920

220 Your 82, January 9, 7 p.m. and 155, January 15, noon, etc.

The settlement outlined therein has been submitted to the President who replies that the decision last communicated by him in Department's 3123, September 14, 8 am. and 3195, September 22,[1] noon remains his final conclusion. You are accordingly requested to convey this information of the President to the French Government and to the British and Italian representatives at Paris for communication to their governments.   Lansing

TS telegram (SDR, RG 59, 763.72119/8833, DNA).
  ¹ The telegrams cited in EBW to RL, Jan. 27, 1920, n. 2.

Edith Bolling Galt Wilson to Albert Sidney Burleson

My dear Mr. Burloson   [The White House, c. Jan. 29, 1920]

The President asks me to thank you for your letter & memorandum about the Senators, and also asks that you give very serious consideration to the enclosed¹

Cordially,   Edith Bolling Wilson

ALS (A. S. Burleson Papers, DLC).
  ¹ The enclosure is missing. Perhaps she sent him a copy of the draft of WW to GMH, Jan. 26, 1920.

Robert Lansing to Edith Bolling Galt Wilson, with Enclosure

My dear Mrs. Wilson: Washington January 29, 1920.

I enclose herewith a letter which I have just received from Robert Underwood Johnson, with reference to the President's desire to designate him as Ambassador to Italy.

I will appreciate it if you will inform me of the President's wishes in order that I may make reply to Mr. Johnson's inquiry.

Faithfully yours,   Robert Lansing

TLS (WP, DLC).

E N C L O S U R E

Robert Underwood Johnson to Robert Lansing

My dear Mr. Secretary: New York, January 28, 1920.

I have the honor to acknowledge receipt of your courteous letter of yesterday apprising me of the President's wish to designate me as Ambassador to Italy. I thank you cordially for the kind and friendly terms in which you convey the information of this distinction, the high compliment of which I fully appreciate.

I can say without affectation that the news comes to me as a surprise, for, although some months ago I consented to the desire of friends that my name should be presented for the post, I had concluded that the exigencies of the public service had demanded and provided a better man, and I had dismissed the matter as a closed incident. I have since taken on certain new activities which

I must arrange to relinquish if I accept the appointment, as I certainly wish to do.

In order that I may adjust my affairs to that end and make a final reply to the President's gracious wish, will you be so good as to let me know, first, how long without inconvenience to you I can have for consideration, and, secondly, how long it would be before you would wish me to take up the duties of the embassy.

I am, indeed, my dear Mr. Lansing, with high regard,

Faithfully yours,   Robert Underwood Johnson.

TCL (RSB Coll., DLC).

To Gilbert Fairchild Close

My dear Close: [The White House] January 30th, 1920.

I part with you with the greatest reluctance, because my association with you, both here and in Princeton, has taught me to repose in you the utmost confidence. I am glad you have an opportunity to prove your qualities in a freer field.[1]

My heartiest good wishes go with you.

Cordially and sincerely yours,   Woodrow Wilson

TCL (WP, DLC).
[1] Close had accepted a position with the Commonwealth Steel Company of St. Louis.

From Robert Lansing

My dear Mr. President: Washington, January 30, 1920.

On January 26th the French Ambassador handed Mr. Polk a Note[1] containing the following telegram to our Government from the Supreme Council:

"The Allied Governments have waited several months in the matter of the Peace Treaty with Turkey with the object of letting the United States have all the time it needed to decide upon the policy it will pursue on the Eastern question.

"The Allies are indeed extremely desirous of securing America's advice and cooperation but, beside the large military outlay entailed upon the countries concerned, Great Britain and France particularly, the delay has afforded the disturbing elements antagonistic to the Allies an opportunity to recover much of their sway in Turkey and to open with the Bolsheviks relations that are fraught with danger. It is therefore important that the negotiations be no longer delayed.

"On the other hand, there clearly would be no hope of conducting them with the needed speed and directness if, because of the absence of a fully empowered American plenipotentiary the many questions awaiting settlement must be referred to the American Government.

"It is needless to say that the Allied Governments attach the utmost importance to the assistance and cooperation of America. They would be glad to have such a plenipotentiary in their council. However should the American Government be unable to take that course, the Allied Governments see no other way open to them than the immediate opening of peace negotiations with Turkey, while keeping the United States fully acquanited [acquainted] with the progress of the parleys and earnestly endeavoring to elicit the views of the American Government in so far as it may be consistent with an early conclusion of peace. But, in the present world conditions, time is the essential factor."

The last instruction sent on January 9th to Mr. Wallace on the Turkish Treaty was that he might, if invited, attend the meetings of heads of governments, but should state that he would not be in a position to give the views of this Government unless in any specific instance they were requested and then only after submission of the matter to Washington.

In view of the French Ambassador's Note, I would be glad to know whether you desire the United States to participate in the Turkish Treaty in the present circumstance and if so on what basis the participation should be placed.

You will note from the text of the telegram from the Council that a speedy decision is of the utmost importance.[2]

Faithfully yours,   Robert Lansing

TLS (SDR, RG 59, 763.72119/9150, DNA).
[1] J. J. Jusserand to RL, Jan. 25, 1920, TLS (SDR, RG 59, 763.72119/8818, DNA).
[2] Wilson marked the last three paragraphs of this letter, and Mrs. Wilson added the following note to Lansing: "The President wishes me to say the instructions to Ambassador Wallace as outlined in your letter of Jan. 30 (herewith returned) are, in his judgment quite adequate E.B.W."

Joseph Patrick Tumulty to Edith Bolling Galt Wilson

Personal

Dear Mrs. Wilson: The White House January 30, 1920

I attach a self-explanatory letter from Miss Frances Freeman.[1]

Mrs. Eula McClary, to whom Miss Freeman refers, called upon me in respect to the matter, but I have known her for some time and have observed that all of the undertakings for which she has sought to enlist the President's interest have been schemes for making or collecting money for one purpose or another. I therefore had no hesitation in writing to Miss Freeman, expressing regret that during the President's convalescence it was not feasible to burden him with matters of this nature. I likewise said "no" to the attached letter from C. M. Tremaine in the same matter.[2]

I have just learned that Dr. Grayson took up the matter with the President and that the President has consented to press a button opening the celebration. Of course, I have no wish to interpose objection, but I think I should lay all the facts before you. This "victory chimes" business has all the earmarks of a scheme to collect money under circumstances that bid fair to provoke a scandal.

Scarcely a day passes that some similar request is not received—asking that the President do this or do that in furtherance of one undertaking or another, some good, some bad—and, realizing how fatal it would be to get involved in some of these enterprises, I have replied to them all, stating that under the orders of the President's physician I could not in conscience burden the President with any save the most urgent matters during his convalescence.

Sincerely yours,   Tumulty

The President says of course he will stand by you in this matter—that Dr. G did not know they had seen you E.B.W.

TLS (WP, DLC).
[1] Frances Freeman to JPT, Jan. 29, 1920, TLS (WP, DLC). She was corresponding secretary of the Victory Chimes and Carillon Association, Inc., of New York. She asked Wilson to press a button on February 2 which would ring a miniature carillon in New York, in order to launch a campaign for children to contribute pennies to finance the building of a full-size carillon as a national war memorial.
[2] Charles Milton Tremaine to JPT, Jan. 29, 1920, TLS (WP, DLC). Tremaine, the founder and secretary of the National Bureau for the Advancement of Music of New York, asked that Wilson endorse "New York's Music Week," scheduled for February 1-7, 1920.

Edith Bolling Galt Wilson to Robert Lansing

My dear Mr. Secretary: The White House Jan. 31, 1920

I am returning herewith Mr. Johnson's letter which you sent me for the President to see.

He asks me to say that he feels you can answer the questions Mr. Johnson's asks in regard to the limit of time, better than he can at present, so he confidantly leaves it to your judgment.

Faithfully yours   Edith Bolling Wilson

ALS (RSB Coll., DLC).

From the Diary of Colonel House

January 31, 1920.

The most interesting visitor of the week was Attorney General Mitchell Palmer. He came yesterday and remained for an hour. Palmer and I have never been very close friends and I know him but slightly, however before he left he became confidential and told of his embarrassment because his friends insisted that he permit them to work for his nomination as a presidential candidate. The President's silence is particularly embarrassing to him and to McAdoo. Vance McCormick, Palmer said, spoke to Mrs. Wilson about the matter but received no satisfaction further than "the President has not made up his mind."

Palmer agreed that the President's Jackson Day letter made him the logical candidate if the Treaty is not ratified. However, Palmer believes that with the President a candidate for a third term, that issue will over-shadow every other even that of the ratification of the Treaty. I cannot imagine that the President is seriously thinking of running again. I take it that it is only a continuation in his mind of the understanding we had in Paris, that is, it would be best not to announce his intentions until after the Treaty was ratified. And yet how can his Jackson Day letter be considered in any other light than that of a candidate.

There is so much mystery surrounding the President and his condition that I am wholly at a loss to form an opinion as to the truth. I wish I knew. I am not writing to him or to Mrs. Wilson for the very good reason that I have had no replies to my letters of November 24th and 27th and Mrs. Wilson has seen fit to allow the stories that are rife as to the break between us remain undenied. Denials come from Tumulty every few days, and he has called her attention to the harm he thinks is being done the President, but she has never given anything out from the President and I am forced to the conclusion that she is willing to have the story credited. If she would write me and say the President knows nothing of it and she was sorry such gossip was rife it would be sufficient. I should know then what to do but, as it is, I am helpless and the only thing I can do is to remain aloof until I receive some direct word from the President. I have made offers directly and have sent messages through others that I stand ready to help in any direction. I have publicly announced my continued affection and admiration for the President. More than this I can not do and yet I am afraid he is in a condition totally unfit to appreciate the situation as it has developed.

In retrospect I can see what a mistake the President made when he came to Paris and in not holding the Entente to the Fourteen Points. It was with difficulty I succeeded in having them accepted as a condition of the Armistice with Germany. It has been stated that many of the Fourteen Points were so vague and so general that they were practically meaningless, and the Entente could very well refuse to interpret them in the way they were meant. This is not true for I interpreted each point before the Armistice was made and the interpretations filled many typewritten pages. I cabled them in advance to the President for his approval[1] therefore, Georges Clemenceau, Orlando, Lloyd George and the others were barred from pleading they did not understand what each meant. These interpretations were on the table day after day when we sat in conference in Paris while the Armistice was in the making. Many times they asked the meaning of this or that point and I would read from the accepted interpretation. Therefore the skeleton of the Treaty was made before the President came to Paris, and if he had insisted upon the strict adherence to the Fourteen Points, Clemenceau, George and Orlando could not have evaded the issue. As far as I know, he never once referred to the Armistice or to the interpretation of the Fourteen Points after he came to Paris.[2] He seemed never to realize how important it was that the powers had accepted the Fourteen Points as the basis of peace.

Gregory came last night and spent the entire evening. He said Ray Stannard Baker saw Mrs. Wilson the other day and she is now in favor of a speedy ratification of the Treaty, I take it upon practically the best terms to be had. She said the President was not of her way of thinking.

Gregory said conditions were still chaotic in Washington and he saw no indication of improvement. He believes the President much sicker than is stated. The Government is not functioning but is merely drfiting [drifting]. The Democratic Party is on the rocks and so also is the great reputation of the President. If those around him could but have seen after he was stricken that it was best for him to call in the Vice President to act, much of the present situation might have been avoided. . . .

Raymond Fosdick came Wednesday. He came to tell more of the details of his resignation as Under Secretary General of the League of Nations. The President allowed him to go without protest. Frazier says Mrs. Wilson resented Fosdick's putting up his resignation to the President at all. She resents any responsibility being placed upon him.

---

[1] EMH to WW, Oct. 29, 1918, Vol. 51. For Wilson's approval, see WW to EMH, Oct. 30, 1918, ibid.

[2] House wrote in ignorance. Wilson referred to the Fourteen Points numerous times in the Council of Four, for example.

From David Franklin Houston

Dear Mr. President: Washington February 2, 1920.

As I shall assume the duties of Secretary of the Treasury this afternoon, I have the honor hereby to tender my resignation of the Office of Secretary of Agriculture, to take effect today, February 2, at 12 M. I shall not attempt to tell you how grateful I have been to you for your generous interest, during nearly seven years, in the work of the Department and its plans for improving farming and bettering rural life, and how much I have appreciated your constant courtesy and consideration. The years of your administration have been exceptionally fruitful not only of legislation but also of action to make farming more effective and profitable and to make the conditions of rural life more satisfactory.

I take pleasure in saying that I have found that in the Department of Agriculture the Nation has a very large force of loyal, devoted and efficient men and women to whom it is under many obligations.   Faithfully yours,   D. F. Houston.

TLS (WP, DLC).

To David Franklin Houston

My dear Houston: [The White House] 2 February, 1920

Of course, I accept your resignation as Secretary of Agriculture because I am so anxious to see you in the Treasury, and am quite willing that it should take effect, as you suggest, as of February second (today) at noon.

It has been a great pleasure to cooperate with you in your duties as Secretary of Agriculture and I want to congratulate you on the admirable results which have been achieved during your administration of the department, results from which the whole country will certainly benefit.

Cordially and faithfully yours,   [Woodrow Wilson][1]

CCL (WP, DLC).
[1] Wilson resumed nearly daily dictation to Swem on February 2, 1920.

From Carter Glass

My dear Mr. President: Washington February 2, 1920.

I am sending you a letter from Mr. Leffingwell[1] expressing his willingness to remain at the Treasury for several months, until Secretary Houston shall have familiarized himself with the details of the fiscal bureaus. It simply evinces the fine spirit which Leffingwell has exhibited from the beginning until now, and I am sure you will be pleased to note this further evidence of his devotion to you.

I am leaving the Treasury today for service in the Senate and take the occasion again to express my grateful appreciation of your kindness. It is my understanding that I am not quitting; but, at your expressed desire, going to another post. With cordial regards,

Sincerely yours,   Carter Glass.

TLS (WP, DLC).
    [1] R. C. Leffingwell to C. Glass, Jan. 29, 1920, CCL (WP, DLC).

Breckinridge Long to Edith Bolling Galt Wilson

My dear Mrs. Wilson: Washington February 2, 1920.

On my return to Washington this afternoon Mr. Lansing told me of the President's very kind thought and his desire to appoint me as Minister to Switzerland. I very much appreciate the suggestion of the President as it indicates a confidence in me which leads me to feel that my efforts have not been entirely in vain. I would prefer his confidence to that of any other man and I rejoice that I have had it to the extent which he has manifested before and appreciate sincerely this additional evidence of it.

My ambitions have not been of a diplomatic character and unless there was some urgent need of the Government in a situation where it was felt I could be of practical value I would not consider a post abroad. As I view the situation there seems to be no particular work which I could do in Switzerland. Then, too, I have announced my candidacy for the United States Senate from Missouri for the seat to be filled in the general elections next November. Consequently, I feel that I must decline the honor which the President has seen fit to offer me and, at the same time, to say that it is quite possible that my continued presence here may hamper him in some way. The fact that he has thought of me in some other capacity might indicate that he has in mind some other person to succeed me in office. Most naturally my desire is, as it always has been, to be of as much help to him as possible and to obstruct him in his work as little as possible. Therefore, I would like him to feel free to accept my resignation here without any embarrassment to him if he feels that it would in any way expedite matters or facilitate any arrangements he may have in contemplation.

It has been a great pleasure and a most distinguished honor to have been identified with his administration through such troublesome times and I have looked forward with pleasure to staying near him as long as his convenience would permit and I still feel that way and make the allusion which has been made to the acceptance of my resignation only with the thought that it might help him.

I hope that you will find a favorable opportunity to tell the President how I feel and express to him my appreciation of the honor offered and my most sincere wishes for his recovery from the illness which has resulted so unfortunately and which has given such concern to the entire people of the United States.

Yours very sincerely,   Breckinridge Long

TLS (WP, DLC).

A News Report

[*Feb. 3, 1920*]

Wilson Narrowly Escapes Influenza;
Improves Steadily But Can't Leave Capital Yet

Washington, Feb. 3.—President Wilson contracted a cold several days ago and had a narrow escape from influenza, his physician, Rear Admiral Grayson, said today. Every precaution is now being taken to protect him, Dr. Grayson said, and no person with even the suspicion of a cold is permitted to enter his room.

Dr. Grayson said the President was steadily, though slowly, improving, and was allowed now to walk about the second floor of the White House unassisted.

The President is not likely to leave Washington for some time, Dr. Grayson intimated in discussing reports from various sections of the country concerning impending trips. With the President steadily improving, Dr. Grayson said he thought it would be unwise to change his course of treatment.

Printed in the *New York Times*, Feb. 4, 1920.

To Joseph Patrick Tumulty

Dear Tumulty: [The White House] 3 February, 1920

Will you not be kind enough to issue express directions that no document or paper of any kind is to be sent over from the office or to be accepted at the office for delivery to me that is not in a sealed package or envelope? I think you will see the reasons for this suggestion without my dwelling upon them.

Faithfully,   The President.

TL (J. P. Tumulty Papers, DLC).

To Breckinridge Long

My dear Mr. Long:	The White House 3 February, 1920

Thank you for your letter of February second, but your resignation is the last thing I desire and I beg that you will not think of it for a moment. I offered you the post at Berne because of my appreciation of the services you have rendered the department and the Government and I certainly do not wish to see those services ended, though I am glad, I must say, that you are to contest the seat in the Senate and wish you the best fortune in the contest.

Cordially and sincerely yours,	Woodrow Wilson

TLS (B. Long Papers, DLC).

From Breckinridge Long

My dear Mr. President:	Washington February 3, 1920.

Your very kind letter has just reached me and I of course withdraw my suggestion of resignation. I offered it only that you might feel free—not that I wished to leave. I only want to do what will best help you and thought it might aid in solving some of the many difficulties you labor under, some of which I know.

Your cordial expressions and the manifestations of your confidence are the greatest of encouragement and I sincerely appreciate them.	Most sincerely yours,	Breckinridge Long

TLS (WP, DLC).

Edith Bolling Galt Wilson to Robert Lansing

My dear Mr. Secretary:	[The White House] 3 February, 1920

Enclosed you will find your letter to the President of January twenty-second and Mr. Polk's letter to the President of January twenty-fourth.

The President desires me to say that the second course proposed by Mr. Polk (page 3) is the course he wishes adopted. He foresees many ways in which it can be made very inconvenient to the Italian Government not to have the friendly support and co-operation of the Government of the United States.

The President is keenly aware of the embarrassments which may be created for us should the gentlemen in London and Paris repeat the discourteous and injurious course they have recently followed with regard to the Adriatic question, but that does not affect the President's judgment in regard to it. He considers the Italian claims in the Adriatic unjust and inconsistent with the peace of the world, and means to resist them to the end, no matter what the consequences are or the incidental inconveniences. He thinks that this is the time for plain speaking all around on this question and that nothing but plain speaking can put an end to the things that are going on, which are likely to disturb many international relations.

He hopes to see Mr. Johnson before his departure for Rome, so as to acquaint him very fully with his views with regard to this disturbing matter.

Sincerely yours,   [Edith Bolling Wilson]

P.S. The President quite appreciates Mr. Breckinridge Long's position with regard to the Swiss appointment and, sorry as he is to turn away from the idea, acquiesces in Mr. Long's declination because he is glad to see Mr. Long take the part he is taking in Missouri politics. He wishes to substitute for Mr. Long in the Swiss appointment Mr. Arthur Hugh Fraser [Frazier], not long ago attached to the Embassy in London and very usefully active, as you re[call.]

CCL (WP, DLC).

From the Desk Diary of Robert Lansing

February Tuesday 3 1920

P.S. to letter from Mrs. Wilson says Prest desires to send Frazer to Switzerland. I am horrified at the idea. . . . Preparing reply.[1]

Adm. Grayson came over at my request & I went over Frazer matter with him. Told him it would be most humiliating for me. He asked me to hold up reply for a few days.

[1] For the reasons for Lansing's bitter reaction to this proposed appointment, see his memorandum printed at Feb. 22, 1920.

Joseph Patrick Tumulty to Edith Bolling Galt Wilson, with Enclosure

Dear Mrs. Wilson: [The White House, c. Feb. 3, 1920]

This matter is so vitally important that I send this letter to you so that you may read it to the President when you think fit.

Sincerely,   Tumulty

TLS (WP, DLC).

E N C L O S U R E

From Gifford Pinchot

Sir: Washington, D. C. February 3, 1920.

The failure of a cabinet officer to safeguard the public interest is a sufficient reason, even at this time, to appeal to the President. Attorney General Palmer's failure and refusal to do his clear duty in a matter of large importance to the American people not only justify recourse to you, but make it unavoidable.

On December 5, 1919, Mr. Palmer announced that he would not appeal from the decision, adverse to the government, of the District Court at Los Angeles, rendered August 29, 1919, in a suit to recover from the Southern Pacific 160,000 acres of oil lands said to be worth $500,000,000.[1] The next morning, in the first ten minutes of trading in Wall Street, Southern Pacific stock jumped fourteen points.

The land grant to the Southern Pacific excluded oil land. The so-called Elk Hills case against the Southern Pacific, previously decided against the government in the lower courts, was decided in favor of the government in the Supreme Court on November 17, 1919. The District Judge in the decision of the case now being dropped by Mr. Palmer said that it was parallel to the Elk Hills case. These and other facts led the informed public to believe that the 160,000 acre case would be appealed and won in the Supreme Court.

Mr. Palmer alleges that the case is weak and if appealed can not be won. Whether right or wrong, his opinion is of little import and beside the point. In a matter of so much moment to the public interest it is his obvious duty to appeal the case and never to admit defeat until the Supreme Court has spoken. The Supreme Court, which alone has final authority, is the only tribunal whose decision against the government can rightly be accepted and allowed to stand.

What good can come from dropping this case except to private interests which will thus secure without further contest what the law specifically provided they should never get? What can be lost by appealing the case? If the Supreme Court should be obliged to decide against the public we shall be in a position no whit worse than that in which Mr. Palmer would put us by his refusal to appeal. But if the Supreme Court should reverse the lower courts, as it did in the Elk Hills case, the people will have saved hundreds of millions in value, and the Navy a Petroleum Reserve so important that Secretary Daniels has said of it that "some day it might turn the tide of war."

Mr. Palmer's course is clearly unfaithful to his public duty. If persisted in until the time for an appeal expires, it might readily become suspicious in the view of those who will recall that he has been an active attorney for large oil interests; that as Attorney General he came into a position of unique power in the matter of the discontinuance and dismissal of oil land suits; that immediately upon his appointment he dispensed with the Assistant Attorney General then in charge of the Public Lands Division of the Department of Justice,[2] who had been noted for his activities in suits to recover oil lands; and that not only has he dropped this momentous Southern Pacific suit, but, if I am correctly informed, he is proceeding actively to dismiss other oil suits in the mid-continent fields.

Mr. Palmer has no power except as it is derived from you. His action, unless you change it, will become your own. I urge it upon you as a matter of the clearest public obligation and the highest public importance that you cause your Attorney General to appeal the 160,000 acre suit against the Southern Pacific, and to see to it that the other oil cases shall not be dropped but vigorously prosecuted.

Mr. Palmer originally had six months within which to perfect his appeal. By his dereliction only four weeks remain. On January 9 I wrote him, urging him to do his duty. Having received no reply, I turn to you. Every moment is precious if a good fight for the public interest is still to be made.

Very respectfully,   Gifford Pinchot

TLS (WP, DLC).
[1] Pinchot well describes below the essentials of the case and Palmer's attitude toward it. For accounts of the background of the case and the furor that Palmer's stand stirred up in the press and among conservationists, see Stanley Coben, *A. Mitchell Palmer: Politician* (New York and London, 1963), pp. 192-95, and J. Leonard Bates, *The Origins of Teapot Dome: Progressives, Parties, and Petroleum, 1909–1921* (Urbana, Ill., 1963), pp. 174-79.
[2] Francis Joseph Kearful, who served as Assistant Attorney General from March 19, 1917, to July 15, 1919. About his dismissal, see *ibid.*, pp. 172-74.

Joseph Patrick Tumulty to Edith Bolling Galt Wilson

Dear Mrs. Wilson: [The White House, c. Feb. 3, 1920]

I know the President will not be pleased with some parts of this editorial, but I hope that you will have a chance to read it to him.[1]

Sincerely,   Tumulty

It is from the Springfield Republican

TLS (WP, DLC).
[1] "Taking Account of Stock," *Springfield*, Mass., *Republican*, Feb. 3, 1920. This edi-

torial dealt with the letter concerning American ratification of the Treaty of Versailles which Lord Grey had published in the London *Times* on January 31.

Grey's letter, which was reprinted in the *New York Times* on February 1, 1920, sought to clarify "some aspects of the position in the United States with regard to the League of Nations which are not wholly understood in Great Britain." His observations, Grey said, represented only his own personal opinion and nothing more.

Grey began by stating that there was great impatience and disappointment in the United States over the delay in American ratification of the treaty, just as there was in Europe. "Nowhere," he wrote, "is the impasse caused by the deadlock between the President and the Senate more keenly regretted than in the United States, where there is a strong and even urgent desire in the public opinion to see a way out of that impasse found which will be both honorable to the United States and helpful to the world." No charge of bad faith could be brought against the United States Senate, he continued: "By the American Constitution it is an independent body, an independent element in the treaty-making power." Nor was it fair to say that either partisan politics or considerations of self-interest were the main, or even considerable, elements in the delay of ratification. The real reasons for the Senate's insistence on reservations to the treaty lay elsewhere. First, there was in the United States a true conservative feeling for traditional policy, and one of those traditions consecrated by the advice of Washington was to abstain from foreign and particularly European entanglements. For the United States, entrance into the League of Nations was "not merely a plunge into the unknown, but a plunge into something of which historical advice and traditions have hitherto positively disapproved." Hence the desire for some qualifications and reservations. Second, the American Constitution "not only makes possible, but under certain conditions renders inevitable, a conflict between Executive and Legislatures." "It would be possible," Grey continued, "as the covenant of the League of Nations stands, for a President in some future years to commit the United States through the American representative on the Council of the League of Nations to a policy of which the Legislature at that time might disapprove."

The participation of the United States in the peace settlement and the League of Nations, Grey asserted, was absolutely essential to secure stability in peace. "Without the United States," he said, "the present League of Nations may become little better than a league of the Allies for armed self-defense against a revival of Prussian militarism or against a sinister sequel to Bolshevism in Russia. . . . The great object of the League of Nations is to prevent future wars and to discourage from the beginning the growth of aggressive arguments which would lead to war. For this purpose it should operate at once and begin here and now, in the first years of peace, to establish a reputation for justice, moderation, and strength. Without the United States it will have neither the overwhelming physical nor moral force behind it that it should have, or if it has the physical force it will not have the same degree of moral force, for it will be predominantly European, and not a world organization, and it will be tainted with all the interracial jealousies of Europe."

It was a mistake to suppose that the American people wished to withdraw their influence in world affairs. The spirit which had brought them to participate wholeheartedly in the war was still present. As for the Senate reservations themselves, Grey declared: "I do not deny that some of them are material qualifications of the League of Nations as drawn up at Paris or that they must be disappointing to those who are with that covenant as it stands and are even proud of it, but those who have had the longest experience of political affairs and especially of treaties know best how often it happens that difficulties which seem most formidable in anticipation and on paper never arise in practice. I think this is likely to be particularly true in the working of the League of Nations. The difficulties or dangers which the Americans foresee in it will probably never arise or be felt by them when they are once in the League. And in the same way the weakening and injury to the League which some of its best friends apprehend from the American reservations would not be felt in practice."

Then Grey urged the British government and people to accept American participation in the League even with reservations: "If the outcome of the long controversy in the Senate has been to offer co-operation in the League of Nations it would be the greatest mistake to refuse that co-operation because conditions are attached to it, and when that co-operation is accepted, let it not be accepted in a spirit of pessimism."

Grey devoted the last three paragraphs of his letter to the reservation in regard to the six British and dominion votes in the Assembly of the League of Nations which, he admitted, "must give rise to some difficulty in Great Britain and [the] self-governing dominions." The rights of the self-governing dominions as full members of the League could not be denied or abridged. However, here also, Grey believed that in practice no conflict would arise between the United States and the British Empire.

The editorial writer for the *Springfield Republican*, like most commentators on Grey's letter, proceeded from the assumption that, despite his denial, Grey spoke on behalf of the British government, albeit unofficially. "Mr Lodge," the editorial began, "cannot conceal his pleasure over Lord Grey's acknowledgment that Great Britain would now favor the admission of the United States into the league with almost any reservations rather than have this country stay out entirely; and the acknowledgment undeniably weakens the president in his struggle for a treaty as nearly as possible like the treaty which he signed and which the other powers have ratified. Viscount Grey, it must be admitted, acting unofficially for the British government, and in consequence of a kind of desperation, has become in effect an ally of Lodge, for the senator can now say that reservations to which the British government no longer objects ought no longer to be objectionable to any portion of the American people."

Then the editorial came to its central point: "Especially for President Wilson is this an opportunity to take a fresh account of stock. He cannot have lost all of his old suppleness and dexterity. Grey's letter surely releases him from his obligation to the allies to put the treaty through, if possible, in the form in which they have already ratified it. The viscount admits, as the president has all along contended, that the Lodge reservations 'are material qualifications of the league of nations as drawn up at Paris'; and by plain implication the viscount admits that on paper these reservations are killing in their nature. So far, then, the president is vindicated in his fight for the covenant, and the other signatory powers must credit him with having been virtually abandoned by them before he would yield ground in the matter of the covenant.

"The president's possible opportunity is found in Grey's statement that, while the worst of the Lodge reservations on paper are destructive, in practice they would probably be innocuous. . . . If the president should now accept Viscount Grey's judgment on this point, his consistency would be fully preserved, because his condemnation of the reservations has been necessarily from the standpoint of theory alone—'on paper' they cut out the heart of the covenant. But if, in practice, it should be possible, and even easy, for the league to do business much as its creators intended, the president would get the substance of what he has been heroically struggling for if he should execute a flank movement and make the Grey position his own. . . .

"If the president were now to say: 'Very well! I will put aside personal pride and all thought of personal triumph. I will make any personal sacrifice by ending this quarrel in order to save civilization. I will accept Lord Grey's judgment and join Mr Lodge in welcoming his intervention. Let the treaty be approved with conditions the least harmful that the honorable Senate can agree upon.' Would this not be a master stroke for the peace and stability of the world? We think it might because of the dreadful economic plight into which international affairs are rapidly plunging."

On the question of whether Grey spoke for the British government or only for himself, it is clear from the record that the latter was the case. The possibility that the United States might ratify the treaty with the so-called Lodge reservations had shocked most British leaders, who saw in them a repudiation by the United States of all vital obligations under the Covenant. There then ensued a debate in British governmental circles as to whether His Majesty's Government should make its views known to the United States. British leaders concluded that such action could have only adverse results. By the time Grey wrote his letter to *The Times*, opinion was still divided in governmental circles as to what policy Great Britain should pursue if the United States ratified the treaty with the so-called Lodge reservations or did not ratify it at all. See the discussion of this matter in George W. Egerton, *Great Britain and the Creation of the League of Nations: Strategy, Politics and International Organization, 1914-1919* (Chapel Hill, N. C., 1978), pp. 179-98. Egerton believes that Grey wrote his letter to persuade the British government to accept American ratification of the treaty with the necessary reservations. Egerton also points out that Grey had been in close touch with Lodge since his arrival in the United States, although Egerton does not intimate that Grey wrote his letter to support Lodge or anyone else in the treaty fight. On the question of the British government's knowledge of the Grey letter, see also the telegram from Ambassador Davis printed as an Enclosure with RL to WW, Feb. 7, 1920 (first letter of that date).

Joseph Patrick Tumulty to Edith Bolling Galt Wilson, with Enclosure

Dear Mrs. Wilson: The White House, 3 February, 1920.

Mr. Justice Brandeis has asked me to put the enclosed letter in the hands of the President.   Sincerely,   [J P Tumulty]

CCL (J. P. Tumulty Papers, DLC).

E N C L O S U R E

From Louis Dembitz Brandeis

My dear Mr. President,   New York February 3, 1920.

Negotiations in Paris on the Turkish settlement have reached so critical a state in their effects upon the realization of the Balfour Declaration[1] of a Jewish Homeland in Palestine as to compel me to appeal to you.

My associates of the Zionist organization cable me from Paris that in the conferences on the Turkish Treaty, France now insists upon the terms of the Sykes-Picot agreement[2]—one of the secret treaties made in 1916 before our entrance into the War. If the contention of the French should prevail it would defeat full realization of the promise of the Jewish Homeland; for the Sykes-Picot agreement divides the country in complete disregard of historic boundaries and of actual necessities. Rational northern and eastern boundaries are indispensable to a self-sustaining community and the economic development of the country. On the north, Palestine must include the Litany River and the water sheds of the Hermon. On the east, it must include the plains of the Jaulon and the Hauron. If the Balfour Declaration subscribed to by France as well as the other Allied and Associated Powers is to be made effective, these boundaries must be conceded to Palestine. Less than this would produce mutilation of the Jewish Homeland.

Neither in this country nor in Paris has there been any opposition to the Zionist program. The Balfour Declaration, which you made possible, was a public promise. I venture to suggest that it may be given to you at this time to move the statesmen of Christian nations to keep this solemn promise to Israel. Your word to Millerand and Lloyd George at this hour may be decisive.

Most respectfully and cordially,   Louis D. Brandeis.

TLS (SDR, RG 59, 867N.01/90, DNA).
[1] About which, see n. 2 to the Enclosure printed with WW to RL, Nov. 28, 1917, Vol. 45, and the index references in Vols. 52, 55, 57, 58, 59, and 61.

² About which, see A. J. Balfour to WW, May 18, 1917, n. 1, Vol. 42; n. 7 to the minutes of the Council of Ten printed at Feb. 6, 1919, Vol. 54; and the index references in Vols. 55, 56, 57, 59, and 61.

From the Diary of Ray Stannard Baker

Washington February 3. 20

I came down here Saturday night to see if I could not help in some way to bring about a better spirit of conciliation in connection with the treaty—following up my former conversation with Mrs. Wilson. Had a long talk Sunday with Baruch & Admiral Grayson. The President has had a severe set back—a case of hard cold or influenza. It is evident that he knows very little of what is really going on. A good deal comes through Tumulty: who is incurably political in his reactions & political in no large or clear sense, but only as concerns personalities. He has the Irish instinct for personal politics. I went up Sunday afternoon for a talk with my old friend Senator Lenroot who calls himself a "mild reservationist" but who really stands upon the Lodge position. Yesterday I lunched with Senator Underwood, Senator Gerry & Senator Jones¹ in the Senate lunch room. Senator Underwood sees the situation clearly: he was for the treaty without amendment or reservation but sees the plain fact that the majority in the Senate stands for reservations nearly on the Lodge platform. The Democrats will either have to accept this situation—going [for] merely inconsequential changes—or get no treaty & league. *This is the fact in the case.* Lord Grey's letter to the London *Times* has helped the reservationists. In explaining to the British people the situation in America he has weakened the President's position. Either the Democrats & the President must accept the treaty with reservations or else throw the whole thing into the next campaign with the odium upon them of sticking for what public opinion will believe to be verbal differences of view. They cannot do this: and the best way out for the President is to make a large gesture of willingness to do any thing to get the League speedily into being. His trouble, of course, now, is his previous unbending attitude, especially the Jackson-day letter. The whole thing has now become a bitter struggle for political advantage.

I dropped in to see Justice Brandeis & found Mrs. Brandeis having a tea: I met with many interesting [?] people. I had a short private talk with the Justice (who proves more & more to look like Lincoln) & found him taking just the position I do: that the great thing is to get a League into being & that compromises will be necessary to do it. The President can accept whatever draft the

Senate sends him & transmit to the foreign nations, abiding by whatever they will accept. . . .

The poor President! So nearly a friendless man. Yet beyond all of this yelping pack he is the only man who has had truly constructive ideas: & it is to him & to him alone that the world will owe the League of Nations—*if ever it gets it.* There is something indescribably tragic in the sight of this sick man, now willing to kill his own child rather than to have it misborn in the world! But future generations will not remember these mean bickerings if somehow the *spirit* of a new world association here comes into being. It is the old old tragedy of a man's dearest desire thwarted by the defects of his own temperament, and his own physical weakness. He has done a great work: and suffers in bitterness of spirit. Such rending of him by little mean men as one sees here now in Washington is surely one of the most unlovely exhibits of human nature.

[1] Andrieus Aristieus Jones of New Mexico.

From the Diary of Colonel House

February 3, 1920.

The sensation of the hour is the letter Lord Grey wrote on Friday of last week to the London Times and which was cabled over in full to the New York Times and Philadelphia Public Ledger. The press without exception gives it the front page and have written editorials commenting on it. It is as I feared and the ground is cut from under the President's feet. I suppose the White House entourage will make the President believe I am in some way responsible for the letter. As a matter of fact, I knew nothing of it further than I was informed of Grey's views which he has now given to the public. I had no intimation of his intention to do this. In my opinion, he would not have done this if he had been on good terms with the White House. They treated him so discourteously that he evidently felt free to speak his mind regardless of what was thought. Grey was looked upon by the White House, the State Department and the public as my particular friend and properly so. It is known that he came over largely at my insistence and that he expected to be guided by me. If the President had not fallen ill and our relations had continued as of old, the greatest good might have resulted from Grey's visit. It is possible that even so difficult a problem as the Irish question might have been solved to the satisfaction of all fairminded men. Grey, as this diary relates, was ready to go far in pressing the Lloyd George Government into effective action. The question of naval armaments and building could have been settled.

Then, too, we had in mind to take up the solution of the international financial problems which are weighing so heavily upon the world. By now, the financial question would have reached a solution. Questions relating to the League of Nations and its effective organization and operation were also in Grey's and my mind. I regard the failure of his mission as one of the great misfortunes that have befallen us all. If it had succeeded as planned, it would be hard to estimate its benefits.

A News Item

[*Feb. 4, 1920*]

Wilson, Recovered from Cold,
Is Out on Portico in Storm

Washington, Feb. 4.—Despite a hail, sleet, and wind storm, President Wilson spent some time today on the south portico of the White House.

Apparently he had recovered from the effects of a slight cold he contracted several days ago.

Printed in the *New York Times*, Feb. 5, 1920.

To Robert Lansing

My dear Mr. Secretary: The White House 4 February, 1920

I enclose an impressive letter which I have just received from Mr. Justice Brandeis and which I beg that you will read. I agree with its conclusions and beg that you will instruct Mr. Wallace at Paris to use every means that is proper to impress this view upon the French and English authorities. All the great powers are committed to the Balfour Declaration, and I agree with Mr. Justice Brandeis regarding it as a solemn promise which we can in no circumstances afford to break or alter.[1]

Cordially and sincerely yours,   Woodrow Wilson

TLS (SDR, RG 59, 867N.01/90, DNA).
[1] For the telegram sent, see RL to H. C. Wallace, Feb. 6, 1920.

To Russell Cornell Leffingwell

My dear Leffingwell: The White House 4 February, 1920

Your willingness to remain and assist Secretary Houston is characteristic of you and confirms the very great confidence I have learned to have in you as a man who puts patriotic duty above everything else. I thank you sincerely for your willingness to stay, for I think that your assistance will be indispensable and I am sure it will be as highly appreciated by Mr. Houston as it will be by myself.

With the best wishes,

Cordially and appreciatively yours,   Woodrow Wilson

TLS (received from Mrs. Edward Pulling).

From Russell Cornell Leffingwell

Dear Mr. President: Washington February 4, 1920.

Your kind and thoughtful note has touched and pleased me greatly. It makes it easier for me to defer my resignation as I had offered to do in my letter of January 29th to Secretary Glass.

With assurance of my profound respect, I am,

Faithfully yours,   R C Leffingwell

TLS (WP, DLC).

From the Diary of Ray Stannard Baker

[Washington] February 4 '20

Also [talked] with Admiral Grayson. The White House is much concerned over the Grey letter: it probably prevents entirely the plans I had for a statement from the President, although the President asked that I remain here another day, that he "might have a message" for me. There is something "on."[1] I took a walk late in the afternoon down to the new Lincoln Memorial, which is approaching completion—with a sea of mud of new earthwork all around it. It is a very noble structure & with the two other great monuments of Washington—the Capitol & the Obelisk—gives a magnificent promise of future beauty. Feb 4 1920 dined with Sweetser:[2] Walter Lippman[n] & his wife[3] & William Hard & his wife were there.[4] Tremendous controversies over the treaty & the League—and Russia—until midnight. Lippmann wants the absolute: is not content with working with the incurable old world as it is, but wants to reserve his plans of reform until men are virtuous enough to operate them. He is against the treaty & the League. I think him all wrong, yet agree with him as to the imperfections of the treaty.

I have clear intimations that my work down here has not been without result, that the President has prepared a letter very much along the line of my suggestions & will soon give it out.

[1] The "something on" was Wilson's recent tentative decision to resign. John W. Davis had a long talk with Grayson at the Wardman Park Hotel in Washington on September 2, 1920, and recorded in his diary that day or the next: "Especially interested in advice given Pres. last January to resign, his inclination, & Mrs. W's persuasion to the contrary." The Diary of John W. Davis, Hw bound diary (J. W. Davis Papers, CtY), Sept. 2, 1920. Grayson told Ray Stannard Baker the same thing on November 28, 1920: "He [Wilson] talked with Grayson about resigning last January. Grayson advised it strongly, especially on health grounds. But Mrs W objected." The Diary of Ray Stannard Baker, Hw bound diary (R. S. Baker Papers, DLC), Nov. 28, 1920.

At some time Grayson dictated the following memorandum (an undated T MS in possession of James Gordon Grayson and Cary T. Grayson, Jr.):

NOTE:

Look up notes re President Wilson's intention to go to the Senate in a wheeled chair for the purpose of resigning.

On another occasion he discussed with Admiral Grayson the matter of arranging for a visit by him (President Wilson) to the Senate in a wheeled chair so that he could make a plea to the Senate for the League of Nations.

That Wilson should have been inclined to resign in late January, and that Dr. Grayson advised him to do so, is not surprising. The attack of what Grayson called influenza (it was probably a viral infection) in late January must have weakened Wilson considerably and made him feel that he simply could not cope with the momentous problems that were crowding in upon him. For his part, Dr. Grayson must have thought that Wilson was unable to direct affairs of state; perhaps he also thought that Wilson's resignation was the only hope for the ratification of the Versailles Treaty. On at least one later occasion, Wilson seriously contemplated resigning. He told Grayson on April 13, 1920: "I am seriously thinking what is my duty to the country on account of my physical condition. My personal pride must not be allowed to stand in the way of my duty to the country. When I am well, I feel eager for work. I judge my condition because now I do not have much desire for work." T MS, dated April 13, 1920 (in possession of James Gordon Grayson and Cary T. Grayson, Jr.).

The importance of Mrs. Wilson's role in persuading Wilson not to resign in late January and early February is problematic. She was undoubtedly strongly opposed to resignation at this and other times. But there were probably two other more important reasons for Wilson's decision. Wilson's physical condition improved dramatically in early February, and with that improvement came euphoria and a surge of energy, as has already become evident and will become increasingly evident as this volume progresses. The specific event that put an end to any thought of resignation was Lord Grey's letter to the London *Times*. It made Wilson so furious that he issued the stinging and insulting rebuke that is printed as the next document. It also galvanized his determination to stand firm in the treaty fight to the bitter end.

[2] That is, Arthur Sweetser.

[3] Faye Albertson Lippmann.

[4] Anne Nyhan Scribner Hard. William Hard was at this time a weekly contributor to *The New Republic*.

A Press Release

[The White House, Feb. 5, 1920]

When comment was asked for at the Executive Office upon Viscount Grey's extraordinary attempt to influence the action of the President and the Senate it at once became evident that the Executive had been as completely taken by surprise as the general public itself by Lord Grey's utterance.

It may safely be assumed that had Lord Grey ventured upon any such utterance while he was still at Washington as an ambassador (a post which he has just left with the intimation that he was on leave) his government would have been promptly asked to withdraw him.[1]

T MS (WP, DLC).
    [1] There is an EBWhw draft of this statement dictated by WW, in WP, DLC.

Ellis Loring Dresel to Robert Lansing

Berlin via Paris February 5, 1920.

Urgent 67. The list of war guilty published in this morning's papers[1] was received here through German press correspondent Wertheimer in Paris who secured it in some way unknown to German Foreign Office, apparently from Lersner. The Entente note with official list has not yet reached the Foreign Office.

In conversation with a member of the Commission, Foreign Office official emphasized that Cabinet meeting held after publication of list, reached the unanimous decision that delivery of war guilty was impossible. He stated that Entente demand would have beneficial effect on Government support throughout the country as it has tended to unite all factions behind it. Even some of papers of the Right, such as the RUNDSCHAU, which had been bitterly attacking the Government, now come out in its support. Official stated that all Germany might be occupied by Allied troops but no German Government can be found to deliver these persons to Allies.[2] Appearance of names like that of Hindenburg made this out of the question.

In the eyes of the German people the inclusion on the list of so many of the leading political, military, naval, and diplomatic officials as well as persons of royal families is likely to lend rather a mark of distinction than of opprobrium to inclusion on list. The general attitude is one of amazement not unmixed with ridicule, it is felt that demand is so impossible of execution that it can hardly be taken seriously. The fact that persons dead for some months are included is taken as proof of its hasty and careless compilation.

One phase of present situation that has been exposed to me by a British General on special mission here is that in a great crisis German Government may be inclined to turn to Russia, especially in view of situation in Poland which is pictured here as critical.

The National Assembly will probably be called shortly and Prussian State Assembly is holding to-day a special session of protest.

Paris informed.   Dresel

T telegram (WP, DLC).
    [1] Since the summer of 1919, British and French leaders had indicated less and less eagerness to try Germans for alleged war crimes, but public pressure forced the French

government to appoint a special commission, which came up with a long list of "war criminals" in November. Then followed much discussion among British, French, and Belgian representatives to the Heads of Delegations in Paris about the number of persons to be indicted, etc. Meanwhile the German National Assembly, on December 13, has passed a law that gave exclusive jurisdiction over the trials to the Reichs court at Leipzig.

When the new French Premier, Millerand, presented the list of 854 indicted persons to Baron Kurt von Lersner, German delegate to the peace conference, on February 3, 1920, Lersner refused to accept it and left Paris the next day. The list included virtually the entire political and military leadership of the Imperial regime, and its publication set off a storm of protest and indignation in Germany, particularly against the indictment of Hindenburg. James F. Willis, *Prologue to Nuremberg: The Politics and Diplomacy of Punishing War Criminals of the First World War* (Westport, Conn., 1982), pp. 113-22.

² All underlining by WW.

From the Diary of Ray Stannard Baker

New York Febr 5 [1920].

I had quite a talk with Tumulty, the President's secretary, whom I instinctively doubt. I dropped in for a call on Secretary Lansing who was sitting just as I found him sitting in Paris so often, writing in his diary: what a place is his! He occupies the position of foreign secretary at a moment when foreign affairs were never more important—& has no power. The real foreign secretary lies ill in the White House. Mr. Lansing told me pathetically how he put up problem after problem to Mr. Wilson & never got any answer at all!

"I can do nothing whatever" he said. "We are just drifting."

If he puts his real feelings in his diary, there'll be holes burned in the pages!

He is anxious, above all, to see the treaty ratified & out of the way so that he can get at some of the problems now crowding for consideration. We talked of the Grey letter. He thought it very able & clever & hardly concealed his satisfaction in the thought that it might hasten action in the Senate, however it might offend the President.

All the men around the State Department whom I knew at Paris seemed glad to see me: I was pleased to meet them again. . . .

Grayson came over to the hotel before I left. He said the Grey letter had made a great difference & that the President might now defer sending his letter to Senator Hitchcock. It is all in state of utter confusion heightened by the President's illness & his stubborn temperament. He does not want to hear what is going on apparently.

Edith Bolling Galt Wilson to Robert Lansing

My dear Mr. Secretary: The White House Feb. 6, 1920

The President wishes me to say to you that he feels time is of the Essence now in getting the appointments for the Diplomatic Service confirmed—so he will be obliged if you will let him have the nominations of the recent appointments at your earliest convenience.

Hoping you are quite well again, believe me

Faithfully yours   Edith Bolling Wilson

ALS (RSB Coll., DLC).

Robert Lansing to Edith Bolling Galt Wilson

My dear Mrs. Wilson: [Washington] February 6, 1920.

I have your note of today inquiring in relation to the appointments in the diplomatic service.

The delay in preparing the appointments for the President is due to the fact that I have communicated with the Governments asking them as to the acceptability of the persons whom it is proposed to appoint. As yet I have received no replies but expect them every day. Of course it would be quite wrong to send names until their acceptability was known. As soon as I have the replies I will prepare the nominations.

Thanking you for your inquiry as to my health, which is improved if not quite normal, I am

Faithfully yours,   [Robert Lansing]

CCL (RSB Coll., DLC).

From the Desk Diary of Robert Lansing

1920 Friday 6 February

Cabinet meeting—11-12:45. General discussion of international trade. Conferred in Prest's office with Adm. Grayson as to whether Jusserand had approved Grey's letter. Told him I never heard of it. Also told me he had spoken to Prest about Frazer.[1] Advised sending Prest letter. Will first consult Tumulty. . . .

Adm. Grayson says I should send letter in re Frazer.[2] Also wants me to find out about N[ews] P[aper] story about Jusserand's attitude toward Grey's letter. This he phoned me. . . .

Phoned Adm. Grayson that through a correspondent I learn that

French Amb. says he has received no instructions & will make no statement in re Grey's letter.

[1] See the memorandum by RL printed at Feb. 22, 1920.
[2] About this letter, which seems to be missing, see *ibid.*

From Robert Lansing, with Enclosures

Dear Mr. President: Washington February 6, 1920

I am enclosing herewith a letter addressed to you by Dr. Douglas Johnson, of Columbia University, regarding the Adriatic situation, together with a draft of the reply[1] to the communication recently forwarded by the French and British Premiers. Dr. Johnson reiterates the necessity of standing firm on this matter, and I think that we all agree with him on that point; the suggestion contained in the last paragraph of the draft reply, however, is one which will require your careful consideration. In this relation you may wish to consider the effect of acting on Dr. Johnson's suggestion should it finally become necessary to withdraw the treaties as a result of the solution of the Adriatic question. I cannot help but feel that the withdrawal of the treaties would be fraught with disastrous results. The people of the United States wish the treaty consummated and do not favor long drawn out negotiations with Germany. The existing treaty presents the best available opportunity quickly to change present conditions of unrest to normal conditions and it protects American interests from inroads by the Allies better than a new agreement with Germany could ever do.

In this connection I am also enclosing a draft of a communication on the Adriatic question which Dr. Johnson desires to transmit to Mr. Balfour under his own signature. If you approve of this course, the message can be sent to Mr. Balfour through private and unofficial channels.[2]

I am, my dear Mr. President,

Faithfully yours,   Robert Lansing.

TLS (SDR, RG 59, 763.72119/9767, DNA).
[1] It is printed, with Wilson's changes, as the Enclosure with WW to RL, Feb. 7, 1920 (first letter of that date).
[2] Wilson circled this paragraph, and Mrs. Wilson wrote in the margin "This is approved."

E N C L O S U R E   I

From Douglas Wilson Johnson

Urgent.

My Dear Mr. President: New York January 29th, 1920.

I venture to lay before you for your consideration the following opinion and suggestion based on my long experience in assisting you in the Adriatic negotiations.

It seems to me that the French and British Governments have hoped, by threatening to enforce the Treaty of London, to compel the Jugoslav representatives to assent to a settlement negotiated without our knowledge or approval, and containing a number of features which the French, British and American Governments had all three previously rejected; and then by presenting to us a *fait accompli*, to make our adhesion follow as a matter of necessity. The two most serious features of the new proposal are the establishment of a measure of Italian sovereignty over Fiume, and the achievement of the very geographical device by which Italy has so long sought to pave the way for the ultimate annexation of that port. Both of these features the President has repeatedly and emphatically rejected. With Italy in charge of the foreign affairs of Fiume, with all the natural defenses of the port delivered into Italian hands, with the vital railway forming the only lateral line of communications along Jugoslavia's northwestern frontier controlled by Italian guns, with the main outlet of the Gulf of Fiume dominated by Italy and the Gulf itself transformed into a partly-Italian water body, with Italian territory carried to the very doors of Fiume, and with Italian agitation endlessly knocking at those doors, the stage will be set for a repetition of the Bosnia-Herzegovina affair,[1] on a much smaller scale it is true, but with consequences which may prove no less disastrous. I cannot doubt that Italy's stubborn insistence on these features is due to her unalterable determination to carry out the policy openly avowed by Sonnino's organ, the *Giornale d'Italia*, "to create at Fiume an effectively Italian situation susceptible of being with certainty transformed in due time into annexation to Italy." Nor can I doubt that this policy will in time be executed if the present proposal is allowed to stand.

But this is only one phase of a most dangerous situation. Back of Fiume lies Western Thrace, and back of Western Thrace the whole game of grab in the Near East. France and England stand committed by secret agreements, some formal and written, some verbal but held to be in honor binding, in all three areas. In the absence of America, and on plea of the urgent necessity of speed, the two governments are proceeding to execute their own ideas of the most expedient settlement, previous commitments considered. In doing this they do not hesitate to employ the same method of an ultimatum backed by threats of serious consequences in case of refusal, which precipitated the world war. And in the triple partition of Albania, which partition I do not know that we have accepted even in principle, it is the Franco-British line giving to Greece the Koritza region (the center of the Albanian national movement and the country's richest and most advanced district), and not the American line, which is followed. It is reasonable to suppose that the same history may be repeated in the other cases pending, and that we will in the end find ourselves facing the embarrassing alternative of either rejecting agreements already reached in our absence by our associates, or of pledging ourselves to maintain settlements which we have earlier rejected as both unjust and dangerous.

The whole of our diplomacy in Eastern Europe and the Near East, our great effort to substitute a new order of justice in international dealings for the old game of barter and bargain, is at stake; and nothing but vigorous action by the President will save it. I cannot pretend to advise the President in so serious a matter. The President alone knows all the facts in their complex relationships. I have thought, however, that it might not be impertinent to suggest a possible line along which the President could address the associated governments in case he deems this form of action expedient, and to summarize for his possible use those aspects of the later negotiations to which reference might be necessary. These suggestions I have cast into the form of a tentative draft of a reply from the Secretary of State to the communication recently addressed to him by the French and British Premiers; and I have added at the end a paragraph to suggest that if the President thinks the time has come to make clear to our associates that they must choose between the new order with us, or the old order without us, such a step might finally end the Italian struggle for unfair advantages and clear the way for a solution of other pending problems along lines laid down by the President.

I am, my dear Mr. President,
                    Your obedient servant,   Douglas Johnson.

I am sending this with enclosure to the Secretary of State in order that when it reaches you it may carry his criticisms, and his approval or disapproval.

TLS (SDR, RG 59, 763.72119/9766, DNA).
[1] Austria-Hungary unilaterally announced the annexation of Bosnia and Herzego-

vina, peopled by Serbs and Croats, on October 6, 1908, thus setting off an international crisis which lasted for six months. Although the annexation was eventually legitimized by lengthy negotiations among the great powers, it also created the festering discontent among South Slav nationalists which was a direct cause of the assassinations at Sarajevo in 1914 and, hence, of the outbreak of the World War.

E N C L O S U R E   I I

Suggested cable to Mr. Balfour.

[New York]

The Right Honorable Lord Balfour: February 2nd, 1920.

May I take advantage of your great courtesy to me on the several occasions when we have conferred on the Adriatic question, to beg your attention to one phase of this difficult problem which seems to me of critical importance. I am deeply concerned over the probable consequences of the proposal to concede to Italy enough additional Jugoslav territory to bring the Italian frontier to the gates of Fiume. From the very first this has been the most dangerous of the Italian objectives, and they have pursued it with a skill and a pertinacity which shows how great importance they attach to it. I advised our Government that the demand for Albona was but a step toward this goal, and that if conceded, a new proposal would certainly follow. This occurred in the form of a demand for an additional coast strip to Volosca; and the third step was to carry this strip clear to Fiume. Under the guise of conciliating a strong national sentiment (which sentiment was deliberately excited for the purpose) Italy is preparing the way for the future annexation of Fiume. If she can now with the consent of the Powers annex all the Jugoslav territory between her legitimate frontier and the city, she can in a few years stage a new self determination of Fiume, and give effect to the sacred right of self-determination by proclaiming annexation. She will then advance the plea that no one except Italy and Fiume are concerned since no alien territory intervenes between them. Neither the League of Nations nor the Powers acting separately can make effective protest under such conditions. By this device Italy will have gained possession of the only practicable port of the Jugoslav nation, located in the midst of a Jugoslav population, and possessing no economic interest for Italy save the interest of controlling it to the advantage of Trieste. I do not believe it is an exaggeration to say that Italy will thus acquire a stranglehold upon the economic life of Jugoslavia, and that the political consequences of this act will be disastrous. That Italy herself hopes to profit greatly from the proposed device is clearly indicated by the open avowal of Sonnino's mouthpiece, the Giornale d'Italia, which some months ago stated that one of the four fundamental policies of the Italian Government is "To create at Fiume an effectively Italian situation certain of being in due time transformed into annexation to Italy."

As one who labored earnestly to secure the entrance of America into the war in defense of our Anglo-Saxon ideals of justice and liberty, I appeal to you most earnestly immediately to use your great influence to prevent the stain on Anglo-Saxon honor which must result if either of our Governments should join in forcing on the Jugoslav people a device which is deliberately calculated to enslave them economically and to weaken them politically.

Let me add that this appeal is purely a personal one, made wholly on my own initiative.   Douglas Johnson.

TS MS (SDR, RG 59, 763.72119/9767, DNA).

Three Letters from Robert Lansing

My dear Mr. President: Washington February 6, 1920

In compliance with your instructions of January 26 [27]th, Mr. Wallace has been directed to inform the interested governments that your previous decision in the Adriatic matter remains unaltered and that the final position of this Government was contained in the joint note to the Italian Government of December 9th signed by Messrs. Polk, Crowe, and Clemenceau. This was, as you know, a recapitulation of the whole question in strict accord with your views.

I am now in receipt of your instructions of February 3d in which you reaffirm your previous judgment and express the view that the unjust Italian claims in the Adriatic should be resisted to the end. In this connection I venture to call to your attention certain additional facts regarding the impossibility of bringing any serious economic pressure to bear on Italy. A private loan to Italy has just been granted and aside from the proposed funding of the interest on the advances already made to Italy, which it would be to the advantage of this country to grant, no further advances to Italy are in contemplation. Such coal shipments to Italy as might be stopped are not considerable and an attempted economic blockade of Italy by this Government might have the most far reaching and unfortunate developments in both countries and would undoubtedly encourage the existing notable pro-German sentiment in Italy.

I should be glad to be informed, therefore, if you approve the transmission of the telegram drafted by Dr. Johnson which was submitted to you with suggested alterations in my letter of February 6th. You will note that the amended form of the telegram, in

closing, characterizes the terms of the British-French memorandum of January 14th as unwise and unjust and states that "if such
a solution is to be adopted it must be reached without the approval
of the United States." In this event should not the Jugoslav Government be advised accordingly in order that it may not labor under any misapprehension?

I am, my dear Mr. President,

Faithfully yours,   Robert Lansing.

TLS (WP, DLC).

My dear Mr. President: Washington February 6, 1920.

With reference to my letter of January 30th, I beg to enclose
copy of a telegram from Mr. Wallace concerning a proposed meeting of Premiers to discuss the Turkish question to take place in
London on February 12th.[1] I would, therefore, be glad to have your
decision in regard to the Turkish Treaty negotiations as soon as
possible in order that I may communicate it to Mr. Wallace and
define the American attitude before that date.

Faithfully yours,   Robert Lansing

TLS (SDR, RG 59, 763.72119/8923, DNA).
  [1] H. C. Wallace to RL, Feb. 5, 1920, T telegram (SDR, RG 59, 763.72119/8923,
DNA). The significant sentence of this telegram reads as follows: "I learned that Lloyd
George has suggested that the meeting of premiers to discuss the Turkish question
should take place in London one week from to-day on February twelfth and that Millerand has agreed to be present."

My dear Mr. President: Washington February 6, 1920.

Our Minister at Warsaw[1] has telegraphed the Department on
various occasions on the question of the repatriation of the Polish-
Americans of Haller's Army, of whom there are some ten or twelve
thousand, who have been in concentration camps since November
last.

He says the question is daily assuming more serious aspects as
there is intense dissatisfaction among these troops who feel that
they are being held there against their will and one case of actual
mutiny has occurred. He adds that without the assistance of the
American Government it is idle to expect the return of these men
for many months.

There would seem to be only two ways by which this matter can
be arranged, one, to ask for an appropriation from Congress, or,
two, that you should specifically authorize the War Department to
return these soldiers on transports.

In view of the urgency of the matter I submit for your consideration the advisability of your giving this authorization to the Secretary of War.   Faithfully yours,   Robert Lansing

TLS (SDR, RG 59, 860c.22/97, DNA).
¹ That is, Hugh S. Gibson.

Robert Lansing to Hugh Campbell Wallace

Washington, February 6, 1920.

295 Confidential for the Ambassador.

Justice Brandeis, President of the Zionist Organization of America, has written to the President saying that he is informed by his associates from Paris that in the conferences on the Turkish Treaty France is insisting upon the terms of the Sykes-Picot agreement; that if the contention of the French should prevail it would defeat full realization of the Balfour declaration of the Jewish homeland in Palestine; that rational northern and eastern boundaries are indispensable to make the country self-sustaining. Justice Brandeis claims therefore that on the north Palestine must include the Litany River and the watersheds of the Hermon and on the east the plains of the Jaulon and the Hauron, if the Balfour declaration subscribed to by France as well as the other Allied and Associated Powers is to be made effective.

The President informs me that he agrees with the conclusions stated in the letter mentioned above and asks me to instruct you to impress this view on the English and French authorities. The President adds that all the Great Powers are committed to the Balfour Declaration, and he regards it as a solemn promise which should in no circumstances be broken or altered.

In view of the fact that the American Government is not taking an active part in the discussions regarding this matter your transmission of the President's views should be oral and informal.

Lansing

TS telegram (SDR, RG 59, 867N.01/90, DNA).

From Franklin Knight Lane

My dear Mr. President: Washington February 6, 1920.

It is with deep regret that I feel compelled to resign the commission with which you saw fit to honor me by appointing me to a place in your Cabinet, now almost seven years ago. If it will meet your convenience I would suggest that I be permitted to retire on March 1st.

With the conditions which make this step necessary you are familiar. I have served the public for twenty-one years, and that service appeals to me as none other can, but I must now think of other duties.

The program of administration and legislation looking to the development of our resources which I have suggested from time to time is now in large part in effect, or soon will come into effect through the action of Congress.

I return this Department into your hands with very real gratitude that you have given me the opportunity to know well a working force holding so many men and women of singular ability and rare spirit.

I trust that you may soon be so completely restored to health that the country and the world may have the benefit of the full measure of your strength in the leadership of their affairs. The discouragements of the present are, I believe, only temporary. The country knows that for America to stand outside the League of Nations will bring neither pride to us nor confidence to the world.

Believe me, my dear Mr. President, always,

Cordially and faithfully yours,   Franklin K. Lane

TLS (WP, DLC).

To Franklin Knight Lane

My dear Mr. Secretary: [The White House] 7 February, 1920

I need not tell you with what regret I accept your resignation as Secretary of the Interior, for our association has been very delightful. I have admired the spirit in which you devoted yourself to the duties of your department, as I am sure that all attentive observers have, but the reasons you give for your retirement leave me no choice but to acquiesce and I of course accept your suggestion that the resignation take effect on the first of March, since that will serve your convenience.

May I not add how sincerely I hope that your future career will be as full of honorable success as your past? My best wishes will follow you throughout all the years that apparently must now separate us, and I beg to subscribe myself

Cordially and sincerely your friend,   [Woodrow Wilson]

CCL (WP, DLC).

To Newton Diehl Baker

My dear Mr. Secretary: The White House 7 February, 1920

You will agree with me that the enclosed concerns a very important matter in which we ought to act and act promptly if it is possible for us to do so.[1] I am sending it to you to ask your opinion and
advice with regard to the course the Secretary of State proposes
the War Department should take.

Cordially and faithfully yours,   Woodrow Wilson

TLS (N. D. Baker Papers, DLC).
[1] See RL to WW, Feb. 6, 1920 (fourth letter of that date). For Baker's reply, see the
Enclosure printed with EBW to RL, Feb. 9, 1920.

To Robert Lansing, with Enclosure

My dear Mr. Secretary: The White House 7 February, 1920

Returning your letter of February sixth, let me say that I do approve of Doctor Johnson's transmitting to Mr. Balfour in the way
you suggest the letter of which you were kind enough to send me
a copy.[1]

I also approve Doctor Johnson's draft reply which I herewith return, except that I think the last paragraph ought to be altered in
the way in which I have indicated in pencil between the lines.

Cordially and sincerely yours,   Woodrow Wilson

TLS (SDR, RG 59, 763.72119/9141, DNA).
[1] Actually, Polk, unknown to Wilson, blocked the dispatch of this cablegram. See the
extract from the House Diary printed at March 28, 1920.

E N C L O S U R E

Suggested alterations to Dr. Johnson's text are typed in red.[1]

The ⟨American⟩ Secretary of State has carefully considered the
joint telegram addressed to him by the French and British Prime
Ministers and communicated by the American Ambassador in
Paris, in regard to the negotiations on the Adriatic question. The
American Government notes with satisfaction that the French,
British, and Japanese Governments have never had the intention
of proceeding to a definite settlement of this question except in
consultation with the American Government. This Government
⟨therefore assumes that it was not correctly informed when it

[1] Deletions in Johnson's text in angle brackets; additions printed in italics.

learned⟩ *was particularly happy to receive this assurance as it understood* that Monsieur Clemenceau and Mr. Lloyd George, in agreement with Signor Nitti, had decided upon a solution of the Adriatic question which included provisions previously rejected by the American Government, and had called upon the Jugoslav representatives to accept this solution, on pain of having the Treaty of London enforced in case of rejection. It is glad to feel that its associates would not consent to embarrass it by placing it in the necessity of refusing adhesion to a settlement which in form should be an agreement by both parties to the controversy, but which in fact should not have that great merit if one party was forced to submit to material injustice by threats of still greater calamities in default of submission.

The American Government fully shares the view of the French and British Governments that the future of the world largely depends upon the right solution of this question, but it cannot ⟨agree⟩ *believe* that a solution containing provisions which have already received the well-merited condemnation of the French and British Governments can in any sense be regarded as right. Neither can it share the opinion of the French and British Governments that the proposals contained in their memorandum delivered to the Jugoslav representatives on January 14th leave untouched practically every important point of the joint memorandum of the French, British and American Governments of Dec. 9th, 1919, and that "only two features undergo alterations, and both these alterations are to the positive advantage of Jugoslavia." On the contrary, the American Government is of the opinion that the proposal of December 9th has been profoundly altered to the advantage of improper Italian objectives, to the serious injury of the Jugoslav people, and to the peril of world peace. ⟨Doubtless it was because of the positive advantages thereby accruing to Italy⟩ *The view of this Government that very positive advantages have been conceded to Italy would appear to be borne out by the fact* that the Italian Government rejected the proposal of December 9th and accepted that of January 14th.

The memorandum of December 9th rejected the device of connecting Fiume with Italy by a narrow strip of coast territory as quite unworkable in practice, and as involving extraordinary complexities as regards customs control, coast guard services and cognate matters in a territory of such unusual configuration. The French and British Governments, in association with the American Government, expressed the opinion that "the plan appears to run counter to every consideration of geography, economics and territorial convenience." ⟨Yet this unworkable and unjustifiable⟩ *The*

American Government notes that this annexation of Jugoslav territory by Italy is *nevertheless* agreed to by the memorandum of January 14th.

The memorandum of December 9th rejected Italy's demand for the annexation of all of Istria, on the solid ground that neither strategic nor economic considerations could justify such annexation, and that there remained nothing in defense of the proposition save Italy's desire for more territory admittedly inhabited by Jugoslavs. The French and British Governments then expressed their cordial approval of the way in which President Wilson had met every successive Italian demand for the absorption in Italy of territories inhabited by peoples not Italian and not in favor of being absorbed, and joined in the opinion that "it is neither just nor expedient to annex as the spoils of war territories inhabited by an alien race." Yet ⟨precisely⟩ this unjust and inexpedient annexation of all of Istria is provided for in the memorandum of January 14th.

The memorandum of December 9th carefully excluded every form of Italian sovereignty over Fiume. *The American Government cannot avoid the conclusion that* The memorandum of January 14th opens the way for Italian control of Fiume's foreign affairs, thus introducing a measure of Italian sovereignty over, and Italian intervention in, the only practicable port of a neighboring people; and, taken in conjunction with the extention of Italian territory to the gates of Fiume, ⟨paving⟩ *paves* the way for possible future annexation of the port by Italy, ⟨in defiance of every consideration⟩ *in contradiction of compelling considerations* of equity and right.

The memorandum of December 9th ⟨was so drawn as to afford⟩ *afforded* proper protection to the vital railway connecting Fiume northward with the interior. The memorandum of January 14th establishes Italy in dominating military positions close to the railway at a number of critical points.

The memorandum of December 9th maintained in large measure the unity of the Albanian state. That of January 14th partitions the Albanian people, against their vehement protests, among three different alien powers.

These and other provisions of the memorandum of January 14th, negotiated without the knowledge or approval of the American Government, change the whole face of the Adriatic settlement, *and, in the eyes of this Government,* render it unworkable, and rob it of that measure of justice which is essential if this Government is to coöperate in maintaining its terms. The fact that the Jugoslav representatives ⟨may have felt⟩ *might feel* forced to accept, ⟨under pressure of threats to enforce⟩ *in the face of the alternative of* the Treaty of London, a solution *which appears to this Government* so unfair in principle and so unworkable in practice, ⟨does not⟩ *would not* in any degree alter the conviction of this Government that it cannot give its assent to a settlement which both in the terms of its provisions and in the methods of its enforcement constitutes a ⟨flagrant violation⟩ *positive denial* of the principles for which America entered the war.

Omit ⟨The matter would wear a very different aspect if there were any real divergence of opinion as to what constitutes a just settlement of the Adriatic issue. Happily no such divergence exists. The opinions of French, British and American experts as to a just and equitable territorial arrangement at the head of the Adriatic Sea were strikingly harmonious. Italy's unjust demands have been condemned by the French and British Governments in terms no less severe than those employed by the American Government. Certainly the French and British Governments will yield nothing to their American associate as regards the earnestness with which they have sought to convince the Italian Government that fulfillment of its demands would be contrary to Italy's own best interests, opposed to the spirit of justice in international dealings, and fraught with danger to the peace of Europe. In particular, the French and British Governments have opposed Italy's demands for specific advantages which it is now proposed to yield to her by the memorandum of January 14th, and have joined in informing the Italian Government that the concessions previously made "afford to Italy full satisfaction of her historic national aspirations based on the desire to unite the Italian race, give her the absolute strategic control of the Adriatic, and offer her complete guarantees against whatever aggressions she might fear in the future from her Jugoslav neighbors."⟩

The memorandum of December 9 establishes the fact that there is no real divergence of opinion as to what constitutes a just settlement of the Adriatic issue. While there is thus substantial agreement as to the injustice and inexpediency of Italy's ⟨insistent⟩ claims, there is a difference of opinion as to how firmly Italy's friends should resist her importunate demands for alien territories to which she can present no valid title. It has seemed to the American Government that its French and British associates, in order to ⟨escape the embarrassments into which Italy's attitude has forced her friends and in order to⟩ prevent the development of possibly dangerous complications in the Adriatic region, have felt constrained to go very far in yielding to demands which they have long opposed as unjust. The American Government, while no less ~~keen~~ ~~firm in its desire to accord to Italy~~ every advantage to which she could offer any proper claim, ⟨has consistently refused to⟩ *feels that it cannot* sacrifice the principles for which it entered the war to gratify the improper ambitions of one of its associates, or to purchase a temporary appearance of calm in the Adriatic at the price of a future world conflagration. It ⟨has been⟩ *is* unwilling to recognize either an unjust settlement based on a secret treaty the terms of which *are inconsistent with* ⟨under⟩ the new world conditions, ⟨are condemned by the consciences of every people;⟩ or an unjust settlement ⟨extorted by using⟩ *arrived at by employing* that secret treaty as an instrument of coercion. It would welcome any solution of the problem based on a free and unprejudiced consideration of the merits of the controversy; ⟨but Italy has steadfastly refused to permit such consideration. It would accept any solution the⟩ *or on* terms ⟨of⟩ which the disinterested Great Powers agreed to be just and equitable; ⟨but⟩ Italy, *however,* has repeatedly rejected such solutions. ⟨What this⟩ *This* government cannot accept ⟨is a solution⟩ *a settlement* the terms of which ⟨are admittedly⟩ *have been admitted to be* unwise and unjust, but which it is proposed to ⟨concede⟩ *grant* to Italy in view of her persistent refusal to accept any wise and just solution. *If such a solution is to be adopted, it must be reached without the approval of the United States.*

Omit to end—⟨It is a time to speak with the utmost frankness. The Adriatic issue as it now presents itself raises the funadmental question as to whether the American Government can on any terms coöperate with its European associates in the great work of maintaining the peace of the world by removing the primary causes of war. This Government does not doubt its ability to reach amicable understandings with the associated governments as to what constitutes equity and justice in international dealings; for differences of opinion as to the best methods of applying just principles have never obscured the vital fact that in the main the several governments have entertained the same fundamental conception of what those principles are. But if substantial agreement on what is just and reasonable is not to determine international issues; if the country possessing the most endurance in pressing its demands rather than the country armed with a just cause is to gain the support of the powers; if forcible seizure of coveted areas is to be permitted and condoned, and is to receive ultimate justification by creating a situation so difficult that decision favorable to the aggressor is deemed a practical necessity; if deliberately incited ambition is, under the name of national sentiment, to be rewarded at the expense of the small and the weak; if, in a word the old order of things which brought so many evils on the world is still to prevail, then the time is not yet come when this Government can enter a concert of powers the very existence of which must depend upon a new spirit and a new order. The American people are willing to share in such high enterprise; but many among them are fearful lest they become entangled in international policies and committed to international obligations foreign alike to their ideals and their traditions. To commit them to such a policy as that embodied in the latest Adriatic proposals, and to obligate them to maintain injustice as against the claims of justice, would be to provide the most solid ground for such fears. This Government can undertake no such grave responsibility.

⟨I am therefore authorized by the President to say that if it does not seem feasible to obtain the acceptance of the generous and just concessions offered to Italy by the French, British and American Governments in their joint memorandum of December 9th, 1919, which concessions the President has already clearly stated to be the maximum that this Government can offer, he is prepared to withdraw the two[2] (?) *must seriously consider the withdrawal of*[3] treaties now before the Senate and to permit the associated governments independently to establish and enforce the terms of the European settlement.⟩[4]

T MS (SDR, RG 59, 763.72119/9766, DNA).
   [2] Wilson's strikeout.
   [3] WWhw.
   [4] For the telegram sent and Wilson's part in composing it, see RL to H. C. Wallace, Feb. 10, 1920.

From Robert Lansing, with Enclosure

Dear Mr. President: Washington February 7, 1920.

I call to your attention the enclosed telegram from Ambassador Davis dated the 6th in response to an inquiry which I made as to the British Government's relation to the Grey letter.

Yesterday I indirectly obtained the information, which I communicated to Admiral Grayson, that Jusserand had received no instructions from his Government on the subject and that the Ambassador had no statement to make. I will continue my investigations as to whether Jusserand has expressed himself on the subject. Of course it is, as you will appreciate, a delicate matter to discover what a foreign diplomat has said to a Senator in casual conversation as it is proceeding on the presumption that he has acted contrary to diplomatic usage. However I will do the best I can to find out the facts.

                         Faithfully yours,   Robert Lansing.

TLS (WP, DLC).

E N C L O S U R E

London February 6, 1920.

Important 204. Your 103. Prime Minister today informs me there is no truth whatever in Borah's reported statement.[1] He adds that he was not consulted by Grey in reference to letter prior to its publication and had no knowledge of Grey's intention until he saw the letter in LONDON TIMES. This he wishes the President to know in view of newspaper intimation that letter was brought to light with consent and approval of British Government. On (?) subject of reservations he feels that so long as other powers are not expressly called upon to agree it is for the American Government alone to determine what reservations it desires to make.   Davis

T telegram (WP, DLC).
[1] A news report in the *New York Times*, Feb. 4, 1920, gave the following account of Borah's statement:
"Senator Borah said tonight that Premier Lloyd George tried to reach President Wilson through Viscount Grey with a statement that the Lodge reservations to the treaty would be satisfactory to the British Government and failed, and that therefore he appealed directly to the Senate through the Grey letter.
"In discussing the action of the British Special Ambassador, Mr. Borah said that Mr. Lloyd George would have stated publicly his willingness to accept the Lodge reservations but for the fact that such a statement would have given offense to President Wilson. The Senator declared that the British Premier consulted the best lawyers in London and some in America concerning the effect of the reservations on the activities of the League of Nations. Their verdict, according to Mr. Borah, was that the reservations would be harmless because they would be subject to construction by the League, and no appeal from the construction would be possible.
"That verdict rendered, Mr. Borah said, Mr. Lloyd George promptly cabled to Lord Grey that the Lodge reservations would be satisfactory."
The same article went on to report that a Democratic senator, who declined to be identified, had essentially corroborated Borah's account. We have found no evidence anywhere to substantiate Borah's assertion.

Two Letters from Robert Lansing

My dear Mr. President: Washington February 7, 1920.

Is there anything that can be done to check the Allied Governments in the course which they are taking in regard to the demand for the surrender of Germans charged with violations of the laws of war?

While of course the fact that we have unfortunately not ratified the treaty gives us no legal right to speak, the gravity of the situation and the probable disaster which may result if the demand is insisted upon impose almost a moral duty to intervene and counsel moderation if not abandonment. Would you think it wise for you to make a personal appeal to the Heads of Governments to act with moderation and to avoid forcing the German Government to a submission which may cause a political upheaval in Germany at a time when they are struggling against both radical and reactionary movements?

I am especially disturbed to read that the Chancellor, Lord Birkenhead[1] and the Attorney General, Sir Gordon Hewart, have gone to Paris to represent the British Government. Birkenhead, whose vanity is beyond measure, has imagined himself the central figure in the prosecution of the Kaiser. It was undoubtedly his personal desire for notoriety which induced Mr. Lloyd-George in the elections of December, 1918, to promise to bring the Kaiser to trial. Hewart is probably touched with the same ambition but to no such extent. I fear that Birkenhead will, in order to gratify his inordinate vanity, insist on pressing for immediate delivery of the prescribed Germans regardless of consequences. His presence in the Paris council adds to the gravity of the situation.

Faithfully yours,   Robert Lansing

TLS (WP, DLC).
[1] Frederick Edwin Smith, Baron Birkenhead.

My dear Mr. President: Washington February 7, 1920.

I have just received a cablegram from Ambassador Davis, in London, requesting instructions as to whether he should attend the prospective meeting of Premiers in London, if he should be invited to do so, and if so, under what conditions.[1] This meeting, I understand, is to take place on February 10, 1920, two days prior to the second meeting of the Council of the League of Nations.

From information received through the Embassies both at London and Paris, I understand that this meeting has been convoked for the purpose of discussing the preliminary bases on which the Turkish Treaty is to rest; final negotiations in regard to this Treaty being left for discussion in Paris. Newspaper reports this morning indicate that certain questions arising out of the prospective non-fulfillment by Germany of the Treaty of Versailles with regard to the surrender of certain "war criminals" will likewise be discussed. Aside from these two points, I am not aware of any further questions which may have been determined upon for discussion by the Premiers.

I should be grateful if you would indicate to me whether or not you desire Ambassador Davis to attend this meeting, and, if so, in what capacity. As you are aware, Ambassador Wallace attended the meetings of the Council of the Heads of Delegations as well as the meetings of the Committee of Ambassadors, in an unofficial capacity as an observer; and it is possible that you may wish Ambassador

Davis to attend this contemplated meeting under similar instructions.

Should you think it best for Ambassador Davis to attend this meeting, I venture to call to your attention my letter of January 29, in which certain aspects of the Turkish problem were set forth.[2]

Faithfully yours,   Robert Lansing

TLS (SDR, RG 59, 763.72119/8937, DNA).
[1] J. W. Davis to RL, Feb. 6, 1920, T telegram (SDR, RG 59, 763.72119/8937, DNA).
[2] "The President does not wish Ambassador Davis to attend in any capacity." EBW to RL, c. Feb. 9, 1920, AL (SDR, RG 59, 763.72119/8991, DNA). This was communicated to Davis as RL to J. W. Davis, Feb. 9, 1920, T telegram (SDR, RG 59, 763.72119/8937, DNA).

To Robert Lansing

My dear Mr. Secretary: [The White House] 7 February, 1920

Is it true, as I have been told, that during my illness you have frequently called the heads of the executive departments of the Government into conference? If it is, I feel it my duty to call your attention to considerations which I do not care to dwell upon until I learn from you yourself that this is the fact. Under our constitutional law and practice, as developed hitherto, no one but the President has the right to summon the heads of the executive departments into conference, and no one but the President and the Congress has the right to ask their views or the views of any one of them on any public question.

I take this matter up with you because in the development of every constitutional system, custom and precedent are of the most serious consequence, and I think we will all agree in desiring not to lead in any wrong direction. I have therefore taken the liberty of writing you to ask you this question, and I am sure you will be glad to answer.

I am happy to learn from your recent note to Mrs. Wilson that your strength is returning.

Cordially and sincerely yours,   [Woodrow Wilson]

CCL (WP, DLC).

From the Desk Diary of Robert Lansing

February Saturday 7 1920

Tumulty. I read him my letter to Mrs. W. on Frazer for Switzerland.[1] He said to send it, but regretted I had to make a personal matter. Told him I could not do otherwise. . . .

Tumulty phoned asking if I had sent letter on Frazer. Said I had. He seemed sorry. Advised him to see Mrs. W at once

Prepared letter to Prest on trial of Germans & suggesting delay.

. . .

Received a letter from Prest criticizing me for calling meetings of Cabinet during his illness without his authority.

¹ To repeat, we have not found this letter; for a summary of it, see Lansing's memorandum on the Frazier affair printed at Feb. 22, 1920.

From the Diary of Henry Fountain Ashurst

February 7, 1920.

Democratic Senators caucused. Senator Hitchcock read a letter from W.W. dated January 26th, stating that he wanted the Treaty ratified without amendment or reservation, but that he would not object to "Interpretative Reservations." Senator Carter Glass, Virginia, who left the Wilson Cabinet one week ago, announced that W.W. would refuse to exchange Ratifications with the signatory powers, if the Lodge Reservations were adopted.

Senator Glass then went on to say that W.W. charged that Lord Grey while here had conspired with Senator Lodge; and that he, W.W., was going to make the Treaty the issue in the coming campaign. Senator Walsh, of Montana, inquired how W.W. would make the Treaty an issue. Senator Glass replied that the President possessed sufficient leadership to bring the question before the people.

Senator Pomerene spoke next and said he was disappointed at the attitude assumed by W.W.

Senator John Sharp Williams then lauded W.W.'s attitude and denounced the suggestion that we should enter the League upon different terms than the other signatories.

Oscar Solomon Straus to Joseph Patrick Tumulty

The White House.

Dear Mr. Tumulty   Saturday 10:15 AM [Feb. 7, 1920]

Fine—we have got them. Your and our plan *re* Article X has check-mated the Lodge group. It is a master move. I could tell you more

Congratulations   Yours sincerely   Oscar S. Straus

ALS (J. P. Tumulty Papers, DLC).

From the Desk Diary of Robert Lansing

1920 Sunday 8 February

Received papers from Prest. Among them letter saying he intends to appoint Frazer in spite of my objections.[1] It makes my position almost impossible. I do not see how I can continue in office.

Prepared answer to Prest's letter in re Cabinet meetings saying after explanations that I am ready to tender my resignation.

5:15. Lane, who resigned Friday to take effect March 1st, came to see me and I showed him above letters & my proposed reply, of which he approved. EFL[2] present.

[1] This letter, too, has not been found.
[2] Eleanor Foster Lansing.

From the Diary of Ray Stannard Baker

N. Y. Sunday Feby 8th [1920]

The letter of the President is published this morning—under date of Jan 26th. It follows closely, in its acceptance of the compromises, the line of my suggestion in my memorandum: it emphasizes our obligations and is broadly conciliatory in tone. It will do real good. I am glad also that it is put out as dating before the Grey letter.

A Memorandum by Robert Lansing

February 9, 1920.

THE TIME TO RESIGN HAS ARRIVED.

The most charitable opinion of the President's mental state is that on account of the paralysis, from which he undoubtedly has suffered, his mind is not normal and that as to certain subjects he is affected by a species of mania, which seems to approach irrationality.

In my correspondence with him he shows an irritability, an astounding insolence and a resentfulness of any suggestion of action by him which seem to indicate a lack of mental balance, which takes the form of an exaggerated *ego*.

On the 7th I received a letter, the first one actually signed by the President since he was taken ill, in which he resented my having called the Cabinet together during his illness. It was couched in language which I can only characterize as brutal and offensive. He asked me in the letter if I had called such meetings and stated that, if I answered in the affirmative, he would have some things to tell me.

This question was entirely superfluous as I had on two occasions at least written him, at the direction of my colleagues, expressing our views on certain questions of general policy. He knew, therefore, that we were meeting, unless his memory has gone, and in fact I know that early in his illness he asked about our meetings for Admiral Grayson said so.

The letter then proceeded to dilate on the dangers of disregarding "constitutional law and practice" and of departing from "custom and precedent." In view of the utter disregard which the President has shown to law as well as precedent, this part of the letter would be ludicrous, where [were] it not so tragic. The whole letter was an exhibition of passion and jealousy based on the assumption that I was attempting to usurp his powers. It sounded like a spoiled child crying out in rage at an imaginary wrong. It seemed the product of an abnormal vanity.

Of course this letter gave me the very opportunity I have been looking for to leave the Cabinet. I shall, therefore, write him a letter admitting my calling the Cabinet together and denying any intention of assuming his authority, and I shall close with an offer to resign. If he does not promptly accept the offer, I shall send in my resignation any way. I shall keep my temper, I hope, although my endurance has reached the limit. Woodrow Wilson is a tyrant, who even goes so far as to demand that all men shall *think* as he does or else be branded as traitors or ingrates. When I am free from this unheard-of tyranny I shall be contented and not till then. In hiding my feelings and subordinating my judgment I have felt a hypocrite, possibly I have been one, but what else could I do in these extraordinary conditions?

Thank God I shall soon be a free man!

T MS (R. Lansing Papers, DLC).

From the Desk Diary of Robert Lansing

February Monday 9 1920

Tumulty phoned Prest had talked angrily to him about his allowing Cabinet meetings

From Carter Glass

My dear Mr. President: [Washington] February 9, 1920.

I am sure Democratic Senators now understand quite clearly your determination never to agree to the Lodge reservations to the covenant and are convinced of the futility of any expectation of a conclusion of the matter on the basis of those reservations. They know that you would regard acquiescence in the Lodge reservations as a betrayal of the Democratic party and a betrayal of you. I agree with you.

If, however, we must go to the American people on the issue, it seems to me of supreme importance to the party and of the gravest concern for the treaty also that we should enter the fight fortified not alone by the righteousness of the cause, but able to convince the average citizen that we had exhausted every possible effort to conciliate the adversaries of the administration short of a virtual nullification of the covenant.

You are not more set against the Lodge reservations than Lodge is determined to reject anything which he may suspect you with favoring. Even if he were less implacable, Borah and Hiram Johnson would not let him accept anything which they could imagine would bring about a ratification of the treaty. This was indisputably revealed by Lodge's hasty and compulsory withdrawal from the conference table of the bi-partisan committee the other day when an agreement seemed imminent.

The analysis of the Taft reservation to article 10 which I ventured to make at my interview with you Friday[1] meets the concurrence of Hitchcock, Underwood and every other Democratic Senator to whom I have submitted it, as well as of wary, discerning and uncompromising friends of the Administration on the outside. They agree that it does not in any particular impair the integrity of article 10; it merely states accepted facts and obvious constitutional processes. If offered by us and accepted it could do no harm to the treaty, but would drive Borah and Johnson into revolt against the Republican party for agreeing to it. But it would not be accepted. Lodge would not if he could and could not if he would. If his malignancy should not prevail to reject it, his fear of the Republican "implacables" would prevent him from accepting it.

Thus responsibility for defeat of the treaty would rest with Lodge and his Republican associates. We could go to the country pointing to our willingness to accept a reservation drafted by a Republican ex-President of the United States, but which was rejected by men willing to wreck the world to satiate their hatred of a Democratic President.

This, Mr. President, is my survey of the situation. I appreciate to the fullest extent your refusal to be drawn into making suggested modifications which might extricate Lodge from his dilemma or involve you in any appearance of assenting to any impairment of the real integrity of the covenant. At the same time your true friends who are uncompromising advocates of the treaty in its essential form would be embarrassed to present a modification such, for example, as the Taft reservation to article 10, if it should, perchance, be so at variance with your view as to cause a refusal to exchange ratifications in the unlikely event of its acceptance by the Republicans. If some word might come to some Senator in complete confidence, not to be directly communicated to anybody else, the matter could, I venture to think, go forward without in the least associating you with the legislative event. I submit the suggestion for what it may seem to be worth.

With warmest regards,

Cordially and faithfully,   [Carter Glass]

CCL (C. Glass Papers, ViU).
    ¹ This Friday was February 6. The so-called Taft reservation was the one agreed upon by Lodge and moderate Republicans on about September 22, 1919, for which see W. Phillips to WW, Sept. 22, 1919 (second telegram of that date), Vol. 63.

From Robert Lansing

My dear Mr. President:			Washington February 9, 1920.

It is true that frequently during your illness I requested the heads of the executive departments of the Government to meet for informal conference.

Shortly after you were taken ill in October certain members of the Cabinet, of which I was one, felt that, in view of the fact that we were denied communication with you, it was wise for us to confer informally together on inter-departmental matters and matters as to which action could not be postponed until your medical advisers permitted you to pass upon them. Accordingly I, as the ranking member, requested the members of the Cabinet to assemble for such informal conference; and in view of the mutual benefit derived the practice was continued. I can assure you that it never for a moment entered my mind that I was acting unconstitutionally or contrary to your wishes, and there certainly was no intention on my part to assume powers and exercise functions which under the Constitution are exclusively confided to the President.

During these troublous times when many difficult and vexatious questions have arisen and when in the circumstances I have been deprived of your guidance and direction, it has been my constant endeavor to carry out your policies as I understood them and to act in all matters as I believed you would wish me to act. If, however, you think that I have failed in my loyalty to you and if you no longer have confidence in me and prefer to have another conduct our foreign affairs, I am of course ready, Mr. President, to relieve you of any embarrassment by placing my resignation in your hands.

I am, as always,   Faithfully yours,   Robert Lansing.

TLS (WP, DLC).

Edith Bolling Galt Wilson to Robert Lansing, with Enclosure

To the Secretary of State.   [The White House, c. Feb. 9, 1920]

The President, as you see, submitted your letter of Feb. 6th to the Secretary of War, and he asks that you now read his enclosed reply, and that you cooperate with the Secretary of War in the way he suggests, as the plan meets the President's approval

EBW

ALI (SDR, RG 59, 86oc.22/97, DNA).

E N C L O S U R E

From Newton Diehl Baker

My dear Mr. President: Washington. February 7, 1920.

I return herewith the letter of the Secretary of State. There is no legal authority whereby the War Department could bring these Polish soldiers back to the United States. The law covering our use of transports is strict and definite.

I agree with the Secretary of State that these people ought to be brought back, for while they were not members of the American Army, and were equipped and transported by cooperation between England and France without expense to the United States, nevertheless they are American citizens and were fighting on our side of the general cause. I suggest that the Secretary of State be asked to cooperate with me in securing the passage of an enabling resolution through the Congress which will permit these people to be brought back on returning transports. We have not many trans ports now in the Army service, but such as there are could go from Antwerp to Dantzig, if the Polish Government could arrange the transportation of these men from Warsaw to Dantzig. Some further arrangement would have to be made for their distribution from New York to their respective places of enlistment. I will be glad to cooperate with the Secretary of State in securing congressional authorization, if that course seems wisest to you.

The only alternative would be to have the Polish Government agree to their repatriation at its expense, as the Czecho-Slovakian Government has agreed to bear the cost of the repatriation of the Siberian Czechs. If such an arrangement could be made, the Shipping Board could undoubtedly supply the necessary ships, and the transportation could be managed by the War Department as it is managing the Czech movement from Vladivostok.

Respectfully yours,   Newton D. Baker

TLS (SDR, RG 59, 860c.22/97, DNA).

From Robert Lansing

My dear Mr. President: Washington 9 February 1920

I am enclosing a memorandum which I commend to your attention.[1] It is most interesting as a concrete plan for Japanese control of Siberia. It was considered by the Japanese Government, but whether it has been adopted is not known. However, it is very enlightening as to Japanese mental operations, political aspirations and methods of procedure. Because of the manner in which it has been obtained, it is of a very confidential nature. Colonel Zavoico,[2] in company with a representative of the firm of J. P. Morgan and Company, brought it to the Department and the original was only in our possession for an hour so that it had to be broken up and copied very hurriedly. Consequently, the typographical work is not uniform. Its importance was immediately seen and is somewhat increased in view of the story of Colonel Zavoico. He is very intimately connected in Siberia, and has a great love for his country. He speaks Japanese fluently and, having spent many months during the last year in Japan, he obtained access through a Buddhist monastery to the original document which he copied, and subsequently translated. He has no idea that the Department has a copy of it. He came to America to interest American capital in an activity to counteract this plan which he feels is about to be put in operation. He has a similar plan to interest Japanese and American capital with Russian Capital so as to deprive Japan of the exclusive control which she would have under this proposal.

It is so characteristic of Japanese activity and so indicative of the close coordination between political, economic, financial and industrial organization and centralization which exists in Japan, that I feel it would well repay the time necessary to read it.

Faithfully yours,   Robert Lansing.

TLS (WP, DLC).
    [1] Not found.
    [2] Vasilii Stepanovich Zavoiko, sometimes known as V. Stepan Kourbatoff or Kourbatov. A Cossack, he was formerly manager of the Russian Oil Trust and military aide to Gen. Lavr Georgievich Kornilov at the time of his attempted coup against the Kerensky government in 1917. Zavoiko came to the United States in 1919.

Robert Lansing to Edith Bolling Galt Wilson

My dear Mrs. Wilson: Washington February 9, 1920.

I have just received the attached correspondence regarding the prospective meeting of the Premiers in London, and in accordance with your memorandum, Mr. Davis has been instructed not to attend this meeting in any capacity.

I notice that my letter to the President regarding our participation in the negotiation of the Turkish Treaty was attached to your memorandum, but it is not entirely clear that the President's decision not to be represented at the meeting in London is intended to include participation in the Turkish Treaty negotiations wherever they may take place. Therefore, before replying to the note on the matter from the French Ambassasdor, which was contained in my letter of January 30th, I take the liberty of asking you to give me an expression of the President's wishes on this particular point.

Sincerely yours,   Robert Lansing.

TLS (SDR, RG 59, 763.72119/8991, DNA).

Joseph Patrick Tumulty to Edith Bolling Galt Wilson

Dear Mrs. Wilson: The White House, February 9, 1920.

Director General of Railroads Hines advises me that he has been in consultation concerning the threatened strike of the employees listed in the attached memorandum,[1] and tells me that it is of imperative importance that he should see the President before 10:00 o'clock tomorrow (Tuesday) morning.

Faithfully yours,   Tumulty

TLS (WP, DLC).
    [1] M. B. Clagett to [JPT], [Feb. 9, 1920], ALS (WP, DLC). It reads as follows:
    "All the 2,000,000 railway employees are strongly pressing for increased wages based on the high cost of living. Mr. Hines has promised them a reply tomorrow (Tuesday) at 11 a.m.
    "In addition the Trainmen told Mr. Hines today that they must have an increase at once or they will strike.

"Also, the maintenance of way employees, about 500,000[,] say they will strike if they do not get a raise now.

"Mr. Hines has assembled all the facts and has concluded any increase to be impossible now. He has pointed out that the legislation to be adopted by Congress, effective March 1, provides machinery to settle such questions.

"Mr. Hines thinks it *essential* that he see the President *today* to discuss the matter with him and decide on the proper procedure."

From Franklin Knight Lane

My dear Mr. President: Washington February 9, 1920.

I have been hoping to see you to talk over matters touching this Department, particularly the Honolulu Oil Case.[1] I am ready to decide this case, and can see no way by which it can be decided consistently with the law and the facts save as it was decided twice by the Commissioner of the General Land Office. I heard a three day argument, which also was attended by all the members of our Board of Appeals. The latter advise unanimously the confirmation of the Commissioner's opinion. I have read the briefs and all the many opinions and arguments. In the normal course of business I would at once proceed to decide this case, but because of the desire expressed in your letter of March 1, 1919,[2] for a conference before decision I do not now feel free to do so. You understand, of course, that my decision would be final and that the Attorney General is a party litigant.

                Cordially and faithfully yours,   Franklin K. Lane

TLS (WP, DLC).

[1] For a bibliographical note on the long-standing controversy over the naval oil reserves, in which the Honolulu Oil Company was intimately involved, see AMP to WW, July 18, 1919, n. 1, Vol. 61. For specific discussions of the Honolulu Oil case, see Enclosure I printed with JD to WW, July 30, 1919, Vol. 62, and Bates, *The Origins of Teapot Dome*, pp. 63-77.

[2] WW to FKL, March 1, 1919, TLS (Letterpress Books, WP, DLC).

Henry Mauris Robinson to Edith Bolling Galt Wilson, with Enclosure

My dear Mrs. Wilson: Pasadena, California [Feb. 9, 1920]

As you doubtless saw, I was taken entirely by surprise by the message from the President which you so kindly gave me on last Wednesday afternoon.

To have become a member of his official family[1] in so important a degree would have more than satisfied all my dreams—this because it would have given me an opportunity to work directly under a man for whom I have grown to have the most profound admiration and respect, and, may I properly say, affection.

Unfortunately, within the last few days I had, as I told you, committed myself to a connection with two financial institutions in California, but since you so graciously gave me the President's message I have used every endeavor to so plan that I might accept; unfortunately, no way has appeared for bridging the banks over their need—at least no way that seems satisfactory to them.

I am, therefore, forced to enclose a note to the President stating my sincere regret that I cannot take advantage of his invitation.

May I venture to repeat to you what I have written the President: that it is my very great desire to be helpful wherever possible, and to assure you that anything I am able to do, I will do.

Cordially yours   Henry M. Robinson

ALS (WP, DLC).
[1] To succeed Lane as Secretary of the Interior.

ENCLOSURE

From Henry Mauris Robinson

My dear Mr. President: Pasadena, California 9 February, 1920.

Your kind message of invitation to become a member of your official family was given to me very graciously by Mrs. Wilson, and, viewed from a selfish standpoint, nothing could have appealed to me so strongly since it offered an opportunity for service in a big way under your leadership.

I am proud of having received your consideration, and very greatly regret that only a few days before my interview with Mrs. Wilson I had committed myself to an engagement with two of the financial institutions in California, and the announcement of this had been made.

After my conference with Mrs. Wilson, I attempted to work out a plan under which I might accept the great honor you have tendered me, but, unfortunately for me, I have not been successful.

May I, however, venture to express to you my deep appreciation of the confidence shown me by your invitation and my very great and continuing desire to be helpful wherever possible in the problems with which you are battling in so masterful a way.

Very sincerely yours,   Henry M. Robinson

TLS (WP, DLC).

A News Report and a News Item

[*Feb. 10, 1920*]

SEES PRESIDENT NEAR RECOVERY
Improvement Slow, Sure and Steady,
Says Dr. Young of Johns Hopkins.

Baltimore, Feb. 10.—In a copyrighted dispatch from a staff correspondent in Washington, The Baltimore Sun today prints an interview with Dr. Hugh H. Young of Johns Hopkins on the condition of President Wilson and the various steps by which it has reached the present stage, in which Dr. Young finds the greatest reason for encouragement. For the rarity of Mr. Wilson's appearances outside the White House, Dr. Young declares only the weather is to blame.

"It has been absolutely the worst imaginable weather for a convalescing case," he told the correspondent. The interview (which is reproduced in THE TIMES by permission) proceeds:

"From the very beginning the medical men associated with the case have never had anything to conceal. When I first saw the President, in October, a crisis had arisen of such gravity, owing to the development of prostatic obstruction, that an emergency operation to relieve this situation was contemplated, but by a fortuitous and wholly unexpected change in the President's condition the obstruction began to disappear.

"The improvement in this respect, which has been steady, is now complete. It may have seemed slow to the outside world, but to those of us who have watched the improving conditions day by day and week by week it has seemed little short of marvelous. The President was organically sound when I saw him first, and I found him not only organically sound when I visited him last week but, further, all the organs were functioning in a perfectly normal, healthy manner.

"Pari passu, the President's general condition and, specifically, the slight impairment of his left arm and leg have improved more slowly, it is true, but surely, steadily. There have been no setbacks, no backward steps, and rumors to this effect are rubbish.

"As you know, in October last we diagnosed the President's illness as cerebral thrombosis, (clot in a blood vessel), which affected his left arm and leg, but at no time was his brain power or the extreme vigor and lucidity of his mental processes in the slightest degree abated. This condition has from the very first shown a steady, unwavering tendency toward resolution and complete absorption. The increasing utility of the left arm and leg, greatly impaired at first, have closely followed on this improvement. The

President walks sturdily now, without assistance and without fatigue. And he uses the still slightly impaired arm more and more every day.

"As to his mental vigor, it is simply prodigious. Indeed, I think in many ways the President is in better shape than before the illness came. He is certainly greatly refreshed and strengthened by the uses to which he has put what would have been for so many men merely the tedious, long-drawn-out weeks of convalescence. Then, again, it must be borne in mind that as a result of the care that has been bestowed upon him by his immediate and by his official family he has been relieved for many weeks from the burden of routine that he has carried without an interruption for so many years. His frame of mind is bright and tranquil and he worries not at all. He knows that he is now quite up to his fighting weight; in fact, he weighs quite a few pounds more than he did when we put him to bed. His eyes are bright and his complexion shows the glow of health. Of course, I do not mean to convey the impression that the President does not find his long confinement at times very irksome. Of course, he is champing at the bit, but he has borne up under his trials, including the visitations of his physicians, with a serene philosophy which is not met with in all sickrooms.

"The public documents which the President has written and signed in the past months and his public study and comment on the questions of the day are, of course, known to all. It is, however, perhaps not so well known that the President is taking a progressively greater part in the daily work of the executive offices, and that he is now able without fatigue to devote several hours every day to official business.

"For the failure of the President to appear more frequently, don't let a naturally solicitous public blame the Chief Magistrate, and put in a word if you can for the physicians. We should, I think, all get together on a platform of blaming the weather. Had it not been for the recent succession of wild storms, which makes the White House lot and Potomac Park look like what I imagine the approaches to the North Pole to be, the President would have appeared out of doors much more frequently than it has been possible to permit. But it is only the weather that confines him—the weather and nothing else. We naturally think that the transition from a sickroom, with carefully guarded temperature, to the heart of a blizzard would be too abrupt. That is all there is to this.

"I hope it won't come, but you can rest assured that the President is ready and willing, and, what is more, perfectly able, to dig himself out of that new avalanche of snow and ice that is announced should come along. In a word, you can say to all who are naturally solicitous as to the condition of the President, that all goes well except the weather on the banks of the Potomac. You can say that the President is able-minded and able-bodied, and that he is giving splendid attention to affairs of state, and that we have every assurance that he will become progressively more active in these matters with the advent of Spring and sunshine, which cannot now be long delayed."

Washington, Feb. 10.—Rear Admiral Grayson, President Wilson's attending physician, declined today to comment on The Baltimore Sun's interview with Dr. Hugh H. Young of Johns Hopkins on President Wilson's illness and present state.

Printed in the *New York Times*, Feb. 11, 1920.

To Carrie Clinton Lane Chapman Catt

[The White House] February 10, 1920.

Permit me to congratulate your Association upon the fact that its great work is so near its triumphant end that you can now merge it into a League of Women Voters to carry on the development of good citizenship and real democracy; and to wish for the new organization the same success and wise leadership.[1]

Woodrow Wilson.

T telegram (Letterpress Books, WP, DLC).

[1] This message was written for the occasion of the opening of the annual convention of the National American Woman Suffrage Association in Chicago on February 13. Mrs. Catt read the telegram to the delegates on that date. On the same day, the executive committee of the association recommended that the League of Women Voters, established the previous year as a section of the association, be organized as a separate body, and that the association be gradually absorbed by the league. *New York Times*, Feb. 14, 1920.

The fervor of Wilson's message may have been enhanced by the fact that the New Jersey Assembly, by a vote of thirty-four to twenty-eight in the early morning of February 10, had made that state the twenty-ninth to ratify the Nineteenth Amendment. *Ibid.*, Feb. 10, 1920.

Joseph Patrick Tumulty to Edith Bolling Galt Wilson

Dear Mrs. Wilson: The White House 10 February, 1920

I went over the railroad situation with Mr. Hines last night. He says that it is most critical and involves a general railroad strike. And he says that the men believe that the President is not consulted about these matters, and because of their faith in the President Mr. Hines feels that if the President could for five minutes see a committee of three, he could settle the matter.

It is needless to exaggerate the importance of something definite being done to hold this thing off.   Sincerely,   J P Tumulty

TLS (WP, DLC).

Joseph Patrick Tumulty to Edith Bolling Galt Wilson, with Enclosure

Dear Mrs. Wilson: The White House, February 10, 1920.

I think you will wish to read this to the President.

Faithfully yours,   J.P.T.

TL (WP, DLC).

E N C L O S U R E

Wieringen Island, February 9, 1920

Mr. President: The demand for the delivery of Germans of every walk of life has again confronted my country sorely tried by four years of war and one year of severe internal struggles with a crisis that is without a precedent in the history of the world as affecting the life of a people. That a government can be found in Germany which would carry out the demanded surrender is out of the question; the consequences to Europe of an enforcement of the demand by violence are incalculable, hatred and revenge would be made eternal. As the former successor to the throne of my German Fatherland, I am willing at this fateful hour to stand up for my compatriots. If the Allied and Associated Governments want a victim, let them take me instead of the nine hundred Germans who have committed no offence other than that of serving their country in the war.   Wilhelm[1]

TC telegram (WP, DLC).
[1] Friedrich Wilhelm Viktor August Ernst, the former German Crown Prince.

Joseph Patrick Tumulty to Edith Bolling Galt Wilson

Dear Mrs. Wilson: The White House, 10 February, 1920.

Will you please have the President mark "Accepted" on the Fletcher resignation, so that we might dispose of this matter.

Sincerely,   [J P Tumulty]

CCL (J. P. Tumulty Papers, DLC).

From the Desk Diary of Robert Lansing

1920 Tuesday 10 February

Polk, back from N. Y. Showed him correspondence in re Cabinet meetings and Frazer appointment. Agrees entirely with my attitude but says Prest is not normal and that I must sit tight. Tells me Frazer has sailed for France, so I cannot communicate with him. Appealed to my sense of public duty to continue in office when I said that I was disposed to resign at once. . . .

Haircut & Luncheon. 12:10-1:40. Polk told me that he had talk with Grayson about Prest's attitude, that he told him I was not anxious to stay in office, but that if I went it would be a tragedy for the Prest, as he would receive all the blame. Grayson said he appreciated situation & would attempt to do something.

Robert Lansing to Hugh Campbell Wallace

Washington, February 10, 1920

318 Your 241, January 23, 9 p.m.

Please communicate following to British and French representatives.

The President has carefully considered the joint telegram addressed to this Government by the French and British Prime Ministers and communicated by the American Ambassador in Paris, in regard to the negotiations on the Adriatic question. The President notes with satisfaction that the French, British, and Japanese Governments have never had the intention of proceeding to a definite settlement of this question except in consultation with the American Government. The President was particularly happy to receive this assurance as he understood that Monsieur Clemenceau and Mr. Lloyd George, in agreement with Signor Nitti, had decided upon a solution of the Adriatic question, which included provisions previously rejected by the American Government, and had called upon the Jugoslav representatives to accept this solution, on pain of having the Treaty of London enforced in case of rejection. The President is glad to feel that the associates of this Government would not consent to embarrass it by placing it in the necessity of refusing adhesion to a settlement which in form would be an agreement by both parties to the controversy, but which in fact would not have that great merit if one partly was forced to submit to material injustice by threats of still greater calamities in default of submission.

The President fully shares the view of the French and British

Governments that the future of the world largely depends upon the right solution of this question, but he cannot believe that a solution containing provisions which have already received the well-merited condemnation of the French and British Governments can in any sense be regarded as right. Neither can he share the opinion of the French and British Governments that the proposals contained in their memorandum delivered to the Jugoslav representatives on January fourteenth leave untouched practically every important point of the joint memorandum of the French, British, and American Governments of December 9, 1919, and that QUOTE only two features undergo alterations, and both these alterations are to the positive advantage of Jugoslavia END QUOTE. On the contrary, the President is of the opinion that the proposal of December ninth has been profoundly altered to the advantage of improper Italian objectives, to the serious injury of the Jugoslav people, and to the peril of world peace. The view that very positive advantages have been conceded to Italy would appear to be borne out by the fact that the Italian Government rejected the proposal of December ninth and accepted that of January fourteenth.

The memorandum of December ninth rejected the device of connecting Fiume with Italy by a narrow strip of coast territory as quite unworkable in practice, and as involving extraordinary complexities as regards customs control, coast guard services, and cognate matters in a territory of such unusual configuration. The French and British Governments, in association with the American Government, expressed the opinion that QUOTE the plan appears to run counter to every consideration of geography, economics and territorial convenience END QUOTE. The American Government notes that this annexation of Jugoslav territory by Italy is nevertheless agreed to by the memorandum of January fourteenth.

The memorandum of December ninth rejected Italy's demand for the annexation of all of Istria, on the solid ground that neither strategic nor economic considerations could justify such annexation, and that there remained nothing in defense of the proposition save Italy's desire for more territory admittedly inhabited by Jugoslavs. The French and British Governments then expressed their cordial approval of the way in which the President had met every successive Italian demand for the absorption in Italy of territories inhabited by peoples not Italian and not in favor of being absorbed, and joined in the opinion that QUOTE it is neither just nor expedient to annex as the spoils of war territories inhabited by an alien race END QUOTE. Yet this unjust and inexpedient annexation of all of Istria is provided for in the memorandum of January fourteenth.

The memorandum of December ninth carefully excluded every

form of Italian sovereignty over Fiume. The American Government cannot avoid the conclusion that the memorandum of January fourteenth opens the way for Italian control of Fiume's foreign affairs, thus introducing a measure of Italian soveriegnty over, and Italian intervention in, the only practicable port of a neighboring people; and, taken in conjunction with the extension of Italian territory to the gates of Fiume, paves the way for possible future annexation of the port by Italy, in contradiction of compelling considerations of equity and right.

The memorandum of December ninth afforded proper protection to the vital railway connecting Fiume northward with the interior. The memorandum of January fourteenth establishes Italy in dominating military positions close to the railway at a number of critical points.

The memorandum of December ninth maintained in large measure the unity of the Albanian state. That of January fourteenth partitions the Albanian people, against their vehement protests, among three different alien powers.

These and other provisions of the memorandum of January fourteenth, negotiated without the knowledge or approval of the American Government, change the whole face of the Adriatic settlement, and, in the eyes of this Government, render it unworkable and rob it of that measure of justice which is essential if this Government is to co-operate in maintaining its terms. The fact that the Jugoslav representatives might feel forced to accept, in the face of the alternative of the Treaty of London, a solution which appears to this Government so unfair in principle and so unworkable in practice, would not in any degree alter the conviction of this Government that it cannot give its assent to a settlement which both in the terms of its provisions and in the methods of its enforcement constitutes a positive denial of the principles for which America entered the war.

The matter would wear a very different aspect if there were any real divergence of opinion as to what constitutes a just settlement of the Adriatic issue. Happily no such divergence exists. The opinions of the French, British, and Americans as to a just and equitable territorial arrangement at the head of the Adriatic Sea were strikingly harmonious. Italy's unjust demands had been condemned by the French and British Governments in terms no less severe than those employed by the American Government. Certainly the French and British Governments will yield nothing to their American associate as regards the earnestness with which they have sought to convince the Italian Government that fulfillment of its demands would be contrary to Italy's own best interests, opposed to the spirit of justice in international dealings and fraught with danger to the peace of Europe. In particular, the French and British Governments have opposed Italy's demands for specific advantages which it is now proposed to yield to her by the memorandum of January fourteenth, and have joined in informing the Italian Government that the concessions previously made QUOTE afford to Italy full satisfaction of her historic national aspirations based on the desire to unite the Italian race, give her the absolute strategic control of the Adriatic and offer her complete guarantees against whatever aggressions she might fear in the future from her Jugoslav neighbors. END QUOTE.

While there is thus substantial agreement as to the injustice and inexpediency of Italy's claims, there is a difference of opinion as to how firmly Italy's friends should resist her importunate demands for alien territories to which she can present no valid title. It has seemed to the President that French and British associates of the American Government, in order to prevent the development of possibly dangerous complications in the Adriatic region, have felt constrained to go very far in yielding to demands which they have long opposed as unjust. The American Government, while no less generous in its desire to accord to Italy every advantage to which she could offer any proper claims, feels that it cannot sacrifice the principles for which it entered the war to gratify the improper ambitions of one of its associates, or to purchase a temporary appearance of calm in the Adriatic at the price of a future world conflagration. It is unwilling to recognize either an unjust settlement based on a secret treaty the terms of which are inconsistent with the new world conditions, or an unjust settlement arrived at by employing that secret treaty as an instrument of coercion. It would welcome any solution of the problem based on a free and unprejudiced consideration of the merits of the controversy; or on terms of which the disinterested Great Powers agreed to be just and equitable; Italy, however, has repeatedly rejected such solutions. This Government cannot accept a settlement the terms of which have been admitted to be unwise and unjust, but which it is proposed to grant to Italy in view of her persistent refusal to accept any wise and just solution.

It is a time to speak with the utmost frankness. The Adriatic issue as it now presents itself raises the fundamental question as to whether the American Government can on any terms co-operate with its European associates in the great work of maintaining the peace of the world by removing the primary causes of war. This Government does not doubt its ability to reach amicable understandings with the Associated Governments as to what constitutes equity and justice in international dealings; for differences of opinion as to the best methods of applying just principles have never obscured the vital fact that in the main the several governments have entertained the same fundamental conception of what those principles are. But if substantial agreement on what is just and reasonable is not to determine international issues; if the country possessing the most endurance in pressing its demands rather than the country armed with a just cause is to gain the support of the powers; if forcible seizure of coveted areas is to be permitted and condoned, and is to receive ultimate justification by creating a situation so difficult that decision favorable to the aggressor is deemed a practical necessity; if deliberately incited ambition is, under the name of national sentiment, to be rewarded at the expense of the small and the weak; if, in a word, the old order of things which brought so many evils on the world is still to prevail, then the time is not yet come when this Government can enter a concert of powers the very existence of which must depend upon a new spirit and a new order. The American people are willing to share in such high enterprise; but many among them are fearful lest they become entangled in international policies and committed to international obligations foreign alike to their ideals and their traditions. To commit them to such a policy as that embodied in the latest Adriatic proposals, and to obligate them to maintain injustice as against the claims of justice, would be to provide the most solid ground for such fears. This Government can undertake no such grave responsibility.

The President desires to say that if it does not seem feasible to obtain the acceptance of the generous and just concessions offered to Italy by the French, British, and American Governments in their joint memorandum of December 9, 1919, which concessions the President has already clearly stated to be the maximum that this Government can offer, he must seriously consider withdrawing the treaty with Germany and the Agreement between the United States and France of June 28, 1919, now before the Senate and permitting the associated governments independently to establish and enforce the terms of the European settlement.

Lansing

Compared with original as drafted by Dr. D. W. Johnson. Telegram prepared under President's instructions[1]

TS telegram (SDR, RG 59, 763.72119/8779, DNA).

[1] The plain meaning of this notation is that someone went over Johnson's draft of this note (printed as an Enclosure with WW to RL, Feb. 7 1920) with Wilson, and that Wilson instructed that person to restore the paragraphs of this draft which Lansing or Polk had deleted.

Two News Reports

[*Feb. 11, 1920*]
PUBLIC DIAGNOSIS VEXES PRESIDENT
Incensed at Interview Regarding His Illness
Given by Baltimore Physician
CONFIRMS THROMBOSIS

Washington, Feb. 11.—President Wilson is incensed over the publishing of the diagnosis of his case, it was learned from his intimate friends today.

The diagnosis was given in an interview with Dr. Hugh H. Young, of Johns Hopkins Hospital, who had been one of the physicians in attendance on the President. The interview was contained in a copyrighted despatch from Washington, to the Baltimore Sun.

Friends of the President say the publishing of the diagnosis is bound to leave a doubt in the mind of the public as to the President's future capabilities, which is entirely unfounded. It is understood this is the view the President takes himself.

At no time since his illness, has the President been incapacitated and his friends fear the statements of Dr. Young may arouse new rumors which are baseless. The diagnosis was published without the consent of the President. . . .[1]

[1] Here follow excerpts from the interview with Dr. Young, just printed.

[*Feb. 11, 1920*]
DERCUM WON'T TALK
Says Statements About President
Should Come From Grayson

Dr. F. X. Dercum, 1719 Walnut St., consulting neurologist to President Wilson, declined today to comment on the President's condition.

"I have always taken the position all inquiries about the President should be directed to Dr. Grayson, his personal physician," he said. "He is in constant attendance upon the President and all statements about the President's condition should properly come from him. Out of consideration for him I must decline to make any comment."

He said he had read the statement of Dr. Hugh Young, of Baltimore, in which it was said the President, now rapidly recovering, has suffered a cerebral thrombosis, impairing use of his left arm and leg.

Printed in the *Philadelphia Press*, Feb. 12, 1920.

To Robert Lansing

My dear Mr. Secretary: [The White House] 11 February, 1920

I am very much disappointed by your letter of February ninth in reply to mine asking about the so-called Cabinet meetings. You kindly explain the motives of those meetings and I find nothing in your letter which justifies your assumption of Presidential authority in such a matter. You say you felt that, in view of the fact that you were denied communication with me, it was wise to confer informally together on interdepartmental matters and matters as to which action could not be postponed until my medical advisers permitted me to be seen and consulted, but I have to remind you, Mr. Secretary, that no action could be taken without me by the Cabinet, and therefore there could have been no disadvantage in awaiting action with regard to matters concerning which action could not have been taken without me.

This affair, Mr. Secretary, only deepens a feeling that was growing upon me. While we were still in Paris, I felt, and have felt increasingly ever since, that you accepted my guidance and direction on questions with regard to which I had to instruct you only with increasing reluctance,[1] and since my return to Washington I have been struck by the number of matters in which you have apparently tried to forestall my judgment by formulating action and merely asking my approval when it was impossible for me to form an independent judgment because I had not had an opportunity to examine the circumstances with any degree of independence.

I, therefore, feel that I must frankly take advantage of your kind suggestion that if I should prefer to have another to conduct our foreign affairs you are ready to relieve me of any embarrassment by placing your resignation in my hands, for I must say that it would relieve me of embarrassment, Mr. Secretary, the embarrassment of feeling your reluctance and divergence of judgment, if you would give your present office up and afford me an opportunity to select someone whose mind would more willingly go along with mine.

I need not tell you with what reluctance I take advantage of your suggestion, or that I do so with the kindliest feeling. In matters of transcendent importance like this the only wise course is a course of perfect candor, where personal feeling is as much as possible left out of the reckoning.

Very sincerely yours,   [Woodrow Wilson]

CCL (WP, DLC).
[1] On the question of Lansing's loyalty, see Dimitri D. Lazo, "A Question of Loyalty: Robert Lansing and the Treaty of Versailles," *Diplomatic History*, IX (Winter 1985), 35-53.

From the Desk Diary of Robert Lansing

February Wednesday 11 1920

Lunch 12:35-1:45. Saw Polk who said he'd seen Tumulty but he knew nothing.

Received letter from Prest indicating he would like to have my resignation. Thank God an intolerable situation is ended.

A Draft of a Letter from Edith Bolling Galt Wilson to Carter Glass

[Feb. 11, 1920]

It is with the utmost reluctance that the President turns away from any suggestion made by Sen. Glass but he feels bound in candor to say that his judgment is decidedly against the course Sen. G. proposes. Article 10 is the backbone of the Covenent & Mr. Tafts proposed reservation is not drawn in good faith

Proposals ought not to come from our side & there is surely tactical skill enough among our people to force the Repub. to take or reject the Treaty as it stands or to propose some other course with regard to it. The initiative ought in no case to be taken by our side It ought to be forced upon the Repub

This is the Presidents clear judgment after repeated & careful considerations of the whole situation & he believes that absolute inaction on our part is better than a mistaken initiative

He attaches little importance to party strategy at this juncture & all importance to a clearly defined position taken on principles

EBWhw MS (WP, DLC).

To Franklin Knight Lane

My dear Mr. Secretary: [The White House] 11 February, 1920

I have your letter regarding your proposed course concerning the Honolulu oil case, and I must express my very great and sincere regret that your judgment is what it is in that case. The case was fully appealed at my suggestion, as you know, and in my opinion the judgment of the General Receiver ought to stand.[1]

I feel it my duty to say this because the matter is fraught with so many dangers and is likely to lead, if not handled with the utmost foresight, it may be to serious scandals.

With the best wishes for the future,

Sincerely yours,   [Woodrow Wilson]

406 FEBRUARY 11, 1920

CCL (WP, DLC).

[1] Again, see Enclosure I printed with JD to WW, July 30, 1919, Vol. 62, wherein the "General Receiver" is referred to as the "Register and Receiver." In June 1920, John Barton Payne, Lane's successor, denied the Honolulu Oil Company's applications for patents on the disputed oil lands in the Buena Vista Hills of California. However, in December of that year, Payne granted leases to the Honolulu Oil Company for some of the lands in question. In 1921, Albert B. Fall and Harry M. Daugherty, the Secretary of the Interior and Attorney General, respectively, in the Harding administration, succeeded in having leases granted to the company for all seventeen of the disputed quarter sections of land. See Bates, *Origins of Teapot Dome*, pp. 77, 215-16, 233. See also Edith Bolling Wilson, *My Memoir*, pp. 301-302.

From Walker Downer Hines

Dear Mr. President: Washington February 11, 1920

The letters from the chief executives[1] may create the impression that railroad employees generally are in a state of serious distresss [distress] on account of wages unequal to existing living requirements. If this point arrests your attention I thought you might be interested in looking over the attached statement[2] which I believe shows with fair accuracy the average monthly compensation per employee for the various classes of railroad employees for the month of October, 1919, also the average number of hours worked per employee in each class in that month, and his average hourly compensation.

The average monthly compensation thus shown includes whatever overtime may have been worked. The employees urge that this should be disregarded because the employees ought to be able to make an adequate wage within the limits of their standard day. This is largely true when it comes to fixing a permanent wage scale under normal conditions. But when the point is made that an adjustment must be made immediately in spite of the very early termination of federal control in order to correct an actual hardship, I think it is perfectly fair to look at the total monthly compensation which the employee is receiving.

On the average I believe that the increase in compensation since 1914 has kept pace with the increase in the cost of living, although much more careful analysis would be necessary in order to reach a conclusion upon which further wage increases could properly be granted or denied.

The earnings for January, 1920 and, except for the shortness of the month, for February, 1920, will make, I believe, a more favorable showing than the earnings for October, because various additional provisions have been made for time and a half for overtime for classes theretofore not enjoying it and to some other matters of pecuniary significance which will appreciably increase the wages of the employees to numerous classes.

It is also true that during the winter months it has been essential to work a great deal of overtime for which the employees have been compensated on the favorable basis of time and a half.

Cordially yours,   Walker D Hines

TLS (WP, DLC).
  [1] About which, see W. D. Hines to WW, Feb. 12, 1920, n. 1.
  [2] We have not found this statement.

From Robert Lansing

My dear Mr. President: Washington February 11, 1920.

I am sending you herewith an Aide Memoire which has just been handed me by the Secretary of the Netherlands Legation,[1] regarding the action which the British Government is contemplating in connection with the surrender of the ex-Kaiser.

You will note that this question will probably be discussed at the meeting of the Prime Ministers of the Allied Powers in London, which may take place within the next few days, and, accordingly, I shall be glad to be informed of your wishes in this matter so that, if instructions are to be sent to Mr. Davis, they can go forward promptly.   Faithfully yours,   Robert Lansing

TLS (SDR, RG 59, 862.001W64/105, DNA).
  [1] Netherlands legation, "AIDE-MEMOIRE," [c. Feb. 11, 1920], T MS (SDR, RG 59, 862.00W64/105, DNA). This document gave the substance of a conversation between the Dutch Foreign Minister, Herman Adriaan van Karnebeek, and the British Minister to The Hague, Sir Ronald (William) Graham, in which the latter had warned that continued Dutch refusal to surrender the former German Emperor for trial as a war criminal would result in Holland's exclusion from the League of Nations, the rupture of diplomatic relations between the Netherlands and the Allied nations, and "other coercive measures." Van Karnebeek had replied that no threats could cause Holland "to swerve from the line of conduct which she feels imposed upon her by her respect for the law and by the conscience [consciousness] of her duty."
  The document also revealed that Charles Benoist, the French Minister to The Hague, had indicated that his government supported the British position on the matter.
  In view of the situation, the note concluded, Van Karnebeek expressed the hope that the United States would not remain an indifferent spectator "when, at the commencement of a new era in the history of the world, Holland, the country which has always upheld right and shaped its course in accordance therewith, would be chosen to serve as an example on whom the supremacy of force were to be demonstrated."

Robert Lansing to Edith Bolling Galt Wilson

My dear Mrs. Wilson: Washington February 11, 1920.

I am sending for the President's signature and for transmission to the Senate the nomination of Mr. Robert Underwood Johnson as Ambassador to Italy, having received this morning official information that he is acceptable to the King of Italy.

As to Mr. Phillips, Mr. Crane and Governor Hunt I am awaiting agréments of the several governments to which they are to be accredited, which were asked at the same time as that for Mr. Johnson. As rapidly as I am informed officially of their acceptability I will send the nominations for the President to sign.

I find that Mr. Frazer is on the ocean having sailed for France and, as he has no code and as sending out a message to him by wireless is to send it broadcast, it would seem wise to await his arrival in Paris before communicating the President's direction to tender him the appointment to Switzerland. This, of course, I will do as soon as it is possible to do so without a publicity which would be considered discourteous by the Swiss Government before it had advised the Department of his acceptability.

Faithfully yours,   Robert Lansing.

TLS (WP, DLC).

To Robert Lansing

My dear Mr. Secretary: The White House 12 February, 1920

In reply to your letter of the eleventh, let me say that I am particularly anxious that neither Mr. Davis nor any other representative of ours should take any part in this matter. At the same time, I am anxious to find some means of conveying the plain intimation to Germany that we stand inexorably with our associates in insisting that every item of the treaty be complied with in letter and in spirit. Perhaps you will think of some way to accomplish this which has not occurred to me.

Sincerely yours,   Woodrow Wilson

TLS (SDR, RG 59, 763.72119/10004, DNA).

From Robert Lansing

My dear Mr. President: Washington February 12, 1920.

I wish to thank you sincerely for your candid letter of the 11th in which you state that my resignation would be acceptable to you, since it relieves me of the responsibility for action which I have been contemplating and which I can now take without hesitation as it meets your wishes.

I have the honor, therefore, to tender you my resignation as Secretary of State, the same to take effect at your convenience.

In thus severing our official association I feel, Mr. President, that I should make the following statement which I had prepared recently and which will show you that I have not been unmindful that the continuance of our present relations was impossible and that I realized that it was clearly my duty to bring them to an end at the earliest moment compatible with the public interest.

Ever since January, 1919, I have been conscious of the fact that you no longer were disposed to welcome my advice in matters pertaining to the negotiations in Paris, to our foreign service, or to international affairs in general. Holding these views I would, if I had consulted my personal inclination alone, have resigned as Secretary of State and as a Commissioner to Negotiate Peace. I felt, however, that such a step might have been misinterpreted both at home and abroad, and that it was my duty to cause you no embarrassment in carrying forward the great task in which you were then engaged. Possibly I erred in this, but if I did it was with the best of motives.

When I returned to Washington in the latter part of July, 1919, my personal wish to resign had not changed but again I felt that loyalty to you and my duty to the Administration compelled me to defer action as my resignation might have been misconstrued into hostility to the ratification of the treaty of peace or at least into disapproval of your views as to the form of ratification. I therefore remained silent, avoiding any comment on the frequent reports that we were not in full agreement. Subsequently your serious illness, during which I have never seen you, imposed upon me the duty—at least I construed it to be my duty—to remain in charge of the Department of State until your health permitted you to assume again full direction of foreign affairs.

Believing that that time had arrived I had prepared my resignation, when my only doubt as to the propriety of placing it in your hands was removed by your letter indicating that it would be entirely acceptable to you.

I think, Mr. President, in accordance with the frankness which has marked this correspondence and for which I am grateful to you, that I cannot permit to pass unchallenged the imputation that in calling into informal conference the heads of the executive departments I sought to usurp your presidential authority. I had no such intention, no such thought. I believed then and I believe now that the conferences, which were held, were for the best interests of your Administration and of the Republic, and that belief was shared by others whom I consulted. I further believe that the conferences were proper and necessary in the circumstances and that I would have been derelict in my duty if I had failed to act as I did.

I also feel, Mr. President, that candor compels me to say that I cannot agree with your statement that I have tried to forestall your judgment in certain cases by formulating action and merely asking your approval when it was impossible for you to form an independent judgment because you had not had an opportunity to examine the circumstances with any degree of independence. I have, it is true, when I thought a case demanded immediate action, advised you what, in my opinion, that action should be stating at the same time the reasons on which my opinion was based. This I conceived to be a function of the Secretary of State and I have followed the practice for the past four years and a half. I confess that I have been surprised and disappointed at the frequent disapproval of my suggestions, but I have never failed to follow your decisions, however difficult it made the conduct of our foreign affairs.

I need hardly add that I leave the office of Secretary of State with only good will toward you, Mr. President, and with a sense of profound relief.

Forgetting our differences and remembering only your many kindnesses in the past, I have the honor to be, Mr. President,

Sincerely yours,   Robert Lansing.

TLS (WP, DLC).

From Carter Glass

Dear Mr. President: [Washington] February 12, 1920.

I seem to have been rather unhappy in my note of Monday if it made the impression that I was proposing to initiate modifications of the covenant. On the contrary, as I tried to indicate at our interview last Friday, it is my considered judgment that Lodge has the treaty on his hands and the Democrats should originate no move to relieve his embarrassment. If I could direct the course of events, we would not budge from that position.

However, when the treaty comes up for consideration in the Senate next week and article 10 is reached, modifications will be proposed, possibly by Lodge himself; if not, then by the so-called Republican "mild reservationists," and not unlikely by Democratic Senators who, willing to vote for the treaty as it stands, nevertheless would vote for modifications rather than have ratification fail.

When this stage is reached, with all the Republicans and certain treacherous Democrats set against taking the treaty as it stands, our side must determine whether, in the reservations submitted, our adversaries have proposed some other course which will meet with executive sanction. It is essentially desirable to send nothing from the Senate which would be rejected at the White House; and yet there is danger of this unless, somehow, we may know how proposed reservations impress you. Hence the particular purpose of my note of the 9th was to draw some expression which would indicate whether the suggested Taft reservation or the bi-partisan committee draft was, either of them, impossible; and the word which you have been good enough to send is perfectly clear on this point.

I agree, of course, that we must not, in any event, make any departure from principle, and it did not occur to me that anything of that sort was involved in the strategy of forcing the other side into either an acceptance or rejection of a reservation to article 10, drafted by a Republican ex-President, and which would not, if accepted, touch the integrity of the treaty, but would, if rejected, gravely weaken the opposition in an issue before the people. Very likely I am entirely mistaken about this and shall not pursue the matter.

With warmest regards, Sincerely yours, [Carter Glass]

CCL (C. Glass Papers, ViU).

Frank Lyon Polk to Hugh Campbell Wallace

Washington, February 12, 1920.

357 For the Ambassador.

The Note from the Supreme Council transmitted by the French Ambassador in regard to the appointment of an American Plenipotentiary at the Turkish Peace Negotiations has been submitted to the President.

The President states that he is not inclined to appoint such a Plenipotentiary and that the instructions sent to you on January 9 are adequate, namely that you may, if invited, attend the meetings but should state that you are not in a position to give the views of this Government unless in any specific instance they are requested and then only after submission of the matter to Washington.

Polk Acting

T telegram (SDR, RG 59, 763.72119/8818, DNA).

From Walker Downer Hines

Dear Mr. President: Washington February 12, 1920.

I enclose two letters of 9th instant and 11th instant from the Chief Executives of all but two of the principal railroad organizations.[1] (The two omitted are the Maintenance of Way Organization, which has called a strike, and the Brotherhood of Railroad Trainmen, which has suggested the probability of calling a strike.)

The letter of the 9th instant claims that Congress has failed to adopt the legislation recommended by you as necessary to meet the cost of living emergency, that the efforts of the Government to deal with profiteering have been ineffective and that the cost of living has increased instead of diminishing. The letter urges that railroad labor had a right to expect that you would see that it would receive increases in wages by this time and urges that you promptly adjust wages to equal those in other industries to meet the increased cost of living, and to insure to all railroad employes at least a minimum living wage and urges that you make all these readjustments retroactive to May 1st. 1919.

The letter also asks that you urge Congress to pass necessary legislation to deal with the cost of living through elimination of profiteering and excess profits, prohibition of hoarding and speculations in futures and through proper restriction of exports; and asks that the departments of the Government be organized to secure the fullest cooperation in reducing the cost of living.

The letter of the 11th instant urges that Congress is making full provision for the careful protection of railroad capital but no provision for the protection of railroad labor; insists that railroad employes are not earning a sufficient wage to maintain pre-war standards, and that many are not earning an amount sufficient to maintain a standard of living above a mere subsistence level. The letter urges that it is the solemn duty of the Director General to take action before the termination of Federal control to restore the earning power of railroad employes and establish a basic minimum living wage and also to correspond more nearly with wages paid in other industries. The letter insists that, growing out of the postponement of wage increases last summer, there is an obligation of the Railroad Administration to deal with this matter now.

I have pointed out repeatedly to these Chief Executives that your announcement of last summer specifically contemplated that action might be impossible prior to the termination of Federal control and that in that event your promise was merely to the effect that you would employ the full influence of the Executive to see that justice was done to the railroad employes. In my judgment this promise will be fulfilled by the course recommended by me.

I also inclose a formal report to you on these problems as they now stand, concluding with a definite recommendation as to the way in which this matter should be dealt with.[2]

These Chief Executives express themselves as altogether opposed to my recommendation and insist that nothing will meet the situation except an immediate adjustment of wages by you or by the Railroad Administration, or a positive promise that such an adjustment will be made in the immediate future. I have made it clear to them that I cannot recommend any such course. My best judgment is that despite their pronounced opposition, the employes in general will acquiesce, though unwillingly, in the plan which I propose. But it is entirely possible that they will refuse to acquiesce and that some, if not all, of the important organizations will strike in the next few days, thus producing a serious tieup of rail transportation at a particularly critical time. Nevertheless, I cannot find justification for going beyond my recommendation. I feel it is wholly incompatible with the expiration of Federal control at the end of this month for the Railroad Administration to undertake to deal with these important matters for the future, especially when, as is explained in my report, the matter cannot be handled in such a brief period intelligently and justly, and could only be dealt with by an arbitrary, and I believe largely unwarranted, increase in wages. This increase when once made would, I believe, be permanent, regardless of any conclusions hereafter reached by tribunals authorized to deal with the subject after March 1st.

Sincerely yours,   Walker D Hines

TLS (WP, DLC).
[1] Edward J. Manion *et al.* to W. D. Hines, Feb. 9 and 11, 1920, both TCL (WP, DLC). Hines summarizes them below. Manion was president of the Order of Railway Telegraphers.
[2] W. D. Hines to WW, Feb. 12, 1920, TLS (WP, DLC): (After explaining the impossibility of the Railroad Administration's coming to any fair conclusions on the matter of wages during the remaining seventeen days of federal control) "I therefore recommend that you indicate your purpose to cause the formation at the earliest possible date of a tribunal with power to carry these matters to a conclusion, such tribunal to be formed by voluntary action, if a tribunal is not created by law. I further advise that you promptly appoint a Committee of Wage Experts to take available data and deduce therefrom as soon as practicable the facts pertinent to this problem. The report of such a Committee will serve as a guide to you in carrying out the policy which you announced last summer to see that justice was done to the railroad employes and I believe will greatly expedite the disposition of the matter. I think an effort should be made to get the railroad corporations to cooperate in the formation of this Committee."

Two Letters to Robert Lansing

My dear Mr. Secretary: [The White House] 13 February, 1920

From independent sources, I have gotten some more sidelights on the appointment of a Minister to Switzerland and write to say very frankly that I am willing to reconsider the appointment of Fraser, unless you have already heard from the Swiss Government or shall hear in the next day or two that he is *persona grata*. In that case, we will proceed with the appointment. If you have not heard from the Swiss Government, my present judgment is that it would be just and fair to substitute Mr. Hampson Gary[1] for the post at Berne.

I think that we ought to have a man of considerable experience in Greece, and for that my judgment settles on Grew.[2]

Sincerely yours, [Woodrow Wilson]

[1] Consul General and Diplomatic Agent at Cairo.
[2] Actually, the current Minister to Greece, Garrett Droppers, had not resigned, as Wilson apparently thought. See the memorandum by RL printed at Feb. 22, 1920.

My dear Mr. Secretary: [The White House] 13 February, 1920

Allow me to acknowledge with appreciation your letter of February twelfth. It now being evident, Mr. Secretary, that we have both of us felt the embarrassment of our recent relations with each other, I feel it my duty to accept your resignation, to take effect at once; at the same time adding that I hope that the future holds for you many successes of the most gratifying sort. My best wishes will always follow you, and it will be a matter of gratification to me always to remember our delightful personal relations.

Sincerely yours, [Woodrow Wilson]

CCL (WP, DLC).

From the Desk Diary of Robert Lansing

February Friday 13 1920

Long. Told him I had resigned and showed him correspondence. Agreed I could do nothing else. Raised question of propriety of publicity of correspondence. Said I must justify myself.

Secy Baker. Showed him correspondence. Expressed great regret but said I had acted rightly. Sorry about publishing letter relating to Cabinet meetings. Told him I must do so. . . .

Received Prest's acceptance of resignation to take effect "at once." Will officiate to close of day. . . .

Wrote letter to Prest expressing pleasure that he has followed my advice and turned down Frazer for Switzerland. This is my *last* letter to him.[1]

[1] We have not found this letter.

A Memorandum by Robert Lansing

February 13, 1920.

MY RESIGNATION AND SOME THOUGHTS ON THE SUBJECT.

Friday, the 13th! This is my lucky day for I am free from the intolerable situation in which I have been so long. Yesterday I resigned my commission as Secretary of State, and this afternoon came the President's acceptance "to take effect at once." When I left the Department at 4:45 p.m., I left it for good, and left behind me a burden of responsibility and anxiety, of which no one can have an adequate idea unless it be Frank Polk and my secretaries, Alexander C. Kirk and Richard C. Sweet. They know and can bear witness to the impossible situation which has existed for a long time.

Not the slightest hint had reached the press of my break with the President although his first letter to me was on the 7th. I saw the correspondents as usual this afternoon at 3:30. They apparently never suspected anything unusual was to happen. Now, however, they know, because the letters exchanged between the President and me were given out at 7:30 tonight.

This afternoon I got Polk to telephone Tumulty and ask whether the White House or Department of State should give the correspondence out, indicating that the Department had had it mimeographed. Tumulty said that it was all right and to give out the copies. Thus the proprieties as to publicity were preserved, and the White House cannot charge that I published the letters without asking permission to do so.

I imagine that a pretty good-sized bomb has been exploded, which will cause a tremendous racket in this country and find an echo abroad. Of course I may be mistaken, but my conviction is that public opinion will be in my favor. I am more than willing to go before the country on the correspondence. In fact I am delighted to do so. The chance that the President has given me to tell the truth and the way that he gave it are simply amazing. I never for a moment imagined that such an opportunity as this would ever be given me. If I did not believe in miracles before, I certainly would after this, for this seems like a direct intervention of Divine Providence. The President delivered himself into my hands and of course I took advantage of his stupidity, for it surely was nothing less than stupidity on his part.

The President's irritation and jealousy, which are so manifest in his letters, make me wonder as to whether he is mentally entirely normal. His complaints are so childish and his tone so peevish that it is hard to believe that his malady has not affected his mind. Always considered very astute in laying a case before the public, the way he has handled this affair is almost unbelievably stupid. I think that the people in general will resent his charges and imputations against me, and that it will be needless to add anything to the published letters. At least I will wait until I get the reaction from the country.[1] If it is favorable to me, I will let the White House try to explain. It will tax their ingenuity.

Some will believe that Tumulty is at the bottom of all this, but I do not believe it. I have believed for a long time that he did not like me and thought I did not consult with him as I should. Of course he is not my type anyway. Probably too, as he is a strong Roman Catholic, he did not approve my taking a prominent office in the Inter-Church World Movement.[2] Be that as it may, I am sure of one thing and that is that Joe Tumulty in politics is not a fool; and, if ever there was political idiocy shown, it was in the President's letters to me. If Joe had had a word to say about those letters, they would not have been sent. I cannot suspect Tumulty of being in any way directly responsible for the way the President got rid of me.

It *is* possible, however, that Tumulty talked to Mrs. Wilson and Admiral Grayson about me giving them the impression that I was disloyal to the President and that I was running foreign affairs as I pleased. If he did do that—and it is not at all unlikely—one of them probably told the President, because that is the sort of gossip that the President's family circle seem to like to repeat to him. I regret to say that many men have been the victims of White House gossip. As the President is by nature abnormally suspicious stories like this affect him much more than they would other men. He broods over them and exaggerates their importance until rumor becomes in his mind a fact and he believes a man to be dishonest and treacherous. Gossip, more than anything else, has caused the President to doubt his friends and break relations with them.

---

[1] For Lansing's public commentary on the events leading to his resignation, see his *The Peace Negotiations: A Personal Narrative* (Boston and New York, 1921), pp. 3-13.

[2] Lansing was chairman of the general committee of the Interchurch World Movement of North America. This organization had been established in February 1919 in an effort to unite all the social and missionary agencies of the Protestant churches of North America in a single entity to promote fund raising, recruitment of personnel, and spiritual revival. A committee of the organization had investigated the steel strike of 1919 and had written a lengthy and controversial report on it. See Commission of Inquiry, The Interchurch World Movement, *Report on the Steel Strike of 1919* (New York, 1920). The organization was at this time preparing for a vast fund-raising drive, scheduled to begin in April 1920. Other prominent political and military leaders involved in the movement were Thomas R. Marshall, Frederick H. Gillett, Selden P. Spencer, Warren G. Harding, William G. McAdoo, Josephus Daniels, and John J. Pershing. The standard study of the Interchurch World Movement is Eldon G. Ernst, *Moment of Truth for Protestant America: Interchurch Campaigns Following World War I* (Missoula, Mont., 1972).

In my case, however, I prefer to think that the President's action was the result of our long-standing differences as to the Peace Treaty, particularly the Covenant of the League of Nations. I think too that the President knows in his heart that he treated me very badly in Paris, and that, like many another man who realizes that he acted wrongly, he seeks to salve his conscience by blaming the one who has suffered by his act and by showing through repetition of the treatment that he feels justified in what he did. This process of reasoning is common with arrogant and self-centered men.

I presume that the President debated the matter with himself something after this fashion:

I was entirely warranted at Paris in not consulting Lansing and in refusing him my confidence, because he disagreed with me, and, therefore, was disloyal, and he added to his disloyalty by telling the Senate Committee that I ignored him, while Bullitt's testimony proved how disloyal he was. Since he was disloyal then, he is disloyal now; and, being disloyal, I will prove that I have not changed my opinion of him by forcing him to resign. Thus I will justify my conduct in Paris and be perfectly consistent.

Now that is the way that I think the President argued the case and convinced himself of the justness of his course. But his illness introduced a new factor. Weakened physically and in a measure mentally the ballast of his "one-track" mind appeared to be in pretty bad repair. It may seem strange that he did not come out frankly and state the real reason for wishing me to resign. I think the explanation is that the President imagined that the people would say, "Well, if you felt that way about it, why did you not call for Lansing's resignation last summer?" It would have been a pertinent question and one hard to answer satisfactorily. I assume that this thought entered the President's mind because it would be like him to reason that way; and so he sought to base his desire to get me out on some misconduct *after he became ill*. And here is where his weakened condition became a decided factor, for he settled upon my calling Cabinet meetings and upon my urging his approval of action proposed supplemented by a statement of facts and reasons, which I knew that he could never work out from a voluminous dossier. These pretexts were so manifestly absurd on their face that the impression is almost unavoidable that the President's mind is not working normally or else that his judgment has been swept away by an uncontrollable passion. Of course basing his action on such flimsy reasons made him peculiarly vulnerable.[3]

[3] Mrs. Wilson's and Tumulty's recollections of Wilson's comments on this affair follow. Mrs. Wilson writes: "I begged Mr. Wilson to state both reasons for his acceptance of the proffered resignation, protesting that the letter as written made him look small, because, unless people

Whether weakness or rage was the cause, I presume that the idea that the Cabinet was meeting in the Cabinet Room rankled in the President's mind as such things will in the mind of a man who has been sick for a long time and who lies in bed and thinks and speculates and imagines all sorts of things; and this would be exaggerated by his abnormally suspicious nature. He probably called on Grayson and Tumulty to explain their part in the meetings (I know from Secretary Lane that he called on Tumulty to do so before he sent me the letter of the 7th); and they probably were glad to avoid responsibility by putting the blame on me. Tumulty, I know, found the President excited and angry about the matter. The result was that he turned his wrath upon me; for which God be thanked.

I only record the foregoing speculations and comments as those which entered my mind as I thought over the President's first two letters. They are of interest in showing what was in the back of my mind when I wrote my replies. If the President had been patient for a few days longer, I would have resigned voluntarily and would probably have been the subject of bitter criticisms and reproaches from the President's friends. Of course I may be now, but my critics will not have an easy job to make a convincing argument for the President's conduct. To be forced out of the Cabinet this way

---

knew, as I did, all the other things he had suffered at Lansing's hands, the precipitating incident would seem the first offence, whereas it was the last and almost the least of many. At this my husband laughed: 'Well, if I am as big as you think me I can well afford to do a generous thing. If not I must take the blame. I like Mrs. Lansing, and had great respect for her father, old Mr. John W. Foster. . . . The disloyalty is a personal act; the calling of meetings of the Cabinet is official insubordination; it is my duty to put a stop to that.' " Edith Bolling Wilson, *My Memoir*, p. 301.

Tumulty writes that he tried to persuade Wilson "that in the present state of public opinion it was the wrong time to do the right thing." Tumulty continues: "Although physically weak, he was mentally active and alert. Quickly he took hold of my phrase and said, with a show of the old fire that I had seen on so many occasions: 'Tumulty, it is never the wrong time to spike disloyalty. When Lansing sought to oust me, I was upon my back. I am on my feet now and I will not have disloyalty about me.'

"When the announcement of Lansing's resignation was made, the flood-gates of fury broke about the President; but he was serene throughout it all. When I called at the White House on the following Sunday, I found him calmly seated in his bathroom with his coloured valet engaged in the not arduous task of cutting his hair. Looking at me with a smile in his eye, he said: 'Well, Tumulty, have I any friends left?' 'Very few, Governor,' I said. Whereupon he replied: 'Of course, it will be another two days' wonder. But in a few days what the country considers an indiscretion on my part in getting rid of Lansing will be forgotten, but when the sober, second thought of the country begins to assert itself, what will stand out will be the disloyalty of Lansing to me. Just think of it! Raised and exalted to the office of Secretary of State, made a member of the Peace Commission, participating in all the conferences and affixing his signature to a solemn treaty, and then hurrying to America and appearing before the Foreign Relations Committee of the Senate to repudiate the very thing to which he had given his assent.' " Joseph P. Tumulty, *Woodrow Wilson as I Know Him* (Garden City, N. Y., and Toronto, 1921), p. 445.

Lloyd G. Gardner, *Safe for Democracy: The Anglo-American Response to Revolution, 1913-1923* (New York and Oxford, 1984), pp. 286-87, suggests that Wilson and Lansing's profound differences over policy toward Mexico was another reason for Lansing's dismissal.

was for me the best thing that could happen I think, although I cannot be sure about it until I see the papers tomorrow and Sunday, which will indicate the country's reaction to the correspondence. Perhaps I am too hopeful and over-confident. If so, it is because I have always had a great faith in the sense of justice of the American people.

Well, whatever the result may be my conscience is clear. I strove to do what I considered my duty to the country, yes, and to the President. All I ask is that the people recognize that fact. That will content me. If they go further and thank me for my services, which the President failed to do, I shall be happy. I await the outcome without anxieties or doubts.

T MS (R. Lansing Papers, DLC).

Joseph Patrick Tumulty to Edith Bolling Galt Wilson

Dear Mrs. Wilson: The White House 13 February, 1920.

I do not know who the President intends to appoint to succeed Mr. Lansing. If he should decide in favor of Frank Polk, of course everybody would approve. Bu[t] the thought ran through my mind, after rereading Homer Cummings' speech this morning,[1] what a wonderful exponent of Woodrow Wilson's foreign policy this man would make, if as Secretary of State, he could avail himself of the opportunity of addressing the American people on internation[al] questions.

Our trouble has been that the President's international policies and purposes have not been adequately set forth by the Secretary of State. No one doubts the virtue of his Mexican policy, but the humanity of it has not been set forth. So with the League of Nations, the President has not received that cooperation from the State Department which he ought to receive. I hope you will believe me when I tell you that I have listened to Homer Cummings on different occasions and in many things, he is the best interpreter in this country to the public of the President and his policies. The copy of the speech which I sent you this morning proves this. What is needed in the State Department now is aggressiveness and offensive action on the part of the Secretary of State, instead of apology and indifference.   Sincerely,   JPT.

TLI (H. S. Cummings Papers, ViU).
[1] Tumulty referred to the speech which Cummings had made at a dinner given in the latter's honor by the Democratic National Club in New York on February 5. Cummings had attacked Lodge and the Republican party for having made partisan issues of the peace treaty and the League of Nations and said that the Democratic party was willing and able to take these issues to the country in the coming election. A brief summary of his remarks appears in the *New York Times*, Feb. 6, 1920.

A News Report

[*Feb. 13, 1920*]

President Shows Old Form
In Talk with Railroad Men

Washington, Feb. 13.—Following the conference at the White House today[1] between President Wilson and a committee of the railroad workers word went out that the President's condition was better than at any time since he was taken ill; in fact that his improvement within the last two weeks had been remarkable. The President, it was said, showed much of his old-time vigor in his discussion of labor troubles with the railroad men.

The President was seated in his wheel chair, wearing a sweater and old golf cap and swathed in a blanket. He shook hands with the committeemen and passed facetious remarks.

One of the committee told the President that he was looking very well. The President smiled and rubbed his hand across his chin.

"I have just been shaved and that helps a bit," he said.

The conversation continued for about ten minutes.

Timothy Shea, one of the committee, afterward said:

"The President looks very vigorous."

Secretary Tumulty and Mrs. Wilson were present during the conference and Dr. Cary T. Grayson dropped by to inquire about the President's health.

Printed in the *New York Times*, Feb. 14, 1920.
    [1] Wilson received the committee at 10:30 a.m. and then handed them the letter printed as the next document.

To Bert Mark Jewell and Others[1]

Gentlemen: [The White House] February 13, 1920.

I address you as the Chief Executives of the largest railroad organizations, which are among the most important industrial democracies in the country. I ask you to bring this message and its enclosure[2] to the attention of your members on all the railroads to the end that they, at first hand, may understand the Government's view as to the present situation. I am confident that with this personal understanding on their part they will see that the position of the Government is not only just to all interests, but is, indeed, unalterable, and also protects the interest of the railroad employes. The fundamental theory of labor organizations is that their mem-

    [1] The following letter was written by Walker D. Hines.
    [2] About the enclosure, see W. D. Hines to WW, Feb. 12, 1920, n. 2.

bership is intelligent and capable of reaching enlightened conclusions, and I think it is of paramount importance at the present time that this great body of American citizens shall have the fullest opportunity personally to consider the national problem of railroad wages in its national aspect and shall not in the absence of this opportunity form erroneous impressions on the basis of local or fragmentary information.

I have received two letters on this general subject[3] signed by all but two of the executives to whom this letter is addressed. I have read those letters with the greatest care and have taken them fully into consideration.

On the 25th of last August, I publicly announced[4] the conviction that a large permanent and general increase in railroad wages ought not to be made upon the basis of the level of the cost of living then prevailing if that cost of living level were to be merely temporary, and I counselled railroad employes to hold their demands in abeyance until the time should arrive when it could reasonably be determined whether that level of the cost of living was temporary or not. They have patriotically and patiently pursued this course and in general have shown an admirable spirit in doing so.

I then anticipated and made it clear in my public statement that the time for determining whether or not the level of the cost of living was such as to be the basis of a readjustment of wages might not arrive until after the expiration of Federal control and accordingly gave my assurance to the railroad employes that in that event I would continue to use the influence of the Executive to see that justice was done them.

Federal control will end in sixteen days and in accordance with the policy as explained to the employes, it is now eminently reasonable and proper that I take such steps as will reassure them that their claims will be properly and promptly disposed of. This is all the more necessary because inevitably the change from Federal control to private control will in the absence of special provision involve delay in dealing with these matters which could not be otherwise than disquieting to the employees.

I wish, therefore, to announce to all railroad employees at this time that I propose to carry out the following steps:

1. In the event that in connection with the return to private control provision shall be made by law for machinery for dealing with railroad wage matters I shall promptly use my influence, and so far as such law confers power upon me. I shall promptly exercise that

---

[3] See W. D. Hines to WW, Feb. 12, 1920, n. 1.
[4] See the statement printed at Aug. 25, 1919, Vol. 62.

power, to bring about the earliest practicable organization of the machinery thus provided.

2. In the event that no such provision is made by law for dealing with these matters, I shall employ the influence of the Executive to get the railroad companies and the railroad employees to join promptly in the creation of a tribunal to take up these problems and carry them to a conclusion.

3. I shall at once constitute a Committee of Experts to take the data already available in the various records of the United States Railroad Administration, including the records of the Lane Commission[5] and of the Board of Railroad Wages and Working Conditions, and to analyze the same so as to develop in the shortest possible time the facts bearing upon a just and reasonable basis of wages for the various classes of railroad employees with due regard to all factors reasonably bearing upon the problem and specifically to the factors of the average of wages paid for similar or analogous labor for other industries in this country, the cost of living, and a fair living wage, so as to get the problems in shape for the earliest possible final disposition. The views of this Board will serve as a guide to me in carrying out the assurance I gave to the employees last summer that I would use the full influence of the Executive to see that justice was done them and will, I believe, be a means of avoiding what might otherwise be a long-drawn out investigation of facts. While I propose to act at once in regard to this matter, and to avoid any delay in doing so, I shall, nevertheless, invite the cooperation of the railroad corporations and believe they will appreciate that it is to their interest, as well as to the public interest, to get these matters promptly settled.

I am sure it will be apparent to all reasonable men and women in railroad service that these momentous matters must be handled by an agency which can continue to function after March 1st, and therefore cannot at the present stage be handled to a conclusion by the Railroad Administration.

The accompanying report which the Director General of Railroads has made to me makes it clear that it has been wholly impracticable for the Railroad Administration to dispose of these matters up to the present time. Not only were the demands for general wage increases necessarily held in abeyance by reason of the policy announced by the Government last summer, but the demands for

[5] The Railroad Wage Commission, Franklin K. Lane, chairman, had been established by McAdoo on January 18, 1918, to investigate the wages of railroad workers as compared with those of workers in other industries. The committee made its report on April 30, 1918. For a summary of its findings, see Walker D. Hines, *War History of American Railroads* (New Haven, Conn., 1928), pp. 160-63.

increases to correct inequalities were so general and far-reaching as to become in themselves demands for general wage increases and were so complex and conflicting that despite continuous application on the part of the Board of Railroad Wages & Working Conditions and the other agencies of the Railroad Administration, the subjects could not be presented for even preliminary consideration by the Director General until the present month, and then in an incomplete form and with a lack of ability on the part of the Wage Board, to reach an agreement growing out of the largely conflicting condition of the data as presented.

Not quite six months have elapsed since I expressed my belief and hope that the then high cost of living could be regarded only as temporary.[6] This high cost of living (which in some respects has become even higher but in other respects has already begun to respond to the corrective factors which have been and are at work) is the product of innumerable influences, many of them of world-wide operation. In the nature of things these readjustments could not come with rapidity. The campaign which the Government has inaugurated to aid in controlling the cost of living has been steadily gaining in momentum, will continue to be aggressively conducted, and I believe will have an increasingly beneficial effect, and this notwithstanding the fact that some of the most needed remedial measures which I recommended to Congress have not been adopted. However, preparation, consideration and disposition of these important wage matters ought not in my opinion to be postponed for a further indefinite period, and I believe the matters involved ought to be taken up and disposed of on their merits at the earliest practicable time.

Pending the consideration of these problems by the Director General of Railroads and by me, at least one class of railroad employees has indicated its unwillingness to await a conclusion and has announced its intention of striking. A strike of railroad employees would at any time be highly injurious to the public and particularly at this time would be harmful not only to the entire country, but to the railroad employees as well. Any interruption of transportation will of course have a serious adverse effect upon the industrial life of the nation at a peculiarly critical period.

Under the circumstances, therefore, I have the right to request and I do request that any railroad labor organization which has a strike order outstanding shall withdraw such order immediately and await the orderly solution of this question. The railroad men of

[6] That is, in his address on the high cost of living printed at Aug. 8, 1919, Vol. 62.

America have stood loyally by their government throughout the war—they must in the public interest and in their own interest continue to do so during this delicate period of readjustment.

I believe that every intelligent railroad employee will recognize the extreme importance of continued cooperation with the Government in this matter, and that any other course will prove not only a grave injury to the public, of which railroad labor is such an important part, but a serious blow to the important principle of collective bargaining and will merely delay rather than expedite the just and prompt solution of these important matters.

cordially yours,   (Signed) Woodrow Wilson.

B. M. Jewell,
Actg. Pres. A. F. of L. Bldg., Washington, D. C.
W. S. Stone,
1116 B. of L. E. Bldg., Cleveland, Ohio.
Timothy Shea,
Actg. Pres. 901 Guardian Bldg., Cleveland, Ohio.
L. E. Sheppard,
President, Order of Railway Conductors, Cedar Rapids, Iowa.
W. G. Lee,
President, American Trust Bldg., Cleveland, Ohio.
S. E. Heberling,
President, 326 Brisbane Bldg., Buffalo, N. Y.
E. J. Manion,
Pres., Order of Railroad Telegraphers, 812 Star Bldg.,
St. Louis, Mo.
James W. Kline,
Genl. Pres., Brotherhood of Blacksmiths & Helpers,
1234 Transportation Bldg., Chicago, Ill.
Wm. H. Johnston,
Pres., International Association of Machinists,
A. F. of L. Bldg., Washington, D. C.
Martin F. Ryan,
Genl. Pres., Brotherhood of Railway Carmen of America,
Hall Bldg., Kansas City, Mo.
Louis Weyand, Actg. Pres., Brotherhood of Boilermakers &
Iron Shipbuilders,
Wyondotte Bldg., Kansas City, Kansas.
John J. Hynes,
Pres., Sheet Metal Workers,
122 S. Ashland Blvd., Chicago, Ill.
James Noonan,
Actg. Pres., Electrical Workers of America,
Reisch Bldg., Springfield, Ill.

A. E. Barker,
Grand Pres., United Brotherhood of Maintenance of Way Employees,
27 Putnam Ave., Detroit, Mich.
Jas. J. Forrester,
Genl. Pres., Brotherhood of Railway Clerks,
Room 407 A. F. of L. Bldg., Washington, D. C.
D. W. Helt,
Pres., Brotherhood of Railroad Signalmen of America,
782 13th St. N. W., Washington, D. C.

TCL (WP, DLC).

Charles Richard Crane to Edith Bolling Galt Wilson

Dear Mrs Wilson   [New York] February 13 1920

Please continue to think about the house at Wood's Hole and the next time I am in Washington I shall bring a little book of photographs to show you. I admired it—and the grounds—for thirty years before it came into our family. It is quiet, beautiful and a good place to play.

I dont want the President to trouble about our report[1] but would like to have him read the enclosed comment of one of our best sociologists.[2]

It is delightful to see the happy way in which Dr Young's report is everywhere being greeted.

Affectionate messages to you both.

Always devotedly yours   Charles R. Crane

ALS (EBW Papers, DLC).

[1] That is, the King-Crane Report, about which see C. R. Crane to WW, Aug. 31, 1919, n. 1, Vol. 62.

[2] It is missing, but it was probably the following comment by Edward Alsworth Ross, Professor of Sociology at the University of Wisconsin: "It seemed to me that this report was a more perfect example of mathematical demonstration in the field of human relationships than anything I have ever met with. Never have I seen so scrupulous an endeavor to procure measurements of population desires. Your conclusions are wonderfully convincing and your demonstration leaves me an ardent supporter of your entire program." E. A. Ross to Henry Churchill King, Nov. 24, 1919, quoted in Harry N. Howard, *The King-Crane Commission* (Beirut, 1963), p. 262.

Edith Bolling Galt Wilson to Rudolph Forster, with Enclosures

Dear Mr. Forster   The White House. [c. Feb. 14, 1920]

The President regards this as poorly expressed—but says let it go, as he agrees to the subject matter   EBW

ALI (J. P. Tumulty Papers, DLC).

E N C L O S U R E   I

Rudolph Forster to Edith Bolling Galt Wilson

Dear Mrs. Wilson: The White House. February 14, 1920.

Mr. Tumulty has instructed me to send you the attached draft of a telegram to Mr. Barker, which he states was prepared by Mr. Hines at his request and which has his approval. He made this request of Mr. Hines at the tactful suggestion of the three gentlemen who yesterday saw the President—Messrs. Jewell, Shea and Manion. Mr. Tumulty hoped that you would read this to the President so that if it met with his approval it might be immediately sent to Mr. Barker.   Faithfully yours,   Rudolph Forster

TLS (J. P. Tumulty Papers, DLC).

E N C L O S U R E   I I

February 14, 1920

A. E. Barker,
President, Brotherhood of Maintenance of Way Employees
and Railway Shop Laborers,
Detroit, Michigan.

Yesterday I addressed to the Chief Executives of the principal railroad labor organizations including the one of which you are President, a message, a copy of which has been transmitted to you at Detroit. I have just received a response indicating the purpose of the organizations generally to conform to the principles of my message, to bring it to the attention of their membership and to hold a Convention here on February 23rd for the purpose of carrying the matter into effect. I note with surprise and disappointment that your organization is the only one addressed which has not expressed its concurrence in this method of handling the matter and I understand that no advice has yet been received of withdrawal of your strike order which was sent out several days ago.

The Director General of Railroads explained this situation to your Committee as soon as it presented to him advice of the strike order and he has since summarized the position of the Government in a telegram to you which I fully endorse. I ask you to take at once the necessary steps to withdraw the strike order and to make sure that no interruption whatever to transportation occurs on that account in this critical period. I feel sure that you and your associates upon full consideration will realize that you cannot in justice to your membership and the citizens generally of the United States persist in a course which is opposed to your obvious duty to the country, to the direct and specific request of the Government and also to the attitude of all other railroad labor organizations, all for the mere purpose of objecting to the procedure I have proposed which is the only practicable method of obtaining a prompt and reasonable settlement of the important wage questions now pending. I also ask you to send my message and its inclosure to all your members and give them the opportunity of cooperating with all the rest of railroad labor in handling the matter.[1]   Woodrow Wilson

T telegram (J. P. Tumulty Papers, DLC).
    [1] Barker's reply was A. E. Barker to WW, Feb. 14, 1920, T telegram (J. P. Tumulty Papers, DLC). Barker informed Wilson that the strike called for February 17 by his union had been "indefinitely postponed." He stressed that his organization had been "driven" into the strike order by "conditions of actual suffering among its members due to inadequate wages and the extreme high costs of necessities from which there has been no relief." He urged Wilson to expedite action on a wage increase and promised that his union would be "properly represented" at the convention in Washington on February 23.

From the Diary of Homer Stillé Cummings

Washington D C February 14, 1920.

The Lansing news broke last night. I am glad he is going out, or rather gone. While an amiable person, it also seemed to me that he lacked virility and I am not at all sure about his loyalty to W.W. I never looked upon him as a real Democrat. However, I regret the tone of the President's letters and think the whole thing could have been put on stronger grounds but perhaps it will be only a nine days wonder after all.

Joe Tumulty has been very active of late in my behalf. He got it into his head I ought to be Secretary of State. He got it from reading over again my New York speech, and he sent the speech to the President with a note stating that in his opinion I was the best interpreter the President had and the one most able to express his policies sympathetically and effectively. This was very nice indeed of Joe and is illustrative of his generous and impulsive nature. He told me that to-day he talked with W.W. about it and the latter wanted him to read my speech to him which Joe says he did with proper feeling, especially the peroration. Joe said that the President's eyes filled with tears and he actually broke down so that Joe had to stop for awhile. And then the President said: "Yes, they have disgraced us; they have disgraced America." Then he told Joe to tell me he thanked me for the speech and said it was wonderful. However, he didnt get me into the Cabinet. He told Joe it would seem as if he (W.W.) had forced Lansing out to make a place for me and that it would look like a political appointment and more-over, he could not spare me as Chairman and said "Who could we get who could take his place." So ended my boom for Secretary of State. Indeed no one knows of it except Joe and Mitchell Palmer and Ray Baker and the President and Mrs. Wilson.

T MS (H. S. Cummings Papers, ViU).

From the Desk Diary of Robert Lansing

1920 Saturday 14 February

Warner.[1] Said Sen. McCumber said that the Senators were unanimous in opinion that "President is crazy," that they were all with me and that the Democrats felt they must go on with the treaty without his leadership.

[1] Charles Damuth Warner, formerly chief of the Washington bureau of the *Christian Science Monitor*, at this time a special assistant to Lansing for public relations and also associated with the Washington office of the League to Enforce Peace. From October 8, 1919, until Lansing's resignation, Warner briefed him almost daily on the status of the peace treaty in the Senate.

From Bert Mark Jewell and Others

My dear Mr. President: Washington, D. C., February 14, 1920.

We, the undersigned Chief Executives of the Railway Labor Organizations signatory hereto have been jointly conferring on your letter of February 13th, and note the following conclusions have been reached by you:

1. "Consideration and disposition of these important wage matters ought not in my opinion be postponed for a further indefinite period, and I believe the matters involved ought to be taken up and disposed of on their merits at the earliest practicable time."

We understand from this that you are referring to the policy of the Government as announced August 25th, 1919, and that you now believe that the time has arrived when prompt disposition of general wage increases for railway labor should be made. In the interest of labor in general, and especially railroad labor and railroad operation, we are extremely gratified to note that you now recognize the necessity for promptly disposing of these vexatious problems; also that you recognize that railroad labor has patriotically and loyally complied with your request of August 25th, 1919.

2. We are further gratified to note that you now state that due regard shall be given "to all factors reasonably bearing upon the problem, and specifically to the factors of the average of wages paid for similar or analogous labor for other industries in this country, the cost of living, and a fair living wage."

We have been especially pleased with your recognition of these principles. It has been our feeling that the present movement has been different from what is ordinarily termed a wage movement.

We have felt that our wages should be adjusted to meet radical changes in living conditions, and that the Government was morally bound to consider the situation, and to assure us as far as possible that this would be done before the termination of Federal Control of the railroads.

During the entire period of the war we felt and acted upon the principle that our country's emergency was not a period for demanding an improvement in our economic conditions. We have been reluctant to believe that the Railroad Administration could not finally dispose of these wage matters before the expiration of Government control, and are greatly disappointed that after due consideration you also think that this is impracticable.

We understand from your letter that you have definitely decided that the subject matter must be dealt with in one of the two following methods:

1—"In the event that in connection with the return to private control provision shall be made by law for machinery for dealing with railroad wage matters I shall promptly use my influence, and so far as such law confers power upon me, I shall promptly exercise that power, to bring about the earliest practicable organization of the machinery thus provided."

2—"In the event that no such provision is made by law for dealing with these matters, I shall employ the influence of the Executive to get the railroad companies and the railroad employes to join promptly in the creation of a tribunal to take up these problems and carry them to a conclusion."

In this connection we have been pressing the necessity for immediate relief, and urge that you do not require us to await the creation of a tribunal by legislation to deal with this problem. We feel justified in saying that we do not believe that railroad employes will willingly accept any plan which contemplates delay.

It is our earnest conviction that the situation warrants us urging that you promptly indicate to railroad labor that you will create by agreement a special tribunal to deal with this specific and important problem.

With a full realization of our responsibilities, however, we have decided to submit to our constituencies the advisability of the creation of a special joint commission composed of an equal number of representatives selected by the railroad companies and the railroad labor organizations signatory hereto by agreement, and invested with full authority to deal with this particular controversy on the basis of the following principles:

1—Rates of pay for similar or analogous services in other industries.

2—Relation of rates of pay to increased cost of living.

3—A basic minimum living wage sufficient to maintain a railroad man's average family upon a standard of health and reasonable comfort.

4—That differentials above this basic minimum living wage be established, giving among other things due regard to skill required, responsibility assumed, and hazard incurred; decision of this tribunal to be handed down within 60 days after agreement to establish it, and to be final and binding upon all railroads in the United States and employes whom we represent.

In compliance with your request that we submit your message and its enclosure to the memberships, we have issued a call for the necessary representatives of the organizations to meet in Washington, D. C., February 23rd, when your letter of February 13th and enclosure, together with the above proposal will be presented to them for consideration and determination.

Pending this action on our part, we respectfully request that you take necessary steps to place this proposal before the executives of the railway companies, and secure their agreement thereto, so that when our representatives convene on February 23rd, we will be able to place before them a definite basis for final action.

Sincerely and cordially yours,

E. J. Manion
President,
Order of Railroad Telegraphers.
[blank]
Grand President,
United Brotherhood of M. of W.
Employees and Railroad Shop
Laborers.
D. W. Helt.
President,
Brotherhood of Railroad Signal-
men of America.
Jas J Forrester
Grand President,
Brotherhood of Railway & Steam-
ship Clerks, Freight Handlers,
Express and Station Employees.
Wm H Johnston by Fred Hewitt
International President,
International Association
of Machinists.
J. W. Kline
Grand President,
International Brotherhood of
Blacksmiths, Drop Forgers &
Helpers of America.
Jas. P. Noonan
International President,
International Brotherhood of
Electrical Workers.
Martin F. Ryan
General President,
Brotherhood Railway Carmen of
America.

E. Carrigan
Representing W. S. Stone,
Grand Chief Engineer,
Brotherhood of Locomotive
Engineers.
Timothy Shea
Acting President,
Brotherhood of Locomotive
Firemen and Enginemen.
L. E. Sheppard
President,
Order of Railway Conduc-
tors.
W. G. Lee
President,
Brotherhood of Railroad
Trainmen.
S. E. Heberling.
President,
Switchmen's Union of
North America.
Louis Weyand
Acting International Presi-
dent,
International Brotherhood of
Boilermakers, Iron Ship
Builders and Helpers of
America.
J. J. Hynes
International President,
Amalgamated Sheet Metal
Workers' International
Alliance.

B M Jewell
Acting President,
Railway Employees Department of the
American Federation of Labor.

TLS (WP, DLC).

Two News Reports

[*Feb. 15, 1920*]

PRESIDENT WILL NEVER RECOVER,
IS VIEW OF DR. BEVAN
Ex-President of American Medical Association
Declares Brain Will Always Be Affected.
SHOULD RESIGN, HE FEELS
'Not Competent to Act as Nation's Executive
and Head of Defenses.'

Chicago, Feb. 15.—The universal interest in the condition of President Wilson, revived by the publication of his correspondence with Secretary Lansing and his curt dismissal of his first aid in the Cabinet, prompted an inquiry today for an authentic medical opinion on the subject.

Dr. Hugh Young, a few days ago, as a consultant in the President's case, gave out for the first time during Mr. Wilson's five months' illness a frank but guarded statement of the fact that a blood clot in the brain had caused a paralysis of the left arm and leg, but added that the condition was improving satisfactorily.

Dr. Arthur Dean Bevan, ex-president of the American Medical Association, professor of surgery at Rush Medical College, and recognized throughout the world as one of the leaders in his profession, was asked to make a statement based on the known and officially acknowledged facts.

In accordance with this request, Dr. Bevan said:

"President Wilson about five months ago, while on a speaking tour, was taken suddenly ill. He was at once taken back to Washington, and his personal physician called into consultation noted specialists. These medical men issued bulletins, giving to the public the impression that the President was suffering from nervous breakdown, but that he had no serious illness. It soon became fairly widely known, in spite of every effort at secrecy, that the President had suffered a stroke, with resulting paralysis of one arm and leg. But it has not been until recently that this fact has been publicly admitted by one of his medical consultants.

"From a scientific medical standpoint, what does the President's illness mean to both himself and the country? The President's stroke, with the resulting paralysis of one side of his body, is due to a disease of the arteries of the brain, with a plugging up of the arteries which supply that part of the right side of the brain which controls his left arm and leg.

"The disease of the arteries is permanent, and not a temporary condition. In other words, the President has a permanently damaged brain.

"He is evidently slowly recovering from the paralysis of his arm and leg and may recover fairly well, although never completely, the use of his limbs. But the diseased arteries, which were responsible for the stroke and the damaged brain, remain and will not be recovered from.

"What advice would be the most scientific medical authority, uncontrolled by personal or partisan reasons, given in the President's case, both for his own personal interests and the interests of the country? Let us consider this latter first from the standpoint of the President's own interest.

"A patient who is suffering as the President is, from diseased arteries of his brain, and where the disease has progressed to such a point as to produce paralysis of one side of the body, should under no circumstances be permitted to resume the work of such a strenuous position as that of President of the United States. The strain and responsibility of such a position would bring with them the danger of a recurrence of such attacks, and might hasten a fatal termination.

"The second matter to consider, and one which naturally overshadows the first, is the relation of the President's illness to the interest of our country. Technically, we are still at war. The President is the commander-in-chief of the army and navy of the United States. As such, if he were called before a non-partisan medical board, he would be at once retired as physically incapacitated to perform the duties of the position.

"The present situation is an impossible one, and should be remedied at the earliest possible moment. The proper and normal course of action would be for the President to retire from office under the advice of his physicians and family and friends."

[*Feb. 15, 1920*]

DOCTOR DERCUM DECLARES MIND OF PRESIDENT WILSON IS KEEN, DENYING RELAPSE
Says He Breaks Rule Not to Discuss Case in Order to Allay Fears.

"The President's mentality is today keen," declared Dr. Francis X. Dercum, 1719 Walnut Street, the noted alienist, who has been treating the President for the past six months.

This statement was in contradiction of the rumor that the President had suffered more or less of a relapse, and that his controversy with Mr. Lansing, which ended in his asking for the Secretary of State's resignation, had arisen through Mr. Wilson's condition.

"Should I follow my inclination and habit of not discussing Mr. Wilson's condition," explained Dr. Dercum, when he was requested to give an opinion of the President's condition, "it would be immediately concluded that his condition is not satisfactory. That is just the impression I do not wish to create. You force me to say that the President's mentality is today keen."

When further information regarding the health of the President was requested, Dr. Dercum said, "Ask Dr. Grayson he is the man to talk about the President."

Dr. Dercum was called into consultation soon after the President was taken ill and has made numerous trips to the White House since. He has always been decidedly optimistic in his meagre discussions of Mr. Wilson's condition.

Printed in the *Philadelphia Press*, Feb. 16, 1920.

From the Diary of Ray Stannard Baker

Home again [Amherst, Mass.] Sunday Feby 15 [1920]

I got home Friday evening, all trains late on account of heavy snow. Yesterday I spoke at the Franklin Harvest club at their dinner at Plymouth Inn: a group of men I like very much: the real New England people at their best.

Papers full to-day of President Wilson's summary discharge (for it looks likes nothing else) of Secretary Lansing. It seems the petulant & irritable act of a sick man. Although I do not rate Secy Lansing high, and he has not, indeed, supported the President loyally either in Paris or here, still this sudden & violent action, with the reasons for it that the President gives, does not seem wise or politic. I do not think that the Secretary was ill-advised in calling cabinet meetings. Was there to be no discussion of public business for 4 months? It is 4 months since the President fell ill, & he has himself been able to transact very little public business. It seemed to me as I went around Washington the other day as though our government had gone out of business. Both executive & legislative bodies are scarcely functioning. With enormous problems to solve Congress is frittering away its time in fruitless discussions of the treaty. And the President is ill. It makes one apprehensive to look forward to the next year or two.

With some men illness destroys the controls over the ungovernable elements of a strong nature: it is so with the President. His tendancy to dictate, his stubbornness, his inability to co:operate whole heartedly with his associates now appear at their worst: yet we must not forget the great service he has done the country.

Francis Xavier Dercum to Cary Travers Grayson

Dear Dr. Grayson,   Philadelphia February 16th, 1920.

I do not know whether you have seen the enclosed pronouncement of Dr. Bevan of Chicago.[1] From the ethical point of view it is even more defenceless than that which issued from Baltimore.[2] You will see that the paper publishing this screed has placed my own statement in the immediately adjoining column.

Very Sincerely, F. X. Dercum

TLS (received from James Gordon Grayson and Cary T. Grayson, Jr.).
  [1] He enclosed clippings of the news reports printed at Feb. 15, 1920.
  [2] He enclosed clippings of the news reports printed at Feb. 11, 1920.

Two News Reports

[*Feb. 17, 1920*]

Grayson Reports President Still Gaining;
Makes Statement Because of Relapse Story

Washington, Feb. 17.—President Wilson continues to show improvement, and was up early today, shaving himself and going about his usual routine, Rear Admiral Grayson, his physician, said.

Dr. Grayson's statement was prompted by published reports that the President had suffered a relapse last night and that Dr. Francis X. Dercum, a Philadelphia specialist, had been hurriedly summoned to the White House for a midnight conference.

Dr. Grayson said he had not been in communication with Dr. Dercum since Saturday, when the latter visited the White House and found the President was making steady progress.

The President's Cabinet will probably not meet this week, Dr. Grayson said, but he added that if the President desired to call a meeting his physician would not object.

Philadelphia, Feb. 17.—There is no reason why President Wilson should not attend meetings of his Cabinet, in the opinion of Dr. Francis X. Dercum, Philadelphia nerve specialist, who has been one of the consultants of Doctor Grayson throughout the President's illness.

Dr. Dercum voiced his opinion today when he denied a report that he had been hurriedly summoned into consultation with the President's personal physician.

"There is nothing in his condition that would make it impracticable for him to attend a meeting of the Cabinet, even if one should be called this week, though it probably will not," said Dr. Dercum.

Printed in the *New York Times*, Feb. 18, 1920.

From Newton Diehl Baker

My dear Mr President: Washington, February 17, 1920

The newspapers are gossiping[1] so violently just now that no silence on my part will stop them and I can think of no statement which will null the varieties of their misstatements. Perhaps it can all be disposed of by a message, which I beg you to accept, of affection and of happiness at the rapid progress your recovery is making.

War Department matters are moving smoothly. Our situation in Siberia is simplified and your decision to withdraw our troops from there as the Czechs are moved has, I think, helped the people of Siberia and created a very favorable impression among them toward us.

Heartily and respectfully yours   Newton D. Baker

ALS (WP, DLC).
[1] There were rumors that Baker had submitted his resignation. See, e.g., the *New York Times*, Feb. 17, 1920.

From Frank Lyon Polk, with Enclosure

My dear Mr. President: [Washington] February 18, 1920

I am transmitting herewith the reply of the British and French Governments to the telegram of February 10th regarding the Adriatic question.   Faithfully yours,   [Frank L Polk]

CCL (SDR, RG 59, 763.72119/9119, DNA).

E N C L O S U R E[1]

London. Feb. 17, 1920.

Most Urgent, 266.

Following is general text of report respecting Adriatic.

"Confidential. The Adriatic. Memorandum by the Prime Ministers of France and Great Britain in reply to President Wilson's communication received on February 14, 1920.

London 17th February 1920.

The Prime Ministers of France and Great Britain have given their earnest attention to the communication made to them in regard to the Adriatic settlement on behalf of President Wilson. They are glad that the Government of the United States has set forth its views so fully and with such complete frankness. They do not,

[1] We have made a few corrections in the following telegram from the text printed in *The Adriatic Question*, pp. 25-30.

however, find it altogether easy to understand the steps by which the Government of the United States has arrived at its present attitude.

In the first place they believe that there is no foundation for the assumption which underlies the American communication that the proposed settlement outlined in their telegram of January 20[2] involves a capitulation to the Italian point of view as opposed to the Yugo-Slav and therefore constitutes a settlement with which the Government of the United States can have nothing to do. The memorandum[3] from the United States Government criticises the proposed settlement on four grounds.

Firstly; that it cedes to Italy the narrow strip of territory running along the coast as far as the Corpus Separatum of Fiume.

Secondly; that this strip of territory, coupled with the constitution of Fiume as a Free city, under the guarantee of the League of Nations, clearly paves the way for its annexation to Italy.

Thirdly; that the modification of the Yugo-Slav-Italian frontier operates to the detriment of Yugo-Slavia in its control of the northern railway from Fiume and;

Fourthly; that it provides for the partition of Albania.

The memorandum of the Government of the United States would appear to have entirely ignored the great advantages conferred on Yugo-Slavia at the same time.

The origin of the proposal of January 20 lies in the fact that when the Prime Ministers of Great Britain and France came to deal directly, both with the representatives of Italy and Yugo-Slavia in Paris, they found that nobody desired the constituting of the Free State of Fiume, which had always been an essential part of the American proposals for settlement. They discovered that Yugo-Slavia would prefer a settlement which did away with the Free State including, as it does, a population of 200,000 Slavs and included as much as possible of its territory and population within its own borders. Accordingly the Governments of France and Great Britain, continuing the negotiations from the point at which they had been left on December 7, made the proposal, under discussion, including the rectification of the Wilson Line and the cession to Italy of a strip of territory running along the shore so as to connect it with the Free City of Fiume, the net upshot of which was that Yugo-Slavia was to gain, as compared with the American proposal, an additional 150,000 Yugo-Slavs while agreeing to the inclusion within the Italian frontier of a further 50,000 Yugo-Slavs in addi-

---

[2] Lloyd George and Clemenceau's memorandum conveyed in H. C. Wallace to RL, Jan. 23, 1920.
[3] That is, RL to H. C. Wallace, Feb. 10, 1920.

tion to the 400,000 which President Wilson had already agreed to allot to that country.

As regards the suggestion that the proposal of January 20 clearly paved the way for the annexation of the town of Fiume to Italy, the French and British Governments cannot possibly accept the implication that the guarantee of the League of Nations is worthless and that the Italian Government has no intention of abiding by a Treaty which it enters into. As regards the railway, the proposal of January 20 gives to the Yugo-Slav state the control of the whole line from the point where it leaves the port of Fiume, which is under the control of the League of Nations. This railway is a commercial and not a strategic railway. Under President Wilson's proposals it is commanded by Italian guns. According to either plan nothing could be easier than for Italy to cut it in the event of war. They do not, therefore, see that there is substance in this criticism, a proposal whose real effect is to transfer the whole railway to Yugo-Slavia instead of leaving it in the hands of the Free City of Fiume which no one desires.

There remains the question of Albania. They are glad to receive the criticism of the American Government on this part of their proposal. They would point out, however, that their telegram of January 20 states that 'The details of the administration of this country by Yugo-Slavia, Italy and Greece have yet to be elaborated and in working to this end sight will not be lost of the feelings and future interest of the Albanian people and every endeavor will be made to carry out the arrangements in full consultation with them.' Further, they would point out that so far from this proposal being made in the interests of Italy it was made in the interests of Yugo-Slavia. The Yugo-Slavs pointed out that, though under the proposal of January 20 the northern part of their territory was guaranteed adequate access to the sea through the port of Fiume, the southern part of Yugo-Slavia had no such access and that the natural outlet was to build a line down the Drin River to the mouth of the Boyana River. The French and British Governments thought that there was force in this contention and their proposal in regard to Albania was designed to enable Yugo-Slavia, inasmuch as Albania was unable to undertake the work for itself, to develop under international guarantee, a railway and a port serving the southern part of this territory. Inasmuch as the Albanian people have never been able to establish a settled government for themselves and as the northern part of the population is overwhelmingly Christian and the southern part similarly Mohammedan they thought it best to entrust the responsibility for government and development of these two parts to Yugo-Slavia and Italy respectively. They have, however, agreed that the whole of Albania should be brought under the mandatory system, and they believe that this will make it possible eventually to satisfy aspirations of the Albanian people for unity and self-government.

The Governments of Great Britain and France therefore must repeat that they find difficulty in understanding the present attitude of the United States Government towards the proposals and they hope that in view of these explanations that Government will see its way to reconsider its attitude. In their view, these proposals are the natural outcome of the policy of the joint memorandum of December 9. Once, with the consent of both parties concerned, the idea of the Free State of Fiume was abandoned, in view of the absence of the American representatives, they had no option but to attempt to settle this question by themselves. It is not, however, the desire of the two Governments to force a settlement which is unacceptable to the President of the United States and they will therefore not attempt to insist upon its acceptance until they have heard the view of the United States Government on this dispatch. They have confined themselves, therefore, to asking the Yugo-Slav Government to give a definite answer to their memorandum of January 20, since they must know what the attitude of that Government is.

They feel bound, however, to ask the United States Government to consider the effect of their action. The proposal of December ninth has fallen to the ground because nobody now wants to set up the artificial Free State of Fiume. The proposal of January twentieth is objected to by the United States which had no representative at the deliberations and which cannot therefore be in close touch with the changes of opinion and circumstances which have taken place since its plenipotentiaries returned to America. They cannot help feeling that a large part of the misunderstanding is attributable to the difficulty of reaching a common understanding. In such circumstances how does the United States Government, which, to the regret of the Allies still has no plenipotentiaries at the conference, propose that this dispute, which prevents the reconstruction and threatens the peace of Southeastern Europe and whose settlement is urgently required, should ever be closed?

Further, the British and French Governments must point out that the fears to secure an agreed settlement between Italy and Yugo-Slavia must leave them no choice but to acknowledge the validity of the Treaty of London. They would recall to the United States Government that the Treaty of London was entered into in the spring of 1915, at a most critical and dangerous moment of the war. In thus entering the war on the side of human freedom Italy made it a condition that the Allies should secure for her, as against Austria-Hungary, strategic frontiers which would guarantee her, against retention by the Central Powers, of the strategic command of the northern plains of Italy. Had the Austro-Hungarian Empire remained in existence as the ally of Germany the provisions of the Treaty of London would have been sound. Relying upon the word of her allies Italy endured the war to the end. She suffered a loss in killed of over 500,000 men and in wounded of three times that number while her people are burdened by crushing debt. It was clearly impossible for her Allies to declare at the end of the war that their signature to the Treaty meant nothing but a scrap of paper and that they did not [sic] intend to renounce their bond. They agreed with President Wilson that these circumstances under which the Treaty of London were concluded had been transformed by the war itself, the Austro-Hungarian Empire had disappeared and the menace to Italy against which the terms of the Treaty were intended to provide had largely diminished. They therefore entirely associated themselves with the efforts of President Wilson to negotiate a settlement between Italy and Yugo-Slavia which was more consonant with the new conditions and which was acceptable to both sides. But throughout these proposals they never concealed from him the fact that they regarded themselves as bound by the Treaty of London, in the event of a voluntary agreement not being arrived at. The fact, therefore, that when they made their proposals of January twentieth they informed both the Italian and the Yugo-Slav Governments that, in the event of their not being accepted, they would have no option but to allow the Treaty of London to come into force, can have come as no surprise, and was indeed the obvious method of bringing this long controversy to a close. They would point out that this declaration is not, as the American Government would appear to think, an ultimatum to Yugo-Slavia on behalf of Italy. Under the Treaty of London, Italy has had to abandon Fiume altogether and hand it over to Yugo-Slavia. This part of the Treaty is as unacceptable to Italians as is the transfer of Dalmatia and the islands to Yugo-Slavia. The declaration, therefore, in regard to the enforcement of the Treaty was an attempt to promote a prompt settlement of this dangerous controversy by pointing out to both sides that if they could not agree upon a settlement, which after long negotiation seemed to be a fair compromise between their conflicting views, the only alternative was an arrangement which was less palatable to both.

Finally, the Governments of France and Great Britain feel bound to reply to the general observations contained in the latter part of the United States' memorandum. They know well the sincerity of

President Wilson's desire for the establishment of a better international order providing real guarantees against a repetition of the terrible events of the last five years. They are reluctant to believe that the President can consider that the modifications which they have made in the memorandum of December ninth can constitute in themselves a justification for a withdrawal from all further cooperation with them in the attempt to adjust peaceably the world's affairs. They feel confident that the explanations contained in this reply will remove any misunderstandings as to the nature of the Adriatic proposals. At the same time they are deeply concerned that the United States should even contemplate the action to which they refer. One of the principle difficulties encountered by the Heads of Governments during the negotiations of peace was that of reconciling treaty obligations with national aspirations which had changed or come into being since the date on which the treaties were signed. It was obviously impossible to ignore these latter aspirations, many of them born during the war, and formulated with unexampled clarity and elevation by the President of the United States himself. It was equally clearly impossible to ignore treaties. In fact the war began in order to enforce upon Germany respect for the solemn treaty she had made nearly eighty years before in regard to the neutrality of Belgium. It is the task of the statesmen of the world to endeavor to adjust national aspirations and ideals, many of which are only transitory and ephemeral, with one another and with international treaties. The difficulty of the task, the patience required in order to effect it successfully, the uselessness of endeavoring to enforce preconceived ideas on refractory material has been recognized by no one more clearly than the President of the United States in his address at the opening session of the Peace Conference. He pointed out how impossible it was to expect imperfect human beings and imperfect nations to agree at once upon ideal solutions. He made it clear that in his judgment the only course before the Peace Conference was to do the best it could in the circumstances and to create machinery whereby improvements and rectifications could be effected by reason and common sense under the authority of the League of Nations instead of by resort to war. Accordingly not only was the League of Nations established but Article Nine was specially inserted in the Covenant providing that the Assembly may from time to time advise the reconsideration by members of the League of treaties which become inapplicable and the consideration of international conditions whose continuance might endanger the peace of the world. Thus an essential part of the Treaties of Peace has been the constitution of machinery for modifying and correcting those treaties themselves where experience shows it to be necessary. The Governments of France and Great Britain, therefore, view with consternation the threat of the United States Government to withdraw from the comity of nations because it does not agree with the precise terms of the Adriatic settlement. The difficulty of reconciling ethnographic with other considerations is certainly not greater in the Adriatic case and does not produce more anomalous results that in the case of other parts of the general treaties of peace, difficulties which were recognized by President Wilson and his colleagues where they agreed to the best settlement practicable at the time because their machinery for peaceful readjustment had come into being; also [that] ethnologic reasons cannot be the only ones to be taken into account is clearly shown by the inclusion of three million Germans in Czecho-Slovakia and the proposals so actively supported by the United States delegation for the inclusion within Poland of great Ruthenian majorities, exceeding three million five hundred thousand in number, to Polish rule. Though the British representatives saw serious objections to this arrangement the British Government have not thought themselves justified in reconsidering on that account their membership in the League of Nations. The Governments of France and Great Britain therefore earnestly trust that whatever the final view of the United States Government as to the Adriatic settlement may be they will not wreck the whole machinery for dealing with international disputes by withdrawing from the treaties of 1919 because their view is not adopted in this particular case. That would be to destroy the hopes now entertained by countless millions of people all over the world that the most enduring and most beneficent part of the Treaty of Peace was the constitution of machinery whereby the defects of treaties could be remedied and that changing conditions and requirements of mankind could be adjusted by processes of reason and justice instead of by the balancing of armaments and resort to war. The Governments of France and Great Britain cannot believe that it is the purpose of the American people to take a step so far reaching and terrible in its effects on a ground which has the appearance of being so inadequate. Millerand. D. Lloyd George."

Paris informed. February 17, midnight.   Davis

T telegram (SDR, RG 59, 763.72119/9119, DNA).

From Frank Lyon Polk, with Enclosure

My dear Mr. President: Washington February 18, 1920.

You may not have noticed the attached telegram from Crane.[1] It contains the suggestion that a personal message from President Masaryk to you and Senator Lodge might be helpful in regard to the Treaty.

As this telegram has been sent to you, I hesitate to send an answer through Crane to Mazaryk without getting your views. Personally, I do not think that a message from Masaryk would do any good, but it would probably do no harm.

Yours faithfully,   Frank L Polk

I agree with you W.W.

TLS (F. L. Polk Papers, CtY).
[1] Richard Crane, former Private Secretary to Robert Lansing; now Minister to Czechoslovakia.

E N C L O S U R E

Prague February 14, 1920

From Prague via Paris 32. Personal for the Secretary. Benes informed me on February 9th that President Masaryk is convinced that the ratification of the Peace Treaty by the United States will greatly help the situation in central Europe. First, because authentication of economic and financial measures cannot be undertaken until that time. Second, Bolshevik and reactionary propaganda is using the present situation to the utmost advantage. It is agreed that the next few months are the most critical especially with the uncertainty of Bolshevik plans toward Poland.

He asked my opinion as to whether a personal message from President Masaryk to the President would help. He inquired if another message to Senator Lodge would be of use at the present juncture. I informed him that at this distance it was very difficult to understand the situation in America and that I did not feel able to advise him.   Crane

T telegram (F. L. Polk Papers, CtY).

From the Diary of Colonel House

February 18, 1920.

The sensation of the hour is the forced resignation of Secretary Lansing announced Saturday morning. I was immediately pressed for a statement, principally because in the New York Times and other papers his resignation was credited to differences with me in Paris. I declined to make a statement declaring that both the President and Secretary of State had been my friends and I had never had a disagreeable difference with either.

As a matter of fact, it is hard to tell who has the right of the situation. The President puts himself wholly in the wrong by asking for Lansing's resignation on the ground that he has usurped presidential authority in calling Cabinet meetings during the President's disability. The country has almost unanimously taken Lansing's part. If the President had adopted a different course he might have thrown the odium almost wholly on Lansing and received the sympathy of the country. On the other hand, Lansing's reply to the President was not so effective as it might have been made. He should have called attention to the fact that it was the President who was straining the Constitution by not permitting the Vice President to act during his acknowledged disability. He might also have called attention to the fact that when the President was in Paris for six months, the Cabinet met and the Government functioned at his, the President's, direction as he, Lansing, was trying to have it function during the President's disability. The difference, of course, is that in the one instance the President authorized it and in the other he did not, but since he was too ill to take the initiative, it had to be done in the way it was done.

From all accounts, Lansing has not been loyal to the President either in Paris or here. I am certain that in the memoirs to be published by Lansing and Bliss, or their executors, they will try to make the President's position appear wholly wrong. I, too, will doubtless come in for a measure of criticism.

A. S. Burleson was here yesterday for a long conference and said he saw Lansing just after he received his dismissal and that he told him without seeming rancor toward me, that his friends thought that he should have resigned in Paris when the President asked me to sit in the Council of Four during the President's illness. Lansing told Burleson the President explained the matter by saying that I knew more about the subjects to be discussed than he did. This indicates that Lansing complained to the President and, I take it, that it was from this period the President saw less of me fearing lest Lansing would resign.

Burleson believes it quite possible the President will be a candidate for another term. He has not seen him or communicated with him since before his illness nearly six months. He believes the President feels toward me as he did before but this is an optimistic view which I in no way share. . . .

Oscar Straus in a conversation today thought the President had again made ratification of the Treaty almost impossible by his note to the Powers on the Adriatic question. He said the passage of the Treaty was practically assured until that note was sent. He was now doubtful of it's [its] ever going through. Senators are saying if it is necessary to threaten withdrawal even before the United States has ratified the Treaty, what is the use of our getting in at all. I am sometimes in doubt whether Senator Lodge or the President has been the worst enemy of the Treaty. I gave the palm to Lodge at first but fairness and candor compel me to yield first place at present to the President.

Woolley told me the other day that the President had agreed to accept Taft's draft of Article 10.[1] It would be difficult for anyone to define the difference between the Taft and Lodge drafts but, according to Woolley, the President said he would see both the Treaty and Lodge in Hades before he would give Lodge the satisfaction of having Article 10 labeled with his name. This is an astounding attitude and is similar to Lodge's attitude toward him. I believe if I could see the President for a few minutes I could show him conclusively that he is not only lessening his own reputation and prestige but is directly abetting the republicans in their effort to destroy his administration and the Democratic Party.

[1] One can only wonder where Robert Wickliffe Woolley, Virginia Democrat and member of the Interstate Commerce Commission, received this misinformation.

To Frank Lyon Polk

My dear Polk: [The White House, c. Feb. 19, 1920]

What do you think of our sending the following as our reply or comment upon the latest communication from the Prime Ministers on the Adriatic question:

"The President has no desire whatever to criticise the attitude of the govts of France and Great Britain concerning the Adriatic settlement, but feels that he has no choice but to maintain immutably the position he has taken. He believes it to be the central principle fought for in the war that no govt or group of govts has the right to dispose of the territory or to determine the political allegiance of any free people. The five great powers, though the Govt of the U S constitutes one of them, has in his conviction no more right than had the Austrian Govt to dispose of the free Jugo-Slavic peoples without the free consent and cooperation of those peoples. The President's position is that the powers associated against Germany gave final and irrefutable proof of their sincerity in the war by writing into the treaty of Versailles Article X of the covenant of the League of Nations, which constitutes an assurance that all the great powers have done what they have compelled Germany to do, have foregone all territorial aggression and all interference with the free political self-determination of the peoples of the world. With this principle lived up to, permanent peace is secure and the supreme object of the recent conflict has been achieved, justice and self-determination have been substituted for aggression and political dictation. Without it there is no security for any nation that conscientiously adheres to an unmilitaristic policy.

The object of the war, as the Govt of the U S understands it was to free Europe from that cloud of anxiety which had hung over it for so many generations because of the constant threat of the use of military force of one of the most powerful govts of the continent. The President begs that the Prime Ministers of France, Great Britain and Italy will read his determination in the Adriatic matter in the light of these principles and settlements and will realize that standing upon such a foundation of principle he must of necessity maintain his position without alteration. He confidently counts upon their cooperation in this effort on his part to maintain the direction of affairs initiated by the victory over Germany and the peace conference at Paris."

In brief this maintains absolutely unaltered the note which you and Johnson and others joined in signing and insists upon no alteration of the solution suggested by the U. S.

I am of course assuming that you will suggest any addition to this answer that you deem necessary in the circumstances.

CLST transcript (C. L. Swem Coll., NjP).

From Frank Lyon Polk

My dear Mr. President: [Washington] February 19, 1920.

On February 12th the Hungarian delegation submitted its general reply to the conditions of peace as presented and part of its special observations. Only extracts from this note have been so far received by the Department, but these cover apparently the principal demands. Since this Government will take part in the negotiations, it would appear to be necessary to formulate a general policy to be communicated immediately to Mr. Wallace.

The Hungarian demand resolves itself broadly into a plea for plebiscites in all the districts of the former Hungarian state which have been assigned to Czechoslovakia, Jugoslavia, Austria, and Roumania. This plea is based on the following arguments:

1. Hungary has been a unit for over ten centuries.

2. The frontiers as drawn place eighteen million Magyars under a foreign yoke.

3. The new states will be no more homogeneous ethnologically than was the Kingdom of Hungary.

4. Economic disorganization must follow the severing of the economic union between the interdependent portions of the former Kingdom.

It would appear that to yield to this demand for plebiscites in all the ceded regions would involve insurmountable administrative difficulties and would also be a repudiation of understandings with the states surrounding Hungary. In connection with this, in fact, the Czechoslovaks have already pointed out in a note to Mr. Crane that letters of June 14th and August 8th from the Supreme Council spoke of "frontiers," not of "lines of demarcation" and that therefore they consider the question of any rectification of the line not open to discussion. Since, however, the Hungarians ask only for a plebiscite, the situation appears to me similar if not identical with that in which after the frontier was drawn between Germany and Poland the decision to hold a plebiscite in Silesia was made at the last moment. The Roumanians appear to deserve little consideration since they have consistently ignored the demands of the Supreme Council and have not yet withdrawn their troops from Hungarian territory. Even in this case, however, the Hungarian demand for a plebiscite in Transylvania could hardly be granted, since Roumania has repeatedly been informed that the district would remain permanently under Roumanian jurisdiction.

I would therefore suggest that this Government take the stand that the general plebiscite demanded by Hungary cannot be considered, but that on the other hand, Mr. Wallace be instructed to adopt a sympathetic attitude toward Hungarian requests for plebiscites in restricted areas when such requests appear likely to receive the favorable consideration of the British and French. Examples of these specific instances might well be the Grosse Schutte southeast of Pressburg, an agricultural district inhabited solely by Magyars and demanded by Czechosolvakia primarily for military reasons; the part of Ruthenia adjoining the present Hungarian boundaries, which district includes the sources of the rivers of eastern Hungary, forests which are lacking in the Hungarian state as constituted, and which is inhabited by people who apparently prefer Hungarian to Czech rule; certain purely Magyar cities situated only a few miles back of the present Roumanian frontier. Since the frontiers as now defined were drawn with the unanimous consent of the Supreme Council, it would appear impossible for Mr. Wallace to act independently. It might well, however, be helpful were he authorized to adopt a sympathetic attitude in cases like those mentioned above or similar cases where further consideration of the economic and nationalistic issues involved may have modified the attitude of his colleagues.

I should be grateful to have an expression of your opinion on this subject in order that Mr. Wallace may be informed of the American attitude and that the Department may act promptly on specific questions as they come up for discussion.

Faithfully yours,   Frank L. Polk

CCL (SDR, RG 59, 763.72119/9384, DNA).

Edith Bolling Galt Wilson to Joseph Patrick Tumulty

My dear Mr. Tumlty   [The White House, c. Feb. 20, 1920]
    The President has asked Judge Payne of the Shipping Board to become Sec. of the Interior & he has accepted.
    Will you send him over the nomination to sign—?
    Enclosed is Mr. Fletchers resignation—accepted.   EBW.

ALI (WP, DLC).

To Frank Lyon Polk, with Enclosure

[The White House, c. Feb. 21, 1920]
    I would appreciate suggestions for a note on this subject. The Italian claims I can never assent to and about the Greek I am *very* doubtful   W.W.

ALI (F. L. Polk Papers, CtY).

E N C L O S U R E

From Frank Lyon Polk

My dear Mr. President: Washington February 21, 1920.
    As you know, the Prime Ministers are discussing in London the Turkish question, and as we are not represented, all the information we get comes from the press. It is quite evident that decisions

are being reached which will determine the policy of the French, British and Italian Governments in the final negotiations of the Turkish Treaty, and I am writing to ask whether it is your intention that we should be represented at the final negotiations of this Treaty in Paris next month, and if not, whether you wish to convey your views in any way to the Conference on the serious questions that will have to be settled.

It was clear to us in Paris that the French and British, because of the fact that we probably would not take a mandate of any kind, would permit the Sultan to remain in Constantinople under some sort of international control. It may be that you do not care to be drawn into this discussion. We are, however, on record in favor of Eastern Thrace being part of the International State of Constantinople, but if the Turks are permitted to remain there, a new situation is presented. You will recall that Mr. Venizelos made a strong appeal to you personally in this matter,[1] and it would seem that under these changed circumstances the Greek claim would be hard to resist.

In regard to Smyrna, Venizelos told me that he had some correspondence with you on the subject and he felt that you were sympathetic to the Greek pretensions.[2] The Italians claim economic control over Southern Anatolia and full sovereignty over the Dodecanese, but there is no justice whatever in these claims, as there are no Italians there, and we always took the position that we had never admitted their right to occupy that territory.

You are familiar with the dispute between the British and French as to the northern boundary of Palestine. Lloyd George told me last summer that they had proposed to the French that this question be submitted to you for arbitration, but the French stubbornly maintained their claim to the line laid down in the Sykes-Picot agreement. The claims of the Zionists, I always felt were a little too ambitious, but on the other hand the line laid down by the French would seem to be too far south.

In addition to the questions I have mentioned, there is also the dispute between the French and Emir Faisal as to Syria, the question of the occupation of Mesopotamia, and, most important of all, as far as the public sentiment of this country is concerned, the question of Armenia. The claims of the Armenians in this country for the territory running from the Mediterranean to the Black Sea, and including all of Cilicia, will never be granted by the European Governments, and, in the opinion of our experts, are neither wise nor just. The drawing of the boundaries of Armenia with an access to the Black Sea is going to be one of the most difficult problems of the Conference. After the boundaries have been drawn, the question as to who is to protect the Armenians from the Tartars, Kurds and Turks will be most serious, for even if they were properly armed and equipped, General Harbord, Colonel Haskell[3] and others felt that the Armenians could not stand up against their neighbors without outside help. The various races are so mixed up in North Eastern Asia Minor that it was the unanimous opinion of the experts that without an international police there would be no peace in that part of the world. General Harbord in his interesting report[4] stated that if we should take a mandate of Armenia, it would require a large force to maintain order and to protect the Armenians from their neighbors. It is obvious that the British and French cannot and will not supply the troops necessary to maintain order, and I fear there is no hope of our people feeling this obligation so strongly as to compel Congress to consent to a mandate, and appropriate the necessary money.

I have mentioned the problems that come to my mind, but I am sure there are many others which will occur to you. As we will be called on to make some decision in the very near future, and particularly in view of the tremendous agitation in this country for the Armenians, I feel that these matters should be called to your attention so that you may consider what policy should be pursued.

Yours faithfully,   Frank L Polk

TLS (F. L. Polk Papers, CtY).
    [1] See FLP to RL, Aug. 16, 1919, Vol. 62; E. K. Vénisélos to WW, Sept. 27, 1919, printed as an Enclosure with W. Phillips to JPT, Dec. 8, 1919.
    [2] See FLP to WW, March 6, 1920 (first letter of that date), n. 2.
    [3] Maj. Gen. James Guthrie Harbord, former Chief of Staff of the A.E.F., who headed the American Military Mission to Armenia from August to October 1919, and Col. William Nafew Haskell, U.S.A., the Allied High Commissioner for Armenia since July 1919.
    [4] Published later in the year as Conditions in the Near East: Report of the American Military Mission to Armenia, 66th Cong., 2d sess., Senate Doc. 266 (Washington, 1920). For a concise discussion of the Harbord mission and its report, see Richard G. Hovannisian, The Republic of Armenia (2 vols. to date, Berkeley, Los Angeles, and London, 1971-82), II, 334-65.

From Frank Lyon Polk

My dear Mr. President: Washington February 21, 1920.

I call your attention to a copy of a telegram which has already been sent you,[1] which indicates that Millerand feels it would be unfortunate to give out the correspondence on Fiume.

In view of the fact that the French were responsible for the premature publication, I think their attitude is humorous, to say the least. The British have already consented to the publication, as you will see by the second telegram which I attach, and if you approve, I will send a message to Wallace telling him to say to Millerand that, as they were responsible for the leak, we feel that it is "necessary" to publish the correspondence.

At the same time, I will send a message to Rome and explain to Nitti that we will be extremely sorry if the publication will embarrass him, but at the same time as all these notes are being given out piece-meal and garbled, you feel that public opinion demands that all the facts should be made public.

I am sorry for Nitti as I think, for an Italian, he tried to play fair, and this publication will not make his task any easier.

Yours faithfully,   Frank L Polk

Agreed *W.W.*

TLS (photostat in F. L. Polk Papers, CtY).
¹ This and the enclosure mentioned below are missing.

To Woodrow Wilson Sayre

The White House Feb 22 1920

Many many happy returns of the day for my dear little namesake
Grandfather

T telegram (received from Francis B. Sayre).

Two Memoranda by Robert Lansing

February 22, 1920.

THE FRAZIER AFFAIR AND ITS EXTRAORDINARY ENDING.

The following incident is worth recording because it shows two things, the abnormal jealousy and self-sufficiency of the President, and also a state of mind at the present time which is as alarming as it is strange and inexplicable.

Here are the facts in what I call "The Frazier Affair":

On Tuesday, February 3rd, I received a letter from Mrs. Wilson giving the views of the President on a certain matter as to which I had asked his opinion. In a postscript she stated that the President had decided to name Arthur Hugh Frazier as Minister to Switzerland, which post became vacant on the 1st.

The suggestion of Frazier for a diplomatic mission caused me great concern. He had been one of the leading figures in the "House group" at The Crillon, and, although a diplomatic secretary of the first grade, he had avoided all intercourse with me in Paris clearly relying on Colonel House's influence rather than mine for his future. I found too that he was thought little of by men who knew him and that several questioned his loyalty and trustworthiness. He acted as interpreter for the President in connection with some of his French correspondence, and in that way came into personal touch with him.

When, soon after the German Treaty was signed, Sir Eric Drummond, the chosen Secretary General of the League of Nations, began to select the personnel of the Secretariat, Frazier, at the instance of Colonel House, was slated for a lucrative position. He, therefore, retired from our diplomatic service preparatory to assuming his new duties. When ratification of the Treaty by the Senate became increasingly doubtful and it became evident that Americans could not be employed in the Secretariat for the present at least, Frazier, who had come to the United States, became anxious as to the future and sought reinstatement in the service. After consulting with Phillips I declined to reinstate him feeling that we were well rid of an incompetent man. Early in January, after Polk had returned, Frazier attempted through him to obtain reinstatement but I refused to change my decision and Polk did not urge it.

This was the status of Frazier with the Department when I read Mrs. Wilson's postscript announcing that the President had selected him for Berne. After talking the matter over with Breckenridge Long, who was unfamiliar with the affair, I called up Admiral Grayson and asked him to come and see me. In a short time he arrived and went over the whole matter. He expressed doubts as to Frazier's loyalty in Paris to the President. I read to him the draft of a letter to the President which I had prepared, but he advised my holding it until he could tell the President some things that he knew about Frazier.

Three days later, on Friday, the 6th, Grayson came to the Executive Offices after Cabinet meeting. He said that he had had a talk with the President about Frazier and that he thought that it would be wise now for me to send my letter.[1] He telephoned later to the same effect suggesting that I show it to Tumulty. The objections to Frazier, which I stated in my letter, were his unfitness, the rebuke that it would be to me for refusing to reinstate him, and the very bad effect that it would have on the morale of the regular service to choose a man from the secretaries of the first grade (even assuming Frazier to be still in the service) who was twelfth in the list and whose seniors all surpassed him in ability and general fitness for a ministerial post. For these reasons I asked the President to reconsider his decision.

Following Grayson's suggestion I asked Tumulty to come and see me. He came about ten on Saturday morning, the 7th, and

[1] Again, we have not found this letter or Wilson's reply of February 8, 1920.

after telling him the situation I gave him my letter to read. After reading it carefully he approved sending it. About an hour and a half later he telephoned me and said that, if I had not sent it, I had best hold it till he could see me. I told him that the letter had gone. He said he was sorry because he was going to suggest that I take out of it my personal reason for objecting to Frazier. I was puzzled by this suggestion at the time, but later in the day I comprehended his reason for making it, when I read the President's letter on my calling Cabinet meetings in which he so plainly showed personal antipathy to me. Undoubtedly between the time Tumulty saw me and the time he telephoned me he read the President's letter to me, and felt that the President would in his state of mind find pleasure in humiliating me and would interpret my letter as another attempt to thwart his wishes.

On Sunday morning, the 8th, I received an answer, in which the President said with suave arrogance that he had been able to form from other sources an independent judgment of Frazier's fitness, and that, while he regretted to cause me any personal annoyance (I can imagine with what zest he dictated that) he was unable to comply with my request to reconsider the appointment.

This flat refusal put me in a hard position, but I felt that the matter was really of too little importance to explain a break with the President, so I determined to let it pass until the important correspondence relative to Cabinet meetings had developed, as I hoped it would, into an open rupture. However, in order to be no party to this outrageous appointment, I decided not to notify Frazier, who was in New York, and not to ask the Swiss Government as to his acceptability. Fortunately this was made easier as on Tuesday, the 10th, Frazier sailed for France and could not be reached.

And now for the amazing climax, which is so fantastic that it is hard to explain on the assumption that the President is mentally normal.

With the letter accepting my resignation to take effect "at once" came another letter from the President. Both were dated on the 13th and were evidently dictated at the same time. In this latter letter, which began, just as if nothing had happened, "My dear Secretary," the President said that on further consideration and on having obtained more information concerning Frazier he had decided to reconsider sending him to Berne, unless I had already addressed the Swiss Government as to his acceptability. He then said that he had decided to appoint Hampson Gary to Switzerland and Joseph C. Grew to Greece.

The fact that he had accepted my resignation and yet communicates with me as if nothing had happened is astonishing enough in itself, but there is another fact which makes the whole affair even more extraordinary. In my letter asking him to reconsider the appointment of Frazier, I had suggested the names of three regular service men, of which the first was Grew's, and the names of three men not in the service, of which the first was Gary's. Now what does the President do but accept the first names in each group apparently deferring entirely to my judgment in the selection.

One other thing must be added about this extraordinary letter, and that is that there is no vacancy at Athens. Droppers, though seriously ill for some time, has not resigned.

So, when I replied to the President (my last official letter to him by the way)[2] telling of my pleasure that he had eliminated Frazier and chosen Gary and Grew, I added that the Greek post was not vacant.

Could anything be more grotesque, more unbelievable than this ending of the Frazier affair? Can there be any satisfactory explanation other than that the President's mental faculties are disordered? I wonder how long this erratic state of mind can continue, and the Government properly function. The country may be thrown into grave peril if there is not a decided change for the better. The Frazier affair in itself is of course a little thing, but as evidence of the President's mental condition it is a great thing.

I am forced, in spite of all the physicians say, to the conclusion that the President's mind, if not actually unbalanced, is so warped and distorted by passions, which through his physical weakness he is unable to control, that his attempt to conduct the affairs of state may result in disaster to the nation.

How will it all end? Will the President grow better or worse? Will he ever again possess the self-restraint, the calmness of judgment and the poise to perform efficiently the duties of his great office? The Government cannot go on long under present conditions. Something must happen, and the sooner it does happen so much the better for this Republic and for the world.

[2] Again, this letter has also not been found.

February 23, 1920.

CABINET MEETINGS DURING THE ILLNESS OF THE PRESIDENT.

Although the President's complaint about my calling cabinet meetings during his illness was a pretext, the absurdity of using it is very clear when one considers the facts. From my memoranda and diary I have made up the following record.

On Thursday evening, October 2, 1919, having returned from New York where I had been with my wife and others to welcome the King and Queen of the Belgians, I telephoned Admiral Grayson inquiring as to the President's condition and whether there was a chance of the King seeing him if he came on to Washington. Grayson answered that the President's condition was "bad" and that he could see no one. I asked him what the trouble was, but got no satisfaction. I had a telephone message sent to Breckenridge Long in New York stating what Grayson had said and asking Long to notify the King that a trip to Washington would be useless.

Friday morning, October 3rd, the newspapers under "scare" headlines carried alarming reports concerning the President, so shortly after 11 o'clock I went over to the Executive Office and saw Mr. Tumulty. He appeared to be nervously excited and very much depressed. He told me that on Wednesday, October 1st, the President had become much worse. I asked him in what way. He did not answer me in words, but significantly put his right hand to his left shoulder and drew it down along his left side. Of course the implication was that the President had had a shock and that his left side was paralyzed.

While we were talking Tumulty telephoned Grayson to come to the Executive Office. On his arrival we went into the Cabinet Room. We were there nearly an hour discussing what course should be taken if the President's disability continued. Grayson was extremely reticent as to the President's malady giving no indication of any trouble other than a nervous breakdown. In view of the information gained from Tumulty I did not press the matter.

We discussed the possible necessity of Vice President Marshall taking over the executive authority temporarily and the absence of precedents as to what constituted disability under the Constitution. I remarked that of course in the event that Mr. Marshall temporarily assumed the duties of President there ought to be no change in the officials of the Government. At that Tumulty became excited and declared with much emphasis that he would not remain a day in office in case Marshall had to act for he would not serve under him.

We then considered what steps should be taken to meet the emergency which would arise if the President's condition became worse, and we decided that the Cabinet ought to meet and confer about the matter, as the responsibility for conduct of the executive departments rested with them if the President could not direct action. To this we all three agreed without question. Tumulty thought that the Cabinet should be summoned at once, but I opposed doing so for two reasons, first, because, if we delayed a little, we would be better able to judge how long the President would be incapacitated, and, second, because a summons for the Cabinet to meet immediately would greatly alarm the country and might induce Congress to take action. Both Tumulty and Grayson accepted this point of view, and we separated with the understanding that I would call a meeting the following Monday (October 6th) at 11 a.m.

Following the conference with Tumulty and Grayson and about 2:15 p.m. Secretary Baker came to see me in the Department and I told him that I had learned from Grayson that the President's condition was serious and that he, Tumulty and I had agreed that the Cabinet ought to meet. I also told him why it seemed wise to postpone the meeting until Monday. He entirely approved of the calling of the meeting and agreed that it was wise to delay it for two or three days.

About 4:30 Friday afternoon I issued the call for the meeting, but I have no record to show whether it was issued directly from my office or through the Executive Office. As a rule the notices of Cabinet Meetings were given by telephone from the Executive Office.

The next day, Saturday, the 4th, I chanced to meet Secretary Lane at The Metropolitan Club where he was a guest at a luncheon. We had a long talk over the critical situation caused by the President's condition, and we both held the view that the Government could not function in certain important particulars without an Executive who was able to act. Lane was heartily in favor of calling a Cabinet meeting and said that we must consider what should be done if the President's physicians would not permit him to perform any official duty. During the conversation Lane told me he had intended to resign November 1st. I replied that I had the intention to resign also but the uncertainty as to the Treaty and now the President's illness prevented. We agreed that we must remain until the condition of the President was much improved.

On Monday, October 6th, the Cabinet met at 11 a.m. in the Cabinet Room and conferred for an hour and three quarters. Every member was present, and no question was raised as to the right or wisdom of meeting in the circumstances. Admiral Grayson and Tumulty were present during the early part of the meeting, and Grayson gave a very encouraging report on the President's condition, which, he said, showed decided improvement and seemed to indicate a speedy recovery. We, therefore, asked Grayson to convey to the President our felicitations and best wishes. Because of Grayson's optimistic report the possibility of the Vice President acting was not discussed and only incidentally mentioned before Grayson made his statement. I did not even note the subject at the time as being discussed, although I did note that we discussed departmental estimates, the policy of not asking for increased salaries, and the work of the Industrial Conference. We agreed at the meeting that beginning on October 14th we should meet weekly on Tuesday.

I have a record of the Cabinet meetings which I attended. In all there were twenty-five. There was to my knowledge one meeting held while I was ill, at which Secretary Glass presided, and I believe there was another one when I was absent from Washington.

At one of the meetings early in December it was suggested—by Postmaster General Burleson according to my recollection—that the Cabinet meet twice a week on Tuesday and Friday. It was unanimously agreed to and I requested Tumulty to see that the usual telephonic notices were given.

In connection with the industrial crisis caused by the coal strike I prepared, by direction of the Cabinet at their meeting on December 9th, a letter in their name to the President stating their views on the subject of a letter by Dr. Garfield. Secretary Houston was also directed by the Cabinet to go at once to the White House, hand the letter to Mrs. Wilson and explain to her the situation in order that she might bring the letter without delay to the President's attention. A few hours later the President acted in accordance with the advice contained in the letter, rescinding thereby certain action which he had already taken.

Three days later, December 12th, the Cabinet conferred upon extending the time for the return of the railroads to the owners. The original time fixed was January 1st, 1920, but it had become evident that the necessary legislation could not be passed by that date. After hearing Hines on the subject it was decided by all except Burleson and Daniels that the transfer should be postponed until March 1st, and I was directed to send a letter to the President stating the opinion of the majority of the Cabinet. This I did the same day calling his attention to the fact that Burleson favored the original date of delivery and that Daniels thought an extention to February 1st would be sufficient. About the 22nd the President issued a proclamation fixing March 1st as the date for the return. It is to be presumed that he was influenced by the Cabinet's advice contained in my letter.

From the very first the President knew of the Cabinet meetings because Admiral Grayson told me that when he conveyed our felicitations to him the President had asked what the meeting was about, evidently suspecting that it was to discuss his ability to act. For four months after that first meeting the Cabinet met regularly and communications were sent to him directly, while no doubt Tumulty kept him fully advised of what was discussed, since he either attended the meetings or talked them over afterwards with some of the members.

In view of these facts the President's query in his letter to me on February 7th, 1920, was absurd. He knew the meetings were being held, and yet he never made the least objection. On the contrary he apparently welcomed the advice of the Cabinet as he followed it.[1]

T MSS (R. Lansing Papers, DLC).

[1] Lansing, on the same day, prepared a second longer memorandum entitled "RECORD OF CABINET MEETINGS HELD DURING THE PRESIDENT'S ILLNESS," dated Feb. 23, 1920 (T MS, R. Lansing Papers, DLC), in which he listed every cabinet meeting that he attended between October 6, 1919, and February 6, 1920—twenty-five in all. This record is based upon the entries in the Lansing Desk Diary and adds no new information to what we have already printed.

From Frank Lyon Polk, with Enclosure

My dear Mr. President: Washington February 23, 1920.

I enclose draft of reply to the British and French Prime Ministers on the subject of the Adriatic settlement.[1] You will notice that the memorandum you drafted[2] is used almost word for word as the introduction and conclusion of the proposed note. Messrs. Randolph, Bowman and Johnson all have had a hand at the body of the note[3] and we tried to make it direct so that the public could understand the controversy. There was a question as to whether it was wise to specifically refer to Article 10, in view of the pending fight in the Senate, but it was my view that you did that deliberately in order to give a practical demonstration of the necessity of this Article. I also attach your draft as you may wish to refer to it.

The Italian Ambassador[4] called on me yesterday to find out whether there was any possibility of your modifying your position and also to make a plea on behalf of Italy. I told him that I did not think there was any chance[5] whatever of your yielding to the Italian claims. He begged me most earnestly to present his arguments to you. In order that his views might be correctly reported I suggested that he write me a personal and informal note repeating what he had told me. It was his idea that I should write you giving you the substance of his letter, but in order to do him justice I thought it would be wiser to send you a translation of his letter. The letter was in French and the translation had to be made hurriedly in order that I might send it over to you with the proposed draft of the reply. I may say that in the third paragraph of his letter the Ambassador does not correctly state my views and I shall set him right.

None whatever W.W. They ought to be made to understand this once for all. W.W.

If the proposed reply is not satisfactory please send it back to me with such criticism as you desire to make and I will let you have it back in a very short time. If it, in the main, meets your views it is already set up as a telegram and ready to go to the Prime Ministers in London.

I have telegraphed to London, Paris and Rome insisting that we must publish the correspondence and suggesting that it be given out for publication after they receive your reply, as of course we could not give it out before it reached the Prime Ministers. Tumulty told me you wished a chronological statement of the controversy and I also enclose that.[6] I assumed that you did not wish to go back of December 9th.

Faithfully yours,   Frank L. Polk

TLS (photostat in F. L. Polk Papers, CtY).
   [1] That is, Lloyd George's and Clemenceau's rejoinder, printed as an Enclosure with FLP to WW, Feb. 18, 1920.
   [2] That is, WW to FLP, Feb. 19, 1920.
   [3] A note at the bottom of the note sent on February 24 reads: "Drafted from memoranda submitted by Dr. Bowman, Dr. Johnson, Mr. Ruddock, and Mr. Randolph." There is a copy of the Bowman memorandum in the Isaiah Bowman Papers, MdBJ. The memorandum by Douglas W. Johnson is missing in both the State Department files and the Polk Papers. "Ruddock" was Albert Billings Ruddock, Acting Chief of the Division of Western European Affairs in the State Department. His memorandum is also missing. "Randolph" was Harrison Randolph, President of the College of Charleston, at this time on leave for special duties in the State Department.
   [4] Baron Camillo Romano Avezzana.
   [5] Wilson's underlining and marginalia.
   [6] Wilson returned it. It is a T MS in the Polk Papers.

E N C L O S U R E[1]

Referring to London's 266, February 17, 10 p.m. to Department, copy of which has been furnished you by London, regarding Adriatic question, you are requested [immediately][2] to communicate following to British and French representatives: QUOTE The joint memorandum of February 17 of the Prime Ministers of France and Great Britain has received the careful and earnest consideration of the President. He has no desire whatever to criticize the attitude of the Governments of France and Great Britain concerning the Adriatic settlement, but feels that in the present circumstances he has no choice but to maintain the position he has *all along* taken as regards that settlement. He believes it to be the central principle fought for in the war that no government or group of governments has the right to dispose of the territory or to determine *the* political allegiance of any free people. The five great powers, though the Government of the United States constitutes one of them, have in his conviction no more right than had the Austrian Government to

   [1] Words in italics in the following document WWhw.
   [2] This word inserted in the State Department before telegram dispatched.

dispose of the free Jugoslavic peoples without the free consent and
co-operation of those peoples. The President's position is that the
powers associated against Germany gave final and irrefutable proof
of their sincerity in the war by writing into the Treaty of Versailles
Article X of the Covenant of the League of Nations which constitutes an assurance that all the great powers have done what they
have compelled Germany to do—have foregone all territorial aggression and all interference with the free political self-determination of the peoples of the world. With this principle lived up to,
permanent peace is secured and the supreme object of the recent
conflict has been achieved. Justice and self-determination have
been substituted for aggression and political dictation. Without it,
there is no security for any nation that conscientiously adheres to
a non-militaristic policy. The object of the war, as the Government
of the United States understands it, was to free Europe from that
cloud of anxiety which had hung over it for generations because of
the constant threat of the use of military force by one of the most
powerful governments of the Continent, and the President feels it
important to say again that in the opinion of the American Government the terms of the peace settlement must continue to be formulated upon the basis of the principles for which America entered the war. It is in a spirit of co-operation, therefore, and of
desire for mutual understanding that the President reviews the
various considerations which the French and British Prime Ministers have emphasized in their memorandum of February 17. He
is confident that they will not mistake his motives in undertaking
to make plain what he feels to be the necessary conclusions from
their statements.

The President notes that the objections of the Italians and Jugoslavs were made the basis for discarding the project of the Free
State of Fiume. It would seem to follow, therefore, that the joint
consent of these two powers should have been required for the
substitute project. The consent of Italy has been obtained. He does
not find, however, that the Jugoslavs have also expressed a willingness to accept the substitute plan. Are they to be required now to
accept a proposal which is more unsatisfactory because they have
raised objections to the solution proposed by the British, French,
and American Governments in the memorandum of December 9?
The President would, of course, make no objection to a settlement
mutually agreeable to Italy and Jugoslavia regarding their common
frontier in the Fiume region provided that such an agreement is
not made on the basis of compensations elsewhere at the expense
of nationals of a third power. His willingness to accept such proposed joint agreement of Italy and Jugoslavia is based on the fact

that only their own nationals are involved. In consequence, the results of direct negotiation of the two interested powers would fall within the scope of the principle of self-determination. Failing in this, both parties should be willing to accept a decision of the Governments of Great Britain, France, and the United States.

The British and French Governments appear to find in the President's suggestion that the latest proposals would pave the way for the annexation of the city of Fiume an implication that the guarantee of the League of Nations, is worthless and that the Italian Government does not intend to abide by a treaty into which it has entered. The President cannot but regard this implication as without basis and as contrary to his thought. In his view the proposal to connect Fiume with Italy by a narrow strip of coast territory is quite impracticable. As he has already said, it involves extraordinary complexities in customs control, coast guard services, and other related matters, and he is unable to detach himself from the previous views of the British and French Governments, as expressed jointly with the American Government in the memorandum of December 9, that QUOTE the plan appears to run counter to every consideration of geography, economics, and territorial convenience. END QUOTE. He further believes that to have Italian territory join Fiume would be to invite strife out of which annexation might issue. Therefore, in undertaking to shape the solution so as to prevent this, he is acting on the principle that each part of the final settlement should be based upon the essential justice of that particular case. This was one of the principles adopted by the Allied and Associated Powers as a basis for treaty making. To it has been added the provisions of the League of Nations, but it has never been the policy of either this Government or its associates to invoke the League of Nations as a guarantee that a bad settlement shall not become worse. The sum of such actions would of necessity destroy faith in the League and eventually the League itself.

The President notes with satisfaction that the Governments of Great Britain and France will not lose sight of the future interests and well-being of the Albanian peoples. The American Government quite understands that the three-fold division of Albania in the British-French agreement might be most acceptable to the Jugoslav Government, but it is just as vigorously opposed to injuring the Albanian people for the benefit of Jugoslavia as it is opposed to injuring the Jugoslav people for the benefit of Italy. It believes that the differences between the Christian and Mohammedan populations will be increased by putting the two sections under the control of nations of unlike language, government, and economic strength. Moreover, one part would be administered by the Italian

Government which is represented on the Council of the League, the other part by the Jugoslav Government which has no such representation. Therefore, to alter or withdraw the mandate at some future time would be well-nigh impossible.

Regarding the Treaty of London, the French and British Prime Ministers will appreciate that the American Government must hesitate to speak with assurance since it is a matter in which the French and British Governments can alone judge their obligations and determine their policies. But the President feels that it is not improper to recall a few of the arguments which have already been advanced against this treaty, namely, the dissolution of Austria-Hungary, the secret character of the treaty, and its opposition to the principles unanimously accepted as the basis for making peace. In addition he desires to submit certain further considerations. In the northern Italian frontiers agreements have already been reached which depart from the Treaty of London line and which were made with the understanding that negotiations were proceeding on quite a new basis. It has been no secret that the parties to the treaty did not themselves now desire it and that they have thus far refrained from putting its provisions into effect. In mutually disregarding their *secret* treaty commitments, the parties to the treaty have recognized the change in circumstances that has taken place in the interval between the signing of the secret treaty and its proposed execution at the present time. For nearly eight months, discussion of the Adriatic problem has proceeded on the assumption that a better basis for an understanding could be found than that provided by the Treaty of London. The greater part of the new proposals have already received Italy's assent. These proposals in some cases affected territory beyond the Treaty of London line, as in the Tarvis and Sexten Valleys; in others, the territory fell short of the Treaty of London line, as in the case of the islands of Lussin, Unie, Lissa, and Pelagosa—to mention only a few of the many proposals upon which tentative agreements have long been reached and which would be upset by an application of the treaty at this late day.

The coupling of the Treaty of London as an obligatory alternative to the Adriatic settlement proposed on January 14 came as a surprise to the American Government because this Government had already by the agreement of December 9 entered into a distinct understanding with the British and French Governments regarding the basis of a settlement of the question. By their action of January 14,[3] the Government of the United States was confronted with a definitive solution, to which was added on January 20 a

---

[3] See Enclosure I printed with RL to WW, Jan. 19, 1920.

threat to fall back upon the terms of the Treaty of London.[4] This course was followed without any attempt to seek the views of this Government or to provide such opportunity of discussion as was easily arranged in many other matters dealt with in the same period.

The President notes that the memorandum of February 17 refers to the difficulty of reconciling ethnographic with other considerations in making territorial adjustments, and cites the inclusion of three million Germans in Czechoslovakia and more than three million Ruthenes in Poland as examples of necessary modifications of ethnographic frontiers. He feels compelled to observe that this is a line of reasoning which the Italian representatives have advanced during the course of negotiations but which the British and French have hitherto found themselves unable to accept. There were cases where for sufficient geographical and economic reasons slight deflections of the ethnographical frontier were sanctioned by the Conference, and the American Government believes that if Italy would consent to apply the same principles in Istria and Dalmatia, the Adriatic question would not exist.

The American Government heartily subscribes to the sentiments expressed by the Governments of Great Britain and France regarding Italy's participation in the war. It fully appreciates the vital consequences of her participation and is profoundly grateful for her heroic sacrifices. These sentiments have been repeatedly expressed by the American Government. But such considerations cannot be made the reason for unjust settlements which will be provocative of future wars. A course thus determined would be short-sighted and not in accord with the terrible sacrifices of the entire world, which can be justified and ennobled only by leading finally to settlements in keeping with the principles for which the war was fought. The President asks that the Prime Ministers of France, Great Britain, and Italy will read his determination in the Adriatic matter in the light of these principles and settlements and will realise that standing upon such a foundation of principle he must of necessity maintain the position which he arrived at after months of earnest consideration. He confidently counts upon their co-operation in this effort on his part to maintain for the Allied and Associated Powers that direction of affairs which was initiated by the victory over Germany and the Peace Conference at Paris. END QUOTE.[5]

T MS (F. L. Polk Papers, CtY).
    [4] See Enclosure I printed with RL to WW, Jan. 22, 1920.
    [5] This was sent as FLP to H. C. Wallace, No. 401, Feb. 24, 1920, TS telegram (SDR, RG 59, 763.72119/9119, DNA).

To Frank Lyon Polk

My dear Polk: The White House 24 February, 1920

I wanted you to know first of all and from me whom I have chosen as Secretary of State. I therefore write to tell you that I am asking Mr. Bainbridge Colby to accept the post.[1] I am anxious now to accomplish something in which I know I will have your cooperation and in which your experience and knowledge will count for a vast deal. I want to build the corps of the State Department up into an organized team, devoted to making the principles of liberty, justice and fair dealing prevail in all international transactions with which we have anything to do. I know this will engage your enthusiasm as much as it does mine, and I am sure that in conjunction with Colby, who believes in the things that we believe in and really believes in them, we should be able to make the world a little different.

With warm regard and sincere admiration,
                    Faithfully yours,   Woodrow Wilson

P.S. I think it very important that we should be represented in the London negotiations, if it is indeed true as represented that the Paris negotiations have been transferred from Paris to London, and I am very anxious that you should go to London as our Commissioner. There is no one over there now to whom I am willing to entrust the business. After your experience in Paris, you will know how to tie the ends of strings together and will know how many pitfalls there are into which we must not fall. I hope that you will be able to undertake this for us.

TLS (photostat in F. L. Polk Papers, CtY).
    [1] Tumulty informed reporters of Wilson's decision to nominate Colby on February 25. The available evidence indicates that Colby himself only learned of Wilson's intention when he came to the White House from New York on that date in response to a telephonic summons from Tumulty. After an hour's conference with Wilson, Colby issued a brief statement which indicated that he would accept the position if the Senate confirmed his nomination. See the *New York Times*, Feb. 26, 1920, and Daniel M. Smith, *Aftermath of War: Bainbridge Colby and Wilsonian Diplomacy, 1920-1921* (Philadelphia, 1970), pp. 10-11.

From Frank Lyon Polk, with Enclosure

My dear Mr. President: Washington February 24, 1920.

I enclose a draft of an instruction to Wallace on the subject of the revision of the terms of the Hungarian Treaty. You will recall that you authorized me to have this prepared for you to look over.
                    Yours faithfully,   Frank L Polk

All right. *W.W.*

TLS (SDR, RG 59, 763.72119/9507, DNA).

E N C L O S U R E[1]

Your 515, Feb. 19, urgent.

Your attitude in conference of ambassadors on Hungarian requests for revision of the peace treaty, particularly as to modifications of the frontier in favor of Hungary, should be as follows: The Government of the United States cannot accede to the Hungarian request for general plebiscites in all the territories assigned to neighboring states since this would be repudiation of understandings reached with these states, since the administrative questions involved would appear to be insurmountable and since far-reaching and dangerous political consequences might ensue. The status of West Hungary should not be re-opened since this is indubitably a German speaking district, economically closely allied to Austria and essential for supplying Vienna with foodstuffs. On the other hand you should adopt a sympathetic attitude toward requests for plebiscites in specific areas when, in the opinion of your colleagues, further consideration of ethnographic or economic arguments or change of conditions since the lines were drawn make these requests appear just and possible of fulfilment. Examples of specific areas to the separation of which from Hungary the American experts agreed unwillingly and in which this Government would gladly agree to a plebiscite are the following: (1) the Grosse Schutte, inhabited solely by Magyars and assigned to Czechoslovakia primarily for military considerations; (2) Ruthenia, containing forests greatly needed by Hungary and the sources of the rivers on which the agriculture of East Hungary depends. It appears that the Ruthenians would prefer Hungarian to Czech control and that former Polish opposition to assignment of region to Hungary for fear of the spread of Bolshevism no longer holds good. Furthermore the claim that the important petroleum refining industry of Hungary will be ruined by the fact that crude oil must pass two customs frontiers appears reasonable. (3) Certain portions of the Banat wishing to remain Hungarian might be permitted through plebiscites to revert to Hungary with less resulting friction than through assignment to either Roumania or Jugoslavia. These examples are given you merely as indicating the attitude of this Government and are not intended to be exhaustive. In general you should understand that modifications of boundaries even through plebiscites might seriously affect the political stability of states bordering on Hungary but that if, in your opinion and that of your colleagues, certain changes can still safely be made that will improve ethnographic lines and will tend to make Hungary self-supporting this Government will cordially approve such rectification.

You should keep the Department fully informed of the negotiations and refer to the Department for instruction in specific cases.

T MS (SDR, RG 59, 763.72119/9160, DNA).
  [1] The following telegram was sent to Wallace on February 25.

To Tom C. Waldrep and Martin Edwin Trapp[1]

[The White House] February 24, 1920

May I not take the liberty of expressing my earnest hope that Oklahoma will join the other suffrage states in ratifying the Federal suffrage amendment, thus demonstrating anew its sense of justice and retaining its place as a leader in democracy?[2]

Woodrow Wilson

T telegram (Letterpress Books, WP, DLC).
  [1] Waldrep was Speaker of the Oklahoma House of Representatives. Trapp was Lieutenant Governor of Oklahoma and, *ex officio*, President of its Senate.
  [2] This telegram was drafted by Tumulty and sent to Mrs. Wilson on February 24.

From Gilbert Monell Hitchcock

My Dear Mr President: [Washington] February 24, 1920.

There is a strong disposition on the part of many democratic senators to abandon the fight against the Lodge reservations and vote for a resolution of ratification containing them.

At this time I believe there are 15 or 18 democratic senators who will not do so, including myself, but the probabilities are that enough will surrender to send the treaty to you unless something can be done to regain some of them.

Perhaps a definite and positive public statement from you or a message to the senate might bring about a change.

As it is a number of democratic senators will vote for the Lodge reservations on the theory that you will accept them ultimately. We might hold their votes if they could be made to understand that sending the treaty from the senate to the White House does not mean ratification.

Lodge proposes to keep the treaty before the Senate continuously beginning Thursday and I expect things will move rapidly and with little debate.   Yours sincerely,   G M Hitchcock

TLS (J. P. Tumulty Papers, DLC).

Joseph Patrick Tumulty to Edith Bolling Galt Wilson

Dear Mrs. Wilson: [The White House] 24 February 1920.

This is the summary of the Railroad Bill which the President asked me to get for him.[1]   The Secretary

TL (WP, DLC).
[1] Tumulty enclosed W. D. Hines to JPT, Feb. 24, 1920, TLS (WP, DLC), which in turn enclosed a lengthy summary (T MS [WP, DLC]) of the Esch-Cummins bill, soon to become the Transportation Act of 1920. The Esch-Cummins bill was an extensively revised version of Esch's original bill, H.R. 10,453, described in T. W. Sims to WW, Dec. 17, 1919, n. 1. The final version of the bill, which emerged from prolonged Senate-House conferences, had been passed by the House on February 21 and by the Senate on February 23. It was formally presented to Wilson on February 25, and he signed it on February 28. The Transportation Act provided for thoroughgoing federal control of the nation's railroads. It gave the Interstate Commerce Commission complete control over rates, even those set by state commissions; authorized the I.C.C. to supervise the sale of railroad securities and expenditures of the proceeds; permitted railroads to pool traffic in the interest of economy; and empowered the I.C.C. to consolidate existing lines into a limited number of systems. The provisions of the act in regard to labor are discussed in some detail in WBW to WW, Feb. 28, 1920. For the text of the act, see 41 *Statutes at Large* 456.

From Joseph Patrick Tumulty

Dear Governor: The White House 24 February, 1920

I just had a talk with Mr. Hines about your letter to the Brotherhoods. He feels that in view of the passage of the Cummings-Esch bill by the Senate the Brotherhood delegates might draw from any letter you would write an inference unfavorable to them. He thinks it wiser for you now to take the position that until the bill is before you and you have taken action upon it, you cannot say what your reply will be to the Brotherhood demand that a bi-party board be appointed; and he thinks that a message of this kind ought to be transmitted, either by 'phone[1] or by writing, to the railroad employees.   Sincerely,   Tumulty

OKeh
W.W.

TLS (J. P. Tumulty Papers, DLC).
[1] Wilson's underlining.

From Walker Downer Hines

Dear Mr. President: Washington February 24, 1920

In reply to your inquiry received this morning as to the status of the labor matter, I advise as follows:

You will recall you signed a letter to the Labor Executives, indicating that prior to action upon the Railroad Bill no step appeared appropriate excepting the appointment of the Committee of Experts.[1]

Before that letter could be delivered, the House had passed the Railroad Bill and Mr. Carter,[2] Director of our Division of Labor, suggested, as a result of the debate in the House, some changes in your letter which he thought would give it a more encouraging effect from the labor standpoint. It also appeared that the Labor Convention (which as indicated in the Labor Executives' letter to you of the 14th instant[3] was called to meet in Washington on the 23rd instant) had not organized to a point making it necessary for your letter to be presented yesterday and therefore a redraft was prepared for submission to you.

Before the redraft could be submitted to you, the Senate passed the Bill and it is now coming to you for consideration.

In view of these rapid developments, it has seemed to me that the most appropriate response for you to make at the moment to the Labor Executives is that you are considering the Bill itself and that it will obviously be necessary to await that consideration before confident plans can be made for the creation of a tribunal which can be expected to have final authority.

I attach draft of letter[4] which puts before you in concrete form my suggestion as to the response which seems appropriate to the Labor Executives at the moment. This draft of response brings out the point to which Mr. Carter attached importance, that being that Section 301 of the Bill itself contemplates that the carriers and the employes shall join in a conference of their representatives to endeavor to agree upon the wage problems. It is important, however, in referring to Section 301, to refer also to Section 307, as I do in the draft of letter submitted.

Cordially and sincerely yours,   Walker D Hines

TLS (WP, DLC).
    [1] WW to B. M. Jewell *et al.*, Feb. 23, 1920, TLS (WP, DLC). This letter was prepared by Hines and never sent.
    [2] William Samuel Carter.
    [3] B. M. Jewell *et al.* to WW, Feb. 14, 1920.
    [4] TL, dated Feb. 24, 1920 (WP, DLC). The letter sent is WW to B. M. Jewell *et al.*, Feb. 28, 1920. Wilson slightly emended Hines' draft.

Two Letters from Frank Lyon Polk

My dear Mr. President: [Washington] February 24, 1920.

The Siamese Minister[1] has explained to me the great desire of his Government to break down the regime of extraterritoriality which foreign nations enjoy in Siam and which apparently has been a great barrier to the successful development of its governmental system, particularly the judicial branch.

    [1] Phya Prabha Karavongse.

At the present time the great powers have the right to try their own subjects before their own consuls in Siam or before the Siamese Courts on which an advisor of the nationality of the defendant sits, and whose opinion prevails. One result of this system is that it is difficult, if not in some cases impossible, to enforce highly desirable laws and regulations generally in respect of all persons in Siam. For example, I am advised that, although Siam is a party to The Hague Convention for the suppression of the abuse of opium and other drugs, she is unable to give effect to its provisions through appropriate legislation owing to her lack of jurisdiction over foreigners in Siam under the present judicial system.

Siam, therefore, is very anxious to free herself from this system and to formulate codes of laws along the lines of Western ideas, which will be applied to Siamese and foreigners alike in Siamese Courts. The Minister states frankly that negotiations are now proceeding with other countries with a view to obtaining this result. The purpose of his Government is to obtain a treaty with the United States which will define a certain period after which the enjoyment of extraterritorial rights in Siam shall cease. He desires us to agree to make this period a definite one, say one to five years (preferably as short as possible) from the date of the promulgation and putting into force of all of the Siamese codes; namely, the Penal code, the Codes of Procedure, and Civil and Commercial Codes, and the Law for the Organization of the Courts. Up to the termination of this period Siam is willing to agree that legal proceedings against Americans as defendants be tried in Siamese Courts, in which an American Advisor would sit, and his opinion would prevail. This would supersede, for the transitory period, the present method of trying such cases before American consuls in Siam, and I see no objection to this substitute, as I believe that the rights of American defendants would be fully protected. The important point with Siam is the absolute termination of such "Advisor" Courts and of the Consular Courts after a definite time; for she believes that with such a treaty with us as a model she will be able to obtain similar treaties with other countries having extraterritorial rights in Siam.

The Siamese Minister has discussed with the Department various plans short of absolute termination of our extraterritorial rights at the end of a definite period. The plans which have been discussed are: that the United States will give up extraterritorial rights at the expiration of a certain period after the promulgation of the Codes, if the operation of the Siamese Courts proves to be satisfactory; or that the United States will terminate its extraterritoriality on a definite date after the promulgation of the Codes if the Codes are found upon examination to be satisfactory to the Government of the United States; or that we could give up our extraterritorial rights as soon as all other governments have given up their rights.

None of these plans entirely satisfied the Minister as there is a condition attached to each one of them. He is pressing for a definite date of termination without any conditions. However, I am inclined to think that he may agree to a provision running something like this:

Said system shall absolutely cease and terminate after _____ years from the promulgation and putting into force of all Siamese Codes—namely, the Penal Code, the Codes of Procedure, and Civil and Commercial Codes, and the Law for the Organization of the Courts; it being understood that if the Government of the United States perceives objections to them that the Government of Siam will endeavor to take measures to meet such objections.

The Department has never committed itself with respect to giving up our rights on a certain date without conditions, and the purpose of this letter is to ask how far I may go in this regard. The only objection I can think of to terminating our rights on a certain date without conditions is that the Senate may interpose the objection that we cannot be sure now that the Siamese Courts will at that date in the future be functioning so as to mete out justice to American citizens who become involved in litigation. If this objection is raised we cannot say that it is covered by a reservation. We will have to meet such an objection by pointing out that the relations between the United States and Siam have been friendly for over a hundred years and that the relative strength and influence of the United States will carry weight in our representations to Siam in the event that our confidence in her courts is overestimated, and that so far no citizen of the United States has suffered a wrong at the hands of the Siamese Government which has not been satisfactorily adjusted; that her judicial system bids fair to be as strong and as impartially administered as the systems of some of the Central and South American Republics, and, finally, that in our Treaty of 1898 with Japan we gave up extraterritorial rights in that country on a certain date without any reservation whatever, although the Japanese Codes had not yet been put into effect.

The Siamese Government have made considerable progress in reforming their judicial system. Several years ago the Siamese Government created a Code Drafting Commission, composed of Siamese and foreign jurists, including jurists of Great Britain, France and (for a time) the United States. This Commission is now engaged drafting and revising the codes, which I mentioned above, and has up to the present time completed drafts of the Penal Code, the codes of Procedure, and the Civil and Commercial Codes. I am informed that the Penal Code was in fact promulgated and put into effect on June 1, 1908. Our reports are that the Siamese Courts have in the last few years been functioning in a fairly satisfactory manner. There is probably no doubt that the Siamese Government will be unable to develop its judicial system beyond a certain point unless it is able to free itself from the extraterritorial privileges of foreign nations.

I should add that Japan has agreed definitely to give up extraterritoriality upon the promulgation of all of the codes. I understand also that Denmark has agreed to give up her rights at the same time. Great Britain and France have already made a partial surrender and the former has agreed to make a further concession on the promulgation of all of the codes.

In connection with our surrender of extraterritorial privileges Siam is willing to revise her commercial treaty and in the revision is willing to grant us effective favored nation commercial treatment, free privilege of travel throughout Siam, the right to own property and engage in business throughout Siam on the same footing as natives, etc., none of which rights we enjoy at the present time. This in a sense is a *quid pro quo* for our surrender of extraterritoriality, as Siam is unwilling to revise the Commercial Treaty unless we make this concession.

So far as the American interests in Siam are affected, I may say that American commercial interests in that country are practically negligible, consisting of only two or three business concerns. It is believed, however, that, if the interior of Siam were opened up for travel and commerce, a greater number of Americans would be attracted to that country to our mutual benefit. Our main interest there at present is that of American Missionaries. American Missions hold considerable property in Siam at the suffrance of the Government, and the Minister states that his Government is quite willing that in the new treaty these holdings be confirmed and title be granted to the Missions. There are few Americans in Siam, probably not much over two hundred, made up almost entirely of Missionaries. I am advised by representatives of the Missionaries that they are entirely favorable to the surrender of extraterritorial rights in Siam by the United States. In fact I know of no objection to this suggestion from any quarter.

I am sorry to make this letter so long, but I could not well present the situation fully without doing so. If you desire further details I can send you memoranda on the subject. I will be pleased if you will indicate whether you approve the surrender without conditions of all extraterritorial rights in Siam at the expiration of a stated period following the promulgation of all of the codes, the last of which will probably not be put into effect for about four or five years.   Faithfully yours,   Frank L. Polk

CCL (SDR, RG 59, 711.923/125, DNA).

My dear Mr. President: [Washington] February 25, 1920.

Many thanks for your letter of the twenty-fourth giving me the advance information that you intend to offer the office of Secretary of State to Mr. Colby, and I can assure you that I shall do all I can to assist him as long as I am in the Department.

I appreciate your suggestion that I should go to London as Commissioner, but my understanding is that this meeting of Prime Ministers in London is a preliminary meeting and that after this week the meetings to discuss the Turkish and other questions will be held in Paris. I think it should also be called to your attention that if I should go to Paris, it would be necessary for me to sit as a Plenipotentiary in these discussions and that might be embarrassing under the circumstances, as we would be drawn into the many difficult Near East questions in spite of the fact that owing to the attitude of Congress we can assume absolutely no responsibilities.

Under all the circumstances, I think you would find that it would complicate for you a situation which is already seriously complicated. I felt last fall, and I think that view was shared by General Bliss and Mr. White, that it would be wiser for this Government not to get mixed up in these negotiations. It is also my belief that by sending a Commissioner back to Paris we would be drawn back into a new Supreme Council and the foreign governments would attempt to bring up and settle with him many questions that should be handled through the Ambassador and the Department of State.   Yours faithfully,   [Frank L Polk]

CCL (F. L. Polk Papers, CtY).

A Memorandum by Cary Travers Grayson

Wednesday, February 25, 1920.

At three o'clock this morning I was called to see the President. He had a little coughing spell and was quite restless. I was sitting by the bed talking with him when he said to me: "Do you know of any reason why I should not appoint Bainbridge Colby as Secretary of State?" I replied: "I certainly know of no objection to him. It would really be an unusual appointment." And I went into some detail as to my views. The President said: "All those things are in his favor. We do not want to follow precedents and stagnate. We have to do unusual things in order to progress. I believe he is an able and a fine man."

(The nomination of Mr. Colby as Secretary of State was sent to the Senate on February 25th).

T MS (received from James Gordon Grayson and Cary T. Grayson, Jr.).

From Joseph Patrick Tumulty

Memorandum for the President:

The White House,
February 25, 1920

Acting Secretary of State Polke advises that because of the length of the note and the necessity for decoding it will probably be late Thursday or Friday before it can be delivered in London. He thinks publication of the notes should await the actual delivery of this one.   J.P.T.

TL (J. P. Tumulty Papers, DLC).

Joseph Patrick Tumulty to Edith Bolling Galt Wilson

Dear Mrs. Wilson: [The White House] 25 February, 1920

I am sending over the Oil Leasing Bill,[1] definite action upon which must be taken before midnight tonight. I am also sending you the views of Secretary Daniels, Judge Payne, Mr. Gregory, and Scott Ferris. Briefly, I state their opinions:

While Mr. Gregory thinks that the naval reserve features of the measure do not adequately protect the Government, he does not offer an opinion as to whether the bill ought to be signed or vetoed.

Judge Payne takes issue with Mr. Gregory on his interpretation of Sections 18 and 19, and holds that the Government is adequately protected; that the powers vested in the Secretary of the Interior can be utilized to guard and protect the rights of the Government at every turn.

Daniels discussed the Gregory memorandum with me and wished me to say to you that despite what Mr. Gregory says he thinks it would be a great misfortune if you should veto the bill; that his experts in the Navy Department agree with him that it is really in its main features a great constructive measure and the best that can be had after seven years of hard work. Mr. Daniels also wishes me to call the President's attention to his letter showing that the conservationists, headed by Gifford Pinchot, favor the enactment of this measure.

Scott Ferris says it is the best bill that can be gotten and that it is vitally needed by the whole country. He hopes the President will approve it.[2]   Sincerely,   [J P Tumulty]

CCL (J. P. Tumulty Papers, DLC).
[1] S. 2775, often referred to as the General Leasing bill, had been introduced by Senator Reed Smoot in June 1919. After much revision, a final conference report on the bill had passed in the House of Representatives on February 10 and in the Senate on the next day. It empowered the Secretary of the Interior to lease public lands containing mineral and oil deposits to private parties on terms designed to safeguard the public interest. The sections of the bill dealing with the naval oil reserves were intended to keep them from private exploitation, although the extent to which they did so adequately was a matter of dispute, as the above letter indicates. For a detailed history of the bill and the criticisms made against it, see Bates, *Origins of Teapot Dome*, pp. 181-99. For the text of the bill as enacted, see 41 *Statutes at Large* 437.
[2] Wilson signed the bill on February 25.

From Maurice Francis Egan

My Dear Mr. President: Washington, D. C. February 25, 1920.

I can not leave Washington without thanking [you] for the appointment of my dear friend, Robert Underwood Johnson to Rome. You have never had a warmer or more consisten[t] supporter than Mr. Johnson; I have known and admired him for many years. I can not be too grateful to Admiral Grayson for the good news he recently sent me of you. I have been prevented from leaving cards for Mrs. Wilson by an attack of influenza—and a carbuncle on the nose! If she had asked me to tea, I might have controlled the influenza; but the carbuncle! You would have chuckled at the sight!

I am, Dear Mr. President
                    Yours sincerely   Maurice Francis Egan.

ALS (WP, DLC).

Two Letters from Joseph Patrick Tumulty to Edith Bolling Galt Wilson

Dear Mrs. Wilson: The White House, 26 February, 1920

I have received several petitions from the farmers' alliances and from the railroad employees protesting against the President's approval of the railroad bill. Is it the President's desire to have these sent to him? They are purely formal in character.

                         Sincerely,   Tumulty

No he does not wish to see them

TLS (WP, DLC).

My dear Mrs. Wilson: [The White House] 26 February 1920.

I think the President ought to read this telegram from the American Federation of Labor.[1]   The Secretary

ask opinion of Secy of Labor   W.W.

TL (WP, DLC).
[1] Printed as an Enclosure with WBW to WW, Feb. 28, 1920.

To Joseph Patrick Tumulty

[The White House, Feb. 26, 1920]

Ask Commissioner Daniels[1] for brief, summary opinion of the Act.[2]   W.W.

ALI (WP, DLC).
[1] That is, Winthrop More Daniels.
[2] Wilson enclosed a new summary by Hines of the transportation bill. The summary, a seventeen-page single-spaced T MS, was enclosed in W. D. Hines to WW, Feb. 26, 1920, TLS (WP, DLC).

From David Franklin Houston, with Enclosures

Dear Mr. President: Washington February 26, 1920

The document attached hereto, entitled "A Proposed Message from the Secretary of the Treasury to the British Chancellor of the Exchequer,"[1] has been under consideration by Mr. Norman Davis and me for more than a week. It is in response to a message which came to the Treasury through the British Embassy from the Chancellor about ten days or two weeks ago. It bears principally on a suggestion contained in his message, bearing on the general cancellation of inter-allied debts.

The question with me is whether you would approve my sending such a reply. Mr. Davis and I are of the opinion that a reply should be sent and that this will cover the ground. Perhaps you may prefer that no reply whatever be sent. I should be glad to know your views and to have your instructions.

I am returning Mr. Davis' memorandum of February 21st, which he sent to you at my request, and also his letter to you of February 23d, giving further information bearing on the matter, particularly parts of articles of the Pact of London.

Faithfully yours,   D. F. Houston.

TLS (WP, DLC).
[1] The immediate question involved was that of the funding of short-term certificates of indebtedness of the Allied governments to the United States into long-term gold bonds, as the Allied governments had promised to do when they borrowed the money during and after the war. The British had borrowed a little over $4 billion; the French, about $3 billion; the Italians, over $1.5 billion, etc. Albert Rathbone, Assistant Secretary

of the Treasury, went to Paris in the autumn of 1919 to discuss this matter with French officials, but could not persuade them to enter into serious negotiations. Discussions with the British began in Washington in early 1920 between Assistant Secretary Leffingwell and Ronald Charles Lindsay, Counselor of the British embassy. On February 9, Lindsay sent Houston a letter from Austen Chamberlain, Chancellor of the Exchequer, to Leffingwell, which discussed briefly the financial difficulties of the European governments and ended by saying that they would welcome a proposal of the mutual cancellation of all intergovernmental war debts.

This narrative, based on Houston, *Eight Years with Wilson's Cabinet*, II, 117-23, and on the correspondence between Rathbone, British Treasury officials, and others, in *Loans to Foreign Governments* . . . (Washington, 1921), 67th Cong., 2d sess., Sen. Doc. No. 86, pp. 60-77, brings the story up to Houston's letter to Wilson of February 26.

A copy of Houston's proposed reply to Chamberlain is not in WP, DLC, but Houston printed it in *Eight Years with Wilson's Cabinet*, II, pp. 123-28. Houston said that the United States Government had advanced some $4 billion to the Allied governments since the conclusion of the Armistice and had done all in postwar financial assistance that it was able to do. The indebtedness of the Allied governments to each other and the United States was not at present a burden upon the debtor governments since they were not paying interest on these debts and had not provided for payment of either interest or principal in their budgets. The existence of foreign debts to the United States posed no obstacle to the obtaining of private credits by the European governments in the United States. The British proposal for a mutual cancellation of intergovernmental war debts did not involve mutual sacrifices on the part of the nations concerned: "It simply involves a contribution mainly by the United States." Solution of the problem lay with the debtor governments and peoples themselves; they had not even begun to face their own domestic financial problems. "It is very clear to me," Houston concluded, ". . . that a general cancellation of inter-governmental war debts, irrespective of the positions of the separate debtor governments, is of no present advantage or necessity. A general cancellation as suggested would, while retaining the domestic obligations intact, throw upon the people of this country the exclusive burden of meeting the interest and of ultimately extinguishing the principal of our loans to the Allied governments. This nation has neither sought nor received substantial benefits from the war. On the other hand, the Allies, although having suffered greatly in loss of lives and property, have, under the terms of the Treaty of Peace and otherwise, acquired very considerable accessions of territories, populations, economic and other advantages. It would therefore seem that, if a full account were taken of these and of the whole situation, there would be no desire or reason to call upon the government of this country for further contributions."

Houston says (p. 123) that Wilson "promptly returned the message [to Chamberlain] with his approval noted upon it in his own writing," and that he, Houston, transmitted it to Chamberlain through Lindsay. We have not found the letter with Wilson's notation, but Houston's reply to Chamberlain is printed in *Loans to Foreign Governments, pp.* 78-80.

E N C L O S U R E   I

A Memorandum by Norman Hezekiah Davis

Washington.

MEMORANDUM FOR THE PRESIDENT: February 21, 1920.

As you are aware, efforts beginning with the peace negotiations were made to bring about a cancellation of our debts against the Allied Governments, but the question was not presented in such a definite way as to require us to take any formal action. Much to the surprise of the Treasury, in connection with negotiations which have been under way with the British Treasury regarding the funding of short time obligations of the Allied Governments into long-time obligations and the extension of the interest accruing thereon during the next two or three years, the question has been formally raised by the British Treasury both in a communication to Mr. Rathbone, and also in a message from the Chancellor of the Exchequer sent through the British Embassy in which, among other questions, the Chancellor in effect invites the American Treasury to a consideration of a general cancellation of all intergovernmental war debts.

Before his departure for a three days' absence, Secretary Houston approved the enclosed reply, which he proposes to send to the Chancellor if it meets with your approval. In order not to consume your time in reading the Chancellor's message which deals with many questions between the two Treasuries, I am attaching an extract from that portion of his message dealing with this subject. For some reason of his own, the Chancellor bases his proposal partly on the theory of an alleged probable financial stringency in this market, which would make it impossible to obtain private credits here. Just as the people of Europe were misled into believing German reparations would supply the deficit in budgets, they are being misled into believing a cancellation of their external governmental debts will later solve their other difficulties. While the Allies have never bluntly so stated, their policy seems to be to make Germany indemnify them for having started the war, and to make us indemnify them for not having entered the war sooner.

Will you kindly indicate your approval or such instructions as you care to give in respect to the proposed reply?

Norman H. Davis

TS MS (WP, DLC).

ENCLOSURE   I I

(Last two paragraphs from message of the Chancellor of the Exchequer)

Turning to more general considerations it is evident that a financial crisis in America would gravely endanger the incipient recovery of Continental Europe. It is impossible to forsee the consequences. With the Continent a prey to bankruptcy and possibly to anarchy and the United States unable to provide credits of any sort owing to the internal crisis, the world's position would be indeed serious. If I may venture on what I fear is controversial ground I may say that it is largely because of these dangers that we should welcome a general cancellation of Inter-Governmental War Debts.

The moral effect would even be a greater practical change and fresh hope and confidence would spring up everywhere.

The existence of these International Debts deters Neutrals from giving assistance, checks private credits and will I fear prove a disturbing factor in future International relations.

T MS (WP, DLC).

ENCLOSURE   III

From Norman Hezekiah Davis

My dear Mr. President: Washington. February 23, 1920.

With reference to my memorandum of February 21st, enclosing a proposed reply to the Chancellor of the Exchequer regarding the cancellation of inter-governmental war loans, I desire to submit for your further information the following considerations:

Without any specific proof, I have for some time suspected that the loans made by England to France and Italy have not the same standing as our loans to the Allies. I recall that Mr. Lloyd George told me England could not afford to force those countries to pay her. Article XI of the Pact of London states that

"Italy shall receive a military contribution corresponding to her strength and sacrifices."

I do not know what this means. It may mean corresponding financial assistance to Italy during the war or after the war, or both. In either case it most probably has a direct relation to the obligations of the Italian Government now held by the British Government, and it may well be that the British desire a general cancellation of inter-governmental war debts as a means of discharging secret treaty provisions. If such is the case the British might thus in great part at our expense discharge their treaty obligations.

Article XIV of the Pact of London provides that

"Great Britain undertakes to facilitate for Italy *without delay* and on favorable conditions the conclusion of a loan in the London market amounting to not less than 50,000,000 pounds."

The reference herein to immediate financial assistance may well indicate that Article XI referred to general financial assistance on a larger scale.

Cordially and faithfully yours,   Norman H. Davis

TLS (WP, DLC).

To Frank Lyon Polk

My dear Polk: The White House 27 February, 1920

I had a conference with the Siamese representatives at the Peace Conference on this subject and feel that there is a great deal of force in their contentions. I would like to go as far as is prudent and possible at the present moment in conforming to their wishes and would like your formulation of a suggestion in the matter.

Cordially and faithfully yours,   Woodrow Wilson

TLS (SDR, RG 59, 711.923/126, DNA).

Two Letters from Joseph Patrick Tumulty

Dear Governor: The White House February 27, 1920

I had a long talk with Senators Robinson and Glass the other day regarding the Treaty situation and there is no doubt that it is critical; that our forces are rapidly disintegrating. Both Glass and Robinson say that nothing but a statement from you will prevent a complete collapse. Robinson, who has been a devoted supporter of yours throughout the whole Treaty fight, says that Senators are influenced by an overwhelming sentiment from "back home" demanding immediate action on the Treaty, even with the Lodge reservations. Whether you should make a statement now or await the action of the Senate in ratifying the Treaty with the Lodge reservations, is a problem. There is great danger in taking action now irrevocable in character. There is no doubt that the country is tired of the endless Senate debate. The ordinary man on the street is for ratification even with the Lodge reservations. He yearns for peace and an early settlement of the whole situation. If the Treaty is ratified with the Lodge reservations, brought about with the aid of a majority of the Democrats, the Democratic party might as well not hold a convention this year. It wouldn't be possible under these circumstances to make the Treaty an issue in the next campaign and thus all the advantage would be with the Republicans.

My judgment is that we should accept the ratification of the Treaty with the Lodge reservations with an address by the President to the American people, showing wherein these reservations weaken the whole Treaty and make it a useless instrument; showing what the real essence of Article X is—a checking of imperialism; that the purpose of the President in standing for an unqualified ratification was to keep America's influence in the affairs of the League undiminished; that the imperialists of the world were the real opponents of Article X; that the President's ambition was to have America enter this League with a great moral influence behind her so as to be in a position to check and prevent those things that in the past have been the breeders of war. Now that the Senate had acted, the question is whether the President by his action is going to postpone peace and thus aggravate a world situation which is now very serious.

If we pocket the Treaty, will we not be responsible for all the consequences and all the perils that may come because of the failure to bring about peace?

TL (J. P. Tumulty Papers, DLC).

The White House,
Memorandum for the President: February 27, 1920.

Commissioner Daniels was consulted by Mr. Tumulty about the Railroad Bill. Commissioner Daniels says that while he thinks it a cumbrous and in some respects a poorly devised piece of legislation, it is on the whole a good measure and ought to be approved by the President.   J.P.T.

TL (WP, DLC).

Joseph Patrick Tumulty to Edith Bolling Galt Wilson

Dear Mrs. Wilson: The White House, 27 February, 1920

I have just talked over the 'phone with Secretary Houston and he says that because of the financial situation, the President ought to take action on the railroad bill before the first of March. It would have a most helpful and beneficial effect for him to do so.

Sincerely,   Tumulty

TLS (WP, DLC).

From Frank Lyon Polk, with Enclosure

My dear Mr. President: Washington February 27, 1920

I am transmitting herewith the reply of the British and French Prime Ministers. There are points which obviously must be challenged, such as, for instance, the proposal to withdraw entirely the memorandum of December 9th; the suggestion that Jugoslavia be assured economic outlets in Albania different from those provided in the memorandum of December 9th; the observations on the Treaty of London; and the ready assumption that the application of that Treaty will not seriously involve our whole relation to the Adriatic settlement. I shall be glad to be advised regarding your views.   Faithfully yours,   Frank L Polk

Please draft such a reply as you think ought to be made and let me see it. *W.W.*

They did not let their *associates* (e.g. the U. S.) know anything about the Pact of London

TLS (SDR, RG 59, 763.72119/9284, DNA).

                    E N C L O S U R E

                                London Feb. 26, 1920
Urgent. 335. Following is text of memorandum delivered to me at 8:45 tonight:

"Memorandum by the Prime Ministers of France and Great Britain in reply to President Wilson's communication received on February 25, 1920.[1]

London, 26th February, 1920.

The Prime Ministers of France and Great Britain welcome the communication which they have today received from the President of the United States in answer to their memorandum February 17.[2] They wish to record their appreciation of the recognition given therein by President Wilson to the attitude of the French and British Governments concerning the Adriatic settlement. The French and British Prime Ministers are glad, once again, to repeat their assurance given by them in the memorandum of January 23[3] that they 'have never had the intention of making a definite settlement of the questions raised without obtaining the views of the American Government'; a further explanation of these views which is supplied in the memorandum under reply is therefore for the French and British Governments a matter of very great interest and importance all the more since it shows that the United States Government do not wish to disinterest themselves from the general question of peace. The absence of any American representatives has proved, in practice, an almost insurmountable obstacle to the success of negotiations and to the acceptance, by the parties concerned, of an equitable solution in conformity alike with the principles of the Peace Conference and of the legitimate, though conflicting aspirations, of the Italian and Jugo-Slav peoples.

[1] FLP to H. C. Wallace, Feb. 24, 1920, printed as the Enclosure with FLP to WW, Feb. 23, 1920.
[2] Printed as an Enclosure with WW to FLP, Feb. 18, 1920.
[3] See H. C. Wallace to RL, Jan. 23, 1920.

They note as a fact of the greatest importance that the President of the United States expressed his willingness to accept any 'settlement, mutually agreeable to Italy and Jugo-Slavia regarding their common frontier in the Fiume region provided that such an argument [agreement][4] is not made on the basis of compensation elsewhere at the expense of nationals of at third power.' This, the French and British Prime Ministers agree, would be the ideal way of settling the question at issue and they are willing to do their utmost to reach a settlement by this road. In order to facilitate this process they are ready to withdraw the proposals made both on the 9th December and the 20th [23rd] January[5] for they feel that if the two parties principally concerned believe that the various Allied and Associated Powers are committed to supporting them in any particular solution it will be more difficult to secure a vouch[er] for agreement between them. The French and British Prime Ministers therefore join in a cordial invitation that President Wilson should take part with them in a formal proposal to the Italians and Jugo-Slav Governments urging them to negotiate a mutual agreement on the basis of a withdrawal of all previous proposals.

If, however, this attempt should prove unsuccessful the French and British Prime Ministers agree that the United States, Great Britain and France should once more consider the question in common with a view to arriving at concrete proposals. The French and British Prime Ministers desire further to record the wording of appreciation of the interest taken by the American Government in the future of the Albanian people and they assure President Wilson that they share to the full respect for the principle which he here enunciates. They would remind him of what they said per [on the subject] in their memorandum of February 17th[6] and would state that they are convinced that by a review of the Albanian question a settlement can be reached which will satisfy the aspirations of the Albanian people for full self Government, while taking into consideration the vital interests of all other parties concerned together with the necessity of assuring to Jugo-Slavia an outlet on the Adriatic in the region of Scutari. They are willing to urge upon the governments interested that they should bring their desires into line with the American point of view.

The French and British Prime Ministers must further refer to the observations of President Wilson on the character and applicability of the Treaty of London. With regard to this treaty they feel bound to insist that its secret character, to which he objects, was

---

[4] This and following corrections from text in *The Adriatic Question*, pp. 35-37.
[5] The telegram cited in n. 3.
[6] Cited in n. 2.

due to the exigencies of military strategy. The essence of all success in warfare is to prevent divulgation to the enemy of important plans which [are] of a military or political character and the treaty on the faith of which Italy entered the war was not one which could be published during hostilities without detriment to the Allied cause. With regard to their statement that in the event of an amicable settlement not being arrived at between Italy and Jugo-Slavia the Treaty of London would have to come into force so far as they are concerned, the French and British Prime Ministers feel that they need add little to the explanations they have already given in the memorandum of February 17th. The Italian Government have cooperated most loyally and assiduously with the French and British Governments in endeavoring to substitute for the arrangements for the Treaty of London, a settlement which would be satisfactory alike to them and to Jugo-Slavia. Such an agreement would obviously replace and annul the Treaty of London with the consent of Italy herself. That such an agreement should be reached is the cordial hope of all the Allied Governments, a hope which they know President Wilson shares to the full, but they cannot disguise the fact that should no voluntary settlement of this kind be attained, the Treaty of London to which they set their hand in 1915 would then become the only valid alternative so far as they were concerned. In conclusion the French and English Prime Ministers venture to call the attention of President Wilson to the urgent importance of a speedy settlement of the Adriatic dispute—a dispute which is now gravely threatening the peace and delaying the reconstruction of south eastern Europe."

Davis

T telegram (SDR, RG 59, 763.72119/9284, DNA).

From Frank Lyon Polk

My dear Mr. President: Washington February 27, 1920.

The British Chargé has just been in and left the attached note, informing me of the King's desire to appoint Sir Auckland Geddes[1] Ambassador to the United States.

As you probably have noticed by the papers, this news has leaked out in London, but the British Government have refused to confirm it. If Sir Auckland Geddes is acceptable to you, I think it would probably help if you could let me know as soon as possible, as the newspaper men have already been asking whether we had received any word on this subject.

Yours faithfully,   Frank L Polk

I instinctively dislike what I hear of this man,[2] but have no ground upon which I can object   W.W.

TLS (photostat in F. L. Polk Papers, CtY).

[1] Sir Auckland (Campbell) Geddes, M.D., former Professor of Anatomy at the Royal College of Surgeons, Dublin, and at McGill University; Director of Recruiting at the War Office, 1916-1917; Minister of National Service, 1917-1919; M.P. since 1917; at this time President of the Board of Trade.

[2] As President of the Board of Trade, Geddes had spoken out for an aggressive British effort to recover markets lost in South America during the war.

FROM THE PAPERS OF CARY TRAVERS GRAYSON*

Miscellaneous Notes and Memoranda by Dr. Grayson

INAUGURATION

Mr. Wilson came down to Washington the day before Inauguration. The first time I saw him he and Mrs. Wilson came to the White House in response to an invitation from President and Mrs. Taft on the afternoon of March 3, 1913, for tea. The picture will always be vivid in my mind—how clear-cut Mr. Wilson's features were, how intensely determined he was—completely calm and at ease. It was on this occasion that I had the first glimpse of Mrs. Wilson's cordial, beautiful smile. This was the first thing I noticed about her. Mr. Wilson while conversing with Miss Helen Taft, who was a student at Bryn Mawr, said: "We have many things in common in Bryn Mawr College." They discussed Bryn Mawr at length. Mr. Taft talked for quite a while to Mrs. Wilson, and Mrs. Taft spent most of her time in conversation with Mrs. Wilson telling her about the White House. President Taft told them that it was a good house to live in and that he regretted that his rent bill was up and he had to move. And he then gave one of his chuckle laughs. He expressed the hope that they would enjoy living there as much as he had.

✧ ✧ ✧

INAUGURATION.

Mrs. Howe fell on the evening of Inauguration. Sewed up the wound. First medical experience with the Wilson family. President came to Mrs. Howe's room and asked if there would be any disfigurement from the wound. There was none. Had first-aid material on hand. Just the things I needed. The President commented on how promptly it was done and wanted to know if I was prepared for the operation before the accident occurred. I took him very seriously in that remark. I did not know he was joking. I did not see the President after that for a few weeks. About the second week on a Sunday morning Mrs. Wilson sent for me. I went down to the White House. She wanted me to come in to see the President; said he was sick; laid up with an attack of indigestion and sick headache, slight cold with it; some fever; had to keep him in bed. He got up in a few days and was all right again. In the meantime, I

* All documents and materials in this section received from James Gordon Grayson and Cary T. Grayson, Jr.

had attended Mrs. Howe. The next time I saw the President he asked me what my status was. I think I told him I did not have a status. He made a remark to me about a number of people who had applied to be his doctor, and that he had not heard anything from me. I told him it was too personal a matter to ask anybody to say a word in my behalf. This was all that was said. The next time he asked me to come to lunch and he had Mr. Daniels also as a guest. He said to Mr. Daniels: "This is a part of the Navy that I am going to appropriate." Mr. Daniels said: "If you want to find good things you will have to go to the Navy." He told me then about his condition. Mrs. Wilson also told me of his frailties and how she had been worried about his health. I told him what I thought he ought to do. He said it was out of the question; that he did not have the time to devote to himself in that way. He spoke of the various programs that different individuals had for him to follow. He believed that I demanded more time in taking care of his health than most anyone else that he had met. I told him that mine was the most important program of all; that the other did not amount to anything. For months he rebelled against playing golf. It was in May before I could finally get him to play. I told him that his new duties consisted of a campaign and that he must prepare himself physically for them; that if he appointed me as his health master I did not want to bore him but it was absolutely necessary that he take the time to take care of himself; that it would save time and make for happiness in the long run. He said; "Yes, I think that is good sense and I would like to follow your prescription but really I haven't the time." I got him to start in May for the first time. Nine holes exhausted him very much. I found his blood pressure to be 110 at that time, which is pretty low.

✧   ✧   ✧

PASS CHRISTIAN—1913

While at Pass Christian we attended one of the old school Presbyterian Churches, and I recall the preacher, an elderly man with white hair, before turning to the text, said: "I want to say to this congregation that this is the second proudest moment of my life, the other occasion being when President Grant attended services in the church in which I preached." Shortly after these services, the President expressed a wish for a copy of the Presbyterian Hymnal—the kind he used when he was a boy. Thereupon I called upon this Minister and he gave me a copy of the Hymnal, which was in good condition, except that one side of the back was gone. I turned it over to the President, and the first Sunday night following, he and Mrs. Wilson and the daughters sang these old hymns at a family reunion. I then first realized what a beautiful tenor voice the President has. Frequently after singing these he would sing a solo—"OLD NASSAU."

While the President and I were returning from Gulfport to Pass Christian, where we had been playing golf on the Gulfport coast, a little boy about ten years of age stood in the middle of the road and waved the President's car to a stop, handing the President a basket of oranges, with his name and address written on the handle of the basket. The President thanked him for the oranges, and the next day wrote him a nice letter of appreciation. A few days afterward while coming along this road the little boy waved us down again. He did not have a basket this time, but he told the President that he enjoyed his letter so much that he would like to have him (the President) write him every week after he got back to Washington. The President was very much pleased over this little incident.

✧　　✧　　✧

NOTES.

Mr. Melville Stone, the head of the Associated Press, in January, 1919, while in conversation with me and Colonel Seale Harris of the Army Medical Corps in Paris stated:

"President Wilson has been unjustly accused of not taking counsel with others. A circumstance to refute this occurred soon after the sinking of the Lusitania, which I doubt but a few people except myself know about. As you know, my son went down on the Lusitania, and I was very strongly in favor of America entering the war at once. President Wilson sent for me to come to the White House and he said to me that he had a very serious situation in which he wanted my help. He wanted me to ascertain through the Associated Press throughout the country whether the country would back him up at this time in declaring war against Germany. I expressed my opinion freely at the time—that we should not lose a moment in declaring war against Germany. President Wilson said to me: "I want you to put yourself in my position and after you have gathered the sentiment of the people through your representatives of the Associated Press, I want you to tell me frankly then whether you think the country is prepared and would back me up in declaring war. I complied with his wishes and at the end of a week came back to the White House and told him that much as I personally was in favor of going into the war, I had to inform him that the country was not ready for war, and that if I were in his place　and he had asked me to put myself in his place—I could not declare war now. I told him, however, that the sentiment was growing in favor of intervention but it was not ripe at that time.["]

✧   ✧   ✧

WESTERN TRIP.

While sitting on the rear platform of the train, the President told me that he had been thinking of the men that he had practically made and who had afterwards turned against him—men to whom in some instances he had unbosomed his very soul; who knew his intimate thoughts and who had promised him their undying loyalty. He called by name several of these, both in his college and political experience. And then he spoke of Senator Reed, of Missouri, whom he had not made but to whom he had rendered such favors as had drawn from Senator Reed the strongest expressions of devotion and loyalty. I think he referred to the postmasterships at St. Louis and Kansas City. I am quite sure it was one of these places, if not both of them. The President, it appeared, made these appointments at the urgent, personal request of Senator Reed in opposition to the recommendations of the Postmaster General. It is almost invariably the President's rule to approve the nominations submitted to him by the Cabinet member. But in this instance he deviated from this rule, in the language of Senator Reed, to "save him (the Senator) from political humiliation" in one of the largest cities of his own State. Senator Reed had told the President that he was under undying obligations, promising him (the President) that he would be eternally grateful to him.

The President then cited the case of Senator Gore, of Oklahoma, who, on one occasion, was in dire distress and appealed to the President for help. The President in circumstances which were very distasteful to him, went to Senator Gore's rescue and saved him from great humiliation and possibly political destruction. And now Gore is one of his bitterest enemies. The President feelingly said: "When I think in times like these what the support of every loyal citizen means to individuals and to the world at large, it makes me at times almost doubt my fellowmen, which, of course, I do not. When I reflect on these things I do not know what I would do if I did not have a God to fall back upon."

✧   ✧   ✧

On October 11th [1919] the President was extremely ill and weak and even to speak was an exertion. He had difficulty in swallowing. He was being given liquid nourishment and frequently it took a good deal of persuasion to get him to take even this simple diet. Mrs. Wilson and I were begging him to take this nourishment, and, after taking a number of mouthfuls given to him by Mrs. Wilson with a spoon, he held up one finger and motioned me to come nearer. He said to me in a whisper: "Doctor, I must repeat to you this limerick:

A wonderful bird is the pelican,
His bill will hold more than his bellican,
He can take in his beak enough food for a week,
I wonder how in the hell-he-can.

The President did not have a shave from October 2nd until November 12th and his beard had grown to a considerable length. Just before he was shaved he called for a mirror to take a final look at himself before parting with his beard. He examined himself very carefully in the mirror, turning his head from side to side, and then he turned to me and said:

"Doctor,

"For beauty I am not a star,
There are others more handsome by far,
But my face I don't mind it
For I am behind it,
It's the folks in front that I jar."

On another occasion I wanted to examine the pupils of his eyes, and he amusingly said, in a whisper; "What are you up to now, Doctor." I said: "I simply want to examine your pupils." (I was making the examination with a small electric light.) He said: "You have a large job on your hands, because I have had a great many in my day."

On still another occasion I brought in Admiral Stitt, who is a specialist in bacteriology and blood examinations. The President wanted to know what I proposed to have Dr. Stitt do. I said: "I want him to get a sample of your blood for examination." The President rolled his eyes to one side, and looking up at me, said: "If you are looking for blood, send him down to the Capitol."

At one time Dr. Hugh Young was in consultation in the President's room, and I remarked to him: "Don't you think the President would feel more comfortable if he had his beard cut off?" Dr. Young agreed and said: "Couldn't you shave him? You know, in the olden days the doctors were barbers. And he went on to say that the colors, red and white, on the barber's sign represented the red blood on the white skin. He added: "And doctors were really barbers in those days." The President, looking up at us, said: "And they are barberous yet."

I took his temperature with a thermometer, and I said to him, after taking it: "Your temperature is normal." He said: "If you keep me in this bed much longer, my *temper* will not be normal." This was published in the newspapers next day, and when his cousin, John A. Wilson, of Franklin Pennsylvania read this in the cloud (crowd?) he shouted out to the men there: "The President is all right. Nobody ever could have invented that saying, because those who have known him all his life know that is just exactly the way he talks."

I was percussing him one day. This is simply the doctor's phrase for tapping over the area of an organ to determine whether it is distended, contracted or displaced. While I was undergoing this procedure, he said: "Why knock; I am at home."

On one occasion Secretary Tumulty came in to see the President, and as he was leaving, the President said: "Why leave now?" Mr. Tumulty said: "I must go to see the King of Belgium." The President: "You are wrong; you should say 'The King of the Belgians.'" Mr. Tumulty said: "I accept the interpretation." The President said: "It is not an interpretation but a reservation."

✧   ✧   ✧

Mr. Wilson kept an electric search light on a little stand by his bed during the trying days of his illness in the White House, and throughout the night, when he would awake and call the nurse and frequently his physician, he would pick up the search light and turn it toward a picture of Mrs. Ellen Wilson.[1] He would look at it intently for a few seconds before asking the doctor or the nurse what he would like them to do or what assistance he wished. This was not done a few times but literally hundreds of times. It was a routine matter with him.

T MSS.
[1] Frederic Yates' drawing of Mrs. Wilson, reproduced in Vol. 16. It hangs in the Wilson house on S Street in Washington.

Remarks at a Stag Dinner[1]

[Dec. 28, 1918]

Your unexpected call upon me for a speech reminds me of an amusing incident which once took place near Washington.

As you know, the American Capital is on the Potomac river, and one day a boy was fishing from the end of a raft anchored in the stream a short distance below the city, when the thing happened which very rarely happens on the Potomac river, he got a bite. So excited was he in striving to get the fish out of the water that he lost his balance and fell over into the river. As he was struggling in the water to get back to the raft with the water streaming out of his eyes, nose, mouth and ears, a farmer passing along the bank called out to him: "Hello, my boy, how did you come to fall in?" Quick as a flash the young fellow called back: "I didn't come here to fall in, you darn fool, I came to fish." So I didn't come here to-night to make a speech, but in the language of the signs we read on the railroad tracks, I came to "Stop, Look, and Listen." But since I am on my feet I cannot refrain, as no American or English-man could, from saying a word of felicitation upon the splendid achievement by which your country and mine have just vindicated the courage of free peoples armed in defense of their freedom, and demonstrated not only that liberty and efficiency can function to-gether, but that great democracies can impose such discipline upon themselves as to turn out a war machine that will outmatch the murderous devices of autocracy. In other words, we have not only made the world safe for democracy, but we have done a greater thing, for we have proven that democracy is safe for the world.

It is a privilege to live in this age. The events of the last five years have been the greatest in all recorded times; and the final triumph of civilization over savagery, the victory of right over might, makes of this day and hour an epoch beside which all history is dimmed.

"We are living, we are dwelling
In and grand and awful time,
In an age on ages telling
To be living is sublime."

Hereafter, in my humble judgment, the history of mankind will be put into two grand divisions only, that before, and that after, this great world conflict.

But I am one of those who believe that the greatest good that has come out of this war is the bond of deathless friendship, born in a common cause, and dipped in fraternal blood, which shall forever unite the British empire and the American commonwealth.

It is a curious fact that except for the Boxer uprising in China a few years ago, England and the United States never before, in their separate sovereignties, have fought side by side. We have fought two wars against each other, while in the several controversies which each has had in its own household, or with a third power, the other has often looked on with an unfriendly interest. But now, at last, on land and sea, English and American forces have fought so close together, that the colors of their flags were merged into one banner of the free. Heretofore, the tie that bound us was one language. Hereafter, we shall be one race. All of us must and do hope that this is the last of wars, and that from the waste and ashes of its fields will rise, Phoenix-like, a great covenant of mankind to compose the differences and enforce peace throughout the world. But mutual respect and affection, which come from the comradeship of peril and sacrifice, and the consciousness of the same traditions, the same ideals and the same destiny, are safer guaranties of peace than written treaties or leagues of nations. England and the United States now, at last, see each other "not through a glass darkly, but face to face."

CC MS.

[1] A formal stag dinner given by Lloyd George, perhaps at 10 Downing Street. These intimate and private remarks were not published in the contemporary press or in *Addresses of President Wilson on First Trip to Europe, December 3, 1918 to February 24, 1919* (Washington, 1919).

Cary Travers Grayson to William Gibbs McAdoo

My dear Mr. Secretary: Paris, 12 April, 1919.

My silence is not indicative of the fact that my thoughts fail to turn to you, for I can assure you that a day does not pass but that I wish you were here. There is so much that I would like to tell you, and so little I can put in a letter. But when I get home I will have a store of things to unload on you.

There has never been a time that the President has needed you as badly as he has since he has been over here. Your cooperation, vision, and more than all else, your boldness and your courage and good common-sense are just what the President needs in this crisis. Some of those who are close to him and are supposed to represent him have hurt the situation materially by attempting to compromise or soft-pedal the issue, when by doing so it was contrary to the President's principles. Then when the President would take a bold stand for his principles, this false representation led the French to believe that the President was merely bluffing and caused the loss of valuable time. You cannot imagine what a terrific handicap this has been. And what a strain it has been on the President. He has never worked as hard nor has he ever put in as many working hours in a day. The situation has been so complex and trying that he has had very little time for recreation. He is within fifteen minutes of a golf course and has only played two games since his arrival in France on the 13th of December.

About ten days ago the President was taken violently sick with the influenza,[1] but by promptly going to bed, and with prompt treatment, he was only laid up one week. As you know, the influenza is weakening and even treacherous, and I have had to guard him very carefully for fear of a relapse and complications. He is working beyond his endurance. Yesterday, for instance, he received a delegation immediately after breakfast. The Council of Four met at eleven o'clock and did not adjourn until the lunch hour. He had the Queen of Roumania and party for lunch,[2] and at three o'clock he attended the Plenary Session of the Peace Conference, which adjourned just before dinner. After dinner, at eight o'clock, he went to the League of Nations meeting and did not get to bed until this morning after 1:00 o'clock. Every night he is up until after 11:00 o'clock. You must remember that in addition to his duties here at the Peace Conference, he has a lot of work to attend to from Washington. The strain he is going through is almost beyond superhuman endurance. But he is at a stage where he cannot let up. When I tell him that he needs rest and relaxation, he answers me by saying that in the midst of this imminent crisis he feels that he should participate in the things for which he is responsible; if he were away from these meetings and did not know what was going on, he would worry. He feels that a mess would be made of things in his absence. I agree that worry would do him more harm than physical fatigue. Confidentially, one cannot blame the President for worrying under the conditions which exist here. As you know, I am loyal to the President first and above all, and I am his doctor and friend; but when I see the way some of the others are trading on him, not only acting as weaklings, but blaming him for the delays and errors, for which they themselves are responsible, it simply makes my blood boil. If you were here behind the scenes and could see and hear what I do, your vocabulary of cuss-words would not last ten minutes.

Of course, I don't know anything about finances, but this is an illustration of what has happened: A prominent member of the American Delegation undertook to handle one of the financial problems, but he got so hopelessly entangled that he was compelled to call on a fellow-American who was not a delegate to help him out of the swamp![3]

You must excuse me for writing such a "blue" letter. I feel I would give anything if I could have a confidential talk and could explode without reserve. That I have wished for your presence over here a hundred times but feebly expresses it. With the President's great brain and courage I am confident that everything ultimately is going to come out all right. But I feel that he is going through a lot of unnecessary strain by not having the proper help.

I suppose you have heard the good news from Gertrude as to the new son. The following cable which I received tells the story:

"I salute you. I weigh seven pounds, seven ounces, but am

slightly bald. Mother, Gordon and I are well and send dearest love. Please write to me.

(Signed) Lieutenant Cary T. Grayson, Jr."

When a fellow receives such a wonderful message as this, and has such a true-blue partner as Gertrude, the other things of life for the moment—peace or war, revolutions or Bolshevism—seem of little consequence.

I was deeply distressed to hear of the death of Nona's husband and of her illness.[4] I sent you a telegram and wrote you a letter just before sailing, which I hope you received.

Not knowing your address, I am sending this letter in care of the White House, with the request that it be forwarded to you. It goes forward to you from here in the diplomatic pouch.

I hope you are enjoying good health and that everything is going all right with you. I hear many complimentary things about you in this part of the world.

If the President and Mrs. Wilson knew I were writing I know they would send their love to both Miss Eleanor and yourself.

With warmest regards to you both, believe me,

Affectionately yours,   [Cary T. Grayson]

CCL.
[1] About this episode, see the extract from the Grayson Diary printed at April 3, 1919, and n. 1 thereto, Vol. 56.
[2] For detailed and colorful accounts of this visit, see the extracts from the Grayson and Benham diaries printed at April 11, 1919, Vol. 57.
[3] See the extract from the McCormick Diary printed at April 2, 1919, Vol. 56.
[4] About this matter, see the extract from the Grayson Diary printed at March 5, 1919, Vol. 55, and WW to E. de Mohrenschildt, March 20, 1919, Vol. 56.

Louis Seibold to Cary Travers Grayson

My Dear Admiral: New York, Oct. 6, 1919

I think you have handled the obviously difficult case of the President with great skill. I do not need to say to you that it is the hope of every good Anerican [American] that the President comes through. I am sure he will if intelligent care and doctering can accomplish it. There have been many absurd reports about his conditions and real trouble which I have done everythimg [everything] I could to dissipate and refute. Most of these reports originate in Wall Street and are circulated for outrages [outrageous] business reasons. The most general is that the President has been affected mentally. I have replied to these statements that I wished I were similarly afflicted if I could be as mentally alert as the President. His illness naturally provokes all sorts of reports, but I guess it is just as well not to pay any attention to them. I thought I would write an article showing the absurdity of them, and will do so if you think it advisable.

I would like to have a good biographical sketch of you with your latest picture because I want to write an article telling the people just what a sort of citizen you are. You may not know it but you are a figure of real interest and one in whom there is great confidence. Will you send the material and picture to me here within the next two or three days? Also if the occasion offers will you not convey my best wishes to the President and Mrs Wilson and tell them that I'm praying for his full restoration to complete health which he is sure to find if he obeys his very competent physician and admirably capable nurse

Faithfully Yours,   Louis Seibold

TLS.

Cary Travers Grayson to Louis Seibold

My dear Friend: [Washington] October 9, 1919.

I have read with genuine interest your letter of October 6th. I do not know of any disease that has not been included in the rumors about the President. If I tried to refute all these rumors that have been scattered around, I would not have any time to devote to the President professionally at all. I have not followed this course, and I do not intend to do so. I agree with you—I wish I were similarly afflicted if I could be as mentally alert as the President. I can sincerely say that his mind is as good as it ever was since I have known him. I hope the time will not be far distant when it will be considered safe to permit him to resume his work, when his motions and his words will speak for themselves. As he gains in strength his case is more difficult for me to handle, as he is very anxious to get back to work. All the doctors I have called in agree that absolute rest and quiet is essential to complete recovery. My great difficulty is to keep him from becoming irritated as a result of the rest treatment, for if he should strain himself too soon severe complications might be the result. I believe you can appreciate the trying situation with which I am laboring.

Concerning your desire for a biographical sketch, I refer you to Who's Who and to the article which appeared in the March, 191[9],[1] number of "Physical Culture." I am sending you a copy of this magazine under separate cover. I am also sending you a photograph of myself. I would rather rely on what you prefer to write about me than to send you anything myself.

Words of encouragement from a friend like you help a fellow a great deal in a trying time like this. When you next come to Washington, let me know, as I should like to see you and have a talk with you.

I have had pleasure in conveying your message to the President and Mrs. Wilson. Both of them value your friendship very highly, and both were deeply touched by your solicitude.

With warm regards, believe me,

Sincerely, Your friend,   [Cary T. Grayson]

CCL.
[1] Richard M. Winans, "Admiral Grayson—Medical Physical Culturist," *Physical Culture*, XLI (March 1919), 17-19, 52, 54, 56.

A Memorandum by Dr. Grayson

Memorandum: October 6, 1919. (Monday)

I was called before the Cabinet this morning at 11:00 o'clock at the request of Secretary Lansing. The entire Cabinet was present. Secretary Lansing asked me the direct questions as to what was the matter with the President, what was the exact nature of the President's trouble, how long would he be sick and was his mind clear or not. My reply was that the President's mind was not only clear but very active, and that he clearly showed that he was very much annoyed when he found that the Cabinet had been called and that he wanted to know by whose authority the meeting had been called and for what purpose. Secretary Lansing was somewhat astounded when I spoke thus. From what the French Ambassador had said previously to Mr. Forster it appeared as if Secretary Lansing was particularly anxious to have Vice-President Marshall act in the President's place.

Secretary Baker intervened at the close of my remarks and said that he thought it would meet with the approval of the Cabinet to say that they only met as a mark of affection and to say also that everything was going in the even tenor of its way; that there was nothing to cause him to worry about now; that they were all looking out for the President's interests as best they could. He added: "Please convey our sympathy to the President and give him our assurance that everything is going along all right." This was unanimously concurred in by the other members.   C.T.G.

T MS.

A Statement by Dr. Grayson[1]

[Oct. 15, 1919]

The continued illness of the President and the natural, rightful and intense interest of the American people in the physical condition suggests the following statement by his medical attendants:

The President has always worked intensely hard. As a student he was assiduous and untiring. During his career at Princeton while engaged in active literary work, in addition to the burden of teaching, he used his physical and mental energies to the utmost. He was always an indefatigable teacher and his lectures were exceedingly popular. At this time he manifested signs of impairment in his general health and muscular power. His lack of muscular development in some respects made necessary a surgical operation, which was entirely successful.[2] His incessant work led to an affection of the eye, which produced injury to one of the retinae.[3] He also developed an obstinate neuritis with persistent pain and loss of muscular power from which he has never entirely recovered. At one time his physical condition was so depleted that specialists in this country were gravely concerned about his health. He went abroad for some time and secured additional advice in Europe.[4] His abstemious habits, and his extraordinary self-possession carried him safely through.

On his election to the Presidency he very cheerfully adopted the regimen suggested by his attending physician, and loyally carried it out whenever possible. He gained ten pounds in weight; his physical functions were well performed; he slept well, and seemed in every way naturally stimulated by the great part which he was called upon to play.

During the first year of his Presidency, before he had become accustomed to his new duties, he had marked indigestion, took colds, frequently had derangement of his elimination, and was seen by specialists, who feared for his general health. Because of his great activity as a speaker and his over-taxed condition at times the President has suffered from a relaxed condition of the mucous membrane of the nose and throat, which has required local treatment.

As soon as he became accustomed to his new duties these symptoms gradually disappeared. He continued in good health during the latter part of his first and the first of his second administrations. He bore the strain of the war crisis admirably, and when he sailed for Europe on the first occasion, he was in very good general health.

In Paris he was subjected to a terrific strain. He was almost entirely deprived of exercise, worked during the day and evening in ill-ventilated rooms, weather conditions were often unfavorable, and as a result of the extraordinary strain to which he was subjected, symptoms of general physical impairment developed, which prevented him from obtaining his usual sleep.[5] On his return sea voyage during the second trip he improved remarkably, and when he finally landed he was again in his accustomed general condition.

The work of last summer was quite well borne, although there never has been a return to the general physical vigor which marked the mid-period of his two administrations. His attending physician, who has followed him closely, was convinced that the Western trip would prove a hazardous experiment and earnestly endeavored to dissuade the President from undertaking it.

During the trip the President worked under the most unfavorable conditions. Again he was deprived of exercise; at times subjected to great and sudden changes of climate and altitude. During long motor processions through cities he was obliged to stand for hours at a time; crowds gathered at every railroad station urging him to speak, and he was obliged at least to stand upon the platform. His rest was repeatedly interrupted night and day, and the strain upon him was beyond human endurance.

His strength progressively failed until he could not sleep, could not eat, could not digest his food, suffered from intense headache, and was rapidly failing in physical and nervous energy until complete nervous exhaustion had developed. In spite of this, it was with the greatest difficulty that his physician could induce him to abandon the trip.

So soon as he began to rest he immediately began slowly to gain. Symptoms, however, of muscular impairment and loss of motion had begun to develop, and after his return to the White House these symptoms increased, and a consultation of physicians was called.

His power of digestion was slowly but steadily improving. The essential functions of the body, while sluggish at times, were yet properly performed. There was ability to speak perfectly with the usual enunciation, good vision, his senses were unimpaired. There was, however, loss of muscular motion on the left side with some disturbances of sensation. As these symptoms in such cases are often transitory and of brief duration, it was hoped that they would speedily disappear and that their appearance was not of essential gravity, and the desire to give the public only accurate information concerning the President led the physicians to place no great stress at that time upon these symptoms.

A thorough physical and neurological examination could find no evidence of a large or serious lesion of any important organ. While it is evident that his body shows the effect of tremendous wear, the essential functions of life are fairly well performed. His recumbent posture in bed and his age have brought about swelling of the prostate gland, very common in men of his years, which leads to retention of urine and impairment in the functions of the bladder. The relief of this condition is often trying for the patient and requires considerable time. There is no evidence of an acute inflammation, the growth of a tumor, or the development of malignant disease in any part of the body, and especially in the prostate gland.

At present the President's mind, as it has always been, is clear, keen, logical, incisive and at times showing evidence of his accustomed humor. On several occasions within the past few days it has been necessary to submit to him important international questions. Upon these he has passed judgment promptly and with unerring accuracy. He relishes his food and expresses his appreciation of the attentions of those who minister to him.

In such a case it is absolutely imperative that the patient be put at complete muscular and physical rest. Until digestion and assimilation can go on for some little time, it would be dangerous to allow the patient to undergo any considerable exertion. Drugs are of unessential value, except as they aid in the natural functions of the body. He rarely is obliged to take remedies to procure sleep. Mrs. Wilson's untiring care and the constant attention of his medical attendants, and the fact that he is not allowed to excite or worry himself by a knowledge of minor details, are the essentials in his treatment.

He is steadily, slowly gaining in the essential functions of life, and as this gain proceeds he will gradually take a more active part in the performance of his official functions. He is at present in a condition where any question of international or national importance could be submitted to him for his counsel, advice and decision.

T MS.

[1] A note at the end of this document says that Dr. Grayson "prepared" it on October 15, 1919. It was never published.

[2] An operation for a hernia in the Presbyterian Hospital in New York about December 15, 1904. Wilson subsequently developed phlebitis and went to Palm Beach, Florida, for three weeks of convalescence in January 1906.

[3] A cerebral-ocular accident on May 28, 1906, which blinded Wilson in his left eye. See WW to J. D. Greene, May 30, 1906, n. 1, Vol. 16.

[4] In the summer of 1906, with his family. See the Index reference, "Woodrow Wilson—Health," in ibid.

[5] It is significant that Grayson does not mention Wilson's viral infection in Paris in early April 1919. Here he referred to an episode that he had never mentioned before— some kind of vascular accident, probably a small stroke. It is the subject of the essays on Wilson's health problems printed as appendixes in Vol. 58.

Francis Xavier Dercum to Cary Travers Grayson, with Enclosure

Dear Dr. Grayson,   Philadelphia October 20th, 1919.

I am enclosing a revised statement. This statement may now, I think, be regarded as final and complete. I call your attention particularly to the DIAGNOSIS on pages four and five. I will be glad if you will show it to Admiral Stitt.

I am with kind regards,

Very Sincerely Yours,   F. X. Dercum

TLS.

E N C L O S U R E
DR. DERCUM'S MEMORANDA

October 2nd, arrived at Washington 4.05 P.M., was met at the station by Dr. Grayson and arrived at the White House about 4.20. On our way to the White House Dr. Grayson gave the following account of the President.

He said that some eight days before, that is on Sept. 25th, he had noticed in the morning that the President's pillow had been stained by a little saliva. He examined the President's face and it seemed to be slightly flattened and drooping on the left side but the change was so slight that he was not certain about it and later when he re-examined the face the symptom had disappeared. Notwithstanding the President's vigorous opposition, Dr. Grayson insisted upon an immediate return to Washington. During the rest on the train the President seemed to improve considerably and after arriving in Washington the gain in strength continued. The President was able to take now and then an automobile ride and an occasional short walk. On the afternoon of October 1st, he had taken a short walk about the White House Grounds. In the evening he had attended a moving picture show at the White House. He had apparently enjoyed the pictures. Dr. Grayson noticed that the President now and then wiped the left side of his mouth with his handkerchief as though there was a slight drooling of saliva.

During the night the President apparently slept well. The next morning, Thursday, October 2nd, on rising from his bed he complained of numbness and weakness of the left leg; in attempting to walk about the room he sank to the floor; this weakness slowly and steadily increased. Finally it involved the left arm and left side of the face. There had been no attack of unconsciousness; there had been none of the symptoms suggesting the sudden onset of a cerebral hemorrhage.

Examined by myself at about 4.30 P.M., the President was found in bed. His left leg and left arm were in a condition of complete flaccid paralysis, the lower half of the left side of the face was drooping. The President was conscious though he was somewhat somnolent. He answered questions a trifle slowly, but without evident impairment of articulation and the answers were always entirely responsive.

He was unable to retract the left angle of the mouth as well as the right. The involvement of the face was not as profound as the involvement of the arm and leg. The tongue was protruded in the median line. In addition there was noted a well marked anaesthesia[1] involving the left side of the face, head, neck, trunk, the left arm and the left leg. The anaesthesia was not sharply delimited by the middle line but faded into hypaesthesia[2] and disappeared upon the trunk within three or four inches of the middle line. Upon the left limbs, especially in the distal[3] portions, the anaesthesia was complete.

The knee jerks were elicited upon both sides; that upon the left side was less marked than that upon the right which was about normal. There was no ankle clonus[4] upon either side. There was a well marked Babinski sign[5] upon the left side. It was noted further that both eyes were directed to the right, i.e. there was present a conjugate deviation[6] to the right. There also appeared to be present an impairment of both visual fields. However, owing to the evident fatigue induced, the fields could not be well outlined. The pupils were unequal, the left was distinctly larger than the right. The left pupil responded feebly to light, the right pupil responded about normally. There was no involvement of the sphincters. There was no rise of temperature. The pulse was regular and full and the respiration was regular and normal in frequency, but perhaps a trifle labored.

A general visceral examination, such as was practicable under the circumstances, was negative, save that the bladder was rather full. An examination of the heart failed to reveal any murmurs or

---

[1] Absence of feeling or sensation.

[2] Imperfect power of perception.

[3] Away from the center of the body.

[4] Rhythmical contraction of the calf muscles following a sudden passive dorsal flexion of the foot.

[5] A certain reaction when a sharp object is drawn along the sole of the foot. It indicates some severe disturbance in the upper part of the central nervous system.

[6] The forced and persistent turning of both eyes to one side while their relation to each other remains unaltered.

other conditions such as might give rise to embolism. There was no evidence of involvement of the sphincters.

During the examination the President was fully conscious and cooperated with Dr. Dercum; protruded his tongue, retracted the angles of the mouth, showed his teeth, opened and closed his eyes and performed other gestures in response to various requests and directions.

On Saturday, October 4th, the President was visited by Dr. Dercum and Dr. de Schweinitz and examined about 11.30 A.M. Dr. Dercum made another examination confirming the symptoms previously noted. Dr. de Schweinitz could find no hemianopsic[7] fields. Dr. de Schweinitz noted the conditions in the eye grounds[8] to be practically identical with those which he had observed on former occasions. The fact that the left pupil was somewhat larger than the right was in keeping with the greatly impaired vision of this eye; a fact of long standing.

While the eyes when at rest still deviated to the right, the President was now able to rotate them to the left though he did not perform rotation to the left as well as to the right. Speech and mental faculties were as before save that somnolence was not present.

On October 11th, Dr. Dercum again examined the President shortly after 11 A.M. It was now noted that the anaesthesia had markedly lessened; it had disappeared or had been replaced by a moderate degree of hypaesthesia; the latter was more marked upon the distal portions of the arm and leg. The President was able to recognize light impressions with cotton wool upon the affected side though he did not recognize them as readily or as promptly as upon the right side. This improvement in sensation appeared to be quite general.

The pupils were as at the previous examination. There was a less marked conjugate deviation to the right and about the same ability to rotate the eyes to the left as at the previous examination. There was apparently no involvement of the sphincters. There were no rise of temperature, and no peculiarities of pulse or respiration.

There was still a marked flaccid palsy of both the arm and leg. The left knee jerk was possibly a little more active than at the previous examination. There was no ankle clonus. A well marked typical Babinski sign was present. The tendon reflexes in the left arm could not be elicited. It was stated by Miss Harkins, the nurse in chief, that the President had at various times moved his left arm, carrying it to his face and also that he had at various times moved his left leg. At this point the President interrupted Miss Harkins

---

[7] Loss of half of the usual area of vision.
[8] The part of the eye opposite the pupil.

saying that the movement of the left leg was purely "mechanical"; presumably the President meant "automatic" and that the movements were independent of his volition. Upon my requesting the President to move the affected members, he was unable to comply. Speech and mental faculties as before. Sphincters as before. The bladder was quite full though the record revealed that a normal amount of urine had been voided.

THE DIAGNOSIS made on October 2nd and confirmed at the subsequent examinations was that of a severe organic hemiplegia,[9] probably due to a thrombosis of the middle cerebral artery of the right hemisphere. An ingravescent[10] hemorrhage was deemed unlikely because of the extremely gradual onset, the final arrest of progress of the symptoms, the absence of marked disturbance of respiration and of consciousness and further because ingravescent hemorrhages are usually continuously progressive and finally fatal; an increasing impairment of consciousness, coma and marked respiratory disturbances preceding the outcome. It should be added that Dr. Grayson's statements concerning the urine excluded a uraemic attack as did also the symptoms presented by the patient.

At the time of the first consultation, the diagnosis was communicated to Mrs. Wilson and Miss Margaret Wilson. The subsequent course of the case revealed the hemiplegia to be persistent. Notwithstanding, because of the improvement noted at various times, Dr. Grayson thought it wise to issue general statements only.

The President was visited October 18th, 4.20 P.M. Little change was noted in the nervous symptoms. The motor hemiplegia was as marked as before. No history of the arm or leg having been moved voluntarily by the patient since the previous examination could be elicited.

The knee jerk upon the left side was a little more pronounced than at the last examination. There was also present a faint disappearing ankle clonus. A Babinski sign was present as before. A biceps reflex was now also elicited upon the left side. It was quite decided. None was elicited upon the right side. The President stated that the test for the biceps reflex upon the left side caused him pain, although the tapping upon the biceps tendon was very light and was done with the finger. The President now volunteered the statement that he had a painful or disagreeable tingling in the left arm and left leg.

Sensation was apparently still further improved. The sensory impairment still present included all forms of sensation. The President was able to differentiate to some extent between superficial

9 Paralysis of one side of the body.
10 Gradually increasing in severity.

and deep pressure. It can be readily understood that elaborate studies of sensation were out of the question as the President became very readily fatigued.

Conjugate deviation of the eyes were at this examination not a feature of the case, although the President allowed the eyes to turn—while at rest—to the right. He could, however, when requested rotate them quite well to the left. The pupils though perhaps a trifle smaller than noted previously, revealed no new peculiarities.

Mentally the patient was as at the last examination. He answered questions readily, cheerfully and accurately. At one time when I spoke of the abdominal muscles, he smiled and said those "abominable" muscles.

After my examination had been concluded, the President's bladder was examined by Drs. Young and Fowler. They expressed themselves as satisfied with the amount of urine that had been passed and with the cognate conditions. I was not present during their examination. Miss Harkins, the nurse in chief, stated in regard to the sphincters that the patient did not inform her of a bowel movement until after it had occurred; that he did not seem to be conscious of the desire to move the bowels, did not control the bowels, and did not speak of the bowel movement until after it had occurred.

Dr. Fowler stated that when he had introduced a suppository into the bowel, the sphincter did not grasp the finger; and that the sphincter was evidently weakened. Both Drs. Fowler and Young were unable to express an opinion as to the sphincter of the bladder, inasmuch as the difficulty in voiding the urine due to the enlarged prostate masked the condition.

At the subsequent conference in which Drs. Grayson, Ruffin, Fowler, Young, Stitt and myself participated, Admiral Stitt expressed uneasiness at a fall in the amount of urea eliminated. He also reported that a Wassermann test of the blood had proved negative.

At the time of the first examination, October 2nd, by Dr. Dercum, Dr. Grayson and Miss Harkins were present in the sick room. Admiral Stitt and Dr. Sterling Ruffin of Washington subsequently took part in a conference held in a separate room.

At the second examination by Dr. Dercum, October 4th, Dr. Grayson, Dr. de Schweinitz, Miss Harkins and the assistant nurse were present in the sick room. Subsequently a conference was held in a separate room in which Admiral Stitt participated.

At the examination, October 11th, by Dr. Dercum, Mrs. Wilson, Miss Margaret Wilson, Dr. Grayson, Miss Harkins and the assistant nurse were present in the sick room. Subsequently a conference was held in a separate room in which Admiral Stitt and Dr. Sterling Ruffin participated.

During my examination on October 18th, Mrs. Wilson, Dr. Grayson and Miss Harkins were present.[11]

T MS.

[11] We submitted Dr. Dercum's clinical evidence and diagnosis to Dr. James F. Toole and Dr. Bert E. Park and asked them to comment on them in light of modern medical knowledge. Dr. Toole is director of the Stroke Center of the Bowman Gray School of Medicine; Dr. Park is a neurosurgeon of Springfield, Missouri, and a member of our Editorial Advisory Committee. Both have served as medical consultants to us and have contributed essays on Wilson's neurologic illness in previous volumes.

Dr. Toole's commentary, in a letter to Arthur S. Link, June 12, 1990, follows:

"President Wilson's acute event has to be considered in light of the preceding episodes with which he had suffered. You told me that Drs. John Chalmers DaCosta and George DeSchweinitz were commissioned to examine President Wilson in Paris regarding a neurologic episode which we have discussed previously. In April 1919, they re-examined him and you tell me that Dr. DeSchweinitz felt that there had been no interval change and Dr. DaCosta left no record. In order to encompass the neurologic illness, I would have to consider this portion of President Wilson's illness in special detail before I could make a final opinion regarding the events which began on September 25-26, 1919, while in Colorado. President Wilson, after retiring for the night, developed severe headache and began drooling from the left mouth. He was urged to cancel the rest of his trip and the presidential train went back to Washington. On the 28th, you tell me that he had persistent headache but that he was able to walk from the train through Union Station, although he looked abnormal as he did so. Then, on October 2, at the request of Admiral Grayson, Dr. Francis X. Dercum was asked to consult. On October 2, Dr. Dercum was taken to see the President at about 4:30 in the afternoon.

"Admiral Grayson, according to Dr. Dercum's memorandum, recounted the history of the present illness. The transitory episode on September 25, with slightly flattened left face and drooping of the left side with some drooling which disappeared, suggests a transient ischemic attack. The President did well, including taking short walks, even on the afternoon of October 1. He attended a moving picture at the White House, which he enjoyed, but Dr. Grayson noticed that the President was drooling from the left side of his mouth. During the night and morning of Thursday, October 2, he had progressive weakness, first in the left leg, then the left arm and left face. This sequence of events is very important from a neurologic point of view and may suggest anterior cerebral artery syndrome due to infarction. Dr. Dercum suggested the possibility of a cerebral hemorrhage.

"On his examination, Dr. Dercum observed a flaccid left hemiplegia, a conscious, lucid patient who was slightly somnolent.

"Of importance is the fact that there was well marked anesthesia involving the left side of the face, head, neck, trunk, left arm and left leg in a distribution which is characteristic of organic disease.

"Dr. Dercum elicited stretch reflexes which were increased on the left compared with the right and he recorded a left Babinski sign. Dr. Dercum observed that both eyes were directed to the right and that vision was impaired in both visual fields. The pupils were unequal, the left distinctly larger than the right with the left pupil responding feebly and the right normally. Vital signs were said to be normal except for slightly labored respirations. Of importance is the fact that the examination of the heart is said to be normal. I find no record of blood pressure determinations or of auscultation of the head or neck.

"On Saturday, October 4, the President was visited once more by Dr. Dercum, this time accompanied by Dr. DeSchweinitz. Surprisingly, Dr. DeSchweinitz found no hemianopic fields and said that the conditions of the eye grounds were practically identical with those observed previously (one does not know what the previous examinations had revealed, however). Dr. DeSchweinitz attributed the slightly larger left pupil to the impaired vision in this eye. (I have sought expert advice regarding this from my colleagues in neuro-ophthalmology and they inform me that if the patient had impaired vision in the left eye with normal vision in the right, the pupils would be equal in size in a lighted room. Pupillary inequality would not exist. Therefore, this raises the question of an abnormality of the right pupil caused by Horners Syndrome.)

"Dr. DeSchweinitz did notice that the eyes deviated to the right but that the President could gaze to the left. There was no hemianopia and speech and mental faculties were normal.

"On October 11, Dr. Dercum again examined the patient. Sensory disturbance had disappeared or was markedly improved. The pupillary inequality was unchanged. Gaze preference to the right persisted. Flaccid left hemiplegia persisted. Left Babinski sign was still present.

"On page 4, Dr. Dercum synthesizes his diagnosis which, in fact, was a combination of diagnosis and formulation as to etiology and location of disease. He felt that a hemorrhage was unlikely because of the extremely gradual onset, the final arrest of the symptoms and the absence of marked disturbance of vital signs and of consciousness. I agree with him within limits. He also concludes that the patient had a right middle cerebral artery thrombosis. This is possible but not likely. More likely, is right internal carotid artery occlusion. This is notoriously slowly progressive in onset, often preceded by transient ischemic attacks and sometimes accompanied by Horners Syndrome with small pupil on the side of the carotid occlusion. This would account for the pupillary inequality.

"In his next paragraphs, Dr. Dercum records his visit of October 18, in which some improvement was reported to have taken place. The President now had tingling and unpleasant sensations in the left arm and leg and sensation had apparently improved even further. Gaze preference to the right persisted.

"From all of the above, it is my belief that the patient quite possibly had a right internal carotid occlusion. This would be superimposed on long-standing hypertensive vascular disease with lacunar infarctions. One, of course, must build mainly from symptomatic evidence; at this time, the best evidence I have had to date is that of Dr. Dercum. These notes by a skilled observer are invaluable and are very important source material."

Dr. Park's commentary, embodied in a memorandum which we received on June 19, 1990, follows:

"Dr. Dercum's detailed clinical description on October 20, 1919, and subsequent examinations substantiate that a major portion of Wilson's right hemisphere was affected by his stroke on October 2, including those deeply seated structures in the brain known as the thalamus and internal capsule. (The thalamus transmits sensory impulses to the superficial cortex of the brain from the spinal cord. The internal capsule is a small area contiguous to the thalamus through which nerve fibers controlling motor function pass from the cortex.) The latter observation reduces the cause of Wilson's stroke to one of two possibilities: he either suffered an occlusion of the right internal carotid artery in the neck or one of its two major branches within the brain (specifically, the middle cerebral artery) proximal to the origin of small tributaries supplying the thalamus and internal capsule; or he experienced a hemorrhage deep within the brain that involved these structures.

"Although the weight of the evidence strongly implicates a middle cerebral artery occlusion, as Dr. Dercum concluded, it is still possible that a hemorrhage could have occurred on the basis of Wilson's long-standing hypertension. That the stroke was large in any case is substantiated by the conjugate deviation of the President's eyes to the right during the acute phase of his illness; in neurologic parlance, such stroke victims are typically described as 'looking at their lesion.' Despite the doctor's claims, the fact that Wilson remained conscious throughout does not rule out a hemorrhage. Nor do such hemorrhages necessarily progress to coma or death. With the advent of CT scans and, more recently, MRI scans, we now know that many assumed vascular occlusions of arteries within the brain are actually hemorrhages. Even if strategically placed enough to cause profound deficits, small areas of bleeding invariably resolve and many large ones often do so without surgery.

"That Wilson suffered from poorly controlled high blood pressure for years is well documented inferentially by Dr. De Schweinitz' examinations of Wilson's eyes as early as 1906. Hypertension in fact had been the most likely cause of Wilson's retinal hemorrhage in that year, and not a 'stroke' from the carotid artery in the neck, as was once proposed. To anticipate no further episodes of bleeding either in the retina or the brain over the next thirteen years would be unlikely, particularly if the underlying condition remained untreated, as was true in Wilson's case. The fact remains, then, that the stroke of October 2 might still have been a hemorrhage, Dr. Dercum's surmise notwithstanding.

"Even so, most of the data seem to point to a vascular occlusion. That diagnosis is supported by the occurrence of a transient ischemic attack on September 25 and again on October 1. Most suggestive of all is Dr. Dercum's observation that Wilson's left-sided weakness on October 2 'slowly and steadily progressed.' Such stepwise progression is precisely how vascular occlusions of larger vessels such as the internal carotid and middle cerebral arteries manifest themselves. Insofar as the latter is concerned, 90 per cent of such occlusions occur as a result of small thrombi or debris passing into the distal circulation from a more proximal source, such as a carotid artery plugged with athero-sclerosis.

"That the small lenticulostriate vessels themselves (or the thalamus and internal cap-sule that they supply) were involved is signified by the thalamic deficits Dr. Dercum so precisely described (i.e., a well demarcated loss of sensation on the left side of Wilson's body). Such 'hemianesthesia' does not occur with involvement of the more superficial cortex alone, as would be seen in more distal middle cerebral artery occlusions. It is of particular interest that Wilson later volunteered that he had 'a painful or disagreeable tingling' in his left arm and leg. Neurologists and neurosurgeons would readily recog-nize this as a 'thalamic syndrome' arising from injury to that area. Moreover, a flaccid paralysis of the arm and leg suggests that the contiguous internal capsule supplied by these penetrating vessels was involved, as more distal middle cerebral artery occlusions affect the face and arm with lesser involvement of the leg.

"Why is this distinction so important? Simply because injury to these deeply seated structures on both sides of the brain leads in time to certain recognizable behavioral disturbances that typified Wilson from late 1919 onward. These characteristically result from hypertension, and it has already been suggested that such earlier small strokes on the opposite side of the brain could have accounted for the difficulty Wilson experi-enced in using his right hand. That is precisely why the profound stroke on October 2 had such distressing behavioral implications for the stricken President, a circumstance that may not have arisen had his stroke been limited to the more superficial cortex."

A Memorandum by Dr. Grayson[1]

On [blank] I noticed in the morning a little saliva on the Presi-dent's pillow. I examined his face and it seemed to me to be slightly flattened and drooping on the left side but the change was so slight that I could not be certain about it, and later when I re-examined him it had disappeared. However, notwithstanding, I insisted upon his giving up the trip and immediately returning to Washington. This he strenuously resisted, saying that it was a matter of con-science with him to do his duty. He was exceedingly ⟨exhausted⟩ *prostrated* and for some time previously had ⟨been neuras-thenic⟩ *shown considerable nervous exhaustion*. However, he rested continuously in bed on the train until we reached Washing-ton. By this time he had in a measure recovered his strength.

After his return to the White House his gain in strength contin-ued and he was able to take an occasional automobile ride and a short walk. He was insistent upon this. I thought it wise, however, to communicate with Dr. F. X. Dercum of Philadelphia and ar-

[1] Words in angle brackets deleted by Dr. Grayson; words in italics, CTGhw.

It is impossible to know exactly when Dr. Grayson wrote this memorandum. The following scenario seems probable to us. Dr. Grayson, thinking that a congressional inquiry into the extent of Wilson's disability might soon occur, prepared this statement for submission to a congressional committee. He then sent it to Dr. Dercum, for his use in preparing the memo-randum printed above. Dr. Dercum returned Dr. Grayson's memorandum to him. Grayson then revised it as indicated in our transcript. We believe that Grayson's memorandum was written at the time of the events it describes.

In any event, Dr. Grayson's memorandum makes one important fact clear—that Mrs. Wil-son did veto the divulgence of the fact that Wilson had suffered a stroke and that Grayson, acting in conformity with her wishes, decided to fall back on what he called general state-ments. The second significant fact comes out in Dr. Dercum's letter to Dr. Grayson of Feb-ruary 16, 1920, printed at that date. It is obvious from this letter and its enclosure that the consultants in Wilson's case had agreed not to divulge that Wilson had had a stroke and to refer all questions concerning Wilson's physical condition to Dr. Grayson for public comment.

range for a consultation. The time was fixed for Friday morning, October 3rd.

On Thursday morning, October 2nd, the President complained of some numbness and weakness in his left side. This symptom seemed to become somewhat more marked during the day and I at once consulted my friends Dr. Sterling Ruffin and Admiral Stitt and also phoned to Dr. Dercum to come by the first train. In the meantime the weakness in the left leg became more pronounced and also made its appearance in the left arm. A drooping of the lower half of the left side of the face also became evident.

Dr. Dercum arrived at the White House and made an examination about 4.30 P.M. By that time a well marked loss of power had made its appearance in the left leg, left arm and lower half of the left side of the face. It was also noted that the President had lost sensation in the affected limbs and also in the left side of the trunk and left side of the head, face and neck. In other words a hemiplegia, both motor and sensory, had become established. The palsy was flaccid in character. The knee jerk, however, could still be elicited upon both sides, that upon the left side was less marked than upon the right. There was no ankle clonus. A well marked Babinski sign was also present upon the left side. It was noted that both eyes were directed to the right, i.e. there was conjugate deviation of both globes to the right. There was also an impairment of both visual fields, suggesting a left lateral hemianopsia. However, the fields could not be well outlined. The pupils were *somewhat* unequal, the left pupil ⟨was distinctly⟩ larger than the right. Both pupils, however, responded to light. There was no involvement of the sphincters. There was no rise of temperature, pulse and respiration revealed nothing abnormal.

During the examination the President was fully conscious and cooperated with Dr. Dercum during the examination; protruded his tongue, his lips, showing his teeth, opening and closing his eyes and performing other gestures in response to various requests and directions.

The President was in full command of all of his faculties. He spoke clearly without hesitation and with an unimpaired enunciation.

On Saturday, October 4th, the President was visited by Dr. Dercum and Dr. de Schweinitz and examined about 11.30 A.M. Dr.

We have not found Dr. Stitt's statement on Wilson's general condition in the Grayson Papers or in the Stitt Papers, DLC.

It is ironical that Mrs. Wilson, in her *My Memoir*, p. 288, wrote: "We lifted the President into his bed. He had suffered a stroke, paralyzing the left side of his body. An arm and one leg were useless, but, thank God, the brain was clear and untouched. Such is the story of that tragic morning hour of October 2, 1919, as my memory presents it to me. So far as was possible I checked my recollections with the data of Dr. Grayson, before his lamented death in 1938."

Dercum made another examination confirming the symptoms previously noted. Dr. de Schweinitz reported that no true hemianopsic fields now existed so that this symptom if present had receded.

The dilation of the left pupil was also a little less marked than at the previous examination. While the eyes when at rest still deviated to the right, the President was able to deviate them to the left though he did not perform conjugate deviation to the left as well as to the right. Speech and mental faculties as before.

On October 11th, Dr. Dercum again examined the President shortly after 11 A.M. It was now noted that the hemianaesthesia[2] had lessened so as to have been replaced by a moderate degree of hypaesthesia. The President was able to recognize ⟨light impressions with⟩ *the touch of* cotton wool upon the affected side though he did not recognize ⟨them⟩ *it* as readily or as promptly as upon the right side. This improvement in sensation appeared to be diffuse and was noted over all parts of the affected side.

The pupils were as at the previous examination. There was a less marked conjugate deviation to the right and ⟨about the same⟩ *improvement in the* ability to rotate the eyes to the left ⟨as at the previous examination⟩. There was no involvement of the sphincters. There were no rise of temperature, and no peculiarities of pulse or respiration.

There was still a marked flaccid palsy of both the arm and the leg. The left knee jerk was possibly a little more active than at the previous examination. There was no ankle clonus. A well marked typical Babinski sign was present. The tendon reflexes in the left arm could not be elicited. It was stated by *Mrs. Wilson* Miss Harkins the nurse in chief & *Miss Powderly, assistant nurse* that the President had at various times moved his left arm, carrying it to his face and also that he had at various times moved his left leg. Upon my requesting the President to move the affected members, he was unable to comply. *At the time of Doctor Stitt's making a puncture of a finger of the left hand for a hemocyte count the President jerked his hand away.* Speech and mental faculties as before.

The marked subsidence of the hemianaesthesia and the improvement in some of the associated symptoms justified the inference that these had been distance symptoms and had not been directly due to the lesion.

⟨At the time of the first examination, October 2nd, by Dr. Dercum, Dr. Grayson and Miss Harkins were present in the sick room. Admiral Stitt and Dr. Sterling Ruffin of Washington subsequent[ly] took part in a conference held in a separate room.

⟨At the the second examination by Dr. Dercum, October 4th, Dr.

---

[2] Lack of feeling or sensation on one side of the body.

Grayson, Dr. de Schweinitz, Miss Harkins and the assistant nurse were present in the sick room. Subsequently a conference was held in a separate room in which Admiral Stitt participated.

⟨At the examination October 11th, by Dr. Dercum, Mrs. Wilson, Miss Margaret Wilson, Dr. Grayson, Miss Harkins and the assistant nurse were present in the sick room. Subsequently a conference was held in a separate room in which Admiral Stitt and Dr. Sterling Ruffin participated.⟩

Besides having Dr. Dercum in consultation as to the neurological condition and Dr. de Schweinitz as to ocular manifestations, I have consulted daily with Dr. Sterling Ruffin, a prominent general practitioner of this city & professor of medicine in Geo. Wash. Univ. and Admiral Stitt the head of the Naval Medical School as to his general condition and statements from day to day.

THE DIAGNOSIS made October 2nd and confirmed at the subsequent examinations was that of a ⟨vascular lesion⟩ *thrombosis* involving the internal capsule of the right cerebral hemisphere.

At the time of the first consultation, the diagnosis was at once communicated to Mrs. Wilson and Miss Margaret Wilson and without any reservations. For various reasons it was thought that the hemisplegia might possibly prove transitory in nature; and in spite of the President's rather good mental condition—though he was slightly somnolent—hemiplegia of other origin could not be absolutely excluded. It was thought wise therefore to make only a general statement regarding the President's illness. The subsequent course of the case revealed the hemiplegia to be persistent. Notwithstanding, because of the undoubted improvement noted at various times, I (Dr. Grayson) thought it wise to issue general statements only. Further, Mrs. Wilson, the President's wife was absolutely opposed to any other course.

Use Admiral Stitt's statement for the Genral Statement—add Dr. Dercum's technical statement of the neurological examination, under some such title as, "Dr. Dercum's detailed statement of his neurological examination is as follows:"

In view of the fact that the first manifestation of weakness of the left side of the face, noted supra, had cleared up so rapidly, it was hoped that the same improvement in the involvement of the left face, leg and arm, which occurred on the 2d of October, might have a similar termination. Doctor Dercum's second examination on Oct. 4th made it apparent that such a course could not be expected.

It was then desired by all the consultants in the case to make a full statement of the Presidents condition ⟨to the public⟩ *but in view of the wishes of _____ this was deferred.*

T MS.

A Statement by Dr. Grayson[1]

[c. Oct. 29, 1919]

The President's continued favorable condition makes it seem that no useful purpose is being served by the issuance of daily bulletins. For the present, therefore, announcements will be made Tuesdays, Thursdays and Saturdays. The country may be assured that if at any time, should it become advisable, the daily bulletins will be resumed.

The President's physicians have been acting with what seemed to them the greatest possible degree of frankness in keeping the country informed from day to day, and in consonance with that policy they take opportunity to make this statement:

In a nervous breakdown, such as the President has suffered, it should be borne in mind that recovery is necessarily slow and is stimulated principally by relaxation and complete quiet and rest. It is with continued difficulty that the President's physicians prevail upon him to accept this form of treatment to its fullest extent. He insists upon thinking and talking about public business, and if his progress continues he may be permitted from time to time to take up some light work. There is no foundation whatever for fears that his exhaustion may have impaired his mentality. His appetite continues good, his digestion has been restored to normal and he suffers no organic difficulty. His blood pressure and heart action are normal, his eyesight has shown no impairment in comparison with a year ago, and the degree of physical exhaustion which was the natural reflex action from the drain on his nervous energies has happily almost entirely passed away.

It is impossible to diagnose with complete accuracy the ultimate effects of his nervous disability because they are, so far, being steadily overcome by his favorable physical condition. If the favorable progress continues it seems justifiable to hope that in a few weeks he may be out and about again. It is only possible now, however, to stimulate this progress with complete rest, relaxation, diversion and absence of worry and work. It remains to be seen whether the President's physique is sufficient to recoup him entirely from the rigors of several years of work which have exhausted his nervous energies.

A set back is not expected, but in the case of a man of his age it is always to be regarded as one of the possibilities. The country will be promptly advised if any change in his condition warrants a departure from the program of three announcements a week.

T MS.
[1] Dr. Grayson probably prepared this statement and then decided to issue the following

bulletin, which was published in the *Washington Post*, Oct. 30, 1919, in a story by Robert T. Small, which in turn was obviously inspired by Grayson and Tumulty:

"President Wilson's improvement has reached the point where it would not be surprising to those who know his condition if he should receive in person this afternoon the King and Queen of the Belgians. His progress has been so satisfactory his physicians have decided to discontinue the issuance of daily bulletins. These two facts should set at rest for all time the many erroneous and sometimes malicious statements that have gained currancy regarding the President.

"King Albert and Queen Elizabeth are scheduled officially to have tea with Mrs. Wilson this afternoon. If the President has rested well during the night there is a strong chance that the memorable tea will be served in his bed chamber rather than in the drawing room of the stately mansion. The President has been looking forward keenly to this visit of the king and queen, and unless Rear Admiral Grayson should interpose a veto at the last moment he will have his limited share in the festivities of the unique occasion.

"The bulletin issued yesterday respecting the President was as follows:

" 'The President's improvement steadily continues. He is eating, sleeping, digesting and assimilating well. His present improvement has now reached a point where it is not considered necessary to issue daily bulletins. The people of the country will be promptly advised of any changes in his condition.

" 'Grayson,
" 'Ruffin,
" 'Stitt.'

"This bulletin will be a great disappointment to those volunteer specialists who have attributed every known ill to the President, but it will be a source of extreme satisfaction to the people of the United States as a whole. The misconceptions of the President's illness and the misstatements concerning it have known no bounds. Propriety, ethics and at times even common decency seem to have been forgotten in the spread of alarming reports as to the nature of Mr. Wilson's unhappy collapse.

"Partial excuse has been made for some of these misstatements on the ground that the bulletins issued from the White House were so meager and lacking in detail as to give rise to false conclusions. As a matter of fact the physicians attending the President have claimed from the first that the bulletins have said all there was to say and that nothing had been concealed.

"The most persistent of all the tales that have been peddled about the President is the one that he broke down completely while speaking at Pueblo, Colo., on what proved to be the last active day of his transcontinental tour. This story, false in virtually every particular, has been told all over the country. It pictured the President as stopping in the middle of his Pueblo speech, struggling vainly for words to go on with, and plainly showing symptoms of facial paralysis. One version of the story had Mrs. Wilson bursting into tears on the stage of the Pueblo auditorium.

"It is difficult to understand how these reports could have got abroad except through malicious intent. Certainly they had no start among those who traveled with the President, as I did.

"The President's Pueblo speech was one of the most effective of his entire trip. It is true he was very tired when he reached Colorado, had had a number of sleepless nights and had suffered for eight days from a persistent headache. He had spoken in the forenoon at Denver to an immense crowd in the Denver auditorium and when he got off his special train at Pueblo he promised Mrs. Wilson he would not talk longer than twenty minutes.

"Under the influence of the friendly greeting he received [and] the sympathetic response of his audience, he spoke for nearly an hour. His peroration was a remarkably dramatic one. He told of the mothers who had lost sons in the war and who had greeted him on his trip with a 'God bless you, Mr. President.'

"The President said he had been puzzled at first as to why these grieving mothers should bless him who had advised Congress to declare war, who had ordered their sons overseas, and who had consented to their being put in the most difficult parts of the battle lines. He knew, at last, he said, that it was because they believed their sons had died for something that vastly transcended any of the immediate and palpable objects of the war; they believed their sacrifices had been made that other sons might not be called upon to lay down their lives in other wars.

"The President told also that day of a visit he had paid to the cemetery at Suresnes, near Paris, where so many of the American dead in France are buried; of his meeting the poor old French women who have adopted the graves as their very own, and who tend them with a motherly care and love which knows no bounds.

"There were few dry eyes in the President's audience when he concluded. Mrs. Wilson had heard the story before, but she had never heard the President tell it more effectively, and the tears of those in front deeply affected her. Her own eyes were not undimmed, and it was this circumstance alone which could be held to justify any part of the remarkable Pueblo tale which has been told the country over.

"Before the President stopped at Pueblo Dr. Grayson had arranged that after the train had proceeded several miles out of that city, it would be stopped, so the President could take a long walk. He was sadly in need of exercise.

"During the more than three weeks he had been on the road he had scarcely done more than step from his private car into an automobile, from the automobile to the speaking platform, thence back into the machine and back to the train.

"No President had ever laid out such an exacting itinerary or exhausting program for a long tour as did Mr. Wilson.

"During the walk the afternoon after leaving Pueblo, the President and Mrs. Wilson covered probably 3 miles of a somewhat dusty road.

"The President stopped at several farm houses, giving the Colorado farmers and their families the surprise and thrill of a lifetime. He came back to the train grinning broadly and bearing several souvenirs of his tramp—a cantaloupe, a cabbage and some beets.

"During that night, as the train was traveling toward Wichita, Kans., the President suffered from sleeplessness and an attack of nervous indigestion. He had reached the end of his strength. He had jokingly remarked several days before that having used up his constitution he was living on his 'by-laws.' As the train neared Wichita the President sought permission to go on with his program. The crowd which had gathered in the pretty little Kansas city, he was told, was the largest in its history. The President did not want to disappoint them. He was afraid they would think him a 'quitter.'

"Mr. Wilson did not realize at the time how thoroughly exhausted he was. But Dr. Grayson did and forbade any further effort by the President. Dr. Grayson might not have been strong enough to enforce his will against that of the President, but he won over Mrs. Wilson and Secretary Tumulty, and, in the face of this triple alliance, the Pesident gave up. There were tears in his eyes truly enough when he reluctantly gave his consent that the train should be turned directly back to Washington."

ADDENDA

To Winthrop More Daniels[1]

My dear Daniels,   Baltimore 23 February, 1895

I have just received your letter of yesterday,[2] and hasten to reply.

I hope that you will use my letters, written to you at Wesleyan about your coming to Princeton in any way you think proper.

It has been my confident expectation that, at the end of this year, you would be advanced to the rank of full professor, and I shall be very much disappointed and chagrined if you are not. To me your work has been altogether satisfactory. There can be do [no] doubt about your having filled the place most adequately and ably, and you are not mistaken in believing that my understanding of the arrangement made with you at the outset was, that, the College being satisfied with your work, you should receive the promotion, the salary, of course, being determined by the resources of the College, but not smaller than the smallest salary given with the rank of full professor.[3]

I sincerely hope that Dr. Craven's[4] note does not mean that the Trustees have done anything incompatible with these expectations, and I stand ready to help you in any way open to me. Perhaps, if you see the President,[5] he would like to see this letter.

Faithfully & Cordially Yours,   Woodrow Wilson

ALS (IGK).
[1] He was at this time an Assistant Professor of Political Economy at Princeton. See W. M. Sloane to WW, May 8, 1891, n. 3, Vol. 7. He had been an instructor at Wesleyan University, 1891-1892.
[2] It is missing, as are the letters mentioned in the next paragraph.
[3] He was appointed Professor of Political Economy in the spring of 1895.
[4] Elijah Richardson Craven, D.D., member and clerk of the Board of Trustees of the College of New Jersey.
[5] That is, Francis Landey Patton.

To Frederick A. Duneka[1]

My dear Mr. Duneka: Princeton, N. J. October 23rd, 1909.

I have not written again about the essays simply because a sudden flood of engagements overwhelmed me and I have not had time to turn back to them again. Your opinion that it would not be possible to get the book ready for the trade at Christmas time made me feel that there was no great hurry, inasmuch as they could in any case be made ready for either of the seasons of next year that you thought best to plan for.

I am sincerely obliged to you for your kind letter and will send the essays on as soon as I have had a moment to touch one or two of them up in places where they are in need of repair.

I am obliged to you for your little note about Colonel Harvey.[2] I sincerely hope that he is recuperating successfully.

Cordially and sincerely yours,   Woodrow Wilson

TLS (IGK).
[1] General Manager of Harper & Brothers. Wilson was replying to F. A. Duneka, Oct. 4, 1909, Vol. 19.
[2] This note is missing.

To William C. Liller[1]

My dear Colonel Liller: [Trenton] July 20, 1911.

Thank you sincerely for your letter of July eighteenth.[2] I am glad to have removed from your mind the very erroneous impressions about my relation to the party and its regular organization.

I wish sincerely that it were possible for me to write the article that you ask for. It is a real disappointment to me to be obliged to say that it is literally impossible but I will write to Mr. Stockbridge[3] in New York and ask him if he can supply you with what you want.

Your frequent letters and invaluable information, I am warmly obliged for.   Cordially yours,   Woodrow Wilson

TLS (WC, NjP).
[1] Of Indianapolis, chairman of the National Democratic League of Clubs.
[2] It is missing.
[3] That is, Frank Parker Stockbridge.

Eleven Letters and a Telegram to Charles Wellman Mitchell[1]

My dear Charlie,   Princeton, 16 July, 1898

The announcement of your marriage[2] comes as the completest sort of a surprise; but it is the most delightful surprise I have had in many a long day! I congratulate you with all my heart,—and I no less congratulate Mrs. Mitchell! Her husband is one of the finest fellows, and one of the truest, in the world. It has been my good fortune to know many a splendid fellow, young and old, but I know of none better than he is, or more lovable. I congratulate her with all my heart!

And *you*, my dear boy,— what shall I say to you? I hope, I believe, this is the beginning of your best happiness. It is just what I could have wished, just what I *have* wished, for you. I shall be impatient to *see* you happy, as you deserve to be.

I write in all love and comradeship; Mrs. Wilson joins in the heartiest messages of godspeed to you both; and I am, as always,
Your affectionate friend   Woodrow Wilson

[1] Wilson's classmate and close friend in the Class of 1879 at Princeton; M.D., University of Maryland, 1881; at this time a pediatrician and Professor of Diseases of Children at the University of Maryland Medical School in Baltimore.
[2] To Florence M. Crowe on July 14, 1898.

My dear Charlie,   Princeton, 13 May, 1899
Of course you understand that you, and the rest of the usual gang,[1] are to stay with me at the Reunion. We are counting on your coming, and could not ourselves enjoy the Reunion if we did not have the unbroken crowd here under our own roof. A welcome awaits you of the biggest, warmest, most home-coming sort; and I am,
     As ever,   Affectionately Yours,   Woodrow Wilson

[1] That is, the Witherspoon Gang, Wilson's closest friends among his classmates at Princeton.

My dear Charlie,   Princeton, 18 Feb'y, 1902
Your kind letter has just been handed me. Thank you with all my heart. It would be a genuine pleasure to me to stay with you,[1] and I wish it were possible. But I am already promised,—to the Reids[2] (#608 Cathedral).
Thank Mrs. Mitchell most warmly for me, and keep all affectionate messages for yourself. It looks as if every minute of Friday and Saturday were mortgaged,—but I shall hope *somehow* to see you.
          As ever, affectionately yours,   Woodrow Wilson

ALS (MdHi).
[1] Wilson was to speak at the twenty-fifth anniversary of The Johns Hopkins University. His address and a news report of it are printed at Feb. 21 and 22, 1902, Vol. 12.
[2] That is, to Professor and Mrs. Harry Fielding (Edith Gittings) Reid.

My dear Charlie,   Princeton, New Jersey, 25 February, 1902.
I need hardly tell you what a keen disappointment it was to me to be in Baltimore twenty-eight hours and not have a half hour even in which to look you up.
My dear father is a very old gentleman now (he will be eighty on Friday) and old age has brought a thickening of the arteries. He is liable to have an attack at almost any time, and it is of course my duty to be with him if possible when it comes. I therefore got to Baltimore just before the exercises on Friday and left just after

those on Saturday.[1] In between times I had hardly time to get more than a hurried glimpse of the Reids, with whom I was staying. I saw nobody that I did not see at Music Hall, at Mr. Gildersleeve's[2] dinner, or at the reception of Friday evening.

It was thoughtful of you to send me the clipping. It gave me vastly more praise than I deserved; but the tone of it made the cockles of my heart warm, and I am grateful.

Give my warmest regards to Mrs. Mitchell, and remember that I am always, with deep affection,

Faithfully Your Friend,   Woodrow Wilson

[1] Wilson received the honorary degree of Doctor of Laws from the Johns Hopkins on Saturday morning, February 22, 1902.
[2] Basil Lanneau Gildersleeve, Professor of Greek at the Johns Hopkins.

My dear Charlie,   Princeton, New Jersey, 9 May, 1902.

Thank you most sincerely for your letter of the seventh. I have sent it on to my aunt.[1] It answers her question most satisfactorily. I do not know when she will come, or what arrangements she expects to make; but I thank you for the thoughtful offer you make to meet her, and it may be that I shall have to avail myself of your kindness.

The last paragraph of your letter went to the right spot. I don't think you know, for I have never known how to show, my deep feeling for you, my old comrade, or my constant affectionate thought of you. I hope I shall be here to greet C.W.M., jr. when he comes!

With warmest regards from Mrs. Wilson to you both, As ever,

Faithfully and affectionately Yrs.,   Woodrow Wilson

WWTLS (MdHi).
[1] Marion Woodrow (Mrs. James) Bones.

My dear Charlie: Princeton, New Jersey. 30 January, 1903.

I was very much touched by your affectionate letter of yesterday, and thank you for it with all my heart. My father's death has gone very hard with me.[1] I find myself undergoing a more considerable reaction than I at first realized. The only thoughts with which I can comfort myself are that he had rounded out his days, and that he has left me an inheritance which I can never forget of high ideals and honorable living. My chief comfort, my dear fellow, is the sympathy of my friends, among whom I count you one of the dearest.

Affectionately yours,   Woodrow Wilson

[1] Dr. Wilson died on January 21, 1903.

My dear Charlie: Princeton, N. J. 6 June, 1904.

I do not know what your preference will be about lodging in Princeton at the reunion, but I write to beg that you will be my guest at Prospect so that the old gang may have their individual reunion as before.

I would have written long ago, if I could have sooner made sure that I would not be obliged to have official guests. I now know that I shall be free and I have quite set my heart on your coming to Prospect. We have room enough to make the whole crowd comfortable.   Affectionately yours,   Woodrow Wilson

My dear Charley: Princeton, N. J. May 10th, 1909.

I write for both Mrs. Wilson and myself to say that we eagerly hope that you will be our guest during Commencement and the Reunion of Seventy-Nine. I am inviting the rest of the gang, and we should be very much disappointed if we could not get them together again under our roof. Poor Bob Henderson[1] cannot come, but we are strongly hoping that all the rest can.
                Always affectionately yours,   Woodrow Wilson

   [1] Robert Randolph Henderson.

My dear Charles: Princeton, N. J. Nov. 19th, 1910

Your telegram was delightful and I thank you for it with all my heart. Please accept my love in return.
                Affectionately yours,   Woodrow Wilson

TLS (MdHi).

Dear Charlie,   Princeton, New Jersey 14 Jan'y, 1912

Thank you with all my heart for your invitation. Its affectionate generosity binds me more closely than ever to you.

I do not think I shall attend the Convention.[1] My instinct is against it. But, if I do, you may be sure I will keep your delightful invitation in mind, and accept it,—unless my political managers *command* me otherwise.

I think you must know how my affection for you has grown the years through. It makes me very happy to have you think of me as you do.   Affectionately Yours,   Woodrow Wilson

ALS (MdHi).
   [1] The Democratic National Convention, which was to meet in Baltimore on June 25, 1912.

My dear Charles: The White House November 22, 1915.

I wonder if you would be free to come down to a sort of im-promptu class dinner at the White House on Tuesday next, the thirtieth at seven o'clock.[1] It would give me a great deal of pleasure if you could. Please let me know at your earliest convenience. I want to see as many of the fellows together again as possible.

Cordially and faithfully yours,   Woodrow Wilson

TLS (MdHi).
[1] Wilson held this dinner for seventy-seven of his classmates on November 30, 1915. See Edith B. Galt to WW, Nov. 28, 1915, n. 2, Vol. 35.

The White House Nov 29 1915

Shall expect you to come direct to the White House and stay with me over night   Woodrow Wilson

T telegram (MdHi).

Six Letters to John Grier Hibben

My dear Jack,   Princeton, N. J. 4 June, 1906.

I want to tell you before the Board meets that the Finance Com-mittee will recommend the increase of your salary to $4,000. Of course the recommendation will be adopted.

This was resolved upon by the Committee at a meeting held some weeks ago, when it became evident that we should be obliged to offer at least that amount to get a psychologist, the Com-mittee feeling very strongly that it would be wrong to offer another four thousand dollar salary in a Department in which there are al-ready two salaries of that amount without increasing yours to the maximum, it being clear to everybody that you were the only man in the Department whose usefulness to the University was clearly at a maximum. This is an action of mere justice and good sense. I have told you of it beforehand in the hope that it might simplify some of the plans immediately ahead of you.

Always,   Your devoted friend,   Woodrow Wilson

WWTLS (NjP-Ar).

My dear Jack: Princeton, N. J. May 17th, 1907.

In response to the invitation of Lafayette College that Princeton be represented at the celebration of the 75th anniversary of the founding of the college, I have written to say that you have been designated as the official representative of the University. I hope that you will find it convenient and pleasant to add this function to your other errand.

Always affectionately yours,   Woodrow Wilson

TLS (NjP-Ar).

My dear Jack,   Princeton, N. J. 29 May, '09[1]

Your note reached me last night. I need not tell you how much I regret your feeling that you ought to leave the Committee on Discipline, but I do not feel that I am at liberty to withstand your desire expressed after a mature consideration of the matter; and certainly long, faithful, and efficient service have entitled you to release from a very arduous and trying task. I will act upon your wish with the greatest regret but with the confidence that you are acting for the best.

Always Faithfully Yours,   Woodrow Wilson

[1] Wilson was replying to J. G. Hibben to WW, May 27, 1909, Vol. 19.

My dear Jack,   Princeton, N. J. 28 October, 1909.[1]

You may be sure I understood perfectly what Stockton told me. It disturbed me very much that you should feel so distressed. I think your fears about what might come out of further committee work on your part are quite exaggerated. I do not see how what you apprehend *could* come out of it. But I do not feel that I can decline your request as you put it, and that I must, just because you desire it, excuse you from further service, at any rate for the present—until your fears prove unfounded—on the Committees on Non-Athletic Organizations, on Examinations and Standing, and on The Course of Study. Your service on these committees has been of real value to the University and I wish both personally and officially to thank you warmly for the time and thought you have given them.

To me personally it is a sad change to see you withdraw, but you may be perfectly sure that I interpret the action just as you would wish me to interpret it. I have no right, in the circumstances, to urge my wishes as against your own; and I am earnestly desirous to serve your happiness in any way I can.

Ever Faithfully Yours,   Woodrow Wilson

I hope that you will feel free to discuss with me at any time your future relation to the work of the Graduate School.   W.W.

[1] Wilson was replying to J. G. Hibben to WW, Oct. 28, 1909, Vol. 19.

My dear Jack,   Princeton, New Jersey 21 Apr., 1910.

I dare say you know that it is going to be necessary to reduce the teaching force in Philosophy (I mean the non-professional force, of course) to four preceptors and one instructor. Conferences with Ormond[1] have convinced me that this will be possible without overburdening any one—except, perhaps, Johnson,[2] who is unselfishly willing—; but it will necessarily involve a very careful rearrangement and concentration of the work.

I know how willing you will be to take part in this; but I did not want you to be taken by surprise by any changes that might, directly or indirectly, affect you. I do not know what your plans are for next year; but I was afraid that you might be thinking of renewing your arrangement with the City College, and I feel that it would be unwise for you to do so in the circumstances. Perhaps you know the plans for the Dept already and this note is unnecessary
                    Always Affectionately Yours,   Woodrow Wilson

[1] Alexander Thomas Ormond, McCosh Professor of Philosophy.
[2] Roger Bruce Cash Johnson, Earl Dodge Preceptor in Philosophy.

My dear Mr. President,   Princeton, New Jersey 31 Dec., 1912

Unfortunately I am bound by many imperative engagements to be at my office in Trenton throughout Thursday, and so cannot accept your kind invitation. I am none the less obliged to Mrs. Hibben and you for your kindness.
                    Sincerely Yours,   Woodrow Wilson

ALS (NjP-Ar).

Eight Letters to William Frank McCombs

My dear McCombs,   Sea Girt, New Jersey 23 July, 1912

I am off for a few days, to write my letter of acceptance (it is impossible to write *anything* at Sea Girt), and before going want to send you an earnest (and affectionate) warning to have no dealings, directly or indirectly, with Murphy[1] till I can see you and tell you why I write. I would not do so were I not sure you would understand.
    In haste,   Cordially & faithfully Yrs,   Woodrow Wilson

[1] Charles Francis Murphy, head of Tammany Hall.

My dear McCombs,   Sea Girt, New Jersey 5 Aug., 1912

The statement in the morning papers about Pence[1] will do a great deal of harm and be everywhere misunderstood. Cannot you correct it without hurting Pence?

The newspaper men were told in New York that Crane[2] would be Treas. They got it, they say, from no one connected with headquarters.   Hastily   Woodrow Wilson

ALS (gifts of Mr. and Mrs. John P. Renshaw, CSt-H).
[1] Thomas Jones Pence, former Washington correspondent of the Raleigh *News and Observer* and Wilson's press representative in Washington, 1911-1912; associated with the publicity bureau of the Democratic National Committee during the campaign of 1912. The *New York Times*, Aug. 5, 1912, reported that a job had been found for Pence in the Wilson campaign organization, and that he had been without any "official designation" for "several weeks."
[2] Charles Richard Crane. The intimation that Crane would become treasurer of the Democratic National Committee came from a news report in *ibid.*

My dear McCombs: Trenton, N. J. August 6, 1912.

I have had a talk with Dr. Waldron and Mr. Harkless,[1] who are interested in the movement to draw our negro people into an independent league,[2] which will serve as their halfway station between the Republican and the Democratic parties. After having talked with these gentlemen, it seems to me they are talking very good sense, and I commend them to your attention.
              Faithfully yours,   Woodrow Wilson

[1] The Rev. John Milton Waldron and William C. Harris (not Harkless), both of Washington, D. C. About Wilson's meeting with them, see the news report printed at July 17, 1912, Vol. 24.
[2] The National Independent Political League.

My dear McCombs: Sea Girt, N. J. August 14, 1912.

I am greatly distressed by your illness.[1] I feared from what you said when I was with you last that perhaps it was coming on. I cannot tell you how deeply I sympathize with you. I hope with all my heart that it is only temporary and that the spell will be brief; and I beg, as I begged you before, that you will take the doctor's advice very literally and follow it entirely. It would be an entirely unjustifiable sacrifice to do otherwise now. You have won the honors already and you can afford to let the rest of us do the work now.

In haste, with warmest regard and sympathy,
              Faithfully yours,   Woodrow Wilson

TLS (gifts of Mr. and Mrs. John P. Renshaw, CSt-H)
[1] Wilson was replying to W. F. McCombs to WW, Aug. 13, 1912, Vol. 25.

My dear McCombs: Sea Girt, N. J. August 23, 1912.

Thank you warmly for your little message, dictated to Lyons on August twenty-first.[1] I am distressed that you are not getting well faster, but I would be more distressed still if you forced it too fast and take any risks. I shall take pains to see to it that nothing halts because of your absence and I beg that you will dismiss all anxiety on the subject for, if you do that, you will come back to us so much the sooner.

With affectionate regard,

Faithfully yours,   Woodrow Wilson

TLS (WC, NjP).
[1] Wilson was replying to M. F. Lyons, Aug. 21, 1912, Vol. 25.

My dear McCombs,   The White House, 5 Apr., 1913

I have hardly a minute to myself these days, but I will try to see you at two to-morrow afternoon[1]

In haste   W.W.

ALI (gift of Mr. and Mrs. John P. Renshaw, CSt-H).
[1] Wilson saw McCombs at the White House at 2 p.m. on Sunday, April 6, 1913.

Dear McCombs,   The White House 20 April, 1913

I have had to wait for Sunday to answer your letter,[1] which I deeply appreciated, because I wanted to answer it with my own hand, and on a week day. I now know, that is literally impossible.

I am greatly pleased and relieved to have your final permission to send your name in for the French post, and I shall do it just as soon as I can get some of the other diplomatic posts fixed for certain. The bill to increase salaries will, I believe, pass, but no bill goes through here in less than several weeks, and I cannot keep my list back until the fate of this one is finally determined. You will understand that. You would be deeply gratified if you could know how deeply pleased everyone is that you have found it possible to arrange to go.

Everything essential, everything that really counts, is going very well down here,—in spite of the eagerness of some of the papers that something should go wrong.

Thank you for writing your suggestions as they come to you. They keep us in mind of men we wish to find places for.

Faithfully and Affectionately Yours,   Woodrow Wilson

ALS (gift of Mr. and Mrs. John P. Renshaw, CSt-H).
[1] Wilson was replying to W. F. McCombs to WW, April 13, 1913, Vol. 25.

My dear McCombs: The White House September 9, 1913

I am heartily glad to hear of your great gain in strength.[1] It cheers us all. It is what we have been ardently hoping for, and you may be sure I am quite ready to take up with you again the question of the appointment to Paris if you desire. I have so far done nothing towards selecting another man.

I did not overlook your suggestion about your brother and the Hot Springs Reservation,[2] but I have run up against a very big snag in the attitude of the two Senators from Arkansas.[3] They seem very much set upon having the man of their own choice, who is excellently fitted for the position, as far as I can learn, and I would have to make it an issue with them. Do you think it would be wise to do that, in view of your own probable appointment as Ambassador to France?

In haste, with warmest regards and congratulations,
                    Faithfully yours,   Woodrow Wilson

TLS (gift of Mr. and Mrs. John P. Renshaw, CSt-H).
    [1] Wilson was here replying to W. F. McCombs to WW, Aug. 24, 1913, ALS (WP, DLC), in which McCombs wrote (from Geneva, Switzerland) that his health was much improved and that he would be glad to discuss the matter of his appointment as Ambassador to France within a month or two "if by that time you have been unable to make a selection." About McCombs' vacillation over accepting the appointment, see the letters between Wilson and McCombs printed in Vol. 27.
    [2] W. F. McCombs to WW, Aug. 24, 1913 (second letter of that date from Geneva), about his brother Robert.
    [3] Joseph Taylor Robinson and James Paul Clarke.

APPENDIX

THE AFTERMATH OF WILSON'S STROKE

By Bert E. Park, M.D., M.A.

Previous essays in this series have discussed Woodrow Wilson's underlying medical condition from 1919 onward as an organic brain syndrome induced by long-standing hypertension. The following essay will discuss the contribution of his serious stroke of October 2, 1919 to that condition, with particular emphasis on the President's thought and behavior during the early post-stroke period.

The psychologic manifestations of strokes were poorly defined in Wilson's day and have been intensively studied only during the last two decades. It was not until 1975 that the results of these studies were taken into account in the classification of mental disorders. Only then was what is known as a "focal psychosyndrome" induced by brain injury recognized in this country as a basic organic mental disorder,[1] of which Wilson's behavior by 1920 appears to have been an archetype. It includes disorders of emotion, impaired impulse control, and defective judgment in the presence of relatively well preserved intellectual function. Moreover, what might be called the substrata of the victim's personality are magnified in bold relief. As one medical authority has described them, strokes may induce a "marked and almost grotesque accentuation" of prior personality traits.[2] In Wilson's case, these traits included intransigence, stubbornness, insistence upon having his own way, self-righteousness, a tendency to fall back upon principles as a means of finding some basis for policy-making, and other characteristics described below.

Wilson's case history during the period covered by this volume may be divided into two distinct phases: the period from the occurrence of the stroke to the end of January, during which Wilson was physically too weak to play a directing role in affairs; and the period from early February through the spring of 1920, during which he entered the recovery phase and began to attempt to take aggressive control of domestic and international policies. If he clearly manifested some attributes of an evolving organic brain syndrome in

---

[1] Lipowski, Z. J., "Organic Brain Syndromes: Overview and Classification," in *Psychiatric Aspects of Neurologic Disease*, D. F. Benson and D. Blumer, eds., New York: Grune and Stratton, 1975, p. 11. The term "focal psychosyndrome" is attributed to M. Bleuler, "Psychiatry of Cerebral Diseases," *British Medical Journal*, 2:1233, 1951.

[2] Lipowski, Z. J., "Organic Mental Disorders: Introduction and Review of Syndromes," in *Comprehensive Textbook of Psychiatry*, H. I. Kaplan, A. M. Freedman, and B. J. Sadock, eds., 3d edn., Baltimore: Williams and Wilkins, 1980, pp. 1388-1389.

both phases, they were certainly underscored in bold relief after January 1920.

During the first phase of his illness, Wilson was unable to do much more than react to events and problems, in part because he was so isolated as to be unable to assess issues in context due to the limited amount of information that he received about them. Yet it is doubtful that he could have done much more on account of his prostration and short attention span. When the subject matter proved too complex or detailed, others were obliged to think and act for him; indeed, virtually all of his correspondence and public statements had to be written in his name. Any business that Mrs. Wilson and Tumulty deemed to be not truly urgent (and even some that was) was put in hold; consequently, the cabinet was left to conduct executive business as best it could. The feebleness of Wilson's attempts to marshal his thoughts enough to give general direction to the conduct of public affairs matched what any neurologist would expect from a recent stroke victim.

This phase encompassed the first Senate vote on the Versailles Treaty in November. Wilson's behavior both before and after that vote clearly reflected his illness. That is to say, his refusal to accept the so-called Lodge reservations or even to consider any policy other than one of no concessions and no compromise was a manifestation of his disease-induced intransigence.

Even on those few occasions when Wilson took initiatives, the best that he could do was to fall back upon earlier concepts and ideas that bore no relation to the requirements of the moment. His groping attempt to find some way to bypass the Senate by holding some kind of national referendum on the League was clearly a throwback to his earlier belief in the superiority of the parliamentary system of ministerial responsibility. In this and other matters, Wilson's rigidity, irascibility, and petulance were typical of the organic brain syndrome from which he suffered. The documents in this volume well illustrate the degree to which the stricken President exhibited these traits during both phases of his illness under discussion.

Wilson entered the recovery phase in early February. He resumed dictating letters to Swem on February 2 and was allowed out of his sickroom to take automobile rides. His stamina increasing, Wilson began to take initiatives of his own. For example, he managed to compose some diplomatic notes. In another initiative he discharged his Secretary of State; in another, he drafted or heavily revised the letter to Senator Hitchcock of March 8, 1920, which effectively ended any hope of winning the Senate's consent to the ratification of the Versailles Treaty when it voted for a second time on the treaty on March 19, 1920.

Perhaps consistent with the belief in some circles that, like Wilson's viral illness in Paris, his aggressiveness, irascibility, and pugnacity now signified an improvement in his condition, most neurophychologists today would point out instead that what really deserves notice is the accentuation of what might be called his temperamental defects by his stroke during the recovery period. Wilson's intransigence in all matters now became pervasive. Regarding the Adriatic question, he simply refused to reopen the subject and threatened publicly to withdraw the treaty from the Senate if England and France made any concession on Fiume to Italy. As for Viscount Grey's pronouncement regarding the desirability of accepting reservations, Wilson took it as an affront and administered a stinging rebuke to the former Ambassador.

Still other symptoms of the organic brain syndrome, such as a perplexing degree of "selective" amnesia, manifested themselves. He claimed that he had not known that Lansing had been holding cabinet meetings since October, even though he had been informed of this fact several times. He again blotted out his memory regarding his knowledge of the Treaty of London before 1919. That would be entirely consistent with the psychopathological residua of a major stroke; for such memory lapses reflect the stroke victim's lack of initiative to recall what he actually remembers.[3]

Moreover, Wilson's charge that Lansing had usurped presidential prerogative by holding cabinet meetings signified an increasingly rigid and suspicious individual's obsession with controlling his environment. Whether Wilson's manner in dismissing Lansing was "childish" or even "unbelievably stupid," there is no doubt that his actions were characterized by petulance and peevishness. That, too, is consonant with the behavior of other victims of a stroke-induced psychosyndrome; for impulsiveness is a cardinal manifestation of that disorder.[4] Ray S. Baker was on target, then, when he described Lansing's dismissal as "the petulant and irritable act of a sick man."

Emotional lability is yet another sequela of an organic brain syndrome. Witness Wilson breaking into tears on February 14, 1920, upon hearing Cummings' effusive description of him, only to recover control of his emotions long enough to castigate his opponents for having "disgraced America." As Baker ruefully acknowl-

---

[3] Hecaen, J., and Albert, M., *Human Neuropsychology*, New York: John Wiley and Sons, 1978.
[4] Lipowski, "Organic Mental Disorders," p. 1389.

edged, "illness destroys the controls of the governable elements of a strong nature."

Wilson was never so compromised as to have suffered from overt dementia. He recovered his ability to write and speak coherently, lucidly, and gracefully. Even his intransigent positions make sense if viewed within the perspective of his *a priori* principles, but they still reflected a disease-induced accentuation of his personality. He simply heard what he wanted to hear and acted on what might be called a distorted logic, at least one that took no account of political realities. As such, Wilson was unable to appreciate the consequences of his actions—yet another symptom of his underlying condition.[5] His letter to Hitchcock of March 8, 1920, highlights that fact in poignant, if tragic, prose.

Scholars who seek to understand the causes for the failure of the treaty in the United States would do well to study Wilson's physical and mental state from the perspective of modern medicine's understanding of the organic personality syndrome. That this condition was far advanced in Wilson's case by the spring of 1920 is now a matter of record. The materials in this volume further substantiate the assumption that illness was one of the prime causes of the defeat of the Versailles Treaty.

[5] *Ibid.*

INDEX

NOTE ON THE INDEX

THE alphabetically arranged analytical table of contents at the front of the volume eliminates duplication, in both contents and index, of references to certain documents, such as letters. Letters are listed in the contents alphabetically by name, and chronologically within each name by page. The subject matter of all letters is, of course, indexed. The Editorial Notes and Wilson's writings are listed in the contents chronologically by page. In addition, the subject matter of both categories is indexed. The index covers all references to books and articles mentioned in text or notes. Footnotes are indexed. Page references to footnotes which place a comma between the page number and "n" cite both text and footnote, thus: "418,n1." On the other hand, absence of the comma indicates reference to the footnote only, thus: "59n1"—the page number denoting where the footnote appears.

The index supplies the fullest known form of names and, for the Wilson and Axson families, relationships as far down as cousins. Persons referred to by nicknames or shortened forms of names can be identified by reference to entries for these forms of the names.

All entries consisting of page numbers only and which refer to concepts, issues, and opinions (such as democracy, the tariff, money trust, leadership, and labor problems), are references to Wilson's speeches and writings.

Four cumulative contents-index volumes are now in print: Volume 13, which covers Volumes 1-12, Volume 26, which covers Volumes 14-25, Volume 39, which covers Volumes 27-38, and Volume 52, which covers Volumes 40-49 and 51.

INDEX

A. Mitchell Palmer: Politician (Coben), 354n1

Acosta, Julio, 186

"Admiral Grayson—Medical Culturist" (Winans), 496n1

Adriatic question, 260-61, 263-64; Anglo-French-American proposal on, 168-78; new Anglo-French proposals for settlement, 264-66, 298-99; and Nitti compromise, 264,n4; Wallace on Anglo-French proposal, 300-305, 318-20; Lansing on, 313-14, 340-41, 367, 371-72; Wallace fears Yugoslavia will give in to Anglo-French proposals unless U.S. intervenes, 314-16; Polk on, 323-24, 480-81; and Yugoslavia's reply to Anglo-French proposal on, 331-35; WW's unyielding position on, 335-36, 352-53, 398-402, 445-46; Lansing conveys WW's position to Wallace, 342; D. W. Johnson on, 367, 368-69, 370-71; WW's suggested changes of Johnson's text on, 375-80; WW's decision to withdraw Versailles Treaty if Anglo-French Adriatic proposals are accepted, 402; first British and French reply, 436-42; France and Britain on WW's threat to withdraw treaty, 442; Straus on WW's response to, 445; WW's reply to Anglo-French note on, 459-63; delay in delivery and publication of notes on, 473; second British-French reply, 481-83; Britain and France agree to withdraw previous proposals and let Yugoslavia and Italy negotiate, 482; Dr. Park on WW's health and, 527

Aftermath of War: Bainbridge Colby and Wilsonian Diplomacy, 1920-1921 (Smith), 464n1

agriculture: and WW's Annual Message to Congress, 110

Agriculture, Department of: Houston resigns as Secretary, 349

Aguilar Barquero, Francisco, 95, 153, 186

Albania: and the Adriatic question, 171, 175, 266, 299, 300, 302, 315, 319, 331, 334, 369, 377, 400, 437-38, 439, 461-62, 480, 482; memorandum on form of mandate for, 176-78

Albert, King of the Belgians, 455, 490; two thank-you notes to WW and WW's response, 30, 61; Grayson on public doubt that WW met with, 136; birthday wishes to WW, 230; and visit to WW's sick room, 51n1

Albona (now Labin, Yugoslavia), 169, 175, 370

Albrecht-Carrié, René, 169n3

Alexander, Joshua Willis, 193; appointed Secretary of Commerce, 142, 317; and railroad situation, 184; House on appointment of, 185

Alexandra, Queen Mother: 27-28, 28; birthday greetings to WW and WW's thank you, 235, 237

Allied Maritime Transport Council: and *Imperator* controversy, 8,n1, 34

Alsace, 200, 248

Alsace-Lorraine, 249n1

Amalgamated Sheet Metal Workers' International Alliance, 431

Ambrosius, Lloyd E., 276n1, 328n2

American Express Company: returned to private control, 222,n1, 223

American Federation of Labor, 431, 475; and coal situation, 179-80; and railroad situation, 424

American Medical Association, 432

American Red Cross: and White House sheep, 57n1

Anatolia, 27, 449

Anderson, Albert Barnes, 141,n1, 143

Argyro Castron (Argyrokastron, Greece), 299, 301, 315

Armenia, 27, 56, 309, 449-50; and wheat to, 13-14

Armistice Commission, 150n1

Armistice Day: WW's statement on, 7

arms limitation: *see* disarmament

Army (U.S.): *see* United States Army

Ashurst, Henry Fountain: on Democratic caucus on treaty, 62-64, 384; on Senate votes on treaty, 62-64; on Jackson Day message and banquet, 252, 256, 263

Asia Minor, 26, 27, 158, 450

Assling Triangle, 170

Associated Press, 118n2, 487

Austria: and Hungary's demands, 447

Austria-Hungary, 440; and annexation of Bosnia and Herzegovina, 368n1

Autobiography of William Allen White, 62n2

Avezzana, Camillo Romano, 458,n4

Axson, Stockton (Isaac Stockton Keith Axson II), brother of EAW, 324, 520

Azerbaidjan, 309

Bailey, Thomas A., 276n1, 328n2

Baker, Newton Diehl, 7n1; reaction to WW's no-compromise statement, 193; on withdrawal of U.S. troops from Siberia, 219-21; and Tumulty's draft letter to Hitchcock on reservations, 278n1; on repatriation of Polish Americans in Haller's Army, 373, 375, 389-90; Lansing shares news about his resignation with, 414; rumor of resignation of, 436,n1; and Cabinet meetings during WW's illness, 456, 496

Baker, Ray Stannard, 348, 362, 365, 385, 428; interview with House, 61-62; his book on WW, 320, 325, 335; and WW's health, 320-21, 527, 527-28; on need for compromise in treaty fight, 320-22, 326-27, 359-60; EBW on Baker's observation on the need to preserve the spirit of the League, 335; and WW's tentative decision to resign, 362n1

balance of trade: and WW's Annual Message to Congress, 79, 108

Balfour, Arthur James, 375; and D. W. Johnson's letter on Adriatic question, 367, 370-71
Balfour Declaration, 358, 361
Balkans, The: Vénisélos on, 162
Ball, Lewis Heisler, 200-201, 336
Baltimore *Sun*, 394, 395
Banat, The, 465
Bandholtz, Harry Hill, 150n1
Bankhead, John Hollis, 199n1, 200
Banking and Currency Committee (House of Reps.): and C. Glass, 52
Barker, Allen E., 425, 426-27,n1
Barnes, Julius Howland: and Poland's request for grain, 4, 5-6, 12; and wheat to Armenia, 13-14
Baruch, Bernard Mannes, 270, 359
Bass, Elizabeth Merrill (Mrs. George), 3, 307
Bates, J. Leonard, 354n1, 392n1, 473n1
Belgium: King Albert thanks WW for hospitality and WW responds, 30-31; invited to first meeting of Council of League of Nations, 272; and war criminals, 364n1
Beneš, Eduard, 443
Benoist, Charles, 407n1
Benson, William Shepherd, 228,n1
Berthelot, Philippe-Joseph-Louis, 35,n3, 263, 303
Bevan, Arthur Dean: on WW's health, 432; Dercum on comments of, 435
Birkenhead, Baron (Frederick Edwin Smith), 382,n1
Bituminous Coal Commission, 145-46, 206-209, 246,n1
Bleuler, M., 525n1
Bliss, Tasker Howard, 444, 472; on Turkish situation, 27; recommendation he stay in Paris to represent U.S. government, 117, 118; and U.S. troops in Rhineland, 156
Board of Railroad Wages and Working Conditions, 422
Bolsheviks and Bolshevism, 133, 344, 443; Lansing on, 56; Lansing recommends withdrawal of U.S. troops from Siberia, 219-21; and Hapgood's resignation, 234n1,3,4; Lloyd George on, 308-309
Bones, Helen Woodrow, 325
Bones, Marion Woodrow (Mrs. James), 517,n1
Bonillas, Ignacio, 120n1
Borah, William Edgar: and Mexican situation, 120; and treaty fight, 200-201, 244, 328n2, 336, 338; on Grey's letter, 381,n1; Glass on, 387
Borden, Sir Robert, 163n6
Bosnia, 368,n1
Boué, Amie, 160,n4
Bowman, Isaiah: and Adriatic question, 178,n4, 458,n3
Bowman Gray School of Medicine, 507n11
Boxer Rebellion, 491
Boyana River, 177
Brandegee, Frank Bosworth: and Mexican situation, 120n1, 152n2; and treaty fight, 200-201, 328n2, 336, 338

Brandeis, Alice Goldmark (Mrs. Louis Dembitz), 359
Brandeis, Louis Dembitz: on railroad situation, 222; on prohibition, 262; concern for Balfour Declaration, 358, 361; R. S. Baker meets with, 359
Branting, Karl Hjalmar, 342
Brazil: invited to first meeting of Council of League of Nations, 272
Brotherhood of Locomotive Engineers, 431
Brotherhood of Blacksmiths & Helpers, 424
Brotherhood of Boilermakers & Iron Shipbuilders, 424
Brotherhood of Locomotive Firemen and Enginemen, 198n2, 431
Brotherhood of Maintenance of Way Employees and Railway Shop Laborers, 426
Brotherhood of Railroad Signalmen of America, 425, 431
Brotherhood of Railroad Trainmen, 431
Brotherhood of Railway Carmen of America, 424, 431
Brotherhood of Railway Clerks, 425
Brotherhood of Railway Conductors, 198n2
Brotherhood of Railway and Steamship Clerks, Freight Handlers, Express and Station Employees, 431
Bryan, William Jennings, 256; on treaty ratification, 261,n1; Lansing compares WW's treaty position to, 267, 269; F. I. Cobb on treaty position of, 270n2
"Bryan-Wilson Split on the Treaty" (*Literary Digest*), 270n2
Bryn Mawr College, 485
Buchanan, James, 32
Bulgaren in ihren historischen, ethnographischen und politischen Grenzen, 160,n3
Bulgaria: Lansing on proper U.S. role toward, 68; Vénisélos on, 159-64; and appointments, 205
Bullitt, William Christian, 417
Burleson, Albert Sidney, 274; on WW's Annual Message and his ability to perform his duties, 123-24; and railroad situation, 184, 457; Lansing on reaction to WW's no-compromise statement, 193; suggested as delegate to international conference on communications, 228,n1; and list of senators who hindered treaty ratification, 338-39, 343; meets with House, 444-45; and Cabinet meetings during WW's illness, 457
business: WW on labor and, 84-85, 113-15

Cabinet (U.S.): *see* Wilson, Woodrow—Cabinet
Calder, William Musgrave: and treaty fight, 94, 200-201, 337
Cambon, Jules Martin, 163n6
Capper, Arthur: and treaty fight, 94, 200-201, 337
Capps, Edward, 297
Carlisle, England: WW named citizen of, 184
Carranza, Venustiano, 129, 134,n6, 135, 136, 140n1; talk of severing diplomatic re-

lations with, 120n1, 121; Lansing on oil crisis and, 210-11,n1; Lansing on, 240, 241, 242
Carrigan, E., 431
Carter, William Samuel, 468,n2
Castoldi, Fortunato, 163n6
Catt, Carrie Clinton Lane Chapman (Mrs. George William), 396
Caucasia, 27
Cavalla, Greece, 164
Chamberlain, (Joseph) Austen: on cancellation of inter-Allied war debts, 475,n1, 477, 477-78
chemical and dyestuffs industry, 80-81, 109-10
Cherso (now Cres, Yugoslavia), 264n4, 265
child labor, 98n1
China: and Lodge reservations, 39; and appointments, 205, 296; see also Shantung settlement
Chinese Eastern Railway, 220, 221
Christian Science Monitor, 428n1
Cilicia, Turkey, 449
civil service: discussed in draft of Annual Message to Congress, 76-77
Civil Service Commission: and appointments to, 205
Clagett, Maurice Brice, 16,n1, 21, 391n1
Clark, Champ (James Beauchamp), 185
Clarke, James Paul, 524,n3
Clemenceau, Georges, 26, 227, 348; and Rumania, 35; on departure of U.S. representatives in Paris, 102, 117-18, 151; note of Dec. 9 to Italy on Adriatic question, 168-78, 323; Wallace on Adriatic proposal of, 260,n1, 318-20; and Adriatic proposal of Lloyd George and, 263, 264-66, 298-305, 376, 398; and Russian situation, 307; gives ultimatum to Yugoslavia on Adriatic question, 314
Clerk, Sir George Russell, 101n2
Close, Gilbert Fairchild, 297, 321; resignation of, 344
coal strike situation: Hines on railroad situation and, 23; and strike, 141n1,2,3; WW's proposal to union leaders, 142-45; Garfield on, 145-46; Tumulty on WW's statement and Garfield principle, 153-54; WW on, 154-55, 206-209; Cabinet action on strike, 166, 167, 457; WW thanks union leaders for help in resolving, 178-80; miners accept WW's proposal, 179; Garfield's resignation, 180-82; draft of letter to Bituminous Coal Commission, 206-209; see also Bituminous Coal Commission
Cobb, Frank Irving: on treaty, 66, 270n2
Cobb, Margaret Hubbard (Mrs. Frank Irving), 66
Coben, Stanley, 354n1
Colby, Bainbridge: WW's choice for Secretary of State, 464,n1; Grayson on WW's decision to appoint, 472-73; Polk willing to assist, 472
collective bargaining: WW on, 85, 114-15, 424

College of Charleston, 458n3
College of New Jersey, 514,n4
Colorado coal strike (1914): mentioned, 4
Colt, LeBaron Bradford: and treaty fight, 94, 200-201, 337, 339
Columbia University, 367
Commerce, Department of: McCormick declines appointment as Secretary of Commerce, 95
Commission on Greek Affairs, 163,n6
Comprehensive Textbook of Psychiatry (Kaplan, Freedman and Sadock, eds.), 525n2
Conditions in the Near East: Report of the American Military Mission to Armenia, 450,n4
Congressional Record, 66th Cong., 1st sess., 58n1, 120n1, 126n1
Congressional Record, 66th Cong., 2d sess., 120n1, 259n, 284n1, 338
Constantinople, 26, 27, 56, 161, 449
Constitution (U.S.): see United States Constitution
cost of living: and WW's Annual Message to Congress, 81, 82, 83, 111; and coal strike, 141n2, 146-47, 154; and railroad crisis, 198, 391n1, 406-407, 412, 420-24, 428-30
Costa Rica: issue of recognition of, 65, 94-95, 153,n1, 186, 204, 229-30, 235, 245, 317; and appointments, 205, 317
Council of the Heads of Delegations, 272; and protocol controversy, 118n2, 149n2
Council of the League of Nations: see League of Nations
Council of Ten: and Greece, 163
Crane, Charles Richard, 262-63, 522,n2; and appointments, 296, 317, 407-408; offers vacation home to WW, 425
Crane, Richard, 447; on letter from Masaryk urging ratification, 443,n1
Craufurd-Stuart affair, 3, 88, 90-91, 217, 235, 239
Craven, Elijah Richardson, 514,n4
Croats, 368n1
Crowe, Sir Eyre, 163n6; and Adriatic question, 168, 178, 323
Culberson, Charles Allen, 63
Cumberland, Charles C., 120n1, 128n1
Cummings, Homer Stillé, 527; suggested as Lansing's successor, 419, 427-28
Cummins, Albert Baird: and treaty fight, 94, 200-201, 337; and railroad legislation, 195,n1, 196, 197
Cummins railroad bill, 195,n1, 196, 197
Cummins-Esch bill: see Esch-Cummins bill
Currie, Archibald A., 191n2
Curtis, Charles: and treaty fight, 200-201, 337
Curzon, George Nathaniel, 1st Marquess of Kedleston, 263; and Syria and Turkish Empire issue, 25-26; and Craufurd-Stuart affair, 88, 91
Czech troops in Russia: repatriation of, 220, 390
Czechoslovakia: Vénisélos on, 162; and Adri-

Czechoslovakia: (*cont.*)
atic question, 299, 302, 442, 463; Minister to, 443n1; and Hungary's demands, 447, 465

Da Costa, John Chalmers, 507n11
Dalmatia: and Adriatic question, 170, 172, 265, 266, 299, 301, 302, 305, 318n2, 334, 341, 440, 463
Daniels, Josephus, 16, 93, 216, 416n2, 486; on Mexican situation, 122-23; Cabinet meeting on coal crisis, 141, 166; and railroad situation, 184, 457; reaction to WW's no-compromise statement, 193; Cabinet meeting on railroads, 222; on general leasing bill, 473
Daniels, Winthrop More: on railroad bill, 475,n1, 480; and Princeton professorship, 514
Daugherty, Harry Micajah, 405n1
Davidson College: establishment of WW chair at, 191-92,n2, 213
Davies, Joseph Edward, 205,n3
Davis, John William, 442, 483; on Syria and Turkish Empire, 25,n1, 26; and Craufurd-Stuart affair, 88, 91; and WW's tentative decision to resign, 362n1; on Borah's comments on Grey's letter, 380, 381; question of presence at meeting of Premiers, 382-83, 391; and war crimes, 407, 408
Davis, Norman Hezekiah, 322; on *Imperator* controversy, 7, 33; on Reparations Commission's chairmanship, 10, 11-12,n2; ideas for treaty ratification, 104-105; on general cancellation of inter-Allied debts, 475, 476-77, 478
Davis, Westmoreland, 41-42,n1, 52, 60
Day, Clive, 163n6
De Mohrenschildt, Ferdinand, 494
De Mohrenschildt, Nona Hazelhurst McAdoo (Mrs. Ferdinand), 494
De Schweinitz, George Edmund, 502, 506, 507n11, 509, 510
Déak, Francis, 101n2
Dedeagatch (now Alexandroupolis, Greece), 164
Democratic National Committee, 522n1,2
Democratic National Convention (1912), 518,n1
Democratic party: and reservations situation in Senate, 28, 72, 165-66; WW wants each vote against Versailles Treaty recorded, 43; caucus and vote on Lodge resolution for ratification, 62-64; and Mexican situation, 120,n1; Lansing on effect of WW's no-compromise statement on, 192; and election of Senate minority leader, 192, 194, 273, 274,n1; Hitchcock seeks WW's advice on compromise to avoid split in, 203; WW's hopes that no proposal or compromise will come from caucus of, 206; and Jackson Day message, 247, 252, 257; Bryan on treaty ratification and, 261n1; Lansing on WW's need to compromise on treaty or wreck, 267-69; House on WW's

treaty position and, 270; Hitchcock on bipartisan meeting on treaty, 283-84; bipartisan committee addresses Article X and hopeful of compromise, 311-12, 312-13,n1; WW's list of senators who hindered ratification of treaty reviewed by Burleson and Hitchcock, 336-37, 338-39; House on, 348; R. S. Baker on treaty reservations and, 359; senators caucus on treaty, 384; Glass on Taft reservation and, 387-88,n1; WW on role of regarding treaty proposals, 405; Glass on treaty negotiations and, 410; Cummings on, 419n1; Hitchcock fears Lodge reservations are being supported by more senators from, 466; Tumulty on Democratic support for Lodge reservations, 479; WW on in *1911*, 515; and blacks in *1912*, 522
Denikin, Anton Ivanovich, 308, 309
Denmark: resignation of Hapgood, 233-34,n1-4
Department of: *see* under the latter part of the name, such as Commerce, Department of; State, Department of
Derby, Lord, 17th Earl of (Edward George Villiers Stanley), 318
Dercum, Francis Xavier, 4, 32, 37, 99, 187, 507-508,n11, 509, 510; to stop regular visits due to WW's improvement, 211; declines comment on WW's health, 403; on WW's health, 433-34, 435; clinical reports on Wilson after stroke, 500-507; and Grayson's memorandum on WW's illness, 507n1
Des Moines *Successful Farming*, 330n1
Dillingham, William Paul: and treaty fight, 200, 202, 337
disarmament, 60, 281; and Lodge reservations, 294
Dodecanese Islands, 449
Doheny, Edward L., 134
Dresel, Ellis Loring: on list of war criminals, 364
Drin River Valley, 300, 302, 303
Droppers, Garrett, 414n2, 454
Drummond, Sir Eric, 274, 275, 306, 452
Du Bois, Arthur Wood, 150n1
Duneka, Frederick A., 514-15,n1
Dunne, Peter Finley, 132n1
Dutasta, Paul-Eugène, 118n2

Edge, Walter Evans: and treaty fight, 94, 200-201, 337
Edward (Edward Albert Christian George Andrew Patrick David), Prince of Wales, 28, 42; visits WW, 31-32; thanks EBW and WW for hospitality, 36-37, 71; WW thanks for New Year's wishes, 236
Egan, Maurice Francis: on appointment of R. U. Johnson as Ambassador to Italy, 474
Egerton, George William, 355n1
Egypt, 49
Eight Years with Wilson's Cabinet, 1913-1920 (Houston), 133n2, 249n1, 475n1
Election of 1920, Hines on railroad situation and effect on, 22; Grayson mentions, 135;

treaty as campaign issue, 263, 267, 384; WW not seeking reelection, 267; F. I. Cobb on, 270n2; Grayson on potential candidates, 325; L. Y. Sherman on, 328n2; and A. M. Palmer, 347; Burleson on, 445

election laws: WW's inquiry on and Palmer's answer, 202-203, 214-15

Electrical Workers of America, 424

Eliot, Charles William, 297,n2

Elisabeth (Elisabeth Valerie), Queen of the Belgians, 31, 136, 230, 511n1

Elkins, Davis: and treaty fight, 200, 202, 337

Ellis Island, 9

employment: WW on returning servicemen, 80, 109

Endicott, Henry Bradford, 141,n4

Ernst, Eldon G., 416n2

Esch, John Jacob: and railroad legislation, 195,n1

Esch-Cummins bill and Act, 467,n1, 474, 475n2; Hines on, 468; Houston urges WW's action on, 480; W. M. Daniels on, 480

excess profits tax: and WW's Annual Message to Congress, 78, 107-108

Faisal, Prince, 25-26, 449

Fall, Albert Bacon: and Mexican situation, 120-21,n1, 123, 125, 127-28, 152; meets with WW on Mexican situation, 129-32, 132-33, 139-40; on WW's health, 132, 138; EBW's notes on WW's meeting on Mexico with, 133-35; WW reaction to prayers by, 133n2; sends WW transcript of report on Mexico, 140,n1; and Underwood resolution, 199n1; and treaty, 200-201, 337; and Honolulu Oil case, 405n1

Fall resolution, 131, 132, 133, 134, 140; Pittman on, 127-28; Grayson on spirit behind, 136-37; WW on opposition to, 152,n2

Fatio, Robert, 98

Federal Control Act, 22-23, 226

Federal Reserve Act, 52, 195

Federal Trade Commission: appointments to, 205

Fernald, Bert Manfred: and treaty fight, 200-201, 337, 338

Ferris, Scott: on general leasing bill, 473, 474

Finland: Lansing on recognition of, 236

First International Labour Conference: see International Labour Conference, First

First Presbyterian Church of Gastonia, N.C., 191, 213

Fiume, 170, 172, 173-74, 264-66,n4, 301, 302, 303, 304, 305, 318n2, 341, 399, 400; Anglo-French proposals for, 264-66, 298, 300, 301, 302, 303, 318-20; and Yugoslavia's reply to Anglo-French Adriatic proposal, 331; D. W. Johnson on, 368, 370-71; WW on, 376-77; Anglo-French reply to WW on, 437-38, 439; Polk on France's position on, 450-51; WW on, 460-61

Fletcher, Henry Prather: and Mexican situation, 120n1, 121, 134; resignation of, 310,n1, 397, 448

Foch, Ferdinand, 149,n2

Food Control Act: WW on extension of, 82, 111

food relief: Lloyd George on Russia and, 308-309; Glass on Europe's urgent need, 339-40,n1

Foreign Relations, Committee on (Senate), 54, 277; and Mexican situation, 120-21,n1, 123, 125, 127, 128, 136, 152,n1,2; and Lodge resolution on termination of war, 126n1; Lansing suggests his meeting with, 148; mention of WW's interview with, 165, 206

Forrester, James J., 425, 431

Forster, Rudolph, 36, 52; and railroad situation, 426

Fosdick, Raymond Blaine: resignation as Under Secretary General of the League, 274-76,n1, 286, 306, 310, 348

Foster, John Watson, 417n3

Fourteen Points, 49; House on, 348,n2

Fowler, Harry Atwood, 506

France, Joseph Irvin: and treaty fight, 200-201, 337, 338

France: and Reparations Commission chairmanship, 11; and Rumania, 35; proposals for Adriatic settlement, 168-78, 264-66; invited to first meeting of Council of League of Nations, 272; and list of war criminals, 364,n1; and Palestine, 373, 449; WW's firm position on Adriatic proposals, 375-80, 398-402, 445-46; and demands on Holland for William II, 407n1; response to WW on Adriatic proposals and on his threat to withdraw Versailles Treaty, 436-42; and Turkish treaty, 449; WW's reply to Anglo-French note on proposed Adriatic settlement, 459-63; debt to U.S., 475,n1; in 1913 WW offers McCombs ambassadorship to, 523, 524,n1; see also France and the United States, and under the names of spokesmen for, such as Clemenceau, Georges

France and the United States: and issue of departure of U.S. representatives in Paris, 100, 101-102, 117-18, 148-49, 150-51; Wallace to remain in Paris, 156-57; relations mentioned in Jackson Day message, 248; and French press, 260n1

Frazier, Arthur Hugh, 157,n1; controversy over WW's proposed appointment of, 353, 366, 383-84, 398, 408, 413, 414, 451-54

Freeman, Frances, 345-46,n1

Frelinghuysen, Joseph Sherman: and treaty fight, 200-201, 337

Friedrich, Stephen, 101n2

Friedrich Wilhelm Viktor August Ernst (former Crown Prince of Germany): on Allied demand for German war criminals, 397

Friendly Road, The: New Adventures in Contentment (J) Grayson [R. S. Baker]), 61,n1

Frondichmann, Maurice C. A., 98

Fuel Administration: and Garfield resignation, 181, 181-82, 185, 186

Galindo, Hermila, 134,n5
Galleani, Luigi, 145n1
Galloway, Charles Mills, 205,n2
Gardner, Lloyd G., 417n3
Garfield, Harry Augustus: and coal strike, 3, 141,n2, 143, 144, 145-46, 153-54, 166, 167, 457; on coal commission being of an advisory nature, 180-81, 181-82; resignation of, 181, 181-82, 186; WW on resignation of, 185
Garraty, John A., 328n2
Garrett, John Work: resignation of, 41,n1
Gary, Hampson, 413-14,n1, 453
Gastonia, North Carolina, 191,n2, 213
Geddes, Sir Auckland (Campbell), 483-84n1,2
general leasing bill, 473,n1
George V (of Great Britain), 32, 483; thanks WW for hospitality shown son, 42; birthday wishes to WW, and WW's thank you, 230, 231
George Washington University, 510
Georgia, Russia, 309
Germany: ratification of Versailles Treaty and exchange of ratifications with Allied Powers, 101,n1; and issue of protocol, 148, 149,n2, 150-51; and Allies' demand for war criminals, 364,n1, 381-82, 397; WW on war-crimes issue, 408
Gerry, Peter Goelet, 359
Gibbons, James Cardinal, 237
Gibson, Hugh Simons, 5,n1, 372,n1
Gilchrist, Huntington, 275,n3
Gildersleeve, Basil Lanneau, 517,n2
Gillett, Frederick Huntington, 416n2
Glass, Carter, 141, 325, 457; resigns from Cabinet to accept Senate seat, 41-42, 50, 52, 60, 349-50; desires to see WW, 103; and coal situation, 154n1, 154-55, 166; and railroad situation, 184; Lansing on reaction of WW's no-compromise statement, 193; on urgent need for food relief in Europe, 339-40,n1; and Democratic caucus on treaty, 384; on treaty situation and Taft reservation, 387-88, 410-11; WW rejects suggestions on Taft reservation, 405; concern over ratification with Lodge reservations, 479
Glynn, Henry Martin, 64n1
Gompers, Samuel: and First International Labour Conference, 98n1; on extending government control of railroads, 197-98
Gonzáles, Pablo, 134,n7
Gore, Thomas Pryor: and treaty fight, 94, 200-201, 273, 337, 338; and Oklahoma appointments, 205; WW on, 488
Gout, Jean-Étienne-Paul, 163n6
Graf Waldersee: S.S., 8
Graham, Sir Ronald (William), 407n1
Grain Corporation (U.S.): and wheat to Armenia, 13, 14; and wheat to Poland, 13
Gray, George, 141,n4; appointed to Permanent Court of Arbitration, 216, 273

Grayson, Alice Gertrude (Altrude) Gordon (Mrs. Cary Travers), 320-21, 325, 493-94
Grayson, Cary Travers, 15, 32, 95, 127-28, 256, 270-71, 320, 324-26, 335, 346, 359, 396, 420, 455; health bulletins and comments on WW's continued improvement, 4, 37, 99, 100, 120, 211, 216, 351, 435, 511,n1; on Hitchcock's interview with WW, 43-45; and Craufurd-Stuart affair, 88, 90; and WW's Thanksgiving, 93; announces Jenkins' release, 129-30, 131, 134, 138; on Fall-Hitchcock visit to WW, 133, 135-39; on Republican rumors on WW's health, 135-36; and railroad crisis, 222; on Jackson Day message, 252; on proposed biography-memoir of WW, 324-25; and Frazier, 353, 452; and WW's tentative decision to resign, 362n1; on Grey's letter, 365; and Cabinet meetings held during WW's illness, 386, 455, 456, 457, 496; and Lansing resignation, 398, 416, 418; Dercum on medical queries being directed to, 403, 434; on WW's decision to appoint Colby, 472-73; on first meeting WW, 485; WW's wit and humor, 488-90; wishes McAdoo was in Paris to see WW's physical and political stress, 492-94; on birth of his son, 493-94; Seibold's proposal to write article on, 494-95, 495-96; unpublished statement on WW's health history, 497-99; and diagnosis of and memorandum on WW's illness, 506, 507-10
Grayson, Cary Travers, Jr., 325,n4, 485n; birth of, 493-94
Grayson, David (pseudonym), 61n1
Grayson, James Gordon, 325,n4, 485n, 494
Great Britain: and Syria and Turkish Empire, 25-27; and Egypt, 49; presents proposals for Adriatic settlement, 168-78, 264-66, 370-71, 375; invited to first meeting of Council of League of Nations, 272; Grey on League of Nations and, 355n1; and issue of war criminals, 364,n1, 381-82, 407,n1; and Palestine, 373, 449; WW's firm position on Adriatic proposals, 375-80, 398-402, 445-46; response to WW on Adriatic proposals and threat to withdraw treaty, 436-42; and Turkish treaty, 449; WW's reply to Anglo-French note on proposed Adriatic settlement, 459-63; see also Great Britain and the United States; and under the names of spokesmen for, such as Balfour, Arthur James; Lloyd George, David
Great Britain and the Creation of the League of Nations: Strategy, Politics and International Organization, 1914-1919 (Egerton), 355n1
Great Britain and the United States: and Craufurd-Stuart affair, 3; and Imperator controversy, 7-10, 33-34; Prince of Wales thanks EBW and WW for hospitality, 36-37, 71; concern over Senate action on reservations, 53; Polk on effect of U.S. delegates leaving Paris, 151; Lansing on WW not receiving Lord Grey, 187-88; and

Grey's letter, 355n1, 380, 381,n1; issue of cancellation of debts, 475,n1, 476-78; Geddes recommended as Ambassador to U.S., 483-84,n1,2; WW on friendship between, 491-92; *see also* Great Britain

Greece: and Thrace, 157-64, 297,n1; and Adriatic question, 171, 299, 301, 315, 369; and League of Nations, 272; and appointment of Minister, 414,n2, 453, 454

Greece at the Paris Peace Conference (1919) (Petsalis-Diomidis), 163n5

Green, William: and WW's proposal to end coal strike, 142-45

Gregory, Thomas Watt, 64n1, 322; on Cabinet appointments and resignations, 184-85; concerned over situation in Washington and WW's ability to serve, 217, 243, 348; on general leasing bill, 473

Grew, Joseph Clark: and appointments, 317,n4, 414, 453

Grey, Edward, 1st Viscount of Fallodon, 157; and Craufurd-Stuart affair, 3, 88, 90, 91, 217; on *Imperator* controversy, 33; on treaty being killed by Lodge and Republicans, 44; controversy over WW not receiving, 187-88, 203, 235, 239, 360; WW charges conspiracy between Lodge and, 384; Dr. Park on WW's health and, 527; *see also* Grey's letter

Grey's letter, 355n1; R. S. Baker on, 359, 362, 385; House on, 360; effect on WW's tentative plans to resign, 362n1; press release on White House reaction to, 363-64; Lansing on, 365, 366-67, 380; and Jusserand, 380; Borah on, 381,n1; Dr. Park on WW's reaction to, 527

Gronna, Asle Jorgenson, 200-201, 337, 338

Grouitch (Grujić), Slavko Y., 341,n1

Hague Tribunal: *see* Permanent Court of Arbitration

Haig, Charlotte Augusta Astor Drayton (Mrs. George Ogilvy), 204,n11

Hale, Edward Joseph, 205,n9

Hale, Frederick: and treaty fight, 94, 200-201, 337, 339; Grayson on attitude toward WW's health, 135-36

Haller's Army: repatriation of Polish Americans in, 372-73, 375, 389-90

Hampton, George P., 197-98,n1

Hankey, Sir Maurice Pascal Alers, 263

Hapgood, Norman: resigns as Minister to Denmark, 233-34,n1

Harbord, James Guthrie, 27, 450,n3,4

Harbord Mission, 27

Hard, Anne Nyhan Scribner (Mrs. William), 362,n4

Hard, William, 362,n4

Harding, Warren Gamaliel, 200-201, 416n2

Harkins, Miss, 502-503, 506, 507, 509, 510

Harlan, James Shanklin, 200,n4

Harper & Brothers, 514n1

Harris, Charles H., III, 140n1

Harris, Seale, 487

Harris, William C., 522,n1

Harris, William Julius, 273

Harrison, Leland, 263

Harvard University, 297

Harvey, George Brinton McClellan, 515; on Hapgood, 234,n3

Harvey's Weekly, 234n3

Haskell, William Nafew, 13,n1, 450,n3

Haynes Powder Company, 206n1

Hearst, William Randolph, 123,n1

Heberling, S. E., 424, 431

Hecaen, Albert M., 527n3

Hecaen, J., 527n3

Helt, D. W., 425, 431

Henderlite, James Henry, 191,n3, 213

Henderson, Robert Randolph, 518,n1

Henry Cabot Lodge: A Biography (Garraty), 328n2

Herzegovina, 368,n1

Hewart, Sir Gordon, 382

Hibben, Jenny Davidson (Mrs. John Grier), 521

Hibben, John Grier, 213, 519-21; sends WW desk from Princeton, 246-47; to receive salary increase, 519

Hindenburg, Paul von: and war criminals, 364n1

Hines, Walker Downer, 141, 197, 198, 246, 457, 475n2; and coal strike, 3, 166; on draft message on railroads for WW to present to Congress, 16, 17-21, 21-24; on postponing return of railroads to private ownership, 183, 184, 188-89, 222, 222n1, 223-25; proclamation relinquishing federal control of railroads, 226; and railroad crisis, 391,n1, 396-97, 406-407, 411-13, 420-24, 426, 427; on WW's response to labor since railroad bill's passage, 467-68

Hispanic American Historical Review, 120n1, 140n1

Hitchcock, Gilbert Monell, 103, 104n1, 125, 183, 336, 338; on need for concessions and compromise for treaty to be ratified, 3, 29-30, 58-59, 93-94, 165, 244; Tumulty drafts letter to on danger of reservations, 15; on progress of Lodge reservations, 28-30, 37-38, 50, 70; on proposed substitute reservations, 29-30,n1; on interview with WW on treaty, 43-45, 45-50, 50, 56; on visiting WW after stroke, 45n11; draft of letter opposing Lodge resolution of ratification, 51; Lansing's praise of, 55, 56; WW answers on Lodge resolution, 58, 59; holds Democratic caucus, 62-63, 384; to meet with WW on treaty, 71; House on treaty strategy involving, 89, 90, 96; list of Republican senators willing to compromise, 94; WW's failure to meet with on treaty, 99, 106; and Mexican situation, 120, 123, 125, 127; on WW shifting responsibility for treaty's fate to Senate, 126; meeting with WW and Fall on Mexico, 129-32, 133-35, 139-40; meets with House on Versailles Treaty, 182-83, fight for minority leadership, 192, 194, 273, 274,n1; seeks WW's advice on compromise to avoid split in Democratic party, 203; WW's advice to on treaty, mistake to propose anything,

Hitchcock, Gilbert Monell (*cont.*)
206; Tumulty on WW adopting substitute reservations of, 238; EBW requests WW's earlier memorandum from, 243, 244; approves invitations to first meeting of Council of League of Nations, 272; proposed letter to on reservations, 276; on bipartisan meetings on reservations, 283-84, 311, 312-13,n1; sends copy of Lodge reservations to Tumulty, 285-88; still hopeful of compromise, 327-28; WW answers on various articles of treaty, 329-30; mention of WW deferred letter to, 365; and Taft reservation, 387; on treaty situation in Senate and fear more Democrats will support Lodge reservations, 466; Dr. Park on WW's letter to, 528
Holland: *see* Netherlands, The
Honduras: and appointments, 317
Honolulu Oil case, 392,n1, 405
Honolulu Oil Company, 405n1
Hooker, Richard, 64n1
Hoover, Herbert Clark, 64n1, 235; and wheat shipments to Poland, 5, 12; and wheat to Armenia, 13; mentioned as presidential candidate, 325
Hoover, Irwin Hood, 180n1
House, Edward Mandell, 53, 182-83, 444-45; get-well wishes to WW, 53-54; Lansing on, 57, 193; EBW relays WW's concern over ill health of, 61; R. S. Baker on, 61-62; on strategy for treaty ratification, 88-90, 95-96; on appointment of Palmer to Cabinet, 184-85; meets with Gregory and Tyrrell, 217; on Lansing's concern over WW's inability to perform his duties, 231; on WW's treatment of Lord Grey, 239, 360; on strained relations between Lansing and WW, 243; Polk visits, 270-71; on rumors of break with WW, 347; on visits from Palmer and Gregory, 347-48; on Grey's letter and friendship, 360-61; on Lansing resignation, 444; and Frazier, 451
House, Loulie Hunter (Mrs. Edward Mandell), 61
Houston, David Franklin, 133n2, 141, 193, 269; and coal situation, 154n1, 154-55, 166; and railroad situation, 184, 480; on revised draft of Jackson Day message, 249n1, 250-52; C. R. Crane on, 262; and draft letter from Tumulty to Hitchcock on reservations, 278n1, 282-83; resigns as Secretary of Agriculture to become Secretary of Treasury, 330,n1, 349; Leffingwell willing to assist, 362, 361-62; and Cabinet meetings during WW's illness, 457; on general cancellation of inter-Allied debts, 475
Hovannisian, Richard G., 450n4
Howard, Harry N., 425n2
Howe, Annie Josephine Wilson (Mrs. George, Jr.), sister of WW, 485, 486
Hudson, Manley Ottmer, 275
Human Neuropsychology (Hecaen), 527n2
Hungary. and Rumania, 35n1; new government established in, 101,n2; and Adriatic question, 265, 299, 300, 332; U.S. position on negotiations with, 446-48, 464-66; *see also* Paris Peace Conference—*Hungarian treaty*
Hungary at the Paris Peace Conference: The Diplomatic History of the Treaty of Trianon (Déak), 101n2
Hunt, George Wylie Paul: and appointments, 296,n1, 317, 322, 407-408
Huston, Howard, 275
Huszár, Karoly, 101n2
Hynes, John J., 424, 431

Imperator controversy, 7-10, 33-34, 52, 65, 212, 218
income tax: and WW's Annual Message to Congress, 78, 107-108
Industrial Conference, Second, 185; WW names new members to, 64,n1; WW on, 84, 113
Inter-Allied Mission at Constantinople, 158
Interchurch World Movement of North America, 416,n2
Interior, Department of the: and Lane's resignation, 373-74, 374; Robinson declines appointment to, 392-93; Payne appointed Secretary, 448; and general leasing bill, 473-74
International Association of Machinists, 424, 431
International Brotherhood of Blacksmiths, Drop Forgers & Helpers of America, 431
International Brotherhood of Boilermakers, Iron Ship Builders and Helpers of America, 431
International Brotherhood of Electrical Workers, 431
International Brotherhood of Locomotive Engineers, 198n2
international communications, conference on (proposed), 228-29
International Labour Conference, First, 97-98,n1
International Labour Organization, 98n1
interstate commerce: WW on, 82-83, 111-12
Interstate Commerce Act of 1887, 196,n3
Interstate Commerce Commission, 445n1; and railroad situation, 20, 24, 197; and proposed Cummins and Esch railroad bills, 195n1; appointments to, 205; and Transportation Act of 1920, 467n1
Interstate Commerce, Committee on (Senate): and railroad situation, 18, 20
Interstate and Foreign Commerce, Committee on (House of Reps.): and railroad situation, 19, 20
Iowa: Democratic politics in, 330n1
Irby, Adeline Paulina, 160,n4
Irreconcilables: The Fight Against the League of Nations (Stone), 328n2
isolationism: WW on, 79, 109
Istria, 169, 172, 174, 301, 377, 399, 400, 463
Italia Irredenta, 175, 170, 332
Italy: appointment suggestions and appoint-

ment of Ambassador to, 205, 296, 343-44, 407, 474; and Anglo-French Adriatic proposal, 263-66, 298-305; and Nitti compromise on Adriatic proposal, 264,n4; invited to first meeting of Council of League of Nations, 272; Polk on Adriatic situation and, 323-24; WW on firm position on Adriatic proposals and claims by, 352-53, 398-402; Lansing on effect of economic boycott on, 371; WW's reply to Anglo-French note on proposed Adriatic settlement, 459-63; debt to U.S., 475,n1; *see also* Adriatic question, and under the names of spokesmen for, such as Nitti, Francesco Saverio
Italy at the Paris Peace Conference (Albrecht-Carrié), 169n3

J. P. Morgan and Company, 390
Jackson, Andrew, 249
Jackson Day Dinner, 261,n1
Jackson Day message, 257-59; first draft mentioned, 199n1, 269,n3, 270; redraft mentioned, 199n1; Houston on first revise of, 249n1, 250-52; redraft of, 252-55; Ashurst on 1920 campaign and, 263; F. I. Cobb on, 270n2; W. G. Sharp on, 285-86; R. S. Baker on, 321, 359; as indicator of WW's candidacy, 347
Jacquemaire, Madeleine Clemenceau (Mrs. Numa), 239,n1
Jacquemaire, Numa, 239n1
Jadwin, Edgar, 198n1
Japan: and Lodge reservations, 39; invited to first meeting of Council of League of Nation, 272; and Adriatic question, 375, 398; and Siberia, 390-91; *see also* Shantung settlement
Japan and the United States: decision to withdraw troops from Siberia, 219-21; treaty of 1898, 470
Jenkins, William Oscar, 120n1, 121, 123, 128,n1; Lansing on, 123, 124; release announced, 128n1, 129, 133, 134, 138; Grayson on, 136
Jenkins affair, 103,n1, 127-28,n1, 127, 129-30, 131, 134, 231
"Jenkins Case and Mexican-American Relations" (Cumberland), 120n1, 128n1
Jewell, Bert Mark: and railroad crisis, 420-24, 426, 428-31
Jews: and Mogenthau mission and issue of publication of report on, 198n1, 260,n1,2
Johns Hopkins University, 32, 394, 516n1, 517n2; and Sir William Osler, 237n1
Johnson, Douglas Wilson: and Adriatic question, 367, 368-69, 370-71, 371, 402,n1, 446, 458,n3; WW's suggested alterations to Adriatic text of, 375-80
Johnson, Hiram Warren: and Mexican situation, 120, on WW's health, 195-96; and treaty fight, 200-201, 328n2, 336, 338, 387
Johnson, Homer Hosea: and Morgenthau's mission to Poland, 198n1
Johnson, Robert Underwood: appointed Ambassador to Italy, 296, 317, 322, 343-44, 346, 353, 407, 474
Johnson, Roger Bruce Cash, 521,n2
Johnson, Simeon Moses, 296,n1
Johnston, William H., 424, 431
Jones, Andrieus Aristieus, 359,n1
Jones, T. Sambola, 317
Jones, Thomas Davies: WW offers Cabinet position to, 232,n1
Jones, Wesley Livsey: and treaty fight, 94, 200, 202, 337, 339
Journal of American History, 120n1
Jusserand, Jean Jules, 157; on treaty being killed by Lodge and Republicans, 44; on need for U.S. delegates to remain in Paris, 101-102; and Grey's letter, 366-67, 380

Kansas City Star, Weekly, 340
Karavongse, Phya Prabha, 468,n1, 469
Kearful, Francis Joseph, 355,n2
Kellogg, Frank Billings: and treaty fight, 94, 200-201, 283, 291, 337, 338, 339
Kendrick, John Benjamin: and treaty fight, 199n1, 200, 202
Kenyon, William Squire: and treaty fight, 94, 200-201, 337, 339
Kerr, Philip, 53
Keyes, Henry Wilder: and treaty fight, 94, 200-201, 337, 339
King, Alexander Campbell, 297,n2
King, Henry Churchill, 425n2
King, Stanley, 64n1
King, William Henry: and Mexican situation, 120n1
King-Crane Commission (Howard), 425n2
King-Crane Report, 425,n1,2
Kirby, William Fosgate: and treaty fight, 199n1, 200-201, 336, 338, 339
Kirk, Alexander Comstock, 90
Kline, James W., 424, 431
Knox, Philander Chase: and resolution of June 1919, 192n1; and treaty fight, 200-201, 328n2, 337, 338
Kolchak, Aleksandr Vasil'evich, 308, 309; collapse of government of, 219
Koritza, Albania, 299, 301, 315, 369
Kornilov, Lavr Georgievich, 390n1
Kourbatoff (Kourbatov), V. Stepan: *see* Zavoiko, Vasili Stepanovich

labor: and Versailles Treaty, 49; and reservations to League of Nations, 58,n1; WW names new members to second Industrial Conference, 64,n1; and Annual Message to Congress, 83-86, 113-15; relationship of capital and, 86; international conference on, 97-98,n1; coal miners accept WW's proposal, 179; on extending government control of railroads, 197-98; Bituminous Coal Commission established, 206-209; and Executive Order for half days for government employees, 218; on not delaying resolution of railroad wage issue, 428-31; Hines on WW's response to railroad situation, 467-68; *see also* employment; strikes

Labor, Department of: WW on employment for returning servicemen, 80, 109; and Mooney case, 145n1

labor unions: and coal strike, 141,n1,2, 155; WW on critical railroad situation and government's request to, 420-26; see also coal situation; railroad situation

Lafayette College: Hibben to represent Princeton at, 519-20

La Follette, Robert Marion: and treaty fight, 200, 202, 337, 338

Lagosta (now Lastova Island, Yugoslavia), 172, 174, 264n4, 265, 301, 302

Lamont, Thomas William, 183, 270

land grant schools, 4

Lane, Franklin Knight, 64n1, 274; and coal strike negotiations, 143; and railroad situation, 184; Lansing on reaction to WW's no-compromise statement, 193; resignation of, 204,n1, 232, 373-74, 385, 456; visits Lansing, 385; on Honolulu Oil case, 392, 405; and Lansing resignation, 418; and Railroad Wage Commission, 422,n5; and Cabinet meetings during WW's illness, 456

Lane Commission: see Railroad Wage Commission

Lange, Christian, 342

Lansing, Eleanor Foster (Mrs. Robert), 156,n1, 229, 385,n2, 455; WW on, 417n3

Lansing, Robert, 3-4, 50, 65, 66, 216, 263-66, 273, 275, 361, 375, 385, 386, 414; and Craufurd-Stuart affair, 3, 88, 91, 235; and Poland's grain request, 4, 5-6; on Imperator controversy, 7-10, 212,n1, 218; on situation in Syria and Turkish Empire, 25-27; on Rumanian situation, 34-35, 36; suggests Phillips for Minister to Netherlands, 41, 103, 204, 205; views on treaty, 54-57; reasons for opposing WW's western tour, 55; on WW's falling reputation, 56-57; on continued U.S. involvement in European activities, 66-68, 87; on Bulgarian treaty, 67, 68; on recognition of Costa Rica, 94-95, 153, 186; and issue of withdrawing U.S. representatives in Paris, 100-102, 117, 147-49, 156, 156-57; on appointments, 119, 296, 316-17, 322, 343, 366, 407-408, 413-14; and Jenkins case, 120n1, 121, 124, 129-30; on Mexican situation, 120n1, 121, 123, 127, 239-42; on question of WW's ability to perform his duties, 123-25, 453-54; on ending secrecy about WW's health, 139-40; on Germany not signing protocol, 147-49; on coal situation, 167; saga of resignation of, 179, 255-56, 270, 385-86, 388-89, 398, 404, 408-10, 414, 415-19; and Thrace, 181; on Cabinet's position on returning railroads to private ownership, 183-84; on WW seeing Lord Grey before his return to England, 187-88, 235; on conference on international communications, 190, 228,n1; memorandum on WW's policy of "no

concession and no compromise," 192-94; on struggle between Hitchcock and Underwood for minority leadership, 192, 194; on publication of Morgenthau report on Poland, 198n1, 260; on crisis with Mexico, 210-11; on withdrawal of U.S. troops from Siberia, 219-21; Christmas and New Year greetings to WW, 229; and Hapgood resignation, 234,n1; on Grey and Craufurd-Stuart affair, 235; on recognition of Finland, 236; House on strained relations between WW and, 243; on dangers of WW's uncompromising position compared to Bryan's, 267-69; on invitations to first meeting of Council of League of Nations, 272-73, 275; meets with Tumulty on reservations, 276; and Tumulty's draft letter to Hitchcock on reservations, 278n1, 282; on Adriatic proposals, 298, 313-14, 340-41, 342, 371-72; on Russian situation, 307-308,n1; EBW answers on WW's Adriatic position, 335-36, 352-53; on Turkish treaty negotiations, 344-45, 382, 391; on Frazier affair, 353, 383-84, 398, 413, 451-54; on Grey's letter, 365, 366-67, 380; R. S. Baker on diary of, 365; on D. W. Johnson's proposal on treaty and Adriatic question, 367; on repatriation of Polish Americans in Haller's Army, 372-73, 375, 389; and Balfour Declaration, 373; and war criminals, 381-82, 407, 408; on Davis at meeting of Premiers, 382, 391; on Cabinet meetings during WW's illness, 383, 384, 454-58, 496; on Japan's interest in Siberia, 390-91; on WW's firm Adriatic position, 398-402; WW accepts resignation of, 404, 414; resignation of prompts inquiries into WW's health, 432, 433; House on resignation of, 444; Dr. Park on WW's charges against, 527

Law (Andrew), Bonar, 263

League of Nations, 15; WW on labor and, 84, 85, 113-14, 114; Hitchcock's proposed substitute reservations, 29-30,n1; text of proposed Lodge reservations on, 38-41; Grey and Jusserand on fate of, 44; British reaction to Senate reservations, 53; reservations on equalizing voting power, 58,n1; reservations on labor, 58,n1; various comments on Article X, 59, 59-60, 69, 384, 479-80; Underwood's compromise proposal on, 69-70; House on WW and, 90; Hitchcock on, 94; Vénisélos on Constantinople and, 161-62; Vénisélos on Dedeagatch and, 164; and Fiume, 170, 173, 265, 298-99, 300, 302, 305, 319, 331, 332; and Zara, 170, 172, 299, 331, 333; and mandate for Albania, 176-78; Tumulty on WW's statement on no compromise on treaty, 190; and Knox resolution of June 1919, 192n1; national referendum on, 200, 248, 249n1, 251-52, 254, 258-59, 263, 268, 270n2; and Jackson Day message, 251, 257; Lansing on, 269; invitations sent to first meeting of Council of, 272-73; and Fosdick resignation, 274-76, 286, 306, 310; WW on withdrawal clause, 279, 329-30; WW on Article X, 279-80; WW on financial obligations to, 281; Hitchcock's marked copy of text of Lodge reservations sent to Tumulty, 288-95; R. S. Baker on public opinion on, 326-27; Grey on U.S. position and, 355n1; R. S. Baker on WW's attitude and, 359-60; Lane on, 374; and The Netherlands, 407n1; and Anglo-French Adriatic response and Article IX, 441-42; and Frazier, 452; see also Versailles Treaty

League of Women Voters, 396

Lee, William Granville, 424, 431

Leeper, Alexander Wigram Allen, 178,n4, 263,n1

Leffingwell, Russell Cornell, 475n1; willing to defer resignation, 349-50, 361-62, 362

Lejean, Guillaume-Marie, 160,n4

Lenin, V. I. (Vladimir I'lich Ul'ianov), 234n3

Lenroot, Irvine Luther: and treaty fight, 47, 49, 94, 202, 283, 337; R. S. Baker meets with, 359

Leonard, Clifford Milton, 205,n7

Lersner, Kurt von, 118n2; and list of war criminals, 364n1

Letters on the League of Nations (Fosdick), 274n1

Lever Act, 23, 141n1

Lewis, John Llewellyn: and coal strike, 141n1, 142-45, 179-80, 180

Liller, William C., 515,n1

limitation of arms; see disarmament

Lincoln, Abraham: bed of, 32

Lincoln Memorial: R. S. Baker on, 362

Lindsay, Ronald Charles, 475n1

Link, Arthur Stanley, 324n2

Lipowski, Z. J., 525n1,2

Lippmann, Faye Albertson (Mrs. Walter), 362,n3

Lippmann, Walter, 362

Lissa (now Vis Island, Yugoslavia), 171, 299, 301, 302, 305, 331, 334, 462

Literary Digest, The, 270n2

Lloyd George, David, 348; on *Imperator* controversy, 9, 10, 33, 33-34; and Fiume, 260n1; and Adriatic proposal, 263-66, 298-305, 376, 398; Lansing on draft of telegram on Russia, 307-308; on Russian situation, 308-309; Wallace on Adriatic proposal of, 318-20; and Palestine, 358, 449; Borah on Lodge reservations and, 381,n1; and war crimes, 382; reply to WW on Adriatic proposals, 436-42, 481-83; in 1918 hosts stag dinner, 490n1

Loans to Foreign Governments (Sen. Doc.), 475n1

Lodge, Henry Cabot, 29, 148, 274, 337, 445; Grey and Jusserand on treaty and, 44; will keep Senate in session to dispose of reservations and move for adoption of his resolution for ratification, 45-50; on preamble, 46-47; Hitchcock on meeting with on possible compromise, 58-59; reads WW's letter into *Congressional Record*, 63; and treaty and political campaign, 72; and Mexican situation, 120,n1, 152n2; on WW's health, 135-36; and Fall resolution, 136-37, 152n2; Glass on treaty negotiations and, 193, 410; WW's challenge to concerning treaty, 200-201; Hitchcock on unyielding position of, 244; F. I. Cobb on treaty position of, 270n2; Tumulty on, 277; and bipartisan meeting, 283; *Springfield Republican* and New York *World* on, 287,n1,2; and bitter-enders, 328n2; and Grey's letter, 355n1; WW charges conspiracy with Grey, 384; Glass on Taft reservation and, 387-88,n1; Cummings on, 419n1; suggestion of letter from Masaryk to, 443; see also Lodge reservations; Lodge resolution of ratification

"Lodge Blocks Pact Compromise, Its Friends Insist" (Michelson), 287n2

Lodge reservations, 28,n1, 29, 276n1, 384; Tumulty on, 15; Hitchcock on proposed substitute reservations, 29-30,n1; Hitchcock on Senate's progress on, 37-38; text of, 38-41; WW will not accept, 38,n1, 47-48, 50, 56, 165-66, 387; 14th and 15th rejected by Senate, 50; E. M. House on, 89; N. H. Davis on, 105; senators voting for, 199n1; bipartisan committee on, 283-84, 311-12, 312-13,n1, 328n2; public opinion poll of college students and faculty on, 284n1; Hitchcock's marked copy of text of, 289-95; and Grey's letter, 355n1; Borah on Grey's letter being affirmation of, 381,n1; Hitchcock and Tumulty fear more Democrats are supporting, 466, 479; Dr. Park on WW's health and, 526

Lodge resolution of ratification: Hitchcock on, 29, 46; Underwood on, 42; WW's opposition to, 43, 51, 58; Hitchcock on possible compromise if defeated, 58-59; first roll call vote on, 63; 2nd vote on, 63-64,n2; Burleson on votes of various senators on, 338

Lodge resolution on termination of war, 126,n1

London, Treaty of (1915): threat of enforcement of, 263-64, 264,n1, 298, 302, 304, 305, 313, 314, 315, 319, 341, 376, 377-78, 398, 400, 429-40, 480-81; WW on, 462-63; Britain and France answer WW's charges concerning Adriatic question and, 482-83

London *Times*, 355n1, 359, 360

Long, Breckinridge, 233, 455; on Hapgood's resignation, 234; suggested for appointment, but declines offer, 296, 316-17, 322, 350-51; and quest for senatorial seat, 316-17; withdraws resignation suggestion, 352; WW pleased he will stay in present position, 352, 353; Lansing shows resignation correspondence to, 414; and Frazier, 452

Lorraine, 200, 248

Lubomirski, Prince Kazimierz, 260,n1

Lussino (now Lošinj Island, Yugoslavia), 171, 175, 299, 302, 331, 334, 462

Lyons, Maurice F., 521

McAdoo, Eleanor Randolph Wilson (Mrs. William Gibbs), daughter of WW and EAW, 325

McAdoo, Ellen Wilson, granddaughter of WW, 325

McAdoo, William Gibbs, 307, 347, 416n2; House on Alexander's appointment and, 185; and extension of government ownership of railroads, 197; and Lane Commission on railroads, 422n5; Grayson confides in on WW's health problems in Paris, 492-94

McCall, Samuel Walker, 64n1

McCombs, Robert, 524,n2

McCombs, William Frank, 521-24; and French ambassadorship, 523, 524,n1

McCormick, Cyrus Hall, Jr., 64n1

McCormick, (Joseph) Medill: Grayson on attitude of toward WW's health, 135-36; and treaty fight, 200-201, 336, 338; and bitter-enders, 328n2

McCormick, Vance Criswell, 347; declines position of Secretary of Commerce, 95, 185

McCumber, Porter James: and treaty fight, 49, 94, 338, 339, 428

Macedonia, 164n8

McGrath, Justin, 123,n1

McKellar, Kenneth Douglas: and bipartisan meeting on reservations, 283-84

Mackenzie, Georgina Mary Muir, 160,n4

McLean, George Payne: and treaty fight, 200-201, 336

McNary, Charles Linza: and treaty fight, 94, 200-201, 311-12, 337, 338, 339

Magyars, 465

mandates: and Turkish Empire, 25, 26, 27; Lansing on abandoning idea of, 56; WW on, 330

Manion, Edward J., 411,n1, 424, 426, 431

Margulies, Herbert F., 276n1, 328n2

Marshall, Thomas Riley, 49, 63, 231, 348, 416n2, 455, 456, 496; and Lodge reservations, 37; on delay in treaty ratification, 217

Martin, Lucy Day: death of her father, 24,n1

Martin, Thomas Staples, 104n1; death of, 24,n1; Glass takes Senate seat of, 52, 60

Martin, William Joseph, 191-92,n1, 213

Martino, Giacomo de, 163n6

Mary, Queen (Victoria Mary of Teck), consort of George V, 32, 42, 231

Maryland, University of, Medical School, 515n1

Masaryk, Thomas Garrigue, 443

Matsui, Keishiro, 263, 314,n2

Maury, Lucy, 93

Meredith, Edwin Thomas: appointed Secretary of Agriculture, 330,n1, 330-31

Mesopotamia, 449

Message of the President of the United States ... December ... 1919, 116n

Mexican Americans, 140n1

Mexican Constitution, 240, 241, 242

Mexico and the United States, 122-23, 231, 270; and seizure of foreign-owned oil wells, 120n1, 134, 210-11,n1; and Senate action concerning, 120-21,n1; Lansing on WW's health and, 123, 124, 125; Tumulty's concern over proposed visit to WW by senators on Mexican situation, 125; Lansing on difference between general situation and Jenkins case, 127; Fall and Hitchcock meet with WW on, 127, 129-32, 132-33, 133-35; Pittman on, 127-28; WW on, 131, 152; and Plan of San Diego, 140n1; Lansing's proposals for policy toward Mexico, 239-42; Fletcher resignation, 310,n1, 397; and Lansing resignation, 417n3; Tumulty on new Secretary of State and, 419; *see also* Jenkins case

Michelson, Charles, 287n2

Millerand, Alexandre, 358; and Adriatic question, 314,n1, 436-42, 450, 481-83; and list of war criminals, 364n1; and Turkish treaty, 372,n1

Mineral Point Zinc Company, 232n1

Missouri: and B. Long's senatorial campaign, 350, 352, 353

Mitchell, Charles Wellman, 515-19,n1

Mitchell, Florence M. Crowe (Mrs. Charles Wellman), 515,n2

Mobile, S.S., 8

Moment of Truth for Protestant America: Interchurch Campaigns Following World War I (Ernst), 416n2

Monroe Doctrine: and proposed substitute reservations, 30; and Lodge reservations, 39, 291; WW on, 280

Montenegro: and Yugoslavia, 177

Mooney, Tom, 145n1

Moore, John Bassett: and Permanent Court of Arbitration, 216, 273

Morgan and Company: *see* J. P. Morgan and Company

Morgenthau, Henry: publication of report on Poland, 198n1, 260,n1,2

Moses, George Higgins: and Mexican situation, 120, 128; and WW's stroke, 132, 135, 136, 137, 138; and treaty fight, 200-201, 337, 338; and bitter-enders, 328n2

Murphy, Charles Francis, 521,n1

Murphy, Edward, 97n1, 215

My Memoir (Edith B. Wilson), 133n2, 405n1, 417n3, 507n1

Myers, Henry Lee: and vote on Lodge resolution, 63

National American Woman Suffrage Association, 396,n1

National Bureau for the Advancement of Music of New York, 346n2

National Democratic League of Clubs, 515n1

National Independent Political League, 522,n2

naval oil reserves: Pinchot on need for Palmer to appeal case concerning oil fields, 354-55; and Honolulu Oil case, 392,n1, 405; and general leasing bill, 473n1

Navy (U.S.): *see* United States Navy

Navy, Department of the: and general leasing bill, 473-74

Negroes, 522,n2

Nelson, Knute: and treaty fight, 94, 338, 339

Netherlands, The: Phillips suggested for appointment to, 41, 103, 119, 204, 205, 296, 317, 322; and Britain's demands for William II, 407,n1

Nevada: and land reclamation bill, 4

New, Harry Stewart: and Mexican situation, 120; Grayson on attitude of toward WW's health, 135-36; and treaty fight, 200-201, 337; and bipartisan meeting on reservations, 283; hopeful of treaty compromise, 311-12; and bitter-enders, 328n2

New Jersey: cold storage law in, 82-83, 112; ratifies 19th amendment, 396n1

New Jersey Zinc Company, 232n1

New Mexico Historical Review, 120n1

New York *Evening Post*, 327,n1

New York Times, 4n, 6n, 7n, 37n, 57n, 81n5, 93n, 106n, 118n2, 126n, 133n, 141n1, 142n2, 145n, 149n2, 152n2, 155n1, 187n, 195n1, 206n1, 234n1,4, 260n2, 261n1, 267n, 307n, 310n1, 312n, 330n1, 342n, 351n, 355n1, 360, 381n1, 394, 396n1, 419n1, 420n, 436n1, 444, 464n1, 522n1

New York *World*, 261n1, 270,n2, 287,n2

Newberry, Truman Handy: and treaty fight, 200-201, 337

newspapers: comments on treaty situation in Senate, 287n1,2; and Lansing's resignation, 415; *see also* under the names of specific papers, such as *New York Times, New York World, Springfield Republican*

Nitti, Francesco Saverio: and Adriatic question, 260n1, 263, 264, 304, 313, 318, 376, 398; Adriatic compromise proposal of, 264,n4; and Anglo-French Adriatic proposal, 298, 300, 301; Polk on, 451

Nobel peace prizes: candidates recommended for, 342

Noonan, James P., 424, 431

Norris, George William, 338

Noyes, Pierrepont Burt, 150n1

Obregón, Álvaro, 134n7

oil industry: and Mexico, 210-11,n1; *see also* Jenkins case

oil reserves: *see* naval oil reserves

Oklahoma: appointments in, 205; and woman suffrage, 466,n1

"One Way with Sedition" (New York *Evening Post*), 327n1

Order of Railway Conductors, 424, 431

Order of Railway Telegraphers, 411n1, 424, 431

"Organic Mental Disorders: Introduction and Review of Syndromes" (Lipowski), 525n1, 527n4

Origins of the International Labor Organization (Shotwell), 98n1

Origins of Teapot Dome: Progressives, Parties, and Petroleum, 1909-1921 (Bates), 354n1, 392n1, 405n1, 473n1

Orlando, Vittorio Emanuele, 263, 315, 348

Ormond, Alexander Thomas, 521,n1

Osler, Grace Linzee Revere Gross (Mrs. William): WW's condolences to, 237

Osler, Sir William: death of, 237,n1

Owen, Robert Latham: and reservations, 49, 283, 284, 311; and vote on Lodge resolution, 63; and Oklahoma appointments, 205

Paderewski, Ignace Jan, 5, 198n1

Page, Carroll Smalley: and treaty fight, 200, 202, 337

Palestine, 26, 358, 449

Palmer, Alexander Mitchell, 112, 193, 269, 428; on sedition, 81,n5; and coal strike, 141, 142-45, 145, 166, 179, 206n1; and WW's coal statement, 154n1, 154-55; WW's inquiry on possibility of referendum on League, 202-203; on proposed Talcott appointment, 215-16, 322n1; and railroad crisis and return of ownership, 222-23; and revision of first draft of Jackson Day message, 249n1; on WW not seeking reelection, 267; on judicial appointments and age factor, 296-97; talk of as presidential candidate, 347; visits House, 347; refuses to appeal oil case, 354-55

Pan American Financial Conference, Second, 307; and Costa Rica, 230, 245

Paris *Le Matin*, 341

Paris Peace Conference: issue of departure of U.S. representatives, 66-68, 87, 100-102, 117-18, 119; Anglo-French response on Adriatic proposals mentioned, 441

Paris Peace Conference—Austrian treaty, 101, 126, 150

Paris Peace Conference—Bulgarian treaty, 67, 68, 87, 101

Paris Peace Conference—Hungarian treaty, 101, 148, 150, 157, 446-48; Wallace's instructions concerning negotiations, 464-66

Paris Peace Conference—Rumanian treaty, 148, 150, 157

Paris Peace Conference—Turkish treaty, 27, 52, 65, 261, 372,n1, 382; Vénisélos on, 158; issue of U.S. participation in negotiations, 344-45, 391, 411, 448-50, 472; and Balfour Declaration, 358, 373

Park, Bert E.: diagnosis of WW's illness, 507n11; on aftermath of WW's stroke, 525-29

Pašić, Nikola: and Adriatic question, 298, 303, 314

Pass Christian, Miss.: Wilson's visit to in 1913, 486-87

Patricia, S.S., 8

Patton, Francis Landey, 514,n5

Payne, John Barton: and *Imperator* controversy, 8, 212, 218; and Honolulu Oil case, 405n1; appointed Secretary of the Interior, 448; on general leasing bill, 473

Peace Negotiations: A Personal Narrative (Lansing), 416n1

Peale, Rembrandt: appointed to coal commission, 206, 209n1

Pelagosa (now Pelagruz Islands, Yugoslovia), 171, 174, 299, 302, 331, 334, 462

Pence, Thomas Jones, 522,n1

Pennsylvania History, 199n1

Penrose, Boise: and WW's health, 135-36; and treaty fight, 200-201, 337

Permanent Court of Arbitration: appointments to, 216, 273; and Mexican Constitution, 240, 241

Pershing, John Joseph, 416n2

Petsalis-Diomidis, N., 163n5

Philadelphia Press, 403n, 434n

Philadelphia *Public Ledger*, 360

Phillips, Caroline Astor Drayton (Mrs. William), 204,n1

Phillips, William, 3, 52, 157, 452; suggested as Minister to Holland, 41, 103, 119, 204, 205, 296, 317, 322, 407-408; on Lansing and WW, 243

Phipps, Lawrence Cowle: and treaty fight, 200-201, 336

Physical Culture, 496n1

Pichon, Stéphen-Jean-Marie, 35

Piłsudski, Józef Klemens, 198n1

Pinchot, Gifford, 474; on having Palmer appeal oil case, 354-55

Pittman, Key: on Mexican situation and Jenkins case, 120, 127-28

Plan of San Diego, 134,n3, 140n1

"Plan of San Diego and the Mexican-United States War Crisis of 1916: A Reexamination" (Harris and Sadler), 140n1

Plumb plan, 21

Poindexter, Miles: and WW's health, 135-36; and treaty fight, 196, 200, 202, 337; and bitter-enders, 328n2

Pola (now Pula, Yugoslavia), 174, 175

Poland, 442, 443; grain request from, 4-6, 12-13; Vénisélos on, 162; issue of publication of Morgenthau report on, 198n1, 260,n1,2; and Jews, 198n1; and repatriation of Polish Americans in Haller's Army, 389-90

Polish Americans: repatriation of men in Haller's Army, 372-73, 375, 389-90

Polk, Elizabeth Sturgis Potter (Mrs. Frank Lyon), 57,n1

Polk, Frank Lyon, 5, 11, 234, 235, 243, 249n1, 269, 318, 436; and *Imperator* controversy, 10; on situation in Syria and Turkish Empire, 25-27; on Rumania, 34, 35, 36; Lansing on reasons for opposition to treaty, 54-57; and American delegates in Paris, 102, 117-18, 147, 149, 150-51, 156-57; on Germany not signing protocol, 150-51; on one of the most critical moments in diplomatic history for U.S., 150;

on Adriatic question, 168-78, 323-24, 331, 352, 402n1, 445-46, 458-59, 473, 480-81; greetings to WW on his return to U.S., 227; on recognition of Costa Rica, 229-30; on Morgenthau report, 260,n2; meets with House, 270; and redraft of Jackson Day message, 270; on H. P. Fletcher resignation, 310; on Lansing's resignation, 398, 415-19; on Turkish treaty negotiations, 411, 448-50, 464, 472; mentioned as Lansing's successor, 419; on R. Crane's suggestion for Masaryk message on ratification, 443; on Hungarian negotiations, 446-48, 464-66; on France's position on Fiume, 450-51; and Frazier, 452; WW informs of new choice for Secretary of State, 464; on extraterritorial rights in Siam, 468-72, 479; on Geddes as British Ambassador to U.S., 483

Pomerene, Atlee: and vote on Lodge resolution, 63; on WW's no-compromise statement, 192n1; and Democratic caucus on treaty, 384

Porto Baross, 304-305, 332

postwar reconstruction: *see* United States: European relief, credits, and postwar reconstruction

Powderly, Miss, 509, 510

Pretoria: S.S., 8

prices and price fixing: and food, 82; Garfield on coal settlement and fuel prices, 146-47; and WW's statement on coal situation, 154

Prince of Wales: *see* Edward

Princeton University, 97n1, 232n1, 297, 515n1; WW requests that his desk be sent to White House, 213, 246-47; WW sings "Old Nassau," 487; Grayson on WW's health at, 497; and W. M. Daniels, 514,n1; Witherspoon Gang, 516n1; WW host to various class reunions and dinners, 516, 517, 518; Hibben to receive salary increase, 519; WW's letters to Hibben, 519-21; Hibben to resign from various committees, 520

Prinz Frederic Wilhelm, S.S., 8

prohibition: WW and Tumulty discuss, 262

Prologue to Nuremberg: The Politics and Diplomacy of Punishing War Criminals of the First World War (Willis), 364n1

Psychiatric Aspects of Neurologic Disease (Benson and Blumer, eds.), 525n1

public opinion: Hitchcock on treaty and, 126, 244; Lansing on treaty and, 149, 367; WW on treaty and, 200; and Jackson Day message, 248, 253, 258; poll of college students and faculty on treaty, 284,n1; W. G. Sharp on, 285; R. S. Baker on, 320-21, 326-27, 359; Lansing on his resignation and, 415, 419; Polk on Adriatic question and, 451; Tumulty on treaty and, 479; and WW's decision to enter into war, 487-88

Railroad Administration (U.S.), 22, 422; Hines on, 412-13,n2; and wage issue, 429 railroad situation, 204; Hines' proposed message for WW, 17-21, 21-24; and WW's Annual Message to Congress, 74-76, 106; controversy over date of return of railroads to private ownership, 183-84, 188-89, 195-96, 197-98, 222, 223-25, 457; proposed Cummins and Esch bills, 195n11; proclamation relinquishing federal control of railroads, 226-27; press release on return of railroads to private ownership, 228; and threatened strike, 391,n1, 423-24; Hines anxious to see WW on, 396-97; and wage issue, 406-407, 411-13, 428-31; WW meets with committee on, 420; WW's request for noncomplying union to withdraw strike order, 426-27,n1; and Transportation Act of 1920, 467,n1; Hines on WW's response to labor on, 467-68; see also Esch-Cummins bill and Act

Railroad Wage Commission (Lane Commission), 422,n5
Raleigh News and Observer, 522n1
Randolph, Harrison, 458,n3
Rathbone, Albert, 10, 11, 12, 475,n1, 477
"Ratify the Treaty!" (New York World), 270n2
Reading, 1st Marquess of (Rufus Daniel Isaacs), 91
Reed, James Alexander, 185, 488; and treaty fight, 49, 63, 94, 200-201, 273, 337
Reid, Edith Gittings (Mrs. Harry Fielding), 516, 517
Reid, Harry Fielding, 516, 517
Reparation Commission: issue of chairmanship, 10, 11-12; and Lodge reservations, 40, 284, 292, 293; Lansing on continuing U.S. unofficial participation in, 91-92; WW on, 281
reparations: and Scapa Flow, 118n2
Republic of Armenia (Hovannisian), 450n4
Republican party: and reservations, 28, 43, 45-50, 71-72, 165-66; Grey and Jusserand on treaty and, 44; and voting in Senate, 48; Lansing on personal animosity toward WW driving force against treaty, 54-55; Underwood on treaty and, 69-70; Hitchcock on senators willing to compromise on treaty, 94; Polk on issue of departure of U.S. representatives in Paris, 117-18; and Mexican situation, 120,n1, 122, 128; Lansing on, 149; and treaty delay, 277, 283; bipartisan committee addresses Article X and hopeful of compromise, 283-84, 311-12, 312-13,n1; W. G. Sharp on, 285; and bitter-enders, 328,n2; WW's list of senators who hindered ratification of treaty reviewed by Burleson and Hitchcock, 336-37, 338-39; Glass on Taft reservation and responsibility of treaty defeat resting with, 387-88,n1; WW feels treaty proposals should come from, 405; Cummings on, 419n1; and blacks in 1912, 522; see also under the names of individual senators, such as, Lodge, Henry Cabot

Revenue Act of 1918, 77-78, 107

Rhineland: and U.S. troops in, 149, 156
Ridley, Thomas, 184
Rizov, Dimitŭr, 160,n3
Robinson, Henry Mauris, 64n1; resignation from Shipping Board, 205,n5; appointed to coal commission, 206-209,n1, 246; declines appointment as Secretary of the Interior, 392-93; concern over ratification with Lodge reservations, 479
Robinson, Joseph Taylor, 524,n3
Rockefeller Foundation, 13
Rogers, Walter Stowell: suggested as delegate to international conference on communications, 228,n1
Rome Giornale d'Italia, 368, 370
Roosevelt, Theodore: and W. A. White, 62
Root, Elihu, 216; appointed to Permanent Court of Arbitration, 273
Rosenwald, Julius, 64n1
Ross, Edward Alsworth: on King-Crane Report, 425,n2
Roumania: see Rumania
Rowe, Leo Stanton: on recognition of Costa Rica, 245,n1
Ruddock, Albert Billings, 458n3
Ruffin, Sterling, 4, 506, 507, 508, 509, 510
Rumania, 265, 332; approval to withdraw U.S. minister if demands are not met, 35, 36; and Hungary, 101n2, 447, 465; Vénisélos on, 162
Rush Medical College, 432
Russia: WW on, 87, 116; Lansing on situation in, 307-308,n1; Lloyd George draft telegram to U.S. on resuming trade with, 308-309
Siberia, intervention in: Lansing recommends withdrawal of U.S. troops from, 219-21; and Japan, 390-91; U.S. decision to withdraw troops, 436
Russian Bureau, Incorporated, 308
Russian Cooperative Societies, 308
Russo-Turkish War (1878), 161
Ruthenia and Ruthenes, 442, 447, 463, 465
Ryan, Martin F., 424, 431

Sadler, Louis R., 140n1
Safe for Democracy: The Anglo-American Response to Revolution, 1913-1923 (Gardner), 417n3
Salonika, 164n8
Salvador: and appointments, 205
San Diego, Texas, 140n1
Sayre, Jessie Woodrow Wilson (Mrs. Francis Bowes), daughter of WW and EAW: greets Prince of Wales, 31
Sayre, Woodrow Wilson, grandson of WW: WW's birthday greetings to, 451
Scapa Flow, 149; and issue of Germany's reparations for, 118n2
Scialoja, Vittorio, 263, 264, 318, 332n2
Scutari, Albania, 302, 303, 482
Second Pan American Financial Conference: see Pan American Financial Conference, Second
sedition: A. M. Palmer's draft bill on, 81,n5

Seibold, Louis: on rumors on WW's health, and desire to write story on Grayson, 494-95, 495-96

Senator Lenroot of Wisconsin: A Political Biography, 1900-1929 (Margulies), 276n1, 328n2

Serbia and Serbs, 162, 368n1

Serbs, Croats and Slovenes, Kingdom of: *see* Yugoslavia

Sextan Valley, 175

Shantung settlement: WW on, 280

Sharp, William Graves: on Jackson Day message, 285-86

Shea, Timothy, 197-98,n2, 420, 424, 426, 431

Sheet Metal Workers, 424

Sheppard, Lucius Elmer, 197-98,n2, 424

Sherley, Joseph Swagar, 21,n1

Sherman Antitrust Act, 141n1,2

Sherman, Lawrence Yates: and WW's health, 135-36; and treaty fight, 200-201, 328n2, 336, 338

Shidehara, Kijuro, 219,n1

Shields, John Knight: and treaty fight, 49, 200-201, 273, 337, 338; and Mexican situation, 120

shipping: WW on disposition of merchant ships, 80

Shipping Board (U.S.): *see* United States Shipping Board

Shotwell, James Thomson, 98n1

Siam: and appointments, 205, 296; and extraterritorial rights issue, 468-72, 479

Siberia: *see* Russia—*Siberia, intervention in*

Silesia, 447

Simmons, Furnifold McLendel: and reservations, 283, 284, 311

Simms, Dan W., 141n1

Sims, Thetus Wilrette: on keeping government control over railroads, 195-96

Slade, George Theron, 64n1

Small, Robert T., 511n1

Smith, Daniel M., 464n1

Smith, Frederick Edwin: *see* Birkenhead, Baron

Smith, Hoke: WW on, 45; and treaty fight, 200-201, 273, 274n1, 336, 338

Smith, Marcus Aurelius: and Mexican situation, 120n1

Smoot, Reed: and treaty fight, 94, 200, 202, 337; and general leasing bill, 473n1

Smyrna (now Izmir, Turkey), 449

Sonnino, Sidney, 368, 370

Soto, José Maria, 186

Southern Pacific Railroad, 354-55

Spain: invited to first meeting of Council of League of Nations, 272

Spencer, Selden Palmer, 316, 416n2; and treaty fight, 94, 200-201, 337, 339; on rumors of WW's health and inability to make decisions, 124-25

Springfield, Mass., Republican, 277, 287,n1, 355,n1

Ståhlberg, Kaarlo Juho, 236,n1

Standard Oil Company: and the *Imperator* controversy, 212

State, Department of: Lansing fears for emergency fund, 67; Lansing on Phillips' service in, 103; suggestions for Lansing's successor, 419; WW's plans for, 464

steel strike of 1919, 416n2

Sterling, Thomas: and treaty fight, 94, 200-201, 337, 339

Stitt, Edward Rhodes, 4, 489, 506, 507n1, 507, 508, 509, 510

Stockbridge, Frank Parker, 515

Stone, Melville: advises WW on entry into war, 487

Stone, Ralph, 328n2

Stone, Warren Sanford, 197-98,n1, 424, 431

Straus, Oscar Solomon, 64n1, 141,n4, 216, 384; appointed to Permanent Court of Arbitration, 273; on negative effect on treaty of WW's Adriatic response, 445

strikes: WW on, 86, 115; *see also* coal strike situation; railroad situation

Stuart, Charles Kennedy Craufurd-: *see* Craufurd-Stuart, Charles Kennedy

Stuart, Henry Carter, 64n1

suffrage: *see* woman suffrage

Supreme Council (Inter-Allied Conference of Prime Ministers), 26, 149, 168, 307; and issue of German tankers, 34; and Rumania, 34-35; issue of U.S. representation on, 67, 67-68, 87, 148; and new Hungarian government, 101n2; on negotiations on Turkish treaty, 344

Suresnes Cemetery, 511n1

Sušak (now in Yugoslavia), 304, 305, 332

Sutherland, Howard: and treaty fight, 200, 202, 337

Swanson, Claude Augustus: and Mexican situation, 120

Sweetser, Arthur, 275,n2, 362

Swem, Charles Lee, 526; and Tumulty's draft letter to Hitchcock on reservations, 278n1

Switchmen's Union of North America, 431

Switzerland, 98, 205; Long declines appointment to, 296, 316-17, 350-51; and Grew, 317n4; and Frazier affair, 383-84, 408, 413, 414, 451-54; Gary appointment to, 453, 454

Sykes-Picot Agreement, 358, 449

Syria, 25-26, 449

Taft, Helen, 485

Taft, Helen Herron (Mrs. William Howard), 485

Taft, William Howard: Grayson's recollections of, 485

Taft reservation, 387-88,n1, 405, 411, 445

Talcott, Charles Andrew, 97,n1, 215-16 322,n1

Tammany Hall, 521n1

Tariff Commission: *see* United States Tariff Commission

tariff legislation: and chemical and dyestuffs industry, 80-81, 109-10, and WW's Annual Message to Congress, 80-81, 108-109

Tarvis (now Tarvisio, Italy), 175

Taussig, Frank William, 64n1, 205,n6

taxation: and WW's Annual Message to Congress, 77-78, 107-108
Taylor, Clara Sears (Mrs. Eugene Whitman), 3,n1
Teschen Plebiscite Commission, 150,n1
Thanksgiving Day: WW observes, 93; WW thanks for turkey, 97
Thanksgiving Proclamation: Lansing and authorship of, 231
Thomas, Charles Spalding: on WW's no-compromise statement, 192n1; and treaty fight, 200-201, 336, 338
Thommen, Edward, 98
Thompson, William Oxley, 64n1
Thrace: Vénisélos on, 157-64, 182; college professors support unification with Greece, 297,n1; D. W. Johnson on western Thrace, 368; Polk on, 449
Tinoco Granadas, Féderico, 186, 229, 245, 317
" 'Tired of Waiting': Senator Albert B. Fall's Alternative to Woodrow Wilson's Mexican Policies" (Trow), 120n1
Tittoni, Tommaso: and Adriatic question, 174-75, 178, 300, 304
Toole, James F., 507n11
Townsend, Charles Elroy: and treaty, 94, 200-201, 337, 339
Trammell, Park: and treaty fight, 200-201, 336, 338-39
Trans-Baikal Railroad, 221
Trans-Siberian Railway, 220, 221
Transportation Act of 1920; see Esch-Cummins bill and Act
Transylvania, 299, 447
Trapp, Martin Edwin, 466,n1
Travels in the Slavonic Provinces of Turkey-in-Europe (Mackenzie and Irby), 160,n4
Treasury, Department of the: Glass leaves, 42, 350; mentioned in Annual Message, 107; Houston becomes Secretary of, 349; Leffingwell willing to defer resignation from, 349-50, 361-62, 362
Treaty of London (1915): see London, Treaty of
Tremaine, Charles Milton, 346,n2
Trieste, 174, 299, 301, 370
Trimble, South, 93, 97
Trotsky, Leon (Leib or Lev Davydovich Bronstein), 234n3
Trow, Clifford W., 120n1
Trumbić, Ante: and Adriatic question, 298, 303-305, 313, 314, 315, 340, 341-42
Tumulty, Joseph Patrick, 1-4, 7n1, 87, 94-95, 97, 130, 141, 216, 261-62, 270, 286, 327,n1, 351, 353, 355, 366, 384, 386, 397, 420, 459, 473-74, 480, 490, 511n1; and EBW as conduit to WW, 4, 6, 10, 14, 42, 65, 66, 93, 97, 103, 156, 198, 204-205, 233, 245, 246; involvement in WW's Annual Message to Congress, 6, 16, 72, 90, 123, 125; and Imperator controversy, 7; and wheat to Armenia, 13 14; suggests letter to Hitchcock on dangers of reservations, 15; on railroad crisis and controversy over date of return to private ownership,

16, 21, 189n1, 222, 222,n1, 228, 391, 396-97, 467; on appointments, 52n1, 142n2, 296, 330, 448; on U.S. unofficial participation on Reparation Commission, 91-92; and WW's health, 99, 100, 125, 455; Lansing on political decision making and, 124; and coal strike negotiations, 142, 143, 144, 154-55, 206n1; and Mooney case, 145; and recognition of Costa Rica, 153, 229-30; on rumors of W. B. Wilson's resignation, 167; and Thrace, 181; and treatment of Lord Grey, 188n1, 235, 239; on WW's statement on no compromise being "body blow," 190; and draft of WW's challenge to opposition senators, 199n1; seeks advice from WW for Hitchcock, 203; submits list of issues for WW to consider, 204-205; birthday greetings to WW, 233; on need to compromise on reservations, 238, 276-77,n1; relationship with Lansing, 243; draft and redraft of Jackson Day message, 247-49, 259n1, 269,n3, 270; on prohibition, 262; Lansing on as conduit to WW, 269; and Fosdick dilemma and resignation, 274n1, 310; drafts letter to Hitchcock on reservations, 276, 278-82; on WW's opportunity to act on treaty, 287; receives marked copy of Lodge reservations, 288-95; on requests for WW to participate in fund raising "schemes," 345-46; R. S. Baker on, 359, 365; and Frazier affair, 383, 384, 452; on Fletcher's resignation, 397; on Lansing's resignation, 415, 416, 417,n3, 418; suggestions for Lansing's successor, 419, 427-28; and Cabinet meetings during WW's illness, 455-56; on possibility of Marshall taking over, 455; and woman suffrage, 466,n2; on Adriatic question, 473; and railroad bill, 474, 475, 480; on treaty situation in Senate and concern over ratification with Lodge reservations, 479-80
Turkey, 26, 27, 344-45, 358, 448-50; Vénisélos on Greece and, 157-64; see also Paris Peace Conference—Turkish treaty
Turkish Empire, 25-27
Tyrrell, Sir William (George), 53, 217

Underwood, Oscar Wilder, 336, 338; on defeat of Lodge resolution and vote for unconditional ratification, 42, 63, 63-64; compromise proposal for ratification, 69-70; and battle for minority leadership, 192,n1, 194, 273, 274n1; R. S. Baker on treaty views of, 359; and Taft reservation, 387
Underwood resolution: list of senators voting against, 199n1
Unie (now Unije Island, Yugoslavia), 171, 302, 462
unions (labor): see labor unions
United Brotherhood of Maintenance of Way Employees, 425
United Brotherhood of Maintenance of Way Employees and Railroad Shop Laborers, 431

United Mine Workers of America, 141,n1, 143, 207, 208

United States: European relief, credits, and postwar reconstruction: and Poland's request for grain, 4-6, 12-13; and wheat to Armenia, 13-14; and U.S. continued role on Reparation Commission, 91-92; Glass on urgent need for food relief in Europe, 339-40; Houston on inter-Allied debts and, 475,n1

United States Army: WW on employment for returning servicemen, 80, 109; Lansing on German protocol issue and use of, 149,n2

United States Congress: information and suggestions gathered for Annual Message to, 6, 16,n1, 89; Hines' proposed congressional message for WW on railroad situation and needed legislation, 17-21, 21-24; draft of Annual Message to, 73-87; suggestions for budget and audit system in Annual Message, 77, 106-107; concern over WW's ability to perform his duties, 106, 120, 139, 140; WW's Annual Message, 106-16; and railroad crisis, 183-84, 188-89, 195-96, 224, 391n1, 412; and WW's railroad proclamation, 228; Lansing on sending report on Russian situation to, 307,n1; and need for food relief in Europe, 340

House of Representatives: and Esch bill, 195n1; and Esch-Cummins bill, 467n1, 468; *see also* under the names of the specific committees, such as Interstate and Foreign Commerce, Committee on

Senate: Reparations Commission's chairmanship and, 12,n2; Glass accepts seat of T. S. Martin, 41-42, 52, 60; Lansing fears appropriations will be withheld if U.S. continues activities in Europe, 67; action of leads to decision to withdraw U.S. delegates from Paris, 100, 102, 118-19; WW's draft statement on Germany's protocol obligations affected by action of, 118,n2; and Mexican situation, 120-21,n1; WW on foreign affairs advisory power of, 152; and bill for international conference on communications, 190; fight for Democratic leadership in, 192, 194, 273, 274,n1; and Cummins and Esch bills, 195n1; WW denies request of to send Morgenthau's report to, 198,n1; WW on referendum on League and, 199-202, 248, 258-59; WW inquires about effect of resignation of senators from specific states and Palmer answers query, 202-203, 214-15; and resignation of Hapgood as Minister to Denmark, 234,n2; Long's candidacy for seat in, 350; and Esch-Cummins bill, 467n1, 468; *see also* under the names of specific committees, such as Interstate Commerce, Committee on, and under the names of individual senators, such as Hitchcock, Gilbert Monell; Lodge, Henry Cabot, and under the entry Versailles Treaty—*fight for ratification*

United States Constitution, 30, 200, 278, 279, 281; and War-making power, 30, 39, 278, 329; and senatorial appointments, 214-15; and Article X, 287n1; Grey on, 355n1; WW charges Lansing with violating, 383; Lansing answers WW's charges, 388; Lansing on discussions with Tumulty and Grayson on WW's disability and, 455

United States Grain Corporation: *see* Grain Corporation (U.S.)

United States Navy: WW on employment for returning servicemen, 80, 109

United States Railroad Administration: *see* Railroad Administration (U.S.)

United States Shipping Board, 390; and *Imperator* controversy, 7-10, 33, 33-34, 212; and appointments to, 205

United States Supreme Court: and Elk Hills case, 354; Pinchot on oil cases and, 354-55

United States Tariff Commission: appointments to, 205

Valona, Albania, 171, 174, 175, 299, 302, 315

Van Karnebeek, Herman Adriaan, 407n1

Velleman, Antoine, 97-98,n1

Vénisélos, Eleutherios Kyrios, 300, 449; on Thrace, 157-64, 182,n1

Versailles Treaty: and preamble, 46, 46-47, 48; WW on reservations being function of negotiations not ratification, 65; WW calls meeting with Hitchcock, 71; and German ratification and exchange of ratifications with Allied Powers, 101,n1; draft of WW's statement on German protocol on, 118,n2; Ashurst on 1920 campaign and, 263; Lansing compares WW's and Bryan's position on, 267-69; WW on reasonable interpretations of treaty, 278-82; Tumulty on WW's opportunity to act on, 287; editorial comments on, 287,n1,2; R. S. Baker on, 326-27; issue of withdrawal of because of Adriatic proposal, 367; Straus on negative effect on treaty of WW's Adriatic response, 445; *see also* League of Nations

fight for ratification: Hitchcock's substitute reservations, 3, 28-30, 238; Tumulty's proposed letter to Hitchcock on dangers of reservations and delaying ratification, 15; and Article X, 28-29,n2, 43, 46, 47, 48, 283, 287,n1, 446, 450; Hitchcock on progress of Lodge reservations, 37-38, 45-50, 58-59; texts of Lodge reservations, 38-41, 288-95; Underwood's strategy, 42, 69-70; with exception of interpretations, WW not willing to make any compromise, 43-44; Hitchcock interview with WW on, 43-45; Senate controversy intensifies, 45-50, 71-72; WW urges vote against Lodge resolution of ratification or will withdraw treaty, 45, 48, 50, 56, 58; Hitchcock gives hint of compromise from WW, 46, 47; Senate rejects 14th and 15th Lodge reservations, 50, Hitchcock's draft letter opposing Lodge resolution of ratification, 51; Britain

distressed over reservations, 53; Hitchcock's strategy for compromise, 59, 70, 93-
94, 203, 244; Senate votes on treaty, 63-
64,n2,3 64,n3, 526-27, 528; Ashurst on
votes on Lodge resolution of ratification,
63-64; House's strategy for treaty passage
in, 89-90, 96; N. H. Davis on, 104-105;
fate of Lodge resolution on for termination
of the war, 126n1; responsibility rests with
Senate, not WW, 126, 148-49, 187; WW
will not agree to Lodge reservations, 165-
66; comments on WW's uncompromising
attitude toward, 183, 190, 192-94,n1, 267-
69, 321, 327,n1; WW's draft of public letter challenging specific senators to resign,
199-202; WW's advice to Hitchcock, 206;
Tumulty advocates WW adopt Hitchcock's
substitute reservations as compromise
plan, 238; and Jackson Day message, 247-
48,n1, 250-52, 252-55, 257-59; Houston
on interpretive reservations not being objectionable, 251-52; Bryan on, 261n1; F. I.
Cobb on need for compromise, 270n2; bipartisan committee meets, 276,n1, 283-84,
311-12, 312-13,n1; Tumulty on proposed
letter to Hitchcock on interpretive reservations, 276-77; WW on reasonable interpretations, 278-82; bitter-enders cause
end of bipartisan committee, 328n2; WW
accepts Hitchcock's reservations, 329;
Burleson and Hitchcock review WW's list
of senators who hindered ratification of
treaty, 336-37, 338-39; and Grey's letter,
355n1, 381,n1; comments on effect of
Grey's letter, 365, 381,n1; Democratic senators caucus on treaty, 384; and Taft reservation, 387-88,n1, 405, 410-11; Glass on
Taft amendment and searches for WW's
reactions to reservations, 410; Warner up-
dates Lansing on treaty situation, 428,n1;
R. Crane suggests Masaryk send message
on need for ratification, 443; concern over
Democrats approving treaty with Lodge
reservations, 466, 479-80; Dr. Park on effect of WW's letter to Hitchcock, 526; see
also League of Nations, and under the
names of the individual senators, such as
Lodge, Henry Cabot; Hitchcock, Gilbert
Monell
Victory Chimes and Carillon Association,
Inc., of New York, 345n1, 346
Virginia: and empty Senate seat, 24, 41-42,
52
Vittorio Emanuele II, 407
Volosca (now Opatija, Yugoslavia), 172, 370

Wadsworth, James Wolcott, Jr.: and treaty
fight, 200-201, 337
Wagner, Charles C., 324,n1
Waldrep, Tom C., 466,n1
Waldron, John Milton, 522,n1
Wall Street, 328n2, 494
Wallace, Hugh Campbell: as unofficial ob-
server, 148, 156, 156-57, 261, 261,n2, 382;
and Adriatic question, 178, 260-61,n1,

263-66, 323, 340, 341-42, 342; and Turkish treaty, 261,n1, 345, 361, 372,n1, 373,
411; on Anglo-French Adriatic proposal,
298-305, 314-16, 318-20; and Yugoslavia's
reply to Anglo-French Adriatic proposal,
331-35, 340, 341-42; instructions on Adriatic question, 371; receives WW's note on
firm Adriatic position, 398; instructions for
Hungarian treaty negotiations, 446, 447,
448, 464-66; and Fiume, 450-51
Walsh, David Ignatius: and treaty fight, 200-
201, 337
Walsh, Thomas James, 273, 338; on Article
X, 59, 59-60; on WW's no-compromise
statement, 192n1; and bipartisan meeting
on reservations, 283; and Hitchcock's copy
of text of Lodge reservations and, 291,
292, 293, 294; and Democratic caucus on
treaty, 384
war crimes and war criminals, 364-65,n1,
382; Lansing on, 381-82; former Crown
Prince Friedrich Wilhelm on, 397; and
Britain's demands for William II, 407,n1;
WW on, 408
War, Department of: and repatriation of Pol-
ish Americans in Haller's Army, 389-90
War Finance Corporation: and appointments
to, 205
Warner, Charles Damuth, 428,n1
Warren, Francis Emroy: and treaty fight, 94,
200, 202, 337
Washington Post, 32n, 100n, 138, 149n2,
187n, 192n1, 511n1
Waters, Henry Jackson, 64n1
Watson, James Eli: and WW's health, 135-
36; and treaty fight, 200-201, 336
Ways and Means, Committee on (House),
340
Wertheimer, Mr. (German press correspon-
dent), 364
Wesleyan University, 514,n1
Westermann, William Linn, 163n6
Weyand, Louis, 431
What Wilson Did at Paris (R. S. Baker),
320,n1, 325,n5, 335
wheat: and shipments to Poland, 4-6, 12-13;
and shipments to Armenia, 13-14
Wheeler, Clayton L., 322n1
White, Henry, 472
White, John Philip: appointed to coal com-
mission, 206, 209n1
White, William Allen, 62,n2
Wickersham, George Woodward, 64n1
William II (of Germany): and war crimes,
382, 407,n1
Williams College: and H. A. Garfield, 181n1
Williams, John Sharp, 156,n2; and Mexican
situation, 120; and Democratic caucus on
treaty, 384
Willis, James F., 364n1
Wilson, Edith Bolling Galt (Mrs. Woodrow),
12n3, 42, 44, 50, 57, 61, 66, 71, 87, 130,
227, 229, 237, 245, 274, 320, 325, 345 46,
350-51, 353, 355, 397, 405n1, 420, 428,
467, 473-74, 480, 488-89, 495, 511n1;

Wilson, Edith Bolling Galt (*cont.*)
  conduit for WW, 4, 6, 10, 12n3, 14, 16, 37-
  38, 42, 50-51, 52n1, 53, 58-59, 61, 72, 88-
  89, 90, 95-96, 97, 100, 103, 104n2, 119,
  145, 147, 156, 166, 167, 189n1, 190n1,
  190, 198, 202, 203, 204, 206, 218, 228,
  230n1, 232, 233-34, 235, 243, 244, 246,
  274, 276-77,n1, 282-83, 297, 330, 330n1,
  332, 335-36, 343, 345n2, 346, 352-53,
  366, 389, 391, 405, 448, 457; and Queen
  Mother of England, 28; greets Prince of
  Wales, 31; thank you from Prince of
  Wales, 36-37; Thanksgiving Day, 93; Lansing on political decision making and, 124;
  notes on WW's meeting with Hitchcock
  and Fall on Mexico, 130-31, 133-35; and
  draft of WW's statement on treaty, 199n1;
  and railroad situation, 222,n1, 223n1;
  Lansing on role of during WW's illness,
  231; on WW's health, 232-33; House on
  discourteous treatment of Lord Grey by,
  239; relationship with Lansing, 243; C. R.
  Crane's advice to, 262; and Lansing's resignation, 270, 416, 417,n3; mentioned as
  WW's adviser, 270; R. S. Baker on, 320-
  21; R. S. Baker's offer to help WW with
  compromise position, 326-27; to R. S.
  Baker on having the "right spirit" of the
  treaty, 335; House on, 347, 348; House on
  treaty position of, 348; and WW's tentative
  decision to resign, 362n1; draft letter to
  Glass on Taft reservation, 405; C. R. Crane
  offers vacation home to, 425; Grayson on
  care of WW by, 499; and WW's health,
  503, 507, 509, 509-10; vetoes divulgence
  of WW's stroke, 507n1, 510; on WW's
  stroke, 507n1; told of diagnosis of WW's
  illness, 510
Wilson, Ellen Louise Axson (Mrs. Woodrow), 516; Grayson on, 485; and place-
  ment of her picture during WW's illness,
  490
Wilson, Florence, 275
Wilson, Janet Woodrow (Mrs. Joseph Ruggles), mother of WW: and Carlisle, England, 184
Wilson, John Adams, first cousin of WW,
  320, 490
Wilson, Joseph Ruggles, father of WW, 515;
  WW on death of, 517
Wilson, Margaret Woodrow, daughter of WW
  and EAW, 57, 93, 320, 325; greets Prince
  of Wales, 31; and WW's health diagnosis,
  503, 507, 510
Wilson, William Bauchop, 64, 193; and First
  International Labour Conference, 98n1;
  and Mooney case, 145,n1; and coal strike,
  147, 154, 166, 167, 207-208; rumor of resignation of, 166, 167, 184-85; draft letter
  to H. M. Robinson, 206n1

WOODROW WILSON

Armistice Day statement, 7; with exception
  of interpretations not willing to make any

Woodrow Wilson, cont.
  compromise on treaty, 43-44; Lansing
  on personal animosity of Republican
  senators against, 54-57; on no reservations, 55; White House sheep, 57n1;
  R. S. Baker on House-WW relationship,
  62; on reservations being function of
  negotiations not ratification, 65; and Tumulty's draft of Annual message to Congress, 72, 73-87; House offers strategy
  for treaty passage, 89; Annual Message
  on the State of the Union, 106-16; draft
  of statement on protocol concerning
  treaty, 118,n2; authorship of Annual
  Message questioned, 123; Lansing on
  WW's ability to perform duties, 123-25;
  statement on coal situation, 153-54,n1,
  154-55; will not accept Lodge reservations, 165-66; relationship between Lansing and, 179, 243; made citizen of Carlisle, England, 184; statement that he
  will not compromise on treaty, 187; chair
  at Davidson College named after, 191-
  92,n2, 213; questions effect of a U.S.
  senator's resignation in certain states,
  202-203; appoints Bituminous Coal Commission, 206-208; Christmas, 211; vacation in Bermuda, 214,n1; issues Executive Order for half days for government
  employees, 218; proclamation ending federal control of railroads, 226-27; birthday
  wishes from George V, and WW's thank
  you, 230, 231; birthday wishes from King
  Albert and WW's thank you, 230; Princeton University sends his desk to, 246-47;
  Jackson Day message, 247-49, 257-59;
  advocates direct referendum on treaty,
  248, 254; and election of 1920, 267; refuses to endorse candidate for Democratic
  minority leadership, 274,n1; letter to
  Hitchcock on reasonable interpretation,
  278-82; R. S. Baker on futility of situation of, 321-22; nominated for Nobel
  Peace Prize, 342; and numerous requests
  to support fund raising 'schemes,' 345-46;
  requests all documents be delivered in
  sealed envelopes, 351; effect of Grey's letter on, 362,n1; tentative decision to resign, 362,n1; decision to withdraw Versailles Treaty if Anglo-French Adriatic
  proposals are accepted, 380, 402; on calling of Cabinet meetings by Lansing, 383,
  384; won't object to "interpretative reservations," 384; position on treaty with "interpretative reservation" published in
  newspapers, 385; on Lansing's resignation, 417n3; emotional reaction to Cummings' speech, 428; unyielding on Adriatic question, 458-63; Grayson on
  inauguration memories, 485-86; seeks
  public opinion on entry into war, 487; remarks in 1918 at a stag dinner at 10
  Downing Street, 490-92; on essays to be
  published, 514-15; willing to assist W. M.
  Daniels in Princeton University position, 514

Woodrow Wilson, cont.
APPEARANCE AND IMPRESSIONS

Hitchcock on after stroke, 45n1; Hitchcock and Fall on, 131, 132; R. S. Baker on, 360; in wheel chair wearing sweater and old golf cap, 420; grows beard during illness, 489

APPOINTMENT SUGGESTIONS,
APPOINTMENTS AND RESIGNATIONS

Glass resigns to take Senate seat, 41-42, 50, 52, 103; Phillips suggested as Minister to Netherlands, 41, 103, 119; to second Industrial Conference, 64,n1; McCormick declines Secretaryship of Commerce, 95; Talcott and district judgeship, 97,n1, 215-16, 322,n1; appointment of Secretary of Commerce, 142,n1,2; rumors of W. B. Wilson's resignation, 166, 167, 184-85; Lansing responds to WW's charges and resigns, 179, 255-56, 385, 385-86, 388-89, 398, 405, 408-10, 415-19; resignation of H. A. Garfield, 181, 181-82, 185, 186; House on J. W. Alexander's appointment, 185; Tumulty submits list of vacancies, 204-205; and Bituminous Coal Commission, 206,n1; Daniels on important missions to be filled, 216; and reappointments to Hague Tribunal, 216, 273; on delegates to international conference on communications, 228,n1; Secretaryship of Interior offered to T. D. Jones, 232; resignation of Hapgood as Minister to Denmark, 233-34; Fosdick resignation from League Secretariat, 274, 286, 306, 310; Palmer on judicial appointments and age factor, 296-97; and some "terrible" appointments, 296; WW and Lansing on several diplomatic appointments, 296, 316-17, 322, 366, 407-408; resignation of H. P. Fletcher, 310, 397; Houston's resignation and new appointment, 330, 349; R. U. Johnson appointed to Italy, 343-44, 346, 474; resignation of Close, 344; Long declines appointment as Minister to Switzerland, 350-51, 352, 353; Frazier suggested as Minister to Switzerland, 353, 383-84, 398, 413, 414, 451-54; Leffingwell willing to defer resignation, 361-62, 362; Lane's resignation, 373-74, 374; Robinson regrets he cannot accept Secretaryship of Interior, 392-93; WW accepts Lansing's resignation, 404, 414; and appointment to Greece, 414,n2; Tumulty's suggestions for Lansing's successor, 419; Cummings on not getting an appointment, 427-28; Lansing resignation prompts inquiries into WW's health, 432, 433; rumors of N. D. Baker's resignation, 436; J. B. Payne as Secretary of the Interior, 448; Colby as Lansing's replacement, 464,n1, 472-73; McCombs as Ambassador to France, 1913, 523, 524n1

Woodrow Wilson, cont.
CABINET

3, 50, 57, 274, 366; proposed history of women in war work, 3; and *Imperator* controversy, 8; and preparations for WW's message to Congress, 16,n1; Glass resigns from Treasury, 52, 60; McCormick declines Secretaryship of Commerce, 95; on coal crisis, 141, 153n1, 166, 167; J. W. Alexander appointed Secretary of Commerce, 142,n1,2, 185; rumors of W. B. Wilson's resignation, 166, 167; Lansing determined to resign, 179, 255-56; and railroad situation, 183-84, 222n1, 222, 223, 224; WW offers Secretaryship of Interior to T. D. Jones, 232; Secretaries of Treasury and Agriculture appointed, 330,n1, 330-31; Houston's resignation as Secretary of Agriculture to become Secretary of Treasury, 349; Lane's resignation, 373-74, 374; various comments on controversy over Lansing's calling Cabinet meetings during WW's illness, 383, 384, 385-86, 386, 388-89, 398, 404, 405, 408-10, 418, 444, 454-58, 496; Robinson regrets he cannot accept appointment to, 392-93; WW accepts Lansing's resignation, 404, 414; Lansing defends his actions in letter of resignation, 408-10; Tumulty on Lansing's successor, 419,n1; Cummings on his not being appointed to, 427-28; Lansing's resignation prompts inquiries into WW's health, 432, 433; physicians on WW's ability to attend meetings, 435; rumors of N. D. Baker's resignation, 436; Payne appointed Secretary of the Interior, 448; B. Colby appointed Secretary of State, 464,n1, 472-73; Dr. Park on WW's health and secret meetings of, 527

FAMILY AND PERSONAL LIFE

observes Thanksgiving, 93, 97; and Carlisle, England, 184; college life at Davidson, 191-92; birthday greetings from Queen Mother Alexandra, 235; discusses with Grayson future use of notes for memoir, 324-25; birthday greetings to grandson, 451; examples of sense of humor and wit, 488-90; Grayson on WW and EAW's picture, 490n1; on his father's ill health and death, 517

HEALTH

leaves sickbed for wheel chair on Armistice Day, 6, 32; comments on continued improvement, 31, 37, 105-106, 307, 325, 351, 435, 495; goes outdoors, 32-33, 37, 50, 57, 100; spirits rise after visit from Prince of Wales, 42; not weakened but strengthened against his opponents, 44; Hitchcock on, 45n1, 133; issue of ability to perform duties, 52, 123-25; press

Woodrow Wilson, cont.

speculates ill health reason for Hitchcock's failure to see WW, 99-100; handwriting indicator of, 105-106, 125; Fall and Hitchcock agree on WW's ability to meet country's emergencies, 131; uses right hand, 131; and retort to Fall's prayer for, 133,n1; Grayson on Fall-Hitchcock visit and, 135-39; Fall on, 139; Lansing on ending secrecy concerning, 139-40; House on, 183; walks about room, negates rumors of paralysis, 187; Polk on, 227; Lansing on, 229, 269, 385; Lansing on WW's mental state, 231, 415-16, 417, 453-54; EBW on, 232-33; contracts viral infection, 325, 351, 362n1; recovers, spends time outside, 361; R. S. Baker on, 365; Dr. Young's interview on, mentions diagnosis of cerebral thrombosis, weather only factor in keeping WW from public appearances, says Young, 394-96; weight gain, 395; Dr. Dercum declines comment on, 403; publication of cerebral thrombosis diagnosis incenses WW, 403; WW's reaction to Dr. Young's interview on, 403; Dr. Bevan on diagnosis of WW's illness, recommends WW's resignation, 432-33, 435; Lansing's resignation prompts inquiry over WW's health, 432, 433; Dr. Dercum on WW's being mentally alert, 433-34; Dr. Dercum on, 435; restless night, coughing spell, 472; Grayson on WW's search for personal physician in 1913, 486; Grayson on long working hours and stress in Paris, 492; violently ill with influenza in Paris, 492-93; Seibold on rumors about, 494-95; Grayson on rumors about, 495; health during first year of presidency, 497; Grayson's unpublished statement on WW's health history, 497-99; neuritis, 497; in Paris, 497-98; phlebitis, 497n2; hernia operation in 1904, 497,n2; cerebral-occular accident in 1906, 497,n3; prostate problems, 499, 506; Dr. Dercum's clinical reports after stroke of 1919, 500-507; diagnosis of paralysis, 503,n9; decision to issue general statements on WW's health, 507n1, 510; diagnoses by Drs. Park and Toole, 507n11; exaggerated rumors on, 511n1; Grayson's bulletins on, 511,n1; Park on aftermath of stroke, 525-29

OPINIONS AND COMMENTS

I am a sick man, lying in this bed, but I am going to debate this issue with these gentlemen in their respective states whenever they come up for re-election if I have breath enough in my body to carry on the fight. I shall do this even if I have to give my life to it, 43; I have no hostility towards these gentlemen but an utter contempt, 43; on isolationism, 79, 109; on representative government as way to

Woodrow Wilson, cont.

reform, 116; on following the Constitution regarding Mexican situation and Senate subcommittee, 152; on various articles of treaty, 329-30; on Sir Auckland Geddes, 484; on men who have turned against him, 488; on friendship between U.S. and Great Britain, 491-92

RECREATION

wheel chair rides outdoors, 57; sings hymns with family in 1913, 487; sings "Old Nassau," 487; golf, 492

RELIGION

WW on comfort of, 488

WESTERN TOUR

Lansing on reasons for opposing, 55; mentioned, 276n1, 277; Grayson on, 488

End of Woodrow Wilson entry

Wimer, Kurt, 199n1
Winans, Richard M., 496n1
Wisconsin, University of, 425n2
Wiseman, Sir William: concern over Senate action on reservations, 53
woman suffrage: creation of League of Women Voters, 396,n1; New Jersey ratifies 19th amendment, 396n1; and Oklahoma, 466,n1
Women: proposed history of war work of, 3,n1; and labor, 98n1
Wood, Leonard: mentioned as presidential candidate, 325
Woodrow Wilson and the American Diplomatic Tradition: The Treaty Fight in Perspective (Ambrosius), 276n1, 328n2
Woodrow Wilson and the Great Betrayal (Bailey), 276n1, 328n2
Woodrow Wilson as I Know Him (Tumulty), 417n3
"Woodrow Wilson and the Mexican Interventionist Movement of 1919" (Trow), 120n1
Woodrow Wilson's Eloquence (Wescott), 232n2
"Woodrow Wilson's Plan for a Vote of Confidence" (Wimer), 199n1
Woolley, Robert Wickliffe, 445,n1

Yates, Frederic, 490n1
Young, Hugh Hampton, 32, 489, 506; gives interview on WW's stroke, 394-96; WW incensed over interview by, 403; interview mentioned, 425, 432
Young, Owen D., 64n1
Yugoslavia, 465; Venizélos on, 162; and Adriatic question, 168-78, 264-66, 376;

and Albania, 177; Anglo-French Adriatic proposals, 298-305, 313-16, 318-20; reply to Anglo-French proposal, 331-35; Lansing and Wallace on U.S. course of action on Adriatic proposal and, 340-43; WW's reply to Anglo-French proposals, 398-402, 459-63; Anglo-French reply to WW on, 437-39; and Hungary's demands, 447, see also Adriatic question

Zara (now Zadar, Yugoslavia), 170, 172, 264n4, 265, 299, 300, 301, 302, 305, 333
Zavoiko, Vasilii Stepanovich, 390-91,n2
Zionism, 358, 449